Taking a Stand

A Guide to the Researched Paper with Readings

IRENE LURKIS CLARK

University of Southern California

HarperCollins*Publishers*

Dedication

To my husband, Bill, and my children, Elisa, Louisa, Clifton, and Justin, whose presence informs all of my writing, and with many thanks to my insightful and supportive colleagues at the Freshman Writing Program.

Sponsoring Editor: Patricia A. Rossi
Development Editor: Vicky Anderson Schiff
Project Coordination, Text and Cover Design: Ruttle, Shaw & Wetherill, Inc.
Cover Illustration: Anne O'Donnell
Photo Researcher: Judy Ladendorf
Production Manager: Michael Weinstein
Compositor: Ruttle, Shaw & Wetherill, Inc.
Printer and Binder: R.R. Donnelley & Sons Company
Cover Printer: The Lehigh Press, Inc.

Taking a Stand: A Guide to the Researched Paper with Readings

Library of Congress Cataloging-in-Publication Data

Clark, Irene L.
    Taking a stand : a guide to the researched paper with readings /
Irene Lurkis Clark.
        p.   cm.
    Includes index.
    ISBN 0-673-46027-4 (Student edition)
    ISBN 0-673-46610-8 (Instructor edition)
    1. English language—Rhetoric. 2. Report writing. I. Title.
PE1478.C55 1991
808'.042—dc20   91-26589
                                                                      CIP

92 93 94 9 8 7 6 5 4 3 2

Contents

3 *Developing an Argument for a Researched Paper*   *64*

4 *Evaluating Information*   *90*

5 *Working with Information*   *117*
Summary, Paraphrase, Quotation

6 *Developing Structure* *158*
The Purpose and the Plan

9 *Search and Seizure* 307
or *"Keep Your Hands Out of My Garbage!"*

10   *Equal Opportunity*   372
or "A Good Idea, But Some Are More Equal than Others"

11   *Men and Women in Society*   **437**
or "Who's Cooking Tonight?"

Preface

Taking a Stand is designed to help students learn to write a **"researched"** paper, that is, a paper that

1. is relatively short (less than ten pages),
2. helps students work through the research process,
3. develops a purposeful position about a controversial topic, and
4. uses, not simply displays or assembles, outside sources as a means of support.

Of course, whenever I use the term "researched" paper, someone always questions why I say "researched" rather than "research," implying either that I harbor a predilection for meaningless jargon or that I am foolishly impressed by the pseudo-originality of pasting new labels on old bottles. Let me establish, then, that I use the term "researched" paper deliberately, because I wish to distinguish the sort of paper this book is concerned with from the traditional information-based "research" paper, which usually results in depressingly unsatisfactory student writing. As my own experience and that of many composition instructors strongly suggest, traditional student research papers are often excessively long and pointless, not to mention hackneyed, uninspired, generalized, and occasionally plagiarized, a mere pasting together of sources rather than a coherent presentation of a thesis that uses outside sources for additional breadth and support. Thus, I use the term "researched" rather than "research" to emphasize that *Taking a Stand* is oriented toward what I believe is a more effective model of a paper incorporating outside sources, a thesis-driven model that represents, I believe, what most college instructors actually mean when they assign a research paper in an undergraduate class.

INSTRUCTIONAL VERSUS CONTENT CHAPTERS

The chapters in this book are of two types: those that give instruction on various skills associated with the writing and research process and those that provide content material to be used as secondary sources. The instructional chapters explain how to perform some necessary tasks such as finding a topic, evaluating and organizing information, locating a controversy, comparing points of view, developing an argument, taking notes, and incorporating quotations. The content chapters provide material, similar to what can be found in a library, that students can use to develop a position or argument, including background information, definitions, or opinions. Thus, students will be able to write about these topics without necessarily having to go to the library, although instructors may wish to supplement some of this material with library sources.

This book is also based on the idea that in order to learn to write, one must write about **something;** the acquisition of a knowledge base enables students to build a context for writing that, in turn, facilitates the development of writing ability. The first six chapters of the book address the skills needed for developing a position and incorporating outside sources into a text. The substantive area selected for this textbook is concerned with ethical, social, and political dilemmas of our culture. The rationale is that these topics are both **controversial** and **significant;** that is, they **generate conflict** and they **matter.** Taking a position on these issues does not simply reflect personal taste or curiosity; these are issues with which every concerned citizen has to grapple in order to decide how society is or ought to be. I believe these topics will fuel exciting class discussions and provide many possibilities for assignments. Also, I think that when students work with these topics, which appear frequently in the newspaper and are always being discussed in the media, they not only will learn research skills, they also will become more involved in current issues, surely an important goal of education. Of course, many other topics are both controversial and significant, and I would certainly encourage instructors to find additional ones in which students might have a special interest.

THE RESEARCH PROCESS AND STAGED ACQUISITION

The researched paper model developed in this book reflects current thinking about composition pedagogy and, in particular, its emphasis on process teaching, sequenced assignments, and collaborative learning, as well as its concern with generating student awareness of invention, audience, and purpose. Over the past twenty years, composition pedagogy has focused on the complexities of the writing process; yet, little scholarly attention has been devoted to the equally complex process students engage in when they undertake research. This book enables students to work through a model of the research process as part of their composition class, a model that they can replicate when they write papers for other courses. This model includes selecting a topic suitable for developing a position, understanding the controversy within a topic, comparing opposing viewpoints, and working with information to understand background and define key terms. The concepts and skills presented here are pertinent to student research efforts both within and beyond the university, whether or not the assignment includes the use of the library.

The skills necessary for writing a researched paper are presented here in accord with the idea of "staged acquisition." Before students are assigned to write a complete paper on a substantive issue, they first complete preliminary activities and assignments related to the topic, which are sequenced according to level of difficulty. For example, when students work with an issue, ultimately they must develop a position using secondary sources for support. However, before they grapple with the topic as a whole, they complete several preparatory assignments, such as defining key terms essential for understanding the issue, locating significant historical information, summarizing and paraphrasing several articles, locating different points of view, and perhaps writing a dialogue incorporating these points of view. After students have worked through several preliminary assignments, they are prepared to develop a position using secondary sources as support.

I have worked with many of these topics and assignments in my own classes and find that they provide rich forums for discussion and infinite topics for assignments involving secondary research. Assignments concerned with controversial topics require students to develop a breadth of information and to make connections between past and present. Thus, when students have worked with the assignments and methods discussed in this text, they not only will have learned a portable skill, they also will have become aware of some of the important controversies of our culture, an awareness that can continue to develop.

THE RESEARCHED PAPER AND UNDERGRADUATE EDUCATION

Too often, instructors in upper division courses complain that students do not know how to write "research" papers, meaning that they do not know how to develop positions and use information in support of those positions. Students, too, often feel tremendous anxiety about papers involving research; many of them are confused about the intention of research paper assignments and have never acquired the skills necessary for writing one. Incorporating the "researched" paper into the composition course, that is, enabling students to work through the research process under the guidance of a composition instructor, is likely to dissipate some of this anxiety and confusion, helping students achieve greater success throughout their academic careers. *Taking a Stand* is aimed toward facilitating this success.

Irene Lurkis Clark

1 Introduction to the Researched Paper

The Characteristics of a Researched Paper

Let me tell you about Scott, a college student who works hard in his classes and usually earns good grades. Scott attends classes faithfully, studies hard, hands his work in on time, and performs well on exams. However, in one of his courses, Scott was given an assignment to write a "research paper," which required him to choose a subject which particularly interested him, find at least five secondary sources, and write a paper that was at least 20 pages long, suitably documented. "No problem," he thought, after studying the assignment. So Scott went to the library and found several sources describing an old Indian burial custom, which he thought was interesting. He then read the information, incorporated it into a paper that included many facts and quotations, and submitted a 25-page paper, suitably documented, of course.

However, when Scott received his paper back, he was disappointed to discover that he had not received as high a grade as he had hoped. His instructor explained that although it was obvious that Scott had worked hard on his paper, apparently he had not understood the requirements of the assignment. "You have a lot of really interesting information, Scott," his instructor said. "And the paper is organized and clearly written. But you didn't focus your information in support of a main point or a clear purpose." In other words, Scott had not **developed a position.**

"I should have clarified what I expected," the instructor continued, "and so it's only fair that I give you the opportunity to revise this paper. Although it might be acceptable in some disciplines for a research paper to consist simply of a lot of well-organized and documented information, research papers in most disciplines, and particularly in the humanities, use outside information **purposefully** in support of a thesis. I expected your research paper to **develop a position.**"

I am recounting this story because Scott's misunderstanding of what is expected in a research paper is one which is shared by many college students. The *Calvin and Hobbs* cartoon on the next page illustrates one commonly held mis-

Calvin and Hobbes

by Bill Watterson

Students often have misconceptions about research papers. (Calvin and Hobbes. Copyright 1989 Universal Press Syndicate. Reprinted with permission. All rights reserved.)

conception—the idea that a clear plastic binder will ensure a good grade—and while most college students do not share this particular belief, many of them think that writing a research paper means simply collecting a lot of interesting information, pasting it together with clever transitions, and documenting references carefully. And yet, when they receive their papers back, they discover that the instructor had expected them to have a clear purpose for their research and to have developed a strong argument.

This book is concerned with helping students write a **"researched"** paper, a **purposeful** position paper that develops a strong argument, **utilizing,** not simply displaying, outside sources. A "researched" paper is what most college teachers mean when they say they are assigning a "research" paper (I am using the term "researched" simply to focus attention on the sort of paper you will be writing in this book). Unlike Scott's (and many students') misconception of a research paper, a "researched" paper has the following characteristics:

1. It is a relatively short paper (less than 10 pages).
2. It has the purpose of developing a position on a controversial issue, one which generates controversy.
3. It integrates outside sources as a means of developing and supporting its main point.

When you write a researched paper, you will be practicing the following activities:

1. Selecting a suitable topic for an argument,
2. Determining the conflict within that topic,
3. Evaluating information,
4. Working with information (notetaking, summarizing, paraphrasing),
5. Organizing information,
6. Understanding how value assumptions influence your position on a topic,

7. Developing a position on a complex topic,
8. Quoting and documenting information.

These activities are divided into manageable components and incorporated into the assignments in this book. Thus, in working with these assignments, you will be learning skills that you can transfer to many different research tasks.

In looking over the table of contents, you might notice that the content areas are all concerned with ethical, social, and political dilemmas of our culture, and you might wonder why these particular areas were chosen. The reason these issues were selected is that they are both **controversial** and **significant;** that is, they generate **conflict,** and they **matter.** Taking a position on these issues does not simply reflect personal taste or curiosity; these are issues with which every concerned citizen has to grapple in order to decide how society is or ought to be. Thus, these topics can fuel exciting class discussions and provide many possibilities for assignments. Also, when you work with these topics, which appear frequently in the newspaper and are always being discussed in the media, you will not only learn research skills; you will also become more involved in current issues, surely an important goal of education Of course, many other topics are both controversial and significant, and I would certainly encourage you to find additional ones in which you might have a special interest.

INSTRUCTIONAL VERSUS CONTENT CHAPTERS

The chapters in this book are of two types: those giving instruction on various skills associated with the writing and research process and those providing content material to be used as secondary sources. The instructional chapters are "how to" chapters, in that they explain how to perform some necessary tasks—finding a topic, evaluating and organizing information, developing an argument, or notetaking, for example. The content chapters provide you with material that you will use to develop your position or argument, and they contain material that is similar to what you would find if you went to a library—background information, definitions, or opinions—so that you will be able to write about these topics without necessarily having to go to the library. Your teacher, however, may wish you to supplement some of this material with library sources, and so suggestions are also provided for additional research.

WRITING THE RESEARCHED PAPER: WORKING THROUGH THE PROCESS

To help you understand what is meant by "developing a position" in a "researched" paper, I will work through an encapsulated version of the writing process of Elisa, another student in a college composition course. I say "encapsulated" because when you read about how someone completes a task, you sometimes get the impression that the task was completed neatly and easily. In reading about Elisa's experience with a researched paper assignment, then, you might think that Elisa's work is too good to be true, since it appears as if she wrote her paper without taking too many wrong turns. I say "appears" because in actuality the task of writing a researched paper is not one that most students can complete without spending a lot of time revising and rethinking. In fact, I would like to stress the following two points about all kinds of writing whether or not outside research is included. The first point is this:

1. **Writing takes time.** As you watch Elisa work through her assignment, it may seem as if she somehow managed to leave enough time to write several drafts, get help from others, rethink her position, and polish her sentences. And you might say to yourself that this organized approach is something you, yourself, could never manage. Most of us have difficulty leaving enough time for writing, even though, ideally, it is very helpful to leave time for thinking, locating information, writing multiple drafts, and editing.

Related to the first point, the second point is this:

2. **Writing is a recursive, messy process.** The process of writing rarely occurs in the neat linear sequence that some textbooks and teachers recommend. You may have been taught that the process occurs by first thinking of an idea, then writing an outline, then writing your paper, and finally, editing for correctness and style. However, I know that for most people, the writing process does not happen this way. When I write, for instance, I may have an idea, start to write, then change my idea, discover that I need different or additional sources, begin to write again, change my idea once again, and even rethink my position after several drafts. Even experienced and professional writers spend a lot of time rewriting, rethinking, rearranging, adding, and deleting their texts. Writing does not usually occur in a neat or orderly fashion.

With these qualifications in mind, then, let us observe how Elisa writes her paper. Elisa was assigned to write a "researched" paper on the following topic:

In a prominent American town of moderate size, many parents are concerned that the local high school library contains books that they feel are unsuitable for their children to read. In particular, they point to many modern novels that, they say, contain explicit sex and gratuitous violence. They feel that exposure to such books will contribute to what they perceive as an already violent and promiscuous society. To prevent the library from acquiring additional books of this nature, these parents have requested that a committee of concerned parents be formed to screen new acquisitions.

Writing Task:

Develop a position on whether or not you feel this committee should be formed. Be sure that you present strong evidence in support of your position, and include in your response a discussion of whether such a committee would be consistent with the values stated in the United States Constitution, particularly the First Amendment. To help you to formulate your opinion and to serve as additional support, please read the following:

The First Amendment to the Bill of Rights
Loudon Wainwright, "A Little Banning Is a Dangerous Thing"
Frank Trippett, "The Growing Battle of the Books"
Susan Brownmiller, "Pornography Hurts Women"
Ruth McGaffey, "Porn Doesn't Cause Violence, but a Fear of New Ideas Does"
Stanley Kauffmann, "Pornography and Censorship"
Garry Wills, "In Praise of Censure"

Elisa's assignment is typical of the assignments you will find in this book. It asks the writer to address a question that is controversial and significant. Note, too, that the assignment requires Elisa to develop a position on her topic. Although in order to express an informed opinion she will have to consider both sides of this question, her paper will be primarily concerned with arguing a point of view; it will not simply show how much information she has found. Finally, Elisa's assignment is based on the idea that one does not form a position in a vacuum— the ideas of others are important in helping us develop a perspective—and skill at incorporating and acknowledging the positions of others is essential to doing research. Elisa, then, will write a "researched" paper in which she "develops a position."

APPROACHING THE RESEARCHED PAPER ASSIGNMENT

Planning Your Time

Sometimes, when students are presented with a writing assignment, they read it through, but remain removed from it until the last night, when the pressure mounts to begin writing. All of us know that terrible, last-minute feeling of panic. We stare at the blank page and nothing comes to mind as the hours tick away into the night. Some people experience this inability to write because they suffer from writer's block; these people find that any writing assignment causes them to panic. But most of us experience inability to write because we have not thought seriously about the assignment; we have not involved ourselves in the topic by raising questions, thinking, talking, reading, and writing about it, so that over a period of time we can develop a position. When you involve yourself in a topic, your mind percs away at it, even when you don't realize it. Then, when you begin to write, you find that you have more to say about your subject than you had anticipated. To avoid last-night writer's block, then, I suggest that you plan your time as follows:

1. **List all of the activities you will engage in when you write your research paper.** These could include talking with someone about the topic, brainstorming, reading, summarizing and comparing sources, writing early drafts, revising, and printing the final draft.
2. Now **estimate the time you think you will need for each of these activities.** Then decide when and where you will actually complete these activities so that you can leave enough time.
3. **Add up the total.** If possible, add at least an hour to each estimate.

Making a Plan

Assuming that Elisa has two weeks to write her paper, here is her researched paper time management plan:

1. Read the assignment, write an exploratory draft.	Monday—in class
2. Compare the drafts of other students.	Wednesday—in class
3. Read and summarize the assigned essays.	Saturday—all day at home
4. Brainstorm and come up with a brief outline.	Sunday (1–5)—at home
5. Write a first draft.	Monday (6–11)—computer center
6. Go to Writing Center and get feedback on draft.	Wednesday (1–2)
7. Rewrite draft.	Thursday afternoon (1–6)—at home
8. Find out about documentation form.	Friday—in class
9. Revise for style and correctness.	Saturday (start at 11)—computer center
10. Print.	Saturday—computer center

Although the paper was due on Monday, Elisa tried to finish it by Saturday, in case she came across difficulties she hadn't anticipated. Again, you may be saying, "It is impossible to plan ahead like this. Elisa is unreal." I understand how difficult such planning is. However, when you receive your next assignment, you might think about what sort of plan you might aim for, one which might actually work for you. On page 7 is a research paper "time management" form, which you might find useful.

Researched Paper Time Management Form

Research Activity	*When?*	*Where?*
Reading assignment		
Writing exploratory draft		
Reading sources		
Brainstorming		
Developing preliminary topic		
Creating an outline		
Writing first draft		
Getting feedback on first draft		
Writing second draft		
Revising second draft		
Editing second draft		
Checking documentation		
Printing and copying		

Then, immerse yourself in your topic by doing the following:

1. Think about the purpose of the assignment.
2. Clarify the key terms.
3. Consider your immediate reaction to the topic.
4. Ask key questions.
5. Share questions and ideas with classmates.
6. Understand the value conflicts in the assignment.
7. Read and compare some opinions on the subject.

These activities will enable you to get involved in your topic so that you will be able to develop a position.

Understanding the Purpose, or What Am I Expected to Do?

To try to understand the purpose of this assignment, Elisa reread it several times looking for terms that would indicate to her what she was required to do. As she read, she noted the terms "develop a position" and "formulate an opinion." Elisa decided then that she was being asked to take a position in the controversy over whether or not the screening committee ought to be formed. The other part of the assignment Elisa noted was that she had to decide if such a committee would or wouldn't be consistent with the values stated in the United States Constitution. Thus, as an important first step in beginning her paper, Elisa carefully considered the overall purpose of her task.

Clarifying Key Terms in the Assignment

The key terms in the assignment help you decide which terms or concepts need additional clarification or definition. In looking over the assignment, Elisa focused on the terms she felt she needed to define: "unsuitable," "explicit sex," and "gratuitous violence." Although she had heard of some of the terms before, she decided that she would have to figure out what these terms meant to her in the context of this assignment before she could decide if she were in favor of the screening committee (her purpose). She was not sure about the meaning of the word "gratuitous," so she looked it up in the dictionary and discovered that it meant "not required, called for, or warranted by the circumstances." She also looked up the word "explicit," just to make sure that she understood it, and found that it meant "plain in language, distinctly expressed, clearly stated, not obscure or ambiguous." The word "unsuitable," she decided, was a matter of interpretation that she would have to think about. Also, she noted that she would have to find out what the First Amendment actually said.

Considering Your Immediate Reaction to the Topic

To engage in research in any topic, it is important to try to get an overview of what you already may "feel" about the topic. Of course, part of the value of doing research is that it can often lead you to change your mind. Nevertheless, when you begin working on an assignment, it is a good idea to assess your first reaction.

How do you find out what you already think about the topic? Talking and thinking about it are good methods. But an excellent way to discover what you already know about a topic is to write about it. Realizing the importance of using writing as a means of discovering ideas, Elisa's writing instructor asked the class to write a preliminary response to some questions concerning their own feelings and experiences on the topic. These are the questions the teacher assigned:

> Think about your own experience as a high school student. Did your mother and father monitor what you read? Did you ever find books in the school library that school authorities might have thought were inappropriate in some way? Did you ever read a book secretly because you felt your parents or teachers would disapprove of it? Do you believe that books influence behavior? Do you have strong feelings about monitoring books?

Elisa thought about these questions and then wrote the following response:

> When I was a high school student, I read books that my parents and teachers disapproved of all the time, although I was never really "forbidden" to read any particular book. I think actually that I kind of liked reading something that I thought my parents would disapprove of and that was part of the fun of it. My mother was always telling me that I was reading "junk." She hated all my romance novels and teenaged soap opera type stuff. She was always saying I should read "good" literature, although she never told me exactly why.
>
> I remember once finding a book called *Peyton Place* in my mother's bookcase that I couldn't believe. It was pretty old, written in the fifties, I think, and it was real dog eared, like it had been really read a lot, some parts over and over. It was pretty easy to find the parts in it that had been read most often, and some of them had some spicy sex scenes, not real raunchy the way books have today, but pretty suggestive for that time. It was funny for me to think that my mother or father used to read these sections, probably over and over again. I also remember the afternoon I "discovered" *The Catcher in the Rye* in my brother's bookcase. I picked it up and couldn't put it down. But I read somewhere that this terrific book had been banned.

I guess that's why I'm probably basically against book monitoring of any kind. I haven't really been monitored and I would be pretty angry if someone started telling me what I could and couldn't read. Even in high school I felt that way. On the other hand, I never read anything really violent or pornographic with lots of explicit sex and gratuitous violence and maybe books like that do have a bad influence on society and cause men to think of women as sex objects or have nasty feelings. If I thought that were really true, I think I might be in favor of screening books, even if it did interfere with freedom to some extent.

But I also wonder who would be on the screening committee and how they would decide which books are suitable. Some books that we think are really good literature like *Ulysses* and *Catcher in the Rye* were banned at one time. I wouldn't want lots of books banned just because someone on the committee felt uncomfortable about them in some way and I know plenty of people who feel uncomfortable about anything—really uptight types. Next thing you know they'd start banning TV shows or movies or dating or whatever, even telling us how to dress.

Elisa looked over her preliminary response and noted a few main ideas: She, herself, had never been monitored about what she should or shouldn't read, although her mother had made suggestions and indicated disapproval. She realized that her immediate feeling about monitoring books was that she was probably against it. She noted that, in general, she was probably against being told what to do and wouldn't like it if the ban on books (one form of censorship) were to carry over into other forms (banning TV shows or telling people how to dress). She was also worried that censoring books could affect really good literature, as it had in the past. Moreover, she felt uneasy about who might be on such a committee and about their criteria for admitting or not admitting books. Still, she also realized that she felt strongly about the possibility that violent or pornographic books could have an adverse effect on women, and she discovered that she would be more likely to advocate the screening committee if she felt that there was a direct cause and effect relationship between reading books and committing violent actions.

Actually, at this point, Elisa felt a bit frustrated, because she really hadn't decided how she felt about the issue. She, herself, didn't like being told what to do, and if someone told her absolutely that she was not allowed to read a particular book, she would immediately feel like reading it. On the other hand, she didn't want to be in favor of something that would be detrimental to women. How could she decide what sort of essay to write?

At this stage in the writing process, Elisa's confusion is to be expected. She had not read anything about the subject and had written only an exploratory draft. That exploratory draft had enabled her to see several aspects of the topic and had therefore made her a bit confused. Nevertheless, it also enabled her to start asking important questions about the topic, and asking questions is an important step in developing a position.

Asking Key Questions

Elisa's initial writing enabled her to formulate some key questions that she would have to answer before she could take a stand or come up with a position. She could answer these questions both by additional thinking and by outside reading. Here are the questions Elisa felt she needed to answer before deciding what sort of response she would write:

Can reading books influence behavior? In what way?

Can violent or pornographic books influence men to feel negatively or violently about women? Can pornographic books cause promiscuous behavior? Are there other factors to consider?

Is it likely that a screening committee will be able to make the right decision about which books to include?

Is the censoring of high school books likely to affect other freedoms?

Sharing Ideas and Questions with Others

Sharing ideas and questions with others can also help you understand your assignment so that you can formulate your own position on a topic. Working in a group, Elisa had an opportunity to learn about how some of her classmates had responded to the preliminary questions, to see how their responses compared to her own.

Here is James's response to the preliminary questions:

```
Although our society is becoming more lenient, there are
still a large part of the population that holds onto
old-fashioned values and are teaching their kids the
difference between right and wrong. My parents always
stressed that we go along with family values and not be
influenced by radical ideas about morality, so they were
very careful to tell us what they felt was suitable or
```

unsuitable for us to read. I think they were right,
because it seems to me that people are influenced by
what they read. For example, my younger brother's
friends all read *Sports Illustrated, Car and Driver,* and
American Guns, and then they beg me to take them to the
rifle range and the batting cages and they love to look
and talk about cars. I think they get their ideas about
how to behave and about what they like to do, at least
some of them, from what they read.

    If I had to choose one word to describe how I was
raised, the word would be "traditional," and I never was
allowed to bring a book or a magazine into the house
that my parents thought was unsuitable. I guess I can
understand the attraction of some of these "modern"
novels, though, but I would worry how they would affect
young people, particularly the men. There is so much
violence these days anyway and so much junk on the
television and the videos, that kids don't need to read
about this stuff in books too. If I were a parent, I
would want to know that kids in the high school are not
reading anything that is going to make them even more
violent than they already are. And I certainly wouldn't
want my daughter reading books with a lot of sex in them
because she might get the wrong ideas.

At first, when Elisa read James' essay, she felt a bit disturbed. Here was a classmate of hers easily accepting a position on censorship without even worrying about loss of freedom or questioning if a relationship really exists between reading and behavior. She noticed that he seemed to accept that connection very easily, but that he never considered that the violence in our society, negative attitudes toward women, or tendencies toward promiscuity could possibly have very little or nothing to do with what people read. In fact, she thought, maybe it is possible that people read violent and pornographic stuff **because** they have these attitudes already. Then Elisa realized that reading James' response had helped her to understand that the issue of whether or not books can generate violent or demeaning attitudes toward women was really crucial to whether or not she was in favor of the screening committee. Unlike the argument about promiscuity, which she felt was unimportant, the issue of how books could affect men's attitudes toward women was the one she would have to focus on before she could develop her own position.

James' response helped Elisa understand her own idea of the topic more thoroughly. Then she read the response of another classmate, Angela, and became aware of another perspective:

```
My son is only five years old and isn't old enough to go to
high school yet. But I know that I wouldn't want him
reading some trash he found in the school library. When
I send my son to school, I expect that he will get a
good education and the right idea about how to behave. I
don't send him to school to pick up whatever turns him
on, and I know that trashy novels sometimes do appeal to
young kids, especially young men.
     When I think of a school, I think of a place where
someone is in charge of my child. Otherwise I wouldn't
send my child to that school. So I think it is a good
idea for a committee to make sure that filth and trash
don't get into the school library. Kids have plenty else
to read without reading that sort of thing in the
school. When they get older, then they can decide for
themselves what they want to read, and there won't be
anyone to stop them. I was raised with strict morals and
wasn't allowed to read junk.
     I don't let him watch violence on the TV either for
the same reasons. If parents don't take care of their
kids, the kids will turn out wild.
```

Reading Angela's preliminary thoughts on the topic, Elisa learned about how a parent might feel about this issue. She also realized that Angela had raised two other issues: the responsibility of the school toward upholding moral and behavioral values and the question of age in relation to freedom from censorship. Elisa had said that she, herself, as a high school student, would have felt angry if anyone had restricted her from reading something that interested her. But didn't her high school restrict her in other ways? She had had to adhere to a dress code, sit in certain areas of the cafeteria, attend classes at certain times, obey the rules. Maybe the high school did have the right to restrict her because they had assumed responsibility for her during the time she attended. If so, did that mean that they also had the right to restrict what she read?

Elisa also decided that she would talk to her father about some of the issues in the assignment. He was a member of a neighborhood yard beautification committee and had experience in working with groups of people. Here is what Elisa's father had to say:

I don't know much about the effect of pornography or violence. But I do know about committees. I can tell you—they attract some pretty weird people—usually people with an ax to grind of some sort. That guy down the street, McGafferty—he attends every meeting and every time he raises objections to every suggestion that anyone makes. He's got some set idea in his head about what this neighborhood should look like and he's driving us all crazy. I think that a screening committee at the school could probably attract the same kind of people.

Elisa's father helped her think about one of her preliminary questions: whether or not the screening committee would be able to make good decisions. Her father obviously did not think so.

Another person that Elisa talked to was Mrs. Phillips, the librarian at her local high school. Elisa wanted to find out how decisions were made about whether certain books were ordered and if books were regularly screened for "gratuitous violence" and "explicit sex." This is what the librarian had to say:

Most of our books are ordered for us because we are part of a state system. But sometimes I will go through a catalogue (I receive a large number of catalogues) and see a few books that I think would be particularly helpful. And if the budget allows, I'll order some of these. Sometimes, teachers will specifically request a book, or someone donates a pile of books when they move. But frankly, I can't possibly read all of the books that come in here, and my guess is that some of them might be considered "unsuitable" by some people. And I guess that's a problem. But my feeling is that even really trashy books are less harmful than movies and video, and I'm just glad when students read at all.

The librarian helped Elisa understand how books actually get admitted into a school library. She realized that to a certain extent books were already judged as "suitable" or "unsuitable" on the basis of catalogue descriptions. She also realized that the librarian did not seem concerned about "gratuitous violence" and "explicit sex" in books; she worried more about the effect of TV, videos, and films.

Understanding the Value Conflicts in the Assignment

The development of a position usually depends on a person's **values,** which may be defined as abstract ideas or standards of behavior that one considers important. Some common values that many of us probably share are tradition, ambition, security, honesty, responsibility, and freedom of speech. One might ask, then, if we all agree on fundamental values, how can we disagree on so many issues? The answer is that, although people may agree broadly that these values are important, they often disagree about the importance assigned to one value over that of another when controversial issues arise. Values, then, frequently come into conflict. In thinking about her position, Elisa noted that several of her own values came into conflict. On one hand, she very much valued freedom of speech. Yet she also felt that young people should be safe from harmful influences. Thus, for Elisa, the value she placed on freedom was in direct conflict with the value she placed on security. James and Angela, however, seemed to have less of a conflict. They did not seem worried about freedom, because they felt that security was more important. In times of stress or danger, many of us would also choose security over freedom. If, for example, a gang of killers were loose in the neighborhood and if, in the interest of public safety, a law has been passed that no one was allowed out on the street after ten P.M., we might feel that our freedom had been curtailed, but we might not mind very much because we might be more worried about safety.

What Elisa had to decide was whether or not she viewed books with "explicit sex" and "gratuitous violence" as threatening to safety in some way. Possibly, such books could have the effect of threatening the safety of women, and Elisa realized that this was a key issue for her. Thus, Elisa understood that in developing her position, she would have to decide which of her values was more important to her on this issue. Understanding the value conflicts in an assignment will help you develop a position for your paper.

READING OUTSIDE MATERIAL: SEQUENCED ASSIGNMENTS

Elisa's assignment is typical of the assignments in this book in that it required her to read several outside sources that would help her develop a position. Outside reading is usually helpful in giving you new ideas and perspectives, but it is important that you not only read the sources, but think about them and work with them so that you can use the ideas in them effectively. Elisa began to read outside sources after she had written an exploratory draft and thought seriously about her topic. Therefore, for Elisa, reading outside sources was a way of helping her to answer key questions about the topic.

Getting the Most Out of a Source

As will be discussed in a later chapter, incorporating sources for a researched paper does not mean simply that you sit down and read as many sources as possible, starting at the beginning of each one. Using a source in a paper means that you interact with it until you can either reject it or integrate it into your own point of view. One way to interact with an outside reading is to work with it—to paraphrase it, summarize it, and take notes on it; these skills are presented in some detail later in this book. Another way to enhance your understanding of a reading and of the issue in general is to write a response to it or to compare one source with another. A response to a reading or a set of readings might be found in an assignment such as the following:

Read Susan Brownmiller's essay "Pornography Hurts Women" and Ruth Mc-Gaffey's article "Porn Doesn't Cause Violence, But a Fear of New Ideas Does." Summarize each article. Then write a paragraph comparing the perspective of the two articles.

Here is the summary Elisa wrote of the Brownmiller article:

In her essay, "Pornography Hurts Women," Susan Brownmiller points out that although liberals are usually in favor of verbal freedom, even in cases of pornography, the "woman's perspective" makes it necessary for them to rethink that position, because pornography poses a real threat to women. Brownmiller asserts that most pornography dehumanizes women; it presents females as dirty and ridiculous simply to make men feel more powerful. Women today are in danger of rape, and it is quite possible that pornography contributes to crimes of sexual violence. Brownmiller feels that women should stop worrying about being pro-censorship on the issue of pornography.

This essay gave Elisa considerable pause for thought. Brownmiller apparently feels strongly that pornography does have the effect of threatening the safety of women. Yet, as Elisa thought further about this essay, she noticed that Brownmiller referred specifically to "stag" films. She hadn't mentioned books at all. Was it possible that reading books would not have the same effect as watching stag films? Anyway, Elisa thought, she didn't really believe that a school library would have a lot of books containing hard-core pornography. Elisa also discovered that the essay came from a book called *Against Our Will: Men, Women, and Rape.* She decided that since the aim of that book was to talk about rape, the position in the essay was probably somewhat extreme.

Elisa summarized Ruth McGaffey's article as follows:

McGaffey states that although she, herself, is not in favor of pornography or of advertisements that demean women or minorities, there is no scientific link between pornography and violent crimes against women. Men commit crimes against women because women are demeaned in our culture; pornography is simply an excuse. What is more dangerous than pornography is a fear of ideas.

After summarizing McGaffey's essay, which she noted had been written in 1986, Elisa noted that it claimed that no study had directly linked pornography with violent crimes against women. Elisa decided, then, that if she felt that McGaffey were correct, her essay would probably take a position *against* the idea of the screening committee. Writing summaries of these articles helped Elisa to understand them. She was then able to write the following paragraph comparing the two points of view:

```
Susan Brownmiller indicates that women ought to be firmly
against pornography, even if it violates their liberal
principles, because pornography dehumanizes women and
contributes to violent crimes against them. In contrast,
McGaffey feels that although pornography is indeed
demeaning to women, many other aspects of the culture
are equally demeaning, such as TV ads or the general
acceptance of men's power over women. McGaffey points
out that there is no proven link between pornography and
violent crime against women; moreover, she feels that
censorship of pornographic material would pose too great
a threat to freedom.
```

In preparation for writing her paper, Elisa also read the additional assigned readings. As she read, she summarized each source briefly and took notes. (These activities will be discussed in subsequent chapters.) She then found some information about the First Amendment.

At this point, Elisa decided that she was ready to formulate a preliminary position, and after giving the issue a lot of thought, she decided that her position would be something like the following:

```
I am against the formation of the screening committee
because I think it is dangerous to personal freedom. I
also do not think that reading books, even those with
"gratuitous violence" and "explicit sex," have been
shown to cause violent behavior.
```

After formulating that preliminary working thesis, Elisa jotted down some ideas she would address in her first draft. Some students, of course, like to write a formal outline. Elisa found that she was more comfortable jotting down the following ideas:

1. Discuss the First Amendment and the guarantee of freedom of speech and of the press to all citizens.

2. Discuss the question of whether or not high school students are citizens.
3. Discuss the possibility that one form of censorship can lead to another. (Use the Trippet article.)
4. Raise the question of whether a book can have a strong influence on behavior. (Use the McGaffey article.)

Here, then, is Elisa's first draft:

The First Amendment to the United States Bill of Rights states that "Congress shall make no law prohibiting or abridging the freedom of speech or of the press; or the right of the people peaceably to assemble, and to petition the Government for a redress of grievances." That amendment, which is so important to the concept of democracy, has come to mean that citizens of the United States should not be restricted about what they read. Therefore, I am against the screening committee because it would be in violation of the United States Constitution.

First of all, how many books are we talking about anyway? In my high school library, I have never seen a book that could even remotely be considered "unsuitable" in any way at all. Furthermore, Mrs. Gwendolyn Phillips, the librarian in the local high school, states that books are usually ordered by the state, by specific teachers, or librarians and that they act as a sort of screening committee anyway. If we think that another screening committee is necessary, doesn't that say something about our faith in our local school board, our librarians, and our teachers? After all, their main job is to examine the books for the library. Why would we think that we would need an additional committee?

Another point to consider is whether books really can influence human behavior, since there is a lot of doubt about whether or not this is really true. Ruth McGaffey points out that no link has been established "between pornography and violent crimes against women" (34) and that messages cannot "magically make people do things they wouldn't otherwise do" (34). If books cannot change behavior, then there seems to be no point to worrying about "explicit sex" and "gratuitous violence" in the school library.

Moreover, a screening committee to decide on books for the school library is a step in the direction of censorship. We think we live in a freedom—loving society. Yet, according to Frank Trippett in "The Growing Battle of the Books," "censorship has been on the rise in the United States for the past ten years. Every region of the country and every state has felt the flaring of the censorial spirit" (39). Because human beings tend to be suspicious of anything new or different from what they believe, people are all too ready to try to censor anything they perceive as threatening.

History has shown us that past attempts to censor books have resulted in the banning of some fine works of literature: *Catcher in the Rye, A Farewell to Arms, The Fixer,* just to name a few examples. We may be surprised that these fine works were judged as "unsuitable," but those who favor the censoring of books often have weird ideas about what is appropriate. Unfortunately, these are just the sort of people who would be in favor of a screening committee.

Young people are exposed to all sorts of influences. Television, rock videos, and movies all contain material that could possibly be judged "unsuitable." To worry about books in the school library seems silly.

In order for young people to become thinking, questioning adults who can function in a free society, they must be able to deal with a variety of ideas, even those with which they might disagree or find "unsuitable." Our country was founded on the principle of freedom of expression. The proposed screening committee for the high school library would not be consistent with the principles of a democratic society.

When Elisa looked over her first draft, she felt somewhat dissatisfied with it. Although it had a main point and several reasons in support of it, the paper seemed too short, not nearly detailed enough, as if she had left something out. It also didn't seem very interesting. She thought of herself as a lively person, with a distinct personality; yet most of the writing in this paper did not seem lively. Reading over her paper, she felt as if that paper could have been written by anyone. She had covered a lot of issues, but had not developed them very much. Also, her paper did not seem to have her own personal flavor of writing.

If, like Elisa, you are not pleased with your first drafts, you should be comforted by realizing that many first drafts, and sometimes even second and third drafts are unsatisfying in just these ways. But writing a first draft is a good beginning. Once you have that first draft, you can begin to revise it so that it will be more satisfying.

WHAT IS REVISION?

Many students think that revision means correcting the spelling, punctuation, grammar, and typographical errors. And that type of editing is certainly important at the final stage. But true revision of early drafts means what it says—a re-vision, that is, seeing the draft in a new way and rethinking how it could be improved. Thinking about the following questions might help your revision process:

Questions for Revisions

1. Are there **thesis problems?** Is the thesis too broad or too narrow? This is a very common problem, sometimes resulting in students giving only superficial attention to each supporting point. Is it possible to shape the thesis by assuming a particular point of view or direction? Is the thesis a statement of your individual perspective? The thesis statement should reflect the particular ideas of the writer.
2. Has the **context** or the background of the paper been adequately described or summarized, so that even a reader who knows nothing about the assignment would be able to understand the purpose of the paper?
3. Has the **audience** been taken into consideration? Is the paper written with a particular audience in mind? Does the paper address the concerns of that audience?
4. Are **reasons** given for the position? Do the reasons directly refer back to the thesis? Are those reasons supported with examples?
5. Is there a **personal voice?** Writing becomes interesting when the reader can sense a writer behind the prose. Do the style and the examples reflect a real person writing? Is the tone appropriate to the task?
6. Is there an acknowledgment of the **opposing point of view?** If not, the

reader may get the feeling that the writer either hasn't thought of the opposing viewpoint or is unable to deal with it.

7. Is there a need for additional **facts or information?** Papers weak on information and facts seem spongy. When you finish reading them, you feel as if you have been wallowing around in a tub of marshmallow.

Getting Help with a Revision

Many students have a great fear of showing their early drafts to anyone; they fear that the other person will think that the writing is poor or that the writer is not very intelligent. Yet sharing an early draft with another reader can be extremely useful in helping you to decide how to revise. Some colleges and universities have Writing Labs or Centers where you can bring your paper and work with a writing consultant or tutor on how to revise it. If no Writing Center is available, you might have a friend read it. Often, you, yourself, are so close to a paper that you cannot see where it has loose ends or needs further development. But an outside person will be able to detect such problems more easily.

Before she revised her paper, Elisa brought her first draft and the revision questions to her college Writing Center. There, she and a writing consultant looked over the revision questions and talked about how to revise the paper. They decided that the thesis statement did not really reflect what Elisa, herself, wanted to say, in that it gave the impression that the entire paper would be concerned with how the screening committee would violate the rights specified in the U.S. Constitution. Yet Elisa wanted her paper to address several issues beyond that particular idea, in particular the idea that young people cannot become thinking adults if someone does their thinking for them. Elisa and the writing consultant also agreed that her thesis did not reflect her individual perspective, in that it seemed to be concerned only with the Constitution. They also noted that in her paper's introduction she had not adequately prepared the reader for what the paper was about. In reading her first paragraph, someone not familiar with the situation would be likely to say, "What screening committee?"

In response to the question about personal voice, Elisa and the writing consultant agreed that she had not incorporated any of the material from her prewriting questions and decided that if she did so, her draft might feel more "personal." Elisa thought that she might use some of this material as examples (in response to Question 3). In showing her paper to the writing consultant, Elisa also noted that in some places her tone seemed inappropriate, somewhat strident, as if she were having a real argument.

An important question, which the writing consultant asked Elisa, was concerned with the question of audience. "Who are you writing this paper for?" the consultant asked, and at first Elisa was tempted to answer flippantly that, of course, she was writing the paper to fulfill the requirements of a writing class. But then, she considered the question more seriously and realized that her audience would most likely be parents in the community who would be voting on whether or not to establish a screening committee. These parents might be like Angela, who, Elisa recalled, had written that she didn't send her son to school "to pick up whatever turns him on." To address an audience of concerned adults, then, Elisa might wish to refer to fears they might have about the effects of unrestricted reading.

Furthermore, the writing consultant pointed out that she had not dealt at all with the opposing viewpoint (the Brownmiller perspective, for example) nor had she even discussed reasons why anyone would feel the need for a screening committee. After her discussion with the writing consultant, Elisa also decided that she would look over the readings again to see if there was anything she had overlooked.

Revising, then, means to make **substantial changes,** not just to correct surface error. Sometimes you can reread a draft and decide right away how to make substantial changes. Frequently, though, you will get suggestions or **feedback** about revising a draft, if you read it aloud to someone else or let someone else read it. Exchanging drafts with a classmate or roommate or working with a consultant in a Writing Center as Elisa did might give you some ideas for revision. Fortunately, Elisa was able to receive a great deal of feedback, both from her classmates and from the writing consultant she saw. As a result of that feedback, and after much rethinking and rewriting, Elisa decided to revise her paper as follows:

1. Introduce a personal voice right in the beginning.
2. Introduce the situation so the reader understands it. (Set the context.)
3. Develop some additional ideas beside those of the Constitution.
4. Consider the audience.
5. Address the opposing viewpoint and argue against it.

Here is a copy of Elisa's first draft, with some notes and marks that indicate what she and the writing consultant wanted to change:

```
The First Amendment to the United States
Bill of Rights states that "Congress shall
make no law respecting or abridging the
freedom of speech." That amendment, which
is so important to the concept of democ-
racy, has come to mean that citizens of the
United States should not be restricted
about what they read. Therefore, I am
against the screening committee because it
would be in violation of the United States
Constitution.
      First of all, how many books are we
```

*No context set.
What screening committee*

*Too strident
a tone*

talking about anyway? In my high school library, I have never seen a book that could
even remotely be considered "unsuitable" in   *nothing to do with issue*
any way at all. Furthermore, Mrs. Gwendolyn
Phillips, the librarian in the local high
school, states that books are usually ordered by the state, by specific teachers, or
librarians and that they act as a sort of
screening committee anyway. If we think
that another screening committee is necessary, doesn't that say something about our
faith in our local school board, our librarians, and our teachers? After all,
their main job is to examine the books for
the library. Why would we think that we
would need an additional committee?

Another point to consider is whether
books really can influence human behavior,   *Develop idea in terms of violence and promiscuity*
since there is a lot of doubt about whether
or not this is really true. Ruth McGaffey
points out that no link has been established "between pornography and violent
crimes against women" (34) and that messages cannot "magically make people do
things they wouldn't otherwise do" (34). If
books cannot change behavior, then there
seems to be no point to worrying about "explicit sex" and "gratuitous violence" in
the school library.

Moreover, a screening committee to decide on books for the school library is a
step in the direction of censorship. We
think we live in a freedom—loving society.
Yet, according to Frank Trippett in "The
Growing Battle of the Books," "censorship   *develop this idea*
has been on the rise in the United States

for the past ten years. Every region of the
country and every state has felt the flaring of the censorial spirit" (39). Because
human beings tend to be suspicious of anything new or different from what they believe, people are all too ready to try to
censor anything they perceive as threatening.

History has shown us that past attempts
to censor books have resulted in the banning of some fine works of literature such as
Catcher in the Rye, A Farewell to Arms, and
The Fixer. We may be surprised that these
fine works were judged as "unsuitable," but
those who favor the censoring of books of-
ten have weird ideas about what is appro-   *vague term—*
define it
priate. Unfortunately, these are just the
sort of people who would be in favor of a   *doesn't address*
thesis
screening committee.

Young people are exposed to all sorts of   *No opposing view*
influences. Television, rock videos, and   *considered*
movies all contain material that could pos-
sibly be judged "unsuitable." To worry   *this idea is not*
about books in the school library seems   *mentioned in*
silly.   *Poor word choice*   *the thesis*

In order for young people to become
thinking, questioning adults who can function in a free society, they must be able
to deal with a variety of ideas, even those
with which they might disagree or find "unsuitable." Our country was founded on the
principle of freedom of expression. The
proposed screening committee for the high
school library would not be consistent
with the principles of a democratic
society.

Then, after thinking about the changes she wanted to make, and perhaps redrafting it several more times, Elisa rewrote her paper as follows:

When I was about 14 years old, I was looking for a dictionary in my brother's bookcase, when I came upon a well-thumbed novel, *The Catcher in the Rye.* I was already familiar with the title, because one of my brother's friends had mentioned it. But since I had not read it myself, I opened it and began reading it. That afternoon, when I discovered *The Catcher in the Rye,* was one of the most wonderful reading experiences of my life, and I always remember it when I think about the issue of censoring books for young people.

Recently, a group of concerned parents has proposed the idea of a committee to screen recent acquisitions to the local high school library. These parents claim that several recently acquired books contain explicit sex and gratuitous violence and that these books are unsuitable for their children to read. My feeling, though, is that although this proposal may be motivated by genuine parental concern, there is little evidence to suggest that unrestricted reading is a direct cause of violent or promiscuous behavior. More importantly, such a screening committee would be a dangerous step in the direction of censorship and would also generate a restrictive educational climate, which is unsuitable for preparing students to function in a democratic society. Finally, it would deprive students of the pleasures of discovering books for themselves.

The First Amendment to the United States Bill of Rights states that "Congress shall make no law respecting an establishment of religion or prohibiting the free exercise thereof, or abridging the freedom of speech." That amendment, fundamental to the concept of a free society, has come to mean that citizens of the United States have the liberty of reading anything they choose. High school students are only a few years away from assuming full rights as citizens, with all of the responsibilities that citizenship brings. Very soon after high school graduation, these students will be eligible to vote and to serve in the military, and many of them will have full-time jobs. By censoring what students are able to read, therefore, the proposed screening committee would deprive the local high school students of their rights as citizens.

Some may argue, of course, that screening a few books in a local high school library is a very small violation of First Amendment rights. Yet even a small violation such as this can be regarded as a step in the direction of censorship, and any form of censorship jeopardizes free thought. We think we live in a liberal age, in which freedom is taken for granted. Yet, according to Frank Trippett in "The Growing Battle of the Books," "censorship has been on the rise in the United States for the past ten years. Every region of the country and every state has felt the flaring of the censorial spirit" (39). Because human beings tend to be suspicious of anything new or different from what they believe, people are all too ready to censor anything they perceive as threatening. Surely, this is not an example that should be set in high school.

One form of censorship can very easily lead to another, perhaps more dangerous, form because of the suspiciousness of human nature. History has shown us that past attempts to censor books has resulted in the banning of some famous and highly acclaimed works of literature, *Catcher in the Rye*, *A Farewell to Arms*, and *The Fixer*, just to name a few examples. We may be surprised that these fine works were judged as "unsuitable," but each age has its own particular notions of propriety and suitability. Those who advocate censoring books are usually those who have very fixed ideas about what is appropriate; often it is only a very small group that feels strongly enough to argue for censorship, and it is this minority that attempts to impose its own views on the majority. Minority rule is also in direct opposition to the concept of democracy.

To some extent, high school is the place where students receive their preparation for becoming citizens, since, for many, this is their last opportunity for formal education. Being a citizen in a democracy means being able to make decisions, to decide for oneself between right and wrong. As Ruth McGaffey points out, "a self-governing people must be able to discuss all ideas regardless of how repulsive they might be" (52). "Instead of worrying about all the dangerous ideas and pictures and films in the world, we should be worrying about developing minds that are comfortable with uncertainty and complexity, not obedient minds" (52). The idea of a screening committee is in direct opposition to the idea of developing minds because it implies that students are incapable of dealing with ideas that might make them uncomfortable. This is not an environment that is likely to prepare its citizens for responsible participation in society.

Moreover, it is highly unlikely that high school students are exposed to much "gratuitous violence" and "explicit sex" in the school library. Mrs. Gwendolyn Phillips, school librarian, states that books are usually ordered by the state, by specific teachers, or librarians, and that the selection process is very much like a screening anyway. We have delegated responsibility for our children to school boards, teachers, and school librarians because their education and experience have qualified them for our trust. This is not a trust we can assume that a self-selected group of parents can handle as well.

Of course, those in favor of the screening committee may point to the increasing violence in our society, particularly that against women, which, some say, can be triggered by pornographic material. Susan Brownmiller points out that "pornography is the undiluted essence of anti-female propaganda," (7) and she suggests that pornographic material could well be "a causative factor in crimes of sexual violence" (7). However, in that same article, Brownmiller also states that the President's Commission on Obscenity and Pornography "maintained that it was not possible at this time to scientifically prove or disprove such a connection." (7) This position is supported by a Danish study (*New York Times,* Nov. 9, 1970), which "finds that sex crimes have sharply declined in Denmark . . . in the three years since censorship laws have been eased there" (Kauffmann 136). Given that there is no proof that reading about sex and violence directly leads to the commission of sexually related violent crimes or to promiscuous behavior, it would seem unwise for the high school library to jeopardize the First Amendment rights of its students by the formation of a screening committee.

My "discovery" of *The Catcher in the Rye* when I was 14 years old is just one example of the pleasure I now associate with books. Moreover, I am very glad that my own reading was not restricted in high school, since I now feel capable of dealing with a variety of ideas, even those with which I might disagree or find "unsuitable." As a college student who will soon be considered a legal adult, I feel strongly that the proposed screening committee for the high school library would not be beneficial either for students or for the quality of society.

For Consideration

Compare Elisa's final draft with her first. Can you point to the features of the final draft that you feel are an improvement over the first one? Is there any aspect of the final draft that you feel needs additional revision?

Following is an example of another student paper. Compare this with Elisa's paper as well.

Samantha Rizzo   Composition 102

                    Book Banning

Due to our rights stated in the First Amendment and
because of the complexity of determining what is
obscene, no committee should ever be formed to censor or
ban books that presumably contain violence and/or
sexually explicit material. Although individual families
have the right to distinguish what is good from what is
evil for their own children, they do not have the right
to distinguish this for everyone else's children. What
is considered offensive reading to some does not apply
to all. What influences one child may or may not
influence another. Parents should relay a variety of
books to their children so that the children,
themselves, will be able to decide what is worthwhile
reading.

     The first amendment of our Constitution, our Bill of
Rights, states that we have freedom of speech. There are
certain inalienable rights that we all have to protect.
Banning books infringes upon these rights. If this right
to freely express a view in a book is taken away, then
nothing can protect us from the repression of new ideas.

Frank Trippet, author of "The Growing Battle of the Books," refers to this repression as a chill. He states, ". . .the chill, whether intellectual, political, moral, or artistic, is invariably hazardous to the open traffic in ideas that not only nourishes a free society but defines its essence" (195). The First Amendment allows us to debate ideas that may or may not be offensive to us. Books allow different authors to express their ideas for the enrichment of our life as members of American society.

With so many different authors and their books, there are many ideas revealed that reader interpret. Similarly, readers have many different interpretations of books. Which reader has the correct interpretation? There are those who want to ban books because they believe them to be obscene or pornographic. Each person has his own definition of pornography. To one, it may be reading about dehumanizing sex acts often seen in XXX movies. To another, it may be the mention of the word "sex." The point is, where does one draw the line, that is, if one had that right to begin with? No one person can decide what book should or should not be banned. A consequence of banning could be the slow installment of one person's ideas. If this were to occur, there would be no more free flow of ideas.

Who are those people who think they can decide what books should be banned? Most are trying to protect others' children from something they know little or nothing about. As Loudon Wainwright points out, most censors never read what it is they want to ban. In "A Little Banning is a Dangerous Thing," Wainwright states that "Vonnegut (author of controversial book *Slaughterhouse-Five*) among others, suspects that a lot of censors never even get around to reading the books they suppress" (490). In the essay, "The Growing Battle of the Books," it was revealed that "one school board banned 'Making It With Mademoiselle,' but reversed the decision after finding out it was a how-to pattern book for youngsters hoping to learn dress making" (Trippet 195). It has also been seen that censors primarily represent the Moral Majority and want to control what is close to their lives, even though they may feel it is uncontrollable. As stated by the essayist, Frank Trippet, ". . .the ultimate purpose of all censorship is mind control, just as surely as the burning of books dramatizes a yearning latent in every consecrated censor" (197).

Of course, one may argue that the censors try to control the traffic of books in schools because they value the integrity of a community good and assume that what a person reads influence his or her behavior. Susan Brownmiller, a strong feminist and author of "Pornography Hurts Women," states that "public opinion seems to be swinging to the position that explicit violence in the entertainment media does have a deleterious effect" (387) as her proof that people are influenced by what they see. Although she is referring to media and not books, the same concept of pornography's influence applies, and the only proof she has is a weak "public opinion seems to be. . .." The fact is that there is no real proof that watching, hearing, or reading explicitly violent or sexual material influences a child. Ruth McGaffey reveals that "modern communication research indicates that the response of any audience to a message depends more upon the predisposition of the audience than upon the power of the speaker, writer, or film-maker (181). In my childhood experience, I can honestly say that my friends and I were not influenced to hurt other children after reading some book or watching a cartoon for that matter. The only kid I knew who left school because he had uncontrolled behavior also had a personality problem that led him to act out. It is an easy excuse to blame a book for the behavior of someone who is innately uncontrollable.

The best way to positively influence a child is not by banning books, but by a family's love and support. Banning books will only make children want to read them more. A family with set values that a child recognizes will be enough support to let him choose what to read. Two sociologists on the Lockhart commission, a Danish study of sex crimes, said they "would rather rely on informal social controls and improvements in sex education and better understanding of human sexual behavior than on ambiguous and arbitrary administrative laws" (Kauffmann 137). If children were given a more open view of human sexuality, censors would not have to be afraid of a dehumanizing sexually explicit influence in books, because children would know the reality of sex. Books should offer children a chance to experience the rich, complicated, and difficult aspects of life. Reading about sex and violence could spark discussions allowing personal values to form or change. That is something book banning should not be allowed to squelch.

Works Cited

Brownmiller, Susan. "Pornography Hurts Women." *Against Our Wills*. New York: Simon & Schuster, 1975.
Kauffmann, Stanley. "Pornography and Censorship." *The Public Interest* 22 (Winter 1971): Copyright by National Affairs, Inc.
McGaffey, Ruth. "Porn Doesn't Cause Violence, but a Fear of New Ideas Does." *The Milwaukee Journal* 28 Sept. 1986.
Trippett, Frank. "The Growing Battle of the Books." *Time* 31 July 1989: 71–72.
Wainwright, Loudon. "A Little Banning Is a Dangerous Thing." *Life* 1982.

▶ **Writing Assignment:** Recently there has been considerable discussion about whether or not rock videos ought to bear labels, making it a crime for them to be sold to anyone under 18 years old. Develop a position in which you argue either for or against the use of such labels.

POINTS TO CONSIDER

Discuss your familiarity with rock videos. Do you think that exposure to sex and violence in rock videos is more harmful than that experienced in books?

Do you think that the label requirement is a dangerous step in the direction of censorship?

Can you use any of Elisa's reasons to develop your position? If not, what additional reasons can you find?

FOR FURTHER RESEARCH

Find three articles in the library concerned with the issue of censorship for rock videos. Consider the extent to which they support your position.

A Little Banning Is a Dangerous Thing

Loudon Wainwright

My own introduction to sex in reading took place about 1935, I think, just when the fertile soil of my young mind was ripe for planting. The exact place it happened (so I've discovered from checking the source in my local library) was the middle of page 249, in a chapter titled "Apples and Ashes," soon after the beginning of Book III of a mildly picaresque novel called *Anthony Adverse*. The boy Anthony, 16, and a well-constructed character named Faith Paleologus ("Her shoulders if one looked carefully were too wide. But so superb was the bosom that rose up to support them. . . .") made it right there in her apartment where he'd gone to take a quick bath, thinking (ho-ho) that she was out.

Faith was Anthony's sitter, sort of, and if author Hervey Allen was just a touch obscure about the details of their moon-drenched meeting, I filled in the gaps. "He was just in time," Allen wrote, "to see the folds of her dress rustle down from her knees into coils at her feet.... He stood still, rooted. The faint aroma of her body floated to him. A sudden tide of passion dragged at his legs. ... He was half blind, and speechless now. All his senses had merged into one feeling.... To be supported and yet possessed by an ocean of unknown blue depths below you and to cease to think! Yes, it was something like swimming on a transcendent summer night."

Wow! Praying that my parents wouldn't come home and catch me reading this terrific stuff, I splashed ahead, line after vaguely lubricious line, exhilarated out of my mind at Anthony's good fortune. "After a while he was just drifting in a continuous current of ecstasy that penetrated him as if he were part of the current in which he lay." I still don't understand *that* line, but I sure feel the old surge of depravity. And reading it again, I thank God there was no righteous book banner around at the time to snatch it from me. *Anthony Adverse* doesn't rank as literature, or even required reading, but I'm convinced it served a useful, even educational, purpose for me at the time.

Alert vigilantes of the printed word worked hard to suppress the novel then. The wretched little war to keep the minds of children clean is always going on. In fact, it has heated up considerably since President Reagan came to power, with libraries around the country reporting a threefold increase in demands that various volumes even less ruinous than *Anthony Adverse* be withdrawn. School boards, too, are feeling the cleansing fire of assorted crusaders against dirty words and irreverent expressions of one sort or another. Protesters range from outraged individual parents to teachers to local ministers to such well-organized watchdog outfits as the Gabler family of Texas, Washington's Heritage Foundation and, of course, the Moral Majority.

The victims are fighting back. Writers are leading public "read-ins" of their banned works. One school board case, which actually dates to 1976, has gone all the way to the U.S. Supreme Court. Before the end of the current term, the court is expected to rule on whether or not the First Amendment rights (to free expression) of five students in Island Trees, N.Y., were denied when the board took nine books out of circulation. A far more personal thrust against censorship was made recently by author Studs Terkel. At the news that his book *Working* was in danger of being banned in Girard, Pa., Terkel went there and standing before the whole school in assembly made his own eloquent case for the book, for the so-called bad language in it and for reading in general. Six weeks later the school board voted unanimously to keep *Working* in the reading program where it had initially been challenged. Presumably they were persuaded, in part at least, that Terkel was *not,* as Kurt Vonnegut wrote in a furious and funny defense of his own *Slaughterhouse-Five,* one of those "sort of ratlike people who enjoy making money from poisoning the minds of young people."

What gets me is the weird presumption that the book banners actually know something about the minds of young people. Vonnegut, among others, suspects that a lot of censors never even get around to reading the books they suppress. And just the briefest scanning of the list of titles currently banned or under threat in various communities calls the banners' credentials to rude question. *The Scarlet Letter, The Great Gatsby, A Farewell to Arms, Huckleberry Finn, The Grapes of Wrath* are a few of the variously seminal works challenged as somehow being dangerous to the stability of impressionable young minds. *Mary Poppins* and *The American Heritage Dictionary* have been under attack, too, the former after protests that its black characters were stereotypes, the latter presumably as a storehouse of words that shouldn't be viewed by innocent eyes, much less defined.

More critically, the censors forget, if they ever knew, many of the needs of childhood. One, obviously, is the need for privacy, for a place to get away from the real world, a place where one is safe from—among other things—difficult or boring adult demands. The world that a reader makes is a perfect secret world. But if its topography is shaped by adults pushing their own hardened views of life, the secret world is spoiled.

Yet the world of the young human mind is by no means a comfy habitat, as much as a lot of interfering adults would like to shape it that way. In *The Uses of Enchantment,* Bruno Bettelheim's book about the great importance of folk and fairy tales to child development, the author writes: "There is a widespread refusal to let children know that the source of much that goes wrong in life is due to our very own natures—the propensity of all men for acting aggressively, asocially, selfishly, out of anger and anxiety. Instead, we want our children to believe that, inherently, all men are good. But children know that *they* are not always good; and often, even when they are, they would prefer not to be." In the fantasies commonly churned out in the mind of a normal child, whatever that is, bloody acts of revenge and conquest, daredevil assaults and outlandish wooings are common currency. To achieve the bleak, cramped, sanitized, fear-ridden state of many adults takes years of pruning and repression.

Books, as everyone but the censors knows, stimulate growth better than anything—better than sit-coms, better than *Raiders of the Lost Ark,* better than video games. Many books, to be sure, are dreadful heaps of trash. But most of these die quickly in the marketplace or become best-sellers incapable of harming the adults who buy them.

It's often the best books that draw the beadiest attention of the censors. These are the books that really have the most to offer, the news that life is rich and complicated and difficult. Where else, for example, could a young male reader see the isolation of his painful adolescence reflected the way it is in *The Catcher in the Rye,* one of the *most* banned books in American letters. In the guise of fiction, books offer opportunities, choices and plausible models. They light up the whole range of human character and emotion. Each, in its own way, tells the truth and prepares its eager readers for the unknown and unpredictable events of their own lives.

Anthony Adverse, my first banned book, was just a huge potboiler of the period. Still, it tickled my fantasy. And it sharpened my appetite for better stuff, like *Lady Chatterley's Lover.* Actually I didn't read that tender and wonderful book until I was almost 50. I wish I'd read it much sooner while we were both still hot.

The Growing Battle of the Books

Frank Trippett

Written words running loose have always presented a challenge to people bent on ruling others. In times past, religious zealots burned heretical ideas and heretics with impartiality. Modern tyrannies promote the contentment and obedience of their subjects by ruthlessly keeping troubling ideas out of their books and minds. Censorship can place people in bondage more efficiently than chains.

Thanks to the First Amendment, the U.S. has been remarkably, if not entirely, free of such official monitoring. Still, the nation has always had more than it needs of voluntary censors, vigilantes eager to protect everybody from hazards like ugly words, sedition, blasphemy, unwelcome ideas and, perhaps worst of all, reality. Lately, however, it has been easy to assume that when the everything-goes New Permissiveness gusted forth in the 1960s, it blew the old book-banning spirit out of action for good.

Quite the contrary. In fact, censorship has been on the rise in the U.S. for the past ten years. Every region of the country and almost every state has felt the flaring of the censorial spirit. Efforts to ban or squelch books in public libraries and schools doubled in number, to 116 a year, in the first five years of the 1970s over the last five of the 1960s—as Author L. B. Woods documents in *A Decade of Censorship in America—The Threat to Classrooms and Libraries, 1966–1975.* The upsurge in book banning has not since let up, one reason being that some 200 local, state and national organizations now take part in skirmishes over the contents of books circulating under public auspices. The American Library Association, which has been reporting an almost yearly increase in censorial pressures on public libraries, has just totted up the score for 1980. It found, without surprise, yet another upsurge: from three to five episodes a week to just as many in a day. Says Judith Krug, director of the A.L.A.'s Office for Intellectual Freedom: "This sort of thing has a chilling effect."

That, of course, is precisely the effect that censorship always intends. And the chill, whether intellectual, political, moral or artistic, is invariably hazardous to the open traffic in ideas that not only nourishes a free society but defines its essence. The resurgence of a populist censorial spirit has, in a sense, sneaked up on the nation. National attention has focused on a few notorious censorship cases, such as the book-banning crusade that exploded into life-threatening violence in Kanawha County, W. Va., in 1974. But most kindred episodes that have been cropping up all over have remained localized and obscure. The Idaho Falls, Idaho, school book review committee did not make a big splash when it voted, 21 to 1, to ban *One Flew Over the Cuckoo's Nest*—in response to one parent's objection to some of the language. It was not much bigger news when Anaheim, Calif., school officials authorized a list of *approved* books that effectively banned many previously studied books, including Richard Wright's classic *Black Boy.* And who recalls the Kanawha, Iowa, school board's banning *The Grapes of Wrath* because some scenes involved prostitutes?

Such cases, numbering in the hundreds, have now been thoroughly tracked down and sorted out by English Education Professor Edward B. Jenkinson of Indiana University in a study, *Censors in the Classroom—The Mind Benders.* He began digging into the subject after he became chairman of the Committee Against Censorship of the National Council of Teachers of English. His 184-page report reviews hundreds of cases (notorious and obscure), suggests the scope of censorship activity (it is ubiquitous), discusses the main censorial tactics (usually pure power politics) and points to some of the subtler ill effects. Popular censorship, for one thing, induces fearful teachers and librarians to practice what Jenkinson calls "closet censorship." The targets of the book banners? Jenkinson answers the question tersely: "Nothing is safe."

Case histories make that easy to believe. The books that are most often attacked would make a nice library for anybody with broad-gauged taste. Among them: *Catcher in the Rye, Brave New World, Grapes of Wrath, Of Mice and Men, Catch-22, Soul on Ice,* and *To Kill a Mockingbird. Little Black Sambo* and *Merchant of Venice* run into recurring protests based on suspicions that the former is anti-black, the latter anti-Semitic. One school board banned *Making It with Mademoiselle,* but reversed the decision after finding out it was a how-to pattern book for youngsters hoping to learn dress-making. Authorities in several school districts have banned the *American Heritage Dictionary* not only because it contains unacceptable words but because some organizations, the Texas Daughters of the American Revolution among them, have objected to the sexual intimations of the definition of the word bed as a transitive verb.

Censorship can, and often does, lead into absurdity, though not often slapstick absurdity like the New Jersey legislature achieved in the 1960s when it enacted a subsequently vetoed antiobscenity bill so explicit that it was deemed too dirty to be read in the legislative chambers without clearing out the public first. The mother in Whiteville, N.C., who demanded that the Columbus County library keep adult books out of the hands of children later discovered that her own daughter had thereby been made ineligible to check out the Bible. One group, a Florida organization called Save Our Children, has simplified its censorship goals by proposing to purge from libraries all books by such reputed homosexuals as Emily Dickinson, Willa Cather, Virginia Woolf, Tennessee Williams, Walt Whitman and John Milton.

Most often, censors wind up at the ridiculous only by going a very dangerous route. The board of the Island Trees Union Free School District on Long Island, N.Y., in a case still being contested by former students in court, banned eleven books as "anti-American, anti-Christian, anti-Semitic and just plain filthy." Later they discovered that the banished included two Pulitzer prizewinners: Bernard Malamud's *The Fixer* and Oliver La Farge's *Laughing Boy.* For censors to ban books they have never read is commonplace. For them to deny that they are censoring is even more so. Said Attorney George W. Lipp Jr., announcing plans to continue the legal fight for the Island Trees board: "This is not book burning or book banning but a rational effort to transmit community values."

Few censors, if any, tend to see that censorship itself runs counter to certain basic American values. But why have so many people with such an outlook begun lurching forth so aggressively in recent years? They quite likely have always suffered the censorial impulse. But they have been recently emboldened by the same resurgent moralistic mood that has enspirited evangelical fundamentalists and given form to the increasingly outspoken constituency of the Moral Majority. At another level, they probably hunger for some power over something, just as everybody supposedly does these days. Thus they are moved, as American Library Association President Peggy Sullivan says, "by a desperation to feel some control over what is close to their lives."

Americans are in no danger of being pushed back to the prudery of the 19th century. The typical U.S. newsstand, with its sappy pornutopian reek, is proof enough of that, without even considering prime-time TV. But the latter-day inflamed censor is no laughing matter. One unsettling feature of the current censorial vigilantism is its signs of ugly inflammation. There is, for instance, the cheerily incendiary attitude expressed by the Rev. George A. Zarris, chairman of the Moral Majority in Illinois. Says Zarris "I would think moral-minded people might object to books that are philosophically alien to what they believe. If they have the books and feel like burning them, fine." The notion of book burning is unthinkable to many and appalling to others, if only because it brings to mind the rise of Adolf Hitler's Germany—an event marked by widespread bonfires fed by the works of scores of writers including Marcel Proust, Thomas Mann, H.G. Wells and Jack London.

Unthinkable? In fact, the current wave of censorship has precipitated two of the most outrageous episodes of book burning in the U.S. since 1927, when Chicago Mayor William ("Big Bill") Thompson, an anglophobe miffed by a view sympathetic to the British, had a flunky put the torch on the city hall steps to one of Historian Arthur Schlesinger Sr.'s books. In Drake, N. Dak., the five-member school board in 1973 ordered the confiscation and burning of three books that, according to Professor Jenkinson, none of the members had read: Kurt Vonnegut's *Slaughterhouse Five,* James Dickey's *Deliverance* and an anthology of short stories by writers like Joseph Conrad, John Steinbeck and William Faulkner. Said the school superintendent later: "I don't regret it one bit, and we'd do it again. I'm just sorry about all the publicity that we got." In Warsaw, Ind., a gaggle of citizens in 1977 publicly burned 40 copies of *Values Clarifications,* a textbook, as a show of support for a school board that decided to ban both written matter and independent-minded teachers from its system. Said William I. Chapel, a member of that board: "The bottom line is: Who will control the minds of the students?"

An interesting question. It baldly reveals the ultimate purpose of all censorship—mind control—just as surely as the burning of books dramatizes a yearning latent in every consecrated censor. The time could not be better for recalling something Henry Seidel Canby wrote after Big Bill Thompson put Arthur Schlesinger to the flame. Said Canby: "There will always be a mob with a torch ready when someone cries, 'Burn those books!'" The real bottom line is: How many more times is he going to be proved right?

Porn Doesn't Cause Violence, but a Fear of New Ideas Does

Ruth McGaffey

I must respond to the Meese Commission's Report on Pornography as well as several comments that have appeared in these pages regarding pornography and censorship. My purpose is not to defend pornography, but if my commitment to the First Amendment makes that necessary, I am willing to do so.

I find much pornography disgusting as well as demeaning to women. The same is true of much commercial advertising, including the ring-around-the-collar commercial. Both depict a woman I do not like.

I also find racist stereotypes offensive. I think uninformed people, ignorant students and religious bigots are offensive. When I taught at Northwestern University last semester and had to live in Chicago, I found Chicago Bear fans repulsive. Neither the First Amendment nor any other part of the Constitution, however, guarantees me a right to live without being offended. Those who would ban sexually explicit material are no different from those who would censor Huckleberry Finn because of racist stereotypes, those who criticize other books because of sexist stereotypes and still others who object to curriculum materials because of offensive ideas on religion or values.

Americans are scared stiff of ideas and people with whom they disagree. We have presecuted all sorts of religious and political groups. We are afraid that these strange groups will influence us and, worst of all, will influence our children.

Those who fear sexually explicit material rejoice in the Meese Commission's report because it agrees with their intuitive fear of pornography. They believe that it has established a link between pornography and violent crimes against women. Yet no respectable social scientist would agree.

Fear of pornography or any other sort of message is based on the theory that messages can magically make people do things they wouldn't otherwise do. That theory is not true. People don't change their behavior very easily. After 30 years of research, scholars have not been able to prove that even subliminal persuasion works. Nor has research on brainwashing shown that to be effective. Modern communication research indicates that the response of any audience to a message depends more upon the predisposition of the audience than upon the power of the speaker, writer, or film-maker. People generally search out information that supports what they already believe. The danger is much more acute when people are not exposed to all kinds of ideas. Then, without experience in questioning ideas, without a "critical mind," they may be more easily persuaded. Researchers believe, for example, that the apparent success of some totalitarian propaganda results not from some magic techniques but from a monopoly control over information.

Ruth McGaffey, "Porn Doesn't Cause Violence, but a Fear of New Ideas Does," *The Milwaukee Journal,* September 28, 1986. Reprinted by permission of the author.

What kind of ideas do rapists and child abusers and wife beaters already have? What we might find by looking at their testimony is that this society really believes that men have the right to make decisions for women. Analysis of the background of wife beaters does not reveal pornography, but rather parents who considered women's role to be appropriately subordinate to men. I have met very well-educated women who don't work or go to school because "My husband won't let me." Grown women who think they have to have permission to do something for themselves are sick, and the men who assert that dominance are sicker. It is not much of a jump from that attitude to believing that men have a right to control women sexually. An amazing number of men admit that they would rape if they could get away with it. Date and marital rape are common. It is highly simplistic to say that pornography either caused this widespread cultural attitude or that it causes acts of violence.

Furthermore, that claim is counterproductive. It allows men to excuse their actions. We laugh when we hear "the devil made me do it," but saying that "pornography made me do it" is exactly the same thing.

Instead of worrying about all the dangerous ideas and pictures and films in the world, we should be worrying about developing minds that are comfortable with uncertainty and complexity, not obedient minds. We must teach our children to question what they are told even when it comes from us. In this society we have rejected the elitist notion that some should make choices for others. That at least is the theory of the First Amendment.

Our Founding Fathers did not envision a nation of cowards. Freedom of expression was put in a primary position in the Bill of Rights because a self-governing people must be able to discuss all ideas regardless of how repulsive they might be. Anti-Jewish, anti-black or anti-Catholic statements offend most decent Americans. Swastikas as well as the white sheets of the KKK and the pornography of *Hustler* are not only offensive but also frightening to the majority of our people. These ideas we hate, however, must be protected if the marketplace of ideas is to survive for those ideas we love.

Pornography Hurts Women

Susan Brownmiller

Pornography has been so thickly glossed over with the patina of chic these days in the name of verbal freedom and sophistication that important distinctions between freedom of political expression (a democratic necessity), honest sex education for children (a societal good) and ugly smut (the deliberate devaluation of the role of women through obscene, distorted depictions) have been hopelessly confused. Part of the problem is that those who traditionally have been the most vigorous opponents of porn are often those same people who shudder at the explicit mention of any sexual subject. Under their watchful, vigilante eyes, frank and free dissemination of educational materials relating to abortion, contraception, the act of birth, and female biology in general is also dangerous, subversive and dirty. (I am not unmindful that frank and free discussion of rape, "the unspeakable crime," might well give these righteous vigilantes further cause to shudder.) Because the battle lines were falsely drawn a long time ago, before there was a vocal women's movement, the antipornography forces appear to be, for the most part, religious, Southern, conservative and right-wing, while the pro-porn forces are identified as Eastern, atheistic and liberal.

But a woman's perspective demands a totally new alignment, or at least a fresh appraisal. The majority report of the President's Commission on Obscenity and Pornography (1970), a report that argued strongly for the removal of all legal restrictions on pornography, soft and hard, made plain that 90 percent of all pornographic material is geared to the male heterosexual market (the other 10 percent is geared to the male homosexual taste), that buyers of porn are "predominantly white, middle-class, middle-aged married males" and that the graphic depictions, the meat and potatoes of porn, are of the naked female body and of the multiplicity of acts done to that body.

Discussing the content of stag films, "a familiar and firmly established part of the American scene," the commission report dutifully, if foggily, explained, "Because pornography historically has been thought to be primarily a masculine interest, the emphasis in stag films seems to represent the preferences of the middle-class American male. Thus male homosexuality and bestiality are relatively rare, while lesbianism is rather common."

The commissioners in this instance had merely verified what purveyors of porn have always known: hard-core pornography is not a celebration of sexual freedom; it is a cynical exploitation of female sexual activity through the device of making all such activity, and consequently all females, "dirty." Heterosexual male consumers of pornography are frankly turned on by watching lesbians in action (although never in the final scenes, but always as a curtain raiser); they are turned off with the sudden swiftness of a water faucet by watching naked men act upon each other. One study quoted in the commission report came to the unastounding conclusion that "seeing a stag film in the presence of male peers bolsters masculine esteem." Indeed. The men in groups who watch the films, it is important to note, are *not* naked.

When male response to pornography is compared to female response, a pronounced difference in attitude emerges. According to the commissions, "Males report being more highly aroused by depictions of nude females, and show more interest in depictions of nude females than [do] females." Quoting the figures of Alfred Kinsey, the commission noted that a majority of males (77 percent) were "aroused" by visual depictions of explicit sex while a majority of females (68 percent) were not aroused. Further, "females more often than males reported 'disgust' and 'offense.' "

From whence comes this female disgust and offense? Are females sexually backward or more conservative by nature? The gut distaste that a majority of women feel when we look at pornography, a distaste that, incredibly, it is no longer fashionable to admit, comes, I think, from the gut knowledge that we and our bodies are being stripped, exposed and contorted for the purpose of ridicule to bolster that "masculine esteem" which gets its kick and sense of power from viewing females as anonymous, panting playthings, adult toys, dehumanized objects to be used, abused, broken and discarded.

This, of course, is also the philosophy of rape. It is no accident (for what else could be its purpose?) that females in the pornographic genre are depicted in two cleanly delineated roles: as virgins who are caught and "banged" or as nymphomaniacs who are never sated. The most popular and prevalent pornographic fantasy combines the two: an innocent, untutored female is raped and "subjected to unnatural practices" that turn her into a raving, slobbering nymphomaniac, a dependent sexual slave who can never get enough of the big, male cock.

There can be no "equality" in porn, no female equivalent, no turning of the tables in the name of bawdy fun. Pornography, like rape, is a male invention, designed to dehumanize women, to reduce the female to an object of sexual access, not to free sensuality from moralistic or parental inhibition. The staple of porn will always be the naked female body, breasts and genitals exposed, because as man devised it, her naked body is the female's "shame," her private parts the private property of man, while his are the ancient, holy, universal, patriarchal instrument of his power, his rule by force over *her.*

Pornography is the undiluted essence of anti-female propaganda. Yet the very same liberals who were so quick to understand the method and purpose behind the mighty propaganda machine of Hitler's Third Reich, the consciously spewed-out anti-Semitic caricatures and obscenities that gave an ideological base to the Holocaust and the Final Solution, the very same liberals who, enlightened by blacks, searched their own conscience and came to understand that their tolerance of "nigger" jokes and portrayals of shuffling, rolling-eyed servants in movies perpetuated the degrading myths of black inferiority and gave an ideological base to the continuation of black oppression—these very same liberals now fervidly maintain that the hatred and contempt for women that find expression in four-letter words used as expletives and in what are quaintly called "adult" or "erotic" books and movies are a valid extension of freedom of speech that must be preserved as a Constitutional right.

To defend the right of a lone, crazed American Nazi to grind out propaganda calling for the extermination of all Jews, as the ACLU has done in the name of free speech, is, after all, a self-righteous and not particularly courageous stand, for American Jewry is not currently threatened by storm troopers, concentration camps and imminent extermination, but I wonder if the ACLU's position might change if, come tomorrow morning, the bookstores and movie theaters lining Forty-second Street in New York City were devoted not to the humiliation of women by rape and torture, as they currently are, but to a systematized, commercially successful propaganda machine depicting the sadistic pleasures of gassing Jews or lynching blacks?

Is this analogy extreme? Not if you are a woman who is conscious of the ever-present threat of rape and the proliferation of a cultural ideology that makes it sound like "liberated" fun. The majority report of the President's Commission on Obscenity and Pornography tried to pooh-pooh the opinion of law enforcement agencies around the country that claimed their own concrete experience with offenders who were caught with the stuff led them to conclude that pornographic material is a causative factor in crimes of sexual violence. The commission maintained that it was not possible at this time to scientifically prove or disprove such a connection.

But does one need scientific methodology in order to conclude that the antifemale propaganda that permeates our nation's cultural output promotes a climate in which acts of sexual hostility directed against women are not only tolerated but ideologically encouraged? A similar debate has raged for many years over whether or not the extensive glorification of violence (the gangster as hero; the loving treatment accorded bloody shoot-'em-ups in movies, books and on TV) has a causal effect, a direct relationship to the rising rate of crime, particularly among youth. Interestingly enough, in this area—nonsexual and not specifically related to abuses against women—public opinion seems to be swinging to the position that explicit violence in the entertainment media does have a deleterious effect; it makes violence commonplace, numbingly routine and no longer morally shocking.

More to the point, those who call for a curtailment of scenes of violence in movies and on television in the name of sensitivity, good taste and what's best for our children are not accused of being pro-censorship or against freedom of speech. Similarly, minority group organizations, black, Hispanic, Japanese, Italian, Jewish, or American Indian, that campaign against ethnic slurs and demeaning portrayals in movies, on television shows and in commercials are perceived as waging a just political fight, for if a minority group claims to be offended by a specific portrayal, be it Little Black Sambo or the Frito Bandido, and relates it to a history of ridicule and oppression, few liberals would dare to trot out a Constitutional argument in theoretical opposition, not if they wish to maintain their liberal credentials. Yet when it comes to the treatment of women, the liberal consciousness remains fiercely obdurate, refusing to be budged, for the sin of appearing square or prissy in the age of the so-called sexual revolution has become the worst offense of all.

Pornography and Censorship

Stanley Kauffmann

One pleasant aspect of pornography discussions is that they never end, even within oneself. No set of arguments can be air-tight, and one can always think of

Stanley Kauffmann, "Pornography and Censorship." Reprinted with permission of the author from: *The Public Interest*, No. 22 (Winter 1971), pp. 28–32. © 1971 by National Affairs, Inc.

points to be added or changed in one's own arguments. But here are some of my present views:

I dislike pornography; and I dislike censorship laws.

I dislike pornography because after the excitements there comes tedium; and with the tedium comes a sense of imperfection. After sex itself comes no such tedium (languor is something else) and no such basic sense of inappropriateness. Porno excites me because all my neural systems seem to be adequately hooked up, but after the shock of crossing the threshold into that "world" wears off, which doesn't take so long, I begin to think that porno represents an ideal—essentially male—of sexual freedom and power, unrelated to reality as is, or as is desirable. I am an anti-idealist; ideals seem morally and functionally corruptive. I am against this ideal as well.

I dislike censorship laws because they intrude on personal rights. Most laws operate between at least two people: they protect me from you and vice-versa. Laws against pornography, like laws against drinking and drug-taking and suicide, come between me and myself. I object to the state's arrogance.

People want pornography.

This has been true of many cultures, especially for men, in many areas. Porno producers are not philanthropists or missionaries; they're in business because people want what they produce. What right have some of us to tell others that they may not have what they want? (I know some intelligent, cultivated men—and a few such women—who delight in porno.) I disbelieve in the legislation of taste.

DEFENSE AGAINST REPRESSION

The question of theatrical productions like *Oh! Calcutta!* is self-solving. If you want to go, go; if not, don't. The concept of "the dram of eale" is a puritan delusion. Gresham's Law doesn't operate in art. If bad art drove out good, there would not be any good art at all because for centuries there has been more bad art than good.

Most films are now clearly labeled by the ratings system of the Motion Picture Association of America. That system has manifest defects, but I have argued for it—and would still—as the best defense against repression. The X rating is, as is often said, a license for opportunists, but numbers of people want what the opportunists offer and I don't recognize anyone's right to deny it to them. More important, the X rating is a license for the serious film maker who wants to deal with sexual subjects. I'm glad that *Midnight Cowboy* (whatever its faults) was made and widely distributed, something that was difficult anyway and would have been nearly impossible without the protection of the X rating.

DANISH SURVEY

The concept of the state's interest in pornography, possibly related to the Roman concept of the republic of virtue, is gradually being eroded by scientific research. The researches in the Lockhart report, incomplete though they are, support the belief that there is no connection between porno and sexual crime. A Danish study (*New York Times,* Nov. 9, 1970) finds that sex crimes have sharply declined in Denmark—coincidentally?—in the three years since censorship laws have been eased there. The data and conclusions of the British Arts Council report on obscenity laws (full text in the *New Statesman,* August 8, 1969) support a recommendation for repeal of the Obscene Publications Acts. The state surely has a legitimate interest in the moral welfare of the community, but every ground for including porno in that interest is weakening.

The only real legal question is the protection of children. And it is a *question*. I can't define what a child is—six, yes, but sixteen?—and I can't define what "protection" is. I'm simply not convinced that a young person without sexual experience and some maturity of judgment can see pornography as pornography: that is—aside from understanding the acts themselves and understanding the unconventionality (even impossibility) of some of them—can see the relation of porno to experience, as commentary and stimulant and revenge. "Depravity and corruption" are supposed to be considerations, too, though no one seems to know much about them. I have no wish to be blithe about parents' concern for a child (particularly since I have no children), but my guess is that a parent's attitude toward his child's exposure to porno is as much secret embarrassment at revelation of his own fantasies as it is protection of the young.

PROTECTION FOR MINORS

Censorship legislation for minors, however, only moves the semantic and moral problem to a different locus. Two sociologists on the Lockhart commission recommended the abolition of *all* statutory legislation, for young persons as well as adults, on the ground that obscenity and pornography have long proved undefinable. They would rather rely on "informal social controls" and "improvements in sex education and better understanding of human sexual behavior" than on "ambiguous and arbitrarily administered laws."

Nevertheless I confess that, even without scientific data to prove harm, I'm uneasy at the thought of children being exposed to pornography before those "improvements" are realized.

Porno is of two distinct kinds.

I don't mean the difference between porno and erotic art nor the argument that sections of recognized classics—Rabelais, Joyce, etc.—are pornographic. (An argument I cannot accept. A sexual portion of a genuine artwork cannot—in my understanding—be pornographic. The latter means, for me, material devised *only* for sexual stimulation.)

The real difference is between imagined porno—written or drawn or painted—and performed porno, done in actuality or on film or in still photographs. The latter entails the degradation of human beings. It doesn't seem to me to matter that these performing men and women always seem cheerful and busily engaged, or that (reportedly) some of the occupants enjoy it or that some of them perform public sex acts as part of lives that are otherwise quite conventional. Obviously conditionings and rationales can vary widely, but I cannot believe that the use of human beings for these purposes is socially beneficial or morally liberating. On the contrary, I think it socially stultifying and morally warped.

I'm not talking about nudity and simulated intercourse in such plays as *Che!*, which are frequently done quite self-righteously as an attempt to *épater le bourgeois*. I mean (currently available in person and on film in New York and other cities) the public performance of coition, fellatio, cunnilingus, and mutual masturbation—with the coition usually interrupted so that the male ejaculation can be seen.

ACTS OF VINDICTIVENESS

I've been as excited by watching some of those films as a human being ought presumably to be. But essentially those films seem to me acts of vindictiveness by men against women in return for the sexual restrictions and taboos of our society and for the cruelties of women toward men that those restrictions have produced. The vindictiveness is essentially mean-spirited and exploitative. I would hope that the socio-sexual improvements on which the Lockhart sociologists rely may affect performed porno first.

In any event, I think that the lumping-together of all porno—imagined and performed—is a conceptual error. The one-to-one relation of writer and reader is a different matter, in psychic and social senses, from the employment of people to enact fantasies.

Conclusions, *pro tem*.

I am not a swinger. I don't believe in pornography as a healthful reminder of the full genital life amidst a pallid and poky society, or as an extender of consciousness in any beneficial way. These views seem to me phony emancipation— in fact, a negation of the very fullness of life that is ostensibly being affirmed. Much better to concentrate on our silliness about the romanticized restrictions of love and the shortcomings of marriage, on the humiliations of both men and women in our rituals of courtship and bedding and wedding, that make pornography such a popular form of vengeance.

But the legal suppression of pornography seems to me anticivil and anticivilized (because it misses the anticivilizing reasons for porno), and also shows a failure in sense of humor. (If the idea of sex is funny, as it often is, the idea of porno is funniness multiplied.) I'm against censorship laws just as I'm against laws against certain kinds of sexual practice, or against any sexual practice between unmarried people, that still exist in many parts of this country. I want to be able to have porno if I want it. The purely personal opinion that I don't happen to want it very often should not be made the law of the land.

To put it entirely subjectively, I think that one way to cure my uneasiness on the subject of porno is to repeal all the laws restricting it, except possibly the ones forbidding the advertising and sale to minors. The more mature the individual, the more he resents the idea of being forbidden something that affects him alone; and the more mature individuals there are, the better the polity.

In Praise of Censure

Garry Wills

Rarely have the denouncers of censorship been so eager to start practicing it. When a sense of moral disorientation overcomes a society, people from the least expected quarters begin to ask, "Is nothing sacred?" Feminists join reactionaries to denounce pornography as demeaning to women. Rock musician Frank Zappa declares that when Tipper Gore, the wife of Senator Albert Gore from Tennessee, asked music companies to label sexually explicit material, she launched an illegal "conspiracy to extort." A *Penthouse* editorialist says that housewife Terry Rakolta, who asked sponsors to withdraw support from a sitcom called *Married . . . With Children,* is "yelling fire in a crowded theater," a formula that says her speech is not protected by the First Amendment.

But the most interesting movement to limit speech is directed at defamatory utterances against blacks, homosexuals, Jews, women or other stigmatizable groups. It took no Terry Rakolta of the left to bring about the instant firing of Jimmy the Greek and Al Campanis from sports jobs when they made racially denigrating comments. Social pressure worked far more quickly on them than on *Married . . . With Children,* which is still on the air.

The rules being considered on college campuses to punish students for making racist and other defamatory remarks go beyond social and commercial pressure to actual legal muzzling. The right-wing *Dartmouth Review* and its imitators have understandably infuriated liberals, who are beginning to take action against them and the racist expressions they have encouraged. The American Civil Liberties Union considered this movement important enough to make it the principal topic at its biennial meeting last month in Madison. Wis. Ironically, the regents of the University of Wisconsin had passed their own rules against defamation just before the ACLU members convened on the university's campus. Nadine Strossen, of New York University School of Law, who was defending the ACLU's traditional position on free speech, said of Wisconsin's new rules. "You can tell how bad they are by the fact that the regents had to make an amendment at the last minute exempting classroom discussion! What is surprising is that Donna Shalala [chancellor of the university] went along with it." So did constitutional lawyers on the faculty.

If a similar code were drawn up with right-wing imperatives in mind—one banning unpatriotic, irreligious or sexually explicit expressions on campus—the people framing Wisconsin-type rules would revert to their libertarian pasts. In this competition to suppress, is regard for freedom of expression just a matter of whose ox is getting gored at the moment? Does the left just get nervous about the Christian cross when Klansmen burn it, while the right will react only when Madonna flirts crucifixes between her thighs?

The cries of "un-American" are as genuine and as frequent on either side. Everyone is protecting the country. Zappa accuses Gore of undermining the moral fiber of America with the "sexual neuroses of these vigilant ladies." He argues that she threatens our freedoms with "connubial insider trading" because her husband is a Senator. Apparently her marital status should deprive her of speaking privileges in public—an argument Westbrook Pegler used to make against Eleanor Roosevelt. *Penthouse* says Rakolta is taking us down the path toward fascism. It attacks her for living in a rich suburb—the old "radical chic" argument that rich people cannot support moral causes.

There is a basic distinction that cuts through this free-for-all over freedom. It is the distinction, too often neglected, between censorship and censure (the free expression of moral disapproval). What the campuses are trying to do (at least those with state money) is use the force of government to contain freedom of speech. What Donald Wildmon, the free-lance moralist from Tupelo, Miss., does when he gets Pepsi to cancel its Madonna ad is censure the ad by calling for a boycott. Advocating boycotts is a form of speech protected by the First Amendment. As Nat Hentoff, journalistic custodian of the First Amendment, says, "I would hate to see boycotts outlawed. Think what that would do to Cesar Chavez." Or, for that matter, to Ralph Nader. If one disapproves of a social practice, whether it is racist speech or unjust hiring in lettuce fields, one is free to denounce that and to call on others to express their disapproval. Otherwise there would be no form of persuasive speech except passing a law. This would make the law coterminous with morality.

Equating morality with legality is in effect what people do when they claim that anything tolerated by law must, in the name of freedom, be approved by citizens in all their dealings with one another. As Zappa says, "Masturbation is not illegal. If it is not illegal to do it, why should it be illegal to sing about it?" He thinks this proves that Gore, who is not trying to make raunch in rock illegal, cannot even ask distributors to label it. Anything goes, as long as it's legal. The odd consequence of this argument would be a drastic narrowing of the freedom of speech. One could not call into question anything that was not against the law—including, for instance, racist speech.

A false ideal of tolerance has not only outlawed censorship but discouraged censoriousness (another word for censure). Most civilizations have expressed their moral values by mobilization of social opprobrium. That, rather than specific legislation, is what changed the treatment of minorities in films and TV over recent years. One can now draw opprobrious attention by gay bashing, as the Beastie Boys rock group found when their distributor told them to cut out remarks about "fags" for business reasons. Or by anti-Semitism, as the just disbanded rap group Public Enemy has discovered.

It is said that only the narrow-minded are intolerant or opprobrious. Most of those who limited the distribution of Martin Scorsese's movie *The Last Temptation of Christ* had not even seen the movie. So do we guarantee freedom of speech only for the broad-minded or the better educated? Can one speak only after studying whatever one has reason, from one's beliefs, to denounce? Then most of us would be doing a great deal less speaking than we do. If one has never seen any snuff movies, is that a bar to criticizing them?

Others argue that asking people not to buy lettuce is different from asking them not to buy a rocker's artistic expression. Ideas (carefully disguised) lurk somewhere in the lyrics. All the more reason to keep criticism of them free. If ideas are too important to suppress, they are also too important to ignore. The whole point of free speech is not to make ideas exempt from criticism but to expose them to it.

One of the great mistakes of liberals in recent decades has been the ceding of moral concern to rightwingers. Just because one opposes censorship, one need not be seen as agreeing with pornographers. Why should liberals, of all people, oppose Gore when she asks that labels be put on products meant for the young, to inform those entrusted by law with the care of the young? Liberals were the first to promote "healthy" television shows like *Sesame Street* and *The Electric Company.* In the 1950s and 1960s they were the leading critics of television, of its mindless violence, of the way it ravaged the attention span needed for reading. Who was keeping kids away from TV sets then? How did promoters of Big Bird let themselves be cast as champions of the Beastie Boys—not just of their *right* to perform but of their performance itself? Why should it be left to Gore to express moral disapproval of a group calling itself Dead Kennedys (sample lyric: "I kill children, I love to see them die")?

For that matter, who has been more insistent that parents should "interfere" in what their children are doing. Tipper Gore or Jesse Jackson? All through the 1970s, Jackson was traveling the high schools, telling parents to turn off TVs, make the kids finish their homework, check with teachers on their performance, get to know what the children are doing. This kind of "interference" used to be called education.

Belief in the First Amendment does not pre-empt other beliefs, making one a eunuch to the interplay of opinions. It is a distortion to turn "You can express any views" into the proposition "I don't care what views you express." If liberals keep equating equality with approval, they will be repeatedly forced into weak positions.

A case in point is the Corcoran Gallery's sudden cancellation of an exhibit of Robert Mapplethrope's photographs. The whole matter was needlessly confused when the director, Christina Owr-Chall, claimed she was canceling the show to *protect* it from censorship. She meant that there might be pressure to remove certain pictures—the sadomasochistic ones or those verging on kiddie porn—if the show had gone on. But she had in mind, as well, the hope of future grants from the National Endowment for the Arts, which is under criticism for the Mapplethrope show and for another show that contained Andres Serrano's *Piss Christ,* the photograph of a crucifix in what the title says is urine. Owr-Chall is said to be yielding to censorship, when she is clearly yielding to political and financial pressure, as Pepsi yielded to commercial pressure over the Madonna ad.

What is at issue here is not government suppression but government subsidy. Mapplethorpe's work is not banned, but showing it might have endangered federal grants to needy artists. The idea that what the government does not support it represses is nonsensical, as one can see by reversing the statement to read: "No one is allowed to create anything without the government's subvention." What pussycats our supposedly radical artists are. They not only want the government's permission to create their artifacts, they want federal authorities to supply the materials as well. Otherwise they feel "gagged." If they are not given government approval (and money), they want to remain an avant-garde while being bankrolled by the Old Guard.

What is easily forgotten in this argument is the right of citizen taxpayers. They send representatives to Washington who are answerable for the expenditure of funds exacted from them. In general these voters want to favor their own values if government is going to get into the culture-subsidizing area at all (a proposition many find objectionable in itself). Politicians, insofar as they support the arts, will tend to favor conventional art (certainly not masochistic art). Anybody who doubts that has no understanding of a politician's legitimate concern for his or her constituents' approval. Besides, it is quaint for those familiar with the politics of the art world to discover, with a shock, that there is politics in politics.

Luckily, cancellation of the Mapplethorpe show forced some artists back to the flair-and cheekiness of unsubsidized art. Other results of pressure do not turn out as well. Unfortunately, people in certain regions were deprived of the chance to see *The Last Temptation of Christ* in the theater. Some, no doubt, considered it a loss that they could not buy lettuce or grapes during a Chavez boycott. Perhaps there was even a buyer perverse enough to miss driving the unsafe cars Nader helped pressure off the market. On the other hand, we do not get sports analysis made by racists. These mobilizations of social opprobrium are not examples of repression but of freedom of expression by committed people who censured without censoring, who expressed the kinds of belief the First Amendment guarantees. I do not, as a result, get whatever I approve of subsidized, either by Pepsi or the government. But neither does the law come in to silence Tipper Gore or Frank Zappa or even that filthy rag, the *Dartmouth Review*.

2 Choosing an Issue
A Debatable Topic That Matters

When you develop a position for your **researched** paper, it is important to choose an issue that is both **controversial** and **significant;** that is, it should generate **conflicting opinions** and it should **matter,** not only to you, but to others as well. When you write about debatable and relevant issues, your writing is likely to have an impact on your readers, influencing the way they think or feel. Many of the assignments in this book are already focused for you so that you will not have to spend much time selecting an issue. However, in many instances, you may wish to select your own issue or to focus on one of the issues in this book more specifically to your own perspective.

This chapter focuses on several ways of selecting and focusing an issue, including **brainstorming, freewriting, clustering, asking questions about a problem, writing dialogues,** and **role playing.** All of these methods are based on the idea that the process of selecting an issue begins with the self, that understanding what you know and how you may already feel about a topic is the first step in choosing an issue. Once you understand your own ideas about your topic, you can then move beyond the self, imagining what "other selves" think and focusing on areas of disagreement. Imagining what other selves think and understanding points of controversy will enable you to write a researched paper that will have an impact on your reader.

BEGIN WITH YOUR OWN CONCERNS

To discover issues that are both debatable and relevant, I suggest that you begin by thinking about **what matters to you and to your family.** Most likely, a great many situations and problems that concern you can be generalized to include others. For instance, look at the following questions about seemingly "personal" situations:

Mothers, Fathers, Children, and Careers: Do you come from a home where your mother has chosen to develop a career or go back to school? Was it difficult for her to find babysitters when you or your brothers and sisters were small? Did she find herself having to "do it all"—that is, take care of the house and children, while assuming new responsibilities? Are you, perhaps, in that situation? How did your father feel about your mother's career?

Old People: Do you have an elderly relative—a grandmother or grandfather? Is your family under pressure about the best way to care for them?

Career Choices: As a student, has it been difficult for you to choose a major because you are concerned most of all with the salary you will be able to earn? Have you ever been torn between choosing what interests you and worrying about whether or not you will be able to earn a living?

Maternity and Abortion: Speaking of career choices, do you think women ought to be guaranteed maternity leaves? Should men? Should men have a say in abortion decisions?

Community Service: Have you ever done some form of community service? Do you think that young people ought to do some form of community service after they complete high school?

Part-Time Jobs: Did you have a job when you were in high school? Did you feel this was a good thing to do? Did it affect your performance in school? Did you feel at a disadvantage because you were young or a student?

Students' Rights: Speaking of school, as a student in high school, did you ever feel that you were being treated too much like a child? Were there restrictions in the lunchroom? A dress code? Locker searches? Did you think these were fair? Were they necessary?

Transportation: Do you drive to work or school? Do you take public transportation? Are you completely satisfied with your commuting situation? Who should be responsible for public transportation?

Think, then, about issues in your own life that you feel are **problems.** Often, issues of personal concern can suggest possibilities for a paper because they are also of concern to others. The problem of who should pay for childcare, the difficulties of providing for the elderly, the rights of women and men in the workplace or in abortion decisions, or the rights of students—many of these issues can provide you with the beginning of a topic. After all, if the problem is of concern to you, might it also be of concern to others? Does anyone else have an opinion on this topic? Has anyone written about it?

Of course, there might be some topics that will matter **only** to those personally involved—the question of whether or not the family dog ought to get a haircut, for example (unless you wrote a whimsical essay meant to be entertaining). A topic such as this is probably too specific to your own particular situation and will probably not matter to others, although you might extend the topic by stating that it ought to be required that all dogs get haircuts once a month, or you might use this debate to discuss the issue of how much money is spent on pets versus resources allocated for the poor. Usually, though, you would not want to write about a topic that is of no interest to anyone except for your own family, unless you were writing exclusively for that audience (a family newspaper, for example). However, there are many issues that might be of concern to you and your family and also might matter to others. Think about those.

UNSTRUCTURED METHODS OF FINDING AN ISSUE

Freewriting and Brainstorming

Many students find that writing freely about a topic enables them to understand their own position or feelings about it, particularly if the topic has affected them personally. In Chapter 1, you may recall that Elisa wrote about her experience of finding a "forbidden" book on her parents' bookshelves; recreating that experience helped her find her position on the issue of whether there ought to be a screening committee for the high school library. Jotting down ideas or brainstorming about a topic can also be extremely helpful. Images that come to mind can suggest other images, and frequently students find that they can then generate ideas that they didn't even know they had.

Clustering

Clustering is similar to freewriting and brainstorming in that its aim is to elicit as many ideas as possible. Clustering, however, enables you to group ideas visually and to see possible connections between ideas. To try clustering, place the central idea or topic in the center of the paper and circle it. Around this circled word, write other words that are associated with this central idea and put circles around them as well. Now write other words that are associated with these other ideas and use lines to connect them either to each other or to other words on the page. Clustering helps you develop details and find connections, which you might not have discovered otherwise. On the next page is a cluster one of Elisa's classmates wrote concerning the issue of whether a screening committee ought to be established to screen books for the high school library.

Finding a Link

Choosing an issue to write about often involves creating a link between ideas and perceptions within yourself and those just beyond, and that linkage between yourself and the outside world will enable you to say something meaningful. Therefore, I suggest that you not only look within yourself but that you also look beyond yourself to establish links with issues in the world. For example, the issue

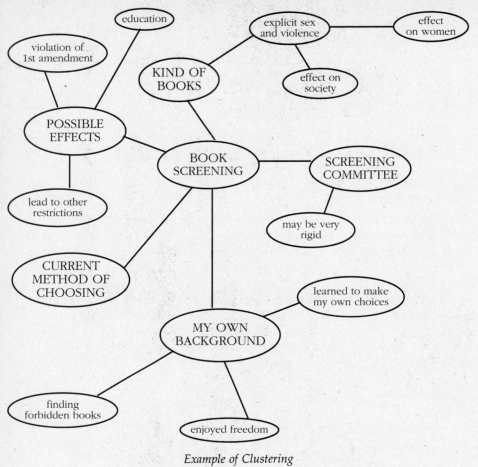

Example of Clustering

of whether or not the family dog ought to get a haircut would not, in and of itself, be of interest to the general population. However, if you used a family-related issue to think about other issues related to pet care or public expense for animal care, you might come up with an interesting and controversial topic.

All around you in the media—the newspapers, TV, and radio—important issues are debated every day. Often these are issues that have endured throughout human history; many of these are issues that have always generated debate. Maybe you will be assigned a topic by your teacher; perhaps a textbook will offer suggestions. But even if you are not provided with ideas significant topics can be found all around: issues concerning abortion, women's and men's rights, the function of education, mandatory busing, antismoking regulations, seatbelt laws, motorcycle helmet laws, handgun legislation, the legalization of marijuana, and the drinking age, for example. All sorts of debates and controversies are concerned with issues such as these, and these make excellent topics to write about, since they lend themselves to multiple points of view.

Read and Listen to What Others Have to Say

In the first chapter, Elisa read some of the responses written by her classmates, which helped her clarify her own ideas and helped her understand how her own perspective differed from those of her classmates. Finding out what others have to say is an excellent way to discover what you, personally, might have to say. The main point is to do something **active** when you are in the process of selecting an issue. Remember, just because you don't think you know much about a topic doesn't mean that you can't eventually write about it. You may know more than you think. And with a little effort, you can learn about it.

STRUCTURED METHODS OF CHOOSING AN ISSUE

Asking Questions About a Problem (What, Who, When, Where, How)

The five questions journalists frequently ask to generate information about a topic can be applied effectively to the process of discovering an issue for a researched paper. Since a researched paper is concerned with a problem, the questions are focused around discovering as much information as possible about that problem. In Chapter 1, Elisa was asked to develop a position about whether or not a screening committee should be established to screen books for the high school library. To help discover ideas and to focus her thinking, Elisa could have framed her questions as follows:

WHAT is the problem?

Parents are concerned that some books in the high school library are unsuitable for their children to read. They want to establish a screening committee for the high school library.

WHO finds this a problem?

Some parents find the books a problem because they are worried about violence and promiscuity in the culture. Other parents worry about the idea of censoring books and about who would be on such a committee. Students find it a problem because they don't want to be restricted in what they read.

WHEN is this a problem?

This is a problem when we are dealing with minors, who may be influenced or disturbed by unsuitable books. It can also be a problem when the idea of censorship is extended beyond the high school.

WHERE is this a problem?

The situation is focused on the high school, but the question of censorship is much larger than this immediate situation. It raises questions about whether restricting books for high school students is a good idea and whether behavior is influenced by reading.

HOW can that problem be solved?

This problem can be solved by understanding that reading books does not necessarily lead to violent behavior and by recognizing that one form of censorship can lead to another. Also, the problem can be solved by recognizing that the screening committee will create more problems than it is likely to solve.

The Topical Questions

In his *Rhetoric,* Aristotle presents the idea of "topics" as a means of discovering material for an argument. Based on these topics, Edward Corbett in *The Little Rhetoric and Handbook* organized questions about these topics according to subject matter, and a few of these sets of questions can help you to choose an issue for a research paper:

Questions About Concepts (e.g., Censorship of Books)

1. How has the term been defined by others?
2. How do you define the term?
3. What other concepts have been associated with it?
4. In what ways has this concept affected the lives of people?
5. How might this concept be changed?

Questions About Propositions (Statements to Be Proved or Disproved)

Example statement: Pornographic literature directly contributes to violent crimes against women.

1. What must be established before a reader will believe the proposition?
2. What are the meanings of key words in the proposition?
3. By what kinds of evidence or argument can the proposition be proved or disproved?
4. What counterarguments must be confronted and refuted?
5. What are the practical consequences of the proposition?

You might find that answering these questions will enable you to think of a topic in a new way and discover a point of view that you had not been aware of before.

YOUR TOPIC AND YOUR READER: WILL ANYONE SAY "SO WHAT"?

In selecting a topic that matters, it is essential to anticipate the reaction of your readers, since no one wants to write a boring paper or to tell readers something they already know or already believe. Sometimes students think that the main basis for choosing a topic is whether or not they or their readers have strong feelings about it. Certainly, if you feel strongly about a topic, you will approach your topic with energy and enthusiasm, and it is a good idea to look first at topics that evoke an emotional reaction. Yet, having strong feelings is not the only criterion for choosing a suitable topic. To use an outrageous example, probably everyone in our culture would agree that it is not a good idea to allow a person to go out into the streets and shoot people randomly, if that person happens to wake up in an unusually violent mood that day. Certainly, if you heard that someone had suggested that everyone should be allowed this kind of license, you would have strong negative feelings about it. In fact, you would probably be outraged or alarmed! Yet, obviously, this topic is *not* suitable for a paper because the student has not thought about the impact of the paper on its readers. Even if the paper were very well written, even if the student found many arguments in support of the main idea, and even if the student used many secondary sources as evidence, anyone reading the paper would be likely to say, *"So what? Everyone already thinks that! only a disturbed person would ever think this is a good idea."*

In our culture, every sane person already believes this. So unless society changed drastically (or unless you were in the unlikely position of writing the paper for gang members who may think it actually is a good idea to go out and shoot at people from cars), you would not write a paper on such a topic. Similarly, you would not want to write a paper proving that the world was round or that the moon is not made of green cheese, because these are not debatable issues. If you found significant evidence to prove that the world is really *flat* or that scientists have discovered that the moon *is* really made of green cheese, then the issue would become debatable, and your paper would be important news to many people.

Unless you found such evidence, though, these topics would not be suitable for a researched paper because there is no point in writing a paper about a topic on which everyone already agrees or knows about. A paper about such topics will not matter to anyone and won't be worth the time you spend writing it. The likely reaction to papers on topics such as these is **"So what?"** If you can anticipate a **"So what"** when considering a paper topic, you might decide to write about something else.

In choosing issues to write about, then, you should choose one that will move your readers to change their minds or at least think about a topic in a new way. So, when you choose a topic for research, it is a good idea to choose one that is sufficiently complex, one about which people have different opinions. Fortunately, most important issues in our society cannot easily be decided upon and have at least two sides. Knowing about different sides of your topic will help you frame a more thoughtful position, enabling you to write your paper successfully.

"So What" Can Lead to a Debatable Issue

Sometimes students begin with topics that are simply statements of fact. They point out that kids usually like sweets or that households consisting of single women with children are usually less financially secure than those containing two parents. They might also generate several supporting points for these statements, backed up with good solid facts. Yet each of these statements could generate a "So what?" because they are not debatable. Everyone agrees that these statements are true. Yet, each of these statements can be the starting points for issues that are both significant and debatable. The statement that kids usually like sweets could be used to begin exploration of whether sweets should be included in school lunches or whether sweet products should be advertised on television. The statement about single mothers could lead to an examination of reasons for this being the case, perhaps to a position that advocates greater governmental assistance for single mothers than for single fathers. Saying "So what?" about a topic doesn't mean that you automatically eliminate it. Perhaps it can be refocused into a topic that is both debatable and relevant.

USING ROLE PLAYING

Who Has a Strong Opinion on the Topic?

A helpful method to understand the issues involved in a topic is to imagine the different people who might be concerned with the topic in some way. For example, suppose that at your university, the administration, concerned about the increase of late-night crime in the neighborhood and also about the large drop-out rate in the freshman class, has proposed that curfews be instituted in all of the freshman dormitories, ten o'clock on weekdays, one o'clock on weekends. Who might have an opinion on this topic? Certainly, in this case, the administration is likely to be strongly in favor of the curfew, since they had proposed it. The students, though, might hold an equally strong opinion that is completely different from that of the administration. Then you might also think about the parents who are paying the bills. With whom would they agree?

CREATING A CHARACTER WITH A STRONG OPINION ON THE TOPIC

A useful way to understand different positions on a topic is to create a character who would have a strong or even an extreme opinion on the topic. To do so, imagine that you are at a party where a guest begins speaking in emotionally charged language about the issue of the school curfew. Give this person a name, a profession, an appearance. Then, assuming the role of this person, write what he or she might say. For example, you might write something like this:

> My character is named Gary Stevens. He is 45 years old, 5′ 10″ tall, has dark hair with flecks of gray at the temples, is tan, and in pretty good shape, though he has a slight tendency to be overweight. He is wearing gray pants with a white shirt, no tie. He makes a lot of money in the computer business and is sending his daughter to an expensive private college. This is what he has to say at the party:

I don't care what students have to say about their so-called "rights." As far as I'm concerned, you get rights when you pay for them. That's the way it was for me, and that's the way it is for my daughter. If she doesn't like the curfew, she can go fund herself for college and live on her own too. I'm paying a lot of money for her to have an education and that doesn't include partying all night, particularly in a dangerous neighborhood. I've seen some of the characters who hang around the school at night and they're a pretty rough bunch. My daughter doesn't like the curfew, but she can just put up with it. As it is, let me tell you, she doesn't overwork. Parties and fun—that's all she knows. If she wants me to pay for her education, she can get herself home on time!

▶ *Exercise:* Imagine you are Gary Stevens's daughter. She is at another party on the same evening, and she, too, has a strong opinion on the topic. Write a heated statement of what she might say about the curfew.

CREATING A BRIEF DIALOGUE ON THE TOPIC

To gain an understanding of your topic, it is helpful to imagine a brief dialogue that might occur among various people who have differing opinions about it. If, in your imagination, you can find several points of **disagreement** among them, you will know that you have selected a controversial topic that is suitable for a researched paper, and you will begin to understand several of the issues concerned with the topic. Scripting the discussion will also help you to begin to think about points you might wish to develop or argue against. For example, on the issue of the curfew, you might imagine a university administrator, a student, and a parent stating the following positions:

> *Student:* Having any sort of curfew is ridiculous! At this point in our lives, we are young adults and can make our own decisions.
>
> *Parent:* Just because you are 18 doesn't mean that you are a young adult. According to my definition, an adult is someone who is self-supporting. I don't see you doing that.
>
> *School official:* I think the main point here is safety and fostering good study habits. Having a curfew means that students cannot stay out late when they should be studying.
>
> *Student:* Safety is our own business. If we think that it's not safe to go out, we'll go out in groups or decide on our own to come home early. And, as far as studying is concerned, just because students are actually inside the dorm doesn't mean that they'll be studying. Students can waste time right in their rooms if they want to. It all comes down to whether or not we have the maturity to discipline ourselves. I think we have, and, if not, we will be the ones to suffer.
>
> *Parent:* You can take on that responsibility when you are paying for your own education.

As you can see, one could debate this topic for a long time, and in the course of the dialogue, many points of disagreement have emerged. These can be stated as questions: Is someone viewed as an adult by age or by economic independence? Does an enforced curfew foster better study habits? Who is responsible for safety—the school or the individual student? Is it the responsibility of the school to foster better study habits? Do parents have rights over their adult children's habits because they are paying for the education? Perhaps you can think of some more.

▶ *Exercise:* **Writing a Brief Dialogue.** Imagining a disagreement will help you understand extreme positions on your topic. Choose one of the topics suggested below and engage in the following activities:

1. Imagine a particular person who might have a strong opinion about the topic. Give that person a name, an age, a profession, and a description.
2. Imagine how that person might feel about the topic. See if you can state that opinion in several sentences.
3. Imagine another person or group of people who might have a different opinion. See if you can state in general terms what these opinions might be.
4. Write a brief dialogue between these people.
5. List points of disagreement as questions.

Some suggested topics follow:

1. Drivers of motorcycles ought to wear helmets.
2. High schools ought to be extremely careful about what books students are allowed to read. Unsuitable material ought to be eliminated from the school library.
3. Fourteen-year-old boys are not old enough to assume the burden of fatherhood. If they father a child, they should not be held responsible.
4. The women's movement has achieved all of its goals and is no longer necessary.
5. College students should not be allowed to sign up for more than five classes. They will be overburdened with work.
6. Employers should be able to test all employees for drugs.
7. Selling drugs should be subject to capital punishment.
8. Smoking should not be allowed in restaurants.

▶ *Exercise:* **Using Extended Dialogue to Understand a Topic.** Scripting **extended** discussions between characters with strong positions can also help you explore a topic and develop your own position. To provide you with opportunities for practice, I have provided scenarios about debatable issues. For each scenario, write an extended dialogue between two characters who have strong opinions on the subject. In writing your dialogue, you should observe the following specifications:

1. No one makes outrageous or insulting statements.
2. No one wins; that is, both views seem intelligent.
3. Each character speaks at least twice, for at least half a page at each turn.
4. Each character's words should be planned and carefully structured.

This is thoughtful, deliberate writing, which is not spontaneous or casual, as if each character had revised and edited their spoken words for publication.

Scenario 1: Helmet or No Helmet? Andrea Wiggins is a second-year university student living in a large metropolitan area. Since housing on campus is difficult to get and is often reserved for freshmen, Andrea lives off-campus, about five miles from school, and commutes to school every day on a motorbike. Andrea doesn't mind living off campus, since she loves the ride to and from school—the lightness and freedom she feels on her bike, the sensation of the wind in her hair, the coolness on her cheeks. Her parents, though, are concerned that Andrea does not wear a helmet when she rides her motorbike. They cite numerous instances in which young people such as Andrea have suffered disabling head injuries from motorcycle injuries. In discussions with her parents, Andrea insists that she is a careful driver and takes care not to ride during busy hours. She feels strongly that a decision to wear a helmet ought to be hers alone.

During the spring semester, a new law has been proposed to the state legislature requiring all riders of motorcycles and motorbikes to wear helmets. Insurance companies are in favor of the law. Motorcycle club members are not.

Write a dialogue between Andrea and her parents in which they discuss the issue of requiring helmets for motorcycle and motorbike drivers.

Scenario 2: Free-Speech Rights. A Supreme Court decision of a few years ago has raised the issue of free speech rights in student publications. The case concerned two articles, written by students in a journalism class at East Hazelwood High School, which were deleted from the student newspaper by the principal. The students felt that their free-speech rights had been violated by the principal. The principal maintained that he had withdrawn the articles because the subjects of the articles, birth control and divorce, were unsuitable for younger readers. His other reason was that the students mentioned in the articles could be easily identified by other students, causing them considerable embarrassment. This case was sent to the Surpreme Court because it raised questions about whether or not high school students should have the same right to free speech as other members of society.

Write a dialogue between the principal and a spokesperson for the students about this issue.

▶ *Assigment: Additional Topics for Extended Dialogue.* Choose one of the following topics about which to write an extended dialogue. Several possible participants have been suggested for you for each topic, but feel free to think about others. Assign each participant at least half a page. Remember, the argument should be well developed, and there should be no winners.

1. Fourteen-year-old boys are not old enough to assume the burden of fatherhood. If they father a child, they should not be held responsible. Write a dialogue between a 14-year-old boy who has fathered a child, the expectant mother of his child, the boy's parents, and the girl's parents.

2. The women's movement has achieved all of its goals and is no longer necessary. Now we need a "men's rights movement." Write a dialogue between a man and a woman on this topic.

3. Students who work should not be allowed to take more than three courses, as they will not be able to complete their work satisfactorily. Write a dialogue between an adult student and a member of the administration.

4. Employers should be allowed to test their employees for drug use periodically. Write a dialogue between an employer and an employee in an organization you are familiar with.

5. College students are still children because they are not economically independent. Write a dialogue between a student and a parent.

Imagining possible participants in a controversy will help you evaluate the relevance of your topic, and writing either brief or extended dialogues will help you decide if the topic is **controversial.** Once you have thought about at least two positions on this topic, you can then decide which one you agree with most and perhaps qualify one of the extreme positions. Then you can begin to think about possible directions for developing your own position.

UNDERSTANDING YOUR POSITION ON INDIVIDUAL RIGHTS

To some extent, your position on controversial issues may be influenced by how much you value the rights of the individual, that is by how strongly you feel that each individual ought to be able to enjoy his or her individual rights as opposed to feeling that individual rights must be secondary to the well being of society as a whole. One extreme position on this topic is that each person in society must be given his or her individual rights under all conditions, that each person counts as an individual above all else. Another extreme position is that the rights of society are much more important than the rights of the individual, that in every society, each individual must give up as many individual rights as necessary for society to function successfully. A moderate position lies somewhere in between.

When laws are passed, an individual might feel as if his or her rights are being infringed upon. Thus, you might say, "I don't need a *law* requiring me to wear a seatbelt, because I always wear one anyway." Someone else might say, "Others are not as responsible as you and they must be required to do what is necessary. Our society can't afford to care for those who are severely injured in automobile accidents." In another instance, you might say, "I shouldn't be required to justify the deductions on my tax form. I am an honest person and would not claim anything unnecessary." The government might say, "*You* may be honest, but there are many who aren't. We have to require proof from everyone in order for our society to function. And if you wish the protection of our government, you must obey its laws."

In order for you to develop a position on significant, debatable issues, you need to examine how many individual rights you are willing to give up in order for society to exist. Almost everyone agrees that obeying red and green signals is necessary for traffic to function smoothly and would support a law requiring all motorists to do so. But probably few would be in favor of a nightly curfew in order to deter criminals who operate during the evening hours. Thinking about where you are willing to compromise will help you develop a position.

▶ **Exercise:** Laws requiring motorists to obey traffic signals and wear seatbelts are designed to help society function more safely; they concern the welfare of society. Yet, there are probably other "laws" that could be passed that might also make society more safe, although some of them might inhibit individual rights more than you would recommend. For example, a law requiring all minors to be accompanied by an adult after certain hours might contribute to child safety; yet at this time, this law does not exist and many would probably be against its passing.

Would you be in favor of such a law? Or would you feel that it would be too much of a restriction on individual freedom? Think about what other "laws" could be passed in the interest of public safety. Write some of these down and compare them with possible "laws" devised by your classmates. Of which ones would you be in favor? In thinking about these "laws," try to determine your position on individual rights versus your concern with public well-being.

BEING ACTIVE IN YOUR SEARCH FOR A TOPIC

If you are having difficulty selecting a position or finding a topic, remember that it is better to **do something actively** than to sit and chew your pencil or fingernails, staring at a blank sheet of paper or computer screen. Freewrite, brainstorm, write responses to questions concerned with problems, but don't just sit staring at the wall. Try writing dialogues and envisioning possible advocates in a debate. Browse through a newspaper or magazine. Listen to the news on the TV or radio; open your eyes to what is happening in your community. Debatable, significant issues are all around you. Searching actively will enable you to find those that are particularly important to you.

3 *Developing an Argument for a Researched Paper*

When some people hear the word "argument," they think of a heated interchange, an emotionally charged disagreement such as the following:

Louisa: It's perfectly obvious that we need a woman for the job. Our department has hired only men for the last 20 years.

Clif: Women can't do a job like this. They have to be able to think clearly, without getting emotional. Hire a woman? That's a joke!

Louisa: You know, that's really a sexist remark! How can you say such a thing to me?

Clif: Look, let's get serious here. Everyone knows that women can't compare to men when it comes to keeping their heads. Any woman who took this job would be an emotional basket case in two weeks.

Louisa: Did anyone ever tell you what a jerk you are? Well, if not, let me be the first!

Clif: You're just mad because you can't face the truth about your own sex! Typical female reaction!

The above dialogue is the sort of interchange we often associate with the word "argument," and, indeed, we do use the word colloquially to refer to this kind of angry discussion. However, when I use the term "argument" in reference to a researched paper, I am using the term to mean a text that develops a reasoned **position,** a thesis statement, which aims to convince the reader that its ideas are true, or, at least, worth considering. The word "argument" in this context implies that **reasons** will be used logically to support a main point. We use arguments when we write about the important issues of our culture—to make a decision, to explain and analyze a situation, to predict potential consequences, or to convince a reader of a position.

Some people think of argument as a specific genre of writing, but, actually, all writing that aims at convincing a reader may be considered argument. Whenever you write for someone other than yourself, which is most of the time, you want your reader to feel that what you have to say is important and worth reading. But to have an effect on a reader, an argument, like all thesis-driven writing, requires demonstration and development. Even a simple statement such as "My roommate is difficult to live with" can be considered an argument in that in order to be convincing, you would have to prove what you said by citing evidence (he blasts his radio, leaves dirty dishes around the house, has a terrible temper, etc.). You would also have to establish that you are a believable person whose word is reliable, that you don't complain about every roommate you have, and that you don't exaggerate or falsify.

This chapter, then, focuses on the important characteristics of a successful argument. In particular, you will learn the following:

1. To distinguish between a topic, an assertion, and an issue.
2. To establish authority or a credible writing "self," so that your reader trusts you and will pay attention to what you have to say.
3. To be aware of your reader or audience and indicate that you have considered both sides of the question.
4. To understand the implications and consequences of your position.
5. To develop an effective argumentative structure.
6. To use evidence effectively in support of your position.
7. To make your writing lively through anecdotes and examples.

THE PURPOSE OF ARGUMENTATIVE WRITING

Writing an argument for a research paper requires you to think critically about a significant issue and to formulate an idea that you want your reader to consider seriously. In attempting to convince your reader of that idea, you will use **evidence,** which you may have obtained from a variety of sources—from your own experience, from what is regarded as "truth" within your culture, from statistics, from articles, and books. But the goal of writing a researched paper is not simply to show how much information you have found. The information is used **purposefully** to convince your reader that something is or is not true, that something will have desirable or undesirable consequences, that something is or is not fair, will or will not work, or has or has not outgrown its usefulness.

It is also important to understand that the issues for a researched paper are concerned with **conflicts in value,** that is, what one considers important or good for society. (See Chapter 4 for a further discussion of values.) Unlike the issue of whether or not one's roommate is difficult to live with, topics concerned with conflicts in value usually cannot easily be supported by simple physical facts, and most of the time, both sides have some merit (which is why they are considered controversial). Writing an argument about a complex social or political issue involves considerable thinking and development, and you might have to use outside sources to explore background material, define terms, or establish criteria or standards for analysis in order to develop a position.

FINDING A POSITION

Beginning with a Topic

As was discussed in Chapter 2, which concerned finding a topic, you can sometimes initiate your search by exploring issues that matter to you personally. Often you can discover an important issue of the culture by looking at your own personal or family situation, since problems that concern you often concern others as well. The heated dialogue at the beginning of this chapter, for example, involved two people arguing about whether or not a woman ought to be hired at a particular firm. They also argued about the stereotypical view of women as emotionally unstable. Yet although the argument concerned specific people and a specific situation, the issues of giving women preference in hiring and the effects of unflattering female stereotypes are of importance to everyone. That "argument" was really concerned with the broader issues of women's position in society, sex discrimination in the workplace, and the related issues of affirmative action and equal opportunity.

Chapter 2 discusses several strategies for selecting and focusing a topic. It emphasizes that your search should be **active** and that debatable, significant issues can be found all around you, beginning with problems in your own life, as well as issues discussed in newspapers and the electronic media. Once you have preliminarily focused on a possible topic, you can then look for issues concerned with that topic.

Distinguishing Among a Topic, an Assertion, and an Issue

Look at the following interchange between two students:

> *Fred:*   Have you found an issue for your paper?
> *Linda:*   Yes. My paper is *about* medical research.

Students often refer to their papers as *"about"* something, or else they will say that they are writing a paper *"on"* something. Yet if you refer to your papers in this way, you may be mistaking a **topic** for an **issue.** A topic is usually a broad area and usually no one either agrees or disagrees just with a topic. Note that the words "medical research" are not a statement and make no assertion. The words alone suggest no particular **position** or **point** to develop.

Now look at Interchange 2:

> *Fred:*   Have you found an issue for your paper?
> *Linda:*   Yes. I'm writing a paper showing that medical researchers sometimes use animals for medical tests.

You will note here that Linda's second statement is also not an issue, since it cannot divide its readers. Because animals are, indeed, used for medical research, everyone will agree with this statement, so there would be no point in developing an argument about it. This statement is an **assertion,** a statement or a fact that is true. An assertion can be used to **support** a position, but it is not an issue or a possible thesis for a paper.

Finally, look at Interchange 3:

> *Fred:* Have you found an issue for your paper?
> *Linda:* Yes, I'm writing a paper that argues that there should be restrictions on
> using animals for medical research.

In this interchange, Linda's statement indicates that now she has found an issue, since her statement is likely to generate different opinions, to divide her readership. Some readers (perhaps those involved in medical research) might feel that restrictions would hamper medical progress. Others might argue that the rights of animals ought to be considered more than they are now. Of course, with a controversial issue, as with any issue, Linda will have to narrow her focus and define carefully what she means. Does she mean that she is against all use of animals for medical research? Or does she mean that there should be rules that limit when or how animals should be used?

An issue for a researched paper, then, ought to be **controversial.** Readers should be divided about how they respond to your position. If you think that all readers will agree with you, you should look for another issue.

Phrasing Your Topic as a Question

An idea for helping you decide whether your preliminary choice is a topic, an assertion, or an issue is to see if you can formulate a question about it. To some extent, one might say that all research begins with a **question,** which leads to exploration of possible answers. Framing a question, then, can lead you in possible directions for searching for information. In Linda's third interchange with Fred, she states, "I'm writing a paper that argues that there should be restrictions on using animals for medical research," a statement that focuses on an issue. That statement could be rephrased as the following question, "**Should there be** restrictions on using animals for medical research?" Note that this question also suggests other questions that can help focus the direction of the paper. Some of these questions might be: **When** should there be restrictions on using animals for medical research? **What** should be the nature of these restrictions? **Where** or in which instances should there be restrictions? and **Why** should there be restrictions on using animals for medical research? Formulating questions can help you decide what additional information you might need to develop your argument.

If we apply the test of formulating a question to Linda's first statement, we can see that it is not an issue. In Linda's first interchange with Fred, above, she states, "My paper is about medical research." But because this is a topic, not an issue, one cannot rephrase her statement as a question. In the second interchange, Linda states, "Medical researchers sometimes use animals for medical tests." If that statement were rephrased as a question, it would read "Do medical researchers sometimes use animals for medical tests?" a question can be answered by a simple "yes," and does not indicate a controversy or suggest a position. One could, of course, move beyond that assertion toward other aspects of the topic that might ultimately lead to the discovery of a controversial issue. One might ask, "Which researchers use animals for medical tests?" or "When do researchers use animls for medical tests?" These are questions that could ultimately lead to the issue-based question, "Should researchers use animals for medical tests?" However, on its own, an assertion cannot be rephrased as a question that will elicit controversy.

CONTROVERSY AND THE CONCEPT OF AUDIENCE

When you think about the audience you are writing for when you write a re-searched paper, you might become somewhat confused. An argumentative paper should be based on a controversial issue, something which divides your readers. However, suppose you were a member of a club aimed at halting the use of animals for medical research, and you decided to write a paper arguing this same position. If members of that club read your paper, they would all agree with you. Does that mean that this issue is not a suitable one for a research paper?

This is a complicated question, but the best answer I can give is that when you think about an issue to write about, you should select one that generates controversy within the broader boundaries of your culture. If you were writing a paper only for members of that club, and if you chose a position that everyone agreed with and supported it with information that everyone already knew, the members would all nod their heads, but they would not have learned anything new or changed their minds about the issue. However, if you presented some new information or a new perspective on the topic, then your audience would have learned something, even if they were already in agreement with your general perspective. When you select a topic for your researched paper, you should aim, if possible, at **changing your readers' minds,** at least a little. If it is unlikely that you will change your audience's mind, then you might aim to **present a new or different perspective** on the subject or to **remind an audience of something important,** about which they may not have thought for some time. The whole purpose of writing an argument is to have at least some form of effect on someone. If your paper is likely to have little effect, there is no point in writing it, except perhaps to clarify your own thinking.

Note, however, that sometimes even a general statement with which everyone seems to agree can be transformed into an issue by using a **qualifying** statement and a careful **definition.** For example, think about the following statement:

Nuclear weapons are bad.

Upon first reading it, most people would probably agree with this statement. They recall the horrors of nuclear explosions, the horribly deformed victims of Hiroshima, the possibility of world destruction. This statement, though, could be turned into a controversial issue if it were phrased as follows:

> Although most people regard nuclear weapons as simply "bad," some people argue that they have served as a deterrent to another world war. Therefore, in their role in preventing world war, nuclear weapons should not be considered all bad.

Note here that the **"although"** part of the statement refers to what people generally think about this topic, while the thesis consists of an arguable statement with which some people will disagree. Many arguments begin with an "although" clause, which presents the current situation, the ideas that are generally believed or the situation that presently exists. Using an "although" clause will help you focus your argument so that you do not write about something that everyone already believes. The although clause presents the position that, *generally*, people think of nuclear weapons as bad; nevertheless, some people might argue that there is something that might be considered good about them in that they seem to have served as a deterrent to additional world wars.

DETERMINING IF A TOPIC IS DEBATABLE

▶ *Exercise:* Decide whether each of the following is a topic, an assertion, or an issue. Then see if you can transform the topics and assertions into controversial issues.

1. All students at the university are required to take two semesters of writing.
2. Computers at the university.
3. Birth control should be easily available to everyone.
4. Both men and women should be granted maternity leave from their jobs.
5. A college degree has become a requirement for most well-paying jobs.
6. Women are generally paid less than men for the same job.

▶ *Assignment:* Read a newspaper for several days and find three controversial issues. See if you can form a statement or a position about each issue. Bring your three issues and three statements into class. Find out whether or not your classmates agree with you on any of your positions.

Facts, Values, and Policies in Argumentative Writing

Annette Rottenberg points out that most arguments are either claims of fact, claims of value, or claims of policy. Actually, though, many argumentative essays could be considered to be all three. A **claim of fact** aims to convince a reader that something is true, as in Louisa's statement (at the beginning of this chapter) that the firm had not hired any women. A **claim of value** attempts to prove that something is right or wrong, just or unjust, or effective or ineffective. Louisa was not aiming to prove simply that no women had been hired in the firm; she was asserting that this condition was not right or desirable. A **claim of policy** usually attempts to show that a policy, rule, custom, or law either is or is not desirable. In the above argument between Clif and Louisa, Louisa was arguing that the current policy was unfair, while Clif was arguing that the policy was based on what he felt was a valid reason: women are emotionally unsuited for such a job.

You will note, though, that neither Louisa nor Clif were particularly convincing in their argument (although I think that most of us would agree that Clif began the argument with his outrageous statements). But neither of them had examined both sides of the question, neither had produced substantial evidence, and neither of them made us feel that they had thoroughly researched the topic or had thought seriously about it. Moreover, since they were both so short tempered and resorted immediately to extreme statements, neither of them made us feel that they knew what they were talking about.

DEVELOPING AN ARGUMENT THAT IS CONVINCING

Unlike Louisa and Clif, you wish to be as convincing as possible when you write a researched paper, so that your readers will consider your ideas seriously. The following five suggestions will help you to develop a position convincingly:

1. Establish authority or a credible "writing self," so that your reader trusts you and will pay attention to what you have to say.
2. Be aware of your reader or audience and indicate that you have considered both sides of the question.
3. Understand the implications and consequences of your position.
4. Develop an effective argumentative structure.
5. Use evidence effectively in support of your position.
6. Make your writing lively through anecdotes and examples.

1. Establishing Authority or a Credible "Writing Self"

There are some people who on a personal level can convince anyone of anything. They have a natural charm and a convincing manner, which make people believe them. Their manner of speaking, their expression and tone of voice, their body gestures—their entire being—create the impression that they are honest and informed. These people are convincing, even those who deliberately attempt to deceive or know little about their subject. If they choose to misuse this talent, they make very successful swindlers.

On the other hand, there are people who have great difficulty convincing anyone of anything. These people can't make up their minds about what they really think and go back and forth between alternatives. Because of their own indecision, they don't inspire confidence. Then there are those who seem overly sure of themselves, so sure that they are abrasive in their manner. These people attempt to dictate what people ought to think, without acknowledging that other people may have ideas, too. Often they are poorly informed about their subject and simply assert their ideas without proof or evidence.

A credible "writing self" is neither indecisive nor over confident; it is one which people will believe and trust. In creating a credible writing self, you are aiming to convince your readers that you have considered different facets of the topic, that you know what you are talking about, and that you are honest, informed, and reasonable.

USING A REASONABLE TONE

If you look at television advertisements, you will note that for most products, the person advocating their use seems to be a reasonable, coherent, thoughtful person. We tend to believe people who seem to be in control of themselves and distrust those who seem out of control or hysterical. In writing an argument for a researched paper, then, you should aim for a forceful, but measured tone. You should indicate that you feel strongly about a topic, but you should avoid inflammatory rhetoric, which can create the impression that you are about to "freak out."

In the following excerpt from an antiabortion editorial, Henry J. Hyde attempts to show that despite many claims to the contrary, the American people are not in favor of abortion. Note that Hyde asserts, rather than substantiates his position:

> But that is the hard fact of the matter. The propaganda campaign has failed. And it has failed because it tried to teach the American people something they know in their hearts is wrong—that the abortion license is congruent with our deep national commitment to liberty and justice for all . . .
>
> The abortion license has led to a terrible coarsening of our public life. Listen to the remarks of my House colleague Rep. Patricia Schroeder (D–Colo.), on the MacNeil/Lehrer News Hour on July 3. "I find it amazing that it should be state and federal policy that absolutely every child should be born, whether they have AIDS, no matter what condition they're in, whether they're wanted, what condition their parents are in. . . ."
>
> This is American liberalism? This is the tradition that freed the slaves, gained women the vote, enacted Social Security, made our streets and public buildings accessible to the handicapped?

Several of the terms used here, in particular "propaganda campaign" and "abortion license," are exaggerated, used to inflame rather than explain. Hyde is implying that anyone in favor of abortion must be against acknowledged "American" traditions, such as freeing the slaves, gaining women the vote, enacting social security, and making streets and public buildings accessible to the handicapped. If you think about these associations, you know they are not valid and do not logically strengthen Hyde's position. In this article, Hyde neither uses a measured tone, nor has he developed his position with good reasons. Therefore, we tend to stand back from accepting his ideas. He has not projected a writing "self" or persona that we are inclined to trust.

Establishing Authority Through Knowledge

Using a reasonable tone and appearing trustworthy are important ways of creating a credible writing self. Another is to establish authority as an author, that is, to appear to your reader as knowledgeable and in control of your material. Advertisers are well aware of this; they know that an authority (a famous person, for example) or even someone who seems to be an authority (an actor dressed up to look like a doctor, for example) can be more convincing than the average person. We all recognize that those who have attained high status in their fields achieve authority simply by the use of their names. However, how do you establish authority, or present a believable writing "self" if you are only a student writing about a topic that is relatively new to you?

THE AUTHORITY OF PERSONAL EXPERIENCE

As a student, you are probably not yet a recognized expert in any field, and so your name on an essay or a reference to yourself within the essay would not help to make your argument convincing. However, for some topics, your personal experience may serve to establish you as knowledgeable, simply by illustrating your personal investment in the topic. In the following opening paragraphs, for example, Anna Quindlen, in her essay arguing against capital punishment,* indicates her familiarity with a series of murders committed by Ted Bundy. She also emphasizes her role as a mother who views the killing of young women with particular horror. Thus, although she is not an acknowledged expert in the field of criminology, Quindlen establishes authority by stressing her personal associations with the topic:

> Ted Bundy and I go back a long way, to a time when there was a series of unsolved murders in Washington State known only as the Ted murders. Like a lot of reporters, I'm something of a crime buff. But the Washington Ted murders—and the ones that followed in Utah, Colorado, and finally in Florida where Ted Bundy was convicted and sentenced to die—fascinated me because I could see myself as one of the victims. . . .
>
> The death penalty and I, on the other hand, seem to have nothing in common. But Ted Bundy has made me think about it all over again, now that the outlines of my 60's liberalism have been filled in with a decade as a reporter covering some of the worst back alleys in New York City and three years as a mother who, like most, would lay down her life for her kids.

*Anna Quindlen, excerpt from "Life in the 30s—Death Penalty's False Promise: An Eye for an Eye," *The New York Times*, September 17, 1986. Copyright © 1986 by The New York Times Company. Reprinted by permission.

Thus, in the beginning of this article, Quindlen's references to her early awareness of the Bundy murders, her days as a reporter in New York City, and her involvement with her children have shown that her own life experiences have qualified her for reflecting on this topic and formulating a position.

THE AUTHORITY OF INFORMATION

Even if you are not an expert in your field, you can establish authority by knowing your subject well. Only when you thoroughly understand your topic will you be able to write about it with conviction. It is therefore important that you examine the background of your topic, define your terms, and read several sources that can give you alternative points of view.

2.   Be Aware of Your Audience

IDENTIFYING WITH YOUR OPPONENT: THE "WE"ATTITUDE

You are more likely to convince your reader of your position if you indicate that you are aware of the opposing position and can even identify with it to some extent. Note the difference in acknowledging the opponent's position in the following two interchanges:

Scenario 1

Steve: Did you get a doctor's appointment for next week?

George: No, the doctor I usually see was on vacation and the only appointment they had for that time was with a woman doctor. I'm not going to a woman doctor! They're never as good as men!

Steve: Why not? Are you living in the Dark Ages? Women are just as good doctors as men.

George: Well, you can say what you like, but I'm still not going.

Scenario 2

Steve: Did you get a doctor's appointment for next week?

George: No, the doctor I usually see was on vacation and the only appointment they had for that time was with a woman doctor. I'm not going to a woman doctor! They're never as good as men!

Steve: I understand how you feel. I used to feel that way myself, even though it was kind of a sexist position. But I've learned that there are many really fine women doctors, and Dr. Smith is particularly good. She has top medical credentials, excellent experience, and a terrific way of putting people at ease. I'm going to her myself.

Now at this point, George might still say "Well, you can say what you like, but I'm still not going." Some people won't change their minds no matter what. But, then again, he might also say this: "Okay, maybe I decided too quickly. If she's that good, and you've used her yourself, maybe I'll give her a try."

The psychologist Carl Rogers has become associated with the idea that before you can convince people of a position, you have to indicate that you are aware of how they feel initially. Rogers points out that people do not like to be told that they are absolutely wrong, and, if you attempt to do so, they are likely to resist what you have to say because they will perceive you as threatening. In this first interchange, Steve told George that he was living in the Dark Ages, and George's reaction was one of resistance. But, according to Rogers, if you show that you understand your opponent's position, you are more likely to be convincing (which is what happened in the second interchange). It makes sense, then, for you to think about how your readers might feel when you present your position. Do not simply present your own point of view and tell readers who think otherwise that they are simply wrong.

THINKING ABOUT YOUR AUDIENCE: AN EXAMPLE

In the following excerpt,* Vera Elleson points out that although all of us were raised to be competitive, some aspects of competition are undesirable. Notice how Elleson indicates to her readers that she, too, shares the competitive spirit. She does not simply lecture to her readers or show them that their thinking is faulty:

> We can have an impact—on the setting in which we work, our friends, family, co-workers, and profession. Each of us must begin with ourselves. Most of us have been acculturated to a competitive mode of behavior. We must recognize how we view and interact with others. It is time now to change what is not positive and growth-enhancing.
>
> Each of us should pause and ask, "Do I put others down or fail to support others in my attempt to get ahead? Do my competitive strivings interfere with my own emotional well-being, with the development of trust between me and others, and with my personal or professional effectiveness?" How often do educators move others by setting them against each other in a vicious struggle for a position at the top? Or do they work cooperatively with students, each learning from and teaching the other?

Using "we" instead of "you" lets readers know that the writer understands their position. It is also a good idea to acknowledge an opponent's position before presenting your own. Let your reader know that you have already considered the opposite position and then cite reasons why you don't think this position is valid.

▶ *An Exercise in Thinking About Your Audience:* Think about a controversial issue. Think about at least two extreme opposing positions. Then formulate your own position (which might be a compromise between the two extremes). Working in groups of three to five, discuss how you might acknowledge the opposite position in a researched paper:

Example

Topic: Smoking in restaurants.

*"Is Competition a Cultural Imperative?" *Education Digest,* November 1984.

Issue: Should smoking be allowed in restaurants?
Issue: Should smoking be allowed in restaurants?

One Extreme Position: Smoking should be outlawed in all restaurants because it is a health hazard. (This has been proposed in the city of Los Angeles.)

An Opposing Extreme Position: Smoking should not be outlawed anywhere, since people have the freedom to do as they please with their own health.

Compromise Position: Smoking should not be allowed in restaurants except in restricted sections (since secondary smoke affects others as well as the smokers).

Acknowledging the Opposite Position: Sample Paragraph

Those who smoke might feel that forbidding smoking in restaurants is an unnecessary restriction of individual freedom and that whether or not people decide to smoke is their own business. They might also argue that if the government passed a law against smoking in restaurants, they could then pass laws restricting all sorts of other activities. However, although I share this concern about the dangers of restricting individual freedom, and recognize that for some people, smoking is an important part of enjoying a meal, I still advocate forbidding smoking in restaurants except in restricted sections. Unlike many activities that only endanger the person involved, smoking in restaurants poses a threat to the health and comfort of everyone around, not just to the smoker.

Analysis of Sample Paragraph

1. Those who smoke might feel that forbidding smoking in restaurants is an unnecessary restriction of individual freedom and that whether or not people decide to smoke is their own business **(first acknowledgment of the opposite position)**.
2. They might also argue that if the government passed a law against smoking in restaurants, they could then pass laws restricting all sorts of other activities **(second acknowledgment of the opposite position)**.
3. However, although I share this concern about the dangers of restricting individual freedom, **(third acknowledgment—indicating that you share these concerns)** and even recognize that for some people, smoking is an important part of enjoying a meal **(fourth acknowledgment)**, I still advocate forbidding smoking in restaurants except in restricted sections **(main position)**.
4. Unlike many activities that only endanger the person involved, smoking in restaurants poses a threat to the health and comfort of everyone around, not just to the smoker **(reason for position)**.

3. Understanding the Implications and Consequences of Your Position

THE COMPLEX NATURE OF PROBLEMATIC ISSUES

Social, ethical, or political dilemmas of our culture usually have no easy answers, no clearly marked right and wrong; by definition a topic for a researched paper is likely to be complex. To take an intelligent **stand** on a complex issue, then, means that we have to acknowledge this complexity and indicate that we are aware that there are no simple answers. Although on some issues, those about which you have especially strong opinions, you might be able to take a clearly defined, emphatically stated stance, sometimes your position on a complex issue might be a **compromise** between two extreme stances. (For example, some people feel that abortion is wrong under *any* circumstances and therefore that all abortions should not be allowed. Others feel that women should have access to abortion whenever they wish and that abortion should be allowed freely. A thoughtful position on this issue might involve a middle ground between these two extremes.)

However, whether you take a strong position on one side of an issue, or develop a position that is a compromise between two extremes, you should be aware of the consequences and implications of your position and realize that it is likely that **any position is likely to favor one group over another.** There are very few policies, legal solutions, plans for living, or schemes for reform that are going to please everyone. Society is diverse, people have different goals and needs, and any policy that is favorable to one group is probably going to be unfavorable to another. Thus, in developing a position, you should consider what effect that position is likely to have and on whom that effect is likely to be most significant.

To illustrate this point, let us examine the Los Angeles proposal formulated earlier, that smoking should not be allowed in restaurants because it constitutes a health hazard. Then let us consider why smoking in restaurants is considered a complex issue and what differences in opinion one might encounter. Finally, let us consider the consequences and implications of a position on this topic.

On first thinking about this topic, one might feel that this topic is not complex at all. It is well known that smoking is dangerous to people's health, and there are many statistics showing the relationship between smoking and a variety of lung diseases, such as lung cancer and emphysema. When one thinks about these statistics, forbidding smoking in restaurants seems like a reasonable idea since the consequences seem completely positive: improvement of people's health. A logical conclusion might be that everyone would be in favor of such a proposal.

If you think about human nature, though, you will realize that the solution is not that simple, since people do not always do what is good for them. You might then consider whether you think that society ought to take on that role. Do you view society in the role of protecting people from themselves? (Chapter 8 contains readings that address this issue.) Perhaps society *ought* to forbid any behavior that is dangerous to people's health. At the present time, marijuana and other drugs are illegal for just this reason. Maybe alcohol should also be forbidden by law. How about other unhealthful habits, such as drinking coffee, eating too many sweets, or not getting enough sleep? Should these be forbidden by law as well? If you feel that smoking should be outlawed on the basis of being unhealthful, why not include other health-endangering habits as well?

▶ *An Exercise in Thinking About Consequences and Implications:* Write a one- to two-page essay responding to the following question: Should something that is dangerous to people's health be outlawed? Why or why not?

Then compare answers with your classmates.

In responding to the above exercise, you have probably come to the conclusion that a position that advocates outlawing *anything* that is dangerous to people's health would be considered extreme in our society. Some of you may have decided that what a person does is his own business, and that people should have freedom to engage in any behaviors they wish, even those which are injurious to health, as long as these behaviors do not harm others. Eating too many sweets or not getting enough sleep, even drinking alcohol, as long as the drinker is not also a driver, does not endanger anyone else's health except that of the person who is doing it. Many of you may feel that in a free society, what a person does to affect his own health is usually that person's own business.

Others of you may have responded in terms of consequences—you may have pointed out that it would be impossible to enforce a law that restricted all behaviors that were injurious to health. If we remember prohibition during the 1920s, and if we recall what we know of human nature, we will realize that a policy that forbids all unhealthful habits would result in numerous people breaking the law, and that unless we had a society in which people were under constant surveillance (as in George Orwell's *1984*), such infractions would be difficult, if not impossible, to detect.

Now let us return to the smoking issue. Here are the two extreme positions: 1. Smoking should be forbidden everywhere since it is dangerous to health, versus 2. What people do to endanger their own health is their own business. However, what makes the smoking issue additionally complex is the fact that smoking doesn't only endanger the health of smokers; it also affects those around them who are breathing the smoke-filled air. This adds another dimension to the argument— the idea that smoking affects others as well. This perspective suggests the idea that if smoking also endangers the health of nonsmokers, then it does not fall into the category of being simply a personal habit. Moreover, what adds even further complexity to the issue is the question of where the smoking is to take place, since restaurants have particular features that are not the same as those in many other places. Restaurants are usually small, enclosed spaces, where other people's smoking is likely to have a greater effect on nonsmokers than it often does elsewhere (such as out on the street). It could also be pointed out that since people go to restaurants to *eat,* and since the smell of smoke to nonsmokers can interfere with their enjoyment of food, that smoking in restaurants creates particular problems for nonsmokers.

Thus, in thinking about a complex issue such as this, one might decide on a **compromise** position—that smoking should be forbidden in restaurants except in certain restricted sections. (Actually, in many restaurants this is already a policy.) Yet even when you develop a position that seems to be a compromise, you will often discover that the position inevitably benefits one side more than another. (For example, requiring smokers to eat in restricted sections probably gives greater consideration to the rights of nonsmokers.) In thinking about the consequences and implications of a potential position for your researched paper, then, you might think about the following questions:

1. What is the area of controversy?
2. Can I state two extreme positions concerning this area of controversy?

Do I believe in one of these two extreme positions? Can I develop a
position that is a qualification or a compromise?

3. Who is likely to benefit from my position? Who is not likely to benefit?

4. Can I predict the consequences and implications of my position? Is it
likely that my ideas can be implemented or enforced?

▶ ***Exercise in Analysis:*** Skim through one or two of the content chapters to
locate a controversial issue. Then, for that issue, see if you can determine at least
two extreme positions, and a possible compromise between the two positions.
Write these positions and your compromise position in complete sentences. Then
think about the consequences and implications of these positions. (Who is likely
to benefit from each one? Can these ideas be implemented or enforced?)

4. Developing an Effective Argumentative Structure

Determining a structure for a researched paper, like that for any text, depends on
what you are trying to accomplish. Form must follow content, not the other way
around. However, over many years, the classical form of argumentation has come
to be accepted, and it is a good idea for you to know what that is. But once you
have studied it, you are then free to modify it to suit your own purposes.

THE CLASSICAL ARGUMENTATIVE STRUCTURE

A classical argument usually contains the following sections:

1. **Introduction.** In this section, which may consist of only one or two
   paragraphs, you introduce your topic, indicate why it is important, and
   present your position.

2. **Background information and definitions.** In this section, you place
   your position within a cultural context, perhaps by showing that it has
   aroused current interest, that it generally stimulates controversy, or that
   is has not been understood adequately. This section might include personal experience that is relevant to the topic and might define important
   key terms.

3. **Acknowledgment of opposing points of view.** In this section, you
   summarize positions that are opposed to your own. Such a summary
   indicates that you understand other positions; in fact, you may concede
   that certain aspects of the opposing argument have merit and also point
   out weaknesses. A discussion of opposing arguments leads naturally into
   the presentation of your main arguments. It also establishes you as someone who has researched the topic thoroughly and shows that you realize
   that the issue is complex.

4. **Presenting your main position.** This is usually the longest and most substantial section of your essay. In this section you present your position or claim, present one or more reasons, and support your reasons logically, either with evidence (examples, facts, statistics, data) or with other reasons, and illustrative examples.

5. **Anticipation and refutation of possible objections to your position.** If you think of your argument as a kind of dialogue, you will be able to envision possible objections to your position. By doing this, you will appear to your reader to be in total control of your subject matter.

6. **Conclusion.** This section will summarize your main argument and perhaps suggests what action, if any, the readers ought to take. Perhaps it indicates why the issue is important or postulates possible implications of a policy or situation. In general, it provides readers with a sense of closure on the topic.

Most formal arguments will include these sections, although they might not be in exactly this order. Read the following essay by Norman Cousins, "How to Make People Smaller Than They Are" (*Saturday Review*, December 1978). Then answer the following questions:

1. Find Cousins' position in this essay. In which paragraph does it appear?
2. How does Cousins establish a credible "writing self" in this essay? How does he indicate concern with the problem he is addressing?
3. Where does Cousins discuss background information?
4. What are Cousins' reasons for his position?
5. Where does Cousins acknowledge an opposing position?

How to Make People Smaller Than They Are

Norman Cousins

Three months ago in this space we wrote about the costly retreat from the humanities on all the levels of American education. Since that time, we have had occasion to visit a number of campuses and have been troubled to find that the general situation is even more serious than we had thought. It has become apparent to us that one of the biggest problems confronting American education today is the increasing vocationalization of our colleges and universities. Throughout the country, schools are under pressure to become job-training centers and employment agencies.

The pressure comes mainly from two sources. One is the growing determination of many citizens to reduce taxes—understandable and even commendable in itself, but irrational and irresponsible when connected to the reduction or dismantling of vital public services. The second source of pressure comes from parents and students who tend to scorn courses of study that do not teach people how to become attractive to employers in a rapidly tightening job market.

It is absurd to believe that the development of skills does not also require the systematic development of the human mind. Education is being measured more by the size of the benefits the individual can extract from society than by the extent to which the individual can come into possession of his or her full powers. The result is that the life-giving juices are in danger of being drained out of education.

Emphasis on "practicalities" is being characterized by the subordination of words to numbers. History is seen not as essential experience to be transmitted to new generations, but as abstractions that carry dank odors. Art is regarded as something that calls for indulgence or patronage and that has no place among the practical realities. Political science is viewed more as a specialized subject for people who want to go into politics than as an opportunity for citizens to develop a knowledgeable relationship with the systems by which human societies are governed. Finally, literature and philosophy are assigned the role of add-ons—intellectual adornments that have nothing to do with "genuine" education.

Instead of trying to shrink the liberal arts, the American people ought to be putting pressure on colleges and universities to increase the ratio of the humanities to the sciences. Most serious studies of medical-school curricula in recent years have called attention to the stark gaps in the liberal education of medical students. The experts agree that the schools shouldn't leave it up to students to close those gaps.

The irony of the emphasis being placed on careers is that nothing is more valuable for anyone who has had a professional or vocational education than to be able to deal with abstractions or complexities, or to feel comfortable with subtleties of thought or language, or to think sequentially. The doctor who knows only disease is at a disadvantage alongside the doctor who knows at least as much about people as he does about pathological organisms. The lawyer who argues in court from a narrow legal base is no match for the lawyer who can connect legal precedents to historical experience and who employs wide-ranging intellectual resources. The business executive whose competence in general management is bolstered by an artistic ability to deal with people is of prime value to his company. For the technologist, the engineering of consent can be just as important as the engineering of moving parts. In all these respects, the liberal arts have much to offer. Just in terms of career preparation, therefore, a student is shortchanging himself by shortcutting the humanities.

But even if it could be demonstrated that the humanities contribute nothing directly to a job, they would still be an essential part of the educational equipment of any person who wants to come to terms with life. The humanities would be expendable only if human beings didn't have to make decisions that affect their lives and the lives of others; if the human past never existed or had nothing to tell us about the present; if thought processes were irrelevant to the achievement of purpose; if creativity was beyond the human mind and had nothing to do with the joy of living; if human relationships were random aspects of life; if human beings never had to cope with panic or pain, or if they never had to anticipate the connection between cause and effect; if all the mysteries of mind and nature were fully plumbed; and if no special demands arose from the accident of being born a human being instead of a hen or a hog.

Finally, there would be good reason to eliminate the humanities if a free society were not absolutely dependent on a functioning citizenry. If the main purpose of a university is job training, then the underlying philosophy of our government has little meaning. The debates that went into the making of American Society concerned not just institutions or governing principles but the capacity of humans to sustain those institutions. Whatever the disagreements were over other issues at the American Constitutional Convention, the fundamental question sensed by everyone, a question that lay over the entire assembly, was whether the people themselves would understand what it meant to hold the ultimate power of society, and whether they had enough of a sense of history and destiny to know where they had been and where they ought to be going.

Jefferson was prouder of having been the founder of the University of Virginia than of having been President of the United States. He knew that the educated and developed mind was the best assurance that a political system could be made to work—a system based on the informed consent of the governed. If this idea fails, then all the saved tax dollars in the world will not be enough to prevent the nation from turning on itself.

---

5.   Using Evidence Effectively

When you cite reasons for your position, you must support them with appropriate, accurate, and relevant evidence. This evidence can be drawn from a number of sources, including examples from experience, the statements of authorities, and statistics.

EXPERIENCE AS EVIDENCE: REAL AND HYPOTHETICAL

A number of topics suitable for a researched paper can be substantiated by examples drawn from your own life or from the lives of other individuals. If you choose a topic of concern to students or to those in the field of education, you may indeed find that you can cite relevant examples based on your own experience or that of other students. Or you might decide to use a hypothetical example to illustrate your point. In his essay "The Case for Torture" (*Newsweek,* 1982), Michael

Levin develops the point that although our society is against torture, there are some extreme cases in which even the most gentle person will be in favor of it. To introduce his position, Levin creates the hypothetical example of a terrorist who has hidden an atomic bomb on Manhattan Island. He then asks whether or not torture should be used to locate the bomb and then moves on to other cases, not quite as extreme to similarly illustrate his point. Citing examples from your own or others' lives or creating appropriate hypothetical examples as illustrations is an effective way of providing support.

THE STATEMENTS OF AUTHORITIES

Showing that authorities in the field agree with your statements is another effective method of gaining support for a position. Of course, these experts should be acknowledged authorities in their field (simply having one's name in print does not automatically indicate expertise) and their statements should be sufficiently current so that they are relevant to the situation under consideration. For example, the effects of secondary smoking have only recently been acknowledged, so if you were writing about the issue of smoking in restaurants, it would be important to cite a recent medical expert on that topic. Stuart Hirschberg* points out that expert testimony usually 1. points out a causal connection, 2. offers a prediction about the future, and 3. offers a solution to a problem. For example, on the topic of smoking in restaurants, the expert might 1. show the connection between smoking and secondary effects (causal connection), 2. point out that it would be impractical to ban smoking altogether (offer a prediction about the future), or 3. propose to ban smoking in restaurants except in restricted sections (offer a compromise solution).

STATISTICS AS EVIDENCE

Statistics can be an extremely forceful way of supporting a position. However, it is important to realize that statistics can also be misleading, if they are not current or representative of the population they are intended to describe. In the issue concerning secondary smoking, the statistics regarding the effect on secondary smokers has only recently been published, so if you were writing about this topic, you would have to be careful that you used only the most recent studies. In citing statistics, it is also important that you use only those published by reliable sources (large, well-known scientific institutions or government agencies such as the U.S. Bureau of Census or the Centers for Disease Control are two examples).

What can be particularly misleading about statistics is the extent to which they actually represent the general population. For example, if you questioned students in one particular class about their feelings concerning required courses, you might find that they were all in favor of them and conclude that students in general have positive feelings about required courses. Yet this one class might have been special in some way and may not be representative of the general population of students

Strategies of Argument, New York: Macmillan, 1990.

at the university. Moreover, some statistics can be misleading because of erroneous sampling methods. One common error in sampling results from using a self-selecting population. For example, if, after a departmental exam, you posted a large sign that said "Please fill out this form to express your feelings about the final examination," it is likely that only students who had negative feelings would respond voluntarily. (The others probably did not have strong enough feelings to bother filling out the form.) You might then conclude that students in general hated the final examination, but this may not have been the case at all since you were not using a representative sample. To obtain meaningful statistics in this situation, you would have to question a **random sample** of students, and include a wide range (men and women, young and old, etc.). Statistics can be an extremely effective means of support, but it is important to think about what they mean when you include them as evidence.

BEING LOGICAL: THE USE OF REASON

An obvious requirement of effective support is that it be logical, that is, that it be based on rational thinking. Those who study formal argument usually identify two types of reasoning: **inductive** and **deductive,** and I include a brief discussion of these to help you gain a better understanding of how you might use logic in support of your position.

Inductive reasoning establishes a conclusion based on incomplete evidence, on a less than a full sample. We actually use this form of reasoning very frequently, since we cannot experience everything. The following interchange is an example of inductive reasoning:

Maria: I'm going over to Smith's market to pick up some fresh fruit for lunch.
Anna: Oh, don't go to Smith's. I've gone there four times this week, and every time they were out of really fresh fruit. All they had left were some wormy-looking apples.

In this interchange, Anna's conclusion that Smith's is not a good store for fresh fruit was reached *inductively,* in that it was based on several visits, although not on visits occurring every day. But because Anna feels that her four visits provide sufficient evidence for her conclusion, she cautions Maria against going there.

Most of the information we have about everyday life we have obtained through induction. Although we have not seen every alligator in the world, the few we have seen, either live or in pictures or films, have lived in swamps. We therefore believe that alligators live in swamps. Similarly, we believe that cats meow and birds sing, although surely we have not seen every cat or bird for ourselves.

In order to evaluate a conclusion reached by induction, you have to feel that your sample provides an **adequate, representative** sample. (This, of course, pertains to statistics that are derived inductively.) If you say, "All women doctors are incompetent. Let me tell you about this awful woman doctor I went to," you are basing a conclusion on an inadequate sample (only *one* woman doctor). If you stand outside the student cafeteria and ask people to fill out a questionnaire aimed at showing how poor the food is, you will not have obtained a sample that is *representative* of the whole student population, since only those students who dislike the food are likely to respond.

Returning to the argument concerning forbidding smoking in restaurants, evidence concerning the relationship between smoking and lung diseases was reached inductively, through controlled experiments conducted under laboratory conditions. Unlike Anna, who based a conclusion on only four visits (and, after all, maybe Smith's was out of fresh fruit *only* during those visits), experiments involving the relationship between smoking and lung disease use thousands of subjects, repeated many times, to ensure that the conclusions are valid. When we use inductive reasoning to reach a conclusion, though, we have to be careful that our experience has really been adequate and representative. Many unfair stereotypes are formulated because people generalize hastily from very limited experience.

DEDUCTIVE REASONING

Deductive reasoning establishes conclusions based on a fundamental truth, belief, or value of the culture. The most important tool of deductive reasoning is the **syllogism,** which consists of a major premise (or fundamental truth, belief, or value), a minor premise, which consists of a particular example of the major premise, and the conclusion, which uses the information in the two premises to assert that what is true of the major premise is also true of the minor premise. A famous syllogism is the following:

> All men are mortal (major premise).
>
> Richard is a man (minor premise).
>
> Therefore, Richard is mortal.

The above syllogism is both valid and true, because both the major and the minor premises are true. However, note that the following syllogism is valid, but not true:

> All students like rock music.
>
> Jonathan is a student.
>
> Therefore, Jonathan likes rock music.

As it is easy to see, the major premise, "All students like rock music" is not true. (Although *many* students may like rock music, not all of them do.) Therefore, although the syllogism is valid in that it fulfills the proper form, it cannot be considered true.

Here is a paragraph based on Elisa's paper in Chapter 1 that uses deductive reasoning:

> The First Amendment to the United States Bill of Rights states that "Congress shall make no law respecting an establishment of religion or prohibiting the

free exercise thereof, or abridging the freedom of speech." That amendment, fundamental to the concept of a free society, may be regarded as a guarantee against censorship, implying that citizens of the United States have the liberty of reading anything they choose. By censoring what students are able to read, the proposed screening committee would deprive students of their rights as citizens.

Here is the deductive pattern:

Censorship is forbidden under the Bill of Rights.

The screening committee is a form of censorship.

Therefore, the screening committee would be forbidden under the Bill of Rights.

FALLACIES OR ERRORS IN LOGIC

Not every argument is developed logically. Many rely on errors in reasoning that do nothing to provide support. Being aware of some of these common **logical fallacies** can help you evaluate the strength of your evidence.

1. **Presuming cause and effect.** The *post hoc* fallacy is one in which one event is said to have caused another simply because they occurred in sequence. This type of thinking presumes a relationship between events without recognizing other factors that may have contributed. It is a very common way of thinking, but it does not incorporate logic. Here are some examples:

   "Don't take Susan on a picnic. Everytime I go somewhere with her, it rains!" (Obviously, Susan could not have had anything to do with the rain despite the coincidence.)

   "We have discovered that all of the criminals in the county jail ate white bread as children. Therefore, white bread leads to criminal behavior." (The white bread obviously did not *cause* the criminal behavior.)

2. **Generalizations from insufficient evidence: hasty generalization.** Related to the fallacy of presuming causality is the hasty generalization, which bases claims on insufficient evidence. An example of a hasty generalization is the following:

   "We shouldn't allow girls from that part of town into our club. I once knew a girl from there and she was a thief."

   Loose generalization. A loose generalization is an overly broad, unqualified statement, which does not allow for exceptions of complexity.

   "Girls are not good in math" is an example of a loose generalization.

3. **False analogy.** This form of argument presumes that if two things or people are alike in one or two ways, they will be alike in other ways also. Here is an example:

   People should be allowed to smoke in restaurants. If they are allowed to drink in restaurants, they should be allowed to smoke as well. (This analogy ignores the fact that smoking in restaurants interferes with others, while drinking, at least in moderation, does not.)

4. **Attacking the person rather than the issue.** An *ad hominem* argument attacks a person, rather than an issue.

   "Don't listen to Fred's ideas for a new computer system. He's a homosexual," is an example of this type of fallacy. In this case, whether or not Fred is a homosexual is irrelevant to the argument.

5. **Appeals to false authority and the bandwagon.** Television ads frequently use well-known stars to advertise products about which they really have no expertise. If a famous movie star endorses a particular product, it does not mean that the product is therefore worth buying. Similarly, if a famous person endorses a particular social or ethical position, it does not mean that the position is therefore right or just.

   The **bandwagon effect** is a type of logical fallacy that maintains that if everyone or a lot of people believe or do something, then it must be right. "Millions of people are in favor of the death penalty. Therefore, it must be right," is an example of using bandwagon thinking.

6. **Circular reasoning.** Circular reasoning is another common form of illogical thinking. It occurs when you state your position and then restate it in different words as your reason. An obvious example of circular reasoning is the following:

   "Excess drinking is *detrimental to health* because it *causes harm to the body.*"

   A more complicated form of circular reasoning is the following:

   Corporations, too, would *benefit from the decrease in taxes* because business *needs the advantages a decrease would bring*.

   Becoming aware of these common errors in logic will help you avoid them in your own writing.

7. **Black and white thinking.** This is a form of reasoning that presumes that there are only two possibilities, when there may be many. Black and white reasoning is exemplified in the following statement:

   Either we must institute a strict dress code or employees will dress inappropriately.

This statement overlooks the possibility that general specifications about dress might be sufficient or that employees may well dress appropriately even without a dress code.

8. **Non sequitur.** This is a fallacy in which a piece of evidence does not relate directly to the idea being supported. Saying that a brand of toothpaste is the best because the company has a wonderful marketing department is an example of this kind of fallacy.

9. **Slippery-slope.** This type of argument presumes a chain of events that is likely to occur from one original event. An example of a slippery-slope argument is as follows:

   I can't allow my son to join that mountain climbing club. If he does, he will be climbing mountains at least once a week, then twice a week. Before you know it, he will spend all of his time climbing mountains and won't be able to keep up with his studies.

Using Details and Examples

No matter how thoroughly you have researched your topic, how carefully you have worked out your reasoning, and how credibly you have created your "writing self," your reader will be bored and unconvinced if you do not write in a lively style with many colorful details, specific examples, and, if appropriate, anecdotes and short narratives. A researched paper about the necessity for antidiscrimination policies to provide women with equal opportunity can be enhanced by a specific reference to a particular woman who is attempting to obtain a particular position. If you write a paper about the necessity of restricting medical research done on animals, you would probably include descriptions of how animals are being mistreated. A paper in favor of liberalized abortion policies might refer to specific instances in the past in which women resorted to illegal methods. Examples and details will bring your writing to life and make it accessible to your reader, even when you are writing about a complex topic.

Writing the Introduction

I suspect that more pencils are chewed over the writing of an introduction than over any other section of a paper. Writers often have problems with introductions because they try to write them first, before they really know what they want to say. If you are having difficulty writing an introduction, my general recommendation is to stop trying to write it and save it for last, after you have written the rest of the paper. Usually, once you have clarified your thinking, your introduction will not be such a problem.

If you think about the purpose of your introduction, you will not be at a loss for ideas. Some of the following suggestions can be included in the introduction:

1. **The topic, the issue, and the controversy.** Readers need to know what subject you are going to write about and why that subject is controversial.

2. **Your position or thesis.** Readers also should be told where you stand on this controversy. State your position clearly in the introduction or, for longer papers, within the first several paragraphs.

3. **The significance of the topic.** Readers need to know why a topic is important or significant.

4. **Background of the topic.** Use the introduction to present relevant background material and define important terms. However, more detailed background and definitions should be discussed in the body of the paper.

5. **Attracting your reader.** The introduction is a good place to interest your reader in what you have to say. Establishing the significance of your topic is a good way of doing this. Another technique is to challenge a prevailing view, present a new piece of information, or use an illustrative example or quotation.

Writing the Conclusion

Conclusions are also difficult. After grinding away at a paper, researching, writing, rewriting, restructuring, and refocusing, the temptation is to say, "Well, that's all I have to say, so good-bye." Don't give in to that temptation, though. Conclusions are important too. They focus the reader's attention back to the problem addressed in the introduction and, most important, emphasize why what you have been discussing is significant. Here are some possibilities for writing conclusions:

Returning to Something in the Introduction

Often, you have introduced your topic with a statement of a particular problem or illustration of a situation that needs to be addressed. If your introduction contains this material, you might wish to return to it in the conclusion. Returning full circle to the introduction can provide your essay with unity. (Elisa's essay in Chapter 1 uses this technique.)

Postulating the Implications of Your Position

You might conclude your researched paper by showing how the issue you have discussed will have an impact on society as a whole, thus placing the issue in a wider context. A paper arguing against restricting smoking in restaurants, for example, might refer to the wider context of individual rights or suggest that if smoking is restricted, other individual liberties could be threatened as well.

Illustrating Your Position with an Anecdote

You might help your reader experience the significance of your position by concluding with an illustrative anecdote or description. For example, an essay arguing in favor of affirmative action policies to provide women with equal opportunity might cite the example of a particular woman who is now successfully launched in a career or the opposite situation of a bright woman who has remained in a dead-end job due solely to lack of opportunity. A paper arguing in favor of restricting smoking in restaurants could conclude with a description of a smoke-filled room, where it is difficult even to see, let alone taste, the food. Of course, in using this method of conclusion, you have to be careful not to be silly or obvious. Clever use of this type of conclusion, though, can be extremely effective.

Summarizing

The most common form of concluding an essay is to summarize your main points, restating why the issue is important. However, unless your essay is fairly complex, this type of conclusion is simply a restatement of the introduction, which many readers may not find effective.

▶ *Exercise:* Look through some of the readings in the second half of this book. Find some introductions and conclusions for discussion in class.

Writing an argument on a complex issue is not simply a matter of technique—it really involves a mode of thinking. This type of thinking can be developed as a habit, which you can cultivate by reading the newspapers, listening to the news, asking questions, and having discussions. The more you ponder the issues of our culture, the wider will be your perspective and the deeper will be your understanding. And writing about these issues will further enrich your point of view.

4　Evaluating Information

In *Through the Looking Glass* by Lewis Carroll, the White Queen claims that believing information is simply a matter of effort and practice, and, of course, we all know that this is nonsense. Actually, what is not usually recognized is that *not* believing what you read or hear sometimes involves effort and practice or at least awareness. This chapter is concerned with helping you consider when to believe and when to doubt, that is, how to decide if a piece of information from an outside source is true or worth considering.

ASSESSING YOUR ATTITUDE TOWARD PRINTED MATERIAL

In order to develop skill at working with outside sources, it is a good idea to consider how you generally react when you read information in articles or books. Do you usually believe what you read? Or do you tend to be skeptical? Think about this question the next time you read a text that you consider to be nonfiction. To help you focus your thinking, consider whether the following statements should be answered "true" or "false."

1. Information from a published work is always true.
2. When a work is published, all statements by the writer are carefully checked by the editor to see if they are true.

3. Articles that cite statistics are more likely to be true than those that do not.
4. An article written by an expert in a field is more likely to be accurate than one written by a nonexpert.
5. Recent publications are more useful than those written longer ago.

Here is a general response to all of these statements concerning reading:

When you read a source, begin with an attitude of acceptance. Then, question what you read by asking critical questions.

More specifically, I suggest the following responses to the above statements:

1. **Information from a published work is always true.**
   False.

   Even published works are subject to error, both intentional or unintentional. Be wary of believing everything you read.

2. **When a work is published, all statements by the writer are carefully checked by the editor to see if they are true.**
   False.

   Reputable publishers do have a staff of people who check information. But even then, errors can occur. And many publishers do not check sources or facts very carefully at all.

3. **Articles that cite statistics are more likely to be true than those that do not.**
   False.

   Although most writers do not actually make up or lie about their figures, they can use them to create an impression that may actually be a distortion of the truth. For example, look at the following set of statements:

   > Increasingly, college men are inclining toward a return to the traditional family structure of the past. A questionnaire given to entering freshmen at State University revealed that 253 wished their future wives to stay at home and care for their children. This is an increase of 50 students over the responses given to the same questionnaire in 1980.

   In this paragraph, the statistics have been distorted to suit the author's purpose because we do not know what percentage of the entering freshmen the number 253 represents. If the enrollment of male freshmen had increased considerably since 1980, then the figure of 253 might actually represent a *decrease*. Moreover, we do not have access to the questionnaire, which may have contained questions designed to elicit certain responses.

4. **An article written by an expert in a field is more likely to be accurate than one written by a nonexpert.**
   True.

   Established experts are more likely to know what they are talking about than nonexperts. Yet even experts may use information to suit their own purposes.

5. **Recent publications are more useful than those written longer ago.**
   Sometimes, but not always.

   In developing fields, such as the sciences or social sciences, recently written articles contain more current information than those written longer ago, and, in these fields, new information may mean that the writer has greater insight into the topic. In fact, sometimes new studies directly contradict older ones. At other times, though, you may be dealing with a subject that generated controversy some years ago, and for that subject, articles and books written longer ago may be more useful to you. For historical topics especially, older source material may be more valuable.

SHOPPING FOR SOURCES: TWO METAPHORIC SCENARIOS

Scenario 1: Paul enters a large men's clothing store. He comes upon a rack of red and blue plaid jackets and selects one without checking the price, size, or fit. Next he sees a display of dress shirts and selects a green one, again without doing any further checking. His eye then lights upon a display of slacks, tennis shoes, underwear, and raincoats; he quickly selects one of each in the same way. Paul pays for everything and leaves the store, satisfied that he has done a good day's shopping and that he will be able to use everything he has purchased.

Scenario 2: Before going shopping, Carol carefully surveys her wardrobe, noting exactly what she needs. She makes a careful list, which includes the name of the item, the quality, the color and size, and the expected price. She then goes to the store, finds everything on her list, and goes home, well satisfied with her shopping excursion.

   Think about these scenarios. You are probably thinking that both scenarios are neither realistic nor desirable. In Scenario 1, it is obvious that Paul knows very little about shopping and is unlikely to have purchased suitable articles. He did not enter the store with a specific **purpose** in mind, he did not **plan** his choices, nor did he **examine and evaluate** his purchases in terms of how appropriate they were for his particular needs. His behavior suggests that he believes that any item he finds will be useful, regardless of the size, color, fit, or price, and most of us would be critical of anyone who shopped in this way.

On the other hand, Carol's narrow list did not allow for much flexibility, nor did it enable her to do much looking around. Most stores are unlikely to have carried every specific item on Carol's list, and since she was focused so narrowly on finding only those particular items, she did not get any ideas from simply browsing. Her behavior suggests that she had thought of everything beforehand and that she was uninterested in anything new or surprising.

These two scenarios represent two extreme metaphors of how students look for sources. Some students, like Paul, scout around the library and as soon as they find a source that is remotely concerned with their topic, they open it up and begin reading it passively, from beginning to end, satisfied that they have found something useful. They then go on to the next source, and when they have found the required number, they feel they have fulfilled their assignment. Other students, like Carol, plan very carefully what they think they need from a library and look only for these items. If the library doesn't have exactly what they are looking for, they feel extremely frustrated, and even if it does, they miss out on valuable opportunities for browsing and getting new ideas.

Actually, an initial search for sources is probably a compromise somewhere between randomly selecting a source and searching for specific sources to fit a specific need. It is a good idea to plan what you might need, but it is also desirable to remain flexible to new possibilities and ideas. After working initially on a topic, you might expect to skim through anywhere from ten to twenty sources in order to find five that are worthy of close attention.

CHOOSE SOURCES PURPOSEFULLY

You would not select clothing at random; you would be unlikely to wear just anything, simply because you happened to come upon it. Neither should you randomly select your sources for inclusion in your researched paper. People who engage in academic research approach their sources with a questioning attitude, and before they read a source, they check several features of it to see if it will be useful. Then they consider whether or not the source is likely to fulfill their particular needs or purposes before reading it through. And as they read, they ask questions, in their minds, in their notes, sometimes in the margins.

Approaching Your Source

Before you begin reading a source, ask the following questions:

What information is this source likely to provide? Is this a source that will provide you with background information? Will it help you understand what happened during a particular time period? Will it familiarize you with key terms and concepts concerning your topic? Will this source provide you with a particular point of view? What can you expect from this source?

What opinions do you already have on this topic? Can your opinion be changed? Is this source likely to change it? Thinking about your own position on a topic will help you set your source into a framework. Perhaps you already have a very strong position, which is unlikely to be changed by anything you read. This is worth knowing if you are thinking about developing an argument and acknowledging alternate points of view. If you can get an advance sense of what impact the source will have on your own opinion, you can then determine how it might help you to formulate ideas or serve as a support.

What can you determine about the source before reading it?

▶ *Clues About Your Source:* In order to get a sense of your text, you should check all of its standard features, as if they were clues. Here are some clues to examine:

▶ *The Title:* Think about the title. What does the title suggest about the author's attitude toward the subject or purpose in writing? Does the title mean anything to you? Can you guess what the article or book is about simply from the title?

▶ *The Author and the Topic:* Is the author addressing a controversial topic or critical question? Are you familiar with different positions on this question? Can you determine the author's attitude about the subject? Is the author well known in the field? Can you determine the status of the author by reading an introduction or information on a back cover? Can you use the resources of your department or library to assess the status of the author?

▶ *The Copyright Date and the Publisher:* Check the copyright date and the publisher to see if the work is current or if you recognize the publisher's name. Is the book a second or third edition? Is this information important to your topic?

▶ *The Table of Contents and the Index:* Look through the table of contents and note the chapter headings. Think about what the chapter headings suggest about the structure of the text. See if there is a chapter summary at the beginning or end of each chapter or group of chapters. Look over the index to see how much information the source contains about your particular topic.

If you are reading an article from a journal, you should similarly note the title, the author, the topic, the publication date, and the journal or periodical in which it appeared. Some journals are known for a particular political orientation, so that you can predict the position of articles on the basis of your knowledge of the journal. Sometimes articles include an abstract, which you can read quickly to get a sense of what it is about. Skimming over section headings or words that appear in bold might provide you with additional insight into the main theme.

Utilizing Available Resources

If you are enrolled at a college or a university, you probably have many resources available to you that you can use to help assess the value of a particular source. Your instructor or professor may know something about the author of a source you have found or may even be familiar with the source itself. Your librarian may also be able to suggest other resources that will help you make this assessment. Many students, though, are reluctant to avail themselves of these resources because they are concerned about appearing foolish or ignorant. They thus refrain from asking questions that could save a lot of work. If you can overcome these very natural fears, though, I suggest that once you have learned something about your topic and have attempted to find out as much as possible about a given source on your own, that you then consult the authorities and resources available to you. Most of the time, I think you will find that instructors and librarians are quite happy to assist you.

BECOMING A CRITICAL READER

Interacting with the Text: Once you have gotten "a sense" of the text, you are then ready to begin reading. However, reading a text for a researched paper does not mean that you simply open to the first page and read steadily until you come to the end. Rather, it means that you read *critically,* maintaining a questioning attitude toward your material and interacting with it as much as possible. Browne and Keeley discuss reading, versus **critical reading,** by using the metaphor of a sponge and a filter. If you read like a **sponge,** you simply absorb everything you read, passively, without questioning whether or not it is true. But if you read like a **filter,** you read actively, "filtering" or straining out impurities—that is, you accept some pieces of information or points of view, but reject others as biased or inaccurate. Becoming a critical reader means that you interact with the information you are reading.

Understanding Context and Meaning: Reading a text critically means being able to question what it says and to place it in the context of other texts concerned with the topic. Very few authors sit down and write an article or book on a controversial issue unless they have a strong reason for doing so, and understanding the situation or context of a piece of writing is the first step in becoming a critical reader. Think, then, about why the author may have written this particular text. Was he or she responding to a particular event or news item? Was it perhaps a response to another piece of writing? Then consider the audience for whom this piece of writing may have been written. For what sort of reader was it intended? Finally, be sure that you really understand the meaning of the text, in particular its main point, the value system it presumes, its means of support, and its method of organization.

Finding the Author's Main Point: What is the controversy? What is the author's position in the controversy?

Understanding the main point of a text means that you understand the issue or controversy it addresses. It also means that you understand the position that the author wishes the reader to accept. Sometimes the author tells you straight out which controversy is being addressed and what his or her position is in reference to it. Often, the main point is found either at the beginning or at the end of the text. Wherever you find it, see if you can determine the main point and the author's position in reference to a controversy before you begin reading carefully, since then you will be in a better position to ask critical questions and evaluate what you read.

Finding the Author's Values and the Conflicts in Values

Understanding the main point of a text frequently involves understanding the author's **values,** that is, those ideas the author considers fundamentally important. Authors often support their position by appealing to values, since questions of "right" and "wrong" usually depend on what one considers to be important. Freedom of speech, equality, and individualism are examples of values that are considered important in our culture, and an author may support a position because it promotes one of these values. Sometimes, though, disagreements on controversial issues occur because a particular value may conflict with another one, and sometimes issues are difficult to decide because of divided values. For example, many of us are in favor of individual freedom. We do not wish the government to tell us what to do, we value being able to come and go as we please, and we worry about the implications of a government that is too controlling. Yet, we are also in favor of living in a safe environment, where we need not worry about being robbed or assaulted, and we feel that it is the role of government to ensure that our society is safe. But if a crime wave developed in our neighborhood and if the police began to enforce a curfew to ensure public safety, many of us would object strenuously. Even though we value individual safety, we also value individual freedom. In this situation, our values would be in conflict, and we would probably have to develop a compromise position, in which one value is sacrificed to another, at least to some extent.

Similarly, a person may value tradition, particularly that of the home and family. Yet she may also value individual self-fulfillment and the opportunity to pursue happiness. Therefore, she might experience a conflict in values if she learned that a friend had left her husband and family for another man. (Although, because she also values friendship, she may support her friend's decision.) Understanding an author's values can help you understand and evaluate what you read.

▶ *Exercise:* Read the essay "Teenagers Need Drug Testing," by Brian Mittman. What is the controversy Mittman is addressing? What is Mittman's position in the controversy? List the values you believe Mittman believes in. Then compare your list with list of your classmates.

Evaluating Reasons

Reading a text critically also means understanding how the author supports his or her position. Such support may take the form of reasons that are, in turn, supported by facts, claims of fact, examples, support from authority, or statistics. The quality of support is crucial to whether or not we accept the author's position; therefore, we must examine carefully any facts or "claims" of facts, which may not actually have been proven.

If we examine the Mittman article, we will see that it gains its support primarily by Mittman's own claim of "inside" information about drug use in high school. Mittman begins his article by stating that he, himself, has seen many high school students "stoned," and he uses his own observations to claim that there is a "massive drug problem" in the schools. He also points out that, according to his experience, most adults are unaware of the problem and that those who are feel incapable of dealing with it. Mittman's tone is one of concern; he presents himself as a responsible young adult who is interested only in solving a serious problem. Yet even if we feel that Mittman is completely trustworthy, and credit him with only the most noble of motives, it does not necessarily mean that we have to accept his suggestion for mandatory drug testing. Our acceptance of his main point depends on the quality of his reasons or support.

If we examine Mittman's reasons carefully, we will see that most of his position depends simply on his claim that a problem exists. Moreover, we can also note that some of Mittman's support is not clearly presented. For example, early in the essay, Mittman makes the following claim: "In interviews conducted by *USA Today*, teenagers themselves were the strongest advocates of hardline legislation to handle drug abuse." On the surface, this statement appears to be straightforward. Yet if we read carefully, we will note that Mittman does not mention which issue of *USA Today* he is referring to nor does he include some important information, such as which and how many teenagers were interviewed, what sort of questions they were asked, or what he means exactly by "the strongest advocates." The omission of this information casts serious doubt on whether most teenagers are in favor of mandatory testing. Moreover, even if most teenagers are in favor of the testing, it does not necessarily mean that testing is the best means of solving the problem. Finally, one might question whether *USA Today* is necessarily the most credible source for information of this type.

Another problem one might find with this essay is that Mittman gives only a passing mention to a possible opposing position, the idea that mandatory drug testing might be considered a violation of students' rights to privacy. With a quick statement that drug abuse, by definition, disqualifies students from the right to privacy, Mittman goes on immediately to discuss how such a policy could be implemented, without considering possible implications and consequences. A careful reader might say, "Wait a minute. If a person breaks the law in one way, does that mean that all rights are forfeited?"

In evaluating the use of support in a source, then, be sure to ask the following questions:

1. What is the main basis of support?
2. Are there any unsupported statements?
3. Is adequate information provided?
4. Are sources adequately documented?
5. Are the sources reliable?

▶ *Exercise:* Read the essay, "The Right to Arms," by Edward Abbey. Evaluate its use of support in terms of the five questions above.

Finding the Organizational Pattern

A helpful method of understanding a text is to create a brief outline of the text to see if you perceive the author's method of organization. After finding the main point, try to locate the first reason in support of that point. Note examples that develop that reason. Then go on to the next, noting whatever evidence the author provides and seeing if you understand how such evidence is functioning within the text.

▶ *Exercise:* Outline the main points of the Mittman article. Compare your outline with that of a partner.

Checking for Ambiguity and Distortion

We are all familiar with ambiguity in the language of advertising. We would be suspicious of an ad for a face cream that claims it will "bring out all of your natural beauty," since we really don't know what "bringing out" or "natural beauty" means. A toothpaste ad that claims that the product "fights cavities in six ways" would mean little if we were not told anything about those six ways. Writers concerned with social or political issues often use abstract words that have different meanings to different people, words such as "freedom," "obscenity," or "privacy," for instance. In reading a source, check to see if the term is adequately defined and if the examples support that definition. In the Mittman article, for example, there was a claim that "teenagers themselves were the strongest advocates of hardline legislation to handle drug abuse," yet the term "strongest advocates" is not clearly defined.

Note also if the author uses inflammatory language, exaggerated comparisons or examples, or inflated statistics to support the main position. Often extreme situations and hysterical language are so compelling that they distract us from questioning their appropriateness. Think about whether such examples are truly representative and whether the author has omitted other equally representative examples.

GETTING IN THE HABIT OF EXAMINING YOUR SOURCES

Below is a form that can assist you in reading your sources with a critical eye.

Reading a Source: Worksheet

Author:

Title:

Publisher:

Copyright date:

What information is this source likely to provide?

What is the controversy?

My opinion on this topic:

Clues about the source:

Title:

Author in relation to the topic:

Main point:

   The controversy:

   Reasons:

Method of organization:

Ambiguous terms?

Inflammatory examples?

Omissions?

Representative quotations:

Read the essay "Presumption of Guilt" by Nat Hentoff. Then note how two students approached their reading. One filled in the "Reading a Source Worksheet" as a means of generating critical thinking about a source. The other interacted with the text by underlining key points and writing questions and comments in the margins. Both methods are useful for better understanding and evaluating your source, although you should not, of course, mark up a source from a school or library.

Reading a Source: Worksheet

Author: Nat Hentoff

Title: "Presumption of Guilt"

Publisher: *The Progressive*

Copyright date: May 1986

What information is this source likely to provide? This article is likely to provide reasons against mandatory drug testing.

My opinion on this topic: I am concerned with possible drug abuses in certain industries in which public safety is at stake. I think I am probably in favor of drug testing, at least for certain industries.

Clues about the source:

    Title: The title refers to the general idea that in our culture, someone is thought innocent until proven guilty. This seems a reversal of that idea.

    Author in relation to the topic: This article was published in a journal called *The Progressive,* so it is likely that the author is in favor of maintaining freedom from government interference. He is probably somewhat "left-wing" and worries about abuses.

    Main point: Mandatory drug testing is a violation of a person's right to privacy under the Fourth Amendment. It can lead to all sorts of abuses.

    The controversy: Some say that there should be mandatory drug testing because there are too many instances in which drug users cannot do their job adequately. Others say that mandatory drug testing will lead to a "Big Brother" society in which the government will know all sorts of things about everyone, which they will be able to use against them.

Reasons: 1. Mandatory urine tests are an invasion of privacy.
           2. They aren't accurate.

3. They violate the Fourth Amendment because they allow searches without probable cause.

4. New tests will soon provide employers with all sorts of private information about employees' body chemicals or their likelihood of catching a disease, information that employers could then use against employees.

Method of organization: Shows how prevalent mandatory drug testing has become both in government and in the private sector. Then presents reasons against it. Then states how more sophisticated tests could lead to further abuses.

Ambiguous terms? Although the author says that drug use might be considered simply a "disability," and although it is forbidden by law to fire someone because of a disability unless it affects job performance, there are no examples of how drug abuse *wouldn't* affect job performance.

Inflammatory examples? Compares drug testing to eavesdropping or hidden microphones. I'm not sure this is the same thing. Brings up Orwell's "Big Brother." "Massive and official attack on workers' privacy." This seems a little exaggerated. "Having one's bodily fluids forcibly and randomly inspected."

Critical questions: Has anything been left out? The author doesn't address industries where it is really necessary for safety to have employees drug-free. Cites only extreme cases of possible abuses.

Representative quotations: As for coming attractions that verify the prescience of George Orwell, *The Washington Post* reported in mid-1984, "Researchers in academia and industry say it is now possible to envision a product that could instantaneously assess whether employees are concentrating on their jobs by analyzing their brain waves as they work."

The worksheet enabled the student to perceive that the author had a strong bias on the question of drug testing and that a balanced argument would have to include at least one other point of view on the subject. Gaining this overall perspective enabled the student to understand the reasoning and viewpoint of the text more thoroughly than if he had simply begun to read it unquestioningly. Now note how the student interacted with the text by writing in the margins.

Being able to understand and evaluate articles and books is an important skill to develop both for working with course material and for selecting outside sources for papers. But becoming a critical reader does not mean simply acquiring a skill; it also means developing a questioning perspective toward information that will enable you to function more effectively as a member of society. Practice in evaluating sources will enable you to gain that perspective.

Teenagers Need Drug Testing

Brian Noal Mittman

As a recent high school graduate I've seen rampant drug use—in schools, where students take a few "hits" before entering class; at parties, from which many kids drive home completely stoned; and even at a high school prom, where cocaine usage was high. Today's younger generation is often too accepting of drugs as a part of its life, and adults are too unwilling to implement necessary anti-drug laws. With the massive drug problem that exists in our schools today, new legislation is necessary to discourage substance abuse. Cities in Texas, New York, California and Tennessee have already implemented mandatory drug testing in some of their public schools. Such a program is needed on a national scale.

Many adults who oppose mandatory drug testing in schools are completely oblivious to the severity of the problem. Students see signs of drug usage in school, with friends, and on the street far more often than their parents. In interviews conducted by USA Today, teenagers themselves were the strongest advocates of hardline legislation to handle drug abuse. Many parents fail to realize how rampant drug addiction is. It is no longer monopolized by problem-plagued students and inner-city schools—good students and promising athletes are often victims as well. I attended an academically-oriented, highly-competitive, affluent, suburban high school. The number of students dealing and using drugs was shocking. Parents of friends on drugs feel incapable of dealing with the problem, while others choose to ignore a child's addiction. Mandatory testing in schools would raise teenage consciousness about drug danger and could reduce students' abuse of toxic substances without depending upon their parents' guidance.

Most opponents of mandatory drug testing in schools argue that such legislation is an invasion of students' pricacy—the mere fact that so many teenagers do abuse drugs is sufficient evidence that they are not mature enough to handle such problems independently.

Mandatory school drug testing should be administered to students beginning at the junior high level where many drug problems start. The test should be given by an outside organization, unassociated with our public schools. Without prior warning, testing should take place for all students at a given school on Mondays, when drugs ingested from weekend partying can still be detected. Repeated testing should be administered before reporting results to parents in order to reduce uncertainties inherent in the drug test itself. This would reduce unfounded parental suspicions of frequent use if a child simply "tried" a drug for the first time before the test date, had recently kicked a drug habit, or if the test result itself was inaccurate. Finally, all information should be kept confidential between parent, child and the administering agency. Results should be kept by the administrating agency—not by the school—to lessen "leaks" of confidential information.

Such drug testing could reduce teen substance abuse in six ways. (1) Younger, more immature students might be deterred from future drug abuse through junior high testing and heightened awareness. (2) Individuals might refrain from drugs due to embarrassment before drug testing personnel. (3) Students would fear that surprise drug testing could result in parent notification of abuse. (4) Parents notified of their children's drug problems would seek help for them. (5) Students already addicted, fearing they might be detected, might seek help on their own. (6) School administration could take action if heavy drug use over a long period of time is detected.

State laws (required inoculations against various diseases and periodic medical checkups) have already affected health mandates for students. Today, drug abuse has become a terrible health menace in our public schools. Any attempt to reduce this growing disease should be implemented. It's time to institute drug testing for teens.

The Right to Arms

Edward Abbey

If guns are outlawed
Only outlaws will have guns
(True? False? Maybe?)

Meaning weapons. The right to own, keep, and bear arms. A sword and a lance, or a bow and a quiverful of arrows. A crossbow and darts. Or in our time, a rifle and a handgun and a cache of ammunition. Firearms.

In medieval England a peasant caught with a sword in his possession would be strung up on a gibbet and left there for the crows. Swords were for gentlemen only. (*Gentlemen!*) Only members of the ruling class were entitled to own and bear weapons. For obvious reasons. Even bows and arrows were outlawed—see Robin Hood. When the peasants attempted to rebel, as they did in England and Germany and other European countries from time to time, they had to fight with sickles, bog hoes, clubs—no match for the sword-wielding armored cavalry of the nobility.

In Nazi Germany the possession of firearms by a private citizen of the Third Reich was considered a crime against the state; the statutory penalty was death—by hanging. Or beheading. In the Soviet Union, as in Czarist Russia, the manufacture, distribution, and ownership of firearms have always been monopolies of the state, strictly controlled and supervised. Any unauthorized citizen found with guns in his home by the OGPU or the KGB is automatically suspected of subversive intentions and subject to severe penalties. Except for the landowning aristocracy, who alone among the population were allowed the privilege of owning firearms, for only they were privileged to hunt, the ownership of weapons never did become a widespread tradition in Russia. And Russia has always been an autocracy—or at best, as today, an oligarchy.

In Uganda, Brazil, Iran, Paraguay, South Africa—wherever a few rule many— the possession of weapons is restricted to the ruling class and to their supporting apparatus: the military, the police, the secret police. In Chile and Argentina at this very hour men and women are being tortured by the most up-to-date CIA methods in the effort to force them to reveal the location of their hidden weapons. Their guns, their rifles. Their arms. And we can be certain that the Communist masters of modern China will never pass out firearms to *their* 800 million subjects. Only in Cuba, among dictatorships, where Fidel's revolution apparently still enjoys popular support, does there seem to exist a true citizen's militia.

There must be a moral in all this. When I try to think of a nation that has maintained its independence over centuries, and where the citizens still retain their rights as free and independent people, not many come to mind. I think of Switzerland. Of Norway, Sweden, Denmark, Finland. The British Commonwealth. France, Italy. And of our United States.

When Tell shot the apple from his son's head, he reserved in hand a second arrow, it may be remembered, for the Austrian tyrant Gessler. And got him too, shortly afterward. Switzerland has been a free country since 1390. In Switzerland basic national decisions are made by initiative and referendum—direct democracy—and in some cantons by open-air meetings in which all voters participate. Every Swiss male serves a year in the Swiss Army and at the end of the year takes his government rifle home with him—where he keeps it for the rest of his life. One of my father's grandfathers came from Canton Bern.

There must be a meaning in this. I don't think I'm a gun fanatic. I own a couple of small-caliber weapons, but seldom take them off the wall. I gave up deer hunting fifteen years ago, when the hunters began to outnumber the deer. I am a member of the National Rifle Association, but certainly no John Bircher. I'm a liberal—and proud of it. Nevertheless, I am opposed, absolutely, to every move the state makes to restrict my right to buy, own, possess, and carry a firearm. Whether shotgun, rifle, or handgun.

Of course, we can agree to a few commonsense limitations. Guns should not be sold to children, to the certifiably insane, or to convicted criminals. Other than that, we must regard with extreme suspicion any effort by the government—local, state, or national—to control our right to arms. The registration of firearms is the first step toward confiscation. The confiscation of weapons would be a major and probably fatal step into authoritarian rule—the domination of most of us by a new order of "gentlemen." By a new and harder oligarchy.

The tank, the B-52, the fighter-bomber, the state-controlled police and military are the weapons of dictatorship. The rifle is the weapon of democracy. Not for nothing was the revolver called an "equalizer." *Egalité* implies *liberté*. And always will. Let us hope our weapons are never needed—but do not forget what the common people of this nation knew when they demanded the Bill of Rights: An armed citizenry is the first defense, the best defense, and the final defense against tyranny.

If guns are outlawed, only the government will have guns. Only the police, the secret police, the military. The hired servants of our rulers. Only the government—and a few outlaws. I intend to be among the outlaws.

Presumption of Guilt

Nat Hentoff

"I don't take drugs and I don't believe I have to piss in a bottle to prove I don't."

—*Bob Stanley, pitcher, Boston Red Sox*

"If you hang all the people, you'll get all the guilty."

—*Tom T. Hall, country singer*

In March, Ira Glasser, executive director of the American Civil Liberties Union, sent a letter to twenty of the nation's largest labor unions inviting them to take part in a series of seminars this fall to work out a strategy for the unions and the ACLU to protect the privacy of Americans where they work.

"Government employees and employees of private industry, railway workers and baseball players," Glasser wrote, "are being required in ever greater numbers to prove their innocence by submitting to intrusive and humiliating urine and blood tests." The seminars, he said, would deal not only with "random drug testing of people not suspected of using drugs" but also with "other violations of the right to privacy of the workplace."

As many workers can testify, privacy rights in the workplace have been eroding for a long time by means that range from management eavesdropping on employee telephone calls to placement of hidden microphones in employee washrooms in order to pick up intelligence concerning "troublemakers." What prompted Glas-

Net Hentoff, "Presumption of Guilt," *The Progressive*, May 1986. Reprinted by permission from *The Progressive*, 409 East Main Street, Madison, WI 53703.

ser's rallying cry, however, ws the proclamation of an unprecedented massive and offical attack on workers' privacy.

On March 2, the President's Commission on Organized Crime strongly recommended—in the name of "national security"—that all Federal employees be tested for drug use. Not particular individuals about whom some reasonable suspicion of drug abuse exists, but *all* employees. Furthermore, the Commmission urged all private employers who have Federal contracts to begin dragnet testing of their workers. If the contractors refuse, they should be denied any further Government business.

The Commission went on to recommend that all private employers, not just those with Federal contracts, start collecting urine samples and otherwise screen their workers from drug use. Peter Rodino, chairman of the House Judiciary Committee and a member of the President's Commission on Organized Crime, objected strenuously, noting that such wholesale testing "raises civil-liberties concerns." Nonsense, said Attorney General Edwin Meese, a mail-order scholar of the Framers' intentions on these matters. No unlawful search and seizure is involved, Meese explained, because, "by definition, it's not an unreasonable seizure because it's something the employee consents to as a condition of employment."

In other words, when the boss tells you to pee in a bottle if you want to keep your job, you consent to the condition if you don't want to lose your job.

At the press conference with the Attorney General was the chairman of the President' Commission, Judge Irving Kaufman of the Second Circuit Court of Appeals. Kaufman was the judge who sent Ethel and Julius Rosenberg to the electric chair after praying earnestly for guidance, thus making God an accomplice in the execution. As the years went on, Kaufman, extremely sensitive to charges that he was the prosecutor's judge in the Rosenberg case, has developed an exceptional reputation as a defender of First Amendment rights of defendants, especially the press, against the Government. But now, in the twilight of his career, Kaufman has again become the prosecutor's judge by supporting dragnet drug testing of millions of Americans.

The testing he and the majority of the Commission advocate, says Kaufman, is no more an invasion of privacy than requiring any American to walk through metal detectors at an airport. However, as Tom Wicker noted in *The New York Times,* "Having one's bodily fluids forcibly and randomly inspected is substantially different from putting one's luggage through an electronic device."

What's more, the drug tests aren't even accurate. "The most commonly used urine test is notoriously unreliable," Ira Glasser noted in an ACLU statement. "It cannot identify specific drugs and it cannot distinguish between common cold medicine and illegal substances like marijuana and cocaine. The test cannot determine when someone used a particular drug, or to what extent. And it cannot measure impairment of the ability to function on the job."

There are also blood tests for drugs, and they reveal much more than the Government or a private employer claims to be testing for. Charles Seabrook, an unusually probing science writer, pointed out in the *Atlanta Journal & Constitution* last year that "from a single ounce of a person's blood, sophisticated computerized tests can determine, or at least strongly suggest, whether a person is predisposed to heart attacks, whether he smokes, drinks to excess, has had a venereal disease, or is epileptic, schizophrenic, or subject to depression. . . . 'Given enough blood and enough lab technicians, I could find out hundreds of things about you—what you eat, what drugs you take, even the kind of booze you drink,' says Dr. James Woodford, a forensic chemist in Atlanta, who is frequently consulted in drug-related cases."

Judge Kaufman and the Attorney General may have unwittingly rendered a considerable service to the nation because their proposal has begun to focus attention on routine invasions of privacy in the workplace. A growing number of large corporations have been doing just what the President's Commission on Organized Crime is pushing.

As an index of the dragnet testing that is already in place, everyone who applies for work at United Airlines, IBM, Exxon, Du Pont, Federal Express, Lockheed, Shearson Lehman, TWA, and a good many other companies has to undergo urinalysis. Indeed, at least a quarter of the *Fortune* 500 companies test all applicants for drugs. Even without prodding from the President's Commission, many other firms, large and small, would have joined the list. Any time management has a chance to control its work force more firmly, it seizes on that chance. Now, the notion that every worker is guilty until proven innocent also has the imprimatur of a blue-ribbon Government commission that insists on regarding urinalysis and other forms of testing workers—before and after they're hired—as essential for national security.

At the ACLU seminars with labor unions to be held in the months ahead, the first distinction to be drawn will be between the Government and private employers. Although Kaufman and Meese claim there are no constitutional problems with regard to testing public employees, case law indicates otherwise. When the State is the employer, the Fourth Amendment prohibition against unreasonable search and seizure comes into play. The Fourth Amendment requires that there be probable cause—or, in some instances, the lower standard of reasonable suspicion—that *particular* individuals may be doing or holding something illegal.

In 1984, for example, the Eighth Circuit Court of Appeals affirmed a decision granting prison guards an injunction against random urinalysis even though they certainly perform crucial security functions. The court ruled that for the bodily fluids of public employees to be seized there has to be an *individualized,* reasonable basis for the search.

In East Rutherford, New Jersey, last year, the school board ordered all students to undergo urine and blood testing for drugs and alcohol as part of an annual physical examination. Any student who tested positive would be suspended or expelled from scool. The ACLU of New Jersey, representing five of the students, took the case to court and the rule was struck down because, said the judge, it violated each student's "legitimate expectation of privacy and personal security" under the Fourth Amendment.

Also in 1985, the school board of the Patchogue-Medford School District on Long Island decided that to be given tenure, a teacher would have to submit to a urine test to determine the presence or absence or illegal drugs. In Suffolk County Supreme Court, Justice Thomas Stark could not have been more clear in his decision declaring that the school board had acted unconstitutionally:

"The Fourth Amendment of the United States Constitution, applicable to state action through the Fourteenth . . . protects individuals from unreasonable searches of the person. The compulsory extraction of bodily fluids is a search and seizure within the meaning of the Fourth Amendment." Such a search is permissible, he added, only when there is particularized, reasonable suspicion "based on objective supportable facts."

Workers in private employment, however, do not have Fourth Amendment protections because the order to give up bodily fluids does not come from the State. Alternative sources of protection are available, however. Union contracts can include, through collective bargaining, provisions extending to workers the equivalent of First Amendment, Fourth Amendment, and other constitutional rights. Some United Auto Workers locals, for example, have won contracts with clauses that make it difficult to fire an employee for anything he says or puts on a bulletin board or wears on a T-shirt.

Until now, most workers and their unions have been slow to recognize the importance of battling for such contract clauses. It may well be that the Meese-Kaufman assault on workers' privacy may spur more collective-bargaining strategy to get language that will give workers the same rights on the job as they have on the streets and at home. As bus driver Randy Kemp of Seattle put it in *Time,* "You've got to have a search warrant to search my house. Well, my body is a lot more sacred than my home."

Another route to protecting privacy is through state constitutions and local statutes. Some state constitutions have stronger privacy provisions than the U.S. Constitution, and if the language covers private employees, dragnet and random searches can be banned. Richard Emergy, a Fourth Amendment specialist with the New York Civil Liberties Union, also points out that under some local human-rights statutes, it is illegal to fire anyone who has a disability if that disability does not affect his job performance. Drug use can be a disability, but not necessarily one that interferes with worker competence. Accordingly, if a local statute includes drug dependence as a disability, and if the worker is doing his job efficiently, he can't be fired if he fails a drug test.

More directly specific is a San Francisco ordinance—the first in the country—that prohibits employers from administering random, dragnet blood and urine tests. And state legislatures in California, Maine, Oregon, and Maryland are considering bills that would limit or regulate testing of employees.

Clearly, there is potential for a natural alliance between workers and civil libertarians to educate local and state legislators and to lobby for protective statutes. Invasion-of-privacy horror stories and realistic remedies ought to be covered in union newspapers, general publications, and—never to be underestimated—letters to the editors of all kinds of papers and magazines.

For many workers, civil liberties have long seemed to be a class issue. If you look at the composition of most ACLU affiliates and chapters, the overwhelming majority of members are lawyers, academics, enlightened businessmen, and a very few union officials. Blue-collar workers are seldom represented. The rights that have appealed most to workers are economic rights, and they don't see the ACLU and other civil liberties organizations as being particularly concerned with take-home pay and benefits. But when a worker can lose his job if he won't piss into a bottle, the Fourth Amendment, at least, becomes much less abstract, and that's why a coalition between the usual civil-liberties activists and workers is not only plausible but potentially effective.

The possibility of protests within certain shops also exists. Job actions not for more pay but to be a free citizen at work could put some heat on certain company officials.

Take the *Los Angeles Times*. Its editorial page has been among the most forceful and lucid in the nation in fighting to keep the Bill of Rights in working order. Yet, according to Daniel Jussim, writing in the ACLU's *Civil Liberties* newsletter, "The *Los Angeles Times,* though its director of employee relations says there's no particular drug problem at his newspaper, recently adopted a mandatory urinalysis program 'to stay current with what other employers are doing.' "

Imagine the impact in Los Angeles if Anthony Day, the civil libertarian who is editor of the *Los Angeles Times*'s editorial page, were to lead a picket line outside the paper with such signs as:

JAMES OTIS, FATHER OF THE FOURTH AMENDEMNT, FOUGHT BRITISH GENERAL SEARCH WARRANTS ON BEHALF OF WORKING PEOPLE—NOT JUST PUBLISHERS.

The need for alliances to preserve what's left of privacy grows greater by the day. Charles Seabrook writes of new tests that can "detect the presence of the abnormal levels of chemicals found in patients with severe depression, schizophrenia, and manic-depression . . . that can detect chemical 'markers' that may mean a person is at high risk of developing diabetes, arthritis, or cancer . . . that can screen for more than 150 genetic diseases, including sickle cell anemia . . . and cystic fibrosis."

Would an employer hire someone who is at risk of developing cancer? Should an employer have access to such private information?

On a more modest level, a new test developed by Werner Baumgartner, a Los Angeles chemist, bypasses such old-time procedures as requiring the random suspect to urinate into a cup or bottle. The new test uses radiation on hair and discloses not only what drugs have been taken but when they were taken, something urinalysis can't do.

As for coming attractions that verify the prescience of George Orwell, *The Washington Post* reported in mid-1984, "Researchers in academia and industry say it is now possible to envision a product that could instantaneously assess whether employees are concentrating on their jobs by analyzing their brain waves as they work."

There isn't much time left to create, in law, the best possible defenses against Government and employer intrusions into privacy, including intrusions that now seem inconceivable.

Presumption of Guilt

Nat Hentoff

"I don't take drugs and I don't believe I have to piss in a bottle to prove I don't."

—*Bob Stanley, pitcher, Boston Red Sox*

"If you hang all the people, you'll get all the guilty."

—*Tom T. Hall, country singer*

In March, Ira Glasser, executive director of the American Civil Liberties Union, sent a letter to twenty of the nation's largest labor unions inviting them to take part in a series of seminars this fall to work out a strategy for the unions and the ACLU to protect the privacy of Americans where they work.

"Government employees and employees of private industry, railway workers and baseball players," Glasser wrote, "are being required in ever greater numbers to prove their innocence by submitting to intrusive and humiliating urine and blood tests." The seminars, he said, would deal not only with "random drug testing of people not suspected of using drugs" but also with "other violations of the right to privacy of the workplace."

As many workers can testify, privacy rights in the workplace have been eroding for a long time by means that range from management eavesdropping on employee telephone calls to placement of hidden microphones in employee washrooms in order to pick up intelligence concerning "troublemakers." What prompted Glasser's rallying cry, however, ws the proclamation of an unprecedented massive and offical attack on workers' privacy.

privacy rights are being eroded

On March 2, the President's Commission on Organized Crime strongly recommended—in the name of "national security"—that all Federal employees be tested for drug use. Not particular individuals about whom some reasonable suspicion of drug abuse exists, but *all*

Net Hentoff, "Presumption of Guilt," *The Progressive*, May 1986. Reprinted by permission from *The Progressive*, 409 East Main Street, Madison, WI 53703.

employees. Furthermore, the Commmission urged all private employers who have Federal contracts to begin dragnet testing of their workers. If the contractors refuse, they should be denied any further Government business.

The Commission went on to recommend that all private employers, not just those with Federal contracts, start collecting urine samples and otherwise screen their workers from drug use. Peter Rodino, chairman of the House Judiciary Committee and a member of the President's Commission on Organized Crime, objected strenuously, noting that such wholesale testing "raises civil-liberties concerns." Nonsense, said Attorney General Edwin Meese, a mail-order scholar of the Framers' intentions on these matters. No unlawful search and seizure is involved, Meese explained, because, "by definition, it's not an unreasonable seizure because it's something the employee consents to as a condition of employment."

In other words, when the boss tells you to pee in a bottle if you want to keep your job, you consent to the condition if you don't want to lose your job.

At the press conference with the Attorney General was the chairman of the President' Commission, Judge Irving Kaufman of the Second Circuit Court of Appeals. Kaufman was the judge who sent Ethel and Julius Rosenberg to the electric chair after praying earnestly for guidance, thus making God an accomplice in the execution. As the years went on, Kaufman, extremely sensitive to charges that he was the prosecutor's judge in the Rosenberg case, has developed an exceptional reputation as a defender of First Amendment rights of defendants, especially the press, against the Government. But now, in the twilight of his career, Kaufman has again become the prosecutor's judge by supporting dragnet drug testing of millions of Americans.

The testing he and the majority of the Commission advocate, says Kaufman, is no more an invasion of privacy than requiring any American to walk through metal detectors at an airport. However, as Tom Wicker noted in *The New York Times,* "Having one's bodily fluids forcibly and randomly inspected is substantially different from putting one's luggage through an electronic device."

What's more, the drug tests aren't even accurate. "The most commonly used urine test is notoriously unreliable," Ira Glasser noted in an ACLU statement. "It cannot identify specific drugs and it cannot distinguish between common cold medicine and illegal substances

— urine testing is invasive

— Drug tests are not always accurate

like marijuana and cocaine. The test cannot determine when someone used a particular drug, or to what extent. And it cannot measure impairment of the ability to function on the job."

There are also blood tests for drugs, and they reveal much more than the Government or a private employer claims to be testing for. Charles Seabrook, an unusually probing science writer, pointed out in the *Atlanta Journal & Constitution* last year that "from a single ounce of a person's blood, sophisticated computerized tests can determine, or at least strongly suggest, whether a person is predisposed to heart attacks, whether he smokes, drinks to excess, has had a venereal disease, or is epileptic, schizophrenic, or subject to depression. . . . 'Given enough blood and enough lab technicians, I could find out hundreds of things about you—what you eat, what drugs you take, even the kind of booze you drink,' says Dr. James Woodford, a forensic chemist in Atlanta, who is frequently consulted in drug-related cases."

—Drug tests can reveal too much

Judge Kaufman and the Attorney General may have unwittingly rendered a considerable service to the nation because their proposal has begun to focus attention on routine invasions of privacy in the workplace. A growing number of large corporations have been doing just what the President's Commission on Organized Crime is pushing.

As an index of the dragnet testing that is already in place, everyone who applies for work at United Airlines, IBM, Exxon, Du Pont, Federal Express, Lockheed, Shearson Lehman, TWA, and a good many other companies has to undergo urinalysis. Indeed, at least a quarter of the *Fortune* 500 companies test all applicants for drugs. Even without prodding from the President's Commission, many other firms, large and small, would have joined the list. Any time management has a chance to control its work force more firmly, it seizes on that chance. Now, the notion that every worker is guilty until proven innocent also has the imprimatur of a blue-ribbon Government commission that insists on regarding urinalysis and other forms of testing workers—before and after they're hired—as essential for national security.

—Drug testing is pervasive

At the ACLU seminars with labor unions to be held in the months ahead, the first distinction to be drawn will be between the Government and private employers. Although Kaufman and Meese claim there are no constitutional problems with regard to testing public employees, case law indicates otherwise. When the State is the employer, the Fourth Amendment prohibition against unreasonable search and seizure comes into play. The Fourth Amendment requires that there be probable cause—or, in some instances, the lower standard of reasonable suspicion—that *particular* individuals may be doing or holding something illegal.

In 1984, for example, the Eighth Circuit Court of Appeals affirmed a decision granting prison guards an injunction against random urinalysis even though they certainly perform crucial security functions. The court ruled that for the bodily fluids of public employees to be seized there has to be an *individualized,* reasonable basis for the search.

In East Rutherford, New Jersey, last year, the school board ordered all students to undergo urine and blood testing for drugs and alcohol as part of an annual physical examination. Any student who tested positive would be suspended or expelled from scool. The ACLU of New Jersey, representing five of the students, took the case to court and the rule was struck down because, said the judge, it violated each student's "legitimate expectation of privacy and personal security" under the Fourth Amendment.

Also in 1985, the school board of the Patchogue-Medford School District on Long Island decided that to be given tenure, a teacher would have to submit to a urine test to determine the presence or absence or illegal drugs. In Suffolk County Supreme Court, Justice Thomas Stark could not have been more clear in his decision declaring that the school board had acted unconstitutionally:

"The Fourth Amendment of the United States Constitution, applicable to state action through the Fourteenth . . . protects individuals from unreasonable searches of the person. The compulsory extraction of bodily fluids is a search and seizure within the meaning of the Fourth Amendment." Such a search is permissible, he added, only when there is particularized, reasonable suspicion "based on objective supportable facts."

Workers in private employment, however, do not have Fourth Amendment protections because the order to give up bodily fluids does not come from the State. Alternative sources of protection are available, however. Union contracts can include, through collective bargaining, provisions extending to workers the equivalent of

— union agitation for private workers

First Amendment, Fourth Amendment, and other constitutional rights. Some United Auto Workers locals, for example, have won contracts with clauses that make it difficult to fire an employee for anything he says or puts on a bulletin board or wears on a T-shirt.

Until now, most workers and their unions have been slow to recognize the importance of battling for such contract clauses. It may well be that the Meese-Kaufman assault on workers' privacy may spur more collective-bargaining strategy to get language that will give workers the same rights on the job as they have on the streets and at home. As bus driver Randy Kemp of Seattle put it in *Time,* "You've got to have a search warrant to search my house. Well, my body is a lot more sacred than my home."

Another route to protecting privacy is through state constitutions and local statutes. Some state constitutions have stronger privacy provisions than the U.S. Constitution, and if the language covers private employees, dragnet and random searches can be banned. Richard Emergy, a Fourth Amendment specialist with the New York Civil Liberties Union, also points out that under some local human-rights statutes, it is illegal to fire anyone who has a disability if that disability does not affect his job performance. Drug use can be a disability, but not necessarily one that interferes with worker competence. Accordingly, if a local statute includes drug dependence as a disability, and if the worker is doing his job efficiently, he can't be fired if he fails a drug test.

More directly specific is a San Francisco ordinance—the first in the country—that prohibits employers from administering random, dragnet blood and urine tests. And state legislatures in California, Maine, Oregon, and Maryland are considering bills that would limit or regulate testing of employees.

Clearly, there is potential for a natural alliance between workers and civil libertarians to educate local and state legislators and to lobby for protective statutes. Invasion-of-privacy horror stories and realistic remedies ought to be covered in union newspapers, general publications, and—never to be underestimated—letters to the editors of all kinds of papers and magazines.

For many workers, civil liberties have long seemed to be a class issue. If you look at the composition of most ACLU affiliates and chapters, the overwhelming majority of members are lawyers, academics, enlightened busi-

— Drug testing should require a search warrant

— compares drug abuse to a disability. One shouldn't be fired for a disability. But is this a good comparison?

nessmen, and a very few union officials. Blue-collar workers are seldom represented. The rights that have appealed most to workers are economic rights, and they don't see the ACLU and other civil liberties organizations as being particularly concerned with take-home pay and benefits. But when a worker can lose his job if he won't piss into a bottle, the Fourth Amendment, at least, becomes much less abstract, and that's why a coalition between the usual civil-liberties activists and workers is not only plausible but potentially effective.

The possibility of protests within certain shops also exists. Job actions not for more pay but to be a free citizen at work could put some heat on certain company officials.

Take the *Los Angeles Times*. Its editorial page has been among the most forceful and lucid in the nation in fighting to keep the Bill of Rights in working order. Yet, according to Daniel Jussim, writing in the ACLU's *Civil Liberties* newsletter, "The *Los Angeles Times,* though its director of employee relations says there's no particular drug problem at his newspaper, recently adopted a mandatory urinalysis program 'to stay current with what other employers are doing.' "

Imagine the impact in Los Angeles if Anthony Day, the civil libertarian who is editor of the *Los Angeles Times*'s editorial page, were to lead a picket line outside the paper with such signs as:

JAMES OTIS, FATHER OF THE FOURTH AMENDEMNT, FOUGHT BRITISH GENERAL SEARCH WARRANTS ON BEHALF OF WORKING PEOPLE—NOT JUST PUBLISHERS.

The need for alliances to preserve what's left of privacy grows greater by the day. Charles Seabrook writes of new tests that can "detect the presence of the abnormal levels of chemicals found in patients with severe depression, schizophrenia, and manic-depression . . . that can detect chemical 'markers' that may mean a person is at high risk of developing diabetes, arthritis, or cancer . . . that can screen for more than 150 genetic diseases, including sickle cell anemia . . . and cystic fibrosis."

Would an employer hire someone who is at risk of developing cancer? Should an employer have access to such private information?

On a more modest level, a new test developed by Werner Baumgartner, a Los Angeles chemist, bypasses such old-time procedures as requiring the random suspect to urinate into a cup or bottle. The new test uses

— It soon will be possible to detect all sorts of other things through testing.

radiation on hair and discloses not only what drugs have been taken but when they were taken, something urinalysis can't do.

As for coming attractions that verify the prescience of George Orwell, *The Washington Post* reported in mid-1984, "Researchers in academia and industry say it is now possible to envision a product that could instantaneously assess whether employees are concentrating on their jobs by analyzing their brain waves as they work."

There isn't much time left to create, in law, the best possible defenses against Government and employer intrusions into privacy, including intrusions that now seem inconceivable.

Drug testing compared to 1984. Big Brother concept

5 *Working with Information*
Summary, Paraphrase, Quotation

In the children's story, "Rumpelstiltskin," a greedy king locks a miller's daughter in a room filled to the ceiling with straw. The king tells her that she has one night to spin all the straw into gold and that if she fails in this task, she will be killed. In utter despair and in complete confusion about how or where to begin, the Miller's daughter cries and wails until the gnome, Rumpelstiltskin, comes to her rescue and performs the task for her.

The plight of the Miller's daughter is very like the situation that confronts many students when they attempt to work with outside information for writing assignments. With greater enterprise, they locate large amounts of information and stack it all around them—on their desks, on the floor, all over the room. But having found it, they are then at a loss about what to do with it—how to understand it or use it. So much information! So little time! What to do? Where to begin? In great confusion and despair, students sit among the piles of papers and books, wishing for someone, even Rumpelstiltskin, to come to their rescue!

Using outside sources in your writing involves transforming disorder into order, creating usable material out of a formless pile of articles and books. In order to do this, it is important that you learn some techniques for **working with information**—learning to **take notes** that include **summaries, paraphrases,** and **direct quotations.** Once you work with information, you will be able to make decisions concerning how you wish to incorporate it into your paper. One important point to remember, though, is that whenever you use material that you have obtained from a source, you must **give credit to the author** of that source. Being careful about acknowledging your sources will help you to avoid plagiarism.

SUMMARIZING

Summarizing means to condense a piece of writing to a shorter form; a summary is always *shorter* than the original source. In writing a summary, you are attempting to grasp the **main points** of your source from the perspective of its **author;** that is, you focus on the author's main point and include what you feel are the important ideas. When you write a summary, you are also gaining an understanding of the relative importance and relationship between the còmponent ideas of the text. Learning to summarize will help your performance in any class you take, even those that do not involve writing, since the act of summarizing can help you understand the main point of a source. A written summary can also help you to remember material long after you have read the original.

Within the scope of this book, you will be working with articles, not with whole books, and the following discussion of summary writing assumes that you will be summarizing *articles*. Actually, when you summarize a whole book, you often focus on the main point of each chapter, relating that chapter to the overall point of the book. Thus, the following suggestions about writing summaries can help you summarize both articles and chapters in a book.

Thinking About the Author's Purpose

Before you write a summary, you might consider what the author of the article or book is trying to accomplish. Is the author arguing for a particular position? Is the author reacting against someone else's position? From the title of the article or book, can you determine where the author's ideas fit among other points of view on the topic? Before you begin to summarize a piece of writing, think about why the author may have written it. Figuring out the author's purpose will help you decide what points to include in your summary.

The Role of Audience in Writing a Summary

Summaries can be written for just yourself or for other readers such as your teacher or other students. Usually, when you are assigned to summarize a source, you assume that your reader has *not* read it. Therefore, you should make sure that even a reader who knows nothing about the topic or the source will be able to understand its main points, and you should mention the author and/or the article's title. Even when you summarize a source for yourself, you should assume that once a period of time has elapsed you may not remember it clearly yourself. Therefore, in writing a summary, you must be sure to include sufficient details so that any reader will be able to understand it without confusion.

Writing the Summary

Writing a summary involves making a lot of decisions about which details to include. Those decisions are based on a number of factors: your own research purpose and the relationship of the article or book to that purpose, your previous knowledge of the topic, what you can figure out about the author's purpose in writing, and your intended use for the text you are summarizing. Thinking about these issues before you begin to write your summary may be useful. The following suggestions, derived from research in reading comprehension, may also help you.

1. **Scan your source before reading it carefully. Do not attempt to write the summary before you understand its main point.** Because a summary represents an overview of what a work is about, it is a good idea to *scan the piece* before writing anything down, even though this method may seem to take more time. See if you can locate the main point the author is trying to prove or explore. Then look for subpoints that might be related to that main point. Are there terms central to the topic that seem to jump out at you from the page? Can you quickly determine how the article is structured?

   Some students think that they can whip off a summary as they discover the meaning of a source; they copy down bits of the text as they read. But when students attempt this sort of shortcut, their summaries are not usually well written, nor do they serve as useful a function. A summary written this way may include elements that are not really central to the main point. Also, students may be so busy writing that they are unable to think about and remember what they are reading.

   To scan an article, look at the first paragraph or two. Often this is where the main argument or thesis may be found. Glance at the conclusion. This might give you an overview of the results or the emphasis of the text. Then look quickly over the subdivisions of the text. Perhaps it uses headings; if not, look at the beginnings of each paragraph. See if you can trace the general line of the argument.

2. **Ask yourself if you understand the purpose of the text.** Look at the title of the excerpt or article you plan to summarize. Does the title give you insight into what the text is about? As you read, think about the main purpose of the text. Is the purpose of the text to present information? Or does its tone suggest that the main purpose is to express an opinion or argue a position? Does the author sound seriously involved with the topic? Or do you feel that the tone is impersonal, which suggests that the author is not terribly involved with the topic?

   Often if you can get a sense of the tone, you can also determine the author's purpose. To decide if you are aware of the author's purpose, see if you can fill in one of the following statements:

   The purpose of this text is to show that _____.
   or

   The purpose of this text is to prove that _____.

   Thinking about the purpose of the text will lead you to think about the **audience** for whom the text was intended. Was this text written for a particular group? Does this group have a particular opinion? Was it designed to change the audience's mind about a particular topic? Did the author assume that the audience knew a lot or a little about the topic?

3. **Examine the "plan" of the text.** Understanding the "plan" of a text can be very helpful for both readers and writers. It can also be very helpful in writing a summary. Like any plan, the plan of a text may be defined as a set of directions about how the overall purpose is to be achieved. In other words, if you understand the purpose of a text, focusing on the plan will help you understand how that purpose is achieved. Thus, as you examine the plan, you are gaining insight into how the source has been "put together" or how it "works."

USING "PLANS" TO UNDERSTAND PARAGRAPH AND TEXT STRUCTURE

Plans are used in texts to help authors accomplish their purpose more effectively, and they are often used to determine the structure. Some of the most common plans are the following:

1. **Antecedent–Consequent or Cause and Effect:** This plan structures information in terms of causal relations, as in the following paragraph:

   > Poor performance during a student's first year at the university cannot always be attributed to lack of ability or inadequate preparation. Even students with excellent high school records can be overwhelmed by the university experience and hence do poorly in their courses. For many students, the difficulties of adjusting to a new environment, the sudden assumption of adult responsibilities, and the necessity of managing one's time without parental guidance create extreme emotional stress, which prevents them from functioning adequately in their classes.

   Examine the structure of this paragraph. Note the main idea—that poor student performance during the first year at a university may be attributed to other factors beside poor ability or inadequate preparation. It begins with the **effect** (poor performance) and analyzes the **cause** (emotional stress caused by other factors).

2. **Comparison–Contrast or Opposing Viewpoints:** This plan structures information in terms of comparison or contrast, as in the following example:

   > Although many women are now working outside the home, they still feel a greater responsibility for traditional housework than do men. Women often feel guilty if they leave beds unmade, dishes stacked in the sink, or carpets unvacuumed, even if their involvement in their work makes it almost impossible for them to attend to these matters. In fact, many women return from a full day at work and then spend their evenings cleaning the house. Men, on the other hand, do not feel re-

sponsible for a messy house and will very rarely use leisure hours for housecleaning. In fact, some married men may feel perfectly justified in complaining to their working wives if the house is not as tidy as they feel it ought to be.

This paragraph presents two perspectives on housekeeping, that of women and that of men.

3. **Description:** This plan is structured around the main characteristics of the subject of the paragraph:

> An ideal pet is one that provides a maximum of companionship yet requires a minimum of responsibility. In complete devotion, it will follow us around the house, never doing any damage, but it doesn't mind being ignored if we are otherwise occupied or just want to be left alone. An ideal pet comes when called, is capable of learning tricks, and is sufficiently intelligent to maintain our interest and attention. (After all, how many of us would be satisfied with a stuffed animal for a pet?) Yet it places no demands on us and doesn't mind being left behind when we go on vacation.

In this paragraph, the first sentence tells what the subject is (an ideal pet) and the rest of the paragraph describes its main characteristics.

4. **Response or Question and Answer:** This plan presents information in terms of a question and answer or problem and solution.

> Why do so many old people accumulate junk? . . . Their tables are piled high with it, their bureau drawers are stuffed with it, their closet rods bend with the weight of clothes not worn for years. I suppose that the piling up is partly from lethargy and partly from the feeling that everything once useful, including their own bodies, ought to be preserved. (From Malcolm Cowley, *The View from Eighty*)

In this paragraph, a question is posed at the beginning. The rest of the paragraph provides the answer.

5. **Time Order:** This plan relates events according to chronology, as in the following example:

> Students' adjustment to living away from home does not usually happen immediately; instead it occurs in stages over the course of about a year. At the beginning of the fall semester, many students are quite homesick. They call home frequently, count the days until the next school holiday, and think longingly of friends and family at home. A transition usually occurs during the Christmas break, when many students find themselves

in a curiously in-between state—they are happy to be home, indeed have been looking forward to it for months. Yet they also miss their friends at school and the autonomy they have when they live on their own. Family and old friends just don't seem the same and many students resent being treated as if they were still in high school. This gradual movement toward independence continues during the second semester. By Easter break, many students find themselves more comfortable at school than at home. Some even prefer to remain at school over the holidays or travel with fellow students, if they can afford it.

This paragraph begins with a description of students' feelings of dependence and homesickness at the beginning of the first year away from home and progresses to their feelings during the Easter break of the second semester.

THE UNION OF FORM AND CONTENT

The above types of plans represent a few of the most common ways of structuring paragraphs and sometimes full texts. However, these are not the only ways paragraphs and texts are developed. Moreover, it is important to clarify that it is usually not a good idea to think of form and content as being totally separate aspects of a text. In examining different paragraph and text structures, students sometimes assume that form can be separated from content, that a writer decides in advance that he is going to write a particular type of paragraph or text and then fits the content into it. And, sometimes writing instructors ask students to do just that. However, my own feeling about the relationship between form and content is that the form of a paragraph or text is usually *determined* by the content a writer wishes to express. In formulating his ideas, a writer perceives the relationship between different aspects of his information and then presents his thoughts in the structure most suitable to that relationship.

Thus, in trying to figure out the plan of a paragraph or text, you should begin by trying to understand the information being presented and how each facet of that information relates to the whole and to the parts. Plans are useful not only in looking at formal structure; they also indicate relationships between different pieces of information by showing that one piece of information is **subordinate** to another, as in the use of an example, or they show when one aspect of a topic makes another aspect more specific. Look at the following excerpt:

Suburbia is as culturally alive as a turnip. It has no great museums or libraries of its own, and so its residents must go to the cities to keep their brains from ossifying. There are no great restaurants in suburbia . . . Suburbia is also racist, and so most of its young people will never know contemporaries who are not socioeconomic duplicates of themselves. (Adapted from Fred Powledge, "Let's Bulldoze the Suburbs," *Penthouse* 1981)

In this paragraph, the lack of museums, libraries, and restaurants are **examples** of the main point—that the suburbs are culturally dead. A second main point is the idea of racism, exemplified by the lack of cultural diversity.

Looking for Cues

The above examples of paragraphs illustrate how plans create structure. But structure is also created by **cues,** which are signals in the text that a change of some sort is about to occur. Cues are commonly used to **introduce new content** while reminding the reader of previous content appearing earlier in the text, and thus functioning as a **transition.** Often in longer texts, readers cannot retain information that has been introduced at an earlier point. The reader must be reminded of this information before new content can be introduced.

Examine the following excerpt adapted from the same essay by Fred Powledge:

> Although the suburbs may be considered cultural wastelands and wasp nests of racism, they have created a great American social institution—the giant shopping center, our most fitting possible memorial to greed and bad taste. Suburbia's young people may be seen loitering day and night at these Eastgates and Westgates and asphalt encrusted Green Acres, their glassy eyes reflecting the vacuity of the suburban landscape, their brains forever softboiled by the Muzak that issues from endless chains of K-Marts and Woolcos. Some young people manage to escape into the real world, but many do not. The only salvation for many of them is rock music and killer weed.

Note that in the first sentence, the writer reminds his reader of his two previous points, the cultural lack and racist characteristic of the suburbs, before introducing his next point—the problems with shopping centers.

Writing Task: Read the article "You New Women Want It All!" by Donald Singletary. See if you can analyze the "plan" that the author uses to present his main point. Write a brief analysis of the plan of this article.

Understanding the "Plan" and Writing the Summary

Knowing the plan of a text helps you to decide its main point and then to determine how other parts of the text relate to that main point. Understanding the interrelationship between the parts will help you know how to condense the ideas presented. Below are some tips, based on the work of Brown and Day (1980), that may help you in your writing of a summary:

Collapse Lists. If you see a list of things, try to think of a word or phrase name for the whole list. For example, if you see a list such as cake, pie, candy, and cookies, you might say "sweets." If you see a list such as books, rulers, pencils, and pens, you might say "school supplies."

Look for Topic Sentences. Often authors use sentences that encapsulate a main idea in the text. Sometimes such a sentence is the topic sentence of a paragraph. Paraphrasing these sentences can help you write your summary.

Eliminate Unnecessary Detail. Not all information in a text is equally important. The author may have included a few trivial examples or repeated some information in several places. In writing a summary, do not include repetitive or trivial information.

Collapse Paragraphs. Some paragraphs expand the ideas in other paragraphs. Some paragraphs may have a transitional function, moving the reader from one idea to another. Other paragraphs may serve to remind readers of previously discussed information. In writing a summary, decide which paragraphs contain the crucial ideas of the text and rephrase the topic sentence of these paragraphs. Eliminate any paragraphs you find unnecessary.

Use Synonyms and Restructure Sentences: You should be writing in your own words and style. You should not copy whole phrases or sentences from the text, particularly if you plan to use the summary in a piece of writing. Rephrasing also helps you understand what you read.

One final step before considering your summary complete:

Rewrite Your Summary so that It Reads Easily and Gracefully. This is particularly important if you plan to include your summary in a piece of writing.

An Example of a Summary: Read the essay at the end of this chapter, "You Men Want It Both Ways!" Then read the summary below:

> Written in a lively style by a black woman, this essay states that although men claim they want educated, independent, money-earning women, their egos cannot handle a true equal. What men really want, Baye states, is a woman who not only works but also does all the housework and cooking and child care.

Practice in Writing Summaries: Write a summary of the article by Donald Singletary, which you analyzed earlier.

PARAPHRASING

Like summarizing, the ability to **paraphrase** can also help you write better papers. To paraphrase means to rephrase a piece of writing, preserving the exact meaning but using your own words. Whereas in a summary, you tend to eliminate some of the information in the original source, in a paraphrase, you retain *all* of the information, of course using your own words. Like summarizing, paraphrasing helps you gain an understanding of what you read so that you can effectively incorporate secondary source information into your writing. Paraphrasing also helps you to avoid excessive quotation. However, when you paraphrase, you must always use your own words and, as in all use of outside sources, acknowledge your source to avoid plagiarism.

When Do You Paraphrase?

It would make no sense for you to paraphrase everything you read. Therefore, unless you are given an assignment that specifically asks you to paraphrase, you would be most likely to paraphrase when:

1. You wish to clarify meaning for yourself.
2. You wish to express an idea in your writing without requiring your readers to have read the source.

Therefore, you would not paraphrase unless you had previewed your source and decided that it pertains directly to your topic. Some of the same suggestions for writing a summary also apply to writing a paraphrase, the following in particular:

1. **Scan your source before reading it carefully. Do not attempt to paraphrase until you understand its main point.**
2. **Ask yourself if you understand the purpose of the text.**
3. **Examine the "plan" of the text.**

Avoiding Plagiarism When Paraphrasing

In writing a paraphrase, the following techniques may help you avoid using the author's own words too heavily:

1. **Substitute synonyms for the words in the text.** Examine the following excerpt:

   > Today, huge television audiences watch surgical operations in the comfort of their living rooms. Moreover, thanks to the animated cartoon, the geography of the digestive system has become familiar territory even to the nursery school set, and the satisfaction of curiosity about almost all matters is a national pastime. Obviously, then, the secrecy surrounding embalming can, surely, hardly be attributed to the inherent gruesomeness of the subject. (Adapted from Jessica Mitford, "Behind the Formaldehyde Curtain," *The American Way of Death*)

   In your paraphrase, you might use the word "large," for "huge," "procedures" for "operations," "structure" for "geography," and so on.

2. **Use different sentence patterns, perhaps reversing the order in which ideas are presented.** In the above sentence, you might begin your paraphrase with the idea that appears at the end, "the secrecy sur-

rounding embalming can, surely, hardly be attributed to the inherent gruesomeness of the subject." Thus, in your paraphrase you might write

> It is unlikely that the lack of media attention given to embalming is due simply to the public's disgust over this subject.

3. **Vary the sentence length. Break up longer sentences into shorter ones or combine short sentences into longer ones.** In the above example, you might break up the second sentence into two sentences as in the following:

> Even children are now familiar with the structure of the digestive system as it is presented in an animated cartoon. In fact, we are a nation that has a great curiosity about such matters.

4. **When you include a paraphrase in your writing, you should mention the source so that the reader knows that you have derived your information from a secondary source.** In using the above paraphrase in a piece of writing, you might phrase it as follows:

> **Mitford indicates** that it is unlikely that the lack of media attention given to the subject of embalming is due simply to the public's unwillingness to learn about it. **She points out that,** after all, we are accustomed to watching all sorts of medical procedures on television and that even children are now familiar with the structure of the digestive system as it is presented in an animated cartoon. In fact, **she says,** we are a nation that has a great curiosity about such matters.

Note here that the first sentence indicates the main point of the paragraph.

DIRECT QUOTING

When you are working with information, you sometimes wish to write down the exact words of your source rather than a summary or a paraphrase. Here are some instances when you would be likely to use direct quotation:

A. If the style of the quotation is so unique that its power would be lost if you paraphrased or summarized.

For example:

> Although the students were not especially interested in American history, all of them found inspiration in Patrick Henry's famous saying, "Give me liberty, or give me death!"

Note the less effective use of paraphrase of this remark:

The students were inspired by Patrick Henry's statement in which he indicated that he must have liberty or else he would prefer to die.

B. If the main importance of a quotation is that it was spoken by a particular authority or famous person. In these cases, you would probably choose to use direct quotation rather than a paraphrase or summary in that it would lend authority to your own position.
For example:

The well-known behavior researchers Masters, Johnson, and Kolodny similarly point out that "school age children are also exposed to obvious gender-role stereotypes on television" (378).

C. If you are discussing someone's first-hand experience. In this case, again, you would probably wish to use direct quotation for the sake of reliability.
For example:

Airline crash survivor, John Rondell, claimed that "the smoke filled the cabin immediately after takeoff."

Punctuating Direct Quotations

Whenever you quote directly, be sure to enclose all quoted material within quotation marks and punctuate as follows:

1. **Commas and periods are placed inside quotation marks, unless you are documenting a source within the text.** Thus:

   The professor stood up quietly and said, "I do not expect to continue at this position any longer."

   Peter Singer states that "according to one estimate, 15 million children under five die every year from the combined effects of malnutrition and infection" (428).

2. **Semicolons and colons are placed outside of the quotation marks.** For example, here is the original:

   Many young adults are confused about what direction they should take. Young women, in particular, are still unclear about their goals and are often torn between the desire to raise a family and the lure of professional ambition (Baker 19).

   Here is an example of how this material could be quoted using a semi-colon:

Baker discusses the confusion young adults often experience in deciding "what direction they should take"; in particular, he focuses on
young women's difficulty in choosing between family and career.

Here is an example of how this material could be quoted using a colon:

Baker focuses on two choices that cause young women "to be unclear
about their goals": their interest in family life and their desire for professional success.

3. **Question marks and exclamation marks are kept within quotation marks if they are part of the original quotation.** For example:

Professor Begley asked, "What is the meaning of life?" (The question
mark is part of original quotation, so question mark is inside.)

Didn't the students feel uncomfortable with that question about
"the meaning of life"? (The question mark is part of the whole sentence. In this sentence, it is placed outside of the quotation marks.)

4. **Single quotation marks are placed inside double quotation
marks for a quote within a quote.**

Professor Jones claimed that he would "never respond to Professor
Begley's question about 'the meaning of life.' "

5. **Use ellipsis when you are omitting part of a quotation.** For example, read this original quotation:

Television is also a powerful force in the gender-role socialization of
young chidren because it provides a window to the rest of the world.
The fictionalized world of Saturday morning children's cartoons is filled
with gender stereotypes: the heroes are almost all males, and the females are shown as companions or as "victims" needed to be rescued
from the forces of evil. Even award winning children's shows such as
Sesame Street have been criticized because women were seldom shown
employed outside the home and male figures predominated. (From
"Gender Roles" by William Masters, Virginia Johnson, and Robert
Kolodny)

This is an example of the use of an ellipsis:

Masters, Johnson, and Kolodny assert that "television is also a powerful
force in the gender-role socialization of young children. . . . Even award
winning children's shows such as Sesame Street have been criticized
because women were seldom shown employed outside the home and
male figures predominated.

6. **Use square brackets whenever you need to substitute or add words to a quotation.** For example:

> Masters, Johnson, and Kolodny indicate that "gender-role socialization of young children [occurs] because [television] provides a window to the rest of the world.

When you copy down quotations directly, be sure you are using the author's exact words and punctuation, including any mistakes or misspellings. To avoid inadvertent plagiarism (that is, including as your own material that has actually been taken from a source), be sure to use quotation marks at the beginning and the end of the quoted material, so that you, yourself, will know that you are quoting, rather than summarizing or paraphrasing.

RECORDING SUMMARIES, PARAPHRASES, AND QUOTATIONS IN YOUR NOTES

Despite the invention of the copy machine, writing down notes in the form of summary, paraphrase, and quotation is still an important part of the research process. Students sometimes think that if they photocopy a sufficient amount of material that they do not have to take notes. My feeling, though, is that simply photocopying a source does not give you the opportunity to think about its meaning and to select material that you wish to include in some form in your own writing. Writing down notes enables you to interact with the text, helping you understand and remember what you read. This section will give you suggestions on methods of recording your notes, so that you can then incorporate them effectively into your paper.

Too Much or Too Little?

Students, understandably, are often concerned with saving time, and they sometimes wonder if they will be more efficient if they write only a few notes, rather than many. My recommendation, however, is for *more,* rather than less. Often, when you begin taking notes, you may not be quite sure of your topic and you may refocus your thesis later to include aspects you hadn't considered in the beginning. Therefore, when in doubt, take more notes than you think you might need. As you work, you might discover that you need them after all.

Recording Your Notes: Notecards Versus Notesheets

Over the past 15 years, a popular method of teaching students to record notes for a research paper involved using notecards, and many students trained in this method may still prefer using them. Notecards are easy to sort and, because they provide only limited room for writing, they can aid students in breaking down a topic into manageable parts. My own experience and that of many other writers and teachers I have asked, however, suggests that taking notes usually requires more room than a notecard provides and that, in fact, part of the notetaking process includes jotting down ideas as they occur, right next to the note. It is therefore necessary to have more room for writing than a notecard allows. Moreover, notecards are easily lost, although, of course, one could lose a notebook as well. In general, though, I recommend using a notebook with detachable pages for taking notes. An inexpensive softcover folder with fasteners to hold the paper is easy to carry around and allows for rearrangement of information as needed. It is also helpful if the folder has side pockets as well for additional storage of information or computer disks.

I recommend two types of sheets for taking notes, the **Source Notesheet,** which may be used for recording notes about a single source and the **Note Synthesis Sheet,** which is used to organize information about one aspect of a topic and may include notes from several sources.

The Source Notesheet

A Source Notesheet is used to record notes about a single source. It includes a summary of the source and contains information only from that source. A Source Notesheet helps you to record your notes easily and can also be used to prepare your bibliography since these sheets can be alphabetized. Below is a sample of a Source Notesheet. You can use your computer to prepare a form for this sheet. Then, using a copying machine, you can prepare many Source Notesheets in advance and fasten them into your notebook.

In creating a Source Notesheet, you begin with the author's last name so that you can easily alphabetize the sheets to create your bibliography. Note that there is also a section for a brief summary of your source, so that you can remember what its overall purpose was. This is particularly useful if you are writing a paper in which you have to compare different points of view on a topic. Note also that there is a space allotted for writing down the page number, a very important piece of information. Too many of us have spent wasted hours in a library hunting for a source for which we forgot to write down a necessary page number. If you remember to include this information as you take notes, you can save yourself a lot of time.

In the section marked "Notes" on the Source Notesheet, you can either paraphrase an idea you want to remember or write it down as an exact quote. If it is an exact quote, remember to put quotation marks around it so that you can document it properly when you write your paper.

Note also the section of the Source Notesheet marked "Idea about Note." As you read, you get ideas that you cannot pursue immediately. You may think to yourself, "This would provide a good argument against that other article I read." So you might write "Compare with _____ article." Or you may think "This is a good example of _____." As you read, many of these ideas will occur to you, but later, when you have finished reading, you may have forgotten them. Using this space to jot down ideas as they occur to you can help you avoid losing your thoughts.

Here is an example of a Source Notesheet used to take notes about the article "You New Women Want It All!"

Source Notesheet

Author(s):   Singletary, Donald

Title: "You New Women Want It All"

Journal Information (if appropriate): *Essence*

Publisher (if appropriate):

Date and Place of Publication: July 1985

Pages: 95–99

Short Summary:

In this humorous article, written from a man's perspective, Singletary accuses modern young women of wanting all the advantages of being liberated women but also wanting many of the advantages of being traditional women. He uses many examples from the dating scene, in which women will take the initiative in approaching a man and selecting a restaurant, but then want men to pay.

Page Number	Note	Idea about note
3	Years ago, men chose women who could cook, take care of a house, and raise children. Women chose men who would make good providers.	Use to show that roles haven't changed much.

The Note Synthesis Sheet

The Note Synthesis Sheet is used to help you organize notes around a particular aspect of a topic. It includes enough information from each source so that you will be able to incorporate it into your paper with relative ease. To see how a Note Synthesis Sheet works, read the two selections at the end of the chapter, "Professions for Women," and "Ms. Givings." Think about the idea that despite increased opportunity for women, other obstacles often prevent women from realizing their potential. One obstacle is the conflict women face about choosing between a career and having a personal life. Then examine the Note Synthesis Sheet prepared below:

Note Synthesis Sheet

Subject of Paper: Obstacles preventing women from realizing potential

Topic: Conflicts between professional and personal life

Source (Author)	Page	Note	Reason for using
Woolf	385	"The consciousness of what men will say of a woman who speaks the truth about her passions had roused her from her artist's state of unconsciousness."	Pre-women's-movement perspective
Cosell	33	"The price of success is high for everyone, but it is especially high for women, and not because they face constant discrimination. For women, the conflicts and the choices involved in dedicating one-self to success are so fundamental, so basic, that sometimes they are unbearable."	Post-women's-movement perspective

The Note Synthesis Sheet allows you to organize information from several sources. Note that the direct quotations here are enclosed in quotation marks, so that you can document them properly if you include them in your paper. (You can also include paraphrase or summary.) Note also that next to each note is a column called "Reason for using." With some topics, you may not know exactly how you are going to use each piece of information until you actually begin to write the paper. With others, though, you may know in advance, and it is a good idea to jot these ideas down before you forget them.

INCORPORATING OUTSIDE INFORMATION INTO YOUR TEXT

When students begin to incorporate their notes into their papers, there is a great danger that they will inadvertently use the ideas of others instead of developing their own ideas. Appropriating others' ideas without proper acknowledgment is a form of plagiarism. Moreover, when students simply take over other peoples' ideas, the paper is usually lifeless and uninteresting to read; it has a "pasted together" flavor. Use the opinions of others, then, to *support* your own position, which you have developed through thinking and reading. Do not use them as substitutes for your own ideas.

Another point to keep in mind is that all sources should be acknowledged by using proper documentation form within the text and correct bibliography form at the end. The new MLA style now requires source citations within the text, making footnotes and endnotes unnecessary (footnotes and endnotes are not necessary for a researched paper). The author and page number are cited within the text and a "works cited" section appears at the end, so that readers can locate your source if they so choose. The appendix to this book contains illustrative examples of this documentation system.

Incorporating Sources Smoothly into Your Text: Avoiding the "Crouton Effect"

Students who have had little experience using outside sources in a paper some-times have difficulty incorporating their sources smoothly within their text. They seem to just sprinkle them in, like croutons in a salad, with the result that the quotations sometimes don't blend in. The reader crunches on them from time to time and may enjoy the flavor, but the information from outside sources always stands out. Unless you deliberately wish to create this effect, you should aim for a smooth blend of quoted material with your own prose.

For example, to take an obvious conversational example, suppose you had used your lunch hour to see your instructor about whether or not she plans to assign a paper at the end of the semester. The teacher responds to your question as follows:

"I have given the matter considerable thought and have decided that I will not assign a paper at the end of the semester."

You then meet a friend who asks where you were during lunch. You would be *un*likely to respond like this;

I went to see the instructor and asked whether or not she was planning to assign a paper at the end of the semester. The instructor said that there would be no paper assigned. *"I have given the matter considerable thought and have decided that I will not assign a paper at the end of the semester."*

Note here that the quoted material is simply thrown in at the end (like a crouton), that it repeats information the student has already said, and that it does not blend in smoothly with the students' own words. If you answered in this way, your friend would probably look at you strangely. Yet, many students present quoted material in just this way because they are unaware that such material should be incorporated into their own prose. They think that quoted material, above all, should be used to support their own statements, and, of course, this is partly true. But it is also important that it be **blended.**

To avoid the "crouton effect," then, try to include quoted material as part of your own sentences. If you include summary and paraphrase as well as direct quotation, you will achieve a smoother effect than if you use only direct quotation.

For example, in the conversational example, above, you would be more likely to respond,

> I went to see the instructor. She said that there will not be a paper assigned at the end of the semester. (This summarizes the instructor's statement.)

or, if you wished to quote exactly,

> I went to see the instructor who said, *"I have given the matter considerable thought and have decided that I will not assign a paper at the end of the semester."*

Below are some possibilities for incorporating quoted material smoothly into your own text. To illustrate these ideas, I will use the following excerpt from an essay in *Time* magazine that is concerned with the issue of whether or not all-male clubs ought to be allowed:

> Yet amid the antique rugs and deep leather chairs, the clubs do furnish a setting for the exertions of professional life: back slapping, ego massage, and one "contact sport"—making business connections. In short, though they offer relaxation, the clubs are places of business too. Meal tabs and annual dues that can run into the thousands of dollars are often picked up by a member's employer as a business expense. (Richard Lacayo, *Time,* July 4, 1988)

Here are several ways to incorporate this material into a paper:

Incorporating Essential Words and Phrases Into Your Text

> Allowing male-only clubs places business women at a disadvantage, since their function is not only recreational. As a recent article in *Time* magazine points out, in addition to being places of relaxation, "the clubs are places of business too." (Lacayo 23)

Note here the placement of the page numbers and the reference to the author's name. As will be discussed in more detail in the appendix, one of the prime functions of systems of documentation is to enable readers to locate your source.

Incorporating Most of the Text by Using an Ellipsis

Sometimes the section you wish to quote contains material that is not essential to your main point. In this case, you may leave out the nonessential piece, but you must insert an ellipsis (three spaced dots) to show that you have left something out. Here is an example of how to use an ellipsis:

> Most businesses recognize the importance of clubs for "making business connections." . . . Meal tabs and annual dues that can run into the thousands of dollars are often picked up by a member's employer as a business expense. (Lacayo 23)

Long Quotations

For a quotation that is more than four lines long, use a block indented ten spaces and do not use quotation marks. Double-space between your own words and the quoted materials, double-space the quoted material, and do not indent the first line of the quoted paragraph. Place the citation reference after the last mark of punctuation. Here is an example:

> The unfairness of male only clubs is pointed out in a recent *Time* magazine article:
>
> > Yet amid the antique rugs and deep leather chairs, the clubs do furnish a setting for the exertions of professional life: back slapping, ego massage, and one "contact sport"—making business connections. In short, though they offer relaxation, the clubs are places of business too. Meal tabs and annual dues that can run into the thousands of dollars are often picked up by a member's employer as a business expense. (Lacayo 23)

SOME GENERAL RECOMMENDATIONS FOR NOTETAKING

1. Paraphrase as much as possible to avoid the possibility of plagiarism.
2. Always acknowledge your source.
3. Use your notes to provide *support* for your own ideas, not in place of them.

▶ **Writing Task:** Based on your reading of the articles included at the end of the chapter, find another obstacle preventing women from realizing their potential. Prepare a Note Synthesis Sheet on this topic.

▶ **Writing Task:** Based on your reading of the four articles included at the end of this chapter and on women you know, write a paper addressing the following topic:

> Do women now have the same freedom of choice as men do in choosing their professions? Do you see many changes occurring in women's opportunities

since the time of Virginia Woolf (1920s)? If so, do you feel that those changes brought any disadvantages?

Use a Source Notesheet for each reading. Use a Note Synthesis Sheet for each aspect of your topic.

You New Women Want It All!

Donald Singletary

A: Why is it always *sex, sex, sex*? Can't a man talk to me as a professional?

B: All men want to do is talk business; there's no romance.

A: These guys are together all day at work; now they come in the club and they're still over there in a group talking to each other.

B: Damn, I can't even come in here to have a quiet drink with my girlfriend without men coming around to hit on us.

A: I feel that as a woman today I can have just as much freedom as a man. That means a casual affair is okay.

B: I don't understand men. They want to jump into bed as fast as they can. They don't want any commitment.

In each of the above, statements A and B were made by the *same woman* at different times. In the second example they were made in the *same evening.*

Imagine eating in an expensive restaurant. You pick up the shaker and it reads: "salt or sugar." Or picture the announcer's voice at the beginning of a boxing match: "In this corner we have the liberated woman. And in the *same* corner we have the woman who wants to be 'kept.' " Let's place the man in the role of referee: How does he judge this fight? Yes, it is confusing, isn't it? Not to mention annoying. It is *very* annoying. What we have here are examples of mixed messages, conflicting signals. And to put it bluntly, it is the women who are sending the confusing signals and the men who are getting confused. Not to mention angry.

In the last few years—since women began their quest for greater personal independence, better jobs and pay comparable to men's and the right to make decisions about what they do with their bodies—men have struggled to understand this "new woman." The signals that we are getting are that women want to take charge of their own destinies. They want to compete alongside men for the fruits of success in society. They no longer wish to rely on men for the things that they want out of life. Instead they have opted to get it themselves. Although these

Donald Singletary, "You New Women Want It All!" *Essence,* July 1985. Reprinted by permission of the author.

changes do in fact create some anxiety among men, many feel that they will ultimately free men from some of the traditional male responsibilities society has imposed upon them. Ideally, this should mean men no longer have to carry the full burden of financial support, decision making and being the aggressor in romantic pursuits. Right?

Wrong! That's one message women send. But there is another message that says, "I'll have my cake and eat yours too."

A perplexed former coworker of mine once said, "You would think that a woman making, say, $35,000 a year could go out with whoever she wants—even the guy in the mail room. But no, she wants somebody who makes $45,000 a year! Why? Because she's still looking to be taken care of."

For this man and for many others, the assumption is that once a woman has the necessary financial security, the need to form relationships on the basis of what a man earns is gone.

Not so.

It's what some of us call the "my money, *our* money" syndrome. Here's a typical example: A man and woman meet through a mutual friend. Both single, they begin chatting about themselves. They are both professionals, make approximately the same money, and each has attended a good college.

SHE: *You're very nice to talk to. It's so refreshing. A lot of men these days can't deal with an independent woman. They seem to always want the upper hand, and if you are making the same bread, they become insecure. I think they still expect women to be impressed with what* they *do.*

HE: *That's true. I even see that in some of my own friends. But I like a professional woman, not one who's dependent on a man.*

SHE: *That's me. Hey, why don't we have dinner sometime? I know a great little place.*

They go out to dinner at an expensive restaurant that *she* chooses. *At last,* he thinks, *a woman who doesn't wait for the man to take the initiative, an independent woman! Wow, I never thought I'd be taken anyplace like this by a woman.*

The check comes, and she waits patiently for *him* to pick it up. Thank goodness our hero has his American Express card up to date. I know guys who've had to excuse themselves from the table and dash out into the streets in search of a bank cash machine. In fact, I've been one of those guys. It's tough. You have to run out in the bitter cold (it's *always* cold) without your coat because you don't want the waiter to think you've left without paying. As one of my cronies put it, "Women want it all today, from soup to nuts—and the man has to pay for the meal."

No one is suggesting, least of all me, that women *have* to pay or date "dutch." But when one professes her liberation, as did this woman, the man has the right to expect her to follow through. The emerging new woman has not only created confusion for men; she has created some problems for women as well. At least one of them, as you might expect, is a paradoxical one. Now that women have more money and more mobility, there don't seem to be any men around. There is, they say, a shortage of men. Not *any* men, mind you, but those with the "right stuff." In conversations between women and men, women and women, coast to coast, the question "Where are all the men?" always rears its head.

I defy you to find one man, one *real* man, who actually believes there is a shortage of men. Yes, I know what the statistics say. But what I and other men see is quite different. We see women who walk around as if they couldn't care less about a man. Women don't have time.

One of my own former girlfriends once told me that she was having a difficult time deciding on what to do with her new status. She had recently passed the New York bar and had gotten a new job. "I don't know what I should be: a socialite, a hard-boiled attorney, or sort of work out a blend of my professional and social life," she mused. Curiously, none of the choices included me, so I asked, "Where do I fit in?" She stared blankly for a moment, as if she'd come home and discovered she'd forgotten to buy catsup. Then she said, "You know, Donald, sometimes I think you really have a place in my life, and sometimes I think if you walked out the door and never came back, it wouldn't faze me at all."

I had to ask.

Had it not been about nine below zero (it's *always* cold) that February night, I would have left right then. (I have since garnered lots more pride.)

Women sit at tables in fours and fives wondering where all the men are, while the men sit a few feet away at the bar. The women almost never initiate anything. Believe me, if there were only ten eligible women in New York, I'd have two of them. If I didn't, it wouldn't be because I didn't try.

It is baffling to men why women are not more aggressive. One has to assume that they are simply not interested. Here are some examples of what "eligible" men are saying.

Women don't have time for you these days. I swear, making a date is like making a business appointment. Everybody's got calendars and datebooks.

While women are in their twenties, they party like cracy and tell you not to pressure them into relationships. Then all of a sudden they hit 30 and uh-oh! Everybody races the clock to get married and make that baby. What are we, sperm factories? I'm supposed to get married so you can have cut crystal?

It's quality I'm looking for, not quantity. I don't care how many women there are out there, it's quality I want. By the time you weed out the workaholics, the ones so bitter about their past lovers that they hate every man, the ones that want you only for your money/prestige, the druggies (yes, women do that too) and star seekers (noncelebrities need not apply) and ones who want fathers for their children, the margin really narrows.

I'll believe women are liberated when one walks up to me, says, 'Hey, good-lookin',' buys me dinner, pats me on the cakes and suggests we go to her place for a nightcap.

It's ironic. Women are always telling me that men are intimidated by independent, assertive women. Where are they? On a recent *Donahue* show dedicated to single men, one man posed this question: "How many women out there would drive two hours to pick me up, take me out and spend $100, bring me back home and leave?" Yes, I'm certain some have done it. Just as I know there are some readers who have figured out the number of angels on the head of a pin. However, although the number of miles and dollar amount might seem exaggerated, the routine is one that is typical and expected of men.

I remember once being headed out the door at about 9:30 on a Saturday night when the phone rang. It was a woman I dated once in a while, and she invited me out that night. Already headed elsewhere, I respectfully declined. "Well, excuse me," she said, obviously miffed. "I guess I have to book ahead."

I remember that I really had something to do that night. I think it was open-heart surgery or something, so I explained that to her. She wouldn't have cared if it really had been open-heart surgery; she felt rejected, humiliated.

I hate to tell you this, but whenever you ask someone out, there is a possibility they will say no. Men know it, they live with it. I'll never like it, but I have gotten used to it.

Oh, you thought we had it easy, huh?

Women, I honestly think, believe it is easy for men to approach them. If that were true, I would be dating Jayne Kennedy *and* Diahann Carroll. Talking to a woman for the first time, especially without an introduction, is always a crap shoot. For me, it is worse. It is tantamount to walking down a dark alley knowing a psychopath with a big baseball bat and little mercy is in there. Approaching someone means you have to bare yourself and lay some of your cards on the table. That's not easy—particularly with the "new woman" who waltzes into a room like it's the set of *Dynasty*. Thumbs up if she likes you; to the lions if not.

I'm certain that it's easier for many men. And I'm equally certain that I've fooled lots of women with my cool, sophisticated facade. It comes with years of practice and experience.

What men are seeing and hearing from women, either directly or indirectly, is that there is a very bad problem with self-image. I'm not quite sure why. It seems contradictory. There are more women than ever before who are well educated, have lucrative careers and are well dressed and good-looking.

Therein may lie the problem. Women are insecure not only about the shortage of men but also about the increasing number of what they see as competition— other women.

I've said it myself. A woman walks into the room and I'm introduced to her and I think, *Okay, you went to a good school, you've got a good job and look good. So what? So do most of the women in this room. In fact, so do most of the ones I meet.* Increasingly, there is nothing exceptional about being young, gifted and cute. It has, in many circles, become a given. Male friends of mine often say, "Why do women place so much emphasis on what they do professionally?" That automatically sets up a false criterion that men fall prey to. It creates a value system that emphasizes material things. Women, of course, are not solely responsible for that. Throughout history men have shown off their uniforms, three-piece suits and jobs since shepherding paid top dollar. However, at the same time, our criteria for women were based largely on hair, ankles, calves—you get the picture.

Nowadays we find ourselves asking more questions about education, career goals and so on. These are valid questions for anyone to ask, mind you, but they are not by any means the sole criterion for what makes a good human being, let alone a good relationship. It does, on the other hand, keep the mind beyond the ankles, which is a step in the right direction.

Years ago men chose women who could cook, take care of a house and raise children. Women chose men who would make good providers. Today more and more men do their own cooking and cleaning, are becoming closer to their children. Women, on the other hand, are becoming more self-supporting. This sounds to me like a marvelous opportunity for people to find some other reasons for relationships and shed some old ones. However, that does not seem to be happening.

It becomes extremely difficult to decipher the signals. One says, "I want a man who's sensitive, caring, spiritual and warm." The other says, "I have this list of things that I feel I should have. I want a man who can help me achieve them and move up in society."

There is a curious side to the pursuit of Mr. Right Stuff. When women settle for less, it is *far* less. I'm not talkin' triflin' here. But for some reason, Brother Rat seems to capture their attention. The story has become a tired soap opera.

I knew a woman, a professional, good school, good job, condo, the whole ball of wax. She could never find a guy good enough. She always broke off the relationships, saying that the men would feel bad because she made more money; their fragile egos would be crushed. She went out with a good guy. A professional, a nice person. They were to be married. At the last minute she shifted gears and decided she wanted more time as a career woman. She left him. She spent her days bemoaning the fact that she had nobody. Then she met a rogue. Not the charming, sophisticated, Billy Dee Williams type, but a sleazy, coke-dealing, never-had-an-honest-job type. She let him move into her apartment; he spent her money and left her in debt and with a great loss of self-esteem. Yet at a given opportunity, whenever he came through town, she would take him in for a few days and, yes, lend him money.

Figure it out.

I have spent nearly all my adult life in the communications business as a writer, journalist and media specialist, and ten years in corporate public relations. None of these things, however, prepared me for the biggest communications gap of all—that between men and women.

It happened so suddenly. Things hadn't changed very much for decades. Then came the middle sixties, while the Black movement was in full fury, and eventually people began questioning, challenging, their sexual roles. Age-old ideas about love, marriage, sex, family and children began to change for women—and for men as well.

When women were fragile little princesses (they never really were, but they played the part), it was a lot more palatable for men to play the role of Prince Charming. There is, at least among college-educated, professional women, little impetus for a man to feel he has to sweep you off your feet as you stand together, pinstripe to pinstripe, Gucci to Gucci, M.B.A. to M.B.A. But there you stand, waiting for him to open the door and take you to dinner. During the day he holds the door at work and she's furious. At night she stands in place until he opens it.

What's a guy to do?

How does one approach the new woman? Should he be forward? more aggressive and to the point? Or should he be more sutble? Should he try to appeal to her intellect through conversation? Or should he be more romantic? Can he assume she is more sexually liberated or that she is seeking only a "meaningful relationship?" How do you separate platonic friendships from romantic inclinations? Who pays the bill? Does the fact that she's "career oriented" mean that she doesn't want or have time for a relationship?

Women are facing a backlash from men that will rival the white blacklash of the seventies and eighties. And, like the white liberals in the sixties, the disenchanted men are the "nice guys"—the guys who feel they have been gentlemanly, supportive, considerate. All of a sudden the message they are getting is one of distrust, as they're portrayed as abusers, ne'er-do-wells, drug abusers and cheats. And after struggling to survive the street, college and/or military service and the day-to-day strife of the work world, they are being sent messages that say women's struggles make theirs pale by comparison. Not only that—they are the ones responsible for it!

Liberation. Independence. They're words that imply hard-won, new-found freedom. Freedom from the shackles of the past. That should include the freedom to look at relationships in a new light. Taking one or two bad experiences into each relationship thereafter is not being liberated. It is being shackled, weighed down, by your past. Understanding that the changes that took place for women also changed the perspective of many men is important. It means that realignments in relationships are necessary.

I once had the experience of working with a group of five women. All of them had previously worked together and had been friends for some time. Their businesslike demeanor made me want to straighten my tie, let alone my files and desk. We would have group meetings prior to every division meeting. They would stress how we would go in as a group, pose a common front. But once inside the meeting, something interesting happened. They broke ranks, and each tried to impress the boss. How? By fluttering eyelashes, flashing toothy smiles and laughing at all his dumb jokes.

It caused one of my male coworkers to remark, "You know who the new woman is? She's the old woman, only she can't cook"—a sexist response evoked by a group of women who lapsed into a stereotypical role.

As bleak as some of this may seem, things are actually getting better. Change did move in very swiftly, and we are all, men and women alike, getting used to it. Certainly most of us over 30 grew up in an America where girls played nurse and boys played soldier. So it will take a while. But regardless of the changes, and the time it takes, there will always be a misread signal somewhere.

And it will *always* be on a cold night.

You Men Want It Both Ways!

Betty Winston Baye

I thought the 1980's would be different, especially after the revolutionary sixties, when it was common to hear some Black men hollering about how Black women should walk ten paces behind their "kings" and have babies for the revolution. I thought that in the eighties, Black men and women had declared a truce in the war between the sexes and that we had reached, or were striving to reach, a level where we could enjoy each other's company as equals.

I know now, however, that I hoped for much too much. Though I don't presume to paint all Black men with one broad brush stroke, it seems to me that there are men—too many—who, for reasons that only they and God understand, find it necessary to lie and pretend that they just love independent women. That's what they say at first, but as their relationships develop, it becomes painfully obvious that what they really want are women who work to help bring home the bacon but also cook, clean and take care of them and their babies on demand. These new men want women who are articulate and forceful when they're taking care of business—but who, behind closed doors, become simpering sycophants who heed their every wish.

I am an independent woman, and I'll tell anybody that what my mother and many of the women of her generation did to keep home and family together I won't do, not for love or money. Whenever I meet a man who says he's interested in me, I tell him up front that I don't do no windows. I don't love housework. I don't love to cook, and I certainly don't reach a climax thinking about having to clean up behind a bunch of kids and some mother's son. If a man wants somebody to make him home bread and fresh collard greens every night, then I'm definitely not the girl of his dreams.

Now, I realize that I'm not every man's cup of tea. But take it or leave it, that's where I'm coming from. I'll gladly work every day to help bring home the money so that my man and I can pool our resources to go out to dinner every once in a while, take a few trips during the year and to pay somebody willing (or needing) to cook, clean and do laundry.

Surprisingly, my attitudes don't turn too many men off—in fact, brothers seem turned on by my honesty and independence. My ex-husband is one case in point. At the dawn of our relationship, he swore to me that I was just what the doctor ordered. Said he'd never met a woman like me—intelligent, witty, educated, self-sufficient and not all that hard on the eyes. He went on about how he was just so thrilled that I had "chosen" him.

At first, everything was wonderful. But soon after I acquired a sweet contract

Betty Winston Baye, "You Men Want It Both Ways," *Essence*, July 1985. Reprinted by permission of the author.

to write my first book, the shit was on. It occurred to me that my beloved husband was just a bit jealous of my success. Before I knew it, I realized that he got some kind of perverse pleasure out of trying to insult me and make me look small in the eyes of my friends and professional colleagues. I remember how one time, for no special reason, he got up and announced in front of my childhood friend, her husband and their children that I was "a stupid bitch." Now, he had already published a novel, and to me he was a fine writer who could handle the English language as smoothly as butter sliding down a hot roll. But my book, and the money I got, just seemed to set him off. Not surprisingly, the marriage was finished before the book hit the shelves.

Had what happened in my marriage been an isolated case, I might have concluded that it was just "my problem"—something we women tend to do a lot. But it wasn't isolated. All around me, women friends of mine were and still are bailing out of relationships with men who say one thing, then do another.

A friend of mine got married a few years ago to a man she'd been dating for more than a year. This was a marriage made in heaven, or so she and we thought. Both she and her husband were talented go-getters who seemed to want the same things out of life. When they first met, she says, he told her he didn't dig her just for her body but also for her sharp mind. Before long, however, it became clear that the only thing he wanted to do with her mind was to cause her to lose it. She says he wanted her to be dynamic by day and servile by night. Finally, after much verbal and physical abuse, she split. Thankfully, her memorable excursion into his insanity didn't last for long. Now she's recovering quite nicely.

Strong, dynamic, intelligent, independent women are what men of the eighties say they want. They claim they want their women to go that extra mile, but what they really mean is that we should work twice as hard but not forget our responsibilities at home. When a woman spends time with *their* children, cleans the house or cooks for *their* family, it often goes unnoticed. No matter how tired she is after a demanding day at work, the expectation is that these are *her* responsibilities. But when a man spends time with *their* children, cooks food for *their* family or cleans *their* house once a month, he acts like he deserves an Academy Award.

Money is another area that has the brothers confused. For example, there are the men who say that if we women want to be truly liberated we should be willing, on occasion, to pick up the tab for dinner or for a night on the town. The fact that many of these same men often get their jaws wired when women, in the presence of a waiter or others at the table, reach for their wallet and pull out the cash or credit card says they're not ready for liberation. They don't mind woman paying but would much prefer that they slip them the money under the table, the way women used to do.

And there are also the double-talking men who claim they can handle a woman who makes more money than they do. At first, everything is all right, but in order to assuage their egos, some men start thinking that "just because" they are men, they must exert control over their women's money and become personal financial managers of sorts. She's smart enough to make the money, he knows, but he believes she doesn't have enough sense to know how to spend it, invest it or manage it. "Are you sure you can afford this?" is a common question, but one rarely asked out of concern for a woman's finances. He knows she can afford it; he'd prefer to think she can't.

Many of the same men rattle on about how if we women want equality, we should buy gifts for them, as they allegedly have always done for us. Gift giving is nice, but for women, it can be a double-edged sword. One well-known singer tells the story of how she bought gifts for her man, which he gratefully accepted. But she says that after a time, the man got real nasty and told her that he couldn't be bought—he wasn't for sale.

And, of course, there are the men who seem to think that success drops out of the sky—that it doesn't require hard work and long hours. I've seen men hotly pursue women who they know are busy and then get bent out of shape if the sister pulls out her datebook to see when she's free. These women say they are tired of feeling guilty and trying to explain to some yo-yo that they can't just saunter off to dinner on the spur of the moment when they've got a report to finish or a meeting to attend.

Brothers are all for liberation when it works to their advantage. Yet, what we have found out is that when men don't want a serious commitment, they encourge us to be independent—to be open-minded enough to accept the terms of an "open relationship." But try that same rap on them, and we're in for trouble. Try saying, "Okay, baby, I don't want a commitment either"; or better yet, beat them to the punch. All of a sudden they've decided that they're in love and want to settle down. They get jealous and accuse us of "using" them.

And what about men who claim they want total honesty with their women? For many men, total honesty means that they want the freedom to talk openly about their prior involvements, including relating to their women intimate details about how many other women they've slept with or how many have aborted their babies. In return, a man like this often demands that his woman tell all her business to keep things in balance. Unfortunately, what many sisters have found— often after they are laid out on a stretcher or when they've had their past sexual exploits thrown in their faces in the heat of an argument—is that many men can't handle total honesty, especially if it's sexual honesty. Many men still seem to buy into the Madonna/whore syndrome. They still believe that their peccadilloes are understandable because everyone knows that "boys will be boys." Women, however, especially *their* women, are supposed to be innocents who somehow, perhaps through osmosis, instinctively know how to turn them on in bed.

There are dozens of other ways that men send out mixed signals to the women in their lives and show, through their words and deeds, that they really want it both ways. They want us to drive the car—but from the backseat. Mostly what they want is for things to be the way they used to be. That, however, is a pipe dream. Black women, like their counterparts of other races, are liberating their minds and their bodies from the shackles of the past. Increasingly, women are refusing to waste their lives trying to decode men's mixed messages and buying into some man's macho fantasies. Instead, many women who are or want to be high achievers are accepting the fact that the price of success may be temporary loneliness. And even that loneliness is relative, since many of us have learned that having a man isn't all there is to life.

Professions for Women
Virginia Woolf

When your secretary invited me to come here, she told me that your Society is concerned with the employment of women and she suggested that I might tell you something about my own professional experiences. It is true I am a woman; it is true I am employed; but what professional experiences have I had? It is difficult to say. My profession is literature; and in that profession there are fewer experiences for women than in any other, with the exception of the stage—fewer, I mean, that are peculiar to woman. For the road was cut many years ago—by Fanny Burney, by Aphra Behn, by Harriet Martineau, by Jane Austen, by George Eliot—many famous women, and many more unknown and forgotten, have been before me, making the path smooth, and regulating my steps. Thus, when I came to write, there were very few material obstacles in my way. Writing was a reputable and harmless occupation. The family peace was not broken by the scratching of a pen. No demand was made upon the family purse. For ten and sixpence one can buy paper enough to write all the plays of Shakespeare—if one has a mind that way. Pianos and models, Paris, Vienna and Berlin, masters and mistresses, are not needed by a writer. The cheapness of writing paper is, of course, the reason why women have succeeded as writers before they have succeeded in the other professions.

But to tell you my story—it is a simple one. You have only got to figure to yourselves a girl in a bedroom with a pen in her hand. She had only to move that pen from left to right—from ten o'clock to one. Then it occurred to her to do what is simple and cheap enough after all—to slip a few of those pages into an envelope, fix a penny stamp in the corner, and drop the envelope into the red box at the corner. It was thus that I became a journalist; and my effort was rewarded on the first day of the following month—a very glorious day it was for me—by a letter from an editor containing a cheque for one pound ten shillings and sixpence. But to show you how little I deserve to be called a professional woman, how little I know of the struggles and difficulties of such lives, I have to admit that instead of spending that sum upon bread and butter, rent, shoes and stockings, or butcher's bills, I went out and bought a cat—a beautiful cat, a Persian cat, which very soon involved me in bitter disputes with my neighbours.

What could be easier than to write articles and to buy Persian cats with the profits? But wait a moment. Articles have to be about something. Mine, I seem to remember, was about a novel by a famous man. And while I was writing this review, I discovered that if I were going to review books I should need to do battle with a certain phantom. And the phantom was a woman, and when I came to know her better I called her after the heroine of a famous poem, The Angel in the House. It was she who used to come between me and my paper when I was writing reviews. It was she who bothered me and wasted my time and so tormented me that at last I killed her. You who come of a younger and happier generation may not have heard of her—you may not know what I mean by the Angel in the House. I will describe her as shortly as I can. She was intensely sympathetic. She was immensely charming. She was utterly unselfish. She excelled in the difficult arts of family life. She sacrificed herself daily. If there was chicken, she took the leg; if there was a draught she sat in it—in short she was so constituted that she never had a mind or a wish of her own, but preferred to sympathize always with the minds and wishes of others. Above all—I need not say it—she was pure. Her purity was supposed to be her chief beauty—her blushes, her great grace. In those days—the last of Queen Victoria—every house had its Angel. And when I came to write I encountered her with the very first words. The shadow of her wings fell on my page; I heard the rustling of her skirts in the room. Directly, that is to say, I took my pen in hand to review that novel by a famous man, she slipped behind me and whispered: "My dear, you are a young woman. You are writing about a book that has been written by a man. Be sympathetic; be tender; flatter; deceive; use all the arts and wiles of our sex. Never let anybody guess that you have a mind of your own. Above all, be pure." And she made as if to guide my pen. I now record the one act for which I take some credit to myself, though the credit rightly belongs to some excellent ancestors of mine who left me a certain sum of money—shall we say five hundred pounds a year?—so that it was not necessary for me to depend solely on charm for my living. I turned upon her and caught her by the throat. I did my best to kill her. My excuse, if I were to be had up in a court of law, would be that I acted in self-defence. Had I not killed her she would have killed me. She would have plucked the heart out of my writing. For, as I found, directly I put pen to paper, you cannot review even a novel without having a mind of your own, without expressing what you think to be the truth about human relations, morality, sex. And all these questions, according to the Angel in the House, cannot be dealt with freely and openly by women; they must charm, they must conciliate, they must—to put it bluntly—tell lies if they are to succeed. Thus, whenever I felt the shadow of her wing or the radiance of her halo upon my page, I took up the inkpot and flung it at her. She died hard. Her fictitious nature was of great assistance to her. It is far harder to kill a phantom than a reality. She was always creeping back when I thought I had despatched her. Though I flatter myself that I killed her in the end, the struggle was severe; it took much time that had better have been spent upon learning Greek grammar; or in roaming the world in search of adventures. But it was a real experience; it was an experience that was bound to befall all women writers at that time. Killing the Angel in the House was part of the occupation of a woman writer.

But to continue my story. The Angel was dead; what then remained? You may say that what remained was a simple and common object—a young woman in a bedroom with an inkpot. In other words, now that she had rid herself of falsehood, that young woman had only to be herself. Ah, but what is "herself"? I mean, what is a woman? I assure you, I do not know. I do not believe that you know. I do not believe that anybody can know until she has expressed herself in all the arts and professions open to human skill. That indeed is one of the reasons why I have come here—out of respect for you, who are in process of showing us by your experiments what a woman is, who are in process of providing us, by your failures and successes, with that extremely important piece of information.

But to continue the story of my professional experiences. I made one pound ten and six by my first review; and I bought a Persian cat with the proceeds. Then I grew ambitious. A Persian cat is all very well, I said; but a Persian cat is not enough. I must have a motor car. And it was thus that I became a novelist—for it is a very strange thing that people will give you a motor car if you will tell them a story. It is a still stranger thing that there is nothing so delightful in the world as telling stories. It is far pleasanter than writing reviews of famous novels. And yet, if I am to obey your secretary and tell you my professional experiences as a novelist, I must tell you about a very strange experience that befell me as a novelist. And to understand it you must try first to imagine a novelist's state of mind. I hope I am not giving away professional secrets if I say that a novelist's chief desire is to be as unconscious as possible. He has to induce in himself a state of perpetual lethargy. He wants life to proceed with the utmost quiet and regularity. He wants to see the same things day after day, month after month, while he is writing, so that nothing may break the illusion in which he is living—so that nothing may disturb or disquiet the mysterious nosings about, feelings round, darts, dashes and sudden discoveries of that very shy and illusive spirit, the imagination. I suspect that this state is the same both for men and women. Be that as it may, I want you to imagine me writing a novel in a state of trance. I want you to figure to yourselves a girl sitting with a pen in her hand, which for minutes, and indeed for hours, she never dips into the inkpot. The image that comes to my mind when I think of this girl is the image of a fisherman lying sunk in dreams on the verge of a deep lake with a rod held out over the water. She was letting her imagination sweep unchecked round every rock and cranny of the world that lies submerged in the depths of our unconscious being. Now came the experience, the experience that I believe to be far commoner with women writers than with men. The line raced through the girl's fingers. Her imagination had rushed away. It had sought the pools, the depths, the dark places where the largest fish slumber. And then there was a smash. There was an explosion. There was foam and confusion. The imagination had dashed itself against something hard. The girl was roused from her dream. She was indeed in a state of the most acute and difficult distress. To speak without figure she had thought of something, something about the body, about the passions which it was unfitting for her as a woman to say. Men, her reason told her, would be shocked. The consciousness of what men will say of a woman who speaks the truth about her passions had roused her from her artist's state of unconsciousness. She could write no more. The trance was over. Her imagination could work no longer. This I believe to be a very common experience with women writers—they are impeded by the extreme conventionality of the other sex. For though men sensibly allow themselves great freedom in these respects, I doubt they realize or can control the extreme severity with which they condemn such freedom in women.

These then were two very genuine experiences of my own. These were two of the adventures of my professional life. The first—killing the Angel in the House—I think I solved. She died. But the second, telling the truth about my own experiences as a body, I do not think I solved. I doubt that any woman has solved it yet. The obstacles against her are still immensely powerful—and yet they are very difficult to define. Outwardly, what is simpler than to write books? Outwardly, what obstacles are there for a woman rather than for a man? Inwardly, I think, the case is very different; she has still many ghosts to fight, many prejudices to overcome. Indeed it will be a long time still, I think, before a woman can sit down to write a book without finding a phantom to be slain, a rock to be dashed against. And if this is so in literature, the freest of all professions for women, how is it in the new professions which you are now for the first time entering?

Those are the questions that I should like, had I time, to ask you. And indeed, if I have laid stress upon these professional experiences of mine, it is because I believe that they are, though in different forms, yours also. Even when the path is nominally open—when there is nothing to prevent a woman from being a doctor, a lawyer, a civil servant—there are many phantoms and obstacles, as I believe, looming in her way. To discuss and define them is I think of great value and importance; for thus only can the labor be shared, the difficulties be solved. But besides this, it is necessary also to discuss the ends and the aims for which we are fighting, for which we are doing battle with these formidable obstacles. Those aims cannot be taken for granted; they must be perpetually questioned and examined. The whole position, as I see it—here in this hall surrounded by women practicing for the first time in history I know not how many different professions— is one of extraordinary interest and importance. You have won rooms of your own in the house hitherto exclusively owned by men. You are able, though not without great labor and effort, to pay the rent. You are earning your five hundred pounds a year. But this freedom is only a beginning; the room is your own, but it is still bare. It has to be furnished; it has to be decorated; it has to be shared. How are you going to furnish it, how are you going to decorate it? With whom are you going to share it, and upon what terms? These, I think, are questions of the utmost importance and interest. For the first time in history you are able to ask them; for the first time you are able to decide for yourselves what the answers should be. Willingly would I stay and discuss those questions and answers—but not tonight. My time is up; and I must cease.

Ms. Givings

Hilary Cosell

I never forgot the commercial.

A montage of fashionable women flashed by in cityscape after cityscape. Woman after woman, each looking more attractive, more important, more in control than her predecessor. Smart tailored suits, attaché cases, shapely pumps, heels clicking on the pavement, legs striding down streets, up stairs, into skyscrapers to rest behind big desks. Makeup perfect, every hair in place in sleek chignons or other graceful, classic hair styles. All projecting an image that said: confident, purposeful, serious. I am a woman who matters. I make a difference.

I think the ad was for a bank and it ran in the early sixties. Needless to say, it made a lasting impression on me. Somehow it fitted right in with the message my collection of Nancy Drews and biographies of Susan B. Anthony, Amelia Earhart, Margaret Bourke-White, and Babe Zaharias sent me. Do something. Be somebody. Grow up to be a woman who counts.

Memory plays tricks, of course, but I think it was the first ad I ever saw in which women weren't portrayed as housewives shilling for cleanser, mothers waxing rhapsodic over detergents or, as little sex kittens, offering themselves as a bonus if you bought their product. Though the women in my ad were obviously models, and there was heavy emphasis on their looks, there was still something different about it. They were businesswomen. Professionals. Successful.

The implications were clear, impressive, and outside the norm of my upper middle class Westchester County world, where mommies didn't work because no mommies "had" to work. So I kept the memory of that ad stored someplace inside me, buried it for future use. A secret, silent motivator. Through my flower-child Fillmore East days, my antiwar years, my style that consisted of two pairs of jeans, a few T-shirts, waist-length hair and no makeup, I never forgot. One day I'll shed this skin and become that. Caterpillar into a butterfly—and I wasn't referring to my looks.

I found a partner to guide me through the tug-of-war taking place inside me during high school, something to remind me that popularity and partying were great, but so was early acceptance by an Ivy League school. I found the women's movement. It reinforced and amplified everything I thought myself, and more.

The days of finding personal reward in being the woman behind the successful man were over. Finished. The days of defining one's worth by the presence of a man, or lack of worth by the absence of one, were over. A woman's place was anywhere she chose to make that place, and if men refused to graciously concede the rightness of our position, we'd take to the streets and the courts to make sure the days of discrimination and second-class citizenry were finished too. In the hearts and minds, as well as the laws, of men. And women.

We had to do it right, though. All the way down the line. Adhere to a position in every part of life. We wouldn't succeed by displaying any traditional kinds of female behavior. No, those had to go, too. What was femininity, anyway, but a male creation? First they shackled our bodies with their silly, restrictive definitions of what was fashion, and what was beauty, and what was the proper height, weight, leg length, breast size, hair color, and eye color. Then they shackled our minds, taught us that ambition, aggression, brains, talent, drive, ruthlessness, independence were all their birthrights. Women who displayed these traits were unfeminine, unattractive, unworthy. The proper province for whatever aggression and drive and competition women had was to compete for male attention and male approval. To win a man and then keep him. By softness, passivity, dependence, nurturing, peacemaking. Control and power by indirect manipulation, all designed to feed the male ego, the male sense of his due, the male definition of his world and everyone else's place in it.

The movement laid it all out for me to see, and when they finished, womankind looked like some washed-up old whore all decked out for one final trick on her bier before retiring to meet her maker. Male, of course. I was aghast. Outraged. So full of righteous anger and indignation I didn't know which way was up or down. Or whom I was more angry with—men for thousands of years of mistreating women, or women for allowing themselves to be willing partners in their own destruction.

And nothing condensed the horror of it all better than the thought that I could wind up condemned to a lifetime of servitude in a kitchen and a nursery. Marriage was a prison, and suburbia death, and children a lifetime of slavery. To end up the dependent and drudge of some man who, if statistics can be trusted, would leave me and our kids six or ten or even twenty years after the ceremony to struggle along on insufficient alimony and child-support payments, most likely in suburbia, was a fate too terrible to contemplate.

No sir, not me. I got the message and the truth set me free. I will be successful. Earn lots of money, be a professional. Ah! I uttered the word in tones usually reserved for brief mentions of the Father, Son, and Holy Ghost. Or a major financial coup. Not a career girl, someone filing her nails at her desk, earning a pittance and marking time between college and a husband. Not a working woman, either, doing unskilled, unglamorous work in the pink-collar ghetto.

No, I got the message right, figured out what was being said amid the shouting, finger-pointing, and epithet-hurling. Women are entitled to success. To a real piece of the action. To the American dream. Upscale and upmarket. Upwardly mobile. Today a Jones, tomorrow a Rockefeller, and everyone will be trying to keep up with you. To the job and the money that will buy a house and two cars, a condo and a boat, the TV, the VCR, the Atari, stocks and bonds, tax shelters, whatever is your pleasure and whatever makes you happy.

It sounds pretty good. It makes sense. Why shouldn't women have a chance at these things? Why should they belong almost exclusively to the white male establishment? Besides, if one becomes successful, one is supposed to reap all sorts of extra rewards besides material goods. Happiness and fulfillment. Respect and recognition. Sometimes even fame. Success will make you more popular, more desirable. An object of other people's envy. At the top of everyone's guest list. In demand. And naturally, more desirable than ever before to the opposite sex. Even though one is no longer supposed to care anything at all about whether they find you desirable or not.

And of course success meant other things, too. It meant freedom from economic and emotional dependence on men. It meant you were a special person, a brave and strong pioneer out there fighting the good fight. Hacking your way through the jungle to beat a path for successive generations of women to follow. It made you superior to women without success, several cuts above them. It was proof that you were USDA Prime, while the others were some inferior cut of person. Hiding behind traditional femininity and clutching the very chains that bound them.

But most of all, for anyone of my generation deeply affected by the women's movement, success would make you active, not passive. You would be in control of your fate and your future, the way men are. You would be safe from victimization. You would be *inviolate*.

Who could turn it down? How seductive. How alluring.

And so I didn't. After studying history and political science for two years at Sarah Lawrence College—and panicking because it was just too liberal arts, and what was I being *prepared* for?—I transferred to New York University to study journalism. To become prepared to be a reporter. I went one step better and got a master's degree in journalism, so that I could perhaps teach if the newspaper I worked for suddenly folded, as they seem wont to do these days. One day you have a by-line, the next day the unemployment line.

That never happened, though. I couldn't get a newspaper job. So many folded that there were seasoned reporters looking for work, people with ten years' experience covering Congress who were willing to spend their days writing obits, if someone would just hire them. So I went into television. It's an expanding market, you see. Also, it pays much, much better.

I began as a production associate for a network news show. I was a "PA" in TV jargon, the lowest of the low, earning a pittance and too often filing my nails, not marking time between Northwestern and marriage, but trying to figure out how to supplant the four people ahead of me who would get promoted to producer first. Not only did I earn a pittance, but there was no overtime, no sixth- or seventh-day pay. But there was lots of overtime and there were lots of sixth and seventh days. On many of those I spent my time logging every word, every gesture, pan, zoom, wipe, and cutaway on Geraldo Rivera videotapes. Or hours on the phone chartering small planes bound for peculiar destinations. Or setting up interviews with people whom I would never meet, for stories I would never help edit, and certainly never come close to producing. In short the job was insufferable but the TV business wasn't. And after all, I was in the "paying your dues" phase of the success mythology.

Almost one year later I got my big break. That's part of the mythology, too. Sooner or later everyone gets the break and I was just lucky. Mine came sooner and I jumped. To another network and another show. At twenty-four I had a new title: network television producer. It seemed to have all paid off: working as a reporter for some Gannett newspapers during college, exchanging de Tocqueville and democracy for Elementary Reporting and the *AP Handbook,* leaving behind the serene academic atmosphere of Sarah Lawrence for the grime and urban blight of NYU. Sure, it was sports, not news or politics, but nothing's ever perfect.

My life changed almost overnight. Not only did my income double, triple and climb even more, but I went from yes-sir-no-sir-anything-you-say-sir to being in charge. Anything you want to do, you just do it, they said, smiling. So I traveled back and forth across the country interviewing athletes, coaches, and team owners. Boxers, promoters, trainers. Athletes on strike, athletes contemplating strikes, athletes who refused to strike. Ones with drug problems, others with alcohol problems. Born-again athletes, retiring athletes, rookies, and veterans. I produced a segment called SportsJournal on a show called "SportsWorld." It was the news part of the show, the journalism, the part that showed we cared about more than who won, or lost, or even how they played the game.

I chose the stories. I researched them. I wrote the scripts. Most of the time I did the interviews. The face people saw, the voice they heard, more often than not never did anything. I picked the music, edited the story, and watched it roll from Studio 6A into millions of homes.

And I understood that I had to look my part. Live my part. Dress for success. The jeans and T-shirts moved to the back of the closet to make way for suits. Designer clothes, all cotton, linen, silk, and wool, as if I wouldn't be real if the fibers weren't too.

So I traveled every week, and talked to famous people, and walked around looking smug, probably. I've got the world on a string. I've done everything differently from my mother's generation. I've done everything right. I have money, and power, and independence, and a profession, and I am inviolate.

So imagine my shock, my near-trauma, when I realized that I wanted something else. Needed something else. When I realized that I loved my job and I hated it. That it was my whole life. That it was no life at all. That somehow, after years of education and what might be called indoctrination into the virtues of success and the worthlessness of female existence without it, I started to feel empty and isolated and desolate. To feel a need for some kind of personal life that was more than casual, or occasional, unstable and rootless.

There I was, coming home from ten or twelve or sometimes more hours at work, pretty much shot after the day, and I'd do this simply marvelous imitation of all the successful fathers I remembered from childhood. All the men I swore I'd never grow up and marry, let alone be like. (Gloria Steinem once said—cheerfuly, I believe—we're becoming the men we were supposed to marry. Great.) The men who would come home from the office, grab a drink or two, collapse on the couch, shovel in a meal and be utterly useless for anything beyond the most mundane and desultory conversation. *Boring.* Burned out. And there I'd be, swilling a vodka on the rocks or two, shoving a Stouffer's into my mouth, and then staggering off to take a bath, watch "Hill Street Blues," and fade away with Ted Koppel. To get up and do it all again.

All the time, of course, in the back of my mind, despite protestations otherwise, was the desire to have something more than my profession. To have a personal life, a future, that somehow included a man and possibly children, although motherhood has never been a big priority of mine. Oh, later on, I'd think, I'll work on it later on, next week after I finish this story, next month when spring training concludes, after the owners' meetings, when the football strike ends, sometime I'll get to it. Just let me get on with this career, it's more important, it's the only vital thing in the world.

But somehow, the life I'd managed to construct for myself—coupled with the prevailing attitudes and popular mythology about success and single professional women—seemed to pretty much preclude the possibility of living much differently from the way I already lived.

First of all, success demands a full-time commitment. Once you become successful, there's no time to relax, or do less than before. Getting in to become successful is only one-third the battle. Staying there takes up most of one's time and energy, and getting even further ahead takes even more.

And then, our culture pretends that creating a social life as an adult in a large metropolitan area—where there is no sense of community and where the old ties of neighborhood, family, and college days have broken down completely—is something people can just go out and do. If they have a mind to. Join a health club! Work on your favorite candidate's political campaign! Take night classes! Talk about feeling foolish. Talk about wearing a neon sign that proclaims: Lonely, need more friends, looking for love. Talk about . . . desperate. And talk about time. Creating a personal life is a task of immense proportion. Like work, it takes time, and it takes energy. How much is there to go around, especially when life is ordered to make success the priority?

And finally, success demands something more from women than it demands from men. And especially from single women, although the demands on married women and working mothers are equally burdensome in different ways. Successful women are asked to continually prove that the company will get a return on its investment. That they will not run off at the first opportunity to wed. Or to have children. That in exchange for the privilege of an employee ID number and a salary that really should be paid to a guy, women will prove that nothing and no one is more important than the job. That life has few, if any other, considerations. That this is the normal, reasonable price one pays for the honor of being admitted to the club.

If it were only that straightforward perhaps it would have been easier to swallow. Unfortunately, it isn't. Because at the same time, women are also pressured constantly about the status of their personal lives. Don't marry, but why aren't you married? You're twenty-eight? What's wrong with you? Oh, you're married? When are you going to have a baby? Why don't you have a baby? You better not have a baby.

In other words, the messages come thick, fast and constantly—and conflicting—from women and men alike: when are you going to act like a woman? Why don't you act like a woman? Don't act like a woman, there's no place for it here.

One isn't supposed to pay attention to things like that. One is supposed to be free from considerations of what people think. Peer pressure is an adolescent problem, something to put away with other childish things. One simply carries on, pays no attention, does the job, delivers what has been promised, and what's all the fuss about?

Nothing, really, until one realizes that "choosing" success, pursuing it through high school and college and graduate school and on into the business world, is not the simple kind of choice between freedom and bondage people have made it out to be. The battles involved don't cover just things such as comparable pay for comparable work, or a question of learning how to dress, or putting a polite damper on your boss, who's trying to sleep with you.

The price of success is high for everyone, but it is especially high for women, and not just because they fight constant discrimination. For women, the conflicts and the choices involved in dedicating oneself to success are so fundamental, so basic, that sometimes they are unbearable. Conflicts about professional life versus family life, career versus husband and children, and even one's most personal and private perceptions of self and sexual identity.

In order to get ahead, one just dismissed or ignored these conflicts. They were cast aside while we got on with the business of work. Perhaps we refused to acknowledge them in hopes that the problems would just disappear in time. Or because to admit them would give aid and comfort to the enemy: the men and the women who insisted that women belonged in the home and nowhere else. That women couldn't handle a professional life, do the work, take the pressure, compete and succeed. That all women ever want—all that ever makes them happy—is a man and a kid and a home to take care of.

So imagine my surprise when I discovered I could no longer dismiss or ignore my own conflicts and questions. When I started to think that if women had erred once before on the side of marriage and motherhood and housewifery, might they be erring again on the side of professionalism, career, and success? That the extreme to which women have gone for the past fifteen-plus years may have been as off base as the idea that all women should ever attempt to do is give birth, wax floors, and watch soaps all day?

I did not like asking myself these questions. I do not like being on the "wrong" side of an issue.

But that is where I am. No longer politically correct, or ideologically pure.

At least I am not alone. Like me, other women who have achieved varying degrees of success are also questioning the tenets of their faith. Trying to redefine and reinterpret success in a way that will permit women to incorporate the so-called "feminine" aspects of themselves into a healthier adult life.

Not that we are sure this can be done.

But it behooves us to try.

"I think we are perceiving a real change in attitude," Kate tells me. She is twenty-nine, married, and a writer for a morning television show in New York. Before joining the show a year ago she was a successful freelance writer, work she continues to do. She has also published two books, one nonfiction, one fiction, with a third due soon.

"At first women were forced to go after success on men's terms alone, because they were the only terms available. We had to grab whatever we could and maneuver our way in and prove we could do it, prove that we could handle whatever they chose to throw at us, and we could do it as well as, or better than, any man could.

"Now that women have proven their abilities and done their jobs without falling apart, I think women in their late twenties and thirties are looking around and asking questions all over again, questions about goals and directions and what's really important to them.

"When the women's movement started up, it was led in part by women who were married and had children and they were mostly housewives. Of course there are notable exceptions to that, Gloria Steinem for instance. But the movement really hit home and talked to women who were bored with their lives, or women who lived the dream of marriage and husband and children and found it lacking. Or women who were forced by divorce to go back to work and who discovered that they weren't qualified to do anything, they didn't have experience, and what work they could get didn't pay anything at all. Those women were caught in a terrible bind, and they were very, very angry. Remember how angry they were?

"And so the whole tone of what followed was colored by their particular experiences and prejudices, and much of it was very negative. It was; don't get caught like I did. Don't be a bored, frumpy housewife chasing kids and driving car pools and waiting hand and foot on a husband. It stinks. Women can do better than that and they should do better than that, and the thing to do is to work. Otherwise you might end up on welfare, trying to make ends meet with food stamps, saddled with custody of the kids while your ex-husband joins Club Med and parties all weekend.

"Now, who could argue with the idea that women should work and earn a lot of money and be able to take care of themselves and their children? No one, really, because it's very reasonable, it's smart thinking and common sense.

"At the same time, because they didn't want to offend housewives and alienate such a large bloc of women, there was lots of talk about choices. The movement was going to free everyone to make choices. If you wanted to work, that was okay, if you preferred to stay at home, that's okay, too, just as long as you're not being forced to stay home by your husband or by a society that won't let you go to law school or medical school. The idea was, do whatever suits you best. We were even going to make it possible to trade places and change roles with men.

"And there was lots of talk, too, about how women should never set out to become like men, because their lives were just as rigid and sex-stereotyped as women's lives were. They were victims too. So we were all going to go off and join the labor force and really humanize it. Then everyone would be better off, men and women alike.

"By the mid-seventies, though, practically all pretense about choices and 'do what pleases you the most' was gone. People still said it occasionally, but they didn't mean it. Instead, everything was success, and success meant, climb the corporate ladder and get as close to the top as you possibly can. Push everything out of your life that might deter you, because most of those things don't matter very much anyway.

"You know, it's very easy for women who have been married and who have had children to lecture younger women who haven't, and tell them that marriage and motherhood are not what they are cracked up to be, and to say, don't be like me, profit from my bad example, go off and do something important, something that counts. And let's face it, some of their examples were pretty bad, and I certainly wouldn't have wanted to grow up to be them.

"So I listened and I followed their advice and I called myself a feminist, and I still do. But I think that for most women a time comes when all this success and career obsession starts to become awfully hollow. I started to want marriage, and I started to think about children, and I was terrified to admit it. Partly because I was afraid my desires would be held over my head as proof that women shouldn't be allowed to work in the first place. But I got scared also because I realized that those women of twenty years ago were no longer talking to me, or about me, in the way I once believed they were. I got scared because I realized that they were so busy trying to get in and get their names on the door, that they never bothered to try to build a model for success that takes the fact that we are female into account. Instead, they built one that *denied* it. There's no provision anywhere that really allows us to integrate a significant working life with a significant personal life. We're faced with lousy choices all the time, which isn't comforting when you realize that you might be talking about something as fundamental as having a child, and that's a function which is the single most important thing that separates a woman's professional needs from a man's.

"I used to listen to critics of feminism say how women didn't know how to act like women anymore. I would think, great, because acting like a woman meant giggling and flirting and batting your eyelashes and deferring to men no matter what. Who wants to act like that?

"But I've thought about that quite a bit lately, and I wonder if those people meant something entirely different, something more basic, a kind of warning, almost. If we weren't smarter or more careful, we might make it very hard on ourselves in a different kind of way. Hard to get married and to have children after so many years of placing so much worth on work as the only way to become a worthwhile person. Hard to be appreciated, respected, really, unless you work at least forty hours a week, and bring home lots of money, as well as do everything else a woman is supposed to do. Now the title of your job affects, or reflects, really, the status of the man you're dating or the man you're married to, the same way a clean house and a good dinner was the measure of a woman's worth, and the man's status, years ago. In other words, we may have trapped ourselves into a new identity that has as many, if not more problems built into it than the traditional female role we all disliked so much.

"Now the measure of worth and the definition of a successful woman seems to be 'a person who works full time at a profession, earns good money, attends to her marriage, runs a home or pays someone else to do it for her, has kids but pays someone else to look after them, too.' I've started to think that it's a crazy definition, and I find myself questioning it all the time.

"What I'd really like to know is, what ever happened to all that talk about freedom and choice? All the conversation about choosing a life that suits you personally—not one that suits other women, or your boss, or the men you date, or the man you marry—seems to have just disappeared. What ever happened to those broader definitions of success we all used to talk about?"

There is something I forgot to mention about Kate. She has a particular interest in redefining herself, and success. She is three months' pregnant with her first child.

6 *Developing Structure*
The Purpose and the Plan

There you sit, surrounded by piles of notesheets or notecards, with books strewn about, highlighted and marked in various ways. Having worked with the topic from several perspectives, you now know the position you plan to develop and have some major points in mind. Now it is time to begin to write.

Thinking about actually beginning to write the paper is sometimes frightening for students. In fact, some students will postpone writing almost indefinitely, finding more sources, taking more notes, anything to avoid writing. But you have to begin sometime, and the process will be less intimidating if you create a preliminary **structure** for your paper and **plan** the sequence of ideas you are going to develop. Although there is a notion in our culture that true creation occurs instantaneously, with a bolt of lightning striking out of nowhere, the truth is that most creative efforts involve a great deal of thinking and rethinking. Of course, some writers claim that they sit down with a blank screen or piece of paper and just "let it happen," but it is likely that most of them have spent a lot of time planning in their heads, mulling over possibilities, changing, substituting, expanding their perspective. The more complex your paper is going to be and the more it utilizes outside information, the more planning you will probably have to do.

Of course, there is another myth about writing that you may have heard— that in order to write, you have to plan every detail in a very complicated outline. That idea is also false for most people. Although it is important to plan your paper somewhat, you do not have to work out each detail meticulously. Discovery occurs at all stages of the writing process, both before, during, and after writing a first draft.

PLANNING THE OVERALL DESIGN OF YOUR PAPER

Before you plan the structure of your paper, read over all of your notesheets or cards and think about your approach to your topic. Reread your position statement so that you are sure you understand the purpose of your paper. Some students find it helpful to read the position statement aloud, or they keep it on a separate sheet for easy referral. If you keep your position statement handy, you can glance at it as you write down each of your main points and ask yourself the following questions, "How does this point relate to my main position? Is it a supporting argument? Is it an example? Is this an opposing argument? Does this idea pertain to my overall conception of the topic?"

Finding Your Main Points

QUESTION, RESPONSE, AND READER EXPECTATIONS

In a researched paper, and in most types of academic writing, formulating a position implies a **question,** whether or not it is stated specifically in that form. If your position is, "Dogs should be banned from public school buildings," the implied question is "*Why* should dogs be banned from public school buildings?" If your position is, "Garbage reveals a great deal about its owner," the implied question is "*How or what* does garbage reveal about its owner?" If your position is, "School newspapers must be censored, at least somewhat, by a responsible adult," the implied quesiton is, "*Why* should school newspapers be censored, at least somewhat, by a responsible adult?"

The position statement thus sets up expectations in the reader that the body of the paper will respond to an implied question and provide an **answer** and a **justification.** If the position is, "Dogs should be banned from public school buildings," the body of your essay would probably establish that dogs were a problem in public school buildings and cite evidence supporting that claim, perhaps information about the damage done by dogs to school buildings, evidence suggesting that dogs can be unpredictable and vicious, possibly harming children, or statistics showing how often attacks by dogs on children occur. Because the body of your paper should contain information that answers the question implicitly posed by your position statement, you select information that is likely to provide some of those answers. Then, as you read, you begin making connections and inferences about the information you find. These connections and inferences help you to select the main points of your paper.

A SEQUENCE FOR FINDING YOUR MAIN POINTS

Below are a few suggestions to help you find your main points:

1. Reexamine your position.
2. Ask what questions are implied in that position.
3. Decide what information will help you answer your questions and provide support.
4. Evaluate the information you have found, and jot down some main points. You will now be able to decide if it is appropriate for your purpose.

If you find that you must modify your main position because you are unable to answer the questions it implies or because the act of rereading has led you to change your mind about your position, you should then repeat this sequence.

MODIFYING YOUR POSITION: WORKING THROUGH THE SEQUENCE

When you begin locating your main points, you may decide to modify your position statement. For example, Clifton, a freshman enrolled in an introductory history course, had been assigned to develop a position about some aspect of Abraham Lincoln. In thinking about his topic, Clifton realized that like most American students, he had been raised with the idea that Lincoln was the epitome of wisdom and goodness, the true humanitarian. However, Clifton did not wish to write a paper that showed how Lincoln freed the slaves or one that was simply a collection of examples of how wonderful Lincoln was, so he decided to approach his topic with the idea that perhaps Lincoln was not as much a humanitarian as everyone thinks. Through his course, Clifton had learned that political concerns were equally important factors in the Civil War, and he hoped that he could focus his paper toward showing that Lincoln was as much concerned with politics as he was with freeing the slaves. He thus began looking through his information, hoping to develop the following position:

> Everyone thinks of Abraham Lincoln as a great humanitarian, as the President who was primarily concerned with freeing the slaves. Yet, that position is somewhat of an exaggeration. Although Lincoln has the reputation for being concerned with slavery purely on moral grounds, his humanitarian views, by modern standards, would be considered moderate, at best. In his campaign against slavery, he was also motivated by political and social concerns.

When he was ready to write, Clifton then went through the four steps outlined above:

1. He **reexamined his position** and decided that he still wanted to write about it. He thought it would have a strong impact on the class if he could show something about Lincoln that few had thought about before.

2. He **asked what questions are implied** in that position. In looking over his position statement, Clifton decided that some of the questions his paper had to address were "*Why* do I say that Lincoln was a moderate by modern standards? *What* do I mean by a 'moderate'? *How* was Lincoln motivated by political and social concerns?"

3. He then decided that **the information he needed** to answer these questions might be concerned with a definition of what is meant by modern humanitarian views, a discussion of Lincoln's political affiliations,

or perhaps an analysis of the political situation during Lincoln's term. For establishing that Lincoln was not as interested in freeing the slaves as he was on settling political differences, Clifton thought he needed some statements Lincoln might have made that would provide support and establish justification.

4. He then **evaluated the information** he had and jotted down some main points contained in that information. Once he reexamined this information, he would then be able to see whether or not it was appropriate.

These are the main points Clifton decided to develop from his notes:

1. Lincoln was a member of the newly formed Republican party, which was strongly against continuing slavery in new territories. Lincoln was expected by party members to adopt a strong antislavery campaign as his party platform.
2. Lincoln was strongly in favor of a united America. He viewed slavery as a divisive force splitting the North and the South. Therefore, he was against slavery because of its effect on the Union.
3. Because he was so strongly in favor of the Union, Lincoln wanted all elements of society to feel as if they had the opportunity to advance. He felt that slavery would prevent workers from obtaining employment, reinforcing class distinctions in the South.
4. England, an important source of income for American products, was objecting to importing from a slave-owning country.
5. Lincoln denied being a Whig, meaning that he did not hold ultraliberal views.

Clifton then reread his main points and looked back at his position. He discovered that he actually had very little information on the first part of his position (Lincoln's humanitarian views were moderate by modern standards) and he realized that if he wished to develop that point, he would have to find some more information on Lincoln's actual position on slavery. He also realized that even if he found additional information on this topic, he would then have to define what he meant by saying "moderate by modern standards." He, therefore, had to decide if he wanted to drop that part of his position statement or modify it in some way. He decided that the more efficient course to take would be to revise his position as follows:

Although Abraham Lincoln has the reputation for being against slavery purely on moral grounds, he was also motivated by political and social concerns.

Thus, Clifton modified his position when he began the process of noting his main points. Structure can influence purpose just as purpose can help to determine structure.

▶ ***Exercise:*** Read the following position statements. In small groups, formulate a question that you would expect the body of the paper to answer. Then, if you know at least something about these topics, discuss subpoints that could serve as support.

1. Eighteen-year-old citizens need further preparation in order to vote wisely.
2. Fast-food establishments generate excessive waste.
3. Young people ought to be required to perform a year of public service.
4. President Kennedy's reputation as a statesman is based more on his personal charisma than on his accomplishments as President.
5. American undergraduates should be exposed to some form of intercultural experience as part of their education.
6. Women are still being socialized to think of careers as secondary to marriage.
7. Computers are going to change our concept of privacy.

ORGANIZATION AND FAMILIARITY WITH YOUR TOPIC

Although many textbooks, including this one, give suggestions about patterns of organization, patterns that students can use as models, the truth is that when you know a lot about a topic, you don't think about organization so mechanically—the mode of organization becomes clear because it is inherent in the topic. The more you know about a topic, the less you will have to consider what sort of structure you will use, because the structure will suggest itself and will develop as you write. However, sometimes it is useful for students to see how other writers have structured information so that they can experiment with these suggestions in their own writing. Here, then, are some methods of presenting information that you might include in your paper:

History, Causality, Definition, Analysis, Comparison

Often, in a researched paper, a discussion of an event or an idea in the present will suggest the need for examining **how it was influenced by past events.** Thus, no paper on the topic of reverse discrimination could be complete without at least some discussion of the discrimination against minorities that occurred in the past. Similarly no analysis of the problems of the aged could be adequately developed without **examining some of the causes of these problems,** the move from a rural to an industrial society, for example. Some of the terms you use may require **definition,** both for meaning and implication. The term "equal opportunity," for example, is one that is open to many interpretations. It is defined in a certain way in the Fourteenth Amendment to the Constitution, but it has had several different implications when applied to employment practices. Perhaps you need to **analyze** how the term "equal opportunity" has been interpreted. Or, you might wish to **compare** the treatment of the aged in American society with the treatment in Samoan society. As you read through the major points of your paper, then, be alert for related areas that would be developed by some of these methods.

▶ *Exercise:* Examine these thesis statements again. For those topics you know something about, decide how you might use history, causality, definition, analysis, or comparison to develop related ideas.

1. Eighteen-year-old citizens need further preparation in order to vote wisely.
2. Fast-food establishments generate excessive waste.
3. Young people ought to be required to perform a year of public service.
4. President Kennedy's reputation as a statesman is based more on his personal charisma than on his accomplishments as president.
5. American undergraduates should be exposed to some form of intercultural experience as part of their education.
6. Women are still being socialized to think of careers as secondary to marriage.
7. Computers are going to change our concept of privacy.

USING NOTE SYNTHESIS SHEETS TO ORGANIZE INFORMATION

Your note synthesis sheets, which are based on related ideas from sources, can often be used as a device to help you develop main ideas. Let us examine a paper Justin is in the process of writing to illustrate how these sheets can be used. Justin's topic is concerned with the topic of old age, and he is writing a paper to fulfill the following assignment:

▶ *Assignment:* To many, old age is a depressing topic. No one wants to experience the feebleness of body and the social neglect that we assume comes with old age. Yet old age is a universal condition that awaits us all.

In a well-organized essay, using at least four outside sources, consider the following question:

What can be done so that the aged in our society can live a more fulfilling life?

As part of your paper, you should demonstrate awareness of some of the problems of the aged in today's culture. Make sure that you narrow your topic so that you can adequately develop your ideas.

In preparing to write this paper, after examining his own feelings and experiences with the topic, Justin noted that one of the key terms in the assignment was the word "fulfilling." In order to decide what a fulfilling life is, he decided, he had better include a definition of that term. In his research, he found several definitions, which he might wish to use in his paper. He recorded them on Note Synthesis Sheet 1.

Note Synthesis Sheet 1

Subject of Paper: Changes to help the old live a more fulfilling life

Subtopic: Defining what is meant by "fulfilling"

Source (Author)	Page	Note	Reason for using
Tuan	145	"Life at any stage" requires a challenge.	to show that the needs of the old are the same as those of any human being
Perera	112	"The secret of success, found so often among those who have bridged their three-score-and-ten in health, serenity, and happiness, pertains to their ability to remain curious and concerned. . . . They possess the common denominator of being self-educable, self-sufficient, and aware of all that is taking place around them."	the need to progress, work at something as a need
Holmes	8	Importance of productivity. "Most older Samoans explain their longevity by the fact that they keep busy every day."	other societies also value productivity
Blau	16	"One pressing need of people in all stages and walks of life is to be useful."	other support for this definition

---

As Justin read about his topic, he kept finding information about problems with the idea of retirement. He learned that although some people looked forward to retirement as a time of freedom, a time when they would no longer have to work long hours, most found it a time of stress. Justin discovered that many old people suffered a loss of identity, a lack of meaningful activity, and a deadly isolation from the mainstream of society when they retired. He, therefore, decided to create a note synthesis sheet to record some of the ideas he found on this facet of the topic. He therefore created Note Synthesis Sheet 2.

Note Synthesis Sheet 2

Subject of Paper: Changes to help the old live a more fulfilling life

Subtopic: Retirement should be rethought.

Source (Author)	Page	Note	Reason for using
Mead	25	Early retirement is wasteful of human resources.	negative idea of retirement
Perera	112	"Retirement! What a distressful word! It smacks of retreat, withdrawal, seclusion, removal from circulation."	isolation of retirement
Jones	57	"For many, the word 'retirement' in the United States means a shift from a busy, active life, to one of idleness and boredom."	Retirement has negative connotations.

As he continued to work on his paper, Justin noted that his assignment specified that he indicate awareness of some of the problems the elderly currently face. He, therefore, created Note Synthesis Sheet 3 to record information he found about this part of his paper.

Note Synthesis Sheet 3

Subject of Paper: Changes to help the old live a better life

Subtopic: The present condition of the elderly in our society

Source (Author)	Page	Note	Reason for using
Blau	21	Advanced industrial society has resulted in enforced idleness for the old.	one problem of old: idleness
Percy	1	"I see no human beings. My phone never rings. I feel sure the world has ended. I'm the only one on earth. How else can I feel? All alone."	another problem of old: loneliness

| DeBeauvoir | 6 | "For the vast majority it is almost tautological to say 'old and poor' " | another problem: poverty |
| Jones | 17 | "Often, they feel as if they have no function in life. Their roles as earners are lost with retirement." | another problem: uselessness |

Often, note synthesis sheets help you see that you have to break down all or part of a topic or create a new emphasis for the information you are discovering. As Justin constructed the above note synthesis sheets, he decided that he needed other note synthesis sheets to narrow his information even further. He recalled that there was a lot of information dealing with the financial problems of the aged. Thus, he decided to create a note synthesis sheet for this idea alone. The note synthesis sheet he created looked like this:

Note Synthesis Sheet 4

Subject of Paper: Changes to help the old live a better life

Subtopic: The present condition of the elderly in our society: financial problems

Source (Author)	Page	Note	Reason for using
DeBeauvoir	6	"For the vast majority it is almost tautological to say 'old and poor' "	support by social commentator
Percy	1	"At a time in their lives when they need more, rather than fewer services, older people suffer drastic drops in income."	support by authority (senator)
Kuhn	41	"Social security payments have increased over the years, but they are not linked to the cost of living or adequate to keep retirees out of near poverty."	(member of gray panthers)

As he read about the problems the aged currently face, Justin decided that he needed to know why these problems existed. He constructed the following note synthesis sheet.

Note Synthesis Sheet 5

Subject of Paper: Changes to help the old live a better life

Subtopic: Causes of problems

Source (Author)	Page	Note	Reason for using
Holmes	20	The situation is due to the following combination of 1) a particular set of values, 2) a particular level of technological development, and 3) a particular form of social organization	causes
Hsu	216	In American society, the fear of dependency is so great that an individual who is not self-reliant is an object of hostility.	causes linked to values
Smith	28	Democracies are societies on the move, and they have little time for ceremony or convention.	to show causes as rooted in democracy

---

As Justin constructed note synthesis sheets for the information he found about his topic, he noted the problems associated with aging and decided that at least some of them were preventable if one prepared adequately. He thus chose to focus on the idea that in order for anyone to live a more fulfilling life as an old person, they would have to prepare for it when they were younger. He decided that part of this preparation would have to be financial, since it is hard to live any kind of life, much less a fulfilling one, without adequate means of support. As he formulated his ideas, he decided that although one could prepare oneself financially on an individual basis, it would probably be better if the government had some programs as well, programs reinforcing or supplementing social security. He also decided that another form of preparation would involve developing interests, activities, and involvement with others, which could be continued in later life. The government could help provide such possibilities also. The key to a successful old age, Justin decided, was in preparing for it, not denying that it ever was going to happen, as so many do. That meant increased awareness for everyone. Once he decided on a preliminary thesis, he was ready to begin constructing his main points.

Your Main Points: Constructing a Plan or Outline

For some writers, the word "outline" is a dirty word since, for them, the idea of creating a structure in advance means limiting possibilities. The outline is viewed as the enemy of creativity as it implies that new ideas cannot be discovered during the writing process.

For other writers, writing an outline is a useful way of creating the paper. It helps them to construct logical relationships between ideas, which sometimes involves discovering new ideas in the process. For these writers, outlining forces consideration of the overall meaning of the paper, which may only have been vaguely formulated before. It also helps to determine the order in which ideas are presented so that the paper's main purpose is more easily conveyed. They see an outline as flexible, as easily changed as one's ideas.

Whether or not you use a plan or outline is your own decision. However, before discussing various methods of doing so, I would like to emphasize the following:

1. **There is no one way to plan a paper.** There are many forms of outlining and planning. You should use the one that works for you.

2. **Outlines are flexible.** Just because you have indicated a particular order in your outline does not mean that you have to stick with it. Your outline will probably change as you write your paper. In fact, some writers write an outline, after, rather than before they write their papers since it helps them find gaps in logic or areas that need further development. However, no one *has* to write an outline at any stage.

Jotting Down Ideas

In Chapter 2, concerned with ways of choosing a topic, I referred to brainstorming or jotting down ideas at random. Jotting down ideas in the order you wish to discuss them is also an easy, informal way to plan a paper. These ideas do not have to be written in complete sentences; in fact, some people argue that writing an outline in complete sentences makes it unlikely that students will make any change in the paper, since they have already invested a great deal in writing the outline. As an example of how jotting down ideas can serve as a plan, look at the ideas Justin jotted down in writing his paper:

Position Statement: Living a more fulfilling life in old age requires financial and educational preparation, on both the government and individual levels.

Introduction: Short sketch of old people sitting uselessly on a park bench. Indication that this is a problem. Then state position to suggest a partial solution.

Problems of the old in contemporary American society. (This establishes that this is an important issue.) Not only physical and financial problems, but enforced idleness leads to feelings of worthlessness and loss of identity.

Definition of a "fulfilling" life as meaning one in which there is a feeling of being needed, of being as productive and independent as possible.

Preparation can help people live a more fulfilling life in their later years.

Financial preparation—government programs, increased emphasis on retirement programs in private industry, attention drawn to the need for preparation.

Preparation by developing interests outside one's job, interests which can occupy one's lifetime.

Using old people to fulfill needs of others. Government programs in which old people work with children or teenagers. Reeducating society to view old people as a resource to enrich society, not as a burden.

No program will work unless society stops thinking of old age as a taboo subject. Need for group rethinking on the topic.

Of course these problems will not be easily solved. Even with the best preparation, old people can become sick or disabled. This is a complex topic.

Conclusion: Important to keep thinking about it.

As Justin jotted down his ideas, he noticed that the preparation he was advocating could be accomplished in two ways: it could be generated by the government or it could be initiated by each individual. He, therefore, regrouped his ideas as follows:

Introduction: Short sketch of old people sitting uselessly on a park bench. Indication that this is a problem. Use position statement to suggest a partial solution.

Problems of the old in contemporary American society (reinforcing claim). Not only physical and financial problems, but enforced idleness leads to feelings of worthlessness and loss of identity.

Definition of a "fulfilling" life as meaning one in which there is a feeling of being needed, of being as productive and independent as possible.

Preparation can help people live a more fulfilling life in their later years.

Government programs:
Financial:
Increased emphasis on retirement programs in private industry.
Attention drawn to the need for financial preparation.
Cultural:
Government programs to sponsor activities for older citizens.
Programs using old people to fulfill needs of others; working with children or teenagers.
Individual preparation:
Financial awareness.
Development of interests that can be continued after retirement.
Reeducating society to view old people as a resource to enrich society, not as a burden. No program will work unless society stops thinking of old age as a taboo subject. Need for group rethinking on the topic.
Of course, these problems will not be easily solved. Even with the best preparation, old people can become sick or disabled. This is a complex topic.
Conclusion: Important to keep thinking about it.

In organizing his jottings in this way, Justin moved toward constructing a more formal outline, which has come to be fairly standard in a variety of disciplines. This form begins with Roman numerals (I, II, III). Then capital letters (A, B, C) are indented under these, and then arabic numbers (1, 2, 3) are indented under these, and then lowercase letters (a, b, c), followed by lowercase roman numbers (i, ii, iii), if necessary. Although many people find this method old-fashioned, others like it because it enables them to see divisions easily and discover parallels and patterns. If Justin had decided to create a formal outline, it might look like this:

I. Introduction: Short sketch of old people sitting uselessly on a park bench.
II. Problems of the old in contemporary American society (shows this as an important issue).
   A. Physical problems.
      1. Illness.
      2. Less energy.
      3. Deterioration of everyday abilities.
         i. Poor eyesight.
         ii. Loss of hearing.
         iii. Loss of muscle coordination.
   B. Psychological problems
      1. Enforced idleness.
      2. Feelings of uselessness.
      3. Loss of identity.
   C. Financial problems.
      1. Inflation reduces buying power.
      2. Loss of income.
III. Definition of a "fulfilling" life.
   A. Being needed.
   B. Being challenged.
   C. Being as independent as possible.

IV. Importance of preparation.
   A. Financial preparation.
   B. Psychological and social preparation.
V. Government programs.
   A. Financial.
      1. Increased emphasis on retirement programs.
      2. Attention drawn to the need for financial preparation.
   B. Psychological and social.
      1. Government programs to sponsor activities for older citizens.
      2. Programs using old people to fulfill needs of others.
         a. Children.
         b. Teenagers.
         c. Single mothers.
VI. Individual preparation.
   A. Financial awareness.
      1. Individual retirement plans.
      2. Discussion among family members.
   B. Development of interests that can be continued after retirement.
VII. Need for reeducating society.
   A. Role of media in promoting the view that old people are a resource.
   B. Elimination of taboo on subject of old age.
VIII. Qualification: the problem is complex.
   A. Old people can become sick or disabled.
   B. Reeducation takes time.
IX. Conclusion: Important to begin work.

INCORPORATING YOUR NOTE SYNTHESIS SHEETS

Once you decide on a form for your main ideas, you can then incorporate your Source Notesheets and Note Synthesis Sheets into your plan. Here is an example of how Justin did it:

Introduction: Short sketch of old people sitting uselessly on a park bench. (*Use Source Notesheet 1 giving statistics on the elderly.*) Indication that this is a problem—establishing importance. Use position statement to suggest a partial solution.

Problems of the old in contemporary American society. Further establishing importance. Not only physical and financial problems, but enforced idleness leads to feelings of worthlessness and loss of identity. (*Use Note Synthesis Sheet 2.*)

Definition of a "fulfilling" life as meaning one in which there is a feeling of being needed, of being as productive and independent as possible. (*Use Note Synthesis Sheet 1.*)

Preparation can help people live a more fulfilling life in their later years. Government programs

    Financial (*Use Note Synthesis Sheet 4.*)

Here is a paragraph from Justin's paper, which he generated from Topic Notesheets 1 and 3. This paragraph is concerned with establishing that the problems of the elderly are not only physical and financial but psychological as well. The notes in the margins indicate how Justin incorporated ideas from sources into his own position.

In addition to enduring physical and financial hardship, many of the elderly also suffer a loss of a sense of purpose in life, which creates feelings of uselessness and loneliness. "Advanced industrial society has resulted in enforced idleness for the old" (Blau 21), which results in the elderly feeling as they "have no function in life" (Jones 17). Since they are no longer earners, no longer a part of the growing, developing part of society, many of them feel as if their lives are over. According to Blau (16) and Perera (112), a fulfilling life means that one is working at something, facing new challenges, and feeling useful. However, the elderly in this society are considered marginal, no longer necessary to society.

[Margin notes: Notesheet 3, Notesheet 3, from Notesheet 3, Notesheet 1]

(Note here that Justin used both direct quotation as well as summary and paraphrase. Also note how quotation marks and source references were used.)

Incorporating references to his source note sheets and note synthesis sheets helped Justin work through a first draft of his paper with relative ease. But remember that, in constructing a plan, the plan is there to help *you;* there is no "best" way to do it and it is not an end in itself. Therefore, you can include anything in the plan that will help you get a better notion of the structure of your paper.

USING CLUSTERING AND TREE DIAGRAMS TO PLAN

Clustering, which is also a tool you can use to discover ideas, can be a way of mapping the structure of your paper. Where jotting down ideas or outlining is basically a linear design (top to bottom), clustering for structure enables you to move horizontally or all over the page. You can then see that some ideas are subordinate to others, while others are not. See Chapter 2 for a sample cluster diagram.

Position Statement: Living a more fulfilling life in old age requires financial and educational preparation, on both the government and individual levels.

A **Tree Diagram** is another form of planning. It has the advantage of enabling you to show levels of generalization and specificity without necessarily dividing ideas into parts. It gives you a visual map of your ideas that can help you understand the relationship of the parts to the whole. If you wished to tree diagram the above topic, you might do it like this:

TREE DIAGRAM

What Can Be Done So That The Aged in Our Society Can Live a More Fulfilling Life?

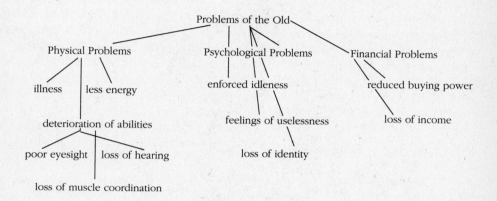

Problems of the Old

Physical Problems   Psychological Problems   Financial Problems

illness   less energy   enforced idleness   reduced buying power

deterioration of abilities   feelings of uselessness   loss of income

poor eyesight | loss of hearing   loss of identity

loss of muscle coordination

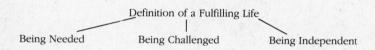

Definition of a Fulfilling Life

Being Needed   Being Challenged   Being Independent

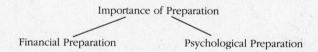

Importance of Preparation

Financial Preparation   Psychological Preparation

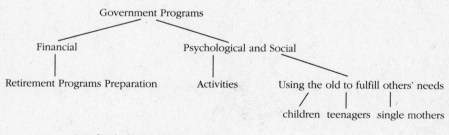

Government Programs

Financial   Psychological and Social

Retirement Programs Preparation   Activities   Using the old to fulfill others' needs

children teenagers single mothers

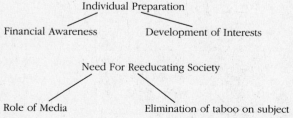

Individual Preparation

Financial Awareness   Development of Interests

Need For Reeducating Society

Role of Media   Elimination of taboo on subject

An Important Qualification: In presenting models and methods of organization, I may have given the impression that successful writers *always* use one method of organization consistently, always keep information organized, and generally write papers in a methodical fashion. Yet as anyone who writes papers frequently will attest to, writers are often less disciplined than they would like to be. Many writers are involved in several research projects at the same time, and they jot down notes not only on carefully constructed notesheets, but also on whatever they happen to have, wherever they happen to be—on the backs of envelopes, in the corners of shopping lists. Sometimes if writers already know a lot about the topic, they can plan a great deal of the paper before beginning to write or search for information. In other words, although you may find that one of the models presented here is a good one to imitate because it enables you to organize information efficiently and coherently, you may also find that another method is more comfortable for you. It is up to you to find the method that works best for you.

Some Assignments in Developing Structure: Read the following essays:

"Injustices Against the Aging"

"Old People on Television"

"The Coming of Age"

"Even Americans Grow Old"

Plan a paper in which you take a position concerned with this topic. Write a position statement, think about reasons and justification for the statement, create at least three note synthesis sheets, and construct a plan.

Some suggestions:

Preparation for old age must begin in youth.

The media promote age stereotypes.

American society discriminates against old people.

Injustices Against the Aging
Elizabeth S. Johnson and John B. Williamson

In recent years television, newspapers, and news magazines have given considerable attention to the plight of the aged. These media often focus on extreme examples of the injustices that some of the elderly are forced to endure. We hear lurid reports of elderly couples found frozen to death in their own apartments, their utilities having been cut off because they were unable to pay the bills. We hear about the elderly who must eat cat food in order to survive on their meager pensions. We are told that even those who were once middle class or even affluent run the risk of poverty in old age. The following is one such report.

> Rose Anderson was 90 years old, wispy and frail. She lived in a room filled with yellowed newspapers, magazines and books; it was filthy. There were cockroaches. There was an ugly permeating stench. She was too weary to clean. She gave her energy to caring for her canary.
>
> She had been the wife of a prominent physician but she had the "misfortune" of living to a ripe old age and outliving both the $300,000 her husband had carefully provided for her and her only child, a son, who died at the age of 56 when she was 76. She had given over some of her money to support her daughter-in-law and grandchildren. But most of it went for her own extensive medical expenses. She ended up living on welfare.[1]

Although well-meaning, those who seek to underscore the plight of the aged sometimes contribute to the creation or perpetuation of inaccurate stereotypes. The aged are a heterogeneous group, and for this reason the impact of such problems as poverty, crime, and inadequate health care varies considerably. The injustices that affect one person are often quite different from those that affect another. In the popular press it is common to find problems that affect a small minority of the aged presented as if they affect the majority. For example, overall, the elderly are no more likely to be victims of crime than are younger age groups, despite what many journalists and television commentators would have us believe.[2] This is not to deny that crime is a problem for the elderly; it very definitely is, but to find out why, we have to look to factors other than age differences in victimization rates.

Many of the social problems associated with aging begin long before a person would appropriately be referred to as elderly. For example, discrimination against older persons seeking employment is more the rule than the exception. In some industries there is evidence of discrimination against job applicants who are over age forty-five and many jobs are closed to applicants over fifty-five.[3] Commercial exploitation based on anxieties about changes in physical appearance due to aging often begins before a person is even middle-aged. Media advertising contributes to a heightening of this anxiety and encourages consumers to deal with their anxiety by purchasing products which purport to minimize the physical signs of the aging process. While many people use cosmetics for reasons other than looking youthful, it is clear from the industry's advertising efforts that the desire to appear younger provides one foundation for this multibillion dollar industry. In view of the tendency for many of the problems associated with aging to begin prior to the onset of old age, our concern in this book will be with the social problems and injustices confronting the aging as well as those confronting the aged.

One objective of this book is to describe the various injustices with which the aging and the aged must contend. In this context we give particular attention to four categories of injustice: exploitation, oppression, discrimination, and victimization. To facilitate this objective our discussion focuses on the various social problems associated with aging. Another equally important objective is to deal with the extent of these problems; that is, to make an effort to separate popular myth from the closer approximation to reality which emerges from a balanced analysis of relevant research findings. The myth typically takes the form of a stereotype that is quite valid for some who are aged, but not valid when used to characterize the typical aged person or the aged as a group. Due to the importance of exploitation, oppression, discrimination, and victimization as aspects of the injustices confronting the aged and aging, it is appropriate to begin with a discussion of what we mean by these terms.

EXPLOITATION

As we grow older our vulnerability to certain forms of exploitation increases. We will be using the term "exploitation" in the sense of economic exploitation. Generally the reference will be to the practice of taking economic advantage of those who are particularly vulnerable for reasons of age. On occasion we will also make use of the Marxist definition of the term which refers to the profit the employer (capitalist) makes on the basis of the worker's labor. All the forms of exploitation we consider are perfectly legal; if a practice is illegal, we find it more appropriate to classify it as victimization.

Later in the chapter we will consider the issue of discrimination against older workers in some detail. However, it is worth noting the Marxist analysis that the problem for the older worker is not so much being exploited as it is not being exploited. This somewhat anomalous conclusion follows from the Marxist argument that there can be no exploitation unless the person is actually employed. A capitalist economy is structured in such a way as to put a high premium on efficiency, productivity, and profit maximization. This emphasis, at least in part, accounts for industry's reluctance to hire older workers and the practice of encouraging or even forcing those who are already employed to retire at a certain age. There are, however, reasons other than having fewer productive years left that contribute to the discrimination against older workers; among the most important are salary expectations and pension considerations. While many workers are affected by these discriminatory practices, the injustice involved does not constitute a form of exploitation, at least in the Marxist sense. However, this is not to say that a Marxist perspective is irrelevant to an analysis of the injustices against older workers. Discrimination against older workers puts those who cannot afford to leave the labor force at a disadvantage. Since most jobs are closed to them, they are forced to take what they can get. Typically, those jobs that are open offer poor working conditions and low wages. The effect of discrimination against older workers by one set of employers is to make them highly vulnerable to exploitation by others.

Another type of problem for the older worker can occur when corporations find that costs can be cut and profits increased by moving their operations from one region of the country to another. This has been illustrated by the exodus of the textile industry from the Northeast to the South where labor costs have been lower. Such relocations can deal a major blow to the entire economy of a community; this is particularly so when a substantial proportion of the jobs in the community are either directly or indirectly dependent on the firm that moves.

While such actions affect all age categories, the impact can be particularly severe for older workers. Those who do not wish to relocate can find that their employability is low or even nonexistent. For some it means they will not be eligible for full pension benefits; for others it means there will be no pension benefits. Some face months or even years of unemployment, while for others the result is forced early retirement. On occasion the company offers jobs to those workers who are willing to relocate. However, this involves a major sacrifice for older workers who have a lifelong investment in a family and friendship network in the area as well as a lifestyle built around the peculiarities of the community and region. For those who remain, it is difficult to start over in a new line of work, giving up years of seniority and specialized skills which are not relevant to jobs which are available.

Workers whose jobs are dependent on looking young have good reason to be concerned about age-linked changes in appearance. In our society no one looks upon change in physical appearance due to the process of aging with pleasure. One response to anxiety about these changes is to purchase cosmetics as well as other goods and services designed to minimize the evidence of aging. Since people have the option not to purchase cosmetics, it is reasonable to ask whether those providing these goods are guilty of exploitation. If people choose to spend their money on cosmetics, hair transplants, face lifts, and the like, who are we to say they are being exploited?

We cannot answer these and related questions about commercial exploitation without making some ethical judgments. Is the supplier of these goods and services in some way violating our sense of fairness? Are high profits being made at the expense of providing adequate services to those in a relatively powerless position as in the case of many nursing homes? Are high profits being made by providing services that people must avail themselves of at a time when they are particularly vulnerable as is often the case when dealing with the funeral industry? When our answer to questions such as these is "yes," it is reasonable to conclude that the practice is an instance of exploitation.

The cosmetics industry has taken advantage of anxiety about the physical signs of aging in an effort to increase demand for its products. But isn't this entirely consistent with accepted business practice in a capitalist economy? Are we to hold those who manufacture cosmetics or provide nursing home services to a different set of standards than we apply to those who supply cars? The answer to these questions will depend in large measure upon one's ideology. The conservative would argue that the only social responsibility of business is to do all it can that is within the law to maximize profits.[4] This includes those who sell cosmetics, the services of a funeral home, or used cars.

However, it is consistent with a liberal ideology (which more accurately describes the perspective of the authors) to make distinctions between more and less ethical business dealings. If one party to an economic exchange is particularly vulnerable, the liberal is likely to question the ethicality of extracting unusually high profits. Such transactions are likely to be considered exploitive.

Most liberals would want to hold the cosmetics consumer partly responsible for his or her decision to buy. Even taking into consideration the vast sums cosmetics manufacturers invest in advertising efforts designed to heighten anxiety about one's appearance, the consumer is viewed as having a choice of whether or not to purchase the goods being offered. This situation can be contrasted with that of a recently bereaved widow who must enter into business dealings with a funeral establishment. In this context, the liberal is more likely to classify a high profit transaction as exploitive, particularly if the person is persuaded to spend more than she can afford.

The case concerning exploitation by the pharmaceutical industry is more compelling than the case for the cosmetics industry. Large sums are spent on the development and testing of new drugs, but the discrepancy between what it costs to produce and market these drugs and what the consumer pays is sufficient to keep the industry consistently among the three most profitable in the United States.[5] While all segments of the population are drug consumers, growing older increases the chances of suffering from conditions that require drug therapy. For some of the elderly, the cost of drugs becomes a major economic burden; however, we must still ask whether the elderly are in any sense being exploited by those who produce and sell these drugs. In answering this question, one factor to consider is the practice of selling the same drug under a brand name at a much higher price than under its generic name. Another factor is the nonvoluntary nature of drug consumption for many of the elderly. Some will counter this last argument by pointing out that the elderly consume many drugs that they really do not need. However, such an argument fails to take into consideration the vast sums the industry spends on advertising. This propaganda has undoubtedly contributed to the expectation that there is a drug which can help with just about any physical or psychological problem. In such a cultural milieu it is not surprising that many get "hooked" on over-the-counter or prescription drugs.[6]

The pharmaceutical industry is just one component of what has come to be referred to as the medical-industrial complex, the third largest industry in the United States. Little needs to be said about the profits being made by doctors, insurance companies, medical vendors (for example, the companies that do required laboratory work), and those who produce the sophisticated equipment hospitals use. Since medical problems arise for persons of all ages, we would not want to argue that the exploitation by the medical establishment is explicitly aimed at the aged. This is particularly true in view of the tendency for such services to be covered by third party payments.[7] However, given the correlation between health problems and the process of growing old, it is reasonable to conclude that the medical establishment does find the health consequences of aging a source of considerable profit.

OPPRESSION

Of the injustices associated with growing old, oppression is the most general and comprehensive. A case can be made that the various forms of discrimination, victimization, and exploitation which we consider are all oppressive aspects of growing old. We will often use the term "oppression" to describe the psychological experience associated with these injustices. This psychic oppression is sometimes the result of the actual experience of discrimination, victimization, or exploitation. It can also result from the fear of such experience, as in the case of an elderly woman who lives in terror of being mugged on the way to the grocery store. There are also sources of oppression such as failing health, social isolation, poverty, and the widespread fear of such fates that are not instances of discrimination, victimization, or exploitation. The restrictions of various age roles and age norms are sources of oppression. In addition to considering the subjective experience of oppression, we will consider the objective sources of this oppression. Of particular interest will be institutional sources such as result from living in a nursing home.

Oppressive Age Norms and Roles

In primitive societies age and sex are two of the major deteminants of social roles. Typically an elaborate set of normative expectations is associated with the sex roles to be fulfilled at each stage in the life span. In many societies elderly adults have a significant role in child care;[8] this is particularly true of those societies with an extended family structure. In such societies grandparents often take on responsibilities for child care while they in turn are relieved of some of the more strenuous roles of young adulthood. It is common for some of the most important roles—such as those relating to various ceremonial and religious functions—to be reserved for the elders. In a preliterate society, those who have lived the longest are often respected for their wisdom. When an unusual event threatens the community, it may be only the older members who have had experience in dealing with it. They also have significant responsibilities in regard to the transmission of the society's oral tradition.

A contrast is often made between modern societies in which there are few roles for the aged, and preliterate societies in which there were (and in some instances still are) a number of important roles for the aged. However, in many preliterate societies the status of the aged was much less enviable than such a comparison would suggest. Although in some, such as the Aleuts of the Aleutian Islands and the Inland Chukchi of Siberia, the aged were accorded a great deal of respect, more common were societies such as the Yakut of Siberia and the Thonga of South Africa in which the dependent aged were viewed as expendable.[9] This was particularly true of societies living under harsh conditions. If limited food supplies were spread too thinly, all would starve. For this reason, in many primitive societies there were norms supporting ritual murder or abandonment of the aged. Among the Koryak of Northern Siberia, a feast was given in honor of the aged parent who was then killed by a son or other close relative toward the end of the festivities. Among the Siriono in the Bolivian forest, the aged were left behind to starve to death while the rest of the community moved on in search of new food supplies.[10]

In our society there is more flexibility with respect to age and sex roles than in most primitive societies, but even so these roles continue to be major determinants of our behavior. When we encounter a person for the first time, among the first attributes we notice are sex and age. These characteristics tell us a great deal about what we can expect of this person and what they are likely to expect of us. There are shared norms that regulate the kinds of behavior which are considered appropriate in a social encounter as a function of the age and sex of the person involved. In a variety of ways, age roles and the related norms facilitate social interaction and benefit us all. These norms and roles are shaped by, and in turn help maintain the social order, but these same roles and norms can in some contexts become a source of oppression.

The oppressiveness that can be associated with certain age roles and norms is well illustrated by the issue of sexuality in old age. Until quite recently, it was generally assumed by the young that sexual activity was of great interest to themselves, of minor interest to the middle-aged, and of no interest to the aged. An exception was made for a few who were rich or famous, but for most it was assumed that there was little or no sexual activity in old age. Any aged man or women who was so bold as to boast of an active sex life could expect to meet with disbelief or ridicule. To have even a serious desire for sexual activity was likely to be considered somewhat improper.

In recent years there has been a dramatic shift in attitudes toward sexuality, including an increase in the acceptance of a variety of forms of sexual behavior which had previously been considered improper, immoral, or perverse. There has been liberalization in attitudes toward premarital sexuality, extramarital sexuality, and homosexuality. As part of a general liberalization in attitudes on such issues, there has been an increase in acceptance of sexuality in old age.[11]

In our society it is considered appropriate for women to select mates who are at least as old as they are and for men to avoid selecting mates who are much older. Minor violations of these norms which do not involve more than a few years generally go without much comment. But any substantial violation becomes an issue worthy of considerable gossip. It would be most interesting to explore why these norms continue with such force today in spite of a marked liberalization in attitudes toward other aspects of sexual behavior. But independent of the reasons why these norms are with us, it is clear that they are no longer functional and that they unnecessarily inhibit the options of both men and women in the selection of mates. The norms result in an unfortunate reduction in the options for persons of both sexes at all ages, but the result is particularly strong for women who outlive their husbands as most women do. For elderly women who wish to find a new mate, men of an "appropriate" age are in very short supply. When this norm is liberalized, a process which may have already begun, there should be an improvement in the options available to elderly women as well as everyone else.

Sexuality is only one sphere of life in which some of the age norms have oppressive consequences. Age norms also regulate and restrict options with respect to friendship formation. We are expected to select our friends from among our associates who are close to us in age. If the age gap between two persons is substantial, in the eyes of many the relationship is suspect. To select as an intimate friend a person of either sex who is either much older or much younger than oneself is not only unusual, it is considered somewhat unnatural. One common interpretation of such relationships is that those involved are acting out certain unresolved early life parent-child fantasies. An even less flattering interpretation is that perverse sexuality is somehow involved.

In addition to the areas of sexuality and friendship formation, labor force participation is also affected by age norms. Some of these norms have been institutionalized as formal regulations, for example, the various mandatory retirement rules. Others operate more informally as subtle or not so subtle pressures on the older worker to retire. The pressure can sometimes result from realistic considerations. For example, in heavy manual work the older worker may no longer carry a full share of the burden; in some situations this increases the burden on the other workers. In bureaucratic organizations there may be younger workers who seek promotions which are not possible until the present division or section heads retire.

Fears: A Source of Oppression

For most crimes, the actual victimization rate for the elderly is not greater than for other age groups, but their lifestyles are affected a great deal more than is reflected in crime statistics.[12] Fear of victimization often leads to a radical curtailment of activities. Many who live in cities are afraid to venture out at night, and in some areas the fear extends to going out alone even during the day.

Fear of victimization can lead to social isolation and to a breakdown in informal mechanisms of social control. In some areas the elderly can be counted on to keep track of what is going on in the neighborhood and to report any crime that occurs. This informal mechanism of social control helps keep crime rates down. However, in other areas, particularly the inner cities, many of the younger generation have moved to the suburbs and have been replaced by persons who differ from those who remain in race or ethnicity. This shift in composition has weakened informal mechanisms of social control which then allow crime rates to increase. Among the elderly who have remained in the inner cities, there has been an intensification of the fear of victimization. The response for many of the elderly has been to retreat behind locked doors and drawn curtains. This has further weakened informal mechanisms of social control and contributed to even higher crime rates.

Fear of victimization is only one of a variety of fears that oppress the aging and particularly the aged. There are a number of fears associated with signs of physical aging and the consequences these signs have for one's ability to attract others.[13] These signs also indicate that we are growing older and therefore closer to death. The fear of death and the fear of dying oppress people of all ages; while the evidence suggests that the aged do not fear death and dying more strongly than do other age groups, they think about these issues more frequently and therefore they may be more oppressed by such fear.[14]

Many of the aged and those approaching old age are oppressed by their fear of poverty. With retirement there is typically a sharp drop in income and a corresponding constriction of opportunities to increase that income in the event of economic need. Some widows live long enough to use up what had been a substantial inheritance left to them and end up on welfare. Expenses due to health problems can wipe out a lifetime of savings in a very short time. Many fear that the day will come when they have nothing to live on except social security or welfare.

The aging can be oppressed by the fear that with old age will come social isolation. Some fear that their children will make little or no effort to keep in contact. Many dread the day when they will be left alone due to the death of a spouse. Another common fear is of spending one's last years in a nursing home or other such institutional environment isolated from friends.

Institutional Experience

Between 20 and 25 percent of the elderly are living in nursing homes when they die or enter the hospital to die.[15] For those who do enter a nursing home it is all too often an oppressive experience. Some suffer a reduction in contact with significant others. Their friends and relatives see less of them once they have made the move to a nursing home, finding it inconvenient and unpleasant to visit such a depressing place. This avoidance of those who have moved into a nursing home is an example of what sociologists refer to as "social death," that is, being treated in some way as dead prior to actual death.[16] The resulting social isolation tends to undermine one's morale and identity.

Another reason life in a nursing home is so oppressive is that it involves regimentation of such activities as waking, going to bed, eating, bathing, and toileting.[17] We all develop routines with respect to these activities, but we are free to make changes in them when we see fit. A routine is generally not considered oppressive if one has a sense of control over it, but one has relatively little control over these routines in many nursing homes. They are established by the staff in an effort to maximize organizational efficiency, not patient autonomy. Loss of control over such basic aspects of one's life can deal a blow to one's sense of self-worth; this impersonal treatment represents a dehumanizing denial of one's individual integrity. The more understaffed the institution, the more oppressive the regimentation, but even the best nursing homes severely restrict resident autonomy in comparison to what it had been prior to institutionalization. Even the most deprived of the elderly poor, those living under deplorable conditions in "welfare hotels" located in the worst of inner city slums, live in dread of the day when they will be forced to move into a nursing home.[18] To move to a nursing home is viewed by many as a sign that "normal" life is over; it is seen as a limbo halfway between life and death.

Fortunately most people are able to avoid residency in an institution. But this does not necessarily mean that those who avoid nursing home placement escape the experience of being oppressed by one or another of the other institutions which provide services to the elderly. Many feel stigmatized at having to deal with the welfare bureaucracy to obtain funds to live on or funds to cover health-related expenses. Others must spend extended periods of time in the hospital, an experience that often involves many of the same oppressive characteristics that are associated with nursing homes.

DISCRIMINATION AND VICTIMIZATION

The logic of a competitive market economy calls for employing workers who are as efficient and productive as can be found. This need becomes a rationale for discrimination against older workers. For those who are not protected by seniority rules it becomes a rationale for dismissal; for those who have become unemployed for any reason, it becomes a rationale not to hire. In many instances workers of fifty-five can perform just as productively as workers of twenty-five, but will be passed over because they have fewer years of high productivity left. Older workers are discriminated against to the extent that they are treated differently and less favorably for reasons of age. In actual practice it is often difficult to distinguish between discrimination based on age and discrimination based on other age-linked characteristics. For example, it is not uncommon to find that an older worker is being paid (or expecting to be paid) substantially more than a younger worker of comparable skill. A case can be made that discrimination against such persons is as much due to their being more expensive as due to their being older.

In much the same way, few would deny the desirability of a policy of assuring workers the *option* of retirement at age sixty-five. The debate has been over the policy of *mandatory* retirement at age sixty-five, seventy, or any other specific age independent of a person's ability to do the job competently.

In many instances mandatory retirement policy has been justified on the basis of economic rationality; for many tasks younger workers are as productive and cheaper. In recent years an effort has been made to get mandatory retirement regulations declared discriminatory. Recently, Congress raised the mandatory retirement age from sixty-five to seventy in the private sector and ended the practice altogether for federal employees. This points to a growing awareness of the discriminatory nature of the existing regulations, but does not eliminate the problem in the private sector. It is easy to see why bureaucratic organizations would prefer a simple policy of retiring all workers at a specific age such as sixty-five or seventy to some alternative that calls for an assessment of the competence of each worker on some periodic basis. While the now common policy of using age as the criterion is administratively simple, it does discriminate against older workers, particularly those who are able to continue working and who want or financially need to do so.

Other forms of discrimination against the aging involve the provision of medical care and various other social services. In his study of dying in a large public hospital catering to lower and working class pateints, David Sudnow observed that more effort was made to resuscitate (revive) the young than the old. If a young person who had recently stopped breathing and whose heart had stopped beating was brought into the emergency room, typically a great deal of effort was made to resuscitate the patient, but when a very elderly person was brought in with the same symptoms, often no effort at resuscitation was made.[19]

It was worth taking "heroic" measures in an effort to save the life of a young patient; however, such measures were deemed less appropriate for the very elderly.

The training of health care specialists often involves inadequate attention to the specific needs of the elderly. Virtually every medical school in the country offers pediatric medicine as a specialty, but very few offer a specialty in geriatric medicine. Discrimination against the elderly in the provision of mental health benefits is illustrated by the preference of psychiatrists for working with younger patients and their hesitancy to suggest long-term psychotherapy for the elderly.[20] Even though the elderly constitute one of the largest population categories for risk of emotional disturbances, they have been in the lowest priority category for need assessment and delivery of community mental health services.

The medical sector is only one of many areas in which the aging are discriminated against in the provision of services. It is often difficult for an older worker to gain admittance to a federally funded job training program, the assumption being that younger workers are in greater need of the limited positions available. The same is true in the provision of educational services. The G.I. Bill, for example, is only available for ten years after a person leaves military service. Children and youth are provided transportation to schools, cultural events, and athletic contests in buses paid for out of public taxes, but most communities have not made a comparable effort to meet the special transportation needs of the elderly.

So far we have considered exploitation, oppression, and discrimination against the aged. We now turn to our fourth and last category of injustice against the elderly, victimization. Included here are those who experience crimes of violence, theft, and various frauds that can in some way be linked to advanced age. Also included are those whose lives are adversely affected by the fear of being so victimized.[21] We will be using the term "victimization" to include criminal victimization and other unethical practices which most would agree should be against the law. For example, consider the legal, but highly disreputable practices used by some land developers in selling "retirement home sites" in swamps and desolate areas without access to roads, to say nothing of public services.

From the attention periodically given to the issue in the mass media, one might be led to conclude that the elderly are more likely to be victimized by crimes of violence than are other age groups; however, this is not the case.[22] Certain subgroups of the elderly, such as those living in the inner city, are disproportionately victimized. In addition, when an elderly person falls victim to a violent crime, the effects of the experience are often more long lasting than in the case of a younger victim. Older people usually take longer to recover and run a greater risk that total recovery will not be possible. The crime statistics also fail to take into consideration the greater precautions, such as not venturing out at night, that the elderly take to protect themselves. The elderly are more likely to be victimized than are equally cautious persons in other age categories.

In addition to violent crime, there are other ways of victimizing the elderly. They are more likely than others to have chronic health problems and for this reason to be highly vulnerable to a variety of health-related frauds. Many entrepreneurs have made fortunes on schemes designed to separate the elderly from their money, some of which are illegal frauds, whereas others are legal but quite disreputable. In some instances a machine or medicine is sold with outlandish promises of effectiveness against everything from arthritis to cancer.[23] Most of these remedies are entirely worthless; some are quite dangerous, as in the case of a quack remedy for cancer which might have been treated successfully with more conventional medical procedures.

Most nursing home residents are not being victimized even though life in such institutions tends to be quite oppressive, but some of those living in very substandard nursing homes are the victims of a wide range of abuses which can be considered criminal. There are a number of laws on the books which were designed to regulate the nursing home industry, but enforcement in many areas has been lax. When nursing home operators have taken advantage of this situation, the outcome has in some cases been appalling living conditions for residents. In such institutions violations of fire and other safety codes are not uncommon.[24] In many of these homes patients are kept highly sedated, not for therapeutic reasons, but rather as a mechanism for social control to make them easier to manage.[25] In her expose of the nursing home industry entitled *Tender Loving Greed,* Mary Adelaide Mendelson documents numerous examples of unsanitary cooking and eating facilities, the use of food that is unfit for human consumption, and a host of flagrant violations of the law, to say nothing of the abuse of personal dignity. In her description of a nursing home in Cleveland she is highly critical of the food the nursing home operator saw fit to feed residents.

> The cook has taken hams, bacon, and wieners and thrown them on Strauss's (the nursing home operator) desk because of their smell, and refused to prepare them. . . . often the cook has thrown away whole baskets of tomatoes Strauss purchased at the market for stewing because they were unfit to eat. And sometimes the cook almost flips a coin to decide whether she should use the contents of a damaged, rusted, and bulging can.[26]

Old People on Television

Richard H. Davis and James A. Davis

Frequency of Appearance

The world of television displays a demographic profile that reflects its structure. No people appear in that television world who are purposeless. Each person on camera has a reason for being there: The plot calls for it. This is true in public affairs shows as well as series comedies and dramas. This is true in documentary specials and movies of the week. It is true as well in news panels.

Richard H. Davis and James A. Davis, "Old People on Television." Reprinted with permission of Lexington Books, an imprint of Macmillan, Inc., from *TV's Image of the Elderly* by Richard H. Davis and James A. Davis. Copyright © 1985 by Lexington Books.

The population of the television world reflects the values of that world. In addition, the length of time any one person (or type, or age) appears on screen also reflects the values of the special world of television.

So it is possible to do a content analysis of programming which is actually a head count. A census can be taken of the population of television's fictive world. Government census counts allow us to know how many men, women, and children and of what ages populate the real world. Does the world of television reflect the demographic facts accurately? Numbers of studies have made such counts, and the answer is a resounding *no*.

How Is Age Determined?

Before counts are taken there has to be a set of criteria established for the designating of on camera characters as old. Researcher Mary Cassata directed a content analysis of thirteen daytime television serials for a two-week period during the summer of 1978. Characters were determined to be older when content defined them as being age 55 or older, they were seen as being the eldest of at least three generations, a grandparent, a resident of an institution for the aged, a retired person, or any character who *appeared* elderly. If the actual age of the actor or actress playing the character was known, that, too, was taken as an indicator that the character was old (if, of course, the actual age was "old" according to the researchers).

In 1981 Joyce Elliott did a similar survey of daytime television—specifically soap operas. She monitored thirteen daytime television serial dramas over a four-week period. For this study an older adult was distinguished by being "about" 65 years old or older, a judgment made on the basis of appearance. In addition, old people were in roles of great-grandparent, parent of a child 30 years old or older, or designated as retired. If the character had lines that self-described him or her as older, or if others described him as older, he was tabulated as being old. Again, if the actual age of the actor or actress was known, this qualified for inclusion in the old category.

Obviously a certain amount of subjectivity is employed on the part of coders on such a survey. In most such studies, coders are carefully coached so that there is consensus on their image of old on television. Often, more than one coding person is assigned to view the same program. One acts as a check against the other.

The Body Count

Several studies have counted old people in various segments of the broadcast day.

Aronoff analyzed data pertaining to age of 2,741 characters in prime time network television drama sampled between 1969 and 1971. From this large number of characters, Aronoff identified 98 older males and 36 older females. Each comprised 4.9 percent of the sample for their sex. It is interesting to note that of the total (television) population, men (regardless of age) numbered 2,017 and women (regardless of age) numbered 724.

Harris and Feinberg gathered data on frequency and type of characterization of the elderly. They used a four-hour random sampling of four time segments during the broadcast day. The programs were selected in a random basis over a six-week period from all seven days of the week and from all three networks. A total of 312 characters were observed and rated. Of these, 24 were classified as being between age 60 and 70. Only two were identified as over 70.

Using a much smaller sample, Peterson analyzed 30 network half hours of prime time in 1972. She counted all people who were known to be at least 65 and who were themselves on the show. In addition, she counted those playing roles she judged to be at least 65. She found 32 people, three of whom were women. This amounted to 13 percent of the television population reviewed.

Ansello analyzed 238 half-hour segments of programs as well as commercials in 1977 and 1978. He found that 6 percent of this population could be identified as elderly.

Commercials are a special genre and will be discussed later. But it is interesting to note that of the sample of 100 television commercials Francher looked at in 1973, only two included an older character.

In 1974 Northcott did a content analysis of prime time drama on the three networks. All role portrayals lasting two minutes or longer were analyzed. This amounted to 464 role portrayals. Of these only seven, or 1.5 percent appeared to be over 65 years of age.

Children's Saturday morning programs have also contributed to these population surveys: Gerbner's group identified only 1.4 percent of all weekend daytime characters being 65 or older. In 1973 Richard Levinson found 4 percent of the human characters in Saturday cartoons to be old. Also looking at cartoons, Bishop and Krause found 7 percent of the characters to be elderly.

Greenberg, Korzenny, and Atkin surveyed for character age (among other variables) in programming in the fall of 1975, 1976, and 1977. Those over age 65 comprised 4 percent of the characters in the first year, 3 percent of the second, and 2 percent of the third. This group analyzed more than 3,500 characters over the three years of the study. Barely 100, or 3 percent, were in the old age bracket.

In the Cassatta study of soap operas, 365 characters were monitored. Of these, 58, or 15.9 percent, were judged to be 55 or older. The majority of these older characters (55 percent) were judged to be in their 60s.

Finally, Elliott's study of daytime soap opera (1981) analyzed 723 characters. Fifty-eight people were determined to be age 60 and above; this constitutes 8 percent of the study population. Estimated as 12.6 percent of the study population were characters who seemed to be in late middle age, age 50 to 59.

Implications

What do these findings tell us? It is obvious that the numbers of older people appearing on television do not correlate with the numbers of older people in society. Of course, there is no rule or regulation that says there should be a correlation beween fiction and reality. Indeed, such an "equal rights" regulation would cause havoc with the various program decision makers, who would then be forced into contriving plots that included percentages of all kinds of people and all kinds of ages. It would be foolish.

The problem, however, with skewed distribution of the elderly rests in the awareness that what is important in our society finds its way onto television. And if an issue or a person appears on television, then by virtue of appearance alone, the issue or person becomes important. When increasing age equals increasing invisibility on television, the message is clear: To be old is to be without importance.

When the elderly are seldom seen on television, this may translate into their seldom being seen in society. Viewers are sensitized to the prevalence of certain physical types as their success on television encourages proliferation of these types. This is evident in the real world, where people strive to resemble the currently popular model. For example, at the height of the popularity of a TV adventure serial, "Charlie's Angels," one could see Farah Fawcett lookalikes on every street. When there are few if any older persons on television, they might, in fact, be on the streets in significant numbers, but remain unseen.

WOMEN ON TELEVISION

It appears that women are more likely to be seen on television if they are in their 20s, and to be seen less frequently with each succeeding decade. The situation differs with males, most of whom are seen in the general age span of 35 to 49. About 20 percent of men on television are in the over-50 category. When a count is made of persons over age 65, this population is more than 90 percent male. We know this does not represent distribution in the real world.

Gerbner's studies show that the likelihood is that older men on television will have a higher level job and a higher socioeconomic status than younger ones. In general, most depiction of the elderly in scripted shows is not that of poverty. In contrast, however, the emphasis in public affairs specials on the elderly is too often on the poor and severely deprived.

Gerbner also finds that the elderly tend to be shown as more comical, stubborn, eccentric, and foolish than other characters. They are more likely to be treated with disrespect. The latter is more true in prime time programming than daytime serials.

Because of the generally negative portrayal of older women, and especially because of their near invisibility on television, several concerns have been raised. Peterson's study indicated that one might expect to see an older man on television every 22 minutes, but an old woman would be seen only every 4 to 5 hours. Gerbner's content analysis shows older women to be in general: silly, stubborn, sexually inactive, and eccentric. And in crime dramas they are the ones killed, almost never the ones doing the killing.

These illustrations of woman's place in the world of television reinforce the generally accepted notion that woman's place in the real world is basically one of romantic interest. Further, it is made clear on television that woman as a romantic partner is more desirable when young than at any other time. In fact, women are portrayed with increasing sexlessness as they age, while men are often attributed enhanced sexual allure. This male attractiveness is based in their having been ascribed power. Men are usually, if not always, depicted as somewhat older and usually smarter in the ways that count than their female companions. The female, according to Beck's 1978 study of older women in television programming, is usually 10 years younger than the lead male, and becomes increasingly unimportant to the plot as she ages. Her role becomes one of adoring attendant upon the "rocking chair sage," or she is cast as a nag.

Past female characters who are "old" come to mind. "Maude," who carried her own show, and Edith Bunker, cheerful mate to the insufferable Archie, were highly visible models of middle age. But what kind of women were these as images to copy for young women who had been listening to the rhetoric of the women's movement for the last 10 years? The grandmother generation fared no better. In past years, Grandma Walton epitomized the patient, enduring, faithful companion, but other older women and mothers-in-law were too often silly to the point of ludicrousness.

In more recent television series the picture of the matriarch has been presented on several series. They seem to fill the role of commentator on the events in the lives of their offspring. They do a lot of warning, shaking of the head, and being generally critical.

This sort of older woman is seen more often in daytime programming. Also the studies of this genre find that the older woman is treated much more favorably than on prime time drama. Although older women may be shown in conventional role behaviors, that is, as housewives or in nonauthoritarian jobs, they are portrayed with respect and sympathetically. Both Downing and Elliott in their extensive studies of older characters on soap operas report that the women tend to be perceived by the coders as being more attractive than people of similar age in the general public. (Being "more attractive" would seem to be requisite for all performers on soap opera, if not television in general.) Elliott also noted that the greater percentage of older females were widowed, which was not the case for the older males who appeared in the serials. Further, the older females tend to live in family settings and to be from the middle to upper classes.

Elliott's soap opera older women were also cast as official and informal advisors. Their male counterparts were authorities in the world of business, so their advising was seen as official. Although older women in these programs tended to have closer friendships with men than with women, their romantic involvement was nil compared to that of younger women. The older women were more likely to be nurturing than were the older men; again, this is true of men and women in general in the fictive world of television.

Implications

What we learn about behaviors of older men and women in television program content is very much like what we learn about other adult males and females on television drama. Women appear less often and in more passive roles. Men hold the power and are active in physical, political, and business senses of the word. Men tend to have interesting and productive roles in the drama of life much longer than do women. For the most part, women act as useful accoutrements to males. They provide romantic interest, and when young they populate the television world in great numbers. They tend to disappear after age 30, except on soap operas, where their numbers diminish after age 50.

Perhaps once again television reinforces commonly held and therefore comfortable stereotypes. The way to behave as males and the way to behave as females is shown over and over again. This cannot help but influence all viewers as they attempt to be socially acceptable persons.

Young people who want to know what the next age stage of life is like and what models there are to pattern themselves after may have some troubles adjusting to harsher realities as they find that human beings are not as simplistically put together as their television heroes and heroines. If they should be curious about what life is like for those in mature adulthood and old age, they will get some input about older males (that is, age 40 and up), but they will have little or no useful information about older women.

Perhaps the most disturbing implication to be drawn from television's presentation of older role models, or rather the lack of role models, is that a disadvantageous stereotype of women is reinforced. As women are instructed to deny their own aging and attempt to create the illusion of youthful appearance and behaviors, they are setting themselves up for some depressing confrontations in later life. As men are conditioned to see older women as second-class citizens through their portrayals on television, they will have difficulty being supportive of the unavoidable consequences of aging in their mates, and in themselves.

IMAGES OF HEALTH AND THE ELDERLY

In the world of television, poor health is often more interesting to the plot than is good health. There are numbers of shows wherein the action is centered in hospitals. The sick person will be the center of attention. In daytime programming health problems often provide a major source of drama. Not all these ill people in both day and night programming are old people. Harris and Feinberg's study showed that a significant percentage of older characters demonstrate moderate to high physical activitiy. In this study 14 percent of the characters between ages 50 and 60, and 12.5 percent of those aged 60 to 70 were tabulated as engaged in highly physical pursuits. Peterson also found that the majority of older characters in programs she reviewed were active, in good health, and independent.

The Harris study charted ill health and age factors showing that poor health increased with age. In the below-50 category, only about 6 percent had health problems; in the 50–60 category, 14 percent showed health problems; and in the 60–70 category, 25 percent of the population had poor health. Harris remarks that, while it is true that in real life, health problems increase with age, it is significant that television chooses to focus on this, the failure aspect, rather than on success in business and politics, which is also demonstrable.

In the world of the soap opera, where it is already demonstrated that the elderly have roles of greater respect and authority than in prime time, it is also indicated that they enjoy better health. It has been pointed out the characters on soap operas do not have diseases and illnesses that viewers are likely to have. This is probably deliberate on the part of writers in order to make the programs nonthreatening. It is doubtful, for example, that any soap opera character battles obesity, much less general excess poundage. Further, not all the illnesses on these kinds of programs are even classified. Cassata found only one fourth of the illnesses to be classifiable and that they were responsible for only one-fifth of the deaths in the programs. People, it seems, are more likely to recover than to die in soap opera. Death may be reserved for those characters who, for one reason or another, must be written out of the script.

Older people on television, therefore, are not necessarily victims of disease, or even holders of disease. In fact, Cassata and Downing both find that over 90 percent of the older characters were in remarkably good health. It is those characters between ages 22 and 45 who have the most health problems.

It is the observation of both Davis and Kubey that television may tend to present a distorted image of health among the aged through a tendency to focus on the exceptional. Calling this "reversed stereotyping," Kubey explains that older people are often seen riding motorcycles, dancing with abandon, or referring to their highly active sex lives. These "exotics" make good video subjects because they are seen doing things thought to be extraordinary for older persons. When young people hang-glide or surf, no one pays much attention. When a 60-year-old does the same thing, it becomes a news item. When a 70-year-old does it, he or she may well become the star of a 10-minute segment of "Real People."

Kubey suggests that when such reverse stereotypes are presented in prime time comedy it is intended to be comical. It is accepted as a joke, and thereby negative stereotypes continue to be reinforced.

In contrast, the usual public affairs special about old people in the community is likely to focus on the visible elderly who have multiple health losses. As the subject of aging has gained media acceptability, public affairs programs are produced and represented almost every season. Since audiences tend to respond to the unusual more readily than the usual, to the tragic rather than joyous circumstance, and to the appalling more than to the appealing, a show about old people easily allows this response to be facilitated. Every city has its derelicts, the down and outers who may look years older than they are. These people make for good "visuals." Most cities have a park where older people come together for a variety of highly valid and useful reasons. Allowing the camera to pan the assembled elderly while a voice-over comments on the pathetic lot of those who do not commute daily to single-family dwellings in the suburbs is a common part of many "community interest" programs.

These two sets of images, the very ill and the very active, are two ends of a spectrum of health in the elderly population. When that is all that is seen, another set of stereotypes is reinforced.

Fortunately, there are also some more realistic images of aging and health available on television. "Over Easy" was a long-running daily half hour program on the Public Broadcasting System. The program format featured thematic examinations of critical issues. Major segment categories included health, nutrition, and exercise. Health segments presented information about heart disease, cataracts, podiatry, stroke, and other pertinent problems. Prevention, detection, and treatment were stressed. Exercise and nutrition segments featured how-to information.

A program analysis of the 1981 season for "Over Easy" represents a typical broadcast year and indicates that there are more segments about the general topic of health than on any other issue. This is because other themes addressed in the programs are closely linked with issues of health and well-being. Family relations, philosophy, psychology, and social issues are all definite aspects of a holistic approach to health maintenance and aging.

Health and the image of aging will receive more positive attention as new broadcast systems search for viable program material. As illustration, the Cable Health Network, which began programming in 1982 devotes all its program schedule to health related issues. Programming for this network follows a thematic concept. Of eleven themes, one is devoted to the health of older persons. Titled "Getting Older, Feeling Younger," this series of programs is designed to contribute to the well-being, fitness, nutrition, medical care, and emotional health of older Americans. It may be assumed that older persons seen in this program and on this cable system will project healthy images.

These two examples, however excellent they may be, still were available only to those who view either public broadcasting or a specialized cable service. Unfortunately, this is not the majority of the viewing population.

Implications

Brotman's report lists the problems of ill health among the elderly, problems of which he says only 14 percent of all older Americans are afflicted. They include arthritis, 44 percent of that group; hearing impairments, 29 percent; and vision impairments, hypertension, and heart conditions, each about 20 percent. Except for the heart conditions, these health problems do not make for very interesting television fare. Since the young populate the world of television, it would be highly unusual (although quite possible) to have a young arthritic admitted to the hospital cast of characters. Most shows deal with acute, not chronic, problems in the first place. In the second place, those problems must have enough elements of the unusual to make for good drama.

Senile behaviors are not mentioned in soap opera, and when used in evening programming, they are usually material for a joke. Other diseases that make life difficult for the elderly are ignored because those who have them do not play central roles in the programs. It is easy to conclude, if one is gathering information about life from television's presentation of it, that there is no midground of health for the elderly. One either suffers from multiple debilitating losses or from none at all. Either way, a rude confrontation with reality is in store.

IMAGES OF AGE IN CHILDREN'S PROGRAMMING

Children are heavy viewers of television. This is especially so of the very young. When they are given a picture of the world and the people who populate it that is biased, then the perception they are forming of reality is likely to be equally biased. In studying a sample of shows viewed by children, Jantz et al. found that not only were older women, children, and minority groups underrepresented, but out of 85 half-hour segments there were only four child–elderly interactions. The researchers concluded that children were not being provided with realistic and accurate portrayals of the elderly.

Other studies of children's attitudes toward the elderly are equally alarming when they show that children say they do not want to be like the elderly or to grow old themselves. Seefeldt surveyed the attitudes of 180 elementary school children in 1978. The children were drawn from a variety of racial, ethnic, and socioeconomic backgrounds. They found that the children stereotyped the elderly, identifying them as being sick, tired, and ugly. The children saw old people as being unable to do anything but sit and rock, go to church, or be pushed in wheelchairs. The physical characteristics of age—white hair, wrinkles, and false teeth—were viewed with horror by the children.

We know that the elderly have a low representation on prime time and evening special shows. This representation is even lower in those weekend daytime television shows that are designed especially for children. The Gerbner figures and those provided by Greenberg indicate weekend shows are mostly populated by characters who are under 20 years of age. This is the age group that is not particularly visible on the usual prime time shows.

The old are seldom seen in cartoon programs. This is a genre specifically targeting younger children. It is concerned with the struggles that children have between one another and with authority. Authority is usually held by the parent generation, not the grandparent generation. So not only are old adults not likely to be seen in cartoon land, but when they are there, they are benign. Negative roles are assigned to younger adults, or to nonhumans who are not old. These findings of content analysis done by Bishop and Krause demonstrate that aging and old age are not dominant themes, or even subordinate themes, in the Saturday morning television programming. This absence of any image at all contributes to the general invisibility of the elderly in the world of children.

Implications

It is estimated that a typical child has watched between 10,000 and 15,000 hours of television by the time he is 16. Children draw on this mediated experience for information to acquaint themselves with the world and to equip themselves to function well within it. There is reason for concern about children's attitudes toward older persons which goes beyond their acceptance of the negative stereotypes and myths that abound in our society. Questions have been raised about the influence of such beliefs on the child's developing self-image and about the effect of such conditioning on productive intergenerational relationships.

Age-segregated housing, dispersed family, and other social conditions tend to isolate today's children from the realities of growing old. This alienation is reinforced by our educational system, as evidenced in the limited curricular on aging. Negative attitudes about aging were present in 90 percent of the sample studied by Seefeldt. The children are quoted as saying they would feel "awful if they were old." They voiced denial, "Oh no, not me, I'm not getting old," and "I won't grow old; it's too terrible."

Mobility has meant that children have fewer opportunities for interaction with aged family members. In addition, for many children, contact with their grandparents means involvement with a relatively young person, someone in their 40s, 50s, or early 60s. Furthermore, because of the proliferation of age-segregated communities, children have limited exposure to older persons outside their family. Children deprived of experiences with a diversity of older persons in a variety of settings may never learn to question the stereotypes they hold about aging.

THE ELDERLY IN TELEVISION COMMERCIALS

When television becomes the primary source of contact with older persons, as is the situation for many children, negative attitudes toward aging are further reinforced. The Gerbner researchers concluded that the main results are clear and consistent: The more young people watch television, the more they tend to perceive old people in generally negative and unfavorable terms.

In the eight televised commercials monitored in the in-depth analysis by Harris and Feinberg, 10.6 percent of the total characters were over 60. This is a different and somewhat larger percentage than others have noted in actual program content. But like program content, the number of males increased as age increased, while the number of females decreased with age increase. The study also indicated that physical activity decreased and health problems increased with age. Statistically, the elderly in commercials experienced ten times the health problems of the young. Even though there is evidence that the elderly are healthy in many important ways, their counterparts in televised commercials do not reflect this.

Commercials often feature advice givers. Older advice givers tend to be male and tend to be celebrities. Older public figures are utilized to enhance a sales message; however, older characters are seldom given that responsibility when cast in story commercials.

Francher's study of television commercials showed that when a single character is used within the commercial it is likely to be a young, very attractive, and usually sexy female. Men are useful in advertising without as much regard to age. In fact, older men with graying temples and a certain macho image of virility and sexual appeal are often valuable to be associated with some products, However, Francher also concluded that older people are more likely to be used when the commercial is either humorous in tone or when there is a health product especially targeting the older age group.

The elderly often function to give reliability to a product. Their presence implies that the product meets the high standards of quality set decades ago. The inference is that only the older person would have the experience to be able to endorse the product.

The words *old* and *older* are seldom used in advertising. The words *young* and *younger,* however, often are used. The message is obvious, the product may be shown with a middle-aged face or an older one, but the words heard or read are those "young" words. The product, it is announced, makes one "younger." This is especially true of beauty products. The promise of youth is the major appeal. And this is a promise made to all those women who don't want people to know they have passed age 30. Younger women sell the beauty products. Older women sell digestion aids, laxatives, denture fixatives, and arthritis remedies.

Implications

The point is well made by this time: The image of aging in all areas of television programming is subject to criticism. However, nowhere might that negative image projection be more damaging than in commercials. Here is where promises are made. That one can buy youth, or at least youthful appearance, endows that state and quality with high value. Television commercials present to a consumer society all that is worth owning. The message inherent in advertising is that we are what we buy. This is what causes resentment and discontent among the disadvantaged, who cannot purchase "the good life." Similar resentments and discontent are likely among those who cannot afford to buy youth, those who find the promises empty; youth cannot be purchased anywhere. The glorification of youth, the Pepsi generation bouncing about the beaches of America, leaves a large majority without validation through the world of television advertising.

STEREOTYPING: CONSEQUENCES AND COUNTERMEASURES

In this discussion of images, it is apparent that what is being dealt with is clusters of stereotypes about men and women and about various age groups. Stereotypes are those conceptions and images which are simplified and inaccurate but which have become standardized and are commonly held. Stereotypes are categorizations. It is a way of thinking that aids in organizing one's world. Psychologists tell us that people find it useful to think in terms of categories, to classify both experiences and people symbolically through language (that is, by using descriptive words). Then these symbolic classifications are used as though they were real and represent truth.

These categorizations then, help to organize human actions toward a particular place, event, or person, regardless of the actual truth. The simplistic ordering of identities enables us to make decisions about how we are going to react to a given situation populated by people about whom we do not have a quantity of personal level experience. For example, when in a neighborhood largely composed of an ethnic group different from our own, we may feel threatened because we believe that all such persons are capable of and even desirous of inflicting harm upon us. If we find ourselves at an entertainment function largely attended by members of another age group than our own, we may feel uneasy because of our conception of them (if they are younger) as irresponsible drug users; or, if they are older, we may feel uneasy because of our conception of them as fragile and humorless. As drivers, we have a set of notions about other drivers and their highway behavior dependent on their age, their sex, their ethnicity, and possibly the kind of car they are driving.

We make decisions about how we are going to behave in each of these situations. More often than not, the motivation for this behavior is fear and mistrust for that which is "different."

In spite of all the statistics we have about aging and being old that would promote a positive image of age, it is evident that these facts are not generally known, or perhaps not generally attended to. Our society perpetuates a mythology about being old. It is possible that some of this mythology is a consequence of truth as it may have existed in decades long past, but which no longer stands as fact. This tells us that much information is passed by word of mouth from generation to generation and given much more validity than what is read in the papers. What we are told at an early age by the authorities in our environment stays with us. Parents and grandparents may pass on information gathered from their parents and grandparents. They may also instruct us through actions even more strongly than through verbalizations. So we are given a set of attitudes about aging, about being old. These attitudes are difficult to overcome even when presented with subsequent packages of more intellectualized information.

The Mythologies of Age

There are numerous commonly held generalities about the elderly. The most common examples are listed here.

1. Old people are rigid and inflexible.
2. Old people decline in intelligence.
3. Old people are less productive as workers.
4. Old people are institutionalized and dependent.
5. Old people are senile.
6. Old people are sexless.

Evidence countering these assertions has been presented in chapter 1, but not everyone has read such evidence.

The Gray Panthers is a national advocacy organization whose members include not only the elderly but young people and middle-aged people. This organization has voiced much concern over media images of aging. They have mounted a "Media Watch" to record evidences of discrimination toward old people. The group has developed a list of characteristics that it considers stereotypes, to guide them in spotting offenses in television program content. The Gray Panthers' list includes the following characteristics.

Appearance. The face is blank and expressionless, and the body is always bent over and infirm.

Clothing. Ill-fitting garments.

Speech. Halting and high-pitched.

Personality. The dominant characteristics are stubbornness, rigidity, and forgetfulness. The "rocking chair" image predominates.

The Gray Panthers pose a series of questions for television's gatekeepers to use in checking against possible distortions of fact:

1. Are older people depicted as intruders or meddlers in the relationships of others?
2. Are older people ridiculed when they show sexual feelings?
3. When there is an age difference in romantic relationships, are older women accorded the same respect as older men?
4. Are old people patronized and treated as children?
5. Are the oppressive conditions under which older people must live in society analyzed? Are alternatives to the existing conditions presented?
6. In any discussion of social and economic issues, are the perspectives of older people included?
7. Are older people directly involved in writing, directing, and producing the program?
8. How about the acting? Are there valid reasons for young actors to play the roles of older people?

These questions asked by the Gray Panthers might cause smiles among network and other programming officials, whose concern is not to act as a public relations agent for any group. Their concern is to present a story that has enough audience appeal to attract large numbers of viewers. They might attend to these guidelines for content review if they thought that by doing so, they would not alienate a significant audience. Nevertheless, such sensitizing of producers, directors, and writers will have eventual results. After all, it is doubtful that any of these creative people deliberately set out to offend through poor taste.

Another set of guidelines has been published by Coronet, a company producing both print and film educational materials. Coronet's target audience is young people, for whom they produce educational materials. The booklet, titled *Guidelines for Creating Positive Images of Persons and Groups,* lists suggestions for the treatment of older persons, including the following:

1. Older adults and children will be included in materials at all levels in all curriculum areas. They will be included both as central characters and as group members.
2. Older citizens will be featured as vital, independent functioning adults. They will be shown living independently, as being successful, doing interesting things, and having interests that are shared by others.
3. Older people will be shown relating positively with each other in realistic, believable situations. Viewers will be shown some positive aspects of a relationship, such as helpfulness, romantic interest, etc. They will be

allowed the full range of human emotions, hopes, and desires. Viewers will be given a feeling that they would like to know characters portrayed.

4. Older adults will be shown as economically productive citizens within a community. They will be shown gainfully employed, participating in community affairs, and as reasonable people to work with.

5. Older persons will be portrayed in positive roles within a family. Their opinions will be respected and their accumulated wisdom will be valued and sought. Their status will be shown as an asset. Families with more than two generations will be shown.

6. Older citizens will be featured interacting in positive relationships with children. Grandparents or foster grandparents will be shown teaching children how to do some task. They will be shown passing on family traditions and values.

A third set of guidelines are those developed by the National Council on Aging by its executive director, Geneva Mathiesen. These guidelines are intended for use in directing program people toward positive depictions of older people. Mathiesen asks that the media portray the current generation of the elderly, not reflect the past in stereotype.

1. Show older people in their current environments and with their current mind sets.

2. Don't portray institutionalization as an inevitable adjunct to old age.

3. Don't give the impression that old people are separated and/or alienated from—and neglected by—their families.

4. Combat the fallacy that emotional or mental departures from the norms by the elderly are evidence of "senility."

5. Don't exaggerate symptoms of mental confusion manifested by older people; they affect people of all age groups.

6. Please, no more cheap jokes about sex in old age.

7. Old people sitting on park benches or in rocking chairs are not prototypes of older people, most of whom are, in fact, busy, active, and useful.

8. Portray the growing significance of the elderly as a political force.

9. Continue an advocacy role on behalf of those elderly who are poor, sick, alone, and afraid, unable to hold their own in a fast-paced society inclined to ignore or to victimize them.

10. Among the many programs depicting violence, dramatize the muggings and murders of the old by youthful gangs or identified bullies, often only for their meager dollars or maintenance checks.

11. To eliminate stereotypes, portray old people as personalities, not types.

All these guidelines help creative people to understand the nature of positive role-modeling in educating about aging. Television decision makers who would not characterize themselves as producers of educational material might still find inspiration in such a set of advisories.

What is important in the mass media is that a balance of images be presented. It is true that some elderly have unappealing mannerisms. The same is true of all ages. It would be reverse stereotyping to present a whitewashed picture. At one time it was acceptable for many minorities to be ridiculed. The handicapped, alcoholics, and members of racial and ethnic minorities were used as the butt of humor. Public awareness has grown so that alcoholic behavior is no longer considered funny, nor is stuttering, limping, or being mentally retarded. As a consequence, there has been a decline in that form of humor. Using the elderly as objects of ridicule is equally inappropriate. But public awareness and sensitivity has yet to rise to the level of expressing concern and limiting such attacks. The Gray Panthers are attempting to do for the elderly what "Black Power" advocates did for blacks. Jamieson's 1977 report to the Senate Committee on Aging says that this sort of activity will "transform the pejorative into the positive while replacing the assumption of powerlessness with the assertion of power."

The Coming of Age

Simone de Beauvoir

When Buddha was still Prince Siddartha he often escaped from the splendid palace in which his father kept him shut up and drove about the surrounding countryside. The first time he went out he saw a tottering, wrinkled, toothless, white-haired man, bowed, mumbling and trembling as he propped himself along on his stick. The sight astonished the prince and the charioteer told him just what it meant to be old. 'It is the world's pity,' cried Siddartha, 'that weak and ignorant beings, drunk with the vanity of youth, do not behold old age! Let us hurry back to the palace. What is the use of pleasures and delights, since I myself am the future dwelling-place of old age?'

Buddha recognized his own fate in the person of a very aged man, because, being born to save humanity, he chose to take upon himself the entirety of the human state. In this he differed from the rest of mankind, for they evade those aspects of it that distress them. And above all they evade old age. The Americans have struck the word death out of their vocabulary—they speak only of 'the dear departed': and in the same way they avoid all reference to great age. It is a forbidden subject in present-day France, too. What a furious outcry I raised when I offended against this taboo at the end of *La Force des choses*! Acknowledging that I was on the threshold of old age was tantamount to saying that old age was lying there in wait for every woman, and that it had already laid hold upon many of them. Great numbers of people, particularly old people, told me, kindly or angrily but always at great length and again and again, that old age simply did not exist! There were some who were less young than others, and that was all it amounted to. Society looks upon old age as a kind of shameful secret that it is unseemly to mention. There is a copious literature dealing with women, with children, and with young people in all their aspects: but apart from specialized works we scarcely ever find any reference whatsoever to the old. A comic-strip artist once had to re-draw a whole series because he had included a pair of grandparents among his characters. 'Cut out the old folks,' he was ordered.* When I say that I am working on a study of old age people generally exclaim, 'What an extraordinary notion! . . . But you aren't old! . . . What a dismal subject.'

And that indeed is the very reason why I am writing this book. I mean to break the conspiracy of silence. Marcuse observes that the consumers' society has replaced a troubled by a clear conscience and that it condemns all feelings of guilt. But its peace of mind has to be disturbed. As far as old people are concerned this society is not only guilty but downright criminal. Sheltering behind the myths of expansion and affluence, it treats the old as outcasts. In France, where twelve per cent of the population are over sixty-five and where the proportion of old people is the highest in the world, they are condemned to poverty, decrepitude, wretchedness and despair. In the United States their lot is no happier. To reconcile this barbarous treatment with the humanist morality they profess to follow, the ruling class adopts the convenient plan of refusing to consider them as real people: if their voices were heard, the hearers would be forced to acknowledge that these were human voices. I shall compel my readers to hear them. I shall describe the position that is allotted to the old and the way in which they live: I shall tell what in fact happens inside their minds and their hearts; and what I say will not be distorted by the myths and the clichés of bourgeois culture.

Then again, society's attitude towards the old is deeply ambivalent. Generally speaking, it does not look upon the aged as belonging to one clearly-defined category. The turning-point of puberty allows the drawing of a line between the adolescent and the adult—a division that is arbitrary only within narrow limits; and at eighteen or perhaps twenty-one youths are admitted to the community of grown men. This advancement is nearly always accompanied by initiation rites. The time at which old age begins is ill-defined; it varies according to the era and the place, and nowhere do we find any initiation ceremonies that confirm the fresh status.† Throughout his life the individual retains the same political rights and duties: civil law makes not the slightest difference between a man of forty and one of a hundred. For the lawyers an aged man is as wholly responsible for his crimes as a young one, except in pathological cases.‡ In practice the aged are not looked upon as a class apart, and in any case they would not wish so to be regarded. There are books, periodicals, entertainments, radio and television pro-

---

* Reported by François Garrigue in *Dernières Nouvelles d'Alsace,* 12 October 1968.
† The feasts with which some societies celebrate people's sixtieth or eightieth birthdays are not of an initiatory character.
‡ Mornet, the public prosecutor, began his indictment of Pétain by reminding his hearers that the law takes no account of age. In recent years the 'inquiry into personality' that comes before the trial can emphasize the age of the accused: but only as one feature among all the rest.

grammes for children and young people: for the old there are none.* Where all these things are concerned, they are looked upon as forming part of the body of adults less elderly than themselves. Yet on the other hand, when their economic status is decided upon, society appears to think that they belong to an entirely different species: for if all that is needed to feel that one has done one's duty by them is to grant them a wretched pittance, then they have neither the same needs nor the same feelings as other men. Economists and legislators endorse this convenient fallacy when they deplore the burden that the 'non-active' lay upon the shoulders of the active population, just as though the latter were not potential non-actives and as though they were not insuring their own future by seeing to it that the aged are taken care of. For their part, the trades-unionists do not fall into this error: whenever they put forward their claims the question of retirement always plays an important part in them.

The aged do not form a body with any economic strength whatsoever and they have no possible way of enforcing their rights: and it is to the interest of the exploiting class to destroy the solidarity between the workers and the unproductive old so that there is no one at all to protect them. The myths and the clichés put out by bourgeois thought aim at holding up the elderly man as someone who is different, as *another being*. 'Adolescents who last long enough are what life makes old men out of,' observes Proust. They still retain the virtues and the faults of the men they were and still are: and this is something that public opinion chooses to overlook. If old people show the same desires, the same feelings and the same requirements as the young, the world looks upon them with disgust: in them love and jealousy seem revolting or absurd, sexuality repulsive and violence ludicrous. They are required to be a standing example of all the virtues. Above all they are called upon to display serenity: the world asserts that they possess it, and this assertion allows the world to ignore their unhappiness. The purified image of themselves that society offers the aged is that of the white-haired and venerable Sage, rich in experience, planing high above the common state of mankind: if they vary from this, then they fall below it. The counterpart of the first image is that of the old fool in his dotage, a laughing-stock for children. In any case, either by their virtue or by their degradation they stand outside humanity. The world, therefore, need feel no scruple in refusing them the minimum of support which is considered necessary for living like a human being.

We carry this ostracism so far that we even reach the point of turning it against ourselves: for in the old person that we must become, we refuse to recognize ourselves. 'Of all realities [old age] is perhaps that of which we retain a purely abstract notion longest in our lives,' says Proust with great accuracy. All men are mortal: they reflect upon this fact. A great many of them become old: almost none ever foresees this state before it is upon him. Nothing should be more expected than old age: nothing is more unforeseen. When young people, particularly girls, are asked about their future, they set the utmost limit of life at sixty. Some say, 'I shan't get that far: I'll die first.' Others even go so far as to say 'I'll kill myself first.'

---

* *La Bonne Presse* has recently launched a periodical intended for old people. It confines itself to giving information and practical advice.

The adult behaves as though he will never grow old. Working men are often amazed, stupefied when the day of their retirement comes. Its date was fixed well beforehand; they knew it; they ought to have been ready for it. In fact, unless they have been thoroughly indoctrinated politically, this knowledge remains entirely outside their ken.

When the time comes nearer, and even when the day is at hand, people usually prefer old age to death. And yet at a distance it is death that we see with a clearer eye. It forms part of what is immediately possible for us: at every period of our lives its threat is there: there are times when we come very close to it and often enough it terrifies us. Whereas no one ever becomes old in a single instant: unlike Buddha, when we are young or in our prime we do not think of ourselves as already being the dwelling-place of our own future old age. Age is removed from us by an extent of time so great that it merges with eternity: such a remote future seems unreal. Then again the dead are *nothing*. This nothingness can bring about a metaphysical vertigo, but in a way it is comforting—it raises no problems. 'I shall no longer exist.' In a disappearance of this kind I retain my identity.* Thinking of myself as an old person when I am twenty or forty means thinking of myself as someone else as *another* than myself. Every metamorphosis has something frightening about it. When I was a little girl I was amazed and indeed deeply distressed when I realized that one day I should turn into a grown-up. But when one is young the real advantages of the adult status usually counterbalance the wish to remain oneself, unchanged. Whereas old age looms ahead like a calamity: even among those who are thought well preserved, age brings with it a very obvious physical decline. For of all species, mankind is that in which the alterations caused by advancing years are the most striking. Animals grow thin; they become weaker: they do not undergo a total change. We do. It wounds one's heart to see a lovely young woman and then next to her her reflection in the mirror of the years to come—her mother. Lévi-Strauss says that the Nambikwara Indians have a single word that means 'young and beautiful' and another that means 'old and ugly'. When we look at the image of our own future provided by the old we do not believe it: an absurd inner voice whispers that *that* will never happen to us— when *that* happens it will no longer be ourselves that it happens to. Until the moment it is upon us old age is something that only affects other people. So it is understandable that society should manage to prevent us from seeing our own kind, our fellow-men, when we look at the old.

We must stop cheating: the whole meaning of our life is in question in the future that is waiting for us. If we do not know what we are going to be, we cannot know what we are: let us recognize ourselves in this old man or in that old woman. It must be done if we are to take upon ourselves the entirety of our human state. And when it is done we will no longer acquiesce in the misery of the last age; we will no longer be indifferent, because we shall feel concerned, as indeed we are. This misery vehemently indicts the system of exploitation in which we live. The old person who can no longer provide for himself is always a burden. But in those societies where there is some degree of equality—within a rural

* This identity is all the more strongly guaranteed to those who believe they have an immortal soul.

community, for example, or among certain primitive nations—the middle-aged man is aware, in spite of himself, that his state tomorrow will be the same as that which he allots to the old today. That is the meaning of Grimm's tale, versions of which are to be found in every countryside. A peasant makes his old father eat out of a small wooden trough, apart from the rest of the family: one day he finds his son fitting little boards together. 'It's for you when you are old,' says the child. Straight away the grandfather is given back his place at the family table. The active members of the community work out compromises between their long-term and their immediate interests. Imperative necessity compels some primitive tribes to kill their aged relatives, even though they themselves have to suffer the same fate later on. In less extreme cases selfishness is moderated by foresight and by family affection. In the capitalist world, long-term interests no longer have any influence: the ruling class that determines the fate of the masses has no fear of sharing that fate. As for humanitarian feelings, they do not enter into account at all, in spite of the flood of hypocritical words. The economy is founded upon profit; and in actual fact the entire civilization is ruled by profit. The human working stock is of interest only in so far as it is profitable. When it is no longer profitable it is tossed aside. At a congress a little while ago, Dr. Leach, a Cambridge anthropologist, said, in effect, 'In a changing world, where machines have a very short run of life, men must not be used too long. Everyone over fifty-five should be scrapped.'*

The word 'scrap' expresses his meaning admirably. We are told that retirement is the time of freedom and leisure: poets have sung 'the delights of reaching port'.† These are shameless lies. Society inflicts so wretched a standard of living upon the vast majority of old people that it is almost tautological to say 'old and poor': again, most exceedingly poor people are old. Leisure does not open up new possibilities for the retired man; just when he is at last set free from compulsion and restraint, the means of making use of his liberty are taken from him. He is condemned to stagnate in boredom and loneliness, a mere throw-out. The fact that for the last fifteen or twenty years of his life a man should be no more than a reject, a piece of scrap, reveals the failure of our civilization: if we were to look upon the old as human beings, with a human life behind them, and not as so many walking corpses, this obvious truth would move us profoundly. Those who condemn the maiming, crippling system of which we live should expose this scandal. It is by concentrating one's efforts upon the fate of the most unfortunate, the worst-used of all, that one can successfully shake a society to its foundations. In order to destroy the caste system, Ghandi tackled the status of the pariahs: in order to destroy the feudal family, Communist China liberated the women. Insisting that men should remain men during the last years of their life would imply a total upheaval of our society. The result cannot possibly be obtained by a few limited reforms that leave the system intact: for it is the exploitation of the workers, the pulverization of society, and the utter poverty of a culture confined to the privileged, educated few that leads to this kind of dehumanized old age. And it is this old age that makes it clear that everything has to be reconsidered, recast from the

---

* This was written in December 1968.
† Racan's phrase.

very beginning. That is why the whole problem is so carefully passed over in silence: and that is why this silence has to be shattered. I call upon my readers to help me in doing so.

Even Americans Grow Old

Richard F. Koubek

Growing old in any culture is a curse; in America we curse the old. Our euphemistically camouflaged "senior citizens" are disturbing reminders that even Americans decay and die. The aged are the nemesis of America's dream—of its boundless youth, limitless resources, endless tomorrows. Since the Founding Fathers first trumpeted their Enlightenment promises some 200 years ago, Americans have believed in their cultural and personal "Manifest Destiny." To be American is to be an individual always changing and growing. Death, infirmity and pain are out of place here. We curse the old because they endure, forcing our attention to the most glaring blind-spot in the American vision—our mortality and our finiteness.

My father has Parkinson's disease. In his youth—the productive half century that preceded his affliction—he was a salesman. His success was living testament to the enduring faith of Jefferson, Hamilton and Franklin. Always punctual, disciplined and hard working, he lived for his company and reveled in its prosperity. Like Cooper's American democrat, he once walked proud and upright; his grip was strong, his gait was quick. Today the business he nurtured is gone. My father, crippled by Parkinson's, barely walks, with a stoop and a palsy that are grim distortions of his youthful strength. He is vulnerable and finite after all. So are his sons. So is his America.

We Americans steadfastly refuse to be humbled by our humanity. Our need to overcome adversity and alter nature's designs has fueled the American production machine. We revere the will of steel, the man or woman who refuses to accept defeat. Rocky, our latest folk hero, is hailed by jubilant theater audiences because he stands the 15 rounds, long after physical exhaustion and the force of gravity should have pinned him to the ring mat. When I was four or five years old, my father used to read me the children's version of "Rocky," a story of a little train that refused to quit and, overcoming insurmountable odds, reached the top of a mountain. Such a mind set is both the source of our strength and the substance of our fantasies. How absent death, defeat and disease are from these scenarios. We are without limits.

Richard Koubek, "Even Americans Grow Old," *Commonweal*, January 20, 1978. Reprinted by permission.

My father's struggle with Parkinson's began in his 65th year; that symbolic turning point when people are supposed to withdraw from the fray. He hardly retired. Rather, he faced seemingly endless assaults—a stroke and the crippling effects of Parkinson's—with willful determination. He took up a cane only when it became impossible to walk without one. He fought off a walker until it was obvious to him that he could not stand without it. To date, there are no plans to purchase a wheel chair. In refusing to accept this strange palsy, he equates resignation with defeat.

Consider this incident which occurred last February. Long after he was told not to drive, my Dad set out on an icy morning to "get gas for the car." My mother pleaded in his monoxide wake for him to turn back. Of course he didn't. The car struck a tree and a street sign. When he finally sputtered into his service station, 20 minutes later, with a fender smashed and a headlight pointing up, he casually said to the astonished attendant, "Fill it up, Frank." "Thank God," my distraught mother later shouted, "No one was hurt!" Proud, reckless, stubborn man. All of us were appalled and stunned by the bravado of his last ride. But in the afterglow, one could detect in his eyes a twinkle that had not been seen for years. And, when asked why he had done so foolish a thing, he only responded with a puckish, adolescent grin that revealed his triumph of his moment. He was "still standing."

My father's is a youthful battle with Parkinson's. Like the culture that spawned his values, he will not come to rest nor will he accept his decline. In his old age, he is an uncomfortable analogue of all that America is and all that it can never be. His restless, defiant courage typifies the American promise, as the degeneration of his body is a stark reminder of its limitations.

I have frequently seen the larger issues of our society reflected in this strong man's struggle. What unshakable confidence we have felt about reaching the moon first, defeating the Vietnamese, or curing cancer. How certain we are that there is no energy crisis and, if there were, that American technology will solve it. How quickly we dismiss the need for national health insurance or a national welfare system because we believe Americans should take care of themselves. Those who can't simply haven't tried. They are quitters.

Our strength as a people is too often weakened by our smugness. We do not age gracefully, nor do we treat our aged graciously, because we arrogantly refuse to accept time's inflexible law. We view ourselves as a nation becoming; eternally evolving into anything but the stagnation we myoptically define as old age. This contradiction, of course, flies in the face of the aging process which eventually overtakes us all. Undoubtedly this is why Americans consign the old to Dickensian nursing homes. We simply cannot reconcile their physical deterioration with our imagined immortality. It is all so at variance with our self-image. So the powerful illusion of America's infinite potential persists, sustaining my father in his pain while, for me, it clouds that most unpleasant reality; even Americans grow old.

Preface to Chapters 7 to 12

The other day I was walking around the campus at USC when I came upon a very lovely and intriguing demonstration of Japanese dancing. Having never seen such dancing before, I stopped and watched it for a while, admiring the brilliance of the costumes and the grace of the movement. I left the scene feeling pleased that I had watched and that I now had at least some idea about what Japanese dancing looked like. However, although I enjoyed the demonstration a great deal and now knew something more about Japanese dancing than I had known before, I would have been unable to express an *informed* opinion about it since I did not have sufficient exposure to it and lacked background information. If someone had asked me to develop a position about the quality of the dancing and the costuming, I would not feel qualified to do so, since I really didn't know enough about it.

My feeling that I did not know enough about Japanese dancing to write about it is similar to the situation of many students when they are asked to develop a position for a researched paper. Often students are assigned to write about topics on which they do not have sufficient information; yet, having a fund of information is *essential* before one can become engaged with a topic and develop an informed position. This second section of *Taking a Stand* provides you with sufficient information about the topics for your writing assignments so that you will be able to develop an informed position.

In the previous chapters you were presented with techniques and strategies that enable you to access information from personal experience and involvement in your community. Yet formulating an opinion on a complex topic and being able to evaluate the opinions of others usually involves a greater knowledge base than most people have. Often students go to the library to accumulate the information necessary for formulating an opinion, and it is likely that your instructors will provide you with writing assignments that require library research. However, in order to help you understand the topics provided in this book without first visiting the library, I begin each of the following chapters with some basic information. Moreover, even if you decide to use the library as well, you will find that you will work more insightfully and confidently if you already know something about the topic.

INFORMATION INCLUDED IN EACH CHAPTER

Each chapter begins with information that will help you understand why this topic is both personally relevant and socially significant. Also included will be an examination of the historical/cultural context of each subject area, emphasizing the extreme positions and controversies that have evolved. I will also define key terms, key questions, and suggest a sequence of assignments that will enable you to absorb information gradually. Thus, each writing assignment can be regarded either as an end in itself or as one that is part of a sequence.

Personal Relevance

In order for you to develop an informed position, you must understand the topic from the perspective of both an individual and a member of the community. After all, how can you find interest in a subject if you don't understand why it is important, why it is relevant for you. In each chapter, then, I will include material that will enable you to perceive of this relevance. Increased understanding of why these topics are important will enable you to become more personally involved with your writing assignments.

Historical/Cultural Background

Being able to formulate a position on a complex social/political controversy means understanding the historical/cultural background from which it developed. Often the controversies we read about in the newspapers and about which we cast our votes had their roots in the past. Frequently, these issues have been controversial since the inception of our country; by definition these topics are probably impossible to resolve absolutely. Because our country is based on the principle of democracy, there is the implication that every citizen is entitled to certain basic rights and freedoms. In other words, all members of society are concerned that they attain what they view as their "rights." And yet, even casting a superficial glance around any community reveals great inequity. Obviously, some people are powerful; others are less so. Some people are rich; others are poor. Presumably, every member of society is entitled to equal opportunity; yet some people's opportunities are greater than those of others.

Developing a position on political and social issues means recognizing the nature of these inequities, understanding how these inequities came into being, and contemplating possible methods of intervention. Therefore, in order to think about these possibilities, it is important to understand how these issues originated and evolved over time. For example, in the chapter concerned with equal opportunity I will trace some of the issues that developed during the Civil Rights movement of the sixties. In the chapter concerned with search and seizure, I will discuss the original meaning of the Fourth Amendment and trace how the meaning of the term "privacy" has evolved with the development of new technologies such as the computer and other sophisticated mechanisms for electronic surveillance. In the chapter concerned with the rights of men and women in society, I will discuss the changing roles of both men and women in the family and the workplace and trace developments occurring as a result of the women's movement of the sixties and seventies. Awareness of the historical and cultural roots of contemporary issues will enable you to approach your writing assignments with increased understanding.

Key Terms

Being aware of the key terms within a given topic and understanding the definitions of these key terms and their relevance to the major issues are essential to developing background information. Therefore, in each chapter, I will highlight certain particularly significant terms and provide a definition and an explanation within the historical/cultural context. For example, in Chapter 9, concerned with search and seizure, I will explain the meaning of terms such as the Fourth Amendment, the right to privacy, and the exclusionary rule. In Chapter 10, concerned with equal opportunity, I will discuss the meaning of such terms as affirmative action and reverse discrimination.

Key Questions

As I discuss each topic, I will highlight the key questions and extreme positions you must take into consideration as you develop your own position. Some of these questions aim simply at helping you think about the topic. Others may have to be addressed within your paper. An important point to keep in mind is that you cannot discover solutions until you are first aware of the important questions.

Laws and Cases

Some of the topics presented in this section have evolved through a series of court cases that established valuable legal precedents. In particular, controversies over such issues as search and seizure, the right to privacy, equal opportunity, and affirmative action were the subjects of important court cases, and you will be better able to develop a position on these issues if you are familiar with at least some of these cases. In a few of these chapters, then, I include a summary of relevant laws and cases pertinent to the topic.

WRITING TO LEARN

In many textbooks, exercises and writing assignments are reserved for the end of each chapter, since they require that the entire chapter be read in advance. My feeling, though, is that when students are presented with a great deal of information, it is important for them to pause periodically in order to review and digest what they have learned. Therefore, as I present information within each chapter, I will pause from time to time to suggest exercises and short assignments that will enable you to assimilate some of this information, that is, to learn by writing. Sometimes these short assignments will be ends in themselves, but sometimes they will be part of a sequence of assignments that will lead to a more complex assignment on the same topic. For example, in Chapter 9, concerned with search and seizure, you may engage in a few short writing assignments that elicit your own response to the topic. Then you may develop a position on a scenario concerned with the right to search curbside garbage. Finally, you may be asked to develop a position on whether or not police have the right to search a suspicious-looking van and use information that they may have found by accident. In other words, each assignment leads to a subsequent one, thereby deepening your understanding of the topic. Of course it is unlikely that your instructor will require you to work with all of these suggestions. However, as you read, you may find it helpful to think about some of them as you build your knowledge base on a given topic. Although it is true that you have to learn about a topic in order to write about it, it is equally true that writing about a topic enables you to learn.

THE RATIONALE FOR THE CHAPTER SEQUENCE

The sequence of Chapters 7 through 12 is designed to enable you to think about what I consider to be fundamental concepts and issues before grappling with contemporary controversies. The early chapters aim to generate thinking about the nature of humanity and varying concepts of government. These chapters may be considered prerequisites to the chapters which later address topics that perpetually have generated controversy.

As members of a democratic society, we have the responsibility of making decisions about how society functions and about how the goods and services of society are distributed. For example, business and educational establishments will often have to decide if they ought to give preference in hiring or admission to one particular group over another. In all aspects of living, people have to make policies that are often based on their ability to trust other people or to delegate responsibility. Many of these decisions, whether we realize it or not, are based on our concept of human nature and on what we consider to be the best way for society to function. Therefore, Chapters 7 and 8 are designed to help you access what you think and believe about these important ideas. Chapter 7, "The Nature of Humanity," will present you with different notions of human nature so that you ultimately will be able to understand and perhaps enhance your own conception of it. Chapter 8, "Individual Versus Societal Rights," similarly aims at helping you think about who should be in charge and about what each individual has to relinquish in order to gain necessary protection. Thus, these two chapters may be regarded as introductions to the topics that follow: Search and Seizure, Equal Opportunity, Men and Women in Society, and Understanding the Abortion Controversy.

A Sequence of Sequences

Because each chapter is sequenced conceptually and because the early chapters in this section of the book may be regarded as prerequisites to the chapters that follow, one might think of this second section of the book as a "sequence of sequences." Thus, my suggestion is that whichever of the last four chapters you choose to or are assigned to work with, that you begin by examining some of the ideas and concepts expressed in Chapters 7 and 8. These may be considered as a conceptual foundation for the complex topics that follow.

A Bridge Between the Past and the Present

Taking a Stand is based on the idea that writing assignments should enable students to create links between the past and the present. Thus, the topics in this section of the book are concerned with problematic social and ethical issues, which are part of our heritage and which continue to be of interest today. Writing about these topics will enable you not only to become more comfortable with using outside sources in your writing, but also to become a more responsible and aware member of the community.

7 The Nature of Humanity or "What's So Good About Being Human?"

"You inhuman beast! Unhand me at once," she cried.

Love in the Wilderness

"Ah well," he said, smiling and scratching his beard. "It's just human nature."

Lovable Old Pa

"I have been studying the traits and dispositions of the "lower animals" (so-called) and contrasting them with the traits and dispositions of man. I find the result humiliating."

Mark Twain

All of the above quotations refer implicitly to the concept of "human nature," that is, to the idea that there are characteristics that may be classified as distinctly "human," traits which can be applied to any human being and which set us apart from animals. For most of us, our everyday conversation suggests that human nature is something we take for granted. We speak of "man's *inhumanity* to man," of criminal acts as "*inhuman*," of the "milk of *human* kindness." This chapter enables you to explore the meaning of the term human, since, to a certain extent, your view of human nature influences the way you believe society should function.

Key Term: The Meaning of "Human"

Most of us believe that we know what is meant by the term human, yet the question of what is really meant by human nature has generated considerable disagreement. Determining the meaning of the term human is not an easy task, since one can often find exceptions even to those features that seem most obvious. For example, man, as distinct from animals, is said to be capable of reason. Yet the history of mankind may be viewed as a chronicle of seemingly irrational, often senselessly brutal acts. Moreover, primates and sometimes other animals, such as dogs and cats, seem to be able to use a form of reason in making choices. Sometimes, characteristics we regard as particularly human do not seem to apply to every human being. Consider the case of Karen Quinlan, who lay in a coma for an unprecedented number of days before she died. For the last part of her life, she was incapable not only of reason, but of thought, speech, volitional movement, of any activity at all. If we use any of these characteristics, then, as distinguishing marks of human nature, does it mean that a chimpanzee capable of a limited amount of reason could be considered more "human" than Karen Quinlan? How about KoKo, the signing gorilla, who apparently can make associations, is quite intelligent, and can even "talk" in some fashion? Would you consider him human? Is he, perhaps, more human than your neighbor?

Other questions concerning the nature of humanity are equally difficult to answer. One question that has been debated for many centuries concerns the extent to which man is inherently an individual as opposed to whether man derives his being from membership in a group. Another question concerns the issue of "human" rights. Is every human being born with "natural rights"? Or do these rights derive from the community into which one is born?

Questions concerning human nature are so difficult to answer that some people have dismissed them entirely. Some say that these questions are irrelevant. Others feel that since people are so different from one another the idea of trying to define human nature is absolutely fruitless. For them, the concept simply doesn't exist.

Yet, political, legal, and ethical systems are ultimately based upon theories of human nature. Whether or not we think there is such a thing as human nature and how we conceive of human nature help determine how we think societies and political systems ought to function. Therefore, because the concept of human nature influences decisions about the nature of society, I feel that it is important to think about the following questions:

1. Is there such a thing as human nature? If so, how would you define it?
2. Are human beings primarily individuals or are they defined primarily by their membership in a group?
3. Do human beings have "natural" rights; that is, are all human beings entitled to human rights, simply on the basis of being human?

The readings and assignments in this chapter are aimed at helping you think about these questions.

HISTORICAL/CULTURAL CONTEXT

Is There a Universal Human Nature?

The concept of human nature is based on the idea that all human beings share some set of attributes or qualities essential to our humanness. Whatever these essential attributes might be, they must be found universally in all human beings regardless of gender, race, time, or place. Some of these qualities are, of course, physical, and, actually, distinguishing human beings from other creatures on the basis of physical characteristics is easier to do than trying to distinguish more abstract characteristics and traits. Scientists have numerous methods of doing so, and most of us believe that we can easily recognize a human being on the basis of physical appearance.

Being able to recognize a human being, though, does not automatically mean that we can define one, at least not without giving the matter careful thought. Examine the two pictures on pages 213 and 214. You, of course, know immediately that one is a picture of a primate (an orangutan) and the other is a picture of outrageous-looking human beings (actually, the picture is from a postcard purchased in London). As a way of thinking about your own ideas about human nature, then, let us assume that a creature from another planet has come to visit the earth and comes upon these two pictures. Not being acquainted with human beings as a species, he is a bit confused about which creature is human and asks you to explain the difference to him.

WRITING TO LEARN: A SEQUENCE OF WRITING ASSIGNMENTS

▶ *Writing Assignment:* Write a short paper in which you compare these two pictures in terms of distinguishing which one is of the human. Use some of the methods for generating ideas discussed in Chapter 2. Assume you are writing for someone who is confused about this (a creature from another planet, for example). On the basis of what you see in the pictures, how can you tell which one is human?

Orangutan, Borneo (Source: Kjell B. Sandved, Sandved & Coleman Photography.)

Greetings from London © WPL 1987
(Photography by Joe Cornish.)

▶ **Writing Assignment:** The visiting alien is a very friendly creature and goes all over the planet looking at a variety of societies. He then writes a letter home telling his fellow creatures about the nature of human beings.

Pretend you are the visiting alien writing to your fellow aliens out in space. Think about those characteristics you consider to be essentially human. Brainstorm the topic either alone, with a partner, or a small group. Then write an essay on the topic, "The Nature of Human Beings." In your response, you should not focus on physical characteristics, but concentrate instead on the qualities, behaviors, and values, which you feel indicate humanness. Be sure to use many examples. Here are some questions that might give you some ideas:

1. What do you think "human nature" is? What do you think we have in common as human beings that is essential to our humanness? The ability to reason? Shared values? Our ability to have relationships? Communication? Religion tells us that we are all created in the image of God. What does this mean?

2. Another question to think about is the following: If there is such a thing as human nature, does that mean that we are all the same?

Questions for Discussion

1. In what way are you, a student and, presumably, a human being, different from KoKo, the signing gorilla?
2. Karen Quinlan, who lay in a coma for a long time, was termed "brain dead," unable to communicate, to relate to others, or be productive. Would you consider her "human?" Often we refer to people in this state as "vegetables." When do you stop being human? When do you stop sharing in a common human nature?
3. Consider a human infant. Is an infant human? Does it partake of human nature? Often we say that an infant "learns" to act as a human being. Yet if that behavior is learned and not innate, is it really human nature?

▶ *Writing Assignment: Human Nature and Everyday Living.* Your concept of human nature is based, to a great extent, on your direct or indirect observances of human action and behavior. Based on your previous paper, in which you discussed characteristics that you feel are associated with humanity, recount an incident in your own life that you feel particularly illustrates the concept of human nature. Such an incident could derive from your family life or from more recent events at school. After you have written a draft of this paper, exchange papers with a partner. Then discuss the extent to which you feel your partner's incident illustrates a basic characteristic of human nature. As a way of evaluating the selection of an incident, you might think about whether the incident would make sense if an animal were substituted in the place of the human beings involved.

▶ *Writing Assignment: Human Nature and Current Events.* Still pretending you are the alien trying to understand human nature, randomly select an issue of a daily newspaper. You are planning to send this issue back to your planet as a representative account of human nature. Write a paper in which you analyze the events depicted in the newspaper in terms of what they seem to reveal about the nature of humanity.

▶ *Writing Assignment: Human Nature and the Media.* Choose two recent films and compare how they depict human nature. Is the nature of humanity depicted as complex, neither good nor bad? Do the films portray easily defined villains and heroes? Can you evaluate the quality of the film in terms of its depiction of human nature?

▶ *Reading and Writing Assignment:* Read Mark Twain's essay "The Lowest Animal." Write an essay in which you respond to Twain's position on the nature of humanity. Explore what he says and how he says it. Use direct quotations, as well as paraphrasing, to support your position on his view. Dissect Twain's sentences and passages. How do his word choices, images, and the comparisons he makes affect the readers?

THE NATURE OF HUMANITY: INDIVIDUAL VERSUS COMMUNITARIAN VIEWS

Key Questions: Is Man an Individual? Does Man Exist Prior to Society?

A key question about the nature of humanity is whether Man is primarily an independent individual whose fundamental nature exists apart from all social–historical relations. This issue is illustrated clearly through the writings of John Locke (1632–1704), who, in his *Second Treatise of Government,* wrote that Man is "by Nature . . . free, equal, independent, no one can be put out of this Estate, and subjected to the Political Power of another, without his own Consent." By "free," Locke meant that all individuals can determine their own actions and dispose of their own property without needing to ask permission of anyone else. By "equal," Locke meant that no one person has any more power or authority over another person than he or she has over him or her self. This freedom and equality, according to Locke, enables Man to be independent.

The individualist perspective views the individual as existing prior to society, which is created by a group of individuals on the basis of rational self-interest. This means that although human beings are individuals motivated primarily by self-interest, they are rational enough to recognize that it is in their self-interest to support government and society, even though such support means that they must give up some of their individual freedom. The state is regarded, therefore, as an instrument to serve individuals, not as an end in itself.

WRITING TO LEARN: A SEQUENCE OF ASSIGNMENTS

▶ *Exercises:*

1. Read the selection by John Locke "Of the State of Nature." Paraphrase Locke's ideas discussed in this excerpt.
2. Write an essay discussing the extent to which you agree with Locke's ideas. Do you feel that Locke has misjudged mankind's capacity for reason?

Key Question: Is the Nature of Man Primarily Determined by His Social Relations?

The communitarian perspective views mankind as defined essentially by his social relationships. It presumes that the individual is fundamentally social or relational and that relations and groups are instrumental in creating human nature; such relations are not regarded simply as an environment that exists externally to the individual. This view of Man as a communitarian being is exemplified in the writings of Karl Marx, who felt that when individuals are truly bonded, they will not relate to each other in terms of separate individual needs and interests but will, instead, work to gain a complementary status with others in order to produce. This communality, according to Marx, is the essence of human nature, since, unlike animals, humans do not produce simply out of physical need. The communitarian view emphasizes that humans need other humans to achieve their humanity. Left alone, without other humans to interact with, humans would have no sense of self since human endeavor is based on relationships with others and since any individual gift or ability still needs the cooperation of others to be effectively used.

This modified conception of the individual self presumes a different view of the nature of society. Unlike Locke, who viewed the creation of society as derived from mutual self-interest, communitarians view society as derived from nurturance, caring attachment, and mutual interestedness. Men as communitarian creatures are defined by their attachments, including social relationships, ties to the community, and their place in history. No single identity can be separated from social relations or community affiliations.

MacIntyre phrases it like this:

> We all approach our own circumstances as bearers of a particular social identity. I am someone's son or daughter, someone else's cousin or uncle; I am a citizen of this or that city, a member of this or that guild or profession. I belong to this clan, that tribe, this nation. Hence what is good for me has to be good for one who inhabits these roles. As such, I inherit from the past of my family, my city, my tribe, my nation, a variety of debts, inheritances, rightful expectations and obligations. These constitute the given of my life. (From *After Virtue,* Notre Dame, Indiana: University of Notre Dame Press, 1981, p. 204.)

▶ *Writing Assignments*

1. Read the excerpt from Karl Marx "The Rights of Man Versus the Rights of the Citizen." Summarize Marx's position. Discuss the extent to which you agree with Marx's position.
2. Write a comparison between Marx's view of human nature and that of Locke.

NATURAL RIGHTS

Key Question: Are Men and Women Born with Natural Rights?

An important question in thinking about the nature of humanity is the extent to which all men and women are born with natural "rights," that is, the idea that human beings are entitled by birth to engage in certain types of behavior without restriction from government. Included in these "rights," which we often term "civil" rights, are freedom of speech, movement, choice of occupation, religion, association or assembly, and freedom from undeserved arrest or imprisonment. The concept of "natural" rights means that these rights are not provided or "allowed" by any government or social system, but are innate to our humanness. In fact, some people believe that these rights are unforfeitable—that is, a person cannot give them up.

A belief in natural rights is sometimes connected with a fundamental belief in human dignity, which suggests that there is something of particular worth in each human being and that it must be valued and respected. For people with religious beliefs, human dignity is derived from the relationship between humanity and God. For those less religiously inclined, human dignity is usually warranted because of our capacity to reason, which sets us apart from all other living things.

Of course, given the complexity of human societies, it is very difficult to find any pure examples of completely "natural" rights, since few live in a "pure" state of nature. Moreover, although many people might assert that all human beings have natural rights, their actual views are often influenced considerably by prejudice and self-interest. For example, a millionaire might feel it is his "right" to earn millions of dollars. The poor may have a different view.

Other critics of the idea of natural rights point out that the idea of natural rights presumes the notion of a universal human nature. Yet, they point out, human beings have no fixed nature since they are constantly in a state of evolution. They feel that the rights of human beings are always based on a particular historical or social context.

UTILITARIANISM

Key Question: Can the Idea of "Good" Be Thought of in Terms of Happiness?

One important justification of the concept of individual or natural rights may be found in the idea of **utilitarianism.** This view presupposes that individuals should be granted only those rights that will lead to the greatest happiness for the greatest number. John Stuart Mill's well-known defense of freedom of speech is an example of how utilitarian thinking can be used to justify the idea of individual rights. Mill states that any society will benefit from a widespread knowledge of the truth regarding social policies and maintains that the truth is more likely to be known in a society in which all individuals are allowed to express their own views, even if they are unpopular, than in one in which this right is denied.

EQUALITY AND EQUALITY OF OPPORTUNITY

Key Questions: Are All Human Beings Equal? Are Human Beings Entitled to Equal Opportunity?

The idea of natural rights presupposes the idea that all human beings are, by nature, equal. Locke maintained that we are by nature equally free and have claim to the same rights given by nature. Thomas Hobbes argued that all persons are equal primarily because even the weakest among us "has strength enough to kill the strongest of body, either by secret machination or by confederacy with others." Some egalitarians have also claimed an economic application of the notion of equality, claiming that there should be an equal distribution of material goods, wealth, or economic power.

The idea that all human beings are equal raises the question of **equal opportunity.** Some people feel that in order for all people to be equal, they must have access to the same possibilities for advancement as everyone else and should be able to compete for goods on an equal basis with everyone else. Yet, for all people to have equal opportunity is very difficult to ensure, since immediately from birth, there are numerous inequalities among people. Some are born weak, sick, or physically handicapped, while others are born strong and healthy. Some are born mentally retarded, while others are geniuses. Moreover, the social structure of society usually creates other forms of inequality of opportunity due to racial, sexual, or economic differences. During the past 25 years, there have been several attempts to ensure social equality of opportunity by means of government intervention. Yet, many of these efforts have been fraught with numerous complexities and difficulties as will be discussed in a later chapter.

THE UNIVERSAL DECLARATION OF HUMAN RIGHTS

The Universal Declaration of Human Rights defines quite clearly what a section of the international community regards as rights necessary to basic human dignity.

▶ *A Sequence of Assignments:* In a small group, read through the Universal Declaration of Human Rights, deciding if any definitions are vague or if any statements could be considered problematic. For example, Article 5 states that "no one shall be subjected to torture or to cruel, inhuman or degrading treatment or punishment." Yet, the idea of "cruel" or "degrading" might differ from person to person.

▶ *Writing Assignment:* Read an issue of the newspaper for your town or city. Note current controversies and choose one or two that particularly interest you. Then write an essay discussing the extent to which these controversies are concerned with presumed violations of human rights.

WRITING TO LEARN: A SEQUENCE OF ASSIGNMENTS

▶ *Exercises*

Read the article "What Rights Do We Have?" by R. Dworkin very carefully. Then answer the following questions:

1. Dworkin discusses two instances in which the government might restrain his freedom: it might prevent him from driving uptown on Lexington Avenue because that street is one-way going downtown, and it might prevent him from speaking his mind on political issues. What does he feel is the connection between these two examples? Why is one an in-

stance in which the right to liberty is infringed upon while the other is not?

2. Read the essay on Utilitarianism by John Stuart Mill. Summarize Mill's ideas.

3. Write an essay discussing Dworkin's dissatisfaction with Utilitarian political philosophy.

▶ ***Reading and Writing Assignment:*** Read the essay interviewing Robert Bellah, "Individualism Has Been Allowed to Run Rampant." Summarize Bellah's position. Then write an essay discussing the extent to which you agree with that position.

For Further Research: Robert Bellah has written a well-received book, *Habits of the Heart,* in which he discusses the effects of individualism in the United States. Read Bellah's book and develop an essay based on your reading. Some possible topics follow:

1. Choose one of Bellah's "representative" cases. To what extent do you feel it really is representative of a distinctly "American" mode of thinking?

2. Bellah discusses several characteristics that he feels are distinctly American. Discuss the extent to which you agree with him.

Calvin and Hobbes. Copyright 1987 Universal Press Syndicate. Reprinted with permission. All rights reserved.

Thinking Further About the Nature of Humanity: Look at the Calvin and Hobbes cartoon. What concept of human nature does it present?

Key Terms

Individualist View

Communitarian View

Equality

Equality of Opportunity

Natural Rights

Utilitarianism

The Lowest Animal

Mark Twain

I have been studying the traits and dispositions of the "lower animals" (so-called), and contrasting them with the traits and dispositions of man. I find the result humiliating to me. For it obliges me to renounce my allegiance to the Darwinian theory of the Ascent of Man from the Lower Animals; since it now seems plain to me that that theory ought to be vacated in favor of a new and truer one, this new and truer one to be named the Descent of Man from the Higher Animals.

In proceeding toward this pleasant conclusion I have not guessed or speculated or conjectured, but have used what is commonly called the scientific method. That is to say, I have subjected every postulate that presented itself to the crucial test of actual experiment, and have adopted it or rejected it according to the result. Thus I verified and established each step of my course in its turn before advancing to the next. These experiments were made in the London Zoological Gardens, and covered many months of painstaking and fatiguing work.

Before particularizing any of the experiments, I wish to state one or two things which seem to more properly belong in this place than further along. This in the interest of clearness. The massed experiments established to my satisfaction certain generalizations, to wit:

1. That the human race is of one distinct species. It exhibits slight variations—in color, stature, mental caliber, and so on—due to climate, environment, and so forth; but it is a species by itself, and not to be confounded with any other.
2. That the quadrupeds are a distinct family, also. This family exhibits varia-

tions—in color, size, food preferences and so on; but it is a family by itself.

3. That the other families—the birds, the fishes, the insects, the reptiles, etc.—are more or less distinct, also. They are in the procession. They are links in the chain which stretches down from the higher animals to man at the bottom.

Some of my experiments were quite curious. In the course of my reading I had come across a case where, many years ago, some hunters on our Great Plains organized a buffalo hunt for the entertainment of an English earl—that, and to provide some fresh meat for his larder. They had charming sport. They killed seventy-two of those great animals; and ate part of one of them and left the seventy-one to rot. In order to determine the difference between an anaconda and an earl—if any—I caused seven young calves to be turned into the anaconda's cage. The grateful reptile immediately crushed one of them and swallowed it, then lay back satisfied. It showed no further interest in the calves, and no disposition to harm them. I tried this experiment with other anacondas; always with the same result. The fact stood proven that the difference between an earl and an anaconda is that the earl is cruel and the anaconda isn't; and that the earl wantonly destroys what he has no use for, but the anaconda doesn't. This seemed to suggest that the anaconda was not descended from the earl. It also seemed to suggest that the earl was descended from the anaconda, and had lost a good deal in the transition.

I was aware that many men who have accumulated more millions of money than they can ever use have shown a rabid hunger for more, and have not scrupled to cheat the ignorant and the helpless out of their poor servings in order to partially appease that appetite. I furnished a hundred different kinds of wild and tame animals the opportunity to accumulate vast stores of food, but none of them would do it. The squirrels and bees and certain birds made accumulations, but stopped when they had gathered a winter's supply, and could not be persuaded to add to it either honestly or by chicane. In order to bolster up a tottering reputation the ant pretended to store up supplies, but I was not deceived. I know the ant. These experiments convinced me that there is this difference between man and the higher animals: he is avaricious and miserly, they are not.

In the course of my experiments I convinced myself that among the animals man is the only one that harbors insults and injuries, broods over them, waits till a chance offers, then takes revenge. The passion of revenge is unknown to the higher animals.

Roosters keep harems, but it is by consent of their concubines; therefore no wrong is done. Men keep harems, but it is by brute force, privileged by atrocious laws which the other sex is allowed no hand in making. In this matter man occupies a far lower place than the rooster.

Cats are loose in their morals, but not consciously so. Man, in his descent from the cat, has brought the cat's looseness with him but has left the unconsciousness behind—the saving grace which excuses the cat. The cat is innocent, man is not.

Indecency, vulgarity, obscenity—these are strictly confined to man; he invented them. Among the higher animals there is no trace of them. They hide nothing; they are not ashamed. Man, with his soiled mind, covers himself. He will not even enter a drawing room with his breast and back naked, so alive are he and his mates to indecent suggestion. Man is "The Animal that Laughs." But so does the monkey, as Mr. Darwin pointed out; and so does the Australian bird that is called the laughing jackass. No—Man is the Animal that Blushes. He is the only one that does it—or has occasion to.

At the head of this article we see how "three monks were burnt to death" a few days ago, and a prior "put to death with atrocious cruelty." Do we inquire into the details? No; or we should find out that the prior was subjected to unprintable mutilations. Man—when he is a North American Indian—gouges out his prisoner's eyes; when he is King John, with a nephew to render untroublesome, he uses a red-hot iron; when he is religious zealot dealing with heretics in the Middle Ages, he skins his captive alive and scatters salt on his back; in the first Richard's time he shuts up a multitude of Jew families in a tower and sets fire to it; in Columbus's time he captures a family of Spanish Jews and—but *that* is not printable; in our day in England a man is fined ten shillings for beating his mother nearly to death with a chair, and another man is fined forty shillings for having four pheasant eggs in his possession without being able to satisfactorily explain how he got them. Of all the animals, man is the only one that is cruel. He is the only one that inflicts pain for the pleasure of doing it. It is a trait that is not known to the higher animals. The cat plays with the frightened mouse; but she has this excuse, that she does not know that the mouse is suffering. The cat is moderate—unhumanly moderate: she only scares the mouse, she does not hurt it; she doesn't dig out its eyes, or tear off its skin, or drive splinters under its nails—man-fashion; when she is done playing with it she makes a sudden meal of it and puts it out of its trouble. Man is the Cruel Animal. He is alone in that distinction.

The higher animals engage in individual fights, but never in organized masses. Man is the only animal that deals in that atrocity of atrocities, War. He is the only one that gathers his brethren about him and goes forth in cold blood and with calm pulse to exterminate his kind. He is the only animal that for sordid wages will march out, as the Hessians did in our Revolution, and as the boyish Prince Napoleon did in the Zulu war, and help to slaughter strangers of his own species who have done him no harm and with whom he has no quarrel.

Man is the only animal that robs his helpless fellow of his country—takes possession of it and drives him out of it or destroys him. Man has done this in all ages. There is not an acre of ground on the globe that is in possession of its rightful owner, or that has not been taken away from owner after owner, cycle after cycle, by force and bloodshed.

Man is the only Slave. And he is the only animal who enslaves. He has always been a slave in one form or another, and has always held other slaves in bondage under him in one way or another. In our day he is always some man's slave for wages, and does that man's work; and this slave has other slaves under him for minor wages, and they do *his* work. The higher animals are the only ones who exclusively do their own work and provide their own living.

Man is the only Patriot. He sets himself apart in his own country, under his own flag, and sneers at the other nations, and keeps multitudinous uniformed assassins on hand at heavy expense to grab slices of other people's countries, and keep *them* from grabbing slices of *his*. And in the intervals between campaigns he washes the blood off his hands and works for "the universal brotherhood of man"—with his mouth.

Man is the Religious Animal. He is the only Religious Animal. He is the only animal that has the True Religion—several of them. He is the only animal that loves his neighbor as himself, and cuts his throat if his theology isn't straight. He has made a graveyard of the globe in trying his honest best to smooth his brother's path to happiness and heaven. He was at it in the time of the Caesars, he was at it in Mahomet's time, he was at it in the time of the Inquisition, he was at it in France a couple of centuries, he was at it in England in Mary's day, he has been at it ever since he first saw the light, he is at it today in Crete—as per the telegrams quoted above—he will be at it somewhere else tomorrow. The higher animals have no religion. And we are told that they are going to be left out, in the Hereafter. I wonder why? It seems questionable taste.

Man is the Reasoning Animal. Such is the claim. I think it is open to dispute. Indeed, my experiments have proven to me that he is the Unreasoning Animal. Note his history, as sketched above. It seems plain to me that whatever he is he is *not* a reasoning animal. His record is the fantastic record of a maniac. I consider that the strongest count against his intelligence is the fact that with that record back of him he blandly sets himself up as the head animal of the lot: whereas by his own standards he is the bottom one.

In truth, man is incurably foolish. Simple things which the other animals easily learn, he is incapable of learning. Among my experiments was this. In an hour I taught a cat and a dog to be friends. I put them in a cage. In another hour I taught them to be friends with a rabbit. In the course of two days I was able to add a fox, a goose, a squirrel and some doves. Finally a monkey. They lived together in peace; even affectionately.

Next, in another cage I confined an Irish Catholic from Tipperary, and as soon as he seemed tame I added a Scotch Presbyterian from Aberdeen. Next a Turk from Constantinople; a Greek Christian from Crete; an Armenian; a Methodist from the wilds of Arkansas; a Buddhist from China; a Brahman from Benares. Finally, a Salvation Army Colonel from Wapping. Then I stayed away two whole days. When I came back to note results, the cage of Higher Animals was all right, but in the other there was but a chaos of gory odds and ends of turbans and fezzes and plaids and bones and flesh—not a specimen left alive. These Reasoning Animals had disagreed on a theological detail and carried the matter to a Higher Court.

One is obliged to concede that in true loftiness of character, Man cannot claim to approach even the meanest of the Higher Animals. It is plain that he is constitutionally incapable of approaching that altitude; that he is constitutionally afflicted with a Defect which must make such approach forever impossible, for it is manifest that this defect is permanent in him, indestructible, ineradicable.

I find this Defect to be *the Moral Sense*. He is the only animal that has it. It is the secret of his degradation. It is the quality *which enables him to do wrong*. It has no other office. It is incapable of performing any other function. It could never have been intended to perform any other. Without it, man could do no wrong. He would rise at once to the level of the Higher Animals.

Since the Moral Sense has but the one office, the one capacity—to enable man to do wrong—it is plainly without value to him. It is as valueless to him as is disease. In fact, it manifestly is a disease. *Rabies* is bad, but it is not so bad as this disease. Rabies enables a man to do a thing which he could not do when in a healthy state: kill his neighbor with a poisonous bite. No one is the better man for having rabies. The Moral Sense enables a man to do wrong. It enables him to do wrong in a thousand ways. Rabies is an innocent disease, compared to the Moral Sense. No one, then, can be the better man for having the Moral Sense. What, now, do we find the Primal Curse to have been? Plainly what it was in the beginning: the infliction upon man of the Moral Sense; the ability to distinguish good from evil; and with it, necessarily, the ability to *do* evil; for there can be no evil act without the presence of consciousness of it in the doer of it.

And so I find that we have descended and degenerated, from some far ancestor—some microscopic atom wandering at its pleasure between the mighty horizons of a drop of water perchance—insect by insect, animal by animal, reptile by reptile, down the long highway of smirchless innocence, till we have reached the bottom stage of development—namable as the Human Being. Below us— nothing. Nothing but the Frenchman.

The State of Nature

John Locke

II. OF THE STATE OF NATURE

4. To understand political power right, and derive it from its original, we must consider what state all men are naturally in, and that is, a state of perfect freedom to order their actions and dispose of their possessions and persons, as they think fit, without the bounds of the law of nature; without asking leave, or depending upon the will of any other man.

A state also of equality, wherein all the power and jurisdiction is reciprocal, no one having more than another; there being nothing more evident, than that creatures of the same species and rank, promiscuously born to all the same advantages of nature, and the use of the same faculties, should also be equal one amongst another without subordination or subjection; unless the lord and master of them all should, by any manifest declaration of his will, set one above another, and confer on him, by an evident and clear appointment, an undoubted right to dominion and sovereignty.

6. But though this be a state of liberty, yet it is not a state of licence: though

man in that state have an uncontrolable liberty to dispose of his person or possessions, yet he has not liberty to destroy himself, or so much as any creature in his possession, but where some nobler use than its bare preservation calls for it. The state of nature has a law of nature to govern it, which obliges every one; and the reason, which is that law, teaches all mankind, who will but consult it, that being all equal and independent, no one ought to harm another in his life, health, liberty, or possessions: for men being all the workmanship of one omnipotent and infinitely wise Maker; all the servants of one sovereign master, sent into the world by his order, and about his business; they are his property, whose workmanship they are, made to last during his, not another's pleasure: and being furnished with like faculties, sharing all in one community of nature, there cannot be supposed any such subordination among us, that may authorize us to destroy another, as if we were made for one another's uses, as the inferior ranks of creatures are for ours. Every one, as he is bound to preserve himself, and not to quit his station wilfully, so by the like reason, when his own preservation comes not in competition, ought he, as much as he can, to preserve the rest of mankind, and may not, unless it be to do justice to an offender, take away or impair the life, or what tends to the preservation of life, the liberty, health, limb, or goods of another.

7. And that all men may be restrained from invading others rights, and from doing hurt to one another, and the law of nature be observed, which willeth the peace and preservation of all mankind, the execution of the law of nature is, in that state, put into every man's hands, whereby every one has a right to punish the transgressors of that law to such a degree as may hinder its violation: for the law of nature would, as all other laws that concern men in this world, be in vain, if there were nobody that in the state of nature had a power to execute that law, and thereby preserve the innocent and restrain offenders. And if any one in the state of nature may punish another for any evil he has done, every one may do so: for in that state of perfect equality, where naturally there is no superiority or jurisdiction of one over another, what any may do in prosecution of that law, every one must needs have a right to do.

8. And thus, in the state of nature, "one man comes by a power over another"; but yet no absolute or arbitrary power, to use a criminal, when he has got him in his hands, according to the passionate heats, or boundless extavagancy of his own will; but only to retribute to him, so far as calm reason and conscience dictate, what is proportionate to his transgression; which is so much as may serve for reparation and restraint: for these two are the only reasons, why one man may lawfully do harm to another, which is that we call punishment. In transgressing the law of nature, the offender declares himself to live by another rule than that of reason and common equity, which is that measure God has set to the actions of men, for their mutual security; and so he becomes dangerous to mankind, the tye, which is to secure them from injury and violence, being slighted and broken by him. Which being a trespass against the whole species, and the peace and safety of it, provided for by the law of nature; every man upon this score, by the right he hath to preserve mankind in general, may restrain, or, where it is necessary, destroy things noxious to them, and so may bring such evil on any one, who hath

transgressed that law, as may make him repent the doing of it, and thereby deter him, and by his example others, from doing the like mischief. And in this case, and upon this ground, every man hath a right to punish the offender, and be executioner of the law of nature. . . .

11. From these two distinct rights, the one of punishing the crime for restraint, and preventing the like offence, which right of punishing is in every body; the other of taking reparation, which belongs only to the injured party; comes it to pass that the magistrate, who by being magistrate hath the common right of punishing put into his hands, can often, where the public good demands not the execution of the law, remit the punishment of criminal offences by his own authority, but yet cannot remit the satisfaction due to any private man for the damage he has received. That, he who has suffered the damage has a right to demand in his own name, and he alone can remit: the damnified person has this power of appropriating to himself the goods or service of the offender, by right of self-preservation, as every man has a power to punish the crime, to prevent its being committed again, "by the right he has of preserving all mankind"; and doing all reasonable things he can in order to that end: and thus it is, that every man, in the state of nature, has a power to kill a murderer, both to deter others from doing the like injury, which no reparation can compensate, by the example of the punishment that attends it from every body; and also to secure men from the attempts of a criminal, who having renounced reason, the common rule and measure God hath given to mankind, hath, by the unjust violence and slaughter he hath committed upon one, declared war against all mankind; and therefore may be destroyed as a lion or a tiger, one of those wild savage beasts with whom men can have no society nor security. And upon this is grounded that great law of nature, "Whoso sheddeth man's blood, by man shall his blood be shed." And Cain was so fully convinced, that every one had a right to destroy such a criminal, that after the murder of his brother, he cries out, "Every one that findeth me, shall slay me"; so plain was it writ in the hearts of mankind.

12. By the same reason may a man in the state of nature punish the lesser breaches of that law. It will perhaps be demanded, with death? I answer, each transgression may be punished to that degree, and with so much severity, as will suffice to make it an ill bargain to the offender, give him cause to repent, and terrify others from doing the like. Every offence, that can be committed in the state of nature, may in the state of nature be also punished equally, and as far forth, as it may in a commonwealth: for though it would be beside my present purpose, to enter here into the particulars of the law of nature, or its measures of punishment, yet it is certain there is such a law, and that too as intelligible and plain to a rational creature, and a studier of that law, as the positive laws of commonwealth: nay, possibly plainer, as much as reason is easier to be understood, than the fancies and intricate contrivances of men, following contrary and hidden interests put into words; for so truly are a great part of the municipal laws of countries, which are only so far right, as they are founded on the law of nature, by which they are to be regulated and interpreted.

The Rights of Man Versus the Rights of the Citizen

Karl Marx

Article 6. "Liberty is the power which man has to do everything which does not harm the rights of others."

Liberty is, therefore, the right to do everything which does not harm others. The limits within which each individual can act without harming others are determined by law, just as the boundary between two fields is marked by a stake. It is a question of the liberty of man regarded as an isolated monad, withdrawn into himself. Why, according to Bauer, is the Jew not fitted to acquire the rights of man? "As long as he remains Jewish the limited nature which makes him a Jew must prevail over the human nature which should associate him, as a man, with other men; and it will isolate him from everyone who is not a Jew." But liberty as a right of man is not founded upon the relations between man and man, but rather upon the separation of man from man. It is the right of such separation. The right of the *circumscribed* individual, withdrawn into himself.

The practical application of the right of liberty is the right of private property. What constitutes the right of private property?

Article 16 (Constitution of 1793). "The right of *property* is that which belongs to every citizen of enjoying and disposing *as he will* of his goods and revenues, of the fruits of his work and industry."

The right of property is, therefore, the right to enjoy one's fortune and to dispose of it as one will; without regard for other men and independently of society. It is the right of self-interest. This individual liberty, and its application, form the basis of civil society. It leads every man to see in other men, not the *realization,* but rather the *limitation* of his own liberty. It declares above all the right "to enjoy and to dispose *as one will,* one's goods and revenues, the fruits of one's work and industry."

There remain the other rights of man, equality and security.

The term "equality" has here no political significance. It is only the equal right to liberty as defined above; namely that every man is equally regarded as a self-sufficient monad. The Constitution of 1795 defines the concept of liberty in this sense.

Article 5 (Constitution of 1795). "Equality consists in the fact that the law is the same for all, whether it protects or punishes."

And security?

Article 8 (Constitution of 1793). "Security consists in the protection afforded by society to each of its members for the preservation of his person, his rights, and his property."

Karl Marx, "The Rights of Man versus the Rights of the Citizen." Excerpted from "On the Jewish Question" in *Karl Marx: Early Writings*, translated and edited by T. B. Bottomore. © T. B. Bottomore, 1963. Reprinted by permission of McGraw-Hill Publishing Company.

Security is the supreme social concept of civil society; the concept of the police. The whole society exists only in order to guarantee for each of its members the preservation of his person, his rights and his property. It is in this sense that Hegel calls civil society "the state of need and of reason."

The concept of security is not enough to raise civil society above its egoism. Security is, rather, the *assurance* of its egoism.

None of the supposed rights of man, therefore, go beyond the egoistic man, man as he is, as a member of civil society; that is, an individual separated from the community, withdrawn into himself, wholly preoccupied with his private interest and acting in accordance with his private caprice. Man is far from being considered, in the rights of man, as a species-being; on the contrary, species-life itself—society—appears as a system which is external to the individual and as a limitation of his original independence. The only bond between men is natural necessity, need and private interest, the preservation of their property and their egoistic persons.

It is difficult enough to understand that a nation which has just begun to liberate itself, to tear down all the barriers between different sections of the people and to establish a political community, should solemnly proclaim (*Declaration* of 1791) the rights of the egoistic man, separated from his fellow men and from the community, and should renew this proclamation at a moment when only the most heroic devotion can save the nation (and is, therefore, urgently called for), and when the sacrifice of all the interests of civil society is in question and egoism should be punished as a crime. (*Declaration of the Rights of Man, etc.* 1793). The matter becomes still more incomprehensible when we observe that the political liberators reduce citizenship, the *political community,* to a mere *means* for preserving these so-called rights of man; and consequently, that the citizen is declared to be the servant of egoistic "man," that the sphere in which man functions as a species-being is degraded to a level below the sphere where he functions as a partial being, and finally that it is man as a bourgeois and not man as a citizen who is considered the *true* and *authentic* man.

"The end of every *political association* is the *preservation* of the natural and imprescriptible rights of man." (*Declaration of the Rights of Man, etc.* 1971, Article 2.) "Government is instituted in order to guarantee man's enjoyment of his natural and imprescriptible rights." (*Declaration, etc.* 1793, Article 1.) Thus, even in the period of its youthful enthusiasm, which is raised to fever pitch by the force of circumstances, political life declares itself to be only a *means,* whose end is the life of civil society. It is true that its revolutionary practice is in flagrant contradiction with its theory. While, for instance, security is declared to be one of the rights of man, the violation of the privacy of correspondence is openly considered. While the "unlimited freedom of the Press" (*Constitution* of 1793, Article 122), as a corollary of the right of individual liberty, is guaranteed, the freedom of the Press is completely destroyed, since "the freedom of the Press should not be permitted when it endangers public liberty."[3] This amounts to saying: the right to liberty ceases to be a right as soon as it comes into conflict with *political* life, whereas

3. Buchez et Roux, "Robespierre jeune," *Histoire parlementaire de la Révolution française,* Tome XXVIII, p. 159. [*Marx*]

in theory political life is no more than the guarantee of the rights of man—the rights of the individual man—and should, therefore, be suspended as soon as it comes into contradiction with its *end,* these rights of man. But practice is only the exception, while theory is the rule. Even if one decided to regard revolutionary practice as the correct expression of this relation, the problem would remain as to why it is that in the minds of political liberators the relation is inverted, so that the end appears as the means and the means as the end? This optical illusion of their consciousness would always remain a problem, though a psychological and theoretical one.

But the problem is easily solved.

Political emancipation is at the same time the *dissolution* of the old society, upon which the sovereign power, the alienated political life of the people, rests. Political revolution is a revolution of civil society. What was the nature of the old society? It can be characterized in one word: *feudalism.* The old civil society had a *directly political* character; that is, the elements of civil life such as property, the family, and types of occupation had been raised, in the form of lordship, caste and guilds, to elements of political life. They determined, in this form, the relation of the individual to the *state as a whole;* that is, his *political* situation, or in other words, his separation and exclusion from the other elements of society. For this organization of national life did not constitute property and labour as social elements; it rather succeeded in *separating* them from the body of the state, and made them *distinct* societies within society. Nevertheless, at least in the feudal sense, the vital functions and conditions of civil society remained political. They excluded the individual from the body of the state, and transformed the *particular* relation which existed between his corporation and the state into a general relation between the individual and social life, just as they transformed his specific civil activity and situation into a general activity and situation. As a result of this organization, the state as a whole and its consciousness, will and activity—the general political power—also necessarily appeared as the *private* affair of a ruler and his servants, separated from the people.

The political revolution which overthrew this power of the ruler, which made state affairs the affairs of the people, and the political state a matter of *general* concern, i.e. a real state, necessarily shattered everything—estates, corporations, guilds, privileges—which expressed the separation of the people from community life. The political revolution therefore *abolished* the *political character of civil society.* It dissolved civil society into its basic elements, on the one hand *individuals,* and on the other hand the *material and cultural elements* which formed the life experience and the civil situation of these individuals. It set free the political spirit which had, so to speak, been dissolved, fragmented and lost in the various culs-de-sac of feudal society; it reassembled these scattered fragments, liberated the political spirit from its connexion with civil life and made of it the community sphere, the *general* concern of the people, in principle independent of these particular elements of civil life. A *specific* activity and situation in life no longer had any but an individual significance. They no longer constituted the general relation between the individual and the state as a whole. Public affairs as such became the general affair of each individual, and political functions became general functions.

But the consummation of the idealism of the state was at the same time the consummation of the materialism of civil society. The bonds which had restrained the egoistic spirit of civil society were removed along with the political yoke. Political emancipation was at the same time an emancipation of civil society from politics and from even the *semblance* of a general content.

Feudal society was dissolved into its basic element, *man;* but into *egoistic* man who was its real foundation.

Man in this aspect, the member of civil society, is now the foundation and presupposition of the *political* state. He is recognized as such in the rights of man.

But the liberty of egoistic man, and the recognition of this liberty, is rather the recognition of the *frenzied* movement of the cultural and material elements which form the content of his life.

Thus man was not liberated from religion; he received religious liberty. He was not liberated from property; he received the liberty to own property. He was not liberated from the egoism of business; he received the liberty to engage in business.

The *formation of the political state,* and the dissolution of civil society into independent *individuals* whose relations are regulated by *law,* as the relations between men in the corporations and guilds were regulated by *privilege,* are accomplished by *one and the same act.* Man as a member of civil society—*non-political* man—necessarily appears as the *natural* man. The rights of man appear as natural rights because *conscious* activity is concentrated upon political *action.* *Egoistic* man is the *passive, given* result of the dissolution of society, an object of *direct apprehension* and consequently a *natural* object. The *political revolution* dissolves civil society into its elements without *revolutionizing* these elements themselves or subjecting them to criticism. This revolution regards civil society, the sphere of human needs, labour, private interests and civil law, as the *basis of its own existence,* as a self-subsistent *precondition,* and thus as its *natural basis.* Finally, man as a member of civil society is identified with *authentic man,* man as distinct from citizen, because he is man in his sensuous, individual and *immediate* existence, whereas *political* man is only abstract, artificial man, man as an *allegorical, moral* person. Thus man as he really is, is seen only in the form of *egoistic* man, and man in his *true* nature only in the form of the *abstract citizen.*

The abstract notion of political man is well formulated by Rousseau: "Whoever dares undertake to establish a people's institutions must feel himself capable of *changing,* as it were, *human nature* itself, of *transforming* each individual who, in isolation, is a complete but solitary whole, into a *part* of something greater than himself, from which in a sense, he derives his life and his being; [of changing man's nature in order to strengthen it;] of substituting a limited and moral existence for the physical and independent life [with which all of us are endowed by nature]. His task, in short, is to take from *a man his own powers,* and to give him in exchange alien powers which he can only employ with the help of other men."[4]

Every emancipation is a *restoration* of the human world and of human relationships to *man himself.*

---

4. J. J. Rousseau, *Du contrat social,* Book II. Chapter VII, "The Legislator." Marx quoted this passage in French, and added the emphases; he omitted the portions enclosed in square brackets.

Political emancipation is a reduction of man, on the one hand to a member of civil society, an *independent* and *egoistic* individual, and on the other hand, to a *citizen,* to a moral person.

Human emancipation will only be complete when the real, individual man has absorbed into himself the abstract citizen: when as an individual man, in his everyday life, in his work, and in his relationships, he has become a *species-being;* and when he has recognized and organized his own powers (*forces propres*) as *social* powers so that he no longer separates this social power from himself as *political* power.

Universal Declaration of Human Rights

Adopted and Proclaimed by General Assembly Resolution 217 A (III) of 10 December 1948

Preamble

Whereas recognition of the inherent dignity and of the equal and inalienable rights of all members of the human family is the foundation of freedom, justice and peace in the world.

Whereas disregard and contempt for human rights have resulted in barbarous acts which have outraged the conscience of mankind, and the advent of a world in which human beings shall enjoy freedom of speech and belief and freedom from fear and want has been proclaimed as the highest aspiration of the common people,

Whereas it is essential, if man is not to be compelled to have recourse, as a last resort, to rebellion against tyranny and oppression, that human rights should be protected by the rule of law,

Whereas it is essential to promote the development of friendly relations between nations,

Whereas the peoples of the United Nations have in the Charter reaffirmed their faith in fundamental human rights, in the dignity and worth of the human person and in the equal rights of men and women and have determined to promote social progress and better standards of life in larger freedom.

Whereas Member States have pledged themselves to achieve, in co-operation with the United Nations, the promotion of universal respect for and observance of human rights and fundamental freedoms.

Whereas a common understanding of these rights and freedoms is of the greatest importance for the full realization of this pledge,

Universal Declaration of Human Rights. Text taken from *A Compilation of International Instructions of the United Nations,* A United Nations publication.

Now, Therefore,

The General Assembly

Proclaims this Universal Declaration of Human Rights as a common standard of achievement for all peoples and all nations, to the end that every individual and every organ of society, keeping this Declaration constantly in mind, shall strive by teaching and education to promote respect for these rights and freedoms and by progressive measures, national and international to secure their universal and effective recognition and observance, both among the peoples of Member States themselves and among the peoples of territories under their jurisdiction.

Article 1

All human beings are born free and equal in dignity and rights. They are endowed with reason and conscience and should act towards one another in a spirit of brotherhood.

Article 2

Everyone is entitled to all the rights and freedoms set forth in this Declaration, without distinction of any kind, such as race, colour, sex, language, religion, political or other opinion, national or social origin, property, birth or other status.

Furthermore, no distinction shall be made on the basis of the political, jurisdictional or international status of the country or territory to which a person belongs, whether it be independent, trust, non-self-governing or under any other limitation of sovereignty.

Article 3

Everyone has the right to life, liberty and the security of person.

Article 4

No one shall be held in slavery or servitude; slavery and the slave trade shall be prohibited in all their forms.

Article 5

No one shall be subjected to torture or to cruel, inhuman or degrading treatment or punishment.

Article 6

Everyone has the right to recognition everywhere as a person before the law.

Article 7

All are equal before the law are entitled without any discrimination to equal protection of the law. All are entitled to equal protection against any discrimination in violation of this Declaration and against any incitement to such discrimination.

Article 8

Everyone has the right to an effective remedy by the competent national tribunals for acts violating the fundamental rights granted him by the constitution or by law.

Article 9

No one shall be subjected to arbitrary arrest, detention or exile.

Article 10

Everyone is entitled in full equality to a fair and public hearing by an independent and impartial tribunal, in the determination of his rights and obligations and of any criminal charge against him.

Article 11

1. Everyone charged with a penal offence has the right to be presumed innocent until proved guilty according to law in a public trial at which he has had all the guarantees necessary for his defence.
2. No one shall be held guilty of any penal offence on account of any act or omission which did not constitute a penal offence, under national or international law, at the time when it was committed. Nor shall a heavier penalty be imposed than the one that was applicable at the time the penal offence was committed.

Article 12

No one shall be subjected to arbitrary interference with his privacy, family, home or correspondence, nor to attacks upon his honour and reputation. Everyone has the right to the protection of the law against such interference or attacks.

Article 13

1. Everyone has the right to freedom of movement and residence within the borders of each State.
2. Everyone has the right to leave any country, including his own, and to return to his country.

Article 14

1. Everyone has the right to seek and to enjoy in other countries asylum from persecution.

2. This right may not be invoked in the case of prosecutions genuinely arising from non-political crimes or from acts contrary to the purposes and principles of the United Nations.

Article 15

1. Everyone has the right to a nationality.

2. No one shall be arbitrarily deprived of his nationality nor denied the right to change his nationality.

Article 16

1. Men and women of full age, without any limitation due to race, nationality or religion, have the right to marry and to found a family. They are entitled to equal rights as to marriage, during marriage and at its dissolution.

2. Marriage shall be entered into only with the free and full consent of the intending spouses.

3. The family is the natural and fundamental group unit of society and is entitled to protection by society and the State.

Article 17

1. Everyone has the right to own property alone as well as in association with others.

2. No one shall be arbitrarily deprived of his property.

Article 18

Everyone has the right to freedom of thought, conscience and religion; this right includes freedom to change his religion or belief, and freedom, either alone or in community with others and in public or private, to manifest his religion or belief in teaching, practice, worship and observance.

Article 19

Everyone has the right to freedom of opinion and expression; this right includes freedom to hold opinions without interference and to seek, receive and impart information and ideas through any media and regardless of frontiers.

Article 20

1. Everyone has the right to freedom of peaceful assembly and association.

2. No one may be compelled to belong to an association.

Article 21

1. Everyone has the right to take part in the government of his country, directly or through freely chosen representatives.

2. Everyone has the right of equal access to public service in his country.

3. The will of the people shall be the basis of the authority of government; this will shall be expressed in periodic and genuine elections which shall be by universal and equal suffrage and shall be held by secret vote or by equivalent free voting procedures.

Article 22

Everyone, as a member of society, has the right to social security and is entitled to realization, through national effort and international co-operation and in accordance with the organization and resources of each State, of the economic, social and cultural rights indispensable for his dignity and the free development of his personality.

Article 23

1. Everyone has the right to work, to free choice of employment, to just and favourable conditions of work and to protection against unemployment.

2. Everyone, without any discrimination, has the right to equal pay for equal work.

3. Everyone who works has the right to just and favourable remuneration ensuring for himself and his family an existence worthy of human dignity, and supplemented, if necessary, by other means of social protection.

4. Everyone has the right to form and to join trade unions for the protection of his interests.

Article 24

Everyone has the right to rest and leisure, including reasonable limitation of working hours and periodic holidays with pay.

Article 25

1. Everyone has the right to a standard of living adequate for the health and well-being of himself and of his family, including food, clothing, housing and medical care and necessary social services, and the right to security in the event of unemployment, sickness, disability, widowhood, old age or other lack of livelihood in circumstances beyond his control.

2. Motherhood and childhood are entitled to special care and assistance. All children, whether born in or out of wedlock, shall enjoy the same social protection.

Article 26

1. Everyone has the right to education. Education shall be free, at least in the elementary and fundamental stages. Elementary education shall be compulsory. Technical and professional education shall be made generally available and higher education shall be equally accessible to all on the basis of merit.

2. Education shall be directed to the full development of the human personality and to the strengthening of respect for human rights and fundamental freedoms. It shall promote understanding, tolerance and friendship among all nations, racial or religious groups, and shall further the activities of the United Nations for the maintenance of peace.

3. Parents have a prior right to choose the kind of education that shall be given to their children.

Article 27

1. Everyone has the right freely to participate in the cultural life of the community, to enjoy the arts and to share in scientific advancement and its benefits.

2. Everyone has the right to the protection of the moral and material interests resulting from any scientific, literary or artistic production of which he is the author.

Article 28

Everyone is entitled to a social and international order in which the rights and freedoms set forth in this Declaration can be fully realized.

Article 29

1. Everyone has duties to the community in which alone the free and full development of his personality is possible.

2. In the exercise of his rights and freedoms, everyone shall be subject only to such limitations as are detemined by law solely for the purpose of securing due recognition and respect for the rights and freedoms of others and of meeting the just requirements of morality, public order and the general welfare in a democratic society.

3. These rights and freedoms may in no case be exercised contrary to the purposes and principles of the United Nations.

Article 30

Nothing in this Declaration may be interpreted as implying for any State, group or person any right to engage in any activity or to perform any act aimed at the destruction of any of the rights and freedoms set forth herein.

What Rights Do We Have?

R. M. Dworkin

I. NO RIGHT TO LIBERTY

Do we have a right to liberty?[1] Thomas Jefferson thought so, and since his day the right to liberty has received more play than the competing rights he mentioned to life and the pursuit of happiness. Liberty gave its name to the most influential political movement of the last century, and many of those who now despise liberals do so on the ground that they are not sufficiently libertarian. Of course, almost everyone concedes that the right to liberty is not the only political right, and that therefore claims to freedom must be limited, for example, by restraints that protect the security or property of others. Nevertheless the consensus in favor of some right to liberty is a vast one, though it is, as I shall argue in this chapter, misguided.

The right to liberty is popular all over this political spectrum. The rhetoric of liberty fuels every radical movement from international wars of liberation to campaigns for sexual freedom and women's liberation. But liberty has been even more prominent in conservative service. Even the mild social reorganizations of the anti-trust and unionization movements, and of the early New Deal, were opposed on the grounds that they infringed the right to liberty, and just now efforts to achieve some racial justice in America through techniques like the busing of black and white schoolchildren, and social justice in Britain through constraints in private education are bitterly opposed on that ground.

It has become common, indeed, to describe the great social issues of domestic politics, and in particular the racial issue, as presenting a conflict between the demands of liberty and equality. It may be, it is said, that the poor and the black and the uneducated and the unskilled have an abstract right to equality, but the prosperous and the whites and the educated and the able have a right to liberty as well and any efforts at social reorganization in aid of the first set of rights must reckon with and respect the second. Everyone except extremists recognizes, therefore, the need to compromise between equality and liberty. Every piece of important social legislation, from tax policy to integration plans, is shaped by the supposed tension between these two goals.

I have this supposed conflict between equality and liberty in mind when I ask whether we have a *right* to liberty, as Jefferson and everyone else has supposed. That is a crucial question. If freedom to choose one's schools, or employees, or neighborhood is simply something that we all want, like air conditioning or lobsters, then we are not entitled to hang on to these freedoms in the face of what we concede to be the rights of others to an equal share of respect and

---

[1] I use 'liberty' in this essay in the sense Isaiah Berlin called 'negative'.

resources. But if we can say, not simply that we want these freedoms, but that we are ourselves entitled to them, then we have established at least a basis for demanding a compromise.

There is now a movement, for example, in favor of a proposed amendment to the constitution of the United States that would guarantee every school child the legal right to attend a 'neighborhood school' and thus outlaw busing. The suggestion, that neighborhood schools somehow rank with jury trials as constitutional values, would seem silly but for the sense many Americans have that forcing school children into buses is somehow as much an interference with the fundamental right to liberty as segregated schooling was an insult to equality. But that seems to me absurd; indeed it seems to me absurd to suppose that men and women have any general right to liberty at all, at least as liberty has traditionally been conceived by its champions.

I have in mind the traditional definition of liberty as the absence of constraints placed by a government upon what a man might do if he wants to. Isaiah Berlin, in the most famous modern essay on liberty, put the matter this way: 'The sense of freedom, in which I use this term, entails not simply the absence of frustration but the absence of obstacles to possible choices and activities—absence of obstructions on roads along which a man can decide to walk.' This conception of liberty as license is neutral amongst the various activities a man might pursue, the various roads he might wish to walk. It diminishes a man's liberty when we prevent him from talking or making love as he wishes, but it also diminishes his liberty when we prevent him from murdering or defaming others. These latter constraints may be justifiable, but only because they are compromises necessary to protect the liberty or security of others, and not because they do not, in themselves, infringe the independent value of liberty. Bentham said that any law whatsoever is an 'infraction' of liberty, and though some such infractions might be necessary, it is obscurantist to pretend that they are not infractions after all. In this neutral, all embracing sense of liberty as license, liberty and equality are plainly in competition. Laws are needed to protect equality, and laws are inevitably compromises of liberty.

Liberals like Berlin are content with this neutral sense of liberty, because it seems to encourage clear thinking. It allows us to identify just what is lost, though perhaps unavoidably, when men accept constraints on their actions for some other goal or value. It would be an intolerable muddle, on this view, to use the concept of liberty or freedom in such a way that we counted a loss of freedom only when men were prevented from doing something that we thought they ought to do. It would allow totalitarian governments to masquerade as liberal, simply by arguing that they prevent men from doing only what is wrong. Worse, it would obscure the most distinctive point of the liberal tradition, which is that interfering with a man's free choice to do what he might want to do is in and of itself an insult to humanity, a wrong that may be justified but can never be wiped away by competing considerations. For a true liberal, any constraint upon freedom is something that a decent government must regret, and keep to the minimum necessary to accommodate the other rights of its constituents.

In spite of this tradition, however, the neutral sense of liberty seems to me to have caused more confusion than it has cured, particularly when it is joined to the popular and inspiring idea that men and women have a right to liberty. For we can maintain that idea only by so watering down the idea of a right that the right to liberty is something hardly worth having at all.

The term 'right' is used in politics and philosophy in many different senses, some of which I have tried to disentangle elsewhere.[1] In order sensibly to ask whether we have a right to liberty in the neutral sense, we must fix on some one meaning of 'right'. It would not be difficult to find a sense of that term in which we could say with some confidence that men have a right to liberty. We might say, for example, that someone has a right to liberty if it is in his interest to have liberty, that is, if he either wants it or if it would be good for him to have it. In this sense, I would be prepared to concede that citizens have a right to liberty. But in this sense I would also have to concede that they have a right, at least generally, to vanilla ice cream. My concession about liberty, moreover, would have very little value in political debate. I should want to claim, for example, that people have a right to equality in a much stronger sense, that they do not simply want equality but that they are entitled to it, and I would therefore not recognize the claim that some men and women want liberty as requiring any compromise in the efforts that I believe are necessary to give other men and women the equality to which they are entitled.

If the right to liberty is to play the role cut out for it in political debate, therefore, it must be a right in a much stronger sense. In Chapter 7 I defined a strong sense of right that seems to me to capture the claims men mean to make when they appeal to political and moral rights. I do not propose to repeat my analysis here, but only to summarize it in this way. A successful claim of right, in the strong sense I described, has this consequence. If someone has a right to something, then it is wrong for the government to deny it to him even though it would be in the general interest to do so. This sense of a right (which might be called the anti-utilitarian concept of a right) seems to me very close to the sense of right principally used in political and legal writing and argument in recent years. It marks the distinctive concept of an individual right against the State which is the heart, for example, of constitutional theory in the United States.

I do not think that the right to liberty would come to very much, or have much power in political argument, if it relied on any sense of the right any weaker than that. If we settle on this concept of a right, however, then it seems plain that there exists no general right to liberty as such. I have no political right to drive up Lexington Avenue. If the government chooses to make Lexington Avenue one-way down town, it is a sufficient justification that this would be in the general interest, and it would be ridiculous for me to argue that for some reason it would nevertheless be wrong. The vast bulk of the laws which diminish my liberty are justified on utilitarian grounds, as being in the general interest or for the general welfare; if, as Bentham supposes, each of these laws diminishes my liberty, they nevertheless do not take away from me any thing that I have a right to have. It will not do, in the one-way street case, to say that although I have a right to drive

[1] See Chapter 7.

up Lexington Avenue, nevertheless the government for special reasons is justified in overriding that right. That seems silly because the government needs no special justification—but only *a* justification—for this sort of legislation. So I can have a political right to liberty, such that every act of constraint diminishes or infringes that right, only in such a weak sense of right that the so called right to liberty is not competitive with strong rights, like the right to equality, at all. In any strong sense of right, which would be competitive with the right to equality, there exists no general right to liberty at all.

It may now be said that I have misunderstood the claim that there is a right to liberty. It does not mean to argue, it will be said, that there is a right to all liberty, but simply to important or basic liberties. Every law is, as Bentham said, an infraction of liberty, but we have a right to be protected against only fundamental or serious infractions. If the constraint on liberty is serious or severe enough, then it is indeed true that the government is not entitled to impose that constraint simply because that would be in the general interest; the government is not entitled to constrain liberty of speech, for example, whenever it thinks that would improve the general welfare. So there is, after all, a general right to liberty as such, provided that that right is restricted to important liberties or serious deprivations. This qualification does not affect the political arguments I described earlier, it will be said, because the rights to liberty that stand in the way of full equality are rights to basic liberties like, for example, the right to attend a school of one's choice.

But this qualification raises an issue of great importance for liberal theory, which those who argue for a right to liberty do not face. What does it mean to say that the right to liberty is limited to basic liberties, or that it offers protection only against serious infractions of liberty? That claim might be spelled out in two different ways, with very different theoretical and practical consequences. Let us suppose two cases in which government constrains a citizen from doing what he might want to do: the government prevents him from speaking his mind on political issues; from driving his car uptown on Lexington Avenue. What is the connection between these two cases, and the difference between them, such that though they are both cases in which a citizen is constrained and deprived of liberty, his right to liberty is infringed only in the first, and not in the second?

On the first of the two theories we might consider, the citizen is deprived of the same commodity, namely liberty, in both cases, but the difference is that in the first case the amount of that commodity taken away from him is, for some reason, either greater in amount or greater in its impact than in the second. But that seems bizarre. It is very difficult to think of liberty as a commodity. If we do try to give liberty some operational sense, such that we can measure the relative diminution of liberty occasioned by different sorts of laws or constraints, then the result is unlikely to match our intuitive sense of what are basic liberties and what are not. Suppose, for example, we measure a diminution in liberty by calculating the extent of frustration that it induces. We shall then have to face the fact that laws against theft, and even traffic laws, impose constraints that are felt more keenly by most men than constraints on political speech would be. We might take a different tack, and measure the degree of loss of liberty by the impact that a particular constraint has on future choices. But we should then have to admit that the ordinary criminal code reduces choice for most men more than laws which forbid fringe political activity. So the first theory—that the difference between cases covered and those not covered by our supposed right to liberty is a matter of degree—must fail.

The second theory argues that the difference between the two cases has to do, not with the degree of liberty involved, but with the special character of the liberty involved in the case covered by the right. On this theory, the offense involved in a law that limits free speech is of a different character, and not just different in degree, from a law that prevents a man from driving up Lexington Avenue. That sounds plausible, though as we shall see it is not easy to state what this difference in character comes to, or why it argues for a right in some cases though not in others. My present point, however, is that if the distinction between basic liberties and other liberties is defended in this way, then the notion of a general right to liberty as such has been entirely abandoned. If we have a right to basic liberties not because they are cases in which the commodity of liberty is somehow especially at stake, but because an assault on basic liberties injures us or demeans us in some way that goes beyond its impact on liberty, then what we have a right to is not liberty at all, but to the values or interests or standing that this particular constraint defeats.

This is not simply a question of terminology. The idea of a right to liberty is a misconceived concept that does a dis-service to political thought in at least two ways. First, the idea creates a false sense of a necessary conflict between liberty and other values when social regulation, like the busing program, is proposed. Second, the idea provides too easy an answer to the question of why we regard certain kinds of restraints, like the restraint on free speech or the exercise of religion, as especially unjust. The idea of a right to liberty allows us to say that these constraints are unjust because they have a special impact on liberty as such. Once we recognize that this answer is spurious, then we shall have to face the difficult question of what is indeed at stake in these cases.

I should like to turn at once to that question. If there is no general right to liberty, then why do citizens in a democracy have rights to any specific kind of liberty, like freedom of speech or religion or political activity? It is no answer to say that if individuals have these rights, then the community will be better off in the long run as a whole. This idea—that individual rights may lead to overall utility—may or may not be true, but it is irrelevant to the defence of rights as such, because when we say that someone has a right to speak his mind freely, in the relevant political sense, we mean that he is entitled to do so even if this would not be in the general interest. If we want to defend individual rights in the sense in which we claim them, then we must try to discover something beyond utility that argues for these rights.

I mentioned one possibility earlier. We might be able to make out a case that individuals suffer some special damage when the traditional rights are invaded. On this argument, there is something about the liberty to speak out on political issues such that if that liberty is denied the individual suffers a special kind of damage which makes it wrong to inflict that damage upon him even though the community as a whole would benefit. This line of argument will appeal to those who themselves would feel special deprivation at the loss of their political and civil liberties, but it is nevertheless a difficult argument to pursue for two reasons.

First, there are a great many men and women and they undoubtedly form the majority even in democracies like Britain and the United States, who do not exercise political liberties that they have, and who would not count the loss of these liberties as especially grievous. Second, we lack a psychological theory which would justify and explain the idea that the loss of civil liberties, or any particular liberties, involves inevitable or even likely psychological damage. On the contrary, there is now a lively tradition in psychology, led by psychologists like Ronald Laing, who argue that a good deal of mental instability in modern societies may be traced to the demand for too much liberty rather than too little. In their account, the need to choose, which follows from liberty, is an unnecessary source of destructive tension. These theories are not necessarily persuasive, but until we can be confident that they are wrong, we cannot assume that psychology demonstrates the opposite, however appealing that might be on political grounds.

If we want to argue for a right to certain liberties, therefore, we must find another ground. We must argue on grounds of political morality that it is wrong to deprive individuals of these liberties, for some reason, apart from direct psychological damage, in spite of the fact that the common interest would be served by doing so. I put the matter this vaguely because there is no reason to assume, in advance, that only one kind of reason would support that moral position. It might be that a just society would recognize a variety of individual rights, some grounded on very different sorts of moral considerations from others. In what remains of this chapter I shall try to describe only one possible ground for rights. It does not follow that men and women in civil society have only the rights that the argument I shall make would support; but it does follow that they have at least these rights, and that is important enough.

2. THE RIGHT TO LIBERTIES

The central concept of my argument will be the concept not of liberty but of equality. I presume that we all accept the following postulates of political morality. Government must treat those whom it governs with concern, that is, as human beings who are capable of suffering and frustration, and with respect, that is, as human beings who are capable of forming and acting on intelligent conceptions of how their lives should be lived. Government must not only treat people with concern and respect, but with equal concern and respect. It must not distribute goods or opportunities unequally on the ground that some citizens are entitled to more because they are worthy of more concern. It must not constrain liberty on the ground that one citizen's conception of the good life of one group is nobler or superior to another's. These postulates, taken together, state what might be called the liberal conception of equality; but it is a conception of equality, not of liberty as license, that they state.

The sovereign question of political theory, within a state supposed to be governed by the liberal conception of equality, is the question of what inequalities in goods, opportunities and liberties are permitted in such a state, and why. The beginning of an answer lies in the following distinction. Citizens governed by the liberal conception of equality each have a right to equal concern and respect. But there are two different rights that might be comprehended by that abstract right. The first is the right to equal treatment, that is, to the same distribution of goods or opportunities as anyone else has or is given. The Supreme Court, in the Reapportionment Cases, held that citizens have a right to equal treatment in the distribution of voting power; it held that one man must be given one vote in spite of the fact that a different distribution of votes might in fact work for the general benefit. The second is the right to treatment as an equal. This is the right, not to an equal distribution of some good or opportunity, but the right to equal concern and respect in the political decision about how these goods and opportunities are to be distributed. Suppose the question is raised whether an economic policy that injures long-term bondholders is in the general interest. Those who will be injured have a right that their prospective loss be taken into account in deciding whether the general interest is served by the policy. They may not simply be ignored in that calculation. But when their interest is taken into account it may nevertheless be outweighed by the interests of others who will gain from the policy, and in that case their right to equal concern and respect, so defined, would provide no objection. In the case of economic policy, therefore, we might wish to say that those who will be injured if inflation is permitted have a right to treatment as equals in the decision whether that policy would serve the general interest, but no right to equal treatment that would outlaw the policy even if it passed that test.

I propose that the right to treatment as an equal must be taken to be fundamental under the liberal conception of equality, and that the more restrictive right to equal treatment holds only in those special circumstances in which, for some special reason, it follows from the more fundamental right, as perhaps it does in the special circumstance of the Reapportionment Cases. I also propose that individual rights to distinct liberties must be recognized only when the fundamental right to treatment as an equal can be shown to require these rights. If this is correct, then the right to distinct liberties does not conflict with any supposed competing right to equality, but on the contrary follows from a conception of equality conceded to be more fundamental.

I must now show, however, how the familiar rights to distinct liberties—those established, for example, in the United States constitution—might be thought to be required by that fundamental conception of equality. I shall try to do this, for present purposes, only by providing a skeleton of the more elaborate argument that would have to be made to defend any particular liberty on this basis, and then show why it would be plausible to expect that the more familiar political and civil liberties would be supported by such an argument if it were in fact made.

A government that respects the liberal conception of equality may properly constrain liberty only on certain very limited types of justification. I shall adopt, for purposes of making this point, the following crude typology of political justifications. There are, first, arguments of principle, which support a particular constraint on liberty on the argument that the constraint is required to protect the distinct right of some individuals who will be injured by the exercise of the liberty. There are, second, arguments of policy, which support constraints on the different ground that such constraints are required to reach some overall political goal, that is, to realize some state of affairs in which the community as a whole, and not just certain individuals, are better off by virtue of the constraint. Arguments of policy might be further subdivided in this way. Utilitarian arguments of policy argue that the community as a whole will be better off because (to put the point roughly) more of its citizens will have more of what they want overall, even though some of them will have less. Ideal arguments of policy, on the other hand, argue that the community will be better off, not because more of its members will have more of what they want, but because the community will be in some way closer to an ideal community, whether its members desire the improvement in question or not.

The liberal conception of equality sharply limits the extent to which ideal arguments of policy may be used to justify any constraint on liberty. Such arguments cannot be used if the idea in question is itself controversial within the community. Constraints cannot be defended, for example, directly on the ground that they contribute to a culturally sophisticated community, whether the community wants the sophistication or not, because that argument would violate the canon of the liberal conception of equality that prohibits a government from relying on the claim that certain forms of life are inherently more valuable than others.

Utilitarian arguments of policy, however, would seem secure from that objection. They do not suppose that any form of life is inherently more valuable than any other, but instead base their claim, that constraints on liberty are necessary to advance some collective goal of the community, just on the fact that that goal happens to be desired more widely or more deeply than any other. Utilitarian arguments of policy, therefore, seem not to oppose but on the contrary to embody the fundamental right of equal concern and respect, because they treat the wishes of each member of the community on a par with the wishes of any other, with no bonus or discount reflecting the view that that member is more or less worthy of concern, or his views more or less worthy of respect, than any other.

This appearance of egalitarianism has, I think, been the principal source of the great appeal that utilitarianism has had, as a general political philosophy, over the last century. In Chapter 9, however, I pointed out that the egalitarian character of a utilitarian argument is often an illusion. I will not repeat, but only summarize, my argument here.

Utilitarian arguments fix on the fact that a particular constraint on liberty will make more people happier, or satisfy more of their preferences, depending upon whether psychological or preference utilitarianism is in play. But people's overall preference for one policy rather than another may be seen to include, on further analysis, both preferences that are *personal,* because they state a preference for the assignment of one set of goods or opportunities to him and preferences that are *external,* because they state a preference for one assignment of goods or opportunities to others. But a utilitarian argument that assigns critical weight to the external preferences of members of the community will not be egalitarian in the sense under consideration. It will not respect the right of everyone to be treated with equal concern and respect.

Suppose, for example, that a number of individuals in the community holds racist rather than utilitarian political theories. They believe, not that each man is to count for one and no one for more than one in the distribution of goods, but rather that a black man is to count for less and a white man therefore to count for more than one. That is an external preference, but it is nevertheless a genuine preference for one policy rather than another, the satisfaction of which will bring pleasure. Nevertheless, if this preference or pleasure is given the normal weight in a utilitarian calculation, and blacks suffer accordingly, then their own assignment of goods and opportunities will depend, not simply on the competition among personal preferences that abstract statements of utilitarianism suggest, but precisely on the fact that they are thought less worthy of concern and respect than others are.

Suppose, to take a different case, that many members of the community disapprove on moral grounds of homosexuality, or contraception, or pornography, or expressions of adherence to the Communist party. They prefer not only that they themselves do not indulge in these activities, but that no one else does so either, and they believe that a community that permits rather than prohibits these acts is inherently a worse community. These are external preferences, but, once again, they are no less genuine, nor less a source of pleasure when satisfied and displeasure when ignored, than purely personal preferences. Once again, however, if these external preferences are counted, so as to justify a constraint on liberty, then those constrained suffer, not simply because their personal preferences have lost in a competition for scarce resources with the personal preferences of others, but precisely because their conception of a proper or desirable form of life is despised by others.

These arguments justify the following important conclusion. If utilitarian arguments of policy are to be used to justify constraints on liberty, then care must be taken to insure that the utilitarian calculations on which the argument is based fix only on personal and ignore external preferences. That is an important conclusion for political theory because it shows, for example, why the arguments of John Stuart Mill in *On Liberty* are not counter-utilitarian but, on the contrary, arguments in service of the only defensible form of utilitarianism.

Important as that conclusion is at the level of political philosophy, however, it is in itself of limited practical significance, because it will be impossible to devise political procedures that will accurately discriminate between personal and external preferences. Representative democracy is widely thought to be the institutional structure most suited, in a complex and diverse society, to the identification and achievement of utilitarian policies. It works imperfectly at this, for the familiar reason that majoritarianism cannot sufficiently take account of the intensity, as distinct from the number, of particular preferences, and because techniques of political persuasion, backed by money, may corrupt the accuracy with which votes represent the genuine preferences of those who have voted. Nevertheless democracy seems to enforce utilitarianism more satisfactorily, in spite of these imperfections, than any alternative general political scheme would.

But democracy cannot discriminate, within the overall preferences imperfectly revealed by voting, distinct personal and external components, so as to provide a method for enforcing the former while ignoring the latter. An actual vote in an election or referendum must be taken to represent an overall preference rather than some component of the preference that a skilful cross-examination of the individual voter, if time and expense permitted, would reveal. Personal and external preferences are sometimes so inextricably combined, moreover, that the discrimination is psychologically as well as institutionally impossible. That will be true, for example, in the case of the associational preferences that many people have for members of one race, or people of one talent or quality, rather than another, for this is a personal preference so parasitic upon external preferences that it is impossible to say, even as a matter of introspection, what personal preferences would remain if the underlying external preference were removed. It is also true of certain self-denying preferences that many individuals have; that is preferences for less of a certain good on the assumption, or rather proviso, that other people will have more. That is also a preference, however, noble, that is parasitic upon external preferences, in the shape of political and moral theories, and they may no more be counted in a defensible utilitarian argument than less attractive preferences rooted in prejudice rather than altruism.

I wish now to propose the following general theory of rights. The concept of an individual political right, in the strong anti-utilitarian sense I distinguished earlier, is a response to the philosophical defects of a utilitarianism that counts external preferences and the practical impossibility of a utilitarianism that does not. It allows us to enjoy the institutions of political democracy, which enforce overall or unrefined utilitarianism, and yet protect the fundamental right of citizens to equal concern and respect by prohibiting decisions that seem, antecedently, likely to have been reached by virtue of the external components of the preferences democracy reveals.

It should be plain how this theory of rights might be used to support the idea, which is the subject of this chapter, that we have distinct rights to certain liberties like the liberty of free expression and of free choice in personal and sexual relations. It might be shown that any utilitarian constraint on these liberties must be based on overall preferences in the community that we know, from our general knowledge of society, are likely to contain large components of external preferences, in the shape of political or moral theories, which the political process cannot discriminate and eliminate. It is not, as I said, my present purpose to frame the arguments that would have to be made to defend particular rights to liberty in this way, but only to show the general character such arguments might have.

I do wish, however, to mention one alleged right that might be called into question by my general argument, which is the supposed individual right to the free use of property. In chapter 11 I complained about the argument, popular in certain quarters, that it is inconsistent for liberals to defend a liberty of speech, for example, and not also concede a parallel right of some sort of property and its use. There might be force in that argument if the claim, that we have a right of free speech, depended on the more general proposition that we have a right to something called liberty as such. But that general idea is untenable and incoherent; there is no such thing as any general right to liberty. The argument for any given specific liberty may therefore be entirely independent of the argument for any other.

What Utilitarianism Is

John Stuart Mill

A passing remark is all that needs be given to the ignorant blunder of supposing that those who stand up for utility as the test of right and wrong use the term in that restricted and merely colloquial sense in which utility is opposed to pleasure. An apology is due to the philosophical opponents of utilitarianism, for even the momentary appearance of confounding them with anyone capable of so absurd a misconception; which is the more extraordinary, inasmuch as the contrary accusation, of referring everything to pleasure, and that, too, in its grossest form, is another of the common charges against utilitarianism: and, as has been pointedly remarked by an able writer, the same sort of persons, and often the very same persons, denounce the theory "as impracticably dry when the word 'utility' precedes the word 'pleasure,' and as too practically voluptuous when the word 'pleasure' precedes the word 'utility'." Those who know anything about the matter are aware that every writer, from Epicurus to Bentham, who maintained the theory of utility, meant by it, not something to be contradistinguished from pleasure, but pleasure itself, together with exemption from pain; and instead of opposing the useful to the agreeable or the ornamental, have always declared that the useful means these, among other things. Yet the common herd, including the herd of writers, not only in newspapers and periodicals, but in books of weight and pretension, are perpetually falling into this shallow mistake. Having caught up the word "utilitarian," while knowing nothing whatever about it but its sound, they habitually express by it the rejection or the neglect of pleasure in some of its forms: of beauty, of ornament, or of amusement. Nor is the term thus ignorantly misapplied solely in disparagement, but occasionally in compliment, as though it implied superiority to frivolity and the mere pleasures of the moment. And this perverted use is the only one in which the word is popularly known, and the one form which the new generation are acquiring their sole notion of its meaning. Those who introduced the word, but who had for many years discontinued it as a distinctive appellation, may well feel themselves called upon to resume it if by doing so they can hope to contribute anything towards rescuing it from this utter degradation.[2]

The creed which accepts as the foundation of morals "utility" or the "greatest happiness principle" holds that actions are right in proportion as they tend to promote happiness, wrong as they tend to produce the reverse of happiness. By happiness is intended pleasure, and the absence of pain; by unhappiness, pain,

---

[2] The author of this essay has reason for believing himself to be the first person who brought the word "utilitarian" into use. He did not invent it, but adopted it from a passing expression in Mr. Galt's *Annals of the Parish*. After using it as a designation for several years, he and others abandoned it from a growing dislike to anything resembling a badge or watchword or sectarian distinction. But as a name for one single opinion, not a set of opinions—to denote the recognition of utility as a standard, not any particular way of applying it—the term supplies a want in the language, and offers, in many cases, a convenient mode of avoiding tiresome circumlocution.

and the privation of pleasure. To give a clear view of the moral standard set up by the theory, much more requires to be said; in particular, what things it includes in the ideas of pain and pleasure; and to what extent this is left an open question. But these supplementary explanations do not affect the theory of life on which this theory of morality is grounded—namely, that pleasure and freedom from pain are the only things desirable as ends; and that all desirable things (which are as numerous in the utilitarian as in any other scheme) are desirable either for the pleasure inherent in themselves, or as means to the promotion of pleasure and the prevention of pain.

Now such a theory of life excites in many minds, and among them in some of the most estimable in feeling and purpose, inveterate dislike. To suppose that life has (as they express it) no higher end than pleasure—no better and nobler object of desire and pursuit—they designate as utterly mean and groveling; as a doctrine worthy only of swine, to whom the followers of Epicurus were, at a very early period, contemptuously likened; and modern holders of the doctrine are occasionally made the subject of equally polite comparisons by its German, French, and English assailants.

When thus attacked, the Epicureans have always answered that it is not they, but their accusers, who represent human nature in a degrading light, since the accusation supposes human beings to be capable of no pleasures except those of which swine are capable. If this supposition were true, the charge could not be gainsaid, but would then be no longer an imputation; for if the sources of pleasure were precisely the same to human beings and to swine, the rule of life which is good enough for the one would be good enough for the other. The comparison of the Epicurean life to that of beasts is felt as degrading, precisely because a beast's pleasures do not satisfy a human being's conceptions of happiness. Human beings have faculties more elevated than the animal appetites and, when once made conscious of them, do not regard anything as happiness which does not include their gratification. I do not, indeed, consider the Epicureans to have been by any means faultless in drawing out their scheme of consequences from the utilitarian principle. To do this in any sufficient manner, many Stoic, as well as Christian, elements require to be included. But there is no known Epicurean theory of life which does not assign to the pleasures of the intellect, of the feelings and imagination, and of the moral sentiments, a much higher value of pleasures than to those of mere sensation. It must be admitted, however, that utilitarian writers in general have placed the superiority of mental over bodily pleasures chiefly in the greater permanency, safety, uncostliness, etc., of the former—that is, in their circumstantial advantages rather than in their intrinsic nature. And on all these points utilitarians have fully proved their case; but they might have taken the other and, as it may be called, higher ground with entire consistency. It is quite compatible with the principle of utility to recognize the fact that some kinds of pleasure are more desirable and more valuable than others. It would be absurd that, while, in estimating all other things, quality is considered as well as quantity, the estimation of pleasures should be supposed to depend on quantity alone.

If I am asked what I mean by difference of quality in pleasures, or what makes one pleasure more valuable than another, merely as a pleasure, except its being greater in amount, there is but one possible answer. Of two pleasures, if there be one to which all or almost all who have experience of both give a decided preference, irrespective of a feeling of moral obligation to prefer it, that is the more desirable pleasure. If one of the two is, by those who are competently acquainted with both, placed so far above the other that they prefer it, even though knowing it to be attended with a greater amount of discontent, and would not resign it for any quantity of the other pleasure which their nature is capable of, we are justified in ascribing to the preferred enjoyment a superiority in quality so far outweighing quantity as to render it, in comparison, of small account.

Now it is an unquestionable fact that those who are equally acquainted with and equally capable of appreciating and enjoying both, do give a most marked preference to the manner of existence which employs their higher faculties. Few human creatures would consent to be changed into any of the lower animals for a promise of the fullest allowance of a beast's pleasures; no intelligent human being would consent to be a fool, no instructed person would be an ignoramus, no person of feeling and conscience would be selfish and base, even though they should be persuaded that the fool, the dunce, or the rascal is better satisfied with his lot than they are with theirs. They would not resign what they possess more than he for the most complete satisfaction of all the desires which they have in common with him. If they ever fancy they would, it is only in cases of unhappiness so extreme that to escape from it they would exchange their lot for almost any other, however undesirable in their own eyes. A being of higher faculties requires more to make him happy, is capable probably of more acute suffering, and certainly accessible to it at more points, than one of an inferior type; but in spite of these liabilities, he can never really wish to sink into what he feels to be a lower grade of existence. We may give what explanation we please of this unwillingness; we may attribute it to pride, a name which is given indiscriminately to some of the most and to some of the least estimable feelings of which mankind are capable: we may refer it to the love of liberty and personal independence, an appeal to which was with the Stoics one of the most effective means for the inculcation of it; to the love of power or to the love of excitement, both of which do really enter into and contribute to it; but its most appropriate appellation is a sense of dignity, which all human beings possess in one form or other, and in some, though by no means in exact, proportion to their higher faculties, and which is so essential a part of the happiness of those in whom it is strong that nothing which conflicts with it could be otherwise than momentarily an object of desire to them. Whoever supposes that this preference takes place at a sacrifice of happiness—that the superior being, in anything like equal circumstances, is not happier than the inferior—confounds the two very different ideas of happiness and content. It is indisputable that the being whose capacities of enjoyment are low has the greatest chance of having them fully satisfied; and a highly endowed being will always feel that any happiness which he can look for, as the world is constituted, is imperfect. But he can learn to bear its imperfections, if they are at all bearable; and they will not make him envy the being who is indeed unconscious of the imperfections, but only because he feels not at all the good which those imperfections qualify. It is better to be a human being dissatisfied than a pig satisfied: better to be Socrates dissatisfied than a fool satisfied. And if the fool, or the pig, are of a different opinion, it is because they only know their own side of the question. The other party to the comparison knows both sides.

It may be objected that many who are capable of the higher pleasures occasionally, under the influence of temptation, postpone them to the lower. But this is quite compatible with a full appreciation of the intrinsic superiority of the higher. Men often, from infirmity of character, make their election for the nearer good, though they know it to be the less valuable; and this no less when the choice is between two bodily pleasures than when it is between bodily and mental. They pursue sensual indulgences to the injury of health, though perfectly aware that health is the greater good. It may be further objected that many who begin with youthful enthusiasm for everything noble, as they advance in years, sink into indolence and selfishness. But I do not believe that those who undergo this very common change voluntarily choose the lower description of pleasures in preference to the higher. I believe that, before they devote themselves exclusively to the one, they have already become incapable of the other. Capacity for the nobler feelings is in most natures a very tender plant, easily killed, not only by hostile influences, but by mere want of sustenance; and in the majority of young persons it speedily dies away if the occupations to which their position in life has devoted them, and the society into which it has thrown them, are not favorable to keeping that higher capacity in exercise. Men lose their high aspirations as they lose their intellectual tastes, because they have not time or opportunity for indulging them; and they addict themselves to inferior pleasures, not because they deliberately prefer them, but because they are either the only ones to which they have access, or the only ones which they are any longer capable of enjoying. It may be questioned whether any one who has remained equally susceptible to both classes of pleasures, ever knowingly and calmly preferred the lower, though many, in all ages, have broken down in an ineffectual attempt to combine both.

From this verdict of the only competent judges, I apprehend there can be no appeal. On a question which is the best worth having of two pleasures, or which of two modes of existence is the most grateful to the feelings, apart from its moral attributes and from its consequences, the judgment of those who are qualified by knowledge of both, or, if they differ, that of the majority of them, must be admitted as final. And there needs be the less hesitation to accept this judgment respecting the quality of pleasures, since there is no other tribunal to be referred to even on the question of quantity. What means are there of determining which is the acutest of two pains, or the intensest of two pleasurable sensations, except the general suffrage of those who are familiar with both? Neither pains nor pleasures are homogeneous and pain is always heterogeneous with pleasure. What is there to decide whether a particular pleasure is worth purchasing at the cost of a particular pain except the feelings and judgment of the experienced? When, therefore, those feelings and judgment declare the pleasures derived from the higher faculties to be preferable *in kind* apart from the question of intensity, to those of which the animal nature, disjoined from the higher faculties, is susceptible, they are entitled on the subject to the same regard.

I have dwelt on this point as being a necessary part of a perfectly just conception of utility or happiness considered as the directive rule of human conduct. But it is by no means an indispensable condition to the acceptance of the utilitarian standard; for that standard is not the agent's own greatest happiness, but the greatest amount of happiness together; and if it may possibly be doubted whether a noble character is always the happier for its nobleness, there can be no doubt that it makes other people happier, and that the world in general is immensely a gainer by it. Utilitarianism, therefore, could only attain its end by the general cultivation of nobleness of character, even if each individual were only benefited by the nobleness of others, and his own, so far as happiness is concerned, were a sheer deduction from the benefit. But the bare enunciation of such an absurdity as this last renders refutation superfluous.

According to the greatest happiness principle, as above explained, the ultimate end, with reference to and for the sake of which all other things are bearable—whether we are considering our own good or that of other people—or an existence exempt as far as possible from pain, and as rich as possible in enjoyments, both in point of quantity and quality; the test of quality and the rule for measuring it against quantity being the preference felt by those who, in their opportunities of experience, to which must be added their habits of self-consciousness and self-observation, are best furnished with the means of comparison. This being, according to the utilitarian opinion, the end of human action, is necessarily also the standard of morality, which may accordingly be defined "the rules and precepts of human conduct," by the observance of which an existence such as has been described might be, to the greatest extent possible, secured to all mankind, and not to them only, but, so far as the nature of things admits, to the whole sentient creation.

Against this doctrine, however, arises another class of objectors who say that happiness, in any form, cannot be the rational purpose of human life and action; because, in the first place, it is unattainable; and they contemptuously ask, What right hast thou to be happy?—a question which Mr. Carlyle clenches by the addition, What right, a short time ago, hadst thou even to *be?* Next they say that men can do *without* happiness; that all noble beings have felt this, and could not have become noble but by learning the lesson of Entsagen, or renunciation; which lesson, thoroughly learnt and submitted to, they affirm to be the beginning and necessary condition of all virtue.

The first of these objections would go to the root of the matter were it well founded; for if no happiness is to be had at all by human beings, the attainment of it cannot be the end of morality or of any rational conduct. Though, even in that case, something might still be said for the utilitarian theory, since utility includes not solely the pursuit of happiness, but the prevention or mitigation of unhappiness; and if the former aim be chimerical, there will be all the greater scope and more imperative need for the latter, so long at least as mankind think fit to live, and do not take refuge in the simultaneous act of suicide recommended under certain conditions by Novalis. When, however, it is thus positively asserted to be impossible that human life should be happy, the assertion, if not something like a verbal quibble, is at least an exaggeration. If by happiness be meant a continuity of highly pleasurable excitement, it is evident enough that this is impossible. A state of exalted pleasure lasts only moments or in some cases, and with some intermissions, hours or days, and is the occasional brilliant flash of enjoyment, not its permanent and steady flame. Of this the philosophers who have taught that happiness is the end of life were as fully aware as those who taunt them. The happiness which they meant was not a life of rapture; but moments of such, in an existence made up of few and transitory pains, many and various pleasures, with a decided predominance of the active over the passive, and having as the foundation of the whole not to expect more from life than it is capable of bestowing. A life thus composed, to those who have been fortunate enough to obtain it, has always appeared worthy of the name of happiness. And such an existence is even now the lot of many, during some considerable portion of their lives. The present wretched education and wretched social arrangements are the only real hindrance to its being attainable by almost all.

The objectors perhaps may doubt whether human beings, if taught to consider happiness as the end of life, would be satisfied with such a moderate share of it. But great numbers of mankind have been satisfied with much less. The main constituents of a satisfied life appear to be two, either of which by itself is often found sufficient for the purpose: tranquility and excitement. With much tranquility, many find that they can be content with very little pleasure; with much excitement, many can reconcile themselves to a considerable quantity of pain. There is assuredly no inherent impossibility of enabling even the mass of mankind to unite both, since the two are so far from being incompatible that they are in natural alliance, the prolongation of either being a preparation for, and exciting a wish for, the other. It is only those in whom indolence amounts to a vice that do not desire excitement after an interval of repose; it is only those in whom the need of excitement is a disease that feel the tranquility which follows excitement dull and insipid, instead of pleasurable in direct proportion to the excitement which preceded it. When people who are tolerably fortunate in their outward lot do not find in life sufficient enjoyment to make it valuable to them, the cause generally is caring for nobody but themselves. To those who have neither public nor private affections, the excitements of life are much curtailed, and in any case dwindle in value as the time approaches when all selfish interests must be terminated by death; while those who leave after them objects of personal affection, and especially those who have also cultivated a fellow-feeling with the collective interests of mankind, retain as lively an interest in life on the eve of death as in the vigor of youth and health. Next to selfishness, the principal cause which makes life unsatisfactory is want of mental cultivation. A cultivated mind—I do not mean that of a philosopher, but any mind to which the fountains of knowledge have been opened, and which has been taught, in any tolerable degree, to exercise its faculties—finds sources of inexhaustible interest in all that surrounds it: in the objects of nature, the achievements of art, the imaginations of poetry, the incidents of history, the ways of mankind, past and present, and their prospects in the future. It is possible, indeed, to become indifferent to all this, and that too without having exhausted a thousandth part of it, but only when one has had from the beginning no moral or human interest in these things, and has sought in them only the gratification of curiosity.

Now there is absolutely no reason in the nature of things why an amount of mental culture sufficient to give an intelligent interest in these objects of contemplation should not be the inheritance of every one born in a civilized country. As little is there an inherent necessity that any human being should be a selfish egotist, devoid of every feeling or care but those which center in his own miserable individuality. Something far superior to this is sufficiently common even now, to give ample earnest of what the human species may be made. Genuine private affections and a sincere interest in the public good are possible, though in unequal degrees, to every rightly brought up human being. In a world in which there is so much to interest, so much to enjoy, and so much also to correct and improve, every one who has this moderate amount of moral and intellectual requisites is capable of an existence which may be called enviable; and unless such a person, through bad laws or subjection to the will of others, is denied the liberty to use the sources of happiness within his reach, he will not fail to find this enviable existence, if he escape the positive evils of life, the great sources of physical and mental suffering—such as indigence, disease, and the unkindness, worthlessness, or premature loss of objects of affection. The main stress of the problem lies, therefore, in the contest with these calamities from which it is a rare good fortune entirely to escape; which, as things now are, cannot be obviated, and often cannot be in any material degree mitigated. Yet no one whose opinion deserves a moment's consideration can doubt that most of the great positive evils of the world are in themselves removable, and will, if human affairs continue to improve, be in the end reduced within narrow limits. Poverty, in any sense implying suffering, may be completely extinguished by the wisdom of society combined with the good sense and providence of individuals. Even that most intractable of enemies, disease, may be indefinitely reduced in dimensions by good physical and moral education and proper control of noxious influences, while the progress of science holds out a promise for the future of still more direct conquests over this detestable foe. And every advance in that direction relieves us from some, not only of the chances which cut short our own lives, but, what concerns us still more, which deprive us of those in whom our happiness is wrapt up. As for vicissitudes of fortune and other disappointments connected with worldly circumstances, these are principally the effect either of gross imprudence, of ill-regulated desires, or of bad or imperfect social institutions. All the grand sources, in short, of human suffering are in a great degree, many of them almost entirely, conquerable by human care and effort; and though their removal is grievously slow—though a long succession of generations will perish in the breach before the conquest is completed, and this world becomes all that, if will and knowledge were not wanting, it might easily be made—yet every mind sufficiently intelligent and generous to bear a part, however small and inconspicuous, in the endeavour will draw a noble enjoyment from the contest itself, which he would not for any bribe in the form of selfish indulgence consent to be without.

And this leads to the true estimation of what is said by the objectors concerning the possibility and the obligation of learning to do without happiness. Unquestionably it is possible to do without happiness; it is done involuntarily by nineteen-twentieths of mankind, even in those parts of our present world which are least deep in barbarism; and it often has to be done voluntarily by the hero or the martyr, for the sake of something which he prizes more than his individual happiness. But this something, what is it, unless the happiness of others or some of the requisites of happiness? It is noble to be capable of resigning entirely one's own portion of happiness, or chances of it; but, after all, this self-sacrifice must be for some end; it is not its own end; and if we are told that its end is not happiness but virtue, which is better than happiness, I ask, would the sacrifice be made if the hero or martyr did not believe that it would earn for others immunity from similar sacrifices? Would it be made if he thought that his renunciation of happiness for himself would produce no fruit for any of his fellow creatures, but to make their lot like his, and place them also in the condition of persons who have renounced happiness? All honor to those who can abnegate for themselves the personal enjoyment of life when by such renunciation they contribute practiced generally, would be generally injurious, and that this is the ground of the obligation to abstain from it. The amount of regard for the public interest implied in this recognition is no greater than is demanded by every system of morals, for they all enjoin to abstrain from whatever is manifestly pernicious to society.

The same considerations dispose of another reproach against the doctrine of utility, founded on a still grosser misconception of the purpose of a standard of morality, and of the very meaning of the words "right" and "wrong." It is often affirmed that utilitarianism renders men cold and unsympathizing; that it chills their moral feelings towards individuals; that it makes them regard only the dry and hard consideration of the consequences of actions, not taking into their moral estimate the qualities from which those actions emanate. If the assertion means that they do not allow their judgement respecting the rightness or wrongness of an action to be influenced by their opinion of the qualities of the person who does it, this is a complaint not against utilitarianism, but against any standard of morality at all; for certainly no known ethical standard decides an action to be good or bad because it is done by a good or a bad man, still less because done by an amiable, a brave, or a benevolent man, or the contrary. These considerations are relevant, not to the estimation of actions, but of persons; and there is nothing in the utilitarian theory inconsistent with the fact that there are other things which interest us in persons besides the rightness and wrongness of their actions. The Stoics, indeed, with the paradoxical misuse of language which was part of their system, and by which they strove to raise themselves above all concern about anything but virtue, were fond of saying that he who has that has everything; that he, and only he, is rich, is beautiful, is a king. But no claim of this description is made for the virtuous man by the utilitarian doctrine. Utilitarians are quite aware that there are other desirable possessions and qualities besides virtue, and are perfectly willing to allow to all of them their full worth. They are also aware that a right action does not necessarily indicate a virtuous character, and that actions which are blamable often proceed from qualities entitled to praise. When this is apparent in any particular case, it modifies their estimation, not certainly of the act, but of the agent. I grant that they are, notwithstanding, of opinion that in the long run the best proof of a good character is good actions; and resolutely refuse to consider any mental disposition as good of which the predominant tendency is to produce bad conduct. This makes them unpopular with many people; but it is an unpopularity which they must share with every one who regards the distinction between right and wrong in a serious light; and the reproach is not one which a conscientious utilitarian need be anxious to repel.

If no more be meant by the objection than that many utilitarians look on the morality of actions, as measured by the utilitarian standards, with too exclusive a regard, and do not lay sufficient stress upon the other beauties of character which go towards making a human being lovable or admirable, this may be admitted. Utilitarians who have cultivated their moral feelings, but not their sympathies, nor their artistic perceptions, do fall into this mistake; and so do all other moralists under the same conditions. What can be said in excuse for other moralists is equally available for them, namely, that, if there is to be any error, it is better that it should be on that side. As a matter of fact, we may affirm that among utilitarians, as among adherents of other systems, there is every imaginable degree of rigidity and of laxity in the application of their standard; some are even puritanically rigorous, while others are as indulgent as can possibly be desired by sinner or by sentimentalist. But on the whole, a doctrine which brings prominently forward the interest that mankind have in the repression and prevention of conduct which violates the moral law, is likely to be inferior to no other in turning the sanctions of opinion against such violations. It is true, the question, "What does violate the moral law?" is one on which those who recognize different standards of morality are likely now and then to differ. But difference of opinion on moral questions was not first introduced into the world by utilitarianism, while that doctrine does supply, if not always an easy, at all events a tangible and intelligible, mode of deciding such differences.

It may not be superfluous to notice a few more of the common misapprehensions of utilitarian ethics, even those which are so obvious and gross that it might appear impossible for any person of candor and intelligence to fall into them; since persons, even of considerable mental endowment, often give themselves so little trouble to understand the bearings of any opinion against which they entertain a prejudice, and men are in general so little conscious of this voluntary ignorance as a defect, that the vulgarest misunderstandings of ethical doctrines are continually met with in the deliberate writings of persons of the greatest pretensions both to high principle and to philosophy. We not uncommonly hear the doctrine of utility inveighed against as a *godless* doctrine. If it be necessary to say anything at all against so mere an assumption, we may say that the question depends upon what idea we have formed of the moral character of the Deity. If it be a true belief that God desires, above all things, the happiness of his creatures, and that this was his purpose in their creation, utility is not only not a godless doctrine, but more profoundly religious than any other. If it be meant that utilitarianism does not recognize the revealed will of God as the supreme law of morals, I answer that a utilitarian who believes in the perfect goodness and wisdom of God necessarily believes that whatever God has thought fit to reveal on the subject of morals must fulfil the requirements of utility in a supreme degree. But others besides utilitarians have been of opinion that the Christian revelation was intended, and is fitted, to inform the hearts and minds of mankind with a spirit which should enable them to find for themselves what is right, and incline them to do it when found, rather than to tell them, except in a very general way, what it is; and that we need a doctrine of ethics, carefully followed out, to *interpret* to us the will of God. Whether this opinion is correct or not, it is superfluous here to discuss: since whatever aid religion, either natural or revealed, can afford to ethical investigation, is as open to the utilitarian moralist as to any other. He can use it as the testimony of God to the usefulness or hurtfulness of any given course of action, by as good a right as others can use it for the indication of a transcendental law, having no connection with usefulness or with happiness.

Again, utility is often summarily stigmatized as an immoral doctrine by giving it the name of "expediency," and taking advantage of the popular worthily to increase the amount of happiness in the world; but he who does it or professes to do it for any other purpose is no more deserving of admiration than the ascetic mounted on his pillar. He may be an inspiriting proof of what men *can* do, but assuredly not an example of what they *should*.

Though it is only in a very imperfect state of the world's arrangements that any one can best serve the happiness of others by the absolute sacrifice of his own, yet, so long as the world is in that imperfect state, I fully acknowledge that the readiness to make such a sacrifice is the highest virtue which can be found in man. I will add that in this condition of the world, paradoxical as the assertion may be, the conscious ability to do without happiness gives the best prospect of realizing such happiness as is attainable. For nothing except that consciousness can raise a person above the chances of life, by making him feel that, let fate and fortune do their worst, they have not power to subdue him; which, once felt, frees him from excess of anxiety concerning the evils of live, and enables him, like many a Stoic in the worst times of the Roman Empire, to cultivate in tranquility the sources of satisfaction accessible to him, without concerning himself about the uncertainty of their duration any more than about their inevitable end.

Meanwhile, let utilitarians never cease to claim the morality of self-devotion as a possession which belongs by as good a right to them as either to the Stoic or to the Transcendentalist. The utilitarian morality does recognize in human beings the power of sacrificing their own greatest good for the good of others. It only refuses to admit that the sacrifice is itself a good. A sacrifice which does not increase or tend to increase the sum total of happiness, it considers as wasted. The only self-renunciation which it applauds is devotion to the happiness, or to some of the means of happiness, of others, either of mankind collectively or of individuals within the limits imposed by the collective interests of mankind.

I must again repeat what the assailants of utilitarianism seldom have the justice to acknowledge, that the happiness which forms the utilitarian standard of what is right in conduct is not the agent's own happiness but that of all concerned. As between his own happiness and that of others, utilitarianism requires him to be as strictly impartial as a disinterested and benevolent spectator. In the golden rule of Jesus of Nazareth, we read the complete spirit of the ethics of utility. "To do as you would be done by," and "to love your neighbor as yourself," constitute the ideal perfection of utilitarian morality. As the means of making the nearest approach to this ideal, utility would enjoin, first, that laws and social arrangements should place the happiness or (as, speaking practically, it may be called) the interest of every individual as nearly as possible in harmony with the interest of the whole; and, secondly, that education and opinion, which have so vast a power over human character, should so use that power as to establish in the mind of every individual an indissoluble association between his own happiness and the good of the whole, especially between his own happiness and the practice of such modes of conduct, negative and positive, as regard for the universal happiness prescribes; so that not only he may be able to conceive the possibility of happiness to himself,* consistently with conduct opposed to the general good, but also that a direct impulse to promote the general good may be in every individual one of the habitual motives of action, and the sentiments connected therewith may fill a large and prominent place in every human being's sentient existence. If the impugners of the utilitarian morality represented it to their own minds in this its true character, I know not what recommendation possessed by any other morality they could possibly affirm to be wanting to it; what more beautiful or more exalted developments of human nature any other ethical system can be supposed to foster, or what springs of action, not accessible to the utilitarian, such systems rely on for giving effect to their mandates.

The objectors to utilitarianism cannot always be charged with representing it in a discreditable light. On the contrary, those among them who entertain anything like a just idea of its disinterested character sometimes find fault with its standard as being too high for humanity. They say it is exacting too much to require that people shall always act from the inducement of promoting the general interests of society. But this is to mistake the very meaning of a standard of morals, and confound the rule of action with the motive of it. It is the business of ethics to tell us what are our duties, or by what test we may know them; but no system of ethics requires that the sole motive of all we do shall be a feeling of duty; on the contrary, ninety-nine hundredths of all our actions are done from other motives, and rightly so done if the rule of duty does not condemn them. It is the more unjust to utilitarianism that this particular misapprehension should be made a ground of objection to it, inasmuch as utilitarian moralists have gone beyond almost all others in affirming that the motive has nothing to do with the morality of the action, though much with the worth of the agent. He who saves a fellow creature from drowning does what is morally right, whether his motive be duty or the hope of being paid for his trouble; he who betrays the friend that trusts him is guilty of a crime, even if his object be to serve another friend to whom he is under greater obligations. But to speak only of actions done from the motive of duty, and in direct obedience to principle: it is a misapprehension of the utilitarian mode of thought to conceive it as implying that people should fix their minds upon so wide a generality as the world, or society at large. The great majority of good actions are intended not for the benefit of the world, but for that of individuals, of which the good of the world is made up; and the thoughts of the most virtuous man need not on these occasions travel beyond the particular persons concerned, except so far as is necessary to assure himself that in benefiting them he is not violating the rights, that is, the legitimate and authorized expectations, of any one else. The multiplication of happiness is, according to the utilitarian ethics, the object of virtue: the occasions on which any person (except one in a thousand) has it in his power to do this on an extended scale, in other words, to be a public benefactor, are but exceptional; and on these occasions alone is he called on to consider public utility; in every other case, private utility, the interest or happiness of some few persons, is all he has to attend to. Those alone the influence of whose actions extends to society in general need concern themselves habitually about so large an object. In the case of abstinences indeed—of things which people forbear to do from moral considerations, though the consequences in the particular case might be beneficial—it would be unworthy of an intelligent agent not to be consciously aware that the action is of a class which, if use of that term to contrast it with principle. But the expedient, in the sense in which it is opposed to the right, generally means that which is expedient for the particular interest of the agent himself; as when a minister sacrifices the interests of his country to keep himself in place. When it means anything better than this, it means that which is expedient for some immediate object, some temporary purpose, but which violates a rule whose observance is expedient in a much higher degree. The expedient, in this sense, instead of being the same thing with the useful, is a branch of the hurtful. Thus it would often be expedient, for the purpose of getting over some momentary embarrassment, or attaining some object immediately useful to ourselves or others, to tell a lie. But inasmuch as the culitvation in ourselves of a sensitive feeling on the subject of veracity is one of the most useful, and the enfeeblement of that feeling one of the most hurtful, things to which our conduct can be instrumental; and inasmuch as any, even unintentional, deviation from truth does that much towards weakening the trustworthiness of human assertion, which is not only the principal support of all present social well-being but the insufficiency of which does more than any one thing that can be named to keep back civilization, virtue, everything on which human happiness on the largest scale depends—we feel that the violation, for a present advantage, of a rule of such transcendent expediency is not expedient, and that he who, for the sake of convenience to himself or to some other individual, does what depends on him to deprive mankind of the good, and inflict upon them the evil, involved in the greater or less reliance which they can place in each other's word, acts the part of one of their worst enemies. Yet that even this rule, sacred as it is, admits of possible exceptions is acknowledged by all moralists; the chief of which is when the withholding of some fact (as of information from a malefactor, or of bad news from a person dangerously ill) would save an individual (especially an individual other than oneself) from great and unmerited evil, and when the withholding can only be effected by denial. But in order that the exception may not extend itself beyond the need, and may have the least possible effect in weakening reliance on veracity, it ought to be recognized and, if possible, its limits defined; and, if the principle of utility is good for anything, it must be good for weighing these conflicting utilities against one another, and marking out the region within which one or the other preponderates.

Again, defenders of utility often find themselves called upon to reply to such objections as this—that there is not time, previous to action, for calculating and weighing the effects of any line of conduct on the general happiness. This is exactly as if any one were to say that it is impossible to guide our conduct by Christianity because there is not time, on every occasion on which anything has to be done, to read through the Old and New Testaments. The answer to the objection is that there has been ample time, namely, the whole past duration of the human species. During all that time, mankind have been learning by experience the tendencies of actions; on which experience all the prudence, as well as all the morality, of life are dependent. People talk as if the commencement of this course of experience had hitherto been put off, and as if, at the moment when some man feels tempted to meddle with the property or life of another, he had to begin considering for the first time whether murder and theft are injurious to human happiness. Even then I do not think that he would find the question very puzzling; but, at all events, the matter is now done to his hand. It is truly a whimsical supposition that, if mankind were agreed in considering utility to be the test of morality, they would remain without any agreement as to what *is* useful, and would take no measures for having their notions on the subject taught to the young, and enforced by law and opinion. There is no difficulty in proving any ethical standard whatever to work ill if we suppose universal idiocy to be conjoined with it; but on any hypothesis short of that, mankind must by this time have acquired positive beliefs as to the effects of some actions on their happiness; and the beliefs which have thus come down are the rules of morality for the multitude, and for the philosopher until he has succeeded in finding better. That philosophers might easily do this, even now, on many subjects; that the received code of ethics is by no means of divine right; and that mankind have still much to learn as to the effects of actions on the general happiness, I admit or rather earnestly maintain. The corollaries from the principle of utility, like the precepts of every practical art, admit of indefinite improvement, and, in a progressive state of the human mind, their improvement is perpetually going on. But to consider the rules of morality as improvable is one thing; to pass over the intermediate generalization entirely and endeavor to test each individual action directly by the first principle is another. It is a strange notion that the acknowledgment of a first principle is inconsistent with the admission of secondary ones. To inform a traveller respecting the place of his ultimate destination is not to forbid the use of landmarks and direction-posts on the way. The proposition that happiness is the end and aim of morality does not mean that no road ought to be laid down to that goal, or that persons going thither should not be advised to take one direction rather than another. Men really ought to leave off talking a kind of nonsense on this subject, which they would neither talk nor listen to on other matters of practical concernment. Nobody argues that the art of navigation is not founded on astronomy because sailors cannot wait to calculate the Nautical Almanac. Being rational creatures, they go to sea with it ready calculated; and all rational creatures go out upon the sea of life with their minds made up on the common questions of right and wrong, as well as on many of the far more difficult questions of wise and foolish. And this, as long as foresight is a human quality, it is to be presumed they will continue to do. Whatever we adopt as the fundamental principle of morality, we require subordinate principles to apply it by; the impossibility of doing without them, being common to all systems, can afford no argument against any one in particular; but gravely to argue as if no such secondary principles could be had, and as if mankind had remained till now, and always must remain, without drawing any general conclusions from the experience of human life, is as high a pitch, I think, as absurdity has ever reached in philosophical controversy.

The remainder of the stock arguments against utilitarianism mostly consist in laying to its charge the common infirmities of human nature, and the general difficulties which embarrass conscientious persons in shaping their course through life. We are told that a utilitarian will be apt to make his own particular case an exception to moral rules, and, when under temptation, will see a utility in the breach of a rule, greater than he will see in its observance. But is utility the only creed which is able to furnish us with excuses for evil doing, and means of cheating our own conscience? They are afforded in abundance by all doctrines which recognize as a fact in morals the existence of conflicting considerations, which all doctrines do that have been believed by sane persons. It is not the fault of any creed, but of the complicated nature of human affairs, that rules of conduct cannot be so framed as to require no exceptions, and that hardly any kind of action can safely be laid down as either always obligatory or always condemnable. There is no ethical creed which does not temper the rigidity of its laws by giving a certain latitude, under the moral responsibility of the agent, for accommodation to peculiarities of circumstances; and under every creed, at the opening thus made, self-deception and dishonest casuistry get in. There exists no moral system under which there do not arise unequivocal cases of conflicting obligation. These are the real difficulties, the knotty points both in the theory of ethics and in the conscientious guidance of personal conduct. They are overcome practically, with greater or with less success, according to the intellect and virtue of the individual; but it can hardly be pretended than anyone will be the less qualified for dealing with them, from possessing an ultimate standard to which conflicting rights and duties can be referred. If utility is the ultimate source of moral obligations, utility may be invoked to decide between them when their demands are incompatible. Though the application of the standard may be difficult, it is better than none at all; while in other systems the moral laws all claiming independent authority, there is no common umpire entitled to interfere between them; their claims to precedence one over another rest on little better than sophistry, and, unless determined, as they generally are, by the unacknowledged influence of consideration of utility, afford a free scope for the action of personal desires and partialities. We must remember that only in these cases of conflict between secondary principles is it requisite that first principles should be appealed to. There is no case of moral obligation in which some secondary principle is not involved; and if only one, there can seldom be any real doubt which one it is, in the mind of any person by whom the principle itself is recognized.

Individualism Has Been Allowed to Run Rampant

Robert Bellah

"Dark Side" of the Self

In many ways, individualism is a positive feature of the American character and culture. But it also has destructive potential.

In the past, its dark side was constrained by society's institutions, like the small town where people knew and helped each other. But because of the enormous social changes that have taken place in the last 100 years, there are now fewer constraints on individualism. In a sense, it has been allowed to run rampant.

At every level, people learn patterns of reward and advancement that focus on their own individual achievement. Career patterns take the middle class out of the place in which they were born—frequently far from their family and relatives. They go to universities, where many of them learn that the things they were taught in Sunday school are not necessarily true.

Our society makes it harder and harder to maintain tight-knit families, small-town environments and other social contexts that can provide support, reinforcement and a moral meaning for individuals—contexts in which they can see that everybody is working for the common good.

Competition vs. Selfishness

Psychology has played a role in this. The language of therapy tends to emphasize almost exclusively the needs, interests, feelings and wishes of the individual and not those of the broader society. Even commitments to others and to community are evaluated in terms of their payoff in personal gratification. Psychology often ends up simply reinforcing the radically inward-turning notion that the only truth is one's feelings.

Current economic thought leads us in the same direction. A deep part of our individualism is a strong belief in the open, competitive system that the market economy generates. But the notion that pure selfishness results in the common good just isn't so.

Reviving "Vocation as a Calling"

Today there's a deep sense in our culture that if you don't reach the pinnacle of radical freedom and control, you haven't validated yourself. That's as true in the university as in the business world. It's almost as if the higher you get in society, the more intense this imperative. Those who don't attain the pinnacle feel misery and alienation.

For example, a man who has spent his whole life on the highest level of scientific research makes a breakthrough discovery only to learn that two weeks earlier at another lab halfway across the country somebody made the discovery first. One wins the Nobel Prize, and the other ends up feeling his life is meaningless.

Many other individuals would like to live in and contribute to society and to work in a job they could really believe in—but don't know how to. They view their jobs strictly as instruments for giving them the wherewithal to live a certain life. Their commitment to work is often marginal and cynical.

That doesn't mean they don't work hard. I know of people at large law firms who work extraordinarily long hours yet are quite alienated from what they do. They enjoy what the money they make buys, but it doesn't seem a terribly happy resolution to feel that your work has little intrinsic meaning.

What we need to do is reappropriate the old notion of vocation as a calling. A career should not be just something in which you reach for ever higher stages of glory and fame but something that allows us to contribute to the good of all.

CRITICISM FOR ITS OWN SAKE

Another part of the picture is that the balance beween doubt and belief has gone awry. Doubt makes sense only if one also believes. If you don't believe anything, then the doubt is just nihilism. But social scientists have managed to call into question the very beliefs on which our public life rests. We've said that people don't operate out of morality but out of psychic drives or power needs. That's intellectually wrong and has serious social consequences.

When the high intellectual cultures becomes one of criticism, dissent and doubt, it doesn't play the role of what Walter Lippmann called "the public philosophy," which gives people confidence that there's something out there they can count on.

George Orwell once said of modern intellectuals:

"For 200 years we had sawed and sawed and sawed at the branch we were sitting on. And in the end, much more suddenly than anyone had foreseen, our efforts were rewarded—and down we came. But unfortunately there had been a little mistake. The thing at the bottom was not a bed of roses after all; it was a cesspool filled with barbed wire."

Criticism for the sake of criticism doesn't create a good society. It has to be balanced with positive moral concern.

IS "THE COMMON GOOD" PASSÉ?

Our political language doesn't really know how to talk about the common good.
The left has focused so heavily on individual rights, women's liberation and

the like that they can't think about the wider community. They think somehow that if we get rid of all restraints on individuals, society would just be great. But what we would have is a bunch of anarchic individuals who would be at each other's throats.

The conservative language, meanwhile, reinforces the status quo. They have some language of common good—of neighborhood, work and family—but it's usually a pretty thin veneer over letting the market have its way.

"WARM, LOVING" CORPORATIONS

In some cases, corporations are trying to re-create something of the moral context of the older community. Even a giant like IBM makes workers feel a part of it.

IBM's style of managerial leadership is not that of an autocratic boss giving orders; it's almost therapeutic, offering support and encouragement. The irony is that their purpose is to increase productivity and the profit margin of the corporation.

It's interesting that corporations have moved from the impersonal—their first model was the military model—to a model of the corporation that's much more like a warm, loving community. But that's a little scary, too, because it's not a real community but a pseudo one in which the therapeutic managerial syndrome becomes a form of social control.

OUR "GENEROSITY IS STILL THERE"

There remains a strong wish to identify with the national community as though it were a local community, to work for the common good. Americans' basic generosity is still there. But people are baffled as to how to translate it into something that won't be distorted.

Organizing effectively as citizens to deal with things that disturb us isn't working very well. The national organization that is simply an office in Washington that sends out letters to raise funds to which people contribute $15 doesn't involve people very deeply. It doesn't give them a sense of participation.

Unlike Europe, we dont have a political party that has a local constituency. Our parties are national coalitions of interest groups. Locally they are only the personal following of particular politicians. So the translation of the still living sense of citizen participation into effective action at the national level is problematical.

AHEAD: "A PERIOD OF SKEPTICISM"

What's happening in the U.S. is also occurring in Western Europe. There, too, a sense of discouragement—not knowing where to go and how to translate one's good impulses into any practical policy—is prevalent. I suspect that we're in for a period of exploring, tentativeness and skepticism.

What we need desperately is the kind of imagination that will translate the positive things in Western culture—our achievements in standard of living and technological advance—into a more coherent conception of what living together really means.

There has to be a recognition that there are resources in our past that if rethought, reworked and imaginatively re-created could help put things back together.

AIMING TOWARD "A SOCIETY WE WANT"

A lot is at stake. If we can't sustain the structures that involve citizens in making decisions about their lives, then somebody's going to make those decisions for us. It'll be the experts and managers. It may be quite benign, but it won't be what the Constitution envisaged.

If we are going to make it in the world and compete with the likes of Japan, we need to have a greater capacity for effective social organization at the same time that we protect our liberties. Ultimately we have to think about community and our common involvement in it if we're going to have a society we want to live in.

8 Individual Versus Societal Rights
or "Whose Society Is It, Anyway?"

Think about groups you have lived or worked with—your family, a club, an office, a neighborhood organization. Maybe you share an apartment with friends or live in a dormitory facility with other students. Perhaps you work in an office or a large company. Now think about how the resources of that group or organization are distributed among its members (salary, status, free time, holidays, material goods, access to keys, decision making, etc.). Is everyone equal? If not, is this inequality accepted? Or is it regarded as unfair or unjust? Does it cause difficulties? Is there a leader? Would you consider this organization to be "good" or "just"?

Reflecting on your own membership in a group will help you think about the central issues in this chapter, those concerned with what characterizes the "good" or "just" society, and with how such a society is likely to be created and sustained. Of course, these issues are extremely complex and controversial; people have been debating about them for centuries.

Key Questions: What Is Meant by a "Good" Society? How Can a Good Society Be Maintained?

To a great extent, your concept of the "good" society depends on the ideas and values with which you were brought up; people from the same community or culture often have similar ideas on this topic. Yet frequently even those whose backgrounds are similar may disagree. One idea that has generated considerable controversy concerns the value of **liberty** and **individuality** versus that of **community** and the **common good.** Many Americans like to think of themselves primarily as individuals who live in the "land of the free." They take pride in the American national political heritage, which boasts of the Declaration of Independence from Britain and claims that all people by "Right ought to be Free and Independent." That Declaration states that we "hold these truths to be self-evident, that all men are created equal, that they are endowed by their Creator with certain unalienable Rights."

At the heart of this political tradition lies the belief that individual freedom is of primary importance and that the state should have only limited power to restrict our liberty. To assure individual liberty, it is claimed that all of us possess certain rights that cannot be violated by the state. It is felt that the main purpose of the state is to regulate, mediate, and maintain our rights in terms of those of other individual citizens.

However, not everyone believes that individual liberty and the possession and exercise of rights should be the primary focus of the political philosophy and system. Some have argued that other values such as **equality, community, duty,** and **justice** are more central to the nation. Others have claimed that our political system is based on racism and patriarchal sexism and that an emphasis on individualism, liberty, and rights has seriously damaged the moral fabric of our society. They claim that we have become overly competitive, that we have lost the ability to engage in moral debate, that we have become alienated, and that we too quickly consider the benefits of immediate self-interest over the long-term interests of society or of the earth. Such people stress that what is important is not our individual ability to sustain liberty, but our obligation to the common good. In other words, the emphasis here is not on separate individualism but on connected community.

WRITING TO LEARN

▶ *Exercise:* What is your position on individual rights? Look at the Calvin and Hobbes cartoon. Write a short summary of what it implies about individual rights.

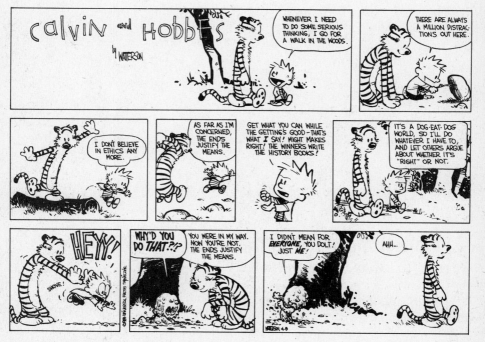

Calvin and Hobbes. Copyright 1989 Universal Press Syndicate. Reprinted with permission. All rights reserved.

Now think about your own position on this topic. Do you believe that your culture emphasizes individual rights? Were you raised with the idea that liberty and individual freedom were important values? Or were you brought up to think that concern for the common good was more important? Write a short essay discussing how those involved in your upbringing viewed these ideas. Use examples from your schooling or childhood. Then share your work with a small group of classmates.

HUMAN NATURE AND SOCIETY

Key Question: How Does Your View of Human Nature Affect Your Concept of the Good Society?

The extent to which you believe in individual rights also depends on your view of human nature. Robert North, in his article "Shaping the Future," states that whether you view people as "innately selfish, competitive, aggressive, and violent" as compared to being capable of "great generosity, integrity, and noble understanding" will determine your concept of society and the degree to which you think society is capable of self-government and improvement.

WRITING TO LEARN: A SEQUENCE OF ASSIGNMENTS

▶ *Writing Assignment:* Think about your concept of human beings. Do you view them as capable of improvement? Do you believe that society has progressed over the society of one hundred years ago? A thousand years ago?

Write an essay exploring your concept of humanity and its capacity for improvement.

▶ *Writing Assignment:* Read the article "Shaping the Future." Rewrite your essay concerned with exploring your concept of humanity and incorporate some of the ideas from that article.

THE ADVANTAGES AND DISADVANTAGES OF FREEDOM

Key Question: What Is the Relationship Between Freedom and Responsibility?

The word "freedom" has positive connotations in our society. "Let freedom ring" and "the land of the free" are catch phrases in well-known patriotic songs. Yet freedom requires responsibility, which, some maintain, could be regarded as a burden.

▶ *Writing Assignment:* Consider an organization or group of which you are a part (family, work, school, living arrangements). Then think about how much freedom you have as a member. Can you come and go as you wish? Do pretty much as you like? Do you have responsibilities to fulfill?

Write a brief essay in which you describe the organization or group and discuss how much freedom you have within it. Does that freedom bring responsibility?

▶ *Writing Assignment:* Read "Arguments Against Freedom" by Scott Gordon. Summarize Gordon's position. Then read the excerpts from Hobbes and Rousseau. Write an essay in which you compare Gordon's position with those of Hobbes and Rousseau.

▶ *Writing Assignment:* Read the following scenario: The residents of the Jamesville Apartment complex have organized a food cooperative in order to reduce food costs to its members. The cooperative was able to purchase nonperishable household items at wholesale prices, savings that they could then pass along to the members. The cooperative is operated by two members who are paid a small salary for their work. However, these members can keep the cooperative open for only a few hours a day, which limits the times when goods can be purchased.

Several members, unable to take advantage of the savings offered by the cooperative because of these limited hours, have suggested that all residents have access to a key to the cooperative. Residents could then sign for the goods they needed and leave the appropriate cash.

This suggestion has caused great controversy among the members. Some are concerned that there would be widespread pilfering of goods and that people, sometimes even members of the same family, cannot always be trusted. Others feel that such a lack of trust is a terrible insult to the integrity of the members since most have lived in the complex for over five years and know one another quite well. They feel that because losses would be felt by everyone, that theft would be minimal.

▶ *Writing Assignment:* Think about your position concerning the nature of humanity. Do you feel that people are capable of self-management? Or do you feel that most people need restrictions in order to function? Then write a paper in which you indicate your position in this controversy, incorporating ideas from the following readings:

Gordon, "Arguments Against Freedom"

Hobbes, "The Need For Security"

Rousseau, "The Social Compact"

Zinn, "Some Truths Are Not Self-Evident"

HISTORICAL/CULTURAL CONTEXT

Principles of the American Political System[1]

The American political system was based on an eighteenth-century concept of humanity and its capacity for self-government, and, to a great extent, our current thinking is still based on that concept. The following key points are central to American political thought:

1. **Individualism.** Individualism is a key principle in American political thought. The individual is conceived of as the basic unit in society and operates in society through rational self-interest. Man is conceived of as rational enough to support government and society, even though such support means a relinquishing of some individual freedoms.

2. **Instrumental view of the state.** Related to the idea of individualism is the view of the state as an instrument to serve individuals, not as an end in itself. The state is conceived of as existing because individuals have agreed that it should exist.

3. **Limited government.** Related to the instrumental view of the state is the view that the state should play a relatively limited role in society. The state is viewed only as a means of protecting individual rights and ensuring that society runs smoothly. In the nineteenth century, this view was referred to as the "nightwatchman" theory of the state. This view conceived of the state as a means of enforcing contracts and providing defense and police protection, in other words, as a guardian.

4. **Individual rights.** Related to the emphasis on individualism is that of individual rights, which are defined as certain fundamental rights that each individual possesses, which cannot be violated by government or other individuals. Some of these rights are "life, liberty, and property." Others that have been included are the right to free expression and behavior. A central expression of the idea of individual rights is contained in John Stuart Mill's *On Liberty*, which argues that society has no right to suppress ideas regardless of how objectionable and that individuals should be allowed to do what they wish, including self-destructive acts, as long as those acts do not harm anyone else.

5. **Equality under the law.** Another central idea in American political thought is that all people are equal; there are no special privileges at-

[1] These principles are stated in William S. Maddox and Stuart Lilie, "Classical Liberalism Is the Basis of American Democracy," *American Government Opposing Viewpoints Series,* ed. David L. Bender (St. Paul Minn.: Greenhaven Press, 1988).

tached to wealth or class determined by heredity. In modern times, this concept of equality has evolved into the idea of "equality of opportunity."

These five principles form the basis of American political thought. However, these are general statements only, and can be interpreted in a number of ways. Even when there is general agreement about these five principles, people debate about what role the state should play in fostering the "good" society, and about what that "good" society should be.

▶ **Writing Assignment:** Read the selections by Rousseau and Hobbes. Summarize each of their positions. Then develop a paper in which you compare how each conceives of the relationship of the individual to the State.

In a small group, discuss which author you agree with most. Which one is most in accord with your view of humanity?

CONSERVATIVE OR LIBERAL? WHAT DO THESE WORDS MEAN?

Key Questions: What Is the Difference Between a Liberal and a Conservative? How Were These Terms Derived from American Political Tradition?

People use the words "conservative" and "liberal" all of the time, often without thinking seriously about what they mean. Stereotypically, we think of a "conservative" as a member of the establishment. Perhaps he is a middle-aged businessman, in a dark suit; he looks prosperous and has a growing paunch. Maybe he wears a pocket watch and is a bit stuffy. In contrast, a "liberal," according to this stereotype, is younger, slimmer, and has longer hair. He may be wearing jeans and is associated with a "free" lifestyle.

Actually, both conservative and liberal political thought derives from nineteenth-century liberal values, which stressed that the individual, rather than the State should be considered most important. It is the way in which contemporary politicians depart from these values that determines their present definitions. Senator Barry Goldwater, who is known to be a "conservative" is actually very close to nineteenth century "liberal" values in that he is opposed to increased government intervention on questions of domestic economic policy. He is, however, in favor of strong government involvement in the military. Senator Edward Kennedy, who is considered a "liberal," is actually not liberal in the nineteenth-century sense; he is, however, liberal in his willingness to revise traditional liberal ideas about the role of government, particularly on the domestic front. In fact, "one can differentiate between contemporary 'conservative' and 'liberal' American politicians on the basis of how they depart from classical liberal thought. Conservatives diverge from the liberal tradition in their support for the expansion of government power in the areas of military and police policy; liberals depart from classical liberal thought in their call for strong government action on economic and welfare problems" (Richard P. Young, *American Politics Reconsidered,* 1973).

WRITING TO LEARN: A SEQUENCE OF ASSIGNMENTS

▶ *Exercises:*

1.   Write an essay in which you discuss whether you feel you are a "liberal" or a "conservative" on social issues. Define what these terms mean to you.

2.   Find a controversial issue in the newspapers. Define the nature of the controversy and the political leaders who have expressed opinions on it. Then compare the "liberal" and the "conservative" positions.

DISTRIBUTIVE JUSTICE: OR WHO GETS WHAT?

Key Question: What Is the Best Method of Determining How Goods and Services Are Distributed in Society?

One area that has generated considerable disagreement is that concerning **distributive justice** or with how the "goods" of a society may be distributed fairly (this includes rights and liberties as well as material possessions). For those who consider freedom and individuality as all important, the only legitimate way fair distribution can be achieved is through total equality of opportunity, since any attempt to redistribute goods according to some predetermined scheme (need, intelligence, superiority) will infringe upon the rights of some individuals. For example, suppose you have two groups: Group A and Group B, Group B being better off financially. Suppose it were decided that in the interest of promoting equality among groups. Group A would be able to purchase goods and services more cheaply than could Group B. Those who feel that each individual is exactly equal to every other individual would probably view this policy as terribly unfair and feel that a society which permitted such a policy was not a "good society." They would probably say that curtailing the rights of any individual or group of individuals even in the interest of a social good (trying to attain equality) does not create the good or just society. For them, a just society is one in which individuals are treated equally and have equality of opportunity.

Others might feel that community values and concern for the common good are more important than equality. According to this view, no individual is worth anything aside from his or her contribution to the group, since no gift or ability is worth anything unless it has an impact on the group. It follows then, according to this view, that the just society is one in which there is an equal sharing of the benefits of society and where the State has power to determine the distribution of these benefits, even if it means that some individuals are given more than others.

▶ *Writing Assignment:* Read the article "The Case Against Helping the Poor" by Garrett Hardin. Summarize the main points of this article.

Revise the essay you wrote concerning the accessibility of food at the apartment house cooperative, incorporating ideas from the Hardin article.

THE CONCEPT OF LEADERSHIP

Key Question: How Does a Leader Influence a Society?

Your concept of humanity also influences your ideas about what sort of leader is best for society. If you view humanity as irrational and incapable of self-government in most instances, it is likely that you would prefer a strong leader who would assume the burden of responsibility for the welfare of society. Although such a leader might assume too much power, you would probably feel that society's need for leadership outweighs the potential for abuse of power. But if you view humanity as inherently noble, capable of self-government and rational behavior, it is unlikely that you would prefer a strong leader, since you would view the potential for abuse of power as a great threat to society's well being.

WRITING TO LEARN

▶ *Writing Assignment:* Read the excerpt from "The Prince" by Machiavelli. Consider how Machiavelli views humanity. Then write an essay in which you compare Machiavelli's view of humanity with that of Hardin.

▶ *Writing Assignment:* Read your local newspaper and select a current controversy. Write a short summary of that controversy. Then write a paper in which you discuss how your view of humanity and of the role of the individual in relation to society will influence your position on this issue. Incorporate readings from this chapter to support your position.

Key Terms
the "good" society
freedom
responsibility
individualism
liberty
conservative
liberal
distributive justice

Shaping the Future

Robert C. North

Bookstores today carry hundreds of publications about current human crises and disturbing problems of the future. Some are pessimistic, spreading gloom and predicting doom. "The future of mankind is at stake," according to many. Others are optimistic, reassuring us that technology will save mankind or that some other solution will turn up.

How about you? Are you an optimist or a pessimist? Do you believe that every day in every way the world is getting better and better? Worse and worse? Six of one and half a dozen of the other? Do you believe in progress? Or that the world is retrogressive, rapidly becoming unraveled? If you believe the latter, there is much to support your viewpoint—energy shortages, taxes, inflation, unemployment, crime in the streets, urban decay, population problems, arms races, monetary crises, and the possibility of nuclear war, to mention only a few. According to economist Robert Heilbroner in his book *An Inquiry into the Human Prospect,* "The outlook is for what we may call 'convulsive change'—change forced upon us by external events rather than by conscious choice, by catastrophe rather than by calculation." Or do you think that the problems can be solved if we just build nuclear reactors, develop better access to solar energy, throw the bad guys out of office, reinvigorate capitalism, establish socialism, increase our military capabilities, or disarm?

What you think about the world and its future may depend upon your view of human nature. Do you view people as innately selfish, competitive, aggressive, and violent—incapable of transforming themselves into something better? Or are people, though often greedy and corruptible, also capable of great generosity, integrity, and noble undertaking? Though sometimes stupid or slavish to habit, do they also have an extraordinary capacity for insight, vision, and invention? Have the great deeds of history been wrought by the rare saint, genius, or prophet? Or is human progress largely fashioned from the day-to-day decisions and harsh experiences of common men and women? Consider Heilbroner's view: "There seems no hope for rapid changes in the human character traits that would have to be modified to bring about a peaceful, organized reorientation of life styles. Men and women, much as they are today, will set the pace and determine the necessary means for the social changes that will eventually have to be made." Are you ready to take on this responsibility?

What do *you* think of the human prospect? Perhaps you see the men and women of the world divided into good guys and bad guys, the enlightened and the unenlightened, heroes and villains, Christians and heathens, Moslems and infidels, progressives and reactionaries (or conservatives and radicals)—locked in a struggle for dominance. Perhaps you agree with Heilbroner's assessment that "no capitalist nation has yet imagined the extent of the alterations it must undergo to attain a viable stationary socioeconomic structure." If you agree with Heilbroner that capitalism is part of the problem, you might also think about his further conviction that "no socialist state has evidenced the needed willingness to subordinate the national interests to supranational ones." Or, if you come from a Third World country that aspires to catch up with the West, you might ponder his conclusion that "no developing country has fully confronted the implications of becoming a 'modern' nation-state whose industrial development must be severely limited, or considered the strategy for such a state in a world in which the Western nations, capitalist and socialist both, will continue for a long period to enjoy the material advantages of their early start."

Paradoxically, among writers, some of the more optimistic seem to view human nature as fundamentally unchangeable (therefore, it is useless, if not dysfunctional, to interfere in what is viewed as a natural course of events), whereas some of the more pessimistic exhort readers, statesmen, and the public at large to do *something*—recycle, establish communes, dissolve the oil companies, reduce economic or population growth to zero, or abolish capitalism. Are you an "interventionist," pessimistic about the present but insistent that there must be a better way? Or are you inclined toward a laissez-faire policy, convinced that many of our difficulties have been brought about, in fact, by bleeding-heart interventionists tinkering with the Constitution? According to Heilbroner, "The drift toward the strong exercise of political power—a movement given its initial momentum by the need to exercise a much wider and deeper administration of both production and consumption—is likely to attain added support from the psychological insecurity that will be sharpened in a period of unrest and uncertainty."

At least the more adamant of the laissez-faire advocates have solutions that are relatively specific. Go back to the old ways, they say, free up the marketplace, put an end to all this welfare nonsense, stop coddling criminals, and our problems will begin to straighten out. Some of the more radical interventionists also have solutions—get rid of the capitalists, they tell us, and all will be well. With few exceptions the hard-core purveyors of doom and gloom, on the other hand, while issuing dire predictions about the future and offering a favorite panacea, present little else that is genuinely futuristic. Few, if any, concrete solutions are offered; seldom, if ever, is it made explicit how the favorite panacea will alter the course of affairs; and rarely is a practical course of action proposed, however crude, for cleaning up the mess they saw we are in.

Agreeing on the condition of the world around them, the interventionists are by no means in universal accord about what should be done. In an essay entitled "The Case Against Helping the Poor" (*Psychology Today*, September 1974), biologist Garrett Hardin asserts that with the continued dwindling of the world's resources, the differences in prosperity between the rich and the poor can only increase. The stake is survival. Should the well-fed people feed the starving? Are the rich responsible for all the rest of humanity? Many critics of aid and welfare programs think not. But since we all share life on this planet, Hardin declares, "no single person or institution has the right to destroy, waste, or use more than a fair share of its resources." He then proceeds with a provocative argument.

Metaphorically each rich nation can be seen as a lifeboat full of comparatively rich people. In the ocean outside the lifeboat swim the poor of the world, who would like to get in. So here we sit, with say 50 people in our lifeboat, while 100 others thrash about in the water outside, begging to be brought aboard—or at least to be thrown a life jacket. What should the lifeboat passengers do? To be generous, argues Hardin, let us assume that there is room for ten more in the boat, making a total capacity of 60. But out of the 100 people struggling against the ocean, how can ten be fairly chosen for rescue; and once aboard, would not their additional weight destroy the margin of safety enjoyed by the 50 as long as the boat is not fully loaded?

Others take a similar viewpoint. The survival of mankind, they argue, depends upon the maintenance of an island of plenty in what amounts to a vast sea of deprivation. Someone must maintain such an island in order to protect the material and intellectual seed grain for the future. Of all places on earth, the United States comes closest to representing an island of plenty; hence we in this country owe its protection and survival not only to our children but to all generations to come.

The perspective of this article is that no answers are evident because they are locked up in you and me and in the minds, hearts, dispositions, and habit patterns of everyone else in the world as well. We all help determine the shape of tomorrow, next year, and the turn of the century by what we have done (or have failed to do) in the past, by what we are doing now, and by what we do in our own homely ways tomorrow and thereafter, day by day, for as long as we live.

SIX BASIC ASSUMPTIONS

We shall proceed from the following six assumptions:

1. Human affairs are not solely, or even primarily, the outcome of economic or other material factors, but neither are they uniquely the result of "free will" or other intellectual, psychological, or spiritual forces. The course of events stems from the intense interaction of both types of influence. Thus, a change in any one important factor is likely to bring about changes in others. But human considerations can effect their own kind of *social determinism*: decisions of the past may limit today's options just as deeply embedded customs and institutions may blind us to promising alternatives.

2. Numbers are not "inhuman," but are closely intertwined with the way we live. They influence our values, just as our beliefs, preferences, and aspirations affect the numbers of people and things we deal with. Large numbers of people and things tend to widen and complicate the scope of our moral responsibility. We cannot confront the future effectively unless we understand the connection between values and numbers, between the quantitative and the qualitative.

3. Our ability to cope successfully with the critical problems of the future will depend a great deal upon both the potential and the limitations of human nature.

But what we commonly refer to as "human nature" is not fixed, and immutable. To a large extent each individual human being *is* what he or she *does,* and over the millennia people's activities have changed enormously. Our predispositions and traits have undergone many changes as alterations have come about in our relations with the physical environment and with each other.

4. Although human beings have achieved progress in some dimensions, we cannot assume that they have progressed in all dimensions, or even in a few of the more important ones. Through the ages people have vastly increased their ability to harness mechanical energy and transform the products of the earth for their special purposes. We have also found ways of maiming and killing each other in greater and greater numbers. It is not at all clear that we have made much moral or ethical progress overall. Progress in one dimension often contributes to retrogression in another.

5. Although each human event is unique and people's ways of doing things are constantly changing, certain general tendencies and broad patterns of behavior have been repeated again and again throughout our prehistory and history. An important key to coping with the future involves an ability to distinguish between what is recurring and what is unique. In order to achieve a perspective of what our possibilities for the future are, we need to review some patterns of the past—not only the relatively recent past, but also the dim past which includes the beginnings of human affairs.

6. The individual is shaped in large part by his or her society, but the society is the outcome of its individual human components. Neither can be understood properly without an understanding of the other. In dealing with the future, then, we should not focus primarily upon the individual, nor primarily upon the society, but upon the dynamic interactions between the two.

One approach to the future advocated in this book involves the building of utopias—not just one or two, but perhaps hundreds or even thousands. You may object that utopia building is a softheaded, imbecilic pastime, a kind of withdrawal from the real world, as useless as daydreaming, although it may be reassuring to learn that at least one utopia influenced the shaping of the United States Constitution. The construction of utopias can help us broaden our perspectives and evaluate alternatives before we commit ourselves to an irrevocable course of action.

THE MEANING AND USEFULNESS OF UTOPIAS

The word *utopia,* coined from the Greek, means "nowhere." It was first used in the sixteenth century by Sir Thomas More in his book *Utopia* as the name of an island, a figment of his imagination, where an ideal commonwealth was said to exist. According to dictionary definitions, a utopia refers to an imaginary country with ideal laws and social conditions, or to an impractical and usually impossibly ideal scheme for social, political, or economic improvement. More broadly, the German sociologist Karl Mannheim, author of *Ideology and Utopia,* writes that the term "may be applied to any process of thought which receives its impetus not from the direct force of social reality but from concepts, such as symbols, fantasies, dreams, ideas, and the like, which in the most comprehensive sense of that term are nonexistent."

Although the concept of utopia has become firmly associated with Sir Thomas More, the genre made its appearance long before his time. Indeed, it was Plato's *Republic* that provided the general model to which all subsequent fictions may have been indebted. Unlike radical reformers of a later day, however, Plato was not proposing an ideal commonwealth that might be brought into existence overnight, by repeating some catch phrases and making a few sweeping changes in the social, political, or economic institutions. Plato's ideal was a counsel of perfection. Ages might be required to bring his envisaged state into being. The purpose of Plato's utopia building, according to Mannheim, was primarily to construct an authoritarian design that would "buttress, in as rational terms as possible, a static and hierarchically ordered political system."

The utopian writings of More and his fellow humanists during the Renaissance, by contrast, were the expression, according to Mannheim, of a powerful "wave of intellectual and social release"—a radical challenge to the more traditional ideas and rigid institutions of the time. A staunch Catholic who suffered execution rather than submit to the demands made upon him by Henry VIII, More was concerned with a revolution that would be much deeper than a mere change in the form of government or even a shift of power from one economic class to another. The only true revolution, he believed, is moral, and hence a change in a society's institutions will be of limited value unless the new arrangement produces good men and good women. His *Utopia* was thus an attempt to infuse a concrete social system with Christian ethical values.

More's criticism of contemporary institutions and the communism of his Utopians have made his book popular with many modern revolutionaries, who have viewed it as a document of social protest. But More himself, unlike many "true believers" before and since, expressed reservations about his own creation. "I admit that not a few things in the manners and laws of the Utopians seemed very absurd to be," he wrote in the last paragraphs of the book, "their way of waging war, their religious customs, as well as other matters, but especially the keystone of their entire system, namely, their communal living without the use of money. . . . Yet I must confess that there are many things in the Utopian Commonwealth that I wish rather than expect to see followed among our citizens." Drawing upon his own travels, as well as his humanistic studies, political theorist James Harrington during the Cromwellian regime used a comparative study of constitutions as a means of identifying that form of govenrment most ideally suited to England. The most realistic of the humanist utopias, Harrington's *The Commonwealth of Oceana* (1656), subsequently exerted a notable influence on makers of the United States Constitution. In *The New Atlantis* Sir Francis Bacon expressed an aggressive faith in science and its liberating role.

During the eighteenth and early nineteenth centuries the widespread social unrest engendered by the industrial revolution as well as the consequent economic and politial readjustments of the time found expression in a succession of somewhat heterogeneous utopias modeled on the work of the earlier humanists. The literary utopias constructed in the decades following the French Revolution were directed more consistently toward a single political ideal. Among them were those of the so-called utopian socialists, such as Saint-Simon, Babeuf, Fourier, and Owen. With variations in individual perspective, these writers believed that unemployment and other undesirable outcomes of the industrial revolution could be eliminated and the economic security of the masses achieved by means of rational planning, through social ownership of the means of production. Moreover, much to the subsequent irritation of Karl Marx and his disciples, these early-nineteenth-century utopia builders thought that propertied groups could be persuaded to surrender their holdings peacefully and even voluntarily.

Specifically, Marx's collaborator, Friedrich Engels, criticized the antibourgeois but idealistic utopians for trying to "evolve out of the human brain" the solution of social problems that lay "hidden in undeveloped social conditions." As a consequence, Engels argued, these new social systems were foredoomed: "The more completely they were worked out in detail, the more they could not help drifting into pure fantasies." Engels rebuked them, Mannheim writes, for perpetuating the "sentimental delusions of the eighteen-century *Philosophes,* who naively fancied that they could bring their fellow men to carry through a reorganization of society merely by placing before them certain abstract ideals." The place to start was with the proletariat, the only class which, in Marxian terms, could bring about a true reorganization of society.

Many utopia builders of the nineteenth century went beyond pen-and-ink creations and created real-life communities. Centered chiefly in the United States, both religious and nonreligious groups established large numbers of model settlements—most of them self-consciously experimental and usually communistic. Among the more notable of these attempts were the Shaker, Hutterite, Zoarite, Owenite, Fourierist, and Perfectionist settlements. Such experimental communities appeared in New England, New York, the Middle West, including Texas, and in various other far-flung localities. The communism of the religious societies was often thoroughgoing. Incoming members normally turned over all property to a common fund. No wages were paid, and every effort was made to ensure that no one in such a community was either rich or poor. Every individual was guaranteed the necessities of life and care in sickness and old age.

In some societies the emphasis was upon eugenics as well as economics. Influenced by Charles Darwin's *The Origin of Species,* the Oneida Community tried to perfect human society by the "scientific" arrangement of sexual unions. Since human beings were perceived as shaped by a combination of heredity and environment, the community hoped to influence the values, moral character, and behavior of future generations by the careful selection of their parents as well as by the molding of the society in which they would live.

Retrospectively, we see how the utopians have often been dismissed as impractical dreamers. Pen-and-ink utopias, such as those of More, Harrington, Bacon, and others, bore little resemblance to reality and had no possibility of being tested. The model communities, on the other hand, could not be effectively tested unless they could be separated from the larger, encompassing society—and despite their most heroic efforts, that was seldom economically, politically, or even socially feasible.

In modern times, the possibility of subjecting experimental, real-life communities to rigorous test through isolation from the encompassing society seems even more remote than in the nineteenth century. Then, at least, settlements could be established on the frontier and a certain degree of independence maintained until the larger society encompassed them. Now, in the latter decades of the twentieth century, there are virtually no frontiers left—none, at least, that cannot be penetrated economically and politically.

The usefulness of pen-and-ink, or purely conceptual, utopias, on the other hand, has been greatly enhanced by the development of computer modeling techniques and other specialized methodologies that make it possible to generate hundreds or even thousands of alternate societies—and then pick and choose among them as we wish. Today, a variety of attempts are already underway, with the aid of computers, to create new utopias designed to help us plan for the future.

Many people object to the idea of trying to model a society. They point out, rightly, that any such attempt is certain to be a gross over-simplification of real life. Even worse, it is likely to overlook the subtle complexity of thought and feeling—as if human beings were themselves machines, no better than electronic computers. Moreover, the major "planned" societies that have been established in the real world—the USSR, for example, or the People's Republic of China—are seen by many as having degraded, even brutalized, people rather than setting them free.

These are important objections, and they need to be taken seriously. But they overlook one fundamental consideration. Each of us carries around in his or her head a "model" of the world, of society, of the local community, of the family—even of oneself—and none of us can deal with any of these entities, even superficially, without reference to the appropriate mental construct or model. It is the only way we have of relating to other people and to our larger surroundings. We draw upon these models whenever we discuss affairs, whenever we vote, and whenever we plan for the future in any way. Such models affect our moral values and choices. In considering possible alternatives, therefore, the central questions are what models are we carrying about and using, what are their implications, and what do we want them to mean for ourselves, our children, and others?

Usually, we know very little about the models we actually use because we do not think about them often. Even when we do think about them, however, we normally ignore the assumptions about people that underlie them, and also the outcomes for ourselves and others that may emerge from them. Any social, economic, or political planning, any policymaking, and any effort to develop future alternatives should therefore begin with a discussion of our basic assumptions about people.

Arguments Against Freedom

Scott Gordon

Describing freedom as a primary social good implies that it is good in itself and not merely instrumental to other ends. A large body of modern thinking, including J. S. Mill's great defense of intellectual freedom in his essay *On Liberty,* the orthodox modern economist's defense of economic freedom, and the orthodox modern political philsopher's defense of political freedom, are essentially instrumentalist in that they are efforts to demonstrate what other desirable things will flow from such freedoms. Yet, very few of the defenders of freedom would deny that they regard freedom as good in itself. Some of those who attack freedom may go so far as to deny this, but the main arguments against freedom are efforts to show that it has undesirable implications or consequences, so the defenders and opponents of freedom enter the lists on the same field. The main arguments against freedom may be classified under four broad headings.

(a) *The choice is burdensome.* If freedom is construed as freedom of choice, it appears to follow that the larger the number of possible choices the greater the degree of freedom. But anyone who has had the bewildering experience of having to choose from among seventeen different brands of canned peas in a modern supermarket knows that the unrestricted proliferation of choice opportunities is not necessarily beneficial. Rational choice requires the acquisition of information and comparative analysis, both of which are costly in terms of time, mental energy, and other scarce resources. The optimum degree of variety is less than infinite and may be quite small if information costs and decision-making costs rise rapidly as the number of potential choices increases. One of the arguments for representative democracy as against plebiscitary government is that the costs of choice under the latter system would be excessive if they had to be borne directly by ordinary people as an addition to their normal activities.

Time magazine, in 1954, reported a discussion between Attlee, Vishinsky, and Mikoyan on the meaning of freedom: "At last, through a bewildered interpreter, the three agreed that in the West it meant 'freedom to choose'; in the Communist East it meant "freedom from having to choose.' "[17] The latter view, despite its form as a definition of freedom, is really a rejection of freedom, but it cannot be dismissed out of hand as simple casuistry. If people were *forced* to choose carefully among seventeen different brands of peas, a large number of candidates for Congress, and so on, one might well conclude that the architect of such a system had invented a new and ingenious form of tyranny. But if people are not forced to expend their time and energy in this way; if what is open to them is the *opportunity* to make such choices, and to devote as much effort to them as they wish; then there is no undesired burden of choice which people cannot avoid by their own individual efforts. This attack on freedom therefore fails to carry, despite the fact that it has to be admitted that making choices is indeed burdensome.

(b) *That responsibility is burdensome.* The classic exposition of this argument against freedom is Ivan's fable of the Grand Inquisitor in Dostoyevsky's *The Brothers Karamazov.* Whenever a man is able to choose among alternative courses of actions he cannot avoid bearing moral responsibility for the consequences of what he does. The argument of the Grand Inquisitor is that this burden is so heavy that, for ordinary men, it greatly outweighs the benefits of freedom. The Church, says the Inquisitor, has labored for centuries to improve man's lot by relieving him of freedom and taking the weight of responsibility upon itself.

One cannot deny that responsibility is burdensome; common empirical experience indicates that most men seek to limit the responsibility they have to bear, and some are evidently willing to contract the scope of their freedom to quite narrow limits if they can thereby escape the responsibility that accompanies the power of choice. However, the weakness of the Inquisitor's argument can be perceived if we shift it from its theological context to a political one. When men give up their freedom to a dictator, does this mean that responsibility is transferred from them to him? If there were a just God, the moral account might be presented in the other world, but in this world it need not be, and it is less likely to be, the greater the power of the dictator. The political meaning of dictatorship is that the empirical connection between power and responsibility is broken. The dictator is not accountable for his actions and, by contrast, his subjects may be made accountable, and heavily so, by whatever standards he chooses to impose.

Freedom is an impure good since it involves the burdens of choice and responsibility, and the optimum amount of it is unlikely to be the same for all. To the extent that a person retains the most vital of all freedoms, the freedom to *change* his choices, he may experiment with different ways of life and suit his own tastes as to how much responsibility he wishes to bear. Political freedom defined as the *opportunity* to participate in the process of collective choice has some of the characteristics of a "public good," which makes it difficult to supply different amounts of it to different persons but, more importantly, since it deals with the exercise of sovereign power, it is not possible to give up freedom of political choice without losing the power to change one's choices. The Grand Inquisitor did not hold an office that was periodically open to popular election.

(c) *That wisdom is not widespread.* Adam Smith's defense of freedom was grounded upon the proposition that each man is the best judge of his own interests. Many others have argued the reverse, and pointing out that people often make unwise choices, have grounded their social philosophies on the need for control of men's actions by those of them who *are* wise. This is not the same as the argument that it is undesirable, for some reason, to minister to men's individual interests; it accepts the merit of doing so, but contends that many (most?) people are incapable of perceiving what their "real" or "true" or "long-run" interests are. The description of this argument as "paternalistic" is indicative of its nature. Humans are altricial animals requiring a lengthy period of both biological and social development before maturity is attained. It is unavoidable that children must be coerced, since they clearly lack the information and judgment that is necessary to the making of decisions which are wise. Nature assures that almost all human organisms become biologically nature at about the same age but there is no reason to believe that all become competent judges of their own interests when they attain a certain age; everyone knows numerous instances of palpable incompetence that lasts indefinitely. If one regards this as characteristic not of special cases, but of the generality of men, it becomes an argument against freedom in the broad sense.

In opposing this argument it is not necessary to cling to Adam Smith's proposition that every man is the best judge of his own interests or even to contend that this is true of most men. It is sufficient to recognize the difficulty of selecting those who would do better. Nature provides parents for children automatically, and does not invariably make a good job of it. Political processes may be more discriminating than procreational ones but there is little warrant for believing that even the best of them can act as an effective selector of governors whose wisdom and benevolence are so great and so reliable that the rest of mankind should place themselves under their paternal control. Adam Smith also pointed out that some activities are not likely to be worse performed than by those who have the audacity to believe that they are the ones who should be entrusted with them. Any political system whose main task is to select a "father of the people" is likely instead to select a slavemaster.

(d) *That freedom conflicts with other social goods.* Some ethical philosophers have argued that the nature of things is such that all good things are harmonious. If that were so there would be no problem of choice at all since this always involves sacrificing some goods in order to obtain others. Some defenders of freedom argue that *freedom* at least has the special characteristic that it cannot be exchanged for anything else that is good.[18] As a general proposition this is difficult to defend since innumerable cases can be cited in which such a trade is clearly possible. The discipline known as "welfare economics" consists largely of the analysis of such cases. The extensive, and growing, restriction of economic freedom in modern democratic societies is based mainly on the argument that such freedom conflicts with the attainment of other social goods.

This is the most important argument against freedom. It cannot, however, be advanced in general terms as an unspecified argument against "freedom" as such. Some freedoms may be in conflict with some other social goods, but other relationships may be characterized by congruence. The issue is an empirical one, not one of principle. The next chapter is an attempt to examine these empirical relationships to some degree.

The Need for Security

Thomas Hobbes

CHAP. XIII. OF THE NATURALL CONDITION OF MANKIND, AS CONCERNING THEIR FELICITY, AND MISERY

Nature hath made men so equall, in the faculties of body, and mind; as that though there bee found one man sometimes manifestly stronger in body, or of quicker mind then another; yet when all is reckoned together, the difference between man, and man, is not so considerable, as that one man can thereupon claim to himselfe any benefit, to which another may not pretend, as well as he. For as to the strength of body, the weakest has strength enough to kill the strongest, either by secret machination, or by confederacy with others, that are in the same danger with himselfe.

And as to the faculties of the mind, (seeing aside the arts grounded upon words, and especially that skill of proceeding upon generall, and infallible rules, called Science; which very few have, and but in few things; as being not a native faculty, born with us; nor attained, (as Prudence,) while we look after somewhat els,) I find yet a greater equality amongst men, than that of strength. For Prudence, is but Experience; which equall time, equally bestowes on all men, in those things they equally apply themselves unto. That which may perhaps make such equality incredible, is but a vain conceipt of ones owne wisdome, which almost all men think they have in a greater degree, than the Vulgar; that is, than all men but themselves, and a few others, whom by Fame, or for concurring with themselves, they approve. For such is the nature of men, that howsoever they may acknowledge many others to be more witty, or more eloquent, or more learned; Yet they will hardly believe there be many so wise as themselves: For they see their own wit at hand, and other mens at a distance. But this proveth rather that men are in that point equall, then unequall. For there is not ordinarily a greater signe of the equall distribution of any thing, than that every man is contented with his share.

From this equality of ability, ariseth equality of hope in the attaining of our Ends. And therefore if any two men desire the same thing, which neverthelesse they cannot both enjoy, they become enemies; and in the way to their End, (which is principally their owne conservation, and sometimes their delectation only,) endeavour to destroy, or subdue one an other. And from hence it comes to passe, that where an Invader hath no more to feare, than an other mans single power; if one plant, sow, build, or possesse a convenient Seat, others may probably be expected to come prepared with forces united, to dispossesse, and deprive him, not only of the fruit of his labour, but also of his life, or liberty. And the Invader again is in the like danger of another.

And from this diffidence of one another, there is no way for any man to secure himselfe, so reasonable, as Anticipation; that is, by force, or wiles, to master the persons of all men he can, so long, till he see no other power great enough to endanger him: And this is no more than his own conservation requireth, and is generally allowed. Also because there be some, that taking pleasure in contemplating their own power in the acts of conquest, which they pursue farther than their security requires; if others, that otherwise would be glad to be at ease within modest bounds, should not by invasion increase their power, they would not be able, long time, by standing only on their defence, to subsist. And by consequence, such augmentation of dominion over men, being necessary to a mans conservation, it ought to be allowed him.

Againe, men have no pleasure, (but on the contrary a great deale of griefe) in keeping company, where there is no power able to overawe them all. For every man looketh that his companion should value him, at the same rate he sets upon himselfe: And upon all signes of contempt, or undervaluing, naturally endeavours, as far as he dares (which amongst them that have no common power to keep them in quiet, is far enough to make them destroy each other,) to extort a greater value from his contemners, by dommage; and from others, by the example.

So that in the nature of man, we find three principall causes of quarrell. First, Competition; Secondly, Diffidence; Thirdly, Glory.

The first, maketh men invade for Gain; the second, for Safety; and the third, for Reputation. The first use Violence, to make themselves Masters of other mens persons, wives, children, and cattell; the second, to defend them; the third, for trifles, as a word, a smile, a different opinion, and any other signe of undervalue, either direct in their Persons, or by reflexion in their Kindred, their Friends, their Nation, their Profession, or their Name.

Hereby it is manifest, that during the time men live without a common Power to keep them all in awe, they are in that condition which is called Warre; and such a warre, as is of every man against every man. For WARRE, consisteth not in Battell onely, or the act of fighting; but in a tract of time, wherein the Will to contend by Battell is sufficiently known: and therefore the notion of *Time,* is to be considered in the nature of Warre; as it is in the nature of Weather. For as the nature of Foule weather, lyeth not in a showre or two of rain; but in an inclination thereto of many dayes together; So the nature of War, consisteth not in actuall fighting; but in the known disposition thereto, during all the time there is no assurance to the contrary. All other time is PEACE.

Whatsoever therefore is consequent to a time of Warre, where every man is Enemy to every man; the same is consequent to the time, wherein men live without other security, than what their own strength, and their own invention shall furnish them withall. In such condition, there is no place for Industry; because the fruit thereof is uncertain; and consequently no Culture of the Earth, no Navigation, nor use of the commodities that may be imported by Sea; no commodious Building; no Instruments of moving, and removing such things as require much force; no Knowledge of the face of the Earth; no account of Time; no Arts; no Letters; no Society; and which is worst of all, continuall feare, and danger of violent death; And the life of man, solitary, poore, nasty, brutish, and short.

It may seem strange to some man, that has not well weighed these things; that Nature should thus dissociate, and render men apt to invade, and destroy one another: and he may therefore, not trusting to this Inference, made from the Passions, desire perhaps to have the same confirmed by Experience. Let him therefore consider with himselfe, when taking a journay, he armes himselfe, and seeks to go well accompanied; when going to sleep, he locks his dores; when even in his house he locks his chests; and this when he knowes there bee Lawes, and publike Officers, armed, to revenge all injuries shall bee done him; what opinion he has of his fellow subjects, when he rides armed; of his fellow Citizens, when he locks his dores; and of his children, and servants, when he locks his chests. Does he not there as much accuse mankind by his actions, as I do by my words? But neither of us accuse mans nature in it. The Desires, and other Passions of man, are in themselves no Sin. No more are the Actions, that proceed from those Passions, till they know a Law that forbids them: which till Lawes be made they cannot know: nor can any Law be made, till they have agreed upon the Person that shall make it.

It may peradventure be thought, there was never such a time, nor condition of warre as this; and I believe it was never generally so, over all the world: but there are many places, where they live so now. For the savage people in many places of *America,* except the government of small Families, the concord whereof dependeth on naturall lust, have no gonverment at all; and live at this day in that brutish manner, as I said before. Howsoever, it may be perceived what manner of life there would be, where there were no common Power to feare; by the manner of life, which men that have formerly lived under a peacefull government, use to degenerate into, in a civill Warre.

But though there had never been any time, wherein particular men were in a condition of warre one against another; yet in all times, Kings, and Persons of Soveraigne authority, because of their Independency, are in continuall jealousies, and in the state and posture of Gladiators; having their weapons pointing, and their eyes fixed on one another; that is, their Forts, Garrisons, and Guns, upon the Frontiers of their Kingdomes; and continuall Spyes upon their neighbours; which is a posture of War. But because they uphold thereby, the Industry of their Subjects; there does not follow from it, that misery, which accompanies the Liberty of particular men.

To this warre of every man against every man, this also is consequent; that nothing can be Unjust. The notions of Right and Wrong, Justice and Industice have there no place. Where there is no common Power, there is no Law; where no Law, no Injustice. Force, and Fraud, are in warre the two Cardinall vertues. Justice, and Injustice are none of the Faculties neither of the Body, nor Mind. If they were, they might be in a man that were alone in the world, as well as his Senses, and Passions. They are Qualities, that relate to men in Society, not in Solitude. It is consequent also to the same condition, that there by no Propriety, no Dominion, no *Mine* and *Thine* distinct; but onely that to be every mans, that he can get; and for so long, as he can keep it. And thus much for the ill condition, which man by meer Nature is actually placed in; though with a possibility to come out of it, consisting partly in the Passions, partly in his Reason.

The Passions that encline men to Peace, are Feare of Death; Desire of such things as are necessary to commodious living; and a Hope by their Industry to obtain them. And Reason suggesteth convenient Articles of Peace, upon which men may be drawn to agreement. These Articles, are they, which otherwise are called the Lawes of Nature: whereof I shall speak more particularly, in the two following Chapters.

CHAP. XIV. OF THE FIRST AND SECOND NATURALL LAWES, AND OF CONTRACTS

THE RIGHT OF NATURE, which Writers commonly call *Jus Naturale,* is the Liberty each man hath, to use his own power, as he will himselfe, for the preservation of his own Nature; that is to say, of his own Life; and consequently, of doing any thing, which in his own Judgement, and Reason, hee shall conceive to be the aptest means thereunto.

By LIBERTY, is understood, according to the proper signification of the word, the absence of externall Impediments: which Impediments, may oft take away part of a mans power to do what hee would; but cannot hinder him from using the power left him, according as his judgement, and reason shall dictate to him.

A LAW OF NATURE, (*Lex Naturalis,*) is a Precept, or generall Rule, found out by Reason, by which a man is forbidden to do, that, which is destructive of his life, or taketh away the means of preserving the same; and to omit, that, by which he thinketh it may be best preserved. For though they that speak of this subject, use to confound *Jus,* and *Lex, Right,* and *Law;* yet they ought to be distinguished; because RIGHT, consisteth in liberty to do, or to forebeare; Whereas LAW, determineth, and bindeth to one of them: so that Law, and Right, differ as much, as Obligation, and Liberty; which in one and the same matter are inconsistent.

And because the condition of Man, (as hath been declared in the precedent Chapter) is a condition of Warre of every one against every one; in which case every one is governed by his own Reason; and there is nothing he can make use of, that may not be a help unto him, in preserving his life against his enemyes; It followeth, that in such a condition, every man has a Right to every thing; even to one anothers body. And therefore, as long as this naturall Right of every man to every thing endureth, there can be no security to any man, (how strong or wise soever he be,) of living out the time, which Nature ordinarily alloweth men to live. And consequently it is a precept, or generall rule of Reason, *That every man, ought to endeavour Peace, as farre as he has hope of obtaining it; and when he cannot obtain it, that he may seek, and use, all helps, and advantgages of Warre.* The first branch of which Rule, containeth the first, and Fundamentall Law of Nature; which is, *to seek Peace, and follow it.* The Second, the summe of the Right of Nature; which is, *By all means we can, to defend our selves.*

From this Fundamentall Law of Nature, by which men are commanded to endeavour Peace, is derived this second Law; *That a man be willing, when others are so too, as farre-forth, as for Peace, and defence of himselfe he shall think it necessary, to lay down this right to all things; and be contented with so much liberty against other men, as he would allow other men against himselfe.* For as long as every man holdeth this Right, of doing any thing he liketh; so long are all men in the condition of Warre. But if other men will not lay down their Right, as well as he; then there is no Reason for any one, to devest himselfe of his: For that were to expose himselfe to Prey, (which no man is bound to) rather than to dispose himselfe to Peace. This is that Law of the Gospell; *Whatsoever you require that others should do to you, that do ye to them*. And that Law of all men, *Quod tibi fieri non vis, alteri ne feceris*.

To *lay downe* a mans *Right* to any thing, is to *devest* himselfe of the *Liberty*, of hindring another of the benefit of his own Right to the same. For he that renounceth, or passeth away his Right, giveth not to any other man a Right which he had not before; because there is nothing to which every man had not Right by Nature: but onely standeth out of his way, that he may enjoy his own originall Right, without hindrance from him; not without hindrance from another. So that the effect which redoundeth to one man, by another mans defect of Right, is but so much diminution of impediments to the use of his own Right originall.

Right is layd aside, either by simply Renouncing it; or by Transferring it to another. By *Simply* RENOUNCING; when he cares not to whom the benefit thereof redoundeth. By TRANSFERRING; when he intendeth the benefit thereof to some certain person, or persons. And when a man hath in either manner abandoned, or granted away his Right; then is he said to be OBLIGED, or BOUND, not to hinder those, to whom such Right is granted, or abandoned, from the benefit of it: and that he *Ought*, and it is his DUTY, not to make voyd that voluntary act of his own: and that such hindrance is INJUSTICE, and INJURY, as being *Sine Jure*; the Right being before renounced, or transferred. So that *Injury*, or *Injustice*, in the controversies of the world, is somewhat like to that, which in the disputations of Scholers is called *Absurdity*. For as it is there called an Absurdity, to contradict what one maintained in the Beginning: so in the world, it is called Injustice, and Injury, voluntarily to undo that, which from the beginning he had voluntarily done. The way by which a man either simply Renounceth, or Transferreth his Right, is a Declaration, or Signification, by some voluntary and sufficient signe, or signes, that he doth so Renounce, or Transferre; or hath so Renounced, or Transferred the same, to him that accepteth it. And these Signes are either Words onely, or Actions onely; or (as it happeneth most often) both Words, and Actions. And the same are the BONDS, by which men are bound, and obliged: Bonds, that have their strength, not from their own Nature, (for nothing is more easily broken then a mans word,) but from Feare of some evill consequence upon the rupture.

Whensoever a man Transferreth his Right, or Renounceth it; it is either inconsideration of some Right reciprocally transferred to himselfe; or for some other good he hopeth for thereby. For it is a voluntary act: and of the voluntary acts of every man, the object is some *Good to himselfe*. And therefore there be some Rights, which no man can be understood by any words, or other signes, to have abandoned, or transferred. As first a man cannot lay down the right of resisting them, that assault him by force, to take away his life; because he cannot be understood to ayme thereby, at any Good to himselfe. The same may be sayd of Wounds, and Chayns, and Imprisonment; both because there is no benefit consequent to such patience; as there is to the patience of suffering another to be wounded, or imprisoned: as also because a man cannot tell, when he seeth men proceed against him by violence, whether they intend his death or not. And lastly the motive, and end for which this renouncing, and transferring of Right is introduced, is nothing else but the security of a mans person, in his life, and in the means of so preserving life, as not to be weary of it. And therefore if a man by words, or other signes, seem to despoyle himselfe of the End, for which these signes were intended; he is not to be understood as if he meant it, or that it was his will; but that he was ignorant of how such words and actions were to be interpreted.

The Social Compact

Jean Jacques Rousseau

CHAPTER I. SUBJECT OF THE FIRST BOOK

Man is born free and everywhere he is in chains. Many a one believes himself the master of others, and yet he is a greater slave than they. How has this change come about? I do not know. What can render it legitimate? I believe that I can settle this question.

If I considered only force and the results that proceed from it, I should say that so long as a people is compelled to obey and does obey, it does well; but that, so soon as it can shake off the yoke and does shake it off, it does better; for, if men recover their freedom by virtue of the same right by which it was taken away, either they are justified in resuming it, or there was no justification for depriving them of it. But the social order is a sacred right which serves as a foundation for all others. This right, however, does not come from nature. It is therefore based on conventions. The question is to know what these conventions are. Before coming to that, I must establish what I have just laid down.

CHAPTER II. PRIMITIVE SOCIETIES

The earliest of all societies, and the only natural one, is the family; yet children remain attached to their father only so long as they have need of him for their own preservation. As soon as this need ceases, the natural bond is dissolved. The children being freed from the obedience which they owed to their father, and the father from the cares which he owed to his children, become equally independent. If they remain united, it is no longer naturally but voluntarily; and the family itself is kept together only by convention.

This common liberty is a consequence of man's nature. His first law is to attend to his preservation, his first cares are those which he owes to himself; and as soon as he comes to years of discretion, being sole judge of the means adapted for his own preservation, he becomes his own master.

The family is, then, if you will, the primitive model of political societies; the chief is the analogue of the father, while the people represent the children; and all, being born free and equal, alienate their liberty only for their own advantage. The whole difference is that, in the family, the father's love for his children repays him for the care that he bestows upon them; while, in the State, the pleasure of ruling makes up for the chief's lack of love for his people.

Grotius denies that all human authority is established for the benefit of the government, and he cites slavery as an instance. His invariable mode of reasoning is to establish right by fact. A juster method might be employed, but none more favorable to tyrants.

It is doubtful then, according to Grotius, whether the human race belongs to a hundred men, or whether these hundred men belong to the human race; and he appears throughout his book to incline to the former opinion, which is also that of Hobbes. In this way we have mankind divided like herds of cattle, each of which has a master, who looks after it in order to devour it.

Just as a herdsman is superior in nature to his herd, so chiefs, who are the herdsmen of men, are superior in nature to their people. Thus, according to Philo's account, the Emperor Caligula reasoned, inferring truly enough from this analogy that kings are gods, or that men are brutes.

The reasoning of Caligula is tantamount to that of Hobbes and Grotius. Aristotle, before them all, had likewise said that men are not naturally equal, but that some are born for slavery and others for dominion.

Aristotle was right, but he mistook the effects for the cause. Every man born in slavery is born for slavery; nothing is more certain. Slaves lose everything in their bonds, even the desire to escape from them; they love their servitude as the companions of Ulysses loved their brutishness. If, then, there are slaves by nature, it is because there have been slaves contrary to nature. The first slaves were made such by force; their cowardice kept them in bondage.

I have said nothing about King Adam nor about Emperor Noah, the father of three great monarchs who shared the universe, like the children of Saturn with whom they are supposed to be identical. I hope that my moderation will give satisfaction; for, as I am a direct descendant of one of these princes, and perhaps of the eldest branch, how do I know whether, by examination of titles, I might not find myself the lawful king of the human race? Be that as it may, it cannot be denied that Adam was sovereign of the world, as Robinson was of his island, so long as he was its sole inhabitant; and it was an agreeable feature of that empire that the monarch, secure on his throne, had nothing to fear from rebellions, or wars, or conspirators.

CHAPTER III. THE RIGHT OF THE STRONGEST

The strongest man is never strong enough to be always master, unless he transforms his power into right, and obedience into duty. Hence the right of the strongest—a right apparently assumed in irony, and really established in principle. But will this phrase never be explained to us? Force is a physical power; I do not see what morality can result from its effects. To yield to force is an act of necessity, not of will; it is at most an act of prudence. In what sense can it be a duty?

Let us assume for a moment this pretended right. I say that nothing results from it but inexplicable nonsense; for if force constitutes right, the effect changes with the cause, and any force which overcomes the first succeeds to its rights. As soon as men can disobey with impunity, they may do so legitimately; and since the strongest is always in the right, the only thing is to act in such a way that one may be the strongest. But what sort of a right is it that perishes when force ceases? If it is necessary to obey by compulsion, there is no need to obey from duty; and if men are no longer forced to obey, obligation is at an end. We see, then, that this word *right* adds nothing to force; it here means nothing at all.

Obey the powers that be. If that means, Yield to force, the precept is good but superfluous; I reply that it will never be violated. All power comes from God, I admit; but every disease comes from him too; does it follow that we are prohibited from calling in a physician? If a brigand should surprise me in the recesses of a wood, am I bound not only to give up my purse when forced, but am I also morally bound to do so when I might conceal it? For, in effect, the pistol which he holds is a superior force.

Let us agree, then, that might does not make right, and that we are bound to obey none but lawful authorities. Thus my original question ever recurs.

CHAPTER IV. SLAVERY

Since no man has any natural authority over his fellow-men, and since force is not the source of right, conventions remain as the basis of all lawful authority among men.

If an individual, says Grotius, can alienate his liberty and become the slave of a master, why should not a whole people be able to alienate theirs, and become subject to a king? In this there are many equivocal terms requiring explanation; but let us confine ourselves to the word *alienate*. To alienate is to give or sell. Now, a man who becomes another's slave does not give himself; he sells himself at the very least for his subsistence. But why does a nation sell itself? So far from a king supplying his subjects with their subsistence, he draws his from them; and, according to Rabelais, a king does not live on a little. Do subjects, then, give up their persons on condition that their property also shall be taken? I do not see what is left for them to keep.

It will be said that the despot secures to his subjects civil peace. Be it so; but what do they gain by that, if the wars which his ambition brings upon them, together with his insatiable greed and the vexations of his administration, harass them more than their own dissensions would? What do they gain by it if this tranquillity is itself one of their miseries? Men live tranquilly also in dungeons; is that enough to make them contented there? The Greeks confined in the cave of the Cyclops lived peacefully until their turn came to be devoured.

To say that a man gives himself for nothing is to say what is absurd and inconceivable; such an act is illegitimate and invalid, for the simple reason that he who performs it is not in his right mind. To say the same thing of a whole nation is to suppose a nation of fools; and madness does not confer rights.

Even if each person could alienate himself, he could not alienate his children; they are born free men; their liberty belongs to them, and no one has a right to dispose of it except themselves. Before they have come to years of discretion, the father can, in their name, stipulate conditions for their preservation and welfare, but not surrender them irrevocably and unconditionally; for such a gift is contrary to the ends of nature, and exceeds the rights of paternity. In order, then, that an arbitrary government might be legitimate, it would be necessary that the people in each generation should have the option of accepting or rejecting it; but in that case such a government would no longer be arbitrary.

To renounce one's liberty is to renounce one's quality as a man, the rights and also the duties of humanity. For him who renounces everything there is no possible compensation. Such a renunciation is incompatible with man's nature, for to take away all freedom from his will is to take away all morality from his actions. In short, a convention which stipulates absolute authority on the one side and unlimited obedience on the other is vain and contradictory. Is it not clear that we are under no obligations whatsoever towards a man from whom we have a right to demand everything? And does not this single condition, without equivalent, without exchange, involve the nullity of the act? For what right would my slave have against me, since all that he has belongs to me? His rights being mine, this right of me against myself is a meaningless phrase. . . .

CHAPTER VI. THE SOCIAL PACT

I assume that men have reached a point at which the obstacles that endanger their preservation in the state of nature overcomes by their resistance the forces which each individual can exert with a view to maintaining himself in that state. Then this primitive condition can no longer subsist, and the human race would perish unless it changed its mode of existence.

Now, as men cannot create any new forces, but only combine and direct those that exist, they have no other means of self-preservation than to form by aggregation a sum of forces which may overcome the resistance, to put them in action by a single motive power, and to make them work in concert.

This sum of forces can be produced only by the combination of many; but the strength and freedom of each man being the chief instruments of his preservation, how can he pledge them without injuring himself, and without neglecting the cares which he owes to himself? This difficulty, applied to my subject, may be expressed in these terms:—

"To find a form of association which may defend and protect with the whole force of the community the person and property of every associate, and by means of which each, coalescing with all, may nevertheless obey only himself, and remain as free as before." Such is the fundamental problem of which the social contract furnishes the solution.

Some Truths Are Not Self-Evident

Howard Zinn

This year Americans are talking about the Constitution but asking the wrong questions, such as, Could the Founding Fathers have done better? That concern is pointless, 200 years after the fact. Or, Does the Constitution provide the framework for a just and democratic society today? That question is also misplaced, because the Constitution, whatever its language and however interpreted by the Supreme Court, does not determine the degree of justice, liberty or democracy in our society.

The proper question, I believe, is not how good a document is or was the Constitution but, What effect does it have on the quality of our lives? And the answer to that, it seems to me, is, Very little. The Constitution makes promises it cannot by itself keep, and therefore deludes us into complacency about the rights we have. It is conspicuously silent on certain other rights that all human beings deserve. And it pretends to set limits on governmental powers, when in fact those limits are easily ignored.

I am not arguing that the Constitution has no importance; words have moral power and principles can be useful even when ambiguous. But, like other historic documents, the Constitution is of minor importance compared with the actions that citizens take, especially when those actions are joined in social movements. Such movements have worked, historically, to secure the rights our human sensibilities tell us are self-evidently ours, whether or not those rights are "granted" by the Constitution.

Let me illustrate my point with five issues of liberty and justice:

§ First is the matter of racial equality. When slavery was abolished, it was not by constitutional fiat but by the joining of military necessity with the moral force of a great antislavery movement, acting outside the Constitution and often against the law. The Thirteenth, Fourteenth and Fifteenth Amendments wrote into the Constitution rights that extralegal action had already won. But the Fourteenth and Fifteenth Amendments were ignored for almost a hundred years. The right to equal protection of the law and the right to vote, even the Supreme Court decision in *Brown v. Board of Education* in 1954 underlining the meaning of the equal

Howard Zinn, "A People's Constitution: Some Truth Are Not Self–Evident," *The Nation*, August 18, 1987. Copyright © 1987 The Nation Co., Inc. Reprinted by permission.

protection clause, did not become operative until blacks, in the fifteen years following the Montgomery bus boycott, shook up the nation by tumultuous actions inside and outside the law.

The Constitution played a helpful but marginal role in all that. Black people, in the political context of the 1960s, would have demanded equality whether or not the Constitution called for it, just as the antislavery movement demanded abolition even in the absence of constitutional support.

§ What about the most vaunted of constitutional rights, free speech? Historically, the Supreme Court has given the right to free speech only shaky support, seesawing erratically by sometimes affirming and sometimes overriding restrictions. Whatever a distant Court decided, the real right of citizens to free expression has been determined by the immediate power of the local police on the street, by the employer in the workplace and by the financial limits on the ability to use the mass media.

The existence of a First Amendment has been inspirational but its protection elusive. Its reality has depended on the willingness of citizens, whether labor organizers, socialists or Jehovah's Witnesses, to insist on their right to speak and write. Liberties have not been given; they have been taken. And whether in the future we have a right to say what we want, or air what we say, will be determined not by the existence of the First Amendment or the latest Supreme Court decision but by whether we are courageous enough to speak up at the risk of being jailed or fired, organized enough to defend our speech against official interference and can command resources enough to get our ideas before a reasonably large public.

§ What of economic justice? The Constitution is silent on the right to earn a moderate income, silent on the rights to medical care and decent housing as legitimate claims of every human being from infancy to old age. Whatever degree of economic justice has been attained in this country (impressive compared with others, shameful compared with our resources) cannot be attributed to something in the Constitution. It is the result of the concerted action of laborers and farmers over the centuries, using strikes, boycotts and minor rebellions of all sorts, to get redress of grievances directly from employers and indirectly from legislators. In the future, as in the past, the Constitution will sleep as citizens battle over the distribution of the nation's wealth, and will be awakened only to mark the score.

§ On sexual equality the Constitution is also silent. What women have achieved thus far is the result of their own determination, in the feminist upsurge of the nineteenth and early twentieth centuries, and the more recent women's liberation movement. Women have accomplished this outside the Constitution, by raising female and male consciousness and inducing courts and legislators to recognize what the Constitution ignores.

§ Finally, in an age in which war approaches genocide, the irrelevance of the Constitution is especially striking. Long, ravaging conflicts in Korea and Vietnam were waged without following Constitutional procedures, and if there is a nuclear exchange, the decision to launch U.S. missiles will be made, as it was in those cases, by the President and a few advisers. The public will be shut out of the process and deliberately kept uninformed by an intricate web of secrecy and deceit. The current Iran/*contra* scandal hearings before Congressional select committees should be understood as exposing not an aberration but a steady state of foreign policy.

It was not constitutional checks and balances but an aroused populace that prodded Lyndon Johnson and then Richard Nixon into deciding to extricate the United States from Vietnam. In the immediate future, our lives will depend not on the existence of the Constitution but on the power of an aroused citizenry demanding that we not go to war, and on Americans refusing, as did so many G.I.s and civilians in the Vietnam era, to cooperate in the conduct of a war.

The Constitution, like the Bible, has some good words. It is also, like the Bible, easily manipulated, distorted, ignored and used to make us feel comfortable and protected. But we risk the loss of our lives and liberties if we depend on a mere document to defend them. A constitution is a fine adornment for a democratic society, but it is no substitute for the energy, boldness and concerted action of the citizens.

The Case Against Helping the Poor

Garrett Hardin

Environmentalists use the metaphor of the earth as a "spaceship" in trying to persuade countries, industries and people to stop wasting and polluting our natural resources. Since we all share life on this planet, they argue, no single person or institution has the right to destroy, waste, or use more than a fair share of its resources.

But does everyone on earth have an equal right to an equal share of its resources? The spaceship metaphor can be dangerous when used by misguided idealists to justify suicidal policies for sharing our resources through uncontrolled immigration and foreign aid in their enthusiastic but unrealistic generosity, they confuse the ethics of a spaceship with those of a lifeboat.

A true spaceship would have to be under the control of a captain, since no ship could possibly survive if its course were determined by committee. Spaceship Earth certainly has no captain; the United Nations is merely a toothless tiger, with little power to enforce any policy upon its bickering members.

If we divide the world crudely into rich nations and poor nations, two thirds of them are desperately poor, and only one third comparatively rich, with the

Garrett Hardin, "The Case Against Helping the Poor." Reprinted with permission from *Psychology Today* Magazine, September 1974. Copyright © 1974 (Sussex Publishers, Inc.).

United States the wealthiest of all. Metaphorically each rich nation can be seen as a lifeboat full of comparatively rich people in the ocean outside each lifeboat swim the poor of the world, who would like to get in, or at least to share some of the wealth. What should the lifeboat passengers do?

First, we must recognize the limited capacity of any lifeboat. For example, a nation's land has a limited capacity to support a population and as the current energy crisis has shown us, in some ways we have already exceeded the carrying capacity of our land.

ADRIFT IN A MORAL SEA

So here we sit, say 50 people in our lifeboat. To be generous, let us assume it has room for 10 more, making a total capacity of 60. Suppose the 50 of us in the lifeboat see 100 others swimming in the water outside, begging for admission to our boat or for handouts. We have several options: we may be tempted to try to live by the Christian ideal of being "our brother's keeper," or by the Marxist ideal of "to each according to his needs." Since the needs of all in the water are the same, and since they can all be seen as "our brothers," we could take them all into our boat, making a total of 150 in a boat designed for 60. The boat swamps, everyone drowns. Complete justice, complete catastrophe.

Since the boat has an unused excess capacity of 10 more passenger, we could admit just 10 more to it. But which 10 do we let in? How do we choose? Do we pick the best 10, the neediest 10, "first come, first served"? And what do we say to the 90 we exclude? If we do let an extra 10 into our lifeboat, we will have lost our "safety factor," an engineering principle of critical importance. For example, if we don't leave room for excess capacity as a safety factor in our country's agriculture, a new plant disease or a bad change in the weather could have disastrous consequences.

Suppose we decide to preserve our small safety factor and admit no more to the lifeboat. Our survival is then possible, although we shall have to be constantly on guard against boarding parties.

While this last solution clearly offers the only means of our survival, it is morally abhorrent to many people. Some say they feel guilty about their good luck. My reply is simple, "Get out and yield your place to others." This may solve the problem of the guilt-ridden person's conscience, but it does not change the ethics of the lifeboat. The needy person to whom the guilt-ridden person yields his place will not himself feel guilty about his good luck. If he did, he would not climb aboard. The net result of conscience-stricken people giving up their unjustly held seats is the elimination of that sort of conscience from the lifeboat.

This is the basic metaphor within which we must work out our solutions. Let us now enrich the image, step by step, with substantive additions from the real world, a world that must solve real and pressing problems of overpopulation and hunger.

The harsh ethics of the lifeboat become even harsher when we consider the reproductive differences between the rich nations and the poor nations. The people inside the lifeboats are doubling in numbers every 87 years, those swimming around outside are doubling, on the average, every 35 years, more than twice as fast as the rich. And since the world's resources are dwindling, the difference in prosperity between the rich and the poor can only increase.

As of 1973, the U.S. had a population of 210 million people, who were increasing by 0.8 percent per year. Outside our lifeboat, let us imagine another 210 million people (say the combined populations of Colombia, Ecuador, Venezuela, Morocco, Pakistan, Thailand and the Philippines), who are increasing at a rate of 3.3 percent per year. Put differently, the doubling time for this aggregate population is 21 years, compared to 87 years for the U.S.

MULTIPLYING THE RICH AND THE POOR

Now suppose the U.S. agreed to pool its resources with those seven countries, with everyone receiving an equal share. Initially the ratio of Americans to non-Americans in the model would be one-to-one. But consider what the ratio would be after 87 years, by which time the Americans would have doubled to a population of 420 million. By then, doubling every 21 years, the other group would have swollen to 354 billion. Each American would have to share the available resources with more than eight people.

But, one could argue, this discussion assumes that current population trends will continue, and they may not. Quite so. Most likely the rate of population increase will decline much faster in the U.S. than it will in the other countries, and there does not seem to be much we can do about it. In sharing with "each according to his needs," we must recognize that needs are determined by population size, which is determined by the rate of reproduction, which at present is regarded as a sovereign right of every nation, poor or not. This being so, the philanthropic load created by the sharing ethic of the spaceship can only increase.

THE TRAGEDY OF THE COMMONS

The fundamental error of spaceship ethics, and the sharing it requires, is that it leads to what I call "the tragedy of the commons." Under a system of private property, the men who own property recognize their responsibility to care for it, for if they don't they will eventually suffer. A farmer, for instance, will allow no more cattle in a pasture than its carrying capacity justifies. If he overloads it, erosion sets in, weeds take over, and he loses the use of the pasture.

If a pasture becomes a commons open to all, the right of each to use it may not be matched by a corresponding responsibility to protect it. Asking everyone to use it with discretion will hardly do, for the considerate herdsman who refrains from overloading the commons suffers more than a selfish one who says his needs are greater. If everyone would restrain himself, all would be well; but it takes only one less than everyone to ruin a system of voluntary restraint. In a crowded world of less than perfect human beings, mutual ruin is inevitable if there are no controls. This is the tragedy of the commons.

One of the major tasks of education today should be the creation of such an acute awareness of the dangers of the commons that people will recognize its many varieties. For example, the air and water have become polluted because they are treated as commons. Further growth in the population of per-capita conversion of natural resources into pollutants will only make the problem worse. The same holds true for the fish of the oceans. Fishing fleets have nearly disappeared in many parts of the world, technological improvements in the art of fishing are hastening the day of complete ruin. Only the replacement of the system of the commons with a responsible system of control will save the land, air, water and oceanic fisheries.

THE WORLD FOOD BANK

In recent years there has been a push to create a new commons called a World Food Bank, an international depository of food reserves to which nations would contribute according to their abilities and from which they would draw according to their needs. This humanitarian proposal has received support from many liberal international groups, and from such prominent citizens as Margaret Mead, U.N. Secretary General Kurt Waldheim, and Senators Edward Kennedy and George McGovern.

A world food bank appeals powerfully to our humanitarian impulses. But before we rush ahead with such a plan, let us recognize where the greatest political push comes from, lest we be disillusioned later. Our experience with the "Food for Peace program," or Public Law 480, gives us the answer. This program moved billions of dollars worth of U.S. surplus grain to food-short, population-long countries during the past two decades. But when P.L. 480 first became law, a headline in the business magazine *Forbes* revealed the real power behind it "Feeding the World's Hungry Millions; How It Will Mean Billions for U.S. Business."

And indeed it did. In the years 1960 to 1970, U.S. taxpayers spent a total of $7.9 billion on the Food for Peace program. Between 1948 and 1970, they also paid an additional $50 billion for other economic-aid programs, some of which went for food and food-producing machinery and technology. Though all U.S. taxpayers were forced to contribute to the cost of P.L. 480, certain special interest groups gained handsomely under the program. Farmers did not have to contribute the grain; the Government, or rather the taxpayers, bought it from them at full market prices. The increased demand raised prices of farm products generally. The manufacturers of farm machinery, fertilizers and pesticides benefited by the farmers' extra efforts to grow more food. Grain elevators profited from storing the surplus until it could be shipped. Railroads made money hauling it to ports, and shipping lines profited from carrying it overseas. The implementation of P.L. 480 required the creation of a vast Government bureaucracy, which then reacquired its own vested interest in continuing the program regardless of its merits.

EXTRACTING DOLLARS

Those who proposed and defended the Food for Peace program in public rarely mentioned its importance to any of these special interests. The public emphasis was always on its humanitarian effects. The combination of silent selfish interests and highly vocal humanitarian apologists made a powerful and successful lobby for extracting money from taxpayers. We can expect the same lobby to push now for the creation of a World Food Bank.

However great the potential benefit to selfish interests, it should not be a decisive argument against a truly humanitarian program. We must ask if such a program would actually do more good than harm, not only momentarily but also in the long run. Those who propose the food bank usually refer to a current "emergency" or "crisis" in terms of world food supply. But what is an emergency? Although they may be infrequent and sudden, everyone knows that emergencies will occur from time to time. A well-run family, company, organization or country prepares for the likelihood of accidents and emergencies. It expects them, it budgets for them, it saves for them.

LEARNING THE HARD WAY

What happens if some organizations or countries budget for accidents and others do not? If each country is solely responsible for its own well-being, poorly managed ones will suffer. But they can learn from experience. They may mend their ways, and learn to budget for infrequent but certain emergencies. For example, the weather varies from year to year, and periodic crop failures are certain. A wise and competent government saves out of the production of the good years in anticipation of bad years to come. Joseph taught this policy to Pharaoh in Egypt more than 2,000 years ago. Yet the great majority of the governments in the world today do not follow such a policy. They lack either the wisdom or the competence, or both. Should those nations that do manage to put something aside be forced to come to the rescue each time an emergency occurs among the poor nations?

"But it isn't their fault!" Some kind-hearted liberals argue. "How can we blame the poor people who are caught in an emergency? Why must they suffer for the sins of their governments?" The concept of blame is simply not relevant here. The real question is, what are the operational consequences of establishing a world food bank? If it is open to every country every time a need develops, slovenly rulers will not be motivated to take Joseph's advice. Someone will always come to their aid. Some countries will deposit food in the world food bank, and others will withdraw it. There will be almost no overlap. As a result of such solutions to food shortage emergencies, the poor countries will not learn to mend their ways, and will suffer progressively greater emergencies as their populations grow.

POPULATION CONTROL THE CRUDE WAY

On the average, poor countries undergo a 2.5 percent increase in population each year; rich countries, about 0.8 percent. Only rich countries have anything in the way of food reserves set aside, and even they do not have as much as they should. Poor countries have none. If poor countries received no food from the outside, the rate of their population growth would be periodically checked by crop failures and famines. But if they can always draw on a world food bank in time of need, their population can continue to grow unchecked, and so will their need for aid.

In the short run, a world food bank may diminish that need, but in the long run it actually increases the need without limit.

Without some system of worldwide food sharing, the proportion of people in the rich and poor nations might eventually stabilize. The overpopulated poor countries would decrease in numbers, while the rich countries that had room for more people would increase. But with a well-meaning system of sharing, such as a world food bank, the growth differential between the rich and the poor countries will not only persist, it will increase. Because of the higher rate of population growth in the poor countries of the world, 88 percent of today's children are born poor, and only 12 percent rich. Year by year the ratio becomes worse, as the fast-reproducing poor outnumber the slow-reproducing rich.

A world food bank is thus a commons in disguise. People will have more motivation to draw from it than to add to any common store. The less provident and less able will multiply at the expense of the abler and more provident, bringing eventual ruin upon all who share in the commons. Besides, any system of "sharing" that amounts to foreign aid from the rich nations to the poor nations will carry the taint of charity, which will contribute little to the world peace so devoutly desired by those who support the idea of a world food bank.

As past U.S. foreign-aid programs have amply and depressingly demonstrated, international charity frequently inspires mistrust and antagonism rather than gratitude on the part of the recipient nation [see "What Other Nations Hear When the Eagle Screams," by Kenneth J. and Mary M. Gerten, PT, June].

CHINESE FISH AND MIRACLE RICE

The modern approach to foreign aid stresses the export of technology and advice, rather than money and food. As an ancient Chinese proverb goes: "Give a man a fish and he will eat for a day; teach him how to fish and he will eat for the rest of his days." Acting on this advice, the Rockefeller and Ford Foundations have financed a number of programs for improving agriculture in the hungry nations. Known as the "Green Revolution," these programs have led to the development of "miracle rice" and "miracle wheat," new strains that offer bigger harvests and greater resistance to crop damage. Norman Borlaug, the Nobel Prize winning agronomist who, supported by the Rockefeller Foundation, developed "miracle wheat," is one of the most prominent advocates of a world food bank.

Whether or not the Green Revolution can increase food production as much as its champions claim is a debatable but possibly irrelevant point. Those who support this well-intended humanitarian effort should first consider some of the fundamentals of human ecology. Ironically, one man who did was the late Alan Gregg, a vice president of the Rockefeller Foundation. Two decades ago he expressed strong doubts about the wisdom of such attempts to increase food production. He likened the growth and spread of humanity over the surface of the earth to the spread of cancer in the human body, remarking that "cancerous growths demand food; but, as far as I know, they have never been cured by getting it."

OVERLOADING THE ENVIRONMENT

Every human born constitutes a draft on all aspects of the environment: food, air, water, forests, beaches, wildlife, scenery and solitude. Food can, perhaps, be significantly increased to meet a growing demand. But what about clean beaches, unspoiled forests, and solitude? If we satisfy a growing population's need for food, we necessarily decrease its per capita supply of the other resources needed by men.

India, for example, now has a population of 600 million, which increases by 15 million each year. This population already puts a huge load on a relatively impoverished environment. The country's forests are now only a small fraction of what they were three centuries ago, and floods and erosion continually destroy the insufficient farmland that remains. Every one of the 15 million new lives added to India's population puts an additional burden on the environment, and increases the economic and social costs of crowding. However humanitarian our intent, every Indian life saved through medical or nutritional assistance from abroad diminishes the quality of life for those who remain, and for subsequent generations. If rich countries make it possible, through foreign aid, for 600 million Indians to swell to 1.2 billion in a mere 28 years, as their current growth rate threatens, will future generations of Indians thank us for hastening the destruction of their environment? Will our good intentions be sufficient excuse for the consequences of our actions?

My final example of a commons in action is one for which the public has the least desire for rational discussion—immigration. Anyone who publicly questions the wisdom of current U.S. immigration policy is promptly charged with bigotry, prejudice, ethnocentrism, chauvinism, isolationism or selfishness. Rather than encounter such accusations, one would rather talk about other matters, leaving immigration policy to wallow in the crosscurrents of special interests that take no account of the good of the whole, or the interests of posterity.

Perhaps we still feel guilty about things we said in the past. Two generations ago the popular press infrequently referred to Dagos, Wops, Polacks, Chinks and Krauts, in articles about how America was being "overrun" by foreigners of supposedly inferior genetic stock [see "The Politics of Genetic Engineering: Who Decides Who's Defective?" PT, June]. But because the implied inferiority of foreigners was used then as justification for keeping them out, people now assume that restrictive policies could only be based on such misguided notions. There are other grounds.

A NATION OF IMMIGRANTS

Just consider the numbers involved. Our Government acknowledges a net inflow of 400,000 immigrants a year. While we have no hard data on the extent of illegal entries, educated guesses put the figure at about 600,000 a year. Since the natural increase (excess of births over deaths) of the resident population now runs about 1.7 million per year, the yearly gain from immigration amounts to at least 19 percent of the total annual increase, and may be as much as 37 percent if we include the estimate for illegal immigrants. Considering the growing use of birth-control devices, the potential effect of educational campaigns by such organizations as Planned Parenthood Federation of America and Zero Population Growth, and the influence of inflation and the housing shortage, the fertility rate of American women may decline so much that immigration could account for all the yearly increase in population. Should we not at least ask if that is what we want?

For the sake of those who worry about whether the "quality" of the average immigrant compares favorably with the quality of the average resident, let us assume that immigrants and nativeborn citizens are of exactly equal quality, how-ever one defines that term. We will focus here only on quantity; and since our conclusions will depend on nothing else, all charges of bigotry and chauvinism become irrelevant.

IMMIGRATION VS. FOOD SUPPLY

World food banks *move food to the people*—hastening the exhaustion of the environment of the poor countries. Unrestricted immigration, on the other hand, *moves people to the food,* thus speeding up the destruction of the environment of the rich countries. We can easily understand why poor people should want to make this latter transfer, but why should rich hosts encourage it?

As in the case of foreign-aid programs immigration receives support from selfish interests and humanitarian impulses. The primary selfish interest in un-impeded immigration is the desire of employers for cheap labor, particularly in industries and trades that offer degrading work. In the past, one wave of foreigners after another was brought into the U.S. to work at wretched jobs for wretched wages. In recent years the Cubans, Puerto Ricans and Mexicans have had this dubious honor. The interests of the employers of cheap labor mesh well with the guilty silence of the country's liberal intelligentsia. White Anglo-Saxon Protestants are particularly reluctant to call for a closing of the doors to immigration for fear of being called bigots.

But not all countries have such reluctant leadership. Most educated Hawaiians, for example, are keenly aware of the limits of their environment, particularly in terms of population growth. There is only so much room on the islands, and the islanders know it. To Hawaiians, immigrants from the other 49 states present as great a threat as those from other nations. At a recent meeting of Hawaiian government officials in Honolulu, I had the ironic delight of hearing a speaker, who like most of his audience was of Japanese ancestry, ask how the country might practically and constitutionally close its doors to further immigration. One member of the audience countered: "How can we shut the doors now? We have many friends and relatives in Japan that we'd like to bring here some day so that they can enjoy Hawaii too." The Japanese-American speaker smiled sympathetically and answered: "Yes, but we have children now, and someday we'll have grandchildren too. We can bring more people here from Japan only by giving away some of the land that we hope to pass on to our grandchildren some day. What right do we have to do that?"

At this point, I can hear U.S. liberals asking: "How can you justify slamming the door once you're inside? You say that immigrants should be kept out. But aren't we all immigrants, or the descendants of immigrants? If we insist on staying, must we not admit all others?" Our craving for intellectual order leads us to seek and prefer symmetrical rules and morals: a single rule for me and everybody else; the same rule yesterday, today and tomorrow. Justice, we feel, should not change with time and place.

We Americans of non-Indian ancestry can look upon ourselves as the descendants of thieves who are guilty morally, if not legally, of stealing this land from its Indian owners. Should we then give back the land to the now living American descendants of those Indians? However morally or logically sound this proposal may be, I, for one, am unwilling to live by it and I know no one else who is. Besides, the logical consequence would be absurd. Suppose that, intoxicated with a sense of pure justice, we should decide to turn our land over to the Indians. Since all our other wealth has also been derived from the land, wouldn't we be morally obliged to give them back to the Indians too?

PURE JUSTICE VS. REALITY

Clearly, the concept of pure justice produces an infinite regression to absurdity. Centuries ago, wise men invented statutes of limitations to justify the rejection of such pure justice, in the interest of preventing continual disorder. The law zealously defends property rights, but only relatively recent property rights. Drawing a line after an arbitrary time has elapsed may be unjust, but the alternatives are worse.

We are all the descendants of thieves, and the world's resources are inequitably distributed. But we must begin the journey to tomorrow from the point where we are today. We cannot remake the past. We cannot safely divide the wealth equitably among all peoples so long as people reproduce at different rates. To do so would guarantee that our grandchildren, and everyone else's grandchildren, would have only a ruined world to inhabit.

To be generous with one's own possessions is quite different from being generous with those of posterity. We should call this point to the attention of those who, from a commendable love of justice and equality, would institute a system of the commons, either in the form of a world food bank, or of unrestricted immigration. We must convice them if we wish to save at least some parts of the world from environmental ruin.

Without a true world government to control reproduction and the use of available resources, the sharing ethic of the spaceship is impossible. For the foreseeable future, our survival demands that we govern our actions by the ethics of a lifeboat, harsh though they may be. Posterity will be satisfied with nothing less.

On Those Things for Which Men, and Particularly Princes, Are Praised or Blamed

Niccolò Machiavelli

Now there remains to be examined what should be the methods and procedures of a prince in dealing with his subjects and friends. And because I know that many have written about this, I am afraid that by writing about it again I shall be thought of as presumptuous, since in discussing this material I depart radically from the procedures of others. But since my intention is to write something useful for anyone who understands it, it seemed more suitable to me to search after the effectual truth of the matter rather than its imagined one. And many writers have imagined for themselves republics and principalities that have never been seen nor known to exist in reality; for there is such a gap between how one lives and how one ought to live that anyone who abandons what is done for what ought to be done learns his ruin rather than his preservation: for a man who wishes to make a vocation of being good at all times will come to ruin among so many who are not good. Hence it is necessary for a prince who wishes to maintain his position to learn how not to be good, and to use this knowledge or not to use it according to necessity.

Leaving aside, therefore, the imagined things concerning a prince, and taking into account those that are true, I say that all men, when they are spoken of, and particularly princes, since they are placed on a higher level, are judged by some of these qualities which bring them either blame or praise. And this is why one is considered generous, another miserly (to use a Tuscan word, since "avaricious" in our language is still used to mean one who wishes to acquire by means of theft; we call "miserly" one who excessively avoids using what he has); one is considered a giver, the other rapacious; one cruel, another merciful; one treacherous, another faithful; one effeminate and cowardly, another bold and courageous; one humane, another haughty; one lascivious, another chaste; one trustworthy, another cunning; one harsh, another lenient; one serious, another frivolous; one religious, another unbelieving; and the like. And I know that everyone will admit that it would be a very praiseworthy thing to find in a prince, of the qualities mentioned above, those that are held to be good; but since it is neither possible to have them nor to observe them all completely, because human nature does not permit it, a prince must be prudent enough to know how to escape the bad reputation of those vices that would lose the state for him, and must protect himself from those that will not lose it for him, if this is possible; but if he cannot, he need not concern himself unduly if he ignores these less serious vices. And, moreover, he need not worry about incurring the bad reputation of those vices without which it would be difficult to hold his state; since, carefully taking everything into account, one will discover that something which appears to be a virtue, if pursued, will end in his destruction; while some other thing which seems to be a vice, if pursued, will result in his safety and his well-being.

On Generosity and Miserliness

Beginning, therefore, with the first of the above-mentioned qualities, I say that it would be good to be considered generous; nevertheless, generosity used in such a manner as to give you a reputation for it will harm you; because if it is employed virtuously and as one should employ it, it will not be recognized and you will not avoid the reproach of its opposite. And so, if a prince wants to maintain his reputation for generosity among men, it is necessary for him not to neglect any possible means of lavish display; in so doing such a prince will always use up all his resources and he will be obliged, eventually, if he wishes to maintain his reputation for generosity, to burden the people with excessive taxes and to do everything possible to raise funds. This will begin to make him hateful to his subjects, and, becoming impoverished, he will not be much esteemed by anyone; so that, as a consequence of his generosity, having offended many and rewarded few, he will feel the effects of any slight unrest and will be ruined at the first sign of danger; recognizing this and wishing to alter his policies, he immediately runs the risk of being reproached as a miser.

A prince, therefore, unable to use this virtue of generosity in a manner which will not harm himself if he is known for it, should, if he is wise, not worry about being called a miser; for with time he will come to be considered more generous once it is evident that, as a result of his parsimony, his income is sufficient, he can defend himself from anyone who makes war against him, and he can undertake enterprises without overburdening his people, so that he comes to be generous with all those from whom he takes nothing, who are countless, and miserly with all those to whom he gives nothing, who are few. In our times we have not seen great deeds accomplished except by those who were considered miserly; all others were done away with. Pope Julius II, although he made use of his reputation for generosity in order to gain the papacy, then decided not to maintain it in order to be able to wage war; the present King of France has waged many wars without imposing extra taxes on his subjects, only because his habitual parsimony has provided for the additional expenditures; the present King of Spain, if he had been considered generous, would not have engaged in nor won so many campaigns.

Therefore, in order not to have to rob his subjects, to be able to defend himself, not to become poor and contemptible, and not to be forced to become rapacious, a prince must consider it of little importance if he incurs the name of miser, for this is one of those vices that permits him to rule. And if someone were to say: Caesar with his generosity came to rule the empire, and many others, because they were generous and known to be so, achieved very high positions; I reply: you are either already a prince or you are on the way to becoming one; in the first instance such generosity is damaging; in the second it is very necessary to be thought generous. And Caesar was one of those who wanted to gain the principality of Rome; but if, after obtaining this, he had lived and had not moderated his expenditures, he would have destroyed that empire. And if someone were to reply: there have existed many princes who have accomplished great deeds with their armies who have been reputed to be generous; I answer you: a prince either spends his own money and that of his subjects or that of others; in the first case he must be economical; in the second he must not restrain any part of his generosity. And for that prince who goes out with his soldiers and lives by looting, sacking, and ransoms, who controls the property of others, such generosity is necessary; otherwise he would not be followed by his troops. And with what does not belong to you or to your subjects you can be a more liberal giver, as were Cyrus, Caesar, and Alexander; for spending the wealth of others does not lessen your reputation but adds to it; only the spending of your own is what harms you. And there is nothing that uses itself up faster than generosity, for as you employ it you lose the means of employing it, and you become either poor or despised or, in order to escape poverty, rapacious and hated. And above all other things a prince must guard himself against being despised and hated; and generosity leads you to both one and the other. So it is wiser to live with the reputation of a miser, which produces reproach without hatred, than to be forced to incur the reputation of rapacity, which produces reproach along with hatred, because you want to be considered as generous.

9 Search and Seizure
or "Keep Your Hands Out of My Garbage!"

The expression "safe at home" suggests the idea that a "home" is a place of security, a place where others cannot enter without your permission. In your own home or room, you probably feel pretty sure that you will be safe from intrusion by the police. If you suddenly heard a knock at the door and several armed policemen began to search the premises without your consent and without a search warrant, you would probably feel violated and outraged. "The security of one's privacy against the arbitrary intrusion by the police," wrote Justice Felix Frankfurter in 1946, "is basic to a free society."

The writing assignments in this chapter are all concerned with the topic of **search and seizure** or **the right to privacy.** They raise questions about when police have or do not have the right to search private property, whether it be a home, a car, or even a bag of garbage. Some assignments will involve your own experience and feelings. Others will require that you become familiar with additional background material and opinions, which are included in the readings.

GARBAGE DISPOSAL OR WHO HAS THE RIGHT TO YOUR TRASH?

It has been said that death and taxes are two experiences universal to humanity. I would suggest that another activity, discarding unwanted material or disposing of trash, is another one. There is no culture in the world, no matter how poor or thrifty, that does not throw away at least *something,* and there is no person you know, male or female, young or old, who has not thrown away at least *something* at some time; actually most people probably throw something away every day. Americans, in particular, are said to be the most wasteful people in the world, frequently discarding old items for new, carelessly tossing away the piles of cardboard, paper, or plastic with which every item purchased seems to be wrapped.

Yet, in some countries, what Americans discard without a thought might be considered to be of value. In some places in the world, the same paper or plastic that Americans throw away so carelessly might not be in such abundance and might actually be considered valuable. And even among members of the same culture, one person's trash might well be another person's treasure. Archaeologists and anthropologists make a business, in fact a science, out of sorting what often appears to be worthless trash. Antique dealers make a profit from selling things that others no longer want.

WRITING TO LEARN: A SEQUENCE OF WRITING ASSIGNMENTS

▶ *Writing Assignment I:* Examine the picture with the saying, "Your Garbage Is You." In small groups, discuss what you think this statement means. In class, write a short essay about this topic. If you are having difficulty getting started, you might think about the wastebaskets in your own home or dorm room. Then think about

Your Garbage is You

trash cans you have seen on the street. What can you learn about people by looking at their trash? In writing your essay, be sure to include many examples.

▶ *Writing Assignment II: Gathering and Classifying Information.* This assignment will help you understand an important part of the research process—gathering and understanding information. Often, the process of gathering, understanding, and sorting information can help you focus and develop a thesis. For most writing assignments, you gather and classify information using notes or notecards. In this assignment, you will gather information you can actually touch, and you will classify it by sorting it into piles.

GATHERING INFORMATION

For one week, collect all of your trash in a brown paper bag (exclude anything really disgusting, please), but be sure to include at least 20 items. Bring these bags to the first class of the week. On your bag, write a number or symbol, which you alone will recognize (maybe your address or your birthday). The students in the class will then exchange bags so that everyone has someone else's. As you can see, gathering information for this assignment will be relatively easy. You might want to have some fun with this assignment by deliberately choosing which objects to include.

DRAWING PRELIMINARY INFERENCES FROM INFORMATION

When information is first gathered, it often seems disconnected—one fact seems isolated from another with little relationship to anything else. As you continue to gather information, however, you begin to see connections and to form hypotheses about what it means. A good way to begin to understand information is first to list it and then to make inferences about each item on the list. To see for yourself how this process works, remove all the objects from the bag of garbage you have received. List these items in a vertical column. Now see if you can draw inferences from these items and write down these inferences in a column next to each item on the list. Do any of these things suggest something to you about the owner of the bag? For example, suppose you find a half-used tube of expensive lipstick. You might draw some of the following inferences:

1. The owner of the bag is probably a woman.
2. The owner of the bag uses cosmetics.
3. Maybe the owner of the bag once used cosmetics and now no longer wants to. That's the reason the lipstick is discarded.
4. The owner of the bag is trying to put together a "new" look and so is discarding previous cosmetics.

Making inferences about each item in the bag can help you understand its contents. But you can learn even more by making inferences based on several items that seem to have a connection. For example, if you also find many other half-used cosmetics, eye shadows, face powders, lip brushes, etc., you might decide that hypotheses number three or four make more sense to you—that is, the owner of the bag is discarding all cosmetics for some reason, which you might be able to determine by looking at the other contents of the bag.

UNDERSTANDING INFORMATION THROUGH CLASSIFICATION

When you are working with a great deal of information, it is often difficult to keep all of it in your mind, to understand it well enough to write about it. This is particularly true when you are working on an unfamiliar topic. A good method to help you understand information, however, is to classify it, that is, to sort it into categories. Sorting information helps you to think about one small part at a time, instead of trying to grasp large amounts of unrelated information all at once. The sorting process also helps you to begin thinking about relationships between groups.

In some ways, understanding information through sorting may be thought of in terms of the following analogy:

Suppose you have a large empty closet with nothing in it at all and a large amount of clothing to put into it. Without hangers or boxes, all you will be able to do is to pile the clothing into the closet as best you can, one thing on top of another. With this method, it will be very difficult for you to find anything without rummaging through everything at once. It will also be very difficult for you to add anything to the pile in any systematic way.

But suppose your closet comes with built in places to put things, a belt rack, a tie holder, trouser and skirt hangers, drawers for small items. These storage places will enable you to gain a better understanding of all the clothing in the closet and help you find things when you want them. When you come upon a new item to be added to the closet, these storage places will help you decide where it should go.

Categorizing or classifying information may be compared to creating these storage aids for your topic. It helps you understand and organize your information, enabling you to decide where to place a new piece of information when you find it.

▶ *Exercise: Classifying Your Trash*

A. List and categorize all the items in the bag you received from a classmate.

B. Write a short paper (one or two pages) **categorizing** and **describing** the contents of the bag. Your thesis for this assignment should be something like this: The contents of the bag consist of the following categories: 1. _____, 2. _____, 3. _____, etc.

C. Write a two- or three-page essay **analyzing** and **interpreting** what the contents the bag reveal about its owner. Some points to consider:

1. Does the bag belong to a male or a female? How do you know?
2. Can you tell how this person spends time? Interests? Hobbies?
3. Can you tell anything about this person's study habits? Value system (what he or she considers worthwhile or not worthwhile)?

▶ **Writing Assignment III: Discovering Other Perspectives.** The essay you have written in response to Assignment II gave you practice in sorting information and using information as evidence. However, often the same information or evidence can be categorized and interpreted in different ways. Writing a researched paper means learning to consider the perspective of others in developing your major arguments. Looking at evidence in a new way or through fresh eyes is especially useful after you have written a first draft. After you have written your essay in which you attempted to learn something about the owner of the trash, complete one of the following activities:

A. Reconsider your own essay. Are there aspects of the topic you might have missed? Are there other ways of organizing the evidence? Other hypotheses you might propose?

B. Exchange trash bags and essays with a partner. Examine your partner's trash bag. Read the essay written about it. Then discuss with your partner whether you agree or disagree with the essay. Would you have chosen similar categories? Did you agree with the analysis?

C. Give a copy of your essay to the original owner of the trash bag, using the codes with which they were originally labelled. You will also receive a copy of the essay that was written about you. Read the essay written about you on the basis of your trash bag. How much do you think the person writing the essay was able to learn about you? Did you agree with his categories? Were his perceptions accurate?

D. Write a short essay evaluating and criticizing the accuracy of the essay which was written about you, based on examination of your trash.

▶ **Writing Assignment IV: New Perspectives Through Reading.** This assignment involves the use of **outside information** to enhance or modify a position. Outside information helps you gain other perspectives on your ideas, much as comparing essays and trash bags with a partner enabled you to look at categories and evidence from another point of view. Even when outside information does not significantly change a position you wish to argue, additional facts or opinions can add to or deepen an argument you already understand and perhaps have already written. Read "What Does Your Garbage Say About You?" the L.A. Times article by Beth Krier, and the article by Stuart Taylor. Take notes on these articles, using one of the notetaking strategies discussed in Chapter 5. Find at least three ideas or quotations that could enhance the essay you have written for Assignment II. Then use these ideas in your essay. Do these readings present a new perspective on your position? Or do they support a position you already have? In using these sources, be sure to alter the text sufficiently so that it reads coherently.

Possible ways to improve your essay by including outside material:

1. Can the use of outside material add strength to one of your main points? Can you quote a statement that can make one of your points seem more authoritative?
2. Do any of these writers use examples that would be appropriate to one of your main points?

3. Do any of these writers make a point or argument that you might include in your own essay?
4. Do any of these writers discuss a point that contradicts your own point of view? Would reshaping your essay to include this perspective result in a better piece of writing?

When you have finished rewriting, document your quoted or paraphrased material using one of the methods discussed in the appendix.

▶ *Variation on Assignment IV:* After you have read the three articles concerned with garbage inspection, exchange essays with a partner. Based on your reading, make suggestions about how your partner could improve his or her essay by including material from outside sources.

▶ *Assignment V:* Read the following scenario:

> In the dormitories on campus, all students place their trash cans outside their rooms on Monday for garbage collection. Mrs. Glenwood-Jones, mother of Cindy Glenwood-Jones, a student at the university, suspects that the dorm in which her daughter is living is not adequately supervised and that the students' conduct is not restricted, permitting students to drink excessively on the weekends. She is worried that her own daugher will do poorly in school because of this permissiveness; moreover, many of the students are only 18, considerably younger than the legal drinking age. One Tuesday morning, when she knew most of the students were in class or else still asleep, Mrs. Glenwood-Jones went to her daughter's dormitory and confiscated the contents of several trash cans, which were left outside the rooms. Just as she had suspected, every can, including that of her own daughter, was filled with liquor bottles and beer cans, as well as other evidence that the weekend had been spent in excessive partying. Furious, Mrs. Glenwood-Jones wants to take her evidence to the school authorities in order to require them to exercise more stringent restraints on student behavior.

Discuss this situation in small groups, considering some of the following questions:

1. What do you think Mrs. Glenwood-Jones ought to do?
2. Was Mrs. Glenwood-Jones violating the students' rights to privacy?
3. Do you think it was right for her to steal the garbage?
4. Do you think it was legal for her to steal the garbage?
5. Do you think she can use the garbage as evidence?
6. What effect do you predict her action will have on the school authorities? On her daughter?
7. How would you feel if you were Mrs. Glenwood-Jones?
8. How would you feel if one of your parents came to your dorm and performed the same action as Mrs. Glenwood-Jones?

▶ *Writing Task:* Using the articles concerned with garbage included in this chapter, write an essay evaluating Mrs. Glenwood-Jones's action from both a social and legal point of view. Do you consider that her action was justified? Was she within her legal rights? Do you think her behavior would be considered "civilized" in our society?

THE RIGHT TO PRIVACY VERSUS PUBLIC SAFETY

Key Question: Does Concern with Safety or Well-Being Justify an Illegal Search?

Imagine the following situation. You are living next door to a family, including a man, a woman, and a young man your own age. The young man seems very pleasant and you sometimes have brief conversations with him when you see him outside. The man and woman, though, have always seemed strange to you. They dress in unusual, almost military costumes. They hold strange meetings at night, and sometimes you hear loud arguments and abusive shouting. One afternoon, you receive a phone call from the young man. He says that he and his parents are at the airport, about to leave the country and that he is calling you because you are unknowingly in great danger. In a frightened whisper, he tells you that his parents, disturbed by a recent government action, have decided to blow up their home as a public protest. Even now, a bomb is ticking away, and it is likely to blow up not only their home but your home and many homes in the neighborhood as well. The bomb is due to go off in one hour!

Of course, you take immediate action. You call the police, who, with no time for a warrant, break into the house and deactivate the bomb.

This, of course, is an extreme and unlikely situation, but it raises, in broad and dramatic terms, the conflict that often exists between individual rights and public safety. Although the Constitution guarantees security from warrantless searches and seizure of private property, there are many occasions when a decision not to intrude may cause great danger to others. In making decisions ensuring public safety, lawmakers often have to infringe on the individual's right to privacy. This conflict is particularly problematic in issues concerning the use of information.

▶ *Assignment VI:* Consider the following scenario:

> You and your best friend leave your hometown and go away to school together.
> Your families have been friends for years. While at school, your best friend
> begins using cocaine and soon becomes involved in selling it to other students.
> When you attempt to discuss the situation, your friend tells you to mind your
> own business.

Write a paper (two or three pages) discussing what you would do. To what extent would you feel that concern for public safety should outweigh concern for your friend's privacy?

WRITING TO LEARN: DISCUSSION QUESTIONS ON SEARCH AND SEIZURE

Discuss the following questions in small groups. You may wish to make one or more of these questions the topic for a short writing assignment.

1. If parents suspect that their high-school-age child has drugs hidden in his room, do they have the right to search the room. Why or why not?
2. Under what circumstances do school officials have the right to search students' lockers?
3. Do police have the right to search suspicious or dangerous looking characters at public functions? How could a policy such as this become a violation of individual rights?
4. If, during a search for one item, police find another illegal item, should they be allowed to use this item as evidence? Why or why not?

THE USE OF EVIDENCE OR NOW THAT I'VE GOT IT, WHAT CAN I DO WITH IT?

Historical/Cultural Background

▶ *Assignment VII:* The original intention of the Fourth Amendment was to prevent police from searching private premises without a warrant and seizing evidence to which they were not entitled. However, throughout history, there have been instances in which the police have obtained evidence in violation of the Fourth Amendment. The question then arose whether or not such evidence could be used in court. Read the sections in the background material concerned with the exclusionary rule and the nature of evidence. Then read the following scenario:

John Davis, a local artist, was driving down the main street of his city in his beat-up van, emblazoned with an array of decals and bumper stickers. One sticker read "Save the Whales," another said "Peace," a third advertised the name of a popular music group. Loud music could be heard blaring from the van from over a block away.

Davis is in his early twenties, has long, streaked blond hair, and wears reflective sunglasses. He wore no shirt as he drove along. Soon he was observed by two local police officers who, while fully aware that he had broken no law, decided to pull him over to "check him out." The two officers, upon stopping Davis, ordered him out of the van and searched it. They found half a pound of marijuana and arrested Davis for possession.

At his trial, Davis' attorney argued that the evidence seized should have been excluded because it had been obtained by officers as a result of an unlawful search. That is, since the Fourth Amendment guarantees people security from unreasonable searches, and since the officers did not have probable cause to suspect that Davis had drugs, then the prosecution should not have been allowed to use the marijuana seized in the search as evidence in court. The end result of this would be that since the prosecution would not be able to show evidence that Davis had marijuana in his possession, such evidence would have to be excluded and the judge would have to dismiss the charges against Davis. The attorney also argued that this unreasonable search violated Davis' right to privacy.

On the other side, the officers maintained that conventional wisdom around the department is that people who fit Davis's description have a 75 percent likelihood of possessing drugs. They also asserted that their first priority as police officers was to maintain law and order, and that Davis was breaking the law by having marijuana in his possession.

At the end of the trial, Judge Smales admitted the evidence. Davis was convicted and sentenced to three years in prison.

Key Question: Does the Recent Increase in Drug Problems Suggest the Need for More Stringent Search and Seizure Laws?

▶ ***Writing Task:*** Assume you are either the president of the "Free John Davis Association" or a member of the "Re-elect Judge Smales Committee." Write a paper arguing that the decision to admit the marijuana was either right or wrong. Support your ideas with reference to the Constitution and any pertinent legislation.

ELECTRONIC SURVEILLANCE: A FORM OF SECRET SEARCHING

When the Bill of Rights was written, actual physical searches and seizures were the only violations of privacy conceived of. However, with the advent of sophisticated technology in this century, a wide variety of unobtrusive methods of searching have become possible. Since the Watergate scandal of the 1970s, there has been considerable controversy concerning the question of electronic surveillance, in particular, the issue of how much wiretapping, planting of secret cameras, keeping of confidential computer files, and general bugging are really going on in our society. At the present time, the government has a great deal of freedom over wiretapping and bugging activities in the interests of national security, although similar activities by private individuals are strictly prohibited. Those advocating such activities view them as vital to the continuing welfare of society. They point to the number of unscrupulous people who care nothing for the harm they do to others—drug pushers, in particular—who prey upon children. Opponents maintain that such intrusions are the tools of a totalitarian state and that the information gained is likely to be misused.

WRITING TO LEARN

▶ ***Assignment VIII:*** In small groups, discuss the electronic surveillance you yourself know about or have experienced. Consider hidden cameras, bank and credit card records, traffic violations, as many examples as you can think of. When you have thought of as many examples as possible, classify them according to type. Discuss whether or not you feel such surveillance is justified. Then write an essay on the following topic: To what extent does electronic surveillance affect your own life? To what extent do you feel such surveillance is justifiable for the well-being of society?

▶ *Assignment IX:* Read the following scenario:

> Government officials have learned that foreign agents, posing as university students, are living on campus attempting to obtain information for their own countries. In order to determine who these agents are and to prevent them from using university resources to locate classified information, the officials have decided to monitor all campus phones.

A. Write a short essay (one or two pages) discussing how you would feel if you thought your phone was being monitored. Would it change who you spoke to or what you talked about?

B. Read the background information and two articles concerned with electronic surveillance. Then, using some of this information, write an essay on the following topic:

> A student has come to you with proof that his phone is being monitored, probably by the government. He believes that as a citizen of the United States, he is entitled to protection from such surveillance. Write a paper discussing what rights this student actually has. Refer specifically to the background information and pertinent cases involving electronic surveillance.

▶ *Assignment X:* Stores routinely use two-way mirrors to monitor shoppers and attempt to curb shoplifting. In grocery stores, these special mirrors are strategically located in the ceiling. In department stores, monitoring routinely occurs in dressing rooms. Banks and some stores use cameras, sometimes hidden, to record the actions of patrons. Today, sophisticated technology permits a high degree of surveillance, both visual and auditory. Often it is argued that surveillance is necessary to crack covert operations (for example, high-level drug dealing) and thus serves to protect the public.

▶ *Writing Task:* Consider your feelings about whether **public safety** and/or the public's right to know is more important than **individual privacy.** Then take a position and argue whether individual rights are jeopardized by increased surveillance (brought about by technology) or whether the need for public safety outweighs the right to individual privacy. In framing your answer, you should refer to rights guaranteed by the **Fourth Amendment.** You should also consider the consequences of both positions and what limits or parameters might be necessary.

▶ *Assignment XI: What Is Happening Now?* Read "Tales of a Computer State," including the foreword by Walter Cronkite. Then over the course of a week, read the newspaper and listen to the news to locate items involving wiretapping, surveillance devices, or the use of secret computerized information. Based on your investigation, how prevalent is electronic surveillance today? Do you feel that our country is moving closer to or further away from the "Big Brother" situation of Orwell's *1984*?

HISTORICAL/CULTURAL BACKGROUND: INFORMATION ON SEARCH AND SEIZURE

The Fourth Amendment

The Fourth Amendment to the Constitution of the United States reads as follows:

> The right of the people to be secure in their houses, papers, and effects against unreasonable searches and seizures, shall not be violated and no warrants shall issue, but upon probable cause, supported by oath or affirmation, and particularly describing the place to be searched, and the persons or things to be seized at the time.

The Fourth Amendment is considered basic to the maintenance of a free society; it is considered essential to protect a fundamental human right. As Justice Felix Frankfurter wrote in 1946, security from unreasonable searches is consistent "with the conception of human rights enshrined in the history and the basic consitutional documents of English-speaking peoples."

The Fourth Amendment may be traced back to American colonial history, when the British King was permitted to take out "general warrants," unlimited in time or scope, which did not list specific persons and were issued without specific or **probable cause.** Often these warrants were used to apprehend critics of the government. Another version of a general warrant were "writs of assistance," which allowed customs inspectors general searching privileges. These were usually used to apprehend colonial smugglers who were seeking to avoid unreasonable British taxes.

The Fourth Amendment requires that a **search warrant** be sufficiently specific concerning place and time, and that no warrant can be issued unless there is a **"probable cause,"** that is, a reasonable belief that a crime is being committed on the premises being searched. In 1933, the case **Nathanson v. United States** set out this requirement:

> Under the Fourth Amendment, an officer may not properly issue a warrant to search a private dwelling unless he can find probable cause therefore from facts or circumstances presented to him under oath or affirmation. Mere affirmation of belief or suspicion is not enough.

The Seizure of Property and Papers: Laws and Cases

As early as 1886, a precedent-setting case, **Boyd v. United States,** established that the Fourth Amendment protected a person from having to produce a private business paper that could be self-incriminating. The case involved a contract between the Boyds and the federal government to furnish plate glass for a post office and courthouse building in Philadelphia. The Boyds agreed to discount the price of the glass if the government agreed to import it duty free. Later, the government charged that the Boyds had imported more glass than had been agreed upon.

To prove its case, the government ordered the Boyds to relinquish the invoice showing the amount of imported glass received. The invoice listed the extra glass, and the Boyds were convicted.

The Supreme Court, however, later reversed their conviction, claiming that forcing someone to produce evidence against himself not only violated Fourth Amendment rights but Fifth Amendment rights as well. Since the Fifth Amendment prohibits anyone from being forced to incriminate himself, the seizure of private papers to be used as incriminating evidence was regarded as against the Constitution.

The Exclusionary Rule: Laws and Cases

In 1914, the case **Weeks v. United States** established that evidence seized in violation of a person's rights will be excluded from use. Weeks had been convicted of using the mails for the purpose of transporting certain coupons or tickets representing chances or shares in a lottery or gift enterprise. He had been arrested without a warrant, federal agents had searched his home also without a warrant, and documents and papers had been seized as evidence.

The Supreme Court, however, found the evidence against Weeks to have been illegally obtained and therefore inadmissible. Justice Day wrote "that if letters and private documents can thus be seized and held and used in evidence against a citizen accused of an offense, the protection of the 4th amendment . . . is of no value and . . . might as well be stricken from the Constitution."

The exclusionary rule has been regarded as a necessary safeguard against illegal practices by the police to gain evidence. However, many agree with Judge Benjamin Cardoza who criticized the law as providing unnecessary leniency for criminals. "The criminal is to go free because the constable has blundered," he stated, objecting to the widespread application of the exclusionary rule in a variety of cases.

In the years following the Weeks case, the exclusionary rule began to have great impact on other areas **(Wolf v. Colorado, 1948).** In 1944, Julius Wolf, a Denver physician, was convicted for performing an illegal abortion on Mildred Cairo. Wolf claimed that the major evidence, an appointment book linking Wolf's name with that of Cairo, had been obtained illegally and thus should be excluded. The trial judge overruled Wolf's claim and the evidence was admitted. In 1948, the Supreme Court reconsidered the case and insisted that no warrantless police search, be it federal, state, or city, is legal under the Constitution. However, in this case, no attempt was made to impose the exclusionary rule upon state or local police. Justice Frankfurter and five other judges maintained that the exclusionary rule was only one possible remedy that could be used to prevent unlawful searches and seizures and that it was up to each individual state to decide which remedy would be best.

The dissenting judges, however, condemned other remedies as unrealistic. Justice Murphy wrote, "Alternatives are deceptive . . . there is but one alternative to the rule of exclusion. That is no sanction [against illegal searches] at all." However, even though the Wolf case did not apply the exclusionary rule in all illegally seized evidence, it did result in state courts reversing convictions when police action was particularly shocking or inappropriate.

In 1961, in the **Mapp v. Ohio** case, the exclusionary rule was extended to cover state trials. In this case, the Ohio police, while searching the home of Dollree Mapp for a bombing suspect, found obscene materials and betting paraphernalia. Mapp was convicted under Ohio law, but challenged the conviction on the grounds that the evidence used against her had been seized illegally. The Supreme Court reversed Mapp's conviction, establishing that the exclusionary rule was an essential part of both the Fourth and Fourteenth Amendments and that state and local police were bound by the same rules that federal agents had been constrained to follow since 1914.

During the 1970s, the exclusionary rule was limited as a means of overturning convictions. In 1971, Chief Justice Warren Burger suggested in the case of **Bivens v. Six Unknown Named Agents** that he preferred an alternative remedy for the problem of the government using illegal means of obtaining evidence. He suggested that anyone whose Fourth Amendment rights had been violated could be authorized by Congress to undertake a lawsuit.

In 1984, the case **Nix v. Williams** added an exception to the exclusionary rule. This case established that if the prosecution could establish that the evidence would have been found eventually by lawful means, then illegally obtained evidence could be used in court. This exception applies exclusively in instances where the police did not intentionally violate a suspect's rights, where they acted in good faith, and where it is certain that the evidence would ultimately have been found.

Stop and Frisk Searches: Laws and Cases

Even within the boundaries of the Fourth Amendment, it is legal for the police to stop suspicious persons and frisk them for weapons. This is a permissible police action even without a search warrant or enough information to be considered "probable cause" for arrest.

In the 1968 case, **Terry v. Ohio,** Chief Justice Earl Warren stated that "there must be a narrowly drawn authority to permit a reasonable search for weapons for the protection of the police officer, where he has reason to believe that he is dealing with an armed and dangerous individual, regardless of whether he has probable cause to arrest the individual for a crime. The officer need not be absolutely certain that the individual is armed; the issue is whether a reasonably prudent man in the circumstances would be warranted in the belief that his safety or that of others was in danger" (Terry v. Ohio, 392 U.S. 1 at 27 {1968}).

In 1972, the case, **Adams v. Williams,** established that an officer is entitled to stop a car and conduct a weapons search, if he has reason to believe that the suspect is armed and dangerous.

Automobile Searches: Laws and Cases

Although the Fourth Amendment guarantees freedom from unreasonable searches and seizures in one's home, it is also recognized that when searching automobiles, boats, airplanes, or other moving objects, it may not be practical to secure a warrant, since the vehicle could easily be moved. Certainly, the founding fathers who wrote the Bill of Rights are unlikely to have considered the special case of automobiles, since, of course, they did not exist at that time. The landmark case of **Carroll v. United States** established that some moving vehicles could be searched without a warrant.

In 1925, George Carroll was convicted of transporting liquor for sale, against the federal prohibition law and the Eighteenth Amendment. The evidence used against him had been taken from his car without a warrant by federal agents. Carroll maintained that his Fourth Amendment rights had been violated by the warrantless search. However, the Supreme Court upheld Carroll's conviction, maintaining that automobiles represent an exception to the search and seizure laws. Chief Justice William Howard Taft wrote the following statement:

> . . . the guarantee of freedom from unreasonable searches and seizures by the Fourth Amendment has been construed, practically since the beginning of the government, as recognizing a necessary difference between a search of a store, dwelling house, or other structure in respect of which a proper official warrant readily may be obtained and a search of a ship, motor boat, wagon, or automobile for contraband goods, where it is not practicable to secure a warrant, because the vehicle can be quickly moved out of the locality or jurisdiction in which the warrant must be sought. (267 U.S. 132 [1925])

The main qualification for such a search is probable cause for believing that the vehicle was carrying something illegal.

The Carroll case was reviewed in 1949 and reaffirmed in the case of **Brinegar v. United States.** In this case, the Supreme Court emphasized that probable cause for the search of an automobile is not identical with the proof needed to establish guilt. Requiring the sort of evidence needed for a trial would make it impossible for the police to search any vehicle. Probable cause, in this instance, rests on probabilities.

RANDOM AUTOMOBILE SEARCHES

In 1978, in the case **Delaware v. Prouse,** the Supreme Court established that the state police are not permitted to stop automobiles randomly without probable cause to check their drivers' licenses and automobile registration. In such cases, any drug violations discovered in randomly searched cars could not be considered evidence in a state court.

Electronic Surveillance: Laws and Cases

During the past 25 years, there has been a tremendous explosion of technology involved with electronic surveillance. Closed-circuit televisions, computers, cordless phones, electronic mail—a wealth of options now exist for surveillance activities. The Fourth Amendment protects against unreasonable searches and seizures; however, when this amendment was written, today's technology did not exist. The principle of the Fourth Amendment still pertains, but its application to new situations is still being decided.

THE USE OF WIRETAPPING

A 1928 case **(Olmstead v. U.S.)** centers on whether evidence obtained by wiretapping of private telephone conversations can be considered a violation of the Fourth and Fifth Amendments. Olmstead and others were convicted of possessing, transporting, importing, and selling alcohol, in violation of the National Prohibition Act. The evidence used for the conviction was obtained by four federal prohibition officers who tapped the wires of Olmstead's telephone lines. The Court found the acquisition of evidence through wiretaps to be legal.

In more recent times, the major public law addressing electronic surveillance is Title III of the Omnibus Crime Control and Safe Streets Act of 1968. This act was designed to protect the privacy of wire and oral communications, although the law specified a list of crimes for which wiretaps could be authorized. However, this law did not cover new technologies, particularly those relying on computer and other electronic communications.

In 1986, the Electronic Communications Privacy Act was passed, revising the Title III act of 1968. This new law increases the list of crimes for which wiretapping would be permitted and generally strengthened the power of the government to engage in overt surveillance in the interest of security.

Key Terms

Privacy

Fourth Amendment

Search and Seizure

Probable Cause

Exclusionary Rule

Admissible Evidence

The Right to Privacy and Trash Collection

What Does Your Garbage Say About You?

Brad Lemley

It's a sparkling afternoon in Tucson, and Barbara Teso, a pretty University of Arizona senior, is up to her elbows in coffee grounds, eggshells, fish bones, cereal boxes, aluminum foil, used paper towels, candy wrappers, sweet-potato peels, TV-dinner trays, carrot tops, soda bottles, grapefruit rinds and other discards. In a word, it's garbage.

And she loves it.

"It's fun," she says, though she concedes that this haul is "pretty average." Nothing on the table today compares with the unusual items she and other students have found in previous garbage-sorting sessions, including false teeth and a cheap diamond ring. "We found a frozen lizard once," says Teso. "We put it in the sun, and it thawed out and ran away."

Welcome to the new science of garbology. Its founder and biggest booster is William Rathje, 41, a professor of anthropology at the University of Arizona and a Harvard Ph.D. whose premise is simple but revolutionary: "If we can learn about ancient civilizations from the debris they left behind, we can learn important information about people today from their garbage."

Propelled by Rathje's vision, some 700 of his students have meticulously sorted and logged 120 tons—more than a million individual items—of Tucson's residential garbage since 1973. They also have examined the refuse of Milwaukee, New Orleans and Mexico City. The information dredged up has been used by the Department of Agriculture, the Environmental Protection Agency and the American Paper Institute, among others. "We supply information they can't get anywhere else," says Rathje proudly.

Garbage, you see, doesn't lie. For example, when people are polled about how much food they throw away, they insist that they discard little or none, says Rathje. "But the garbage bags tell a different story. The first bag I ever opened had a whole T-bone steak in it, fully cooked and wrapped in a paper towel." The project found that Americans waste 15 percent of all solid food brought into the home. "We're talking about $11.7 billion worth of edible food wasted in homes in a year," he adds.

In other words, America throws away enough food to feed Canada.

The subject may be sloppy, but the research is precise and careful. It starts when Tucson residents deposit their garbage at curbside, at which time it legally becomes city property. Garbage collectors under contract with the project collect samples from rich, poor and middle-class neighborhoods and whisk them to the sorting center, a corrugated-steel shed with plywood tables and scales. Here, 20 of Rathje's students inspect and categorize the garbage. For example: "Milk carton, code 011, 64 fluid ounces, cost 87 cents, brand Carnation, type skim, composition paper."

Such results are logged in a computer, which burps out conclusions that are nearly always surprising:

• Conservatives tend to drink Pepsi, while liberals prefer Coke. Rathje reached this conclusion by correlating the cola cans with the political bent of the news-papers also found in a household's trash.

• While Americans do waste food, we waste less than in our past: The current 15 percent figure is down from an estimated 25 percent to 33 percent during World War I. Rathje attributes this to modern America's better refrigeration, transporta-tion, processing and packaging.

• Middle-income families waste more food than upper- or lower-income families. They also buy more name brands. Upper-income families buy more generic brands; lower-income families mix the two.

• Poor people pay more for standard food and household goods than the wealthy do. "In (wealthy) neighborhoods, you find the 181-ounce economy-size laundry detergent," says Rathje. "In poor neighborhoods, where the families have six or seven people, you find the 20-ounce size. Apparently, poorer people just don't have the money to buy ahead."

Some of the trends uncovered are more than surprising—they are cause for concern. Consider:

• The percentage of plastics in garbage increased 40 percent from 1980 to 1985. And plastics are difficult to recycle, don't break down, use up nonrenewable resources (i.e., petroleum) and produce toxic chemicals when burned.

• Increasingly, the chemicals found in wells near landfills used for residential garbage resemble those found near toxic-waste dumps. That's because many of the substances in residential garbage—pesticides, herbicides, paints and caustic cleaners—are toxins. Eventually, they seep into the groundwater and are used for drinking and irrigation.

• The average U.S. household *each year* discards 1800 plastic items, 850 steel cans, 500 recyclable all-aluminum cans, 500 glass bottles and more than 13,000 individ-ual items of paper, most of it packaging, says Rathje. Nationally, our municipal waste totals 180 million tons a year.

What can the average American do about the sheer volume of today's garbage? Rathje suggests that, when we shop, we should keep in mind that garbage does not disappear. "Conveniences like plastics will be with us a long time."

On the subject of recycling, Rathje says: "I can't think of a better place to begin than with kids. We should teach them that recycling improves the quality of the environment—and, in the case of collecting aluminum cans, can get them some money." Many cities are making progress in their programs: Berkeley, Calif., passed a referendum to raise its recycled-trash rate, now 15 percent, to 50 percent by 1991; and there are more than 500 curbside-pickup recycling programs nation-wide.

It seems like a good idea, especially if you spend some time around the sorting tables. Certainly, we should pay more attention to our garbage, because Americans casually toss out not only useless junk but also some of the best products of our civilization. For example, the last item sorted on this particular afternoon was logged as "Newsprint, code 181, 50 grams."

It was a PARADE magazine.

Garbage Man Opens a Can of Social Worms

Jack Smith

Garbage is a more complex product than I thought. It has social implications that go beyond the Supreme Court's recent opinion permitting policemen to pry into it for clues to our behavior.

Louis Lasco confesses that he and his wife found themselves in a game of one-upmanship with a neighbor over the quality of their garbage. Garbage, they discovered, could be a status symbol.

It began when Lasco's wife noticed that their neighbors had dropped two empty Gallo champagne bottles in plain sight on top of their garbage. She regarded this as a flaunting of their superior life style.

I would never have thought of an empty Gallo bottle as a status symbol; however, Lasco overcompensated by seeking out two empty Dom Perignon magnums and placing them on top of *their* garbage, thus restoring his wife's self-esteem.

Next day the neighbors struck back, conspicuously throwing out a worn copy of Horney's "Psychoanalysis and Human Growth" on top of a cracked Caruso record. Lasco retaliated with a biography of Freud and two unplayable Chaliapin records. His wife was appeased.

Obviously there can be no end to this sort of rivalry, and Lasco soon withdrew from the field. He wonders, though, whether there might be some future in garbage items sold merely to establish class.

Carol Nahin's experience has both social and moral implications. Some years ago, she says, she and her husband had to clean out a rental whose tenants were moving out. What they found were hundreds of pornographic books and magazines whose titles are too obscene to print.

They did what anyone would probably do. They put the printed matter in dozens of cardboard boxes, camouflaged their contents with a cover of newspapers, and put them out on the curb for the trash pickup.

First, she said, a little old man came by with a white dog. He looked into one of the boxes. He came to the door and asked permission to take a few books. Nahin's husband said "Sure." An hour later another old man came to the door and the scene was repeated.

The next day six more men and two women helped themselves to stacks of the books and magazines, first asking permission as the first man had done. At the end of the day the first man returned with a small red toy wagon and asked if he could have the remainder. They said yes, and he took the lot.

Nahin concludes that "one man's trash may well be another man's treasure. I believe those books and magazines probably added years to that old gentleman's life. At least I hope so."

John Babcock, executive producer and editorial director, KABC-TV news department, has a problem with garbage that seems extremely simple but that defies solution. He can't get rid of a battered old garbage can.

"The bottom is torn out, but the collectors won't take it away. I tried putting it inside another can; it didn't work. I then put it out alone with a note on it, saying, 'Take me, I'm broken,' but they took the note off and left the can."

Babcock says if it were plastic he could cut it into shreds and dispose of it in another can. But he has nothing to cut the metal can with. He says he doesn't know his trashmen's schedule, so he can't appeal to them personally.

"I just figured that you were about the only source I knew of who had the creative kind of audience which has also had this kind of problem and found a way to deal with it."

It is true that I hear from many intellectuals and creative people, but I'm not sure Hancock's problem is exactly their meat. If nothing else works, I suggest that he dig a hole and bury the can.

Disposing of our waste is becoming more of a problem every day, like traffic congestion, drugs and gang warfare. Notice the sofas and carpeting tossed out on the freeway shoulders. It has been suggested that we shoot our trash into space, but that would simply spoil space even before the death of our planet forces us to take refuge in it.

I'll make Hancock a deal. I'll take his old garbage can if he'll take our defunct Servel refrigerator. Try to get rid of one of *those*.

As Supreme Court Rules Trash Is an Open Book, Garbologists Say How Revealing that Can Be

Beth Ann Krier

Trash . . . garbage . . . rubbish . . . The words have traditionally suggested termination, an ending point, it's over with.

Or is it?

According to this week's Supreme Court ruling, your trash is no longer yours. Once it hits the curb, it's fair—or unfair—game. As the court said, "It is common knowledge that plastic garbage bags left on or at the side of a public street are readily accessible to animals, children, scavengers, snoops and other members of the public."

In decreeing that police officers without search warrants have the right to inspect curb-side rubbish for evidence (but not garbage near a dwelling, which remains personal property), the court also acknowledged that refuse can be extremely revealing. Justice William J. Brennan Jr., offering a dissenting opinion, wrote that "a search of trash, like a search of the bedroom, can relate intimate details about sexual practices, health and personal hygiene. A single bag of trash testifies eloquently to the eating, reading and recreational habits of the person who produced it."

Private detectives and university "garbologists" have known that for years.

FULL OF USEFUL INFORMATION

"It [garbage] is the single most useful tool to obtain information regarding the private lives of individuals," said Armand Grant, president of the Teltec Investigations, a Malibu-based detective agency employing 13 private investigators.

"People do not think of destroying envelopes from the bank. They do not think of destroying telephone numbers they have dialed that are on their phone bills. You would be surprised what one would find in trash."

An investigator for 22 years, Grant claims he has "broken open some monolithic cases by opening up trash. . . . It provides leads you follow on where certain other items might be found. . . . The thing you do is find out when trash is picked up and pick it up before the trash people get there. It's done very quickly."

Archeologist Luanne Hudson, who has taught a garbology class, Modern Material Culture Studies, at USC, pointed out that she and other ethical garbologists typically disregard bills, letters, bank statements and other personal effects when studying trash.

But, even so, it's incredibly revealing.

"What you throw away can reveal your age, whether you have chidren, your economic level, possibly your educational background but at least your intellectual level, your level of health, whether or not you're a stable member of the community and many other things," she said, adding that research obtained by studying garbage is often more accurate than that collected from personal interviews.

"You can reconstruct behavior from actual items. Psychologists, sociologists and anthropologists will go out and ask people, 'How many bottles of beer do you consume a week?' A person will usually tell you what they think you want to hear. At the front door, they tell you one thing; at the back door, their garbage tells you another."

Added archeologist Fred Gorman, a former director of Harvard University's field school and one of the developers of the University of Arizona's Garbage Project: "We can learn a great deal about people's domestic consumption habits that span not only the range of foods consumed, but also medicines, potentially addictive substances, alcohol, tobacco and other types of narcotics. It's possible to gain information even of a financial nature."

As trash pro and former FBI agent John T. Lynch sees it, "What you learn from garbage is that everyone is human. You see *all* the good and *all* the bad."

Lynch, who heads John T. Lynch Inc., a Los Angeles-based investigation firm with offices in New York and Chicago, recalled that former FBI director J. Edgar Hoover once had his garbage stolen from his residence.

"He got himself a trash compactor after that," said Lynch, who was with the FBI from 1943 to 1953. "He was a little unhappy about comments about the type of whiskey he drank—and the number of bottles."

Lynch agrees that garbage inspection is a useful tool in detective work. "I spent many days in the FBI putting together letters that were torn and thrown away. We found a lot of fugitives that way," he recalled.

"People are careless. You find such things as confidential material just crumpled up and thrown away. People [count on] the garbage man and his integrity to quietly and quickly dispose of even their secret information."

But despite the wealth of clues lurking in Hefty bags, Lynch is hesitant to go after them unless other means have been exhausted.

"It [a trash check] is probably not the first thing you do when you get a new case," he said. "You don't just send your investigator out to check the garbage. You do it when all the routine ethical and legal information banks are searched and possibly the neighbors have been talked to about the background of an individual."

According to Lynch, garbage checks are commonly performed in divorce cases when a spouse is having difficulty gathering financial information about a partner's assets. And he said that the technique has long been useful in industrial espionage, particularly in the days before paper shredders were standard equipment.

He told of a "close friend" who worked for a major U.S. automobile company who "used to go and pick up the trash every night where they [a competitor's employees] were working on the designs of cars for the next five years. . . . The fellow would just stop and dump a couple of barrels of trash into the trunk of his car. One night he heard noises in his trunk on the way home, strange sounds. He got out of the car, opened the trunk and a rat jumped out and scared the hell out of him."

SOME RETALIATED

Some who have been harassed by unofficial garbage collectors admit having booby-trapped their trash in retaliation. After singer Bob Dylan's garbage was repeatedly stolen in the late '60s and early '70s by a man who billed himself as "the world's greatest authority on Dylan," Dylan struck back.

In his 1986 Dylan biography, "No Direction Home, The Life and Music of Bob Dylan," former New York Times pop music critic Robert Shelton quoted the artist when he was in the midst of his rubbish frustrations: "We loaded up our garbage with as much dog [feces] as we could—mousetraps, everything—but he still keeps going through my garbage!"

Raking through refuse as a dirty but virtually dead-sure means of obtaining information about an individual even turned up on an episode of television's "L.A. Law" last season. On the show, lawyer Ann Kelsey represented a client who claimed he had invented a tea bag but had received no compensation from a tea bag firm that insisted he did not invent the bag.

"Kelsey enlisted the services of a private investigator on the suspicion that the corporation wasn't producing all the documents relating to the tea bag," recalled "L.A. Law" writer and co-producer David Kelley. "The investigator pulled several garbage bags [from the tea bag corporation] into Kelsey's office, dumped them on the floor. They combed through it and sure enough, Kelsey found the smoking gun memo that allowed her to vindicate her client, win the case and make our viewers happy."

IS IT TIME TO WORRY?

Should those same viewers—or anyone else who places bits and pieces of personal effects on a curb—be concerned? Should they act differently given the prevalence of garbage snooping and the Supreme Court's refusal to prohibit it?

"If you're engaged in criminal enterprise, you should be concerned," said Robert Goldstein, a professor of constitutional law at the UCLA School of Law. "And if there's anything you want to keep private, you should be concerned. . . . One way to protect garbage is that state legislatures or city councils can enact ordinances that protect privacy in garbage. . . . The Supreme Court got into regulating the police because the state legislatures defaulted."

(In Los Angeles, said a Police Department spokesman, there are no laws prohibiting trash picking. But in Beverly Hills, once considered a scavenger's paradise, a city ordinance stipulates that trash can only be collected by firms licensed by the city to do so, a spokesman for the Beverly Hills Police Department said.)

Teltec's Grant advised that those who wish to keep their secrets secret should use paper shredders and then soak what's been shredded.

"The trick with a paper shredder is to be sure that the shredded paper is falling into some type of liquid, not just falling into a trash can," he said. "If you pick up shredded paper, you can often put it back together. The best thing is to have it drop into water or bleach."

FEAR NO GARBOLOGISTS

One group of professional trash analysts that consumers shouldn't have to fear, however, is the garbologists. William Rathje, the University of Arizona archeologist and anthropology professor considered to be the dean of garbology, emphasized that these modern archeologists do not analyze refuse on a dwelling-by-dwelling or individual-by-individual basis. Rather, he said, garbology searches for patterns common to neighborhoods, ethnic groups, cities, regions or entire cultures.

Thus, residents whose trash may be collected by scholars can rest assured that the investigators are not looking to see whether a particular person's reading habits run along the lines of Harper's, Hustler or K mart "Dollar Days" brochures.

"It's unethical, and I personally believe it's inappropriate (to examine personal effects or study individual patterns)," Rathje said, pointing out that the Supreme Court ruling has no effect on his work in that it concerns two areas with which he never deals: individuals and evidence.

In addition, Rathje is careful to work with the cooperation of the local sanitation department for research done through the university's Garbage Project. (Created in the early 1970s, he said, the project is now affectionately known as *Le Projet du Garbage*).

But given all the self-imposed restrictions, Rathje and others in the field still find the country's waste bins reveal far more information than they're equipped to codify and analyze.

This spring, for instance, students participating in the Garbage Project collected Phoenix trash after the city asked the group to determine the quantity, weight and volume of all the household recyclables discarded during a certain period. Rathje said the refuse—sorted into 20 different categories—is still being analyzed.

"The only reason I have any faith in our research is because we have a large number of samples collected over a long period of time," he said, noting that a major problem connected with seeking information about an individual through garbage is that there is no assurance that what is in a bag or can was put there by that person.

"Just because there is a garbage can behind a person's house doesn't mean it's their garbage," Rathje said. "My response to any kind of a law enforcement search is that I would be unsure of the value of the results. If you've put your garbage out in a public area, people can take things out or put things in."

TRASH MANIPULATION MAY RISE

Such activity and other ploys may increase as a result of the high court's ruling and the publicity that trash picking has received.

That's the view of Bill Simcock, a detective who became well versed in obtaining information from garbage when he investigated organized crime cases for the Los Angeles District Attorney's Office. Now the group manager in charge of investigations for CPP/Pinkerton's Los Angeles office, he said he applauds the Supreme Court for clarifying that curb-side trash is not private property. But he also fears ramifications of the decision.

As he put it: "This is going to kill us. You know, everybody's going to secure their garbage now."

Court Rules Police May Search Trash. Says Garbage Placed Outside Home Not Private

Stuart Taylor Jr.

WASHINGTON—The Supreme Court, over an impassioned dissent, ruled Monday that the police may freely search through garbage bags and other refuse containers that people leave outside the home for collection.

Under the court's 6–2 decision, (Justice Anthony M. Kennedy did not take part in the decision) such searches may be conducted without a warrant and without any reason to suspect criminal activity.

The decision, in a Laguna Beach narcotics case, was consistent with rulings by most lower federal and state courts and was expected in light of the court's narrow view in recent years of the Fourth Amendment's protection of the privacy of individuals against "unreasonable searches and seizures."

Justice Byron R. White's opinion for the majority said the privacy of garbage bags left outside the home and its immediate surroundings is not protected by the Fourth Amendment because people have no "subjective expectation of privacy" in their garbage "that society accepts as objectively reasonable."

Justice William J. Brennan Jr., in a dissenting opinion joined by Justice Thurgood Marshall, said, "Scrutiny of another's trash is contrary to commonly accepted notions of civilized behavior."

"A search of trash, like a search of the bedroom, can relate intimate details

Stuart Taylor, Jr., "Court Rules Police May Search Trash," *The New York Times*, May 17, 1988. Copyright © 1988 by The New York Times Company. Reprinted by permission.

about sexual practices, health, and personal hygiene," as well as reading and recreational habits, he wrote.

"I suspect, therefore, that members of our society will be shocked to learn that the court, the ultimate guarantor of liberty, deems unreasonable our expectation that the aspects of our private lives that are concealed safely in a trash bag will not become public," Brennan wrote.

In a rejoinder, White wrote: "Given that the dissenters are among the tiny minority of judges whose views are contrary to ours, we are distinctly unimpressed with the dissent's prediction that 'society will be shocked to learn' of today's decision."

White said that one cannot reasonably expect privacy in one's garbage because "it is common knowledge that plastic garbage bags left on or at the side of a public street are readily accessible to animals, children, scavengers, snoops and other members of the public."

In a footnote placed after the word "snoops," White noted: "Even the refuse of prominent Americans has not been invulnerable. In 1975, for example, a reporter for a weekly tabloid seized five bags of garbage from the sidewalk outside the home of Secretary of State Henry Kissinger." The tabloid, which White did not name, was *The National Enquirer.*

Brennan also referred to the Kissinger episode. "The public response roundly condemning the reporter demonstrates," he wrote, that society recognized as reasonable the reactions of Kissinger and his wife that their privacy had been grossly invaded.

"Most of us, I believe, would be incensed to discover a meddler—whether a neighbor, a reporter or a detective—scrutinizing our sealed trash containers to discover some detail of our personal lives," Brennan said.

In arguing that Monday's decision was a natural outgrowth of the court's precedents, White cited a 1986 decision that the police were free without warrants to spy on the back yards of homes from airplanes flying at 1,000 feet because private planes could legally do the same.

Referring to the California case, White said a trash collector could himself have sorted through the defendants' trash and that "the police cannot reasonably be expected to avert their eyes from evidence of criminal activity that could have been observed by any member of the public."

The case, California vs. Greenwood, No. 86–684, grew out of a police investigation in 1984 of a man in Laguna Beach whose activities at his single-family home has led police to suspect he might be involved in narcotics trafficking.

Police obtained the man's plastic garbage bags from the neighborhood's regular trash collector, found items indicative of narcotics use and used this information to obtain a warrant to search the house. The search of the house found cocaine and hashish.

California courts dismissed the ensuing drug charges against the man and a woman on the ground that the garbage search that had provided the basis for the warrant had been unconstitutional.

The Supreme Court overturned that decision Monday.

SEARCH AND SEIZURE AND THE EXCLUSIONARY RULE

Searching Cars: Court Gives Police More Power

Time Magazine

The trouble started back in Prohibition. Two bootleggers were stopped in their car by federal agents, who ripped out the rumble-seat upholstery and found 68 bottles of gin and whisky. The officers had obtained no warrant allowing the search, but in a 1925 decision, the Supreme Court declared that because cars were mobile, warrantless searches were legal if police had probable cause to believe that contraband was in the vehicle. Ever since, court majorities have been swerving from side to side, trying to define the extent of that exception to the Fourth Amendment's search and seizure rules. In the process, the court has confounded not only police but judges and law professors as well. Last week the Justices swerved again, but they may have cleared up much of the murkiness; they also gave police much greater power. By a 6-to-3 vote, the court ruled that officers without warrants may search anywhere in a car and may open almost any container from paper bag to locked baggage.

The new case involved Albert Ross, who was arrested in Washington, D.C., after an informant tipped police that Ross was selling narcotics kept in his car's trunk. A search of the trunk turned up a small brown paper bag. Inside, the police found heroin—evidence instrumental in Ross's conviction. An appeals court reversed that conviction, and last July the Supreme Court arrived at the same conclusion in a similar case. The Justices had said then that police could not constitutionally undo the opaque plastic wrapped around two bricks of marijuana stashed in the trunk of a California man's car.

But the majority in the case was fractionated, and the author of the prevailing opinion, Potter Stewart, has since retired. Now a new majority, including his replacement, Sandra Day O'Connor, has decided that the Justices erred last July. Since a warrantless auto search (with probable cause) is as legal as a regular search with a warrant, then the same guidelines apply, reasoned Justice John Paul Stevens in last week's decision. "When a legitimate search is under way, and when its purpose and its limits have been precisely defined, nice distinctions between . . . glove compartments, upholstered seats, trunks and wrapped packages . . . must give way to the interest in the prompt and efficient completion of the task at hand."

Stevens noted, however, that limits do remain; for example, "probable cause to believe that undocumented aliens are being transported in a van will not justify a warrantless search of a suitcase." Unless perhaps, it is a very large suitcase.

When the Police Blunder a Little

Bennett Beach, Time *Magazine*

The anonymous letter to police in Bloomingdale, Ill., reported that Lance and Susan Gates had more than $100,000 worth of drugs in their basement and that they "make their living on selling drugs." Prompted by the letter, officers made a preliminary investigation, went to a magistrate, got a warrant, searched the Gates home and car and found more than 350 lbs. of marijuana, along with drug paraphernalia, weapons and ammunition. A good bust of two suspected drug traffickers? Not exactly. Instead, that case turned out to be potentially the most important test of the search-and-seizure rules in two decades.

Before the Gateses went on trial, the Illinois Supreme Court ruled that the anonymous tip and preliminary investigation did not provide probable cause to issue a warrant. The court threw out all the discovered physical evidence because of the much reviled exclusionary rule, which holds that the fruits of an illegal search may not be used against the defendant in court. The U.S. Supreme Court last year considered arguments on the legality of the warrant in the Gates case, but then unexpectedly asked the lawyers to return to debate a proposition not previously at issue in the case: Should there be an exception to the exclusionary rule when law-enforcement officials act illegally but "in good faith"?

Before a crowded, tense courtroom last week, Illinois First Assistant Attorney General Paul Biebel told the Justices that the actions of the Bloomingdale police "can only be characterized as thorough and professional. This is clearly not the kind of activity the exclusionary rule was meant to deter." Speaking against a legal rule that the President has called "absurd," U.S. Solicitor General Rex Lee added that the search was made in the "reasonable good-faith belief" that it was constitutional; second thoughts by an appeals court should not bar use of "highly relevant" evidence. James Reilley, the Gateses' attorney, countered by reciting a long list of state and federal court rulings on the exclusionary rule that seem to brook no major exceptions. But the list may be coming to an end.

The drafters of the Bill of Rights never imagined the current complexity. Their experience with search-and-seizure problems involved writs of assistance, general warrants that allowed the King's agents to conduct wide-ranging searches of the homes of his colonial subjects. To protect citizens from such intrusions by the new Federal Government, the Fourth Amendment specifically prohibits "unreasonable searches and seizures" by authorities and requires detailed warrants. In 1914, the Supreme Court concluded that officials were leaving the amendment in tatters as they routinely tore through privacy rights. The court unanimously ordered federal criminal trial judges to exclude evidence seized unconstitutionally.

Even at its birth, the exclusionary rule seemed to many an overreaction. "The criminal is to go free because the constable has blundered," objected New York Court of Appeals Judge Benjamin Cardozo, who was later to join the high bench. The real howls, however, did not come until 1961, when Earl Warren's Supreme Court ruled that state as well as federal courts were bound by the rule. About half the states had not previously adopted it; they hurriedly set up programs to school patrolmen on the ins and outs of the new requirements. The specifics changed almost monthly as courts grappled with an array of new defense challenges.

In recent years, high crime rates and a more conservative mood have prompted a growing outcry. "People are all mad as the dickens that defendants are freed on technicalities," says Utah Supreme Court Chief Justice Dallin Oaks. The rule, wrote Oaks in 1970 when he was a University of Chicago law professor, "imposes excessive costs on the criminal-justice system." It takes "limitless patience with irrationality" to tolerate the fact that "where there have been two wrongs, the defendant's and the officer's, both will go free." Another problem, says U.S. Appeals Court Judge Malcolm Wilkey of the District of Columbia Circuit, is that "every defense lawyer feels obliged to make a suppression motion in search-and-seizure cases." Wilkey reports that 22% of the criminal cases in his court required analysis of such claims, a process that seriously bogged down the system. Says he: "No other civilized country in the world has a rule excluding relevant material evidence." He contends that the sanction only encourages perjury by police when they testify about the search in question.

New York City Deputy Police Commissioner Kenneth Conboy claims that the rule does not deter much official misconduct. If evidence is discarded at trial, he says, "most officers don't care. You know why? Because the guy rarely goes to jail anyway." Besides, police have no certainty that their best efforts will stand up. "You're talking about sophisticated, subtle distinctions," notes Conboy. "It takes judges months to reach decisions. Police have to make them instantaneously, in alleys, with guns and knives around."

Nonetheless, argue the rule's backers, a judge has to look intently over the policeman's shoulder in order to keep the process as pure as possible. "Law enforcement must be sound and aggressive," insists Maryland Attorney General Stephen Sachs, "but citizens must see law enforcement as law-abiding. The government should not stoop to conquer."

Does this concern for purity cost too much in lost prosecutions? The statistics do not provide a clear-cut answer. According to a 1979 report by the General Accounting Office, Congress's investigatory arm, one in every 250 federal criminal cases is not prosecuted because of the exclusionary rule. A recent study in California, however, found that nearly one in 20 felony cases was not brought because of the rule. The only fact that the figures do clearly demonstrate is that the vast majority of search-and-seizure problems involve drug cases. The impact on cases of violent crimes seems small.

No one considers the rule ideal. "Even civil libertarians sort of hold their noses while arguing for it," says Stanford Law Professor John Kaplan. He would permit the use of any relevant evidence even if it was unlawfully obtained, but only when the offending officer's department has training and disciplinary programs to promote adherence to the Fourth Amendment. Kaplan's approach is also favored by the Police Executive Research Forum, which is made up of police chiefs and county sheriffs.

In a variation of that idea, Judge Wilkey proposes a minitrial after conviction to examine challenged police conduct. If it was ruled illegal, the officer's department would have to punish him adequately or risk having the conviction thrown out. Others suggest that the convicted subject of an unlawful search could sue police for damages. But this idea has never seemed very realistic. Scoffs New York City Defense Lawyer Robert Morvillo: "A defendant is not going to have the money to bring a suit, and he's not going to have credibility with a jury."

The most widely supported alternative is the good-faith exception now before the court. The proposal has already been adopted by at least two federal appeals courts and three states. If the Supreme Court approves such an exception, it could be limited to searches conducted with warrants that turn out to be invalid, as in the Gates case. The exception could also apply any time police were able to prove they had acted in good faith.

"The idea frightens me. Police would be more careless," says Georgetown Law Professor William Greenhalgh, a former prosecutor; on behalf of the American Bar Association, he wrote a *Gates* brief supporting the existing rule. Notes University of Michigan Law Professor Yale Kamisar: "What are we asking here? Whether a police officer reasonably acted unreasonably? If they lower the standard any more, they'll reduce the rule to the vanishing point."

How the Supreme Court will resolve this debate will probably not be known until the end of the term in June. But most court watchers suspect that the exclusionary rule is in for a rough time. Sentiment on the court is thought to be narrowly divided, and the outcome could depend on Justice Sandra Day O'Connor, who succeeded Potter Stewart, an exclusionary-rule backer; O'Connor seemed to favor a good-faith exception at her 1981 Senate confirmation hearing. That change could produce a new majority, one that favors closing a loophole for criminals at the risk of opening a new one for police.

A Peril Not Only to the Press

Marvin Stone

It is starting to sink in—with some in Congress at least—that the recent Supreme Court decision approving search and seizure in a newspaper office has frightening implications. The decision is being rightfully regarded as one more move to cancel safeguards of the First and Fourth amendments, not only for the press, but for all citizens.

The details require a brief review. On April 12, 1971, police came unannounced to the offices of the *Stanford Daily,* armed with a search warrant. They thought the *Daily,* though not itself suspected of crime, might possess photographs showing who helped beat up nine policemen. The invaders ransacked photo labs, cabinets, desks and wastebaskets, found nothing and left. The paper sued local authorities. It won in U.S. district court and appeals court. But the Supreme Court now has ruled that no clause in the Constitution bars what happened to the *Daily.*

The potential peril to every individual became evident in Justice Stevens's dissent: "Doctors, lawyers, merchants, customers, bystanders who may have documents in their possession must relate to an ongoing criminal investigation." You could interpret that to mean that police, armed with search warrants from judges or magistrates—*any* judges or magistrates—could invade the homes of third parties and rummage through their files, letters, photos and documents as if they were no better than common criminals.

The *Boston Globe* saw, as well it might, a "step toward a police state." Sam Dash, once the Senate's chief counsel in investigating Watergate, concluded that the new decision puts innocent people in a worse plight than criminals.

How did we come to such a state?

The Fourth Amendment, written out of bitter experience, declares: "The right of the people to be secure in their persons, houses, papers, and effects, against unreasonable searches and seizures, shall not be violated, and no warrants shall issue, but upon probable cause, supported by oath or affirmation, and particularly describing the place to be searched, and the persons or things to be seized."

For many years, this was interpreted to mean that only weapons or the plunder of crime could be hunted. But in 1967 the Court sanctioned the seizure of "mere evidence." The Stanford raid and other, similar cases followed, broadening the searches to papers and other effects of innocent third parties, and now the Court has approved these also.

The Court's majority—commendably—did invite legislative action. It was not long in coming. Representatives Drinan and Jacobs and Senators Dole and Bayh, occupying a pretty wide political spectrum, are offering legislation to guard the personal privacy made vulnerable by the Court. Cosponsors are many.

Any of these bills would give welcome aid; the only question is whether they go far enough. Drinan's plan, for instance, confines itself to the press—a vital consideration but only part of the problem.

Dole and Bayh would require a hearing for the innocent party before a search could be conducted, but would permit this to be skipped if the police showed that the party, given warning, might destroy the evidence.

This arrangement would provide little safety against the most feared threat, an unscrupulous administration and a compliant magistrate. But the Jacobs bill may have a solution: Where the wanted evidence cannot be found without exposing other private papers to inspection, all must be sealed without examination until after a hearing. If properly structured, this procedure, which parallels the model code of the American Law Institute, averts danger of destruction while protecting the individual.

Whatever the action—and it must be weighed with utmost care—now is the time. Liberties that Americans treasure are being threatened and could easily be stolen away.

A Question of Seizure

Newsweek *Magazine*

When the federal Immigration and Naturalization Service sweeps a factory looking for illegal aliens, teams of agents guard the doors to prevent anyone from leaving. Other agents confront the workers, demanding proof of citizenship or legal residence in the United States. Not everyone is asked: in the West, agents target Hispanics; in the Northeast, they aim more for West Indians and Asians. Any worker who can't produce papers is handcuffed and taken away. Last week the U.S. Supreme Court upheld that procedure by ruling that the Constitution's ban against warrantless searches and seizures did not apply to these episodes because the workers—despite appearances—had not been "seized."

Writing for a 7-2 majority, Justice William H. Rehnquist said that employees were free to leave at any time. Of course, they would first have to answer the agent's questions, but "mere questioning does not constitute a seizure," said Rehnquist. In a sharply worded dissent, Justice William J. Brennan Jr. said that "it is only through a considerable feat of legerdemain that the Court is able to arrive at the conclusion that the respondents were not seized." He accused the majority of signing off on a "jury-rigged enforcement scheme," because security at U.S. borders has "collapsed."

The Court's Ruling on Auto Searches

Newsweek *Magazine*

The Fourth Amendment bars police from searching persons and property without a warrant. When the Founding Fathers drafted that seemingly clear provision, they obviously didn't have the automobile in mind: by the time a policeman gets a warrant for a suspicious car, it may have been driven away. So in 1925 the U.S. Supreme Court invented the "automobile exception" to the Fourth Amendment, allowing police to stop and inspect a car when they have "probable cause" to believe that it contains contraband. But that rule has proved to be murky as well. Can the police look inside the trunk and glove compartment? Can they open up a suitcase or peek inside a package? Last July an exasperated Justice Lewis Powell surveyed the judicial hairsplitting on these questions and branded the rules "intolerably confusing" for the nation's police.

Last week the Court used the case of Albert (Bandit) Ross to reduce the confusion. In November 1978 District of Columbia police received a tip that Ross was selling drugs out of his car. Cruising officers soon spotted him, stopped his car and unlocked the trunk. Inside was an unsealed brown paper bag. The cops opened it and found 30 envelopes of heroin. Ross challenged the search, since if the drug evidence could be suppressed, the case against him would collapse. Writing for a 6-3 majority, Justice John Paul Stevens approved the bag opening and then set out a new general rule: whenever police have probable cause to stop a car they may inspect all containers that "may conceal the object of the search." Justice Thurgood Marshall forcefully dissented, arguing that in Ross's case the cops should have seized the bag and asked a judge for permission to look inside. Efficiency . . . can never be substituted for due process," he wrote. "Is not a dictatorship the more 'efficient' form of government?"

A Matter of Good Faith

Michael S. Serrill, Time *Magazine*

It was a very good year for prosecutors and police as the U.S. Supreme Court sliced away at various precedents to give more leeway to law enforcement. In completing its work for the term, the court last week handed down 19 decisions, including what one law professor called "a real get-out-of-town" ruling on a major Fourth Amendment search-and-seizure issue. Overshadowing their other opinions on such matters as women's rights and free speech, the Justices did what law officials had long hoped for and what civil libertarians had feared. For the first time they created a "good faith" exception to the so-called exclusionary rule, and allowed the use of some illegally obtained evidence in criminal trials.

Although the opinion was less sweeping than some had predicted, the court held 6 to 3 that when judges issue search warrants that are later ruled defective, the evidence gathered by police may still be used at trial in most cases. In 1981 Alberto Leon was one of several people indicted on drug-conspiracy charges in California after police searches of their homes and cars had turned up a large quantity of drugs. A judge had issued the warrant, even though it was based on outdated information provided by an informant of uncertain reliability. Two federal courts later threw out much of the key evidence because the warrant had been issued without a showing of "probable cause" to believe a crime was being committed.

A second case before the court was the classic kind of legal horror story that leads critics to rail against the consequences of the exclusionary rule: a Boston detective, investigating a woman's brutal murder, had good reason to suspect her boyfriend, Osborne Sheppard. Unable to find the proper warrant form, the officer unsuccessfully tried to alter a form normally used in drug cases. A judge okayed the warrant, and Sheppard was convicted. But because of this technical imperfection, Massachusetts' highest court declared the search illegal and threw out the incriminating evidence, including bloody clothing, that had been found in the suspect's house.

The Supreme Court accepted the lower courts' determinations that both warrants were defective, but found that the police had acted in the good-faith belief that the searches they made were lawful. Justice Byron White argued that the principal justification for the exclusionary rule was to deter police misconduct. But when police have obtained what they reasonably think is a valid warrant, "there is no police illegality and thus nothing to deter," wrote White. "Penalizing the officer for the magistrate's error, rather than his own, cannot logically contribute to the deterrence of Fourth Amendment violations."

If the police lie in seeking the warrant, or if the judge granting the warrant is not impartial, the court ruled, evidence in such cases may still be suppressed. But by and large, last week's decision means that if police officers get a warrant, defense attorneys will be unable to persuade trial judges to block the use of the evidence gathered with it. The ruling did not address the question of whether this good-faith exception would apply when police act without a warrant, but the court may look at that issue soon. Dissenter William Brennan thought the majority had done enough already. "In case after case, I have witnessed the court's gradual but determined strangulation of the rule," he wrote. "It now appears that the court's victory over the Fourth Amendment is complete." David Shrager, president of the Association of Trial Lawyers of America, agreed. "Good faith is just a code word for saying we're sick and tired of the exclusionary rule," he complained.

Atlanta District Attorney Lewis Slayton, by contrast, was delighted, because "this ruling takes the technicality out and gives us more practicality, and that's what we need." Massachusetts Assistant Attorney General Barbara Smith argued that the decision would actually protect civil liberties by encouraging more officers to get warrants, because they no longer have to be concerned that "the court is waiting to pounce on them for the slightest error."

The Reagan Administration, which supports a broad good-faith exception, was pleased, particularly by Justice White's statement that "the substantial costs of exclusion" outweigh "the marginal or nonexistent benefits produced by suppressing evidence" in these cases. Said Associate Attorney General D. Lowell Jensen: "It restores a better balance to the criminal justice system."

Whether it is "better balance" or overreach, the court has been tilting decidedly toward the prosecution, especially in search cases. That trend continued last week, prompting Justice John Paul Stevens to decry the majority's "voracious appetite for judicial activism . . . at least when it comes to restricting the constitutional rights of the citizen." In a Virginia case, the court found last week that prison inmates are not protected by the Fourth Amendment. Chief Justice Warren Burger, writing for a 5-to-4 majority, held that an inmate had no right to challenge cell searches. "The recognition of privacy rights for prisoners in their individual cells," Burger wrote, "simply cannot be reconciled with the concept of incarceration." In a dissent that he took the trouble to read aloud when the decision was handed down, Justice Stevens said, "To hold that a prisoner's possession of a letter from his wife, or a picture of his baby, has no protection against arbitrary or malicious perusal, seizure or destruction would not, in my judgment, comport with any civilized standard of decency."

State Wiretap Law Modeled After Federal Statute

Karen E. Klein, News Staff Writer

For 20 years federal agents have relied on electronic eavesdropping devices—bugs and wiretaps—to catch spies, corrupt officials and mobsters.

Last week, California law enforcement officials got their first legislation authorizing the use of wiretaps on suspected drug dealers' telephones. Use of hidden microphones and other bugging devices by law enforcement authorities in California still is illegal.

"There is no better evidence you can put before a jury than the actual words of somebody discussing their part in a criminal scheme," said Assistant U.S. Attorney James L. Sanders.

The state law, signed by Gov. George Deukmejian, is modeled after a 1968 federal statute that prosecutors say is invaluable in investigating and prosecuting criminals.

There are differences, however, between the state and federal legislation. The state law applies only to telephone taps, where the federal law includes hidden microphones.

The state law can be used only in cases where large amounts of drugs are suspected to be involved. The federal law applies in myriad cases, ranging from bribery of public officials to corruption in sporting events to wire fraud to organized crime.

In the case of drug rings or terrorist groups, the leaders usually insulate themselves and the upper echelon cannot be easily infiltrated by undercover agents or informants, federal officials say. That's when secret tape recordings become crucial, they say.

"The people running the show are the ones you want, but they're the hardest to get," Sanders said.

But civil libertarians and defense attorneys say the practice is an invasion of privacy that is too often misused.

"The history of abuses with wiretapping does not lend itself to the belief that they will be used properly now," Dan Stormer, a Los Angeles civil rights attorney, said about the state law.

Eavesdropping on private conversations is often unwarranted, Stormer said. He cited one case in which, he said, investigators planted a hidden microphone in a couple's bedroom.

"The police have no business going in to private conversations, and that is done totally indiscriminately," he said.

U.S. Attorney Robert C. Bonner counters that electronic surveillance is used relatively infrequently in Los Angeles because of its expense and the time-consuming supervision needed. Major narcotics and organized crime are the two kinds of cases that most frequently justify wiretaps, he said.

Checks and balances on the strictly supervised snooping process protect the rights of innocent people caught in the electronic web, prosecutors say.

To conduct a wiretap, a federal prosecutor in Los Angeles must get approval from Bonner's office before submitting an application to Washington. There, it must be approved by a deputy attorney general before it goes on for consideration by a federal judge.

In an affidavit, the prosecutor and agents must convince the judge that they have good cause to believe a crime is being committed and that they cannot investigate it by any other means.

Once a wiretap is approved, on a 30-day basis, most judges require written reports on the progress of the investigation every week or 10 days, Sanders said. An agent must monitor the conversations being taped 24 hours a day, seven days a week.

The entire process is approved secretly and is not made public until three months after the surveillance is completed, Sanders said.

At that point, anyone who was overheard must be informed, even if he or she is not a target of the investigation. During an investigation of terrorists, one of the defendants was monitored making about 15 calls to people who were advertising used cars for sale, Sanders said.

He sent letters to all of the car sellers he could identify, Sanders said, and received calls back from two or three. "Mostly they wanted to know what this was about. As soon as I told them they weren't involved in the investigation, they hung up," he said.

In the case of Richard Miller, the only FBI agent ever to be convicted of espionage, FBI agents planted a hidden microphone under the seat in his car and listened in on Miller and his Russian-immigrant lover discuss a plot to pass classified documents to Soviet officials.

In a Chicago case involving a judge, the man was overheard by a microphone planted in his chambers agreeing to take bribes from defense attorneys who never lost their cases. When confronted with the evidence, the judge pleaded guilty.

In another Chicago case, which Sanders prosecuted, four members of a Puerto Rican terrorist group were convicted of making bombs and planning to blow up U.S. military installations.

Two telephones were tapped during the investigation and hidden microphones and hidden video recorders were planted in an apartment the men used while building the bombs.

"We never would have known they were assembling bombs, and we wouldn't have prevented them from placing them at military bases (without the wiretaps)," Sanders said.

ELECTRONIC SURVEILLANCE

Foreword to Tales of a Computer State

Walter Cronkite

In 1948 George Orwell wrote what turned out to be his final work, the classic *1984*. It drew a picture of a chilling future in which the world had fallen under the sway of three great totalitarian governments.

The country that comprised what had been Western Europe, Britain and the United States was called Oceania and was ruled by Big Brother. The state was all and to serve it, loyally and unthinkingly, its citizens had been divested of all pretense of privacy, and hence liberty.

Books, movies, plays—everything was censored, of course. History was re-written to suit current propaganda needs. Thought police monitored behavior patterns to detect possibly deviant attitudes. Sophisticated listening devices tuned in the most intimate conversations.

And perhaps the most effective means of control was the two-way television set that looked into every room at office, factory or home. The individual never was free from the surveillance of the security forces.

And yet Orwell, with his vivid imagination, was unable to foresee the actual shape of the threat that would exist in 1984. It turns out to be the ubiquitous computer and its ancillary communication networks. Without the malign intent of any government system or would-be dictator, our privacy is being invaded, and more and more of the experiences which should be solely our own are finding their way into electronic files that the curious can scrutinize at the punch of a button.

The airline companies have a computer record of our travels—where we went and how long we stayed and, possibly, with whom we traveled. The car rental firms have a computer record of the days and distances we went afield. Hotel computers can fill in a myriad of detail about our stays away from home, and the credit card computers know a great deal about the meals we ate, and with how many guests.

The computer files at the Internal Revenue Service, the Census Bureau, the Social Security Administration, the various security agencies such as the Federal Bureau of Investigation and our own insurance companies know everything there is to know about our economic, social and marital status, even down to our past illnesses and the state of our health.

If—or is it when?—these computers are permitted to talk to one another, when they are interlinked, they can spew out a roomful of data on each of us that will leave us naked before whoever gains access to the information.

This is the threat, with its many permutations, with which David Burnham deals here. His is not a polemic against the computers or those who program them, and there is full acknowledgment of the great benefits they can and are bringing to mankind. (For instance, we could not have gone to space without them, and they hold the potential for helping scientists conquer disease.)

But we must be vigilant against their misuse, either accidentally or intentionally. The alarm is raised here that, while we are only too aware now of the danger of losing everything in a nuclear holocaust, there also is a danger of losing it all in the green glow from a little phosphor screen.

Tales of a Computer State

David Burnham

Under the hood of the 1981 V8-6-4 Cadillac motorcar, the General Motors Corporation buried a small but sophisticated computer. "Your Cadillac," the owner's manual boasted, "is equipped with a digital fuel injection system which monitors the exhaust stream with an oxygen sensor. The oxygen sensor signals the control unit to adjust the air-fuel ratio as necessary."

The manual further noted that the "Check Engine" light on the instrument panel "is designed to warn you if the system has detected any faults. If the light comes on and stays on while driving, the car should be taken to a Cadillac dealer as soon as possible for system inspection and maintenance. If the light comes on and goes off, it is an indication that a temporary problem has cleared itself. While it is not as critical that the vehicle be brought in to a dealer for inspection immediately, the dealer may at a later date be able to determine what trouble had occurred and if any maintenance is necessary."

But *Electronics Engineering News,* a trade publication, discerned another possible use for the tiny electronic spy: a way to deny Cadillac owners the benefits of their warranties if they have failed to drive according to G.M. standards.

"Any suggestion that there is any equipment in our cars designed to spy on a driver is pure hogwash," said a Cadillac spokesman. "The computer is just to help mechanics repair cars, and the information it provides is used for that purpose only."

The on-board Cadillac computer affects only a handful of people. But it is a symbol of the sweeping computerization of government and industry that is building a world where large organizations routinely collect detailed information about how we drive, where we sleep, what we buy, whom we talk to, where we go and even what we think. Whether the source is a bank, the Internal Revenue

Service, the telephone company, the National Security Agency, a two-way cable television system or an insurance company, computerized surveillance is a largely unacknowledged reality of American life.

The powerful reach of modern surveillance is compounded by the increasing ability of the computers of separate organizations to talk to one another. Computer matching—the automatic correlation of information that has been stored in different data banks for different reasons—is now a widely used and casually accepted practice.

"There is nothing new about matching," said Thomas McBride, until recently the Inspector General of the Labor Department. McBride, who now is a professor at Stanford Law School, is a leading advocate of this investigative technique.

"You do it as a reporter; I did it when I was a prosecutor," he said. "I remember, for example, when I was a member of the special team investigating Watergate and I matched the lists kept by the President's secretary—Rosemary Woods— against the Federal campaign contributions roster. What is new, what is exciting, is that so much more information is now stored on computer tapes. This enables you to match 1,000 names or 100,000 names against telephone numbers, Social Security numbers or whatever in a matter of seconds."

The systematic use of computers to detect fraud in certain Federal programs began under President Carter. But with the election of President Reagan, computer matching has come into vogue. McBride, in fact, was co-chairman of a Presidential committee established to expand the use of the technique.

"There are now about sixty different Federal programs that depend on the income level of the individual to determine eligibility," McBride explained. "Everything from weatherization grants to Head Start. There just isn't any question that this methodology should be widely applied, that it has an enormous potential for eliminating fraud or erroneous payments and saving the taxpayers billions of dollars each year."

McBride acknowledged that computer matching is being used mostly in programs aimed at the poor. "We're now trying to get some matches going that don't have this welfare tilt," he said. "Disaster loans are one example. This is an area where benefits primarily go to business people, agribusiness people, and where some quite wealthy people were into some pretty heavy double dipping. Medical providers, like pharmacists, doctors and hospitals, are another area where big bucks can be saved. I'm quite sure there are a number of areas in the Pentagon where matching might be a big-ticket item."

And he admitted that there are dangers inherent in the widespread use of computer matching. "Making sure that computer data bases are clean and accurate is very difficult," he said. "Social Security, for example, is really a mess. Sure, there is a real potential for abuse. That's why we need very careful controls. I certainly am not prepared to say, for example, that all Federal and state program managers should automatically get access to everyone's income tax return. I think that would be going too far."

In a cream-colored three-story office building in an industrial section of Los Angeles, just off the freeway to Disneyland, is the headquarters of the Bureau of Child Support of the Los Angeles County district attorney's office. With 1,007 investigators, lawyers, technicians and clerks, the bureau employs exactly half of the men and women who prosecute all the crimes that occur within the county's borders.

Robert Kiehl is one of a new category of law enforcement officers whose authority comes from social welfare law rather than criminal statutes. He has developed a computerized system which automatically diverts state tax refunds owed to "runaway parents" to the support of their children. Kiehl, who is 54, has a full gray mustache which dominates his mournful face. He speaks in the quiet monotone of many longtime government employees. "The seizing of tax refunds is just one aspect of our child-support program, and a rather new one at that," he said. "Here is how it works. Once we have a court order on a parent and there are delinquencies built up on that order for support of a child receiving public assistance, we send the name up to the Franchise Tax Board. They run the name through their computer. If the parent is due a refund, it is intercepted and used by the state to offset the support going to the child."

The program appears to be quite efficient. According to Dan Hicks, an analyst with the California Department of Social Services, in the second year of the system's operation the district attorneys of the state's fifty-eight counties submitted 117,000 names to the Franchise Tax Board. The result: more than $10 million in tax refunds was taken from delinquent parents and given to the state to defray the costs of supporting their dependents.

The refund-intercept program is only one way computers help Los Angeles County district attorneys force parents to meet their financial obligations to their children. The computers in the district attorney's office have direct electronic links to the Department of Motor Vehicles, the Employment Development Board and the Criminal Justice Information System and other data banks, providing county investigators with information that helps them locate parents who have left their children without support.

Louis Hays, the director of the Federal Child Support Enforcement Office, provided the perspective from Washington. "This year the whole program will result in support payments being made by about 1 million parents—400,000 who have applied to receive Aid for Dependent Children, 600,000 who have not," he said.

"During roughly the same time period, the states asked us for address information on 200,000 individuals. We put these names on magnetic tapes and periodically submitted them to the Internal Revenue Service, the Social Security Administration, the Defense Department, the Veterans Administration and the National Personnel Record Center. Using their computers, the agencies search their records for information about the people whose names have been submitted by the states. Most of the states have terminals directly linked to us, and when we get a hit—which happens in about 60 percent of the cases—we send the information we have found back to the state."

Hays believes, however, that obtaining the home addresses and places of employment of runaway parents is the simple part of the problem. "You can locate people easily. You can go to court easily. But that doesn't mean you can make them pay," he said.

When I asked him about the possibility that his system might someday be turned against another target, let's say civil rights protesters taking part in legal demonstrations, he became uneasy. "I balk at the implication in your question that parents have a right to avoid their responsibilities," he said. "And besides, the average state doesn't have a very sophisticated computer tracking system yet. I am not saying that we never could get to 1984. I'm just saying that the facts don't support such a premise at the present time."

Michael DuCross, a Canadian-born Indian, lives in Huntington Beach, California, a small city halfway between Los Angeles and San Diego. At about 9 P.M. on March 24, 1980, DuCross, a slight man with a gentle smile and wire-rimmed glasses, decided to drive to a local supermarket for some groceries. Just after he turned his 1976 Pinto into the parking lot of a shopping center near his apartment, the flashing red lights of a police car filled his rear-view mirror. He had made an illegal left turn.

The policeman, using his two-way car radio, asked for a check on DuCross. A clerk in the Huntington Beach police station punched DuCross's name and driver's license number into a terminal. The information was instantly flashed to Sacramento, the state capital. Nothing. Then it was flashed 3,000 miles east to the F.B.I.'s computerized National Crime Information Center in Washington.

Pay dirt. Back across the continent came the answer. The F.B.I.'s records said DuCross was wanted by the Federal government because on Christmas Eve of 1969 he had gone AWOL from the Marine Corps. Based on that information, DuCross was taken to the brig at Camp Pendleton, California. Five months later, the charges were dropped and he was set free to pick up the pieces of his life. The government released DuCross after discovering he had never been AWOL. He had left the Marine Corps in 1969 under a special discharge program for resident aliens.

Thus, an error somewhere in the government's computerized records and surveillance system reached across a vast expanse of time and space and violently interrupted the life of a single Mohawk Indian.

The growing number of privately operated surveillance systems also make errors. In 1977, Harvey Saltz, a former deputy district attorney in Los Angeles, formed a company called U.D. Registry Inc., which provides landlords with information about prospective tenants. Using data obtained from the court records of suits filed by landlords against tenants, Saltz compiled a computerized list of more than a million names from all over the Los Angeles area. Some 1,900 landlords pay him an annual fee ranging from $35 to $60 and a search fee of $7.50 to find out whether potential tenants have been sued by their landlords in the past.

But as Lucky Kellener, Barbara Ward and many others have learned, such information-retrieval systems frequently make mistakes: Kellener, a Los Angeles lawyer, paid his brother's rent on one occasion in 1978. Some months later, when his brother was evicted, Kellener's name was inadvertently included in the papers filed by the landlord in court. U.D. Registry transferred the incorrect information to its computer, and Kellener was recorded as an undesirable tenant. Three years after he paid his brother's rent, in December 1981, Kellener decided he needed a larger apartment. "I went to three apartment houses but was turned away," he said. "They kept saying things like, 'Someone was here before you,' or 'We'll get back to you.' You know, the brushoff."

After the third rejection, a landlord unintentionally let Kellener in on the dark secret: there was a computerized blacklisting service and his name was on its list. "It's creeping McCarthyism," he said. "Actually, it's worse. McCarthy usually did his stuff out in the open. This operation does it under the table."

Barbara Ward was another victim. In 1972 she moved to Los Angeles, rented an apartment and found it was infested with cockroaches and rodents. When her landlord refused to deal with the infestation, she gave him thirty days' notice. He countered with an eviction notice. Ward went to court armed with county health records to support her case. The landlord did not show up. The judge ordered the case dropped from the calendar. A few years later, several landlords refused to rent Ward an apartment because of the listing in U.D. Registry's computer that she had once been served with an eviction notice. Neither Kellener nor Ward knew of U.D. Registry's existence, let alone that it was transmitting false information that would severely damage their reputations.

In the late 1960s President Johnson disturbed by the riots that took place after the assassination of Martin Luther King Jr. and the proliferating antiwar demonstrations, ordered the Army to begin collecting information on potential "subversives" so that the Federal government could prevent civil disturbances. The program became a Frankenstein's monster. In hearings conducted in 1971 by Senator Sam Ervin's Subcommittee on Constitutional Rights, it was revealed that the Army had gathered information on the political activities of about 100,000 people, including members of Congress such as Representative Abner Mikva and members of organizations like the American Civil Liberties Union, the American Friends Service Committee and the N.A.A.C.P.

With few directives to guide them, Ervin said, Army intelligence agents "monitored the membership and policies of peaceful organizations who were concerned with the war in Southeast Asia, the draft, racial and labor problems, and community welfare. Out of this surveillance, the Army created blacklists of organizations and personalities which were circulated to many federal, state and local agencies who were asked to supplement the data provided. Not only descriptions of the contents of speeches and political comments were included, but irrelevant entries about personal finances, such as the fact that a militant leader's credit card was withdrawn. In some cases, a psychiatric analysis taken from the Army or other medical records was included.

Ervin's subcommittee found that the information collected on individuals who opposed the Johnson Administration's policies was filed in four computers, located in the headquarters of the Army Intelligence Command (Fort Holabird, Maryland), the Continental Army (Fort Monroe, Virginia) and the Third Army Corps (Fort Hood, Texas), and at the Pentagon. Not only did the Army gather personal and political information; it had ordered its analysts to code the data so that the individuals could be listed in the computers according to various categories.

Ralph Stein, a young Army analyst, described for the subcomittee the confusing and sometimes arbitrary method used to code data into the Army's computers:

To make the difficult decisions about what category a person belonged in, the analyst was required to examine reports and then resort to a special intelligence code. He had to apply various number combinations which indicated a person's beliefs or status. For instance, 134.295 indicated that a person was a non-Communist, while 135.295—a difference of one digit—indicated Communist Party membership or advocacy of Communism.

Computers are essential to the operation of many of the conveniences of modern life. Without computers, for example, the massive car rental business could not exist. By almost any measure of speed, efficiency and reliability, the service offered by car rental companies is astounding. But the use of computers means that each transaction of each customer involves creating a record that can be stored, modified and retrieved in a matter of seconds.

Officially, F.B.I. agents must obtain administrative summonses for any records they seek. But such summonses are available to them almost automatically. What is more, in most jurisdictions, Federal, state and local law enforcement officers have informal ties with a variety of recordkeepers, so that even this modest restraint is easy to get around. Ready access is guaranteed by the design of computerized credit and reservation networks.

Such a network can be wonderfully handy for the police—and other curious individuals as well. Peter Bronson (a pseudonym) is a first-class reporter I once worked with at *The New York Times*. A few years ago, while he was living in Washington and doing a great deal of traveling for the paper, he became infatuated with a young woman who worked at an Avis desk in Atlanta. "One day I came to Atlanta after being out of Washington for about a week, and I stopped by to see my friend," the reporter recalled. "The first thing she did was ask me what I had been doing in Los Angeles and Houston before coming to Atlanta. I was working on a pretty good story, and I'll tell you her tracking of my movements shook me up. It turns out that when someone has your Avis number, it is very easy to find out where you have been renting cars anywhere in the country. I've quit seeing this lady, by the way."

The five largest credit-reporting companies in the United States have a total of more than 150 million credit records in their computers. The information on file on each individual generally includes his or her full name, Social Security number, address, telephone number, name of spouse, place of work, salary, other sources of income, names of creditors, debt-payment history, arrest and conviction records, bankruptcies, tax liens and lawsuits. Some of this information has been volunteered by the person seeking credit; some has been collected by investigators.

In September 1976, an Ohio man named Bennie Bryant applied for a mortgage through the Hammond Mortgage Company. Before granting the mortgage, Hammond took the routine step of asking TRW Information Service, a credit company, to run a check on him. On September 28, a TRW representative called the mortgage company and said that its written report would show that Bryant had had credit problems with four firms. The mortgage company informed Bryant about the negative report, and he immediately told TRW that its information was not correct. Two days later, according to Federal judge Avern Cohn, who presided in a suit Bryant later brought against TRW, the report was sent to the mortgage company "in its original form," and Bryant was denied the loan. "Subsequently, with a revision in the mortgage report and through the plaintiff's personal efforts, the loan was closed," the judge wrote. In December 1979, a Federal district court jury found that TRW had not followed procedures that would have assured the accuracy of its report, and awarded Bryant $8,000 in damages.

The giant computerized credit company, both during the trial and in a subsequent appeal, contended that Bryant's complaint was unjustified. As a matter of law, TRW argued, it has no obligation to determine the accuracy of the information it receives from businesses about the bill-paying habits of individual consumers. "Put another way," said Judge Cohn, TRW contended "it was an error to allow the jury to consider whether there is an obligation on the defendant to test the truthfulness and/or accuracy of the information it receives."

That is a troubling claim from a company which sells 35 million credit reports each year to 24,000 subscribers throughout the country. A visit to TRW's computer operations center, in a single-story unmarked building about three miles from its corporate headquarters in Anaheim, California, explains why the company has so strenuously opposed being held accountable for the accuracy of the information it collects, organizes and then provides its subscribers. Each month, TRW receives computer tapes from thousands of companies, reporting the status of every one of their customers' accounts. TRW's employees then use its massed computers— the largest commercial concentration of computers in the world—to lift the information from those tapes and organize it alphabetically and by region. The company thus can offer up-to-date data on approximately 90 million people to businesses making credit checks. More than 200,000 times each business day, a TRW subscriber types the name of a customer into its own terminal. Within three seconds, the inquiry reaches Anaheim, the information is located in TRW's computers and a report is flashed back to the waiting subscriber. Obviously, the largely automated system would not be able to function were the courts to force TRW to check the accuracy of the reports it receives from its subscribers.

According to TRW's lawyers, a significant number of reports containing incorrect information are routinely transmitted to clients. Each year, about 350,000 people register formal complaints about the accuracy of TRW's reports with the company's consumer relations department. And each year, as many as 100,000 of these complaints result in TRW changing the information in its computers. But, one must ask, how many incorrect entries are not noticed and how many of those that are noticed go uncorrected?

One other problem must be examined concerning surveillance and TRW. The company's consumer credit reporting system is operated by a single division, one small part of a huge conglomerate which provides a broad range of high-technology services for a variety of customers. One of those customers is the Central Intelligence Agency. Though the relationship between TRW and the C.I.A. is highly classified, it is known to involve the processing of computerized intelligence reports gathered by secret government satellites. TRW prides itself on the independence of its divisions, and there is no known instance when information in one division "strayed" to another. But the decision of the Census Bureau during World War II to give the Army demographic data that pinpointed the residences of Japanese-Americans in California—despite a law prohibiting such sharing of information—is instructive. How much pressure would the chairman of the board and the chief executive officer of TRW have to bring on the vice president in charge of the company's information division to persuade him to give the C.I.A. access to credit reports stored in the division's computers?

Kent Greenwalt, a professor at Columbia University's School of Law, discussed the indirect but powerful effects of computer surveillance in a report he submitted to the White House during the Ford Administration:

> If there is increased surveillance and disclosure and it is not offset by greater tolerance, the casualties of modern society are likely to increase as fewer misfits and past wrongdoers are able to find jobs and fruitful associations. The knowledge that one cannot discard one's past, that advancement in society depends heavily on a good record, will create considerable pressure for conformist actions. Many people will try harder than they do now to keep their records clean, avoid controversial or "deviant" actions, whatever their private views and inclinations. Diversity and social vitality is almost certain to suffer and in the long run independent private thoughts will be reduced.

The question looms before us: Can the United States continue to flourish when the physical movements, the buying habits and the conversations of most citizens are under surveillance by private companies and government agencies? Sometimes the surveillance is undertaken for innocent purposes, sometimes it is not. Does not surveillance, even the innocent sort, gradually poison the soul of a nation? Does not surveillance limit personal options for many citizens? Does not surveillance increase the powers of those who are in a position to enjoy the fruits of that activity?

Alexander Solzhenitsyn wrote about this process some years ago:

> As every man goes through life he fills in a number of forms for the record, each containing a number of questions. . . . There are thus hundreds of little threads radiating from every man, millions of threads in all. If these threads were suddenly to become visible, the whole sky would look like a spider's web, and if they materialized like rubber bands, buses and trams and even people would lose the ability to move and the wind would be unable to carry torn-up newspapers or autumn leaves along the streets of the city.

The Concept of Privacy Applied to the Problem of Monitoring

Charles Fried

Let us return now to the concrete problem of electronic monitoring to see whether the foregoing elucidation of the concept of privacy will help to establish on firmer ground the intuitive objection that monitoring is an intolerable violation of privacy. Let us consider the more intrusive forms of monitoring where not only location but conversations and perhaps other data are monitored.

Obviously such a system of monitoring drastically curtails or eliminates altogether the power to control information about oneself. But, it might be said, this is not a significant objection if we assumed the monitored data will go only to authorized persons—probation or parole officers—and cannot be prejudicial so long as the subject of the monitoring is not violating the conditions under which he is allowed to be at liberty. This retort misses the importance of privacy as a context for all kinds of relations, from the most intense to the most casual. For all of these may require a context of some degree of intimacy, and intimacy is made impossible by monitoring.

It is worth being more precise about this notion of intimacy. Monitoring obviously presents vast opportunities for malice and misunderstanding on the part of authorized personnel. For that reason the subject has reason to be constantly apprehensive and inhibited in what he does. There is always an unseen audience, which is the more threatening because of the possibility that one may forget about it and let down his guard, as one would not with a visible audience. Even assuming the benevolence and understanding of the official audience, there are serious consequences to the fact that no degree of true intimacy is possible for the subject. Privacy is not, as we have seen, just a defensive right. It forms the necessary context for the intimate relations of love and friendship which give our lives much of whatever affirmative value they have. In the role of citizen or fellow worker, one need reveal himself to no greater extent than is necessary to display the attributes of competence and morality appropriate to those roles. In order to be a friend or lover one must reveal far more of himself. Yet where any intimate revelation may be heard by monitoring officials, it loses the quality of exclusive intimacy required of a gesture of love or friendship. Thus monitoring, in depriving one of privacy, destroys the possibility of bestowing the gift of intimacy, and makes impossible the essential dimension of love and friendship.

Monitoring similarly undermines the subject's capacity to enter into relations of trust. As I analyzed trust, it required the possibility of error on the part of the person trusted. The negation of trust is constant surveillance—such as monitoring—which minimizes the possibility of undetected default. The monitored parolee is denied the sense of self-respect inherent in being trusted by the government which has released him. More important, monitoring prevents the parolee from entering into true *relations* of trust with persons in the outside world. An employer, unaware of the monitoring, who entrusts a sum of money to the parolee cannot thereby grant him the sense of responsibility and autonomy which an unmonitored person in the same position would have. The parolee in a real—if special and ironical—sense, cannot be trusted.

Now let us consider the argument that however intrusive monitoring may seem, surely prison life is more so. In part, of course, this will be a matter of fact. It may be that a reasonably secure and well-run prison will allow prisoners occasions for conversation among themselves, with guards, or with visitors, which are quite private. Such a prison regime would in this respect be less intrusive than monitoring. Often prison regimes do not allow even this, and go far toward depriving a prisoner of any sense of privacy: if the cells have doors, these may be equipped with peepholes. But there is still an important difference between this kind of prison and monitoring: the prison environment is overtly, even punitively unprivate. The contexts for relations to others are obviously and drastically different from what they are on the "outside." This itself, it seems to me, protects the prisoner's human orientation where monitoring only assails it. If the prisoner has a reasonably developed capacity for love, trust, and friendship and has in fact experienced ties of this sort, he is likely to be strongly aware (at least for a time) that prison life is a drastically different context from the one in which he enjoyed those relations, and this awareness will militate against his confusing the kinds of relations that can obtain in a "total institution" like a prison with those of freer social settings on the outside.

Monitoring, by contrast, alters only in a subtle and unobtrusive way—though a significant one—the context for relations. The subject appears free to perform the same actions as others and to enter the same relations, but in fact an important element of autonomy, of control over one's environment, is missing: he cannot be private. A prisoner can adopt a stance of withdrawal, of hibernation as it were, and thus preserve his sense of privacy intact to a degree. A person subject to monitoring by virtue of being in a free environment, dealing with people who expect him to have certain responses, capacities, and dispositions, is forced to make at least a show of intimacy to the persons he works closely with, those who would be his friends, and so on. They expect these things of him, because he is assumed to have the capacity and disposition to enter into ordinary relations with them. Yet if he does—if, for instance, he enters into light banter with slight sexual overtones with the waitress at the diner where he eats regularly—he has been forced to violate his own integrity by revealing to his official monitors even so small an aspect of his private personality, the personality he wishes to reserve for persons toward whom he will make some gestures of intimacy and friendship. Theoretically, of course, a monitored parolee might adopt the same attitude of withdrawal that a prisoner does, but in fact that too would be a costly and degrading experience. He would be tempted, as in prison he would not be, to "give himself away" and to act like everyone else, since in every outward respect he seems like everyone else. Moreover, by withdrawing, the person subject to monitoring would risk seeming cold, unnatural, odd, inhuman, to the very people whose esteem and affection he craves. In prison the circumstances dictating a reserved and tentative facade are so apparent to all that adopting such a facade is no reflection on the prisoner's humanity.

The insidiousness of a technique which forces a man to betray himself in this humiliating way or else seem inhuman is compounded when one considers that the subject is also forced to betray others who may become intimate with him. Even persons in the overt oppressiveness of a prison do not labor under the burden of this double betrayal.

As against all of these considerations, there remains the argument that so long as monitoring depends on the consent of the subject, who feels it is preferable to prison, to close off this alternative in the name of a morality so intimately concerned with liberty is absurd. This argument may be decisive; I am not at all confident that the alternative of monitored release should be closed off. My analysis does show, I think, that it involves costs to the prisoner which are easily overlooked, that on inspection it is a less desirable alternative than might at first appear. Moreover, monitoring presents systematic dangers to potential subjects as a class. Its availability as a compromise between conditional release and continued imprisonment may lead officials who are in any doubt whether or not to trust a man on parole or probation to assuage their doubts by resorting to monitoring.

The seductions of monitored release disguise not only a cost to the subject but to society as well. The discussion of trust should make clear that unmonitored release is a very different experience from monitored release, and so the educational and rehabilitative effect of unmonitored release is also different. Unmonitored release affirms in a far more significant way the relations of trust between the convicted criminal and the society which he violated by his crime and which we should now be seeking to re-establish. But trust can only arise, as any parent knows, through the experience of being trusted.

Finally, it must be recognized that more limited monitoring—for instance where only the approximate location of the subject is revealed—lacks the offensive features of total monitoring, and is obviously preferable to prison.

THE ROLE OF LAW

This evaluation of the proposal for electronic monitoring has depended on the general theoretical framework of this whole essay. It is worth noting the kind of evaluation that framework has permitted. Rather than inviting a fragmentation of the proposal into various pleasant and unpleasant elements and comparing the "net utility" of the proposal with its alternatives, we have been able to evaluate the total situation created by the proposal in another way. We have been able to see it as a system in which certain actions and relations, the pursuit of certain ends, are possible or impossible. Certain systems of actions, ends, and relations are possible or impossible in different social contexts. Moreover, the social context itself is a system of actions and relations. The social contexts created by monitoring and its alternatives, liberty or imprisonment, are thus evaluated by their conformity to a model system in which are instantiated the principles of morality, justice, friendship, and love. Such a model, which is used as a standard, is of course partially unspecified in that there is perhaps an infinite number of specific systems which conform to those principles. Now actual systems, as we have seen, may vary in respect to how other ends—for example, beauty, knowledge—may be pursued in them, and they may be extremely deficient in allowing for the pursuit of such ends. But those who design, propose, and administer social systems are first of all bound to make them conform to the model of morality and justice, for in so doing they express respect and even friendship—what might be called civic friendship— toward those implicated in the system. If designers and administrators fail to conform to this model, they fail to express that aspect of their humanity which makes them in turn fit subjects for the respect, friendship, and love of others.

Finally, a point should be noted about the relation between legal structures and other social structures in establishing a rational context such as privacy. This context is established in part by rules which guarantee to a person the claim to control certain areas, his home, perhaps his telephone communications, and so forth, and back this guarantee with enforceable sanctions. These norms are, of course, legal norms. Now these legal norms are incomprehensible without some understanding of what kind of a situation one seeks to establish with their aid. Without this understanding we cannot grasp their importance, the vector of development from them in changing circumstances (such as new technology), the consequences of abandoning them, and so on.* What is less obvious is that law is not just an instrument for bringing about a separately identifiable and significant social result: it is a part of the very situation that it helps to bring about. The concept of privacy requires, as we have seen, a sense of control and a justified, acknowledged power to control aspects of one's environment. In most developed societies the only way to give a person the full measure of both the sense and the fact of control is to give him a legal title to control. A legal right to control is control which is the least open to question and argument, it is the kind of control we are most serious about. Consider the analogy of the power of testamentary disposition. A testator is subject to all sorts of obligations, pressures, and arguments; certain things are so outrageous that he would scarcely dare to do them. Yet, within very broad limits, in the last analysis he is after all free to do the outrageous. And both the fact that certain dispositions are outrageous, immoral, wrong, and the fact that the testator is nevertheless free to make them are *together* important to define the autonomy and personality of a person in the particular

---

* It is a tenet of some forms of positivism that this statement is wrong insofar as it suggests that without appreciation of the context we have no understanding of the meaning of legal norms. This tenet seems wrong for a number of reasons. Legal norms are necessarily phrased in open-ended language, and their specification in actual circumstances needs the aid of the context—that is, the reason for the norm—to determine the appropriate application. This is obviously so when there are changed circumstances and recourse must be had to the principle of the norm. It is less obvious in so-called "central" or "paradigm" cases, but I suggest this is less obvious only because the context is so unproblematic as to require no explicit attention.

situation. In the same way the public and ultimate character of law is part of the definition of the rational context of privacy.

I'll Be Watching You

Gary T. Marx

Popular culture is sometimes far ahead of academic analysis in identifying important social currents. This is true of the hit song *Every Breath You Take**, sung by a celebrated rock group known as The Police. It contains these lines:

every breath you take	(breath analyzer)
every move you make	(motion detector)
every bond you break	(polygraph)
every step you take	(electronic anklet)
every single day	(continuous monitoring)
every word you say	(bugs, wiretaps, mikes)
every night you stay . . .	(light amplifier)
every vow you break . . .	(voice stress analysis)
every smile you fake	(brain wave analysis)
every claim you stake . . .	(computer matching)
I'll be watching you	(video surveillance)

For this song we can draw hints of what can be called "the new surveillance." The surveillance component of social control is changing radically. The rationalization of crime control, which began in the 19th century, has crossed a critical threshold as a result of broad changes in technology and social organization. Surveillance has become penetrating and intrusive in ways that previously were imagined only in fiction.

The information-gathering powers of the state and private organizations are extending ever deeper into the social fabric. The ethos of social control has expanded from focused and direct coercion used after the fact and against a particular target to anticipatory actions entailing deception, manipulation, planning, and a diffuse panoptic vision.

I shall attempt here to (1) describe some of the major types of this new

Gary T. Marx, "I'll Be Watching You: Reflections on the New Surveillances," *Dissent,* Winter 1985.

surveillance; (2) indicate how contemporary forms differ from traditional ones; (3) consider some undesirable consequences of these changes.

The gigantic data banks made possible by computers raise important surveillance questions. Many basic facts about the computerization of credit, banking, medical, educational, employment, tax, welfare, telephone, and criminal-justice records are well known. But beyond the increased amount of information they make available, computers have altered the very nature of surveillance. Record surveillance is routinized, broadened and deepened, and, for practical purposes, records become eternal. Bits of scattered information that in the past did not threaten the individual's privacy and anonymity are now joined. Organizational memories are extended over time and across space. Observations have a more textured, dimensional quality. Rather than focusing on the discrete individual at one point in time and on static demographic data such as date of birth, surveillance increasingly involves more complex transactional analysis, interrelating persons and events (for instance, the timing of phone calls, travel, bank deposits).[1]

A thriving new computer-based, data-scavenging industry now sells information gleaned from such sources as drivers' licenses, vehicle and voter-registration lists, birth, marriage, and death certificates, land deeds, telephone and organizational directories, and census-tract records.

Many issues—such as privacy, civil liberties, uses of and control over information, unauthorized access, errors, and the rights of the person about whom information is gathered—are raised by the computer-matching and profiling operations that have come into increased prominence in the last decade.[2]

Matching involves the comparison of information from two or more distinct data sources. In the United States, more than 500 computer-matching programs are routinely carried out by government at state and federal levels, and the matching done by private interests is far more extensive. Profiling involves an indirect and inductive logic. Often, clues are sought that will increase the probability of discovering violations. A number of distinct data items are correlated in order to assess how close an event or person comes to a predetermined model of known violations or violators. Consider the following examples:

- A Massachusetts nursing-home resident lost her eligibility for government medical assistance because of a match of bank and welfare records. The computer match discovered that she had more than the minimum amount welfare recipients are permitted in a savings account. What the computer did not know was that the money was held in trust for a local funeral director, to be used for her burial expenses. Regulations exempt burial contracts from asset calculations.
- The Educational Testing Service uses profiling to help discover cheating. In 1982 it sent out about 2,000 form letters alleging "copying" to takers of its scholastic aptitude test based partly on computer analysis. A statistical review had "found close agreement of your answers with those on another answer sheet from the same test center. Such agreement is unusual and suggests that copying occurred." Students were told that in two weeks their scores would be canceled and colleges notified, unless they provided "additional information" to prove they had not cheated.

● In New York City, because of computer matching, persons cannot purchase a marriage license or register a deed for a new home if they have outstanding parking tickets.

Some of fiction's imaginary surveillance technology, like the two-way television that George Orwell described, is now reality. According to some observers, video-telephone communication is likely to be widespread in private homes by the year 2000. One-way video surveillance has expanded rapidly, as anyone who ventures into a shopping mall or uses an electronic bank teller should realize. The interior of many stores is monitored by closed-circuit TV. The camera is often inside a ceiling globe with complete 360-degree movement and the ability to tape-record. Amber or mirrored surfaces hide where the cameras are aimed.

Among the new techniques that permit intrusions that only recently were in the realm of science fiction, or not even envisioned there, are new or improved lasers, parabolic mikes and other bugs with still more powerful transmitters, subminiature tape recorders, remote-camera and videotape systems; means of seeing in the dark, detecting heat or motion; odor, pressure, and contraband sensors; tracking devices and voice stress analyzers.

The last decade has seen the increased use of supposedly scientific "inference" or "personal truth technology" based on body clues (such as the polygraph, voice stress analysis, the stomach pump, the "passive alcohol detector," and blood or urine analysis for drugs). These highly diverse forms of detection have at least one thing in common—they seek to verify an implicit or explicit claim put forth by an individual regarding identity, attitudes, and behavior.

"Mini-Awacs" that can spot a car or a person from 30,000 feet up have been used for surveillance of drug traffickers. The CIA has apparently used satellite photographs (with a range of up to 180 miles) for "domestic coverage" to determine the size and activities of antiwar demonstrations and civil disorders. The "starlight scope" light amplifier, developed for the Vietnam War, can be used with a variety of cameras and binoculars. When it amplifies light 85,000 times it turns night settings into daylight. Unlike the infrared devices developed earlier, it does not give off a tell-tale glow.

The highly secretive National Security Agency—using 2,000 staffed interception posts throughout the world, and satellites, aircraft, and ships—monitors all electronic communication from and to the United States. Its computer system permits simultaneous monitoring of about 54,000 telephone calls and cables. The agency is beyond the usual judicial and legislative controls and can disseminate its information to other government agencies without a warrant.[3]

The 1968 wiretap law made it a felony for a third party to place an electronic listening device on a telephone or in a room. Government agents could do this only under strictly defined conditions with a warrant. Yet this law referred only to aurally transmitted "conversations." It said nothing about nonvoice and video communications. Up to 1986, no restrictions were placed on the interception of information transmitted in digital microwave form. As a result of recent technical developments, more than half of all long-distance telephone calls are now transmitted from point to point in digital form and then converted back to a familiar voice sound. Telephone voice communications will increasingly be sent this way. Much computer information is also sent via microwaves. In 1986, laws were passed granting this information the same protection as voice conversations. However, the information can easily be picked up without leaving a trace by anyone with even modest snooping equipment.

Another surveillance use of the telephone involves the expansions of hot lines for anonymous reporting. One of the largest programs is TIP (Turn-in-a-Pusher). The video equivalent of the old reward posters, a program found in hundreds of communities, is called Crime Stoppers USA, Inc. It uses televised reenactments ("The Crime of the Week") to encourage witnesses to unsolved crimes to come forward. There are also radio and newspaper versions. Many companies maintain an internal hot line for anonymous reporting. WeTIP, Inc., a nonprofit organization, offers a general, nationwide 24-hour toll-free hot line for reporting suspicious activities. All 19 federal inspector-generals and some state and local agencies have hot lines for receiving allegations.

The real action, in the future, will be with nonhuman informers: a 400-pound, bulletproof mobile robot "guard" has been developed. It is equipped with a sonar range finder, sonic and infrared sensors, and an odor detector for locating humans. The robot can find its way through a strange building. Should it encounter an intruder, it can say in a stern, synthesized voice, "You have been detected." Another "mobile robotic sentry," resembing a miniature tank, patrols an area and identifies intruders. Users can choose the robot's weaponry and whether or not human permission (from a remote monitoring station) is needed before it opens fire. But not to worry. The manufacturer assures us that in the U.S. the device will not be "armed with lethal weapons"; or if it is, "there will always be a human requirement in the loop."

Telemetric devices attached to a subject use radio waves to transmit information on the location and/or physiological condition of the wearer and permit continuous remote measurement and control. Such devices, along with new organizational forms based on theories of diversion and deinstitutionalization (such as halfway houses and community treatment centers), diffuse the surveillance of the prison into the community.

After over a decade of discussion, telemetric devices are now being tried in the criminal-justice system. Offenders in at least four experimental jurisdictions are serving court-supervised sentences that stipulate wearing a monitoring anklet containing an electronic transmitter. The radio signal it emits is picked up by a receiver connected to the telephone in the wearer's home. This receiver relays the signal to a central computer. If the wearer goes beyond 150 feet from this telephone or tries to remove or unplug the device, the interruption of the signal is displayed on the computer. The judge receives a daily copy of the printout, and any errant behavior must be explained.

In other proposed systems subjects are not restricted to their residence; however, their whereabouts are continuously known. The radio signal is fed into a modified missile-tracking device that graphs the wearer's location and can display it on a screen. In some police departments, an automatic car-locator system has been tried to help supervisors know exactly where patrol cars are at all times.

There also are various hidden beepers that can be attached to vehicles and other objects to trace their movements.

The Hong Kong government is testing an electronic system for monitoring where, when, and how fast a car is driven. A small radio receiver in the car picks up low-frequency signals from wire loops set into streets and then transmits back the car's identification number. The system was presented as an efficient means for applying a road tax to the many cars in Hong Kong's concentrated traffic areas. It can, of course, also be used to enforce speed limits and for surveillance. In the U.S., a parking meter has recently been patented that registers inserted coins and then radios police when the time has run out.

Surveillance of workers, whether on assembly lines or in offices or stores, has become much more severe with computerized electronic measures. Factory outputs and mistakes can be more easily counted and work pace, to a degree, controlled. Employee theft of expensive components or tools may be deterred by embedded sensors that emit a signal when taken through a barrier. Much has been written about the electronic office, where the data processing machine serves both as a work tool and monitoring device. Productivity and employee behavior thus are carefully watched, and even executives are not exempt. In some major American corporations communication flows (memo circulation, use of internal phone systems) now are closely tracked.

In some offices, workers have to inform the computer when they are going to the bathroom and when they return. Employees may be required to carry an ID card with a magnetic stripe and check in and out as they go to various "stations."

Integrated "management systems" offer visual, audio, and digital information about the behavior of employees and customers. Information may be recorded from cash-register entries, voices, motion, or when standing on a mat with a sensor. Audiovisual recordings and alarms may be programmed to respond to a large number of "triggering devices."

Means of personal identification have gone far beyond the rather easily faked signature or photo ID. Thus one new employee security-checking procedure involves retinal eye patterns. Before gaining access, or a benefit, a person's eyes are photographed through a set of binoculars, and an enlarged print of the retina pattern is compared to a previous print on file. Retinal patterns are said to be more individual than thumbprints, offering greater certainty of identification.

Finally, undercover practices—those old, traditional means of surveillance and investigation—have drastically changed in form and expanded in scale during the last decade. The new devices and techniques have enabled police and federal agencies to penetrate criminal, and sometimes noncriminal, milieus in utterly new ways.[4]

In the United States, the federal agency that is most affected is the Federal Bureau of Investigation. In the past, the FBI viewed undercover operations as too risky and costly (for both individuals and the agency's reputation) for use in routine invstigations of conventional criminal activity. Now, however, in the words of an agent, "Undercover operations have become the cutting edge of the FBI's efforts to ferret out concealed criminal activity." In the mid-1970's the FBI began using undercover agents in criminal investigations. The number of such investigations has steadily increased from 53 in 1977, to 239 in 1979, to 463 in 1981.

Beyond well-known cases—such as Abscam, the fake consulting firm run jointly by IBM and the FBI that sold "stolen" data to Japanese companies, the John DeLorean case, police posing as derelicts with exposed wallets or as fences purchasing stolen property—recent cases have involved policewomen posing as prostitutes and then arresting the men who propositioned them; tax agents stationed in banks and businesses posing as prospective buyers or clients to gain information; phony cases entered into the criminal-justice system to test if prosecutors and judges would accept bribes; "bait sales" in which undercover agents offer to sell, at a very low price, allegedly stolen goods to merchants or persons they meet in bars; agents acting as guides for big game hunters and then arresting them for killing protected species or animals out of season. These examples—and we could add many more—surely make clear that it is a new ball game, and that its players are sometimes beyond meaningful restraint.

Although the causes, nature, and consequences of the various new surveillance methods I have described differ from each other, they do share, to varying degrees, nine characteristics that distinguish them from traditional ones.

THE NEW SURVEILLANCE

(1) *It transcends distance, darkness, and physical barriers.* As many observers have noted, the historic barriers to the old, Leviathan state lay in the sheer physical impossibility of extending the rulers' ideas and surveillance to the outer regions of vast empires; through closed doors; and into the inner intellectual, emotional, and physical regions of the individual. Technology, however, has gradually made these intrusions easier. Technical impossibility and, to some extent, inefficiency have lost their roles as unplanned protectors of liberty. Sound and video can be transmitted over vast distances, infrared and light-amplifying technologies pierce the dark, intrusive technologies can "see" through doors, suitcases, fog. Truth-seeking technologies claim to be capable of going beneath surface reality to deeper, subterranean truths.

(2) *It transcends time;* its records can easily be stored, retrieved, combined, analyzed, and communicated. Surveillance information can be "socially freeze-dried."[5] When stored, it is available for instant analysis many years after the fact and in totally different interpretive contexts. Computer records, video and audio tapes and discs, photos, and various "signatures"—like workers or parts used in mass production—have become increasingly standardized and interchangeable. Information can be converted into a form that makes it portable, easily reproducible, and transferable across vast distances. Thus data sharing, on an immense scale, becomes possible.

(3) *It is capital- rather than labor-intensive.* It has become much less expensive per unit watched, because technical developments have dramatically altered the economics of surveillance. Information is easily sent back to a central source. A few persons can monitor a great many things (in contrast to traditional forms, such as the gumshoe tailing a suspect at a discrete distance for many days or manually searching records). The monitor need not literally be attending at the instant of transmission to be able to use it. Economy is further enhanced because

persons have become voluntary and involuntary consumers of much of this surveillance—and are participating in their own monitoring. Many of the points that follow relate to these economic changes that facilitate expanded surveillance.

(4) *It triggers a shift from targeting a specific suspect—to categorical suspicion.* In the technical implementation of Kafka's nightmare, modern society suspects everyone. The camera, the tape recorder, the identity card, the metal detector, the obligatory tax form that must be filled out even if one has no income, and, of course, the computer make all who come within their province reasonable targets for surveillance. The new, softer forms of control are helping to create a society in which people are permanently under suspicion and surveillance. Everyone is assumed to be guilty until proven innocent. As Michel Foucault observed, what is central here is not physical coercion—but neverending "judgements, examinations, and observation."

(5) *One of its major concerns is the prevention of violations.* Thus control is extended to ever more features of society and its surroundings. Rather than simply reacting to what is served up around us, anticipatory strategies seek to reduce risk and uncertainty. Publicity about omnipresent and omnipowerful surveillance is to deter violations. And "target hardening" (for instance, better locks) is to make committing violations more difficult. Where violations cannot be prevented, the surroundings may be so structured that violators are either caught in the act or leave strong evidence of their identity and guilt.

(6) *It is decentralized—and triggers self-policing.* In contrast to the trend of the last century, information can now in principle flow as freely from the center to society's periphery as the reverse. Surveillance is decentralized in the sense that national data resources are available to widely dispersed local officials. (The power of national elites, in turn, may also increase as they obtain instant information on those in the farthest reaches of the network.)

Those watched become (willingly and knowingly or not) active participants in their own monitoring, which is often self-activated and automatic. One aspect of this process is that persons are motivated to report themselves to government agencies and large organizations and corporations in return for some benefit or to avoid a penalty; another is the direct triggering of surveillance systems by its subjects when, for instance, a person walks, talks on the telephone, turns on a TV set, checks a book out from the library, enters or leaves a controlled area.

(7) *It either has low visibility or is invisible.* Thus it becomes ever more difficult to ascertain when and whether or not we are being watched and who is doing the watching. There is a distancing (both socially and geographically) between watchers and watched, and surveillance is increasingly depersonalized. Its instruments are often difficult to discover, either because they are something other than they appear to be or, as with snooping into microwave transmissions, there often are few indications of surveillance. (Contrast this with traditional wire-tapping, which changes electrical currents, or hidden voice analysis with the traditional polygraph, which requires the subject's cooperation.)

(8) *It is ever more intensive—probing beneath surfaces, discovering previously inaccessible information.* Like drilling technology boring ever deeper into the earth, today's surveillance can prod ever deeper into physical, social, and personal

areas. It hears whispers, penetrates clouds, walls, and windows. It "sees" into the body—and attempts to "see" into the soul, claiming to go beneath ostensible meanings and appearances to real meanings.

(9) *It grows ever more extensive—covering not only deeper, but larger areas.* Previously unconnected surveillance threads now are woven into gigantic tapestries of information. Or, in Stan Cohen's imagery, the mesh of the fishing net has not only become finer and more pliable, the net itself now is wider.[6] Broad new categories of persons and behavior have become subjects for information collection and analysis, and as the pool of persons watched expands, so does the pool of watchers. Not only might anyone be watched; everyone is also a potential watcher. And the creation of uncertainty about whether or not surveillance is present is an important strategic element. Mass surveillance has become a reality. The increased number of watchers (whether human or electronic) and self-monitoring devices have recreated, in today's metropolis, some of the dense controls characteristic of the small, closely watched village.

The awesome power of the new surveillance lies in the paradoxical, never before possible combination of decentralized and centralized forms. We are also witnessing an expansion and joining of intensive forms of monitoring traditionally used only in the investigation and surveillance of criminal and espionage suspects, or prisoners, with the more shallow forms of categorical monitoring directed at broad populations.

The new surveillance has been generally welcomed by those in business, government, and law enforcement. It does have many attractive features. Stirring examples of its effectiveness are readily available. For example, the life of an elderly heart-attack victim who lived alone was saved when her failure to open the refrigerator sent an alarm through her telephone to a centralized monitor; a corrupt judge was caught when he took a bribe from a police agent pretending to be a criminal; serious crimes have been solved as a result of tips received on hot lines. Consider also the ease of obtaining consumer goods with a credit card; the savings of taxpayers' dollars because of computer-matching programs; citizens' increased feeling of safety when video surveillance is installed. Indeed, Americans seem increasingly willing, even eager, to live with intrusive technologies because of the benefits they expect to result.

Problems concerning errors, data tampering and misuse can be lessened by government legislation and policies, good program design and sensitive and intelligent management. Furthermore, in a free-market economy, some surveillance can be neutralized (by, for instance, the proliferation of antiradar, debugging, and encryption devices).

My point is not to advance some romantic neo-Luddite world view, or to deny the complexity of the moral judgements and trade-offs involved. Yet in our eagerness to innovate and our infatuation with technical progress and the gimmickry of surveillance, it is easy to miss the time bombs that may be embedded therein. The negative aspects of these new trends have not received sufficient attention.

There is nowhere to run or to hide. A citizen's ability to evade this surveillance is diminishing. There is no escape from the prying eyes and ears and whirring data-processing machines of government and business. To participate in the consumer society and the welfare state, we must provide personal information. To venture into a shopping mall, bank, subway, sometimes even a bathroom is to perform before an unknown audience. To apply for a job may mean having to face lie-detector questioning about intimate details of one's life. Requests for parts of one's personal biography (for birth, marriage, and death certificates, driver's licenses, vehicle and voter registration, information for phone, occupational, educational, and special-interest directories) are invitations to comply with more finely tuned manipulative efforts by a new breed of government and marketing reseachers who combine the enormous quantities of available data with the advantages of computerization.

The new surveillance goes beyond merely invading privacy, as this term has been understood; it makes many of the constraints that made privacy possible irrelevant. Traditionally, privacy depended on certain technically or socially inviolate physical, spatial, or temporal barriers—varying from distance to darkness to doors, to the right to remain silent. To invade privacy required crossing an intact barrier. With much of the new technology, however, many of these simply cease to be barriers. As we discussed, information becomes accessible without the need to resort to traditional coercive forms of intrusion. There is no longer the need to enter a room surreptitiously to plant a bugging device, when a microphone aimed at a window a hundred yards away can accomplish the same end; when microwave phone and computer transmissions can simply be plucked from the air without bothering with direct wire-tapping. Without being opened, mail can be read, purses and briefcases viewed through X-rays or sniffed. Alcohol intake can be assessed without a suspect's consent, and voice stress analysis administered without the subject's awareness.

WHAT OF PRIVACY & AUTONOMY?

In the face of these changes, we must rethink the nature of privacy and create new supports for it. Some of these, ironically, will rely in part on products of the system's technologies (such as coded or scrambled communications, antiradar and debugging devices).

The most desirable support of our individual privacy and autonomy surely is public awareness. At this point, less than one state in five has laws requiring binding standards for the collection, maintenance, and dissemination of personal information.

Yet more is at stake than privacy. Some of the positive anonymity involving the right to be left alone and unnoticed, so characteristic of modern society, is diminished. The easy computer-bank combing and mining of vast publicly available data to yield precise lists (whether of suspects or targets for sales pitches and solicitations) generate a sense of vulnerability that is very different from the feeling experienced on receipt of junk mail addressed to "occupant." Aside from the annoyance factor, the somewhat "personalized" yet standardized word-processed solicitations can leave one asking, "How do they know this about me? How did they find this out? What else do they know? Who are they?" One need not be a Franz Kafka character to feel uneasy.

To mention, briefly, some other, major negative aspects of the new surveillance:

It may violate the spirit of the Fourth Amendment. For it can trigger fishing expeditions and searches where there is no specific evidence of wrongdoing. Thus it might transform the presumption of innocence into one of guilt—shifting the burden of proof from the state to the target of surveillance, the accused. There also is a danger of presumption of guilt by association or statistical artifact. And, because of the technical nature of the surveillance and its distancing aspects, the accused may (at least initially) be unable to face the accuser. The legal basis of some of the new surveillance's crime-prevention actions is also questionable.

The system's focus on prevention can entail the risk of sparking violations that would otherwise not occur. And powerful new mechanisms may invite overloading the system. Far more violations may be uncovered and added to the data banks than can be acted upon. This overabundance of violations in turn may lead to the misuse of prosecutorial discretion, the demoralization of control agents and, perhaps, to favoritism and corruption. And, as our examples suggest, the new surveillance has the potential of fostering repression. The system is invariably less effective and certain, and more subject to manipulation and error, than advocates admit. (Computer matching, for instance, can be no better than the data it is fed, which may be dated or wrong, and is often blunt and acontextual. Chemical analysis, which can detect drugs in a person's body, cannot determine how they got there—if a person, for instance, smoked marijuana or simply was around others who did—or whether a drug was taken on or off the job.)

While deterring or discovering some offenders, the routinization of surveillance, ironically, may grant an almost guaranteed means for successful violations and theft to those who gain knowledge of the system and take action to neutralize and exploit it. This suggests that, over time, it seems likely that many of these systems will disproportionately net the marginal, amateur, occasional violator rather than the master criminal.

The proliferation of the new techniques may create a lowest-denominator morality, which may even affect those who will actively protect privacy and autonomy, who thus will use—indiscriminately—the very tactics of those who seek to lessen them.

The new surveillance increases the power of large organizations (whether governmental or private) over the individual.

Individual freedom and liberty prosper when detailed information about a person's life, for the most part, is private. The permanence and accessibility of computerized records mean that we are all tailed by electronic tale-bearers. As there is the possibility of locking in erroneous or sabotaged data, this may have the unintended consequence of permanent, unjust stigmatization. Thus persons may never cease paying for earlier, or never committed, misdeeds. The issues here go far beyond criminal records and faulty computer banks. As records of education, work, health, housing, civil suits, and the like become ever more important in administering the society, persons may decline needed services (as for mental health), avoid conflictual or controversial action (filing a grievance against a boss or a landlord), shun taking risks and experimenting for fear of what it will look like on the record. Conformity and uniformity may increase—squashing diversity, innovation, and vitality.

The fragmentation and isolation characteristic of totalitarian societies result not only from the state's banning or absorption of private organizations, but because individuals mistrust each other and organizations: trust, the most sacred and important element of the social bond, is damaged.

To be sure, we are far from such a society, but the direction in which the new surveillance points is clear. Making the means of anonymous denunciation easily available can lead to false and malicious accusations, and efforts to create a "myth of surveillance" may backfire and create a degree of inhibition, fear, and anxiety unbecoming a democratic society. The potential for harm may be so great, should social conditions change, that we must hesitate before creating even apparently justified surveillance systems (such as linkages between all federal and state data banks, or a mandatory national identification system). From this perspective, framing the policy debate around how to reform such systems is misguided. The issue, instead, is, Should the system be there to begin with?[8] Once these new surveillance systems are institutionalized and taken for granted in a democratic society, they can be used for harmful ends. With a more repressive government and a more intolerant public—perhaps upset over severe economic downturns, large waves of immigration, social dislocations, or foreign policy setbacks—these devices could easily be used against those with the "wrong" political beliefs, against racial, ethnic, or religious minorities, and those with life style that offend the majority.

Yet should totalitarianism ever come to the United States it would more likely be by accretion than by cataclysmic events. As Sinclair Lewis argued in *It Can't Happen Here,* it would come in traditional American guise, with the gradual erosion of liberties.

Voluntary participation, beneficent rationales, changes in cultural definition and language hide the onerous aspects of the new surveillance. But as Jusice Brandeis warned:

> Experience should teach us to be most on our guard when the government's purposes are beneficent. Men born to freedom are naturally alert to repel invasion of their liberty by evil-minded rulers. The greatest dangers to liberty lurk in insidious encroachment by men of zeal, well-meaning, but without understanding.[9]

The first task of a society that would have liberty and privacy is to guard against the misuse of physical coercion by the state and private parties. The second task is to guard against the softer forms of secret and manipulative control. Because these are often subtle, indirect, invisible, diffuse and deceptive and shrouded in benign justifications, this is clearly the more difficult task.

Notes

This article is drawn from a longer paper available from the author prepared for meetings on George Orwell held by the Council of Europe and the American Sociological Association.

[1] David Burnham, *The Rise of the Computer State* (New York: Random House, 1983) offers a useful discussion of this and other salient themes.

[2] See, for example, G. Marx and N. Reichman, "Routinizing the Discovery of Secrets: Computers as Informants," *American Behavioral Scientist,* March 1984.

[3] J. Bamford, *The Puzzle Palace* (New York: Penguin Books, 1983); K. Krajick, "Electronic Surveillance Makes a Comeback," *Police Magazine,* March 1983.

[4] For example, see G. Marx, "Who Really Gets Stung? Some Issues Raised by the New Police Undercover Work," *Crime and Delinquency,* April 1982; see also U.S. Congress, Select Committee to Study Undercover Activities of Components of the Department of Justice, 97th Congress, Second Session, *Final Report, December 1982* (Washington, D.C.: Government Printing Office, 1982). U.S. Congress, Subcommittee on Civil and Constitutional Rights of the Committee on the Judiciary, House of Representatives, 98th Congress, Second Session, *Report: FBI Undercover Operations* (Washington, D.C.: G.P.O., 1984).

[5] See, for example, G. Goodwin and L. Humphreys, "Freeze-Dried Stigma: Cybernetics and Social Control," *Humanity and Society,* November 1982.

[6] S. Cohen, "The Punitive City: Notes on the Dispersion of Social Control," *Contemporary Crisis,* 1979, no. 3. pp. 339–63.

[7] A large array of control and countercontrol devices, through mail-order catalogues and ads in major national periodicals, are now available for the mass market. One large company offers a "secret-connection briefcase," which among other things includes a "pocket-sized tape-recorder detector that lets you know if someone is secretly recording your conversation," a "micro-miniature hidden bug-detection system, which lets you know if you're being bugged," a "miniature voice stress analyzer, which lets you know when someone is lying," a "built-in scrambler for total telephone privacy," an "incredible 6-hour tape recorder—so small it fits in a cigarette pack." Read to use—or misuse. . . .

[8] See, for example, the thoughtful discussion in J. Rule, D. McAdam, L. Stearns, and D. Uglow, *The Politics of Privacy* (New York: New American Library, 1980).

[9] *Olmstead vs. U.S.,* 277 U.S. (Supreme Court) 438 (1927).

Privacy and the Computer State

Linda Diebel

> *Privacy was a very valuable thing.*
> *Everyone wanted a place where they could be alone occasionally.*
>
> *—Winston Smith*

For Winston Smith, the rebellious hero of *Nineteen Eighty-Four,* there was no privacy. On the landing outside his grubby little flat hung a poster of an enormous face with eyes that followed him everywhere and a caption that read: "Big Brother

Linda Diebel, "Privacy and the Computer State," *Maclean's,* January 9, 1984. Reprinted by permission of *Maclean's,* Canada's Weekly Newsmagazine.

is watching you." Inside, the telescreen with its never-sleeping eye transmitted his movements to the Thought Police. To evade the prying gaze he rented a shabby room over a junk shop to be alone with his lover, but there was no escaping Big Brother. One day an iron voice spoke to them from the wall of their sanctuary. There was a crash of broken glass, and a picture fell to the floor, uncovering the telescreen hidden behind it. It was, Winston knew, "unthinkable to disobey the iron voice from the wall."

Clearly, George Orwell's vision remains largely unfulfilled. As James Rule, a State University of New York sociologist and respected Orwell scholar, recently wrote in an essay on *Nineteen Eighty-Four,* "Contrary to Orwell's gloomy anticipations, the Western democracies have not abandoned their institutions to imitate Nazi Germany or Stalin's U.S.S.R." Still, some of the most respected legal and technical experts in the Western world warn that privacy and freedom are threatened by the ever-expanding capabilities of a device that Orwell did not live to see: the computer. To date, documented cases of computer abuse have been random—certainly none at the hands of a Big Brother—but concern is growing about the potential for widespread, centralized abuse of the information stored in thousands of computer data banks.

In 1984 government and big business will continue to collect, store and distribute details about the private lives of millions of citizens on the world's multiplying networks of computers. There are few effective controls on how that information is used. Explained Grant Hammond, counsel to the University of Alberta's Institute of Law Research and Reform: "Facts by themselves mean little, but the ability to tie immense numbers of facts together—the marriage of data files and the computer—is the name of the game of power." For his part, John Grace, the newly appointed federal privacy commissioner, cautions that, so far, Canadians are "technopeasants," largely ignorant of the extent and power of computers.

There is privacy legislation on the books. The federal Privacy Act of 1982 supplanted and strengthened privacy provisions in the Canadian Human Rights Act of 1977 and increased the privacy commissioner's powers to investigate privacy complaints by citizens against the federal government and to monitor government data banks. The new act regulates the collection, retention, protection, disclosure and disposal of personal information by the federal government. But it does not apply to the private sector.

Quebec is the only provincial government that has introduced public sector data protection. Law 65, passed in June, 1982, established an independent supervisory commission to oversee the protection of privacy in the public sector. But other existing provincial privacy acts in British Columbia (1968), Manitoba (1970) and Saskatchewan (1974) are, according to David Flaherty, a University of Western Ontario history and law professor, "relatively unused and unusable, and would be of no assistance in responding to challenges posed by the new information technology because of their limited scope."

Furthermore, Canadians, unlike Americans, have no constitutional right to privacy. Indeed, in 1981 the joint committee on the Constitution defeated an amendment to the Constitution providing for "freedom from unreasonable interference with privacy, family, home and correspondence." Said Flaherty: "It remains symbolic of the legal status of privacy in Canada that a right to personal privacy was not included in the charter in the first place."

The existence of a modern grid of information banks not only threatens privacy—historically a tenet of liberal democratic society—but it raises disturbing questions about who has access to personal information and why and who should govern its use in both the public and private sectors. In his seminal 1967 book, *Privacy and Freedom,* Columbia University law professor and private theorist Alan Westin said that privacy is the right of individuals to "determine for themselves when, how and to what extent information about them is to be communicated to others." However, Flaherty, who has studied privacy issues in Canada for the past two decades, believes that Canadians have already lost control over who has access to the most intimate details of their private lives. He argues that while there is minimal public sector protection of privacy in Canada, there is nothing governing the private sector's use of its massive banks of information. Said Flaherty: "At least privacy protection issues are still manageable. But if we do not come to grips with them, then the kind of world that Orwell predicted in *Nineteen Eight-Four* will come true by 1994."

The scope of the problem is enormous. The federal government alone has more than 1,500 centralized data banks, overflowing with the details of the day-to-day lives of Canadians. Computers record the passage of people from birth until death, storing a legacy of indelible "electronic tracks"—whether the information is accurate or not. But there is growing evidence to indicate that Canadians are becoming increasingly aware that the most minute details of their lives are being tracked. In 1982 a poll by Bell Canada on public attitudes to new computer technology showed that 65 per cent of 2,000 people polled regarded invasion of privacy as their number 1 concern. Another poll, which Flaherty conducted for the Ontario department of communications last year, revealed that 84 per cent of participants felt that storage of personal information on computers poses a danger to personal privacy. Indeed, there are increasing signals that their fears are justified and that Canadians may be drifting toward Orwell's world.

● In late 1983 Revenue Canada demanded complete access to selected municipal data banks in order, as the agency explained, to search for individual and corporate tax evaders. Consequently, former Tory leader Joe Clark accused Revenue Canada of "setting up a massive detective agency" merely to go on a fishing expedition. Clark warned that the practice would allow the powerful ministry "access to literally any information that any citizen has given any agency at any point in his life."

● In 1981 Alberta Supreme Court Justice David McDonald's royal commission into the affairs of the Royal Canadian Mounted Police urged strict controls on files that the force had opened on 800,000 Canadians during the past two decades. Solicitor General Robert Kaplan promised to have the computerized files destroyed, but to date he has not announced a ministry decision.

● In 1980 two Ontario royal commissions concluded that there was no consistent policy to protect personal information in the province's 117 data banks. More than 20,000 provincial employees with ministry identity cards can scan files containing personal information, according to the Williams Commission on Freedom of Information and Individual Privacy. For its part, the Krever Commission on the Confidentiality of Health Records pointed out that the RCMP routinely receives confidential medical data from provincial health insurance offices and that doctors and hospital employees frequently allow private investigators access to personal medical files. Both commissions recommended privacy protection legislation. Despite a number of promises legislation is still pending.

Few critics fear that the threat to Canadian privacy comes from some malevolent Big Brother. But Osgood Hall Law School Dean John McCamus, for one, who was research director for the Williams commission, warns against governments' insatiable hunger for efficiency and the consequences of a new age of communications. Said McCamus: "We are not there yet but we are sliding down that slippery slope toward *Nineteen Eighty-Four.*" Contrary to many European countries, notably Sweden, France, and West Germany, Canada lacks comprehensive legal protection for the gathering, storage and distribution of data. Even the powers of Privacy Commissioner Grace, appointed on June 2, 1983, depend on moral suasion and the public impact of his annual reports. Grace admitted that it is still too early to determine the extent of his influence.

For more than a decade, Canadian taxpayers have paid for federal reports on the advisability of allowing personal and business data to flow freely to foreign countries. National boundaries are irrelevant to data that leaps from one computer terminal to the next. During the Krever commission sessions, investigators learned that health data on Ontario citizens is routinely stored in the data banks of Equifax Inc., an Atlanta private investigation company which specializes in preparing reports on prospective employees and running credit checks. However, two key questions remain unanswered: should Canadian data, much of it collected by U.S. branch-plant operations, move so freely to foreign countries? And how can Canada maintain its sovereignty when the law does not cover data on Canadians that is stored abroad?

Other countries have recognized the dangers. In 1973 the Swedish government passed tough privacy protection legislation and set up the Data Inspection Board, which monitors personal information that both government and business collect and its distribution in Sweden and abroad. Board President Jan Freese has the power to curtail the dissemination of data that he believes to be intrusive. In Canada there is no legislation pending to protect personal information distributed abroad by either the corporate or public sector. In 1979 a federal committee chaired by John V. Clyne, former chairman of MacMillan Bloedel, studied the implications of telecommunications for Canadian society and then outlined the hazards in a report: "Of all the technologies developing so rapidly today, that of informatics [computer communications] poses possibly the most dangerous threat to Canadian sovereignty."

Western's Flaherty believes that North American subscribers to two-way cable systems already face the possibility that their privacy will be invaded. Recently, the residents of Columbus, Ohio, experienced an ominous demonstration of Orwell's warning. Subscribers to a system called "Qube" send messages to a computerized control centre by means of palm-sized pads. The more they use the service, for everything from watching selected programs to responding to public opinion polls, the more the computer learns about them. A cinema owner who was charged with showing pornographic movies decided to subpoena the company's records to prove that many people, including the city's leading citizens, were already watching pornography on television at home. Only the judge's decision to allow general statistics and not specific names protected the viewers' privacy. In Canada two-way cable is in use on an experimental basis in Victoria, Vancouver, Toronto, Ottawa and Kingston. Said Flaherty, who recently completed a study on two-way systems in Canada: "Organizations such as the KGB would find two-way cable the answer to the difficult problem of making surveillance of an entire population meaningful."

Computers may also be fulfilling Orwell's vision in less dramatic ways. Already, critics charge that social relations and human value systems are subtly changing. As Swedish Data Inspection Board President Freese told *Maclean's,* "If Orwell rose from his grave tomorrow, he would be astonished at the sophisticated methods we have developed for watching each other."

Even if the primary collection of data proceeds in an ethical manner, computer "hackers" have demonstrated the ease with which criminals and vandals can gain access to confidential data. In 1982 officials at the Memorial Sloan-Kettering Cancer Center in New York called in the FBI when they discovered that a group of young hackers, using home computers, had altered computerized patient files controlling radiation treatment. Increasing reports of computer break-ins by hackers and the apparent lack of technology to prevent computer theft have challenged traditional codes of right and wrong. Robert Johnson, a computer expert with the Alberta department of public works, pointed out that "To many people it is not a sin to crack a computer—it is just another level of challenge." Federal Justice Minister Mark MacGuigan announced proposed legislation governing computer crime last summer, but there is still no indication of when it will be enacted.

As the debate about the harmful potential of intrusive technology intensifies, it is becoming clear that technological developments are outstripping the ability of both the public and government to keep pace. What Orwell did not consider, privacy expert Rule submits, is that technology would develop on its own without the "spur of totalitarian intent." He adds, "The only *absolute* safety lies in avoiding the development of systems that concentrate potentially volatile information." But for all practical purposes, those systems are already in place. What is needed now, suggested Osgoode's McCamus, is to set privacy codes for both government and business and to minimize the amount of personal data collected about people in the first place.

Still, information consultant Thomas Riley, an adviser to Canadian commissions on privacy, worries that those who police our data systems could themselves turn into thought police. He declared: "The new technologies are beyond the grasp of most people, so they absolve themselves of responsibility. That could be our downfall." George Orwell would have agreed. After *Nineteen Eight-Four* was published, he summed up his book: "The moral to be drawn from this dangerous nightmare situation is a simple one: 'Don't let it happen. It depends on you.' "

10 Equal Opportunity
or "A Good Idea, But Some Are More Equal than Others"

Think about this situation:

Carol is planning to join a chorus, which during holidays travels all around the country giving performances. Carol has a good singing voice and loves to travel, so the chorus would allow her to engage in two of her favorite activities. However, when Carol is admitted to membership, she is told that although she can sing with the chorus, she will not be allowed to go on any of the trips. "You are over the age of 35," the chorus leader explains, "and we only take the younger women along for performances."

Think about how Carol probably feels and about how you would feel in her place. Would you join an organization that blatantly limited your opportunity in this way? Do you think that Carol's rights have been violated? Do you think an organization can legally say such a thing to Carol?

Carol's situation is fictitious, and, fortunately, is one that, at this time, would not be considered legal. I wanted you to think about it, though, because it raises the issue that will be discussed in this chapter—that of equal opportunity and the impact that this concept has had on our society.

WRITING TO LEARN

1. To begin thinking about this topic, respond with a simple "yes" or "no" to the following question:

Is it important for the U.S. to be a land of equal opportunity?

After this, brainstorm on the phrase "equal opportunity" itself. What things, persons, events does this phrase make you think of?

Now do some twenty minutes of free writing on what the phrase "equal opportunity" means to you.

Save these materials for later use.

2. If you are working as a class or in small groups, do the same things to modify Exercise 1 in the following ways:

Write the answer on a piece of paper.

Have someone collect and tally the results of this "vote."

While that person is tallying, others should brainstorm, putting down the different kinds of things a phrase like "equal opportunity" makes them think of. If there is time, do freewriting on what this phrase means to you.

Report the result of the vote. Did most answer "yes"? Did all answer "yes"? If any answered "no," explore and discuss the differences between these and the others.

Later, publish the results of the brainstorming and freewriting and compare them for differences and as a way to begin developing a definition of this phrase.

Now reconsider the opening question:

Is it important for the U.S. to be a land of equal opportunity?

Probably most Americans—if asked this question—reflexively answer "yes" without too much hesitation. If we consider our upbringing, our own education, the message of various media, and the rest of our daily environment, there is ample support for our responding this way. In fact, many would be surprised at any answer other than "yes."

The fact that we might be surprised is itself an indicator that the question taps into an issue about which we have very deep feelings. This kind of surprise is somewhat like our surprise at other challenges to things that we take as "givens"— that is, as constant and unquestioned parts of our emotional, ethical, and intellectual environment.

Consider a factual "given," such as our belief that the world is round. People respond with similar surprise (and perhaps some amusement) when they first encounter the claims of the Flat Earth Society, which to this day disputes the point, continuing to argue that the world is flat. Presumably, many Renaissance Europeans, some 400 years ago, also responded with this kind of surprise to the audacious claims of the Copernicans that the earth was round and not the center of the universe.

Challenges to ethical givens evoke equally strong, if not stronger responses; the more deeply held or suppressed the belief, the stronger the response. Surprise may then give way to shock. Consider, for example, our beliefs that incest and murder are wrong. The first of these is such a taboo subject that only recently could a public medium like television directly address it (in a made-for-TV movie). Yet the royal house of ancient Egypt routinely practiced it—a fact that, not surprisingly, does not usually show up in our public school books.

The idea that America should be a land of opportunity is also an ethical given, although without quite the shock value of incest or murder. Nevertheless, it is an important part of the fabric of givens that we call our culture, which is why most of us would be appalled at the discrimination Carol faced in joining the chorus.

To deny the value of equal opportunity is to deny an essential ethical and intellectual working assumption of many Americans.

HISTORICAL/CULTURAL BACKGROUND

What forces, activities, events, training, books, etc., contributed to your response to the question concerning equal opportunity? Consider some of the following:

Religious Origins

Since our assumptions about Equal Opportunity are ethical givens, it makes sense that these assumptions would have some of their origins in religion. For example, three of the major world religions—Christianity, Judaism, and Islam—are well represented in contemporary America; all three recognize the significance of the Old Testament as a religious document, and hence the Ten Commandments of Moses. More importantly, within the Judeo-Christian tradition, one of these—the Tenth Commandment—has received special attention, even acquiring a special name, the Golden Rule:

> Do Unto Others As You Would Have Them Do Unto You.

Applied to a culturally homogeneous world of relative equals, the rule works reasonably well. If taken literally, however, the rule poses some problems in a culturally diverse world with inherent social differences between groups. In such a world, literally doing unto others what you would have them do unto you could be offensive (because it violates their cultural givens) or destructive (because of unequal status and power between individuals; the same act applied to two different individuals could have very different, quite unintended results).

The rule cannot be taken too literally. At the least, the rule implies a commitment to a more abstract sense of fair play, of equal treatment—although it leaves open the question of how we address cultural and social differences. And indeed Americans have been claimed to be a people who believe in fair play. The concept of "fair play" might well be considered a concept underlying "equal opportunity."

▶ *Writing Exercise:* Brainstorm on the following question: Are there other general religious principles that might be said to underlie the concept of equal opportunity? What are they? How do they affect or shape the concept of equal opportunity?

Origins in Everyday Life

Cultural, ethical givens are not just learned in the church, synagogue, or mosque. They are absorbed from all the other institutions in a society and through the conduct of what we call everyday life where they are taught and learned more or less unconsciously through example.

Consider the following suggestive examples regarding "equal opportunity."

SPORTS

Fair Play

Above we roughly equated the "Golden Rule" with the concept of fair play. In fact "fair play" as a concept is used to describe proper conduct in many different contexts—in business, personal relationships, school, etc. In fact, as we noted, Americans as a whole are said to believe in fair play. It is no accident that this now very general idea of equality in all conduct had its origins in sports where it literally described what was fair behavior in one's play.

Sports are probably the child's first real experience of having to live by a complex externally shared code—to live by laws that aren't simply those the parents set down. The world of sports is not the jungle-like tooth and fang experience some imagine. On the contrary, it has complex and typically fair rules (laws) that have been constructed and have to be learned and even referees and officials (judges) to administer them. To be sure, some official sports are rough, to say nothing of sandlot football or one-on-one playground basketball, but this roughness is rule-governed, even in the sandlots. This idea is clear enough to any child who knows that outside the sandlot, the neighborhood bully (or perhaps an older sibling) can take away his lunch money without protest, but inside the sandlot or playing field, analogous theft is not nearly so easy. Even if no referee is present, there are still rules that have to be considered and cannot be entirely ignored. If they are, then clearly the action was wrong and there was no "fair play." This itself is a lesson in both equality and opportunity.

The Underdog

Americans have an affection for the "underdog." This is especially obvious in the area of sports. Sportswriters and fans alike get excited when there are upsets: when a small school like St. John's overwhelms a much larger school like George-town in basketball (one of the few sports where smaller schools have an economic chance), or when the spunky American hockey team beats the Russian powerhouse in the Olympics. Not all is nationalism and global politics, though. Americans, for example, can sometimes enthusiastically support an underdog foreign athlete against another athlete, perhaps even one of their own.

One explanation for the tendency to favor the underdog is that the victory of the underdog is the reenactment of one of our most sacred national myths—the myth of great opportunity. We believe in equal opportunity—that it should and, in fact, does to some extent exist. When the underdog wins and we get excited, it is because his victory has provided us with evidence that the apparently weaker, smaller, and less favored does in fact have an opportunity.

This and related mythological scenarios are regularly enacted not only in real fields and stadiums, but also in movies, books, and other works of art. Among movies about baseball alone, there are many serious examples such as the following:

Grover Cleveland Alexander (an early movie with Jimmy Stewart)

The Natural

Field of Dreams

Major League

There are also comic examples such as these:

The Bad News Bears

Bingo Long and the Travelling All-Stars (a comic black variant on the sports underdog movie)

▶ *Writing Exercise: Sports.* Consider the above or other similar examples of the underdog in art. Do they suggest anything further about our concept of equal opportunity? For example, technically is an underdog simply one who is perceived as having little chance of winning? Will just any underdog do for us? What must an underdog be and do to gain our acceptance and love?

▶ *Writing Exercise: Public School.* Public school is sometimes heralded as one of the great democratic institutions of a modern state, with a great deal more to teach than mere subject content. This is because the public school education has been seen as a means of providing a resource (education) and some kind of equal opportunity for all. Do you agree with this ideal role of schools? What is your actual experience with public schools? Does it conform to the ideal view of what should happen? If not, could schools be changed so that they meet this ideal?

▶ *Writing Exercise: You, Your Family, and Friends.* The most seminal and memorable experiences we have are very personal ones. Consider the experiences of you, your family, and friends. Have you or they had a successful or unsuccessful immigrant experience? Have you or they had a successful or unsuccessful experience in changing social class? How have these experiences influenced you and your views about equal opportunity?

▶ *Writing Exercise:* Use your brainstorming and freewriting materials here. From the examples that you chose in earlier exercises, what aspects of your life or experience are connected to the concept "equal opportunity"? Explore these aspects for their influence.

Origins in "Civil Religion"

A number of writers have suggested that America has a "civil religion" (see E. L. Doctorow and Robert Bellah in this chapter). E. L. Doctorow, for example, suggests that America has a civil religion that he provocatively calls "secular humanism," which is enshrined in sacred documents like the Constitution. Robert Bellah also claims that there is a civil religion but that it is much more complementary to rather than in conflict with religion in America. Both largely agree—as I am sure many of us could—on an initial body of sacred texts in an American civil religion: the Declaration of Independence, the Constitution, and Bellah would add "The Gettysburg Address."

WRITING TO LEARN: A SEQUENCE OF ASSIGNMENTS

▶ *Writing Exercises*

1. Three of the most sacred texts in the civil religion are available at the end of this chapter—the Declaration of Independence, the Constitution, and "The Gettysburg Address." Read and compare them.

What kinds of statements do they make about opportunity and equal opportunity? To what extent have you been influenced by these or related ideas in your own thinking? Do you agree with them?

What other things would you add to the canon of sacred texts in the civil religion? What contribution would they make? How would they change our idea of equal opportunity?

2. Aside from the three already mentioned, which texts would you add to the canon of the American civil religion? Why? Would most others agree with you? Do your additions in any way suggest a different concept of "equal opportunity" or comment on it in a different way? If so, how?

3. Texts in civil religions need not be strictly consistent with each other any more than texts in real religions. For example, consider the following from the Declaration of Independence:

> *We hold these truths to be self-evident, that All Men are Created Equal, that they are endowed by their Creator with certain unalienable Rights, that among these are Life, Liberty, and the pursuit of Happiness.*

Compare this bold assertion of equality with some of the realities of our society. Do you find such contradictions between the ideal and the real in yourself? How do you reconcile them?

▶ *Writing Tasks*

1. What things or experiences have most influenced you in developing your initial response to the opening question? How have they shaped your expectation that there should be equal opportunity and your understanding of the phrase itself?

2. What does the phrase equal opportunity mean to you? What do you see as an ideal of equal opportunity? Are there contradictions in your ideal? Are there conflicts between it and other ideals that you have?

Key Question: What Do We Mean by Equal Opportunity?

We have already observed that one of the reasons people may answer yes so readily to the opening question is that they share a kind of civil religion of which this is a common precept. Another reason is that they take the question—and most especially the phrase "equal opportunity"—to mean very different things. It is important for the development of any argumentation around this topic to be clear about some of the dimensions of this phrase.

CONCEPTS OF EQUAL OPPORTUNITY

One of the earliest and best known declarations of the concept is in the Declaration of Independence itself:

> *We hold these truths to be self-evident, that All Men are Created Equal, that they are endowed by their Creator with certain unalienable Rights, that among these are Life, Liberty, and the pursuit of Happiness.*

This bold statement—authored by Thomas Jefferson—focuses 1) on an equality among individuals and 2) on their having unalienable rights (e.g., life, liberty, and the pursuit of happiness).

I shall consider each of these in turn.

Legal Equality

Jefferson's assertion that "all men are created equal" has received considerable attention. What could Jefferson have meant by this? It is obvious that in some sense all "men" are not really created equal; some are smarter than others, some taller, some stronger, and some are healthier. One explanation for this statement is that Jefferson was by no means oblivious to this fact, but viewed the statement as a necessary prerequisite for the kind of government that is being formed— namely, a government based on the common consent of the governed (as in the preamble to the Constitution: We the people of the United States . . .). Consent can only happen among relative equals. Men must be equal to the extent that they join in consent.

Furthermore, once consent is given (with the ratification of a Constitution) this equality persists in the citizens' continuing right to modify or break the "contract" if needed and in their legal equality as citizens under the Constitution.

Origins of Equality

The ideal of equality did not come from nowhere. It emerged out of political struggles and thinking in England as well as native struggles in the budding

Republic. For example, prior to the revolution, as much as 50% of the white population in some states was temporarily enslaved because they were indentured servants who were legally obliged to work for their masters for a period of years to pay for their passage to America. Even the free, unindentured population was often disenfranchised by poll taxes and other more direct restrictions on their rights of citizenship. The revolution brought an end to colonial oppression by England as well as by some of the "home-grown" oppressive institutions. It also brought broad statements of rights like the Declaration of Independence.

However, as has often been noted, the American Revolution, and these declarations of rights—noble as they indeed were and still are—did not in fact apply to women, nor for that matter to all races. Black slaves—both male and female—were deliberately excluded from the protection of the Constitution. Or more correctly, as the Dred Scott decision was to later argue, they were "chattel"—the property of their citizen owners and not citizens themselves.

The Dred Scott case (1857) involved a black slave—Dred Scott—who had been taken by his master to free states (states where slave holding was not permitted) and then returned to Missouri—a slave state (where slave holding was permitted). Scott sued for his freedom. While his case was ultimately rejected on a variety of grounds, some of them technical, the Supreme Court when it reviewed the case nevertheless included as part of its argument the claim that Scott was a slave, a "chattel" (possession) and not a citizen, and therefore had no right to sue at all. In doing this, the court dramatically affirmed the inequality between the races that was implicit in the Constitution all along (for example in its decision to count each black as three-fifths of a person for purposes of determining representation).

The Scott decision came right upon the eve of the Civil War, and was soon to be overturned by one of the more dramatic outcomes of the war—the passage of the Thirteenth, Fourteenth, and Fifteenth Amendments to the Constitution. The Thirteenth outlawed slavery itself; the Fifteenth ensured voting rights for all citizens, but most importantly the Fourteenth—especially, Section 1, redefined the concepts "citizen" and "equality":

> All persons born or naturalized in the United States and subject to the jurisdiction thereof, are citizens of the United States and of the State wherein they reside. No State shall make or enforce any law which shall abridge the privileges or immunities of citizens of the United States; nor shall any State deprive any person of life, liberty, or property, without due process of law; nor deny to any person within its jurisdiction the equal protection of the laws. [Fourteenth Amendment, Section 1]

The opening sentence of Section 1 of the amendment effectively nullified the basis of the Scott decision by asserting that Scott, other blacks, and indeed all persons "born and naturalized in the United States" are citizens of the United States. With this as foundation it then asserts that states cannot abridge their rights as U.S. citizens. Specifically, a state cannot

> "... *deprive any person of life, liberty, or property, without due process of law* [now called the Due Process Clause];

nor deny to any person within its jurisdiction the equal protection of the laws"
[now called the Equal Protection Clause].

Laws and Cases

In its quick broad strokes, the Fourteenth Amendment asserted the existence of a "legal equality" among all "persons" in the U.S., presumably regardless of such things as race, ethnicity, and sex.

However, in the first tests of the amendment—the Slaughterhouse cases, the Civil Rights cases, and Plessy v. Ferguson—the Supreme Court chose to interpret this legal equality very narrowly. In the Slaughterhouse case (1873), it tried to restrict the language of the Equal Protection Clause to blacks only, saying that the clause was to be used only when state laws "discriminated with gross injustice and hardship" against "newly emancipated negroes."

In the Civil Rights cases (1883), the Court struck down a law passed by Congress (Civil Rights Act of 1875), which both prohibited private discriminatory behavior in public accommodations and also assumed federal control over situations in which state and federal governments failed to protect citizens from private discrimination (e.g., discrimination against blacks in the South after the Civil War). The Court held that the amendment was only intended to protect U.S. citizens against discriminatory "State action," but not against the acts of private individuals or organizations.

In the Plessy case (1896), the Court addressed the question of state-mandated segregation—specifically, a Louisiana law requiring railroads to provide "equal but separate accommodations for the races." The Court majority asserted that the segregation law was not explicitly discriminatory and "has no tendency to destroy the legal equality of the races"; given this, they held that the Fourteenth Amendment was only intended to provide legal equality, and not "to abolish distinctions based upon color, or to enforce social as distinguished from political, equality. . . ." Furthermore, they rejected the notion that "social prejudices may be overcome by legislation." The one dissenting vote was that of Justice Harlan who rejected the narrow view of "legal equality." He argued that the Constitution was "color blind." To segregate on the basis of race is a "badge of servitude wholly inconsistent with the civil freedom and the equality before the law established by the Constitution."

With its doctrine of "separate but equal" and its narrow interpretation of both the Fourteenth Amendment and legal equality, the Court laid the base for the evolution of a pervasive network of segregated public and private institutions (buses, schools, restaurants, churches, clubs, prisons, etc.) supported by an equally pervasive network of discriminatory laws called Jim Crow Laws, which restricted the actual freedom of blacks to vote, marry, move about, work, and otherwise conduct their lives (to say nothing of women and other races and ethnic groups who were also excluded by the narrow interpretations of the Constitution). These networks remained more or less intact for six decades after the Plessy case, and did not really begin to change until after World War II.

LIFE, LIBERTY, AND THE PURSUIT OF HAPPINESS

The first hundred years after the Declaration of Independence might be seen as a struggle that yielded a formal equality—in some sense a ratification of Jefferson's declaration that "all men are created equal"—at least legally equal. It ended in declarations that all persons are citizens and all citizens are legally equal. Yet as we noted, that formal equality was undercut by a number of real political actions and decisions.

The second hundred years may be seen as a continuing struggle to see to what extent legal equality does correspond to a *real* equality of opportunity—a struggle that continues to this very day to define what is really meant by "equality of opportunity."

Legal Equality Revisited: The Brown Case

The landmark in the post–World War II transformation of concepts of equality was the case *Brown* v. *Board of Education* (1954). It specifically addressed the issue of segregation in the schools. Like the earlier Supreme Courts in the nineteenth century, the court (frequently referred to as the Warren Court) began by considering whether the authors of the Fourteenth Amendment intended for it to apply to school segregation, but unlike them, found their intentions much more illusory, thus shifting the Court's focus to "the effect of segregation itself on public education." Acknowledging that education was "perhaps the most important function of state and local government," and therefore a fundamental institution, the Court was interested in whether segregation deprived children of equal educational opportunity. It concluded that it did, but not simply because the separate schools were unequal (for this would not have been sufficient grounds for rejecting segregated institutions as a whole). Rather, the Court considered extensive psychological evidence, which showed that segregation "generates a feeling of inferiority as to their status in the community that may affect their minds and hearts in a way unlikely to ever be undone." The Court by unanimous majority overturned Plessy, finding that school segregation violated the Equal Protection Clause of the Fourteenth Amendment. The Court's decision had at least two important implications regarding the concept of equal opportunity.

In its decision, the Court took into consideration a great deal more than earlier courts, which had largely concerned themselves with whether these laws directly undermined legal equality and tended to reinstitute a state of servitude, and felt that they had nothing to do with social equality. The later court saw little difference between social and legal equality, especially in the context of a major social institution like the school. In effect, the concept of legal equality had changed.

In changing its perspective, the Court raised to prominence a range of social and psychological issues—in particular, the impact of inequality on the minds and spirits of those affected. Equal opportunity meant more than mere common access to institutions, positions, and resources; it also meant access to a sense of equality and dignity, a spiritual well-being, which the State could not knowingly or deliberately undermine.

▶ **Writing Exercises**

1. The Court's discussion touched on only one form of social and legal inequality—segregation—which can do spiritual and mental damage. What other inequalities can cause this harm; what other kinds of mental and spiritual harm can be wreaked?

2. Read the selection from Richard Wright, "The Ethics of Living Jim Crow." What does its account of his early life suggest about the damage that accrues from social/legal inequality?

3. Chapter 11 in its discussion of women's issues notes that social stereotypes—in that case stereotypes of men and women—can do serious harm, because they reflect the outlook and expectations of the society as a whole, social "givens" that are always there influencing the one being stereotyped (the "stereotypee"). Look at the discussion of stereotypes there and extend it in the present case to racial and ethnic minorities. First, construct a list of sterotypical traits associated with a minority group; divide these into positive and negative traits. What is the overall effect of these stereotypes? Overall do they support a sense of dignity and social worth?

▶ **Writing Assignments**

1. Describe an experience involving sexism, ageism, racial prejudice, or another form of discrimination in which you were the oppressed. How did it make you feel about yourself? What were its effects? What are the long-term effects of this and similar experiences?

2. What do you see as the major impacts of social and legal inequalities on blacks or some other minority?

3. What do you see as the major impacts of social and legal inequalities on the nominally dominant groups in U.S. society?

BEYOND BROWN

The Brown case opened the floodgate for a whole epoch of legal and social action to change the legal and social status of blacks—and ultimately of other groups that felt discrimination—e.g., other racial and ethnic groups and women.

FURTHER DESEGREGATION AND THE ROLE OF STATE ACTION

Brown of course led to the desegregation of other public institutions and facilities: buses, lunch counters, churches, and housing. The issue here was not just the gradual extension of the Brown ruling to more and more facilities; rather, it was also the steady extension of desegregation into more and more private facilities as the Court changed its concept of state action—and began to rethink the requirement laid down in the Civil Rights case of 1883 that Fourteenth Amendment protections only extend to state and not to private actions.

Key Question: Should Equal Opportunity Legislation Apply to Private Enterprise?

The Court eventually became receptive to assertions that a close relation exists between state authority and discriminatory action in so-called private contexts. For example, in one case the Court found that the state had become a party to discrimination by a restaurant that leased space in a municipal parking facility: namely, the state had not required equal access to all patrons. Further, Congress authored and the Court upheld more stringent legislation such as the Civil Rights Act of 1964 that asserts the right to regulate public accommodations regardless of "state action." The result was an overall extension of the concept of equal opportunity to include access to more and more "privately" owned facilities, so that the law not only promises access to the public library and school, but also to the restaurant and the dress shop nearby.

Desegregation and Remedies

To be sure, the states and institutions affected did not always respond with alacrity, much less "with all deliberate speed" as the Court had directed in Brown. This delay meant that Brown necessarily led to issues of remedies in those cases where no action was taken. In *Swann* v. *Charlotte–Mecklenberg Board of Education,* the board addressed a number of issues in regard to remedies:

1. Although racial balance in schools was not required, ratios of blacks and whites could be considered in shaping a remedy for past segregation.
2. One-race schools were not *per se* unlawful, but school officials had the burden of showing that their racial composition was not the result of discrimination.
3. The redrawing of attendance zones, busing, and assignment of students on the basis of race were proper remedial measures.

In short the Court authorized some strong remedies to overcome past discrimination. In doing so, the Court took a substantial step beyond Brown. Brown had declared a strong form of legal equality between all citizens. The subsequent rulings by authorizing remedies had ensured that the legal rights were more than mere paper rights. Moreover, these remedies applied not only to possible future violations but to past instances as well.

Beyond Desegregation: The Issue of Remedies Again

While segregation was a pervasive system that had to be dismantled, inequality manifested itself in innumerable other ways that were also addressed after Brown. One of these was the general problem of enfranchisement. Blacks (and other minorities) were denied participation and representation in the State. These problems were addressed through a combination of judicial, legislative, and social action. Among the problems addressed were overt and covert restrictions on the right to participate in the political process:

1. The existence of whites-only political parties and primaries (in which blacks could not participate);
2. The existence of cumulative poll taxes and literacy requirements and other requirements or threats that had the effect of restricting or eliminating the black vote;
3. The systematic limitation of the numbers of blacks on juries;
4. Systems of apportionment and representation that diluted or nullified black votes.

These problems were addressed in part through the Voting Rights Act of 1964, which set up a remedial process to end these practices, in some cases through the active intervention of the courts and federal marshalls. To some extent they were addressed in the courts, e.g., through the Supreme Court's "one man–one vote" ruling, which required that systems of apportionment and representation must reasonably correspond to the actual numbers represented and cannot work to undermine the impact of a person's vote.

Other areas that were addressed were housing, public accommodations, and employment. These were dealt with in the Civil Rights Act of 1964, which prohibited discrimination in these and other areas, and set up legal remedies.

Counter-Currents

The period of the late fifties, sixties, and early seventies saw a substantial extension of the legal rights guaranteed in the Brown decision:

1. An extension to include other forms of segregation;
2. An extension of the concept of "state action" to outlaw segregation in more and more "private" facilities;
3. An extension into other areas and forms of discrimination—e.g., in housing, voting, jury selection, public accommodations, and employment.
4. An exploration in all cases of the issue of remedies to eliminate discrimination.

The period of the seventies and eighties, however, saw the evolution of important civil rights counter-currents. While these counter-currents have occurred in many areas of civil rights activity around a variety of issues, not surprisingly they have often focused on the areas of schools and employment (where the impact of decisions is felt the most) and the issue of remedies (which determines the scope and character of the impact), especially affirmative action programs as remedies.

THE BAKKE CASE

One of the earliest and best known cases to raise such questions was *Regents of the University of California v. Bakke* (1978)—the Bakke case for short. In this case, Allan Bakke—a medical school applicant—brought suit against the medical school of the University of California at Davis, challenging the school's voluntarily adopted affirmative action program. While Davis, as a new campus, had no admissions history to speak of and therefore no provable history of race discrimination, it had adopted on its own initiative an affirmative action program that involved admissions quotas. The medical school, which admitted only 100 students annually, reserved 16 of these slots for minority applicants. Bakke, a white applicant, was denied admission twice, even though his credentials were better than those of some of the minority applicants. Bakke argued that the quota system at Davis violated Title VII of the Civil Rights Act of 1964, which prohibited discrimination in programs receiving federal funding. In this case, Bakke was claiming that he was discriminated against because of his race, because he was white. He was asserting that he himself was a victim of racism, of what was to be called by some "reverse discrimination."

The Court responded with a split decision 5–4, which found for both sides in what has been called a "compromise decision." On the one hand, it ruled in favor of Bakke and ordered his admission. Specifically, it rejected the use of quotas (the 16 minority slots) as a violation of the equal protection clause of the Fourteenth Amendment. The defense had argued that the use of race as a classification for admission was in this case "benign" and not subject to sanction. Justice Powell rejected that and other arguments, saying that the "guarantee of equal protection cannot mean one thing when applied to one individual and something else when applied to a person of another color."

On the other hand, while rejecting quotas in this case, the Court did not reject the concept of a race-conscious admissions program. On the contrary, a majority saw the Davis program as an educationally sound one, which among other things sought to attain a diverse student body as a basis for the better training of all its students. These and other goals were deemed sufficiently important to justify a remedial and even race-conscious action. One justice, for example, referred approvingly to Harvard's admissions program, which assigns race or ethnic background a positive value (to be factored in with other information such as interviews, achievements, motivation, and test scores), but still treats each applicant as an individual in the admissions process.

The Response to Bakke: Ideology

The Bakke decision with its 5–4 vote was a close one, standing in sharp contrast to the Brown decision some 24 years earlier, which had been unanimous. Not surprisingly then, the response to it was sharp and divided—with political conservatives finding it far too generous in its support of affirmative action programs, and political liberals finding it far too restrictive. However, while these familiar political divisions generally held, the conflicts were ultimately not all that simple. Apparent political allies often found themselves disagreeing around the issues. Witness for example, the following exchange in the *Civil Liberties Review* between two nominal liberals—both supporters of civil rights:

> Many well-meaning and sincere civil libertarians will still suggest that it is intrinsically wrong to evaluate people on so arbitrary a basis as race. As an abstract proposition, that has a nice ring to it. But in this country people have always been judged on the basis of their race. Most of the black people in the United States are here because their ancestors were brought here as slaves—on the basis of race. Before the Civil War, it was the law of our land that a black person had no rights that a white person was bound to respect—on the basis of race. Most blacks and members of other racial minorities in this country grew up in ghetto neighborhoods and went to segregated schools either because they were legally compelled to do so or because discrimination was so pervasive their families had little opportunity to live elsewhere—all on the basis of race. Is it only when recompense seems imminent that they are to be told that race is no longer a valid criterion? Is it a necessary libertarian principle that, despite all the years of slavery and discrimination against them as a group, black people must now work their way into the American mainstream one by one? . . .
>
> Can it seriously be disputed that the remedy for group exclusion is group inclusion? To say now that members of those formerly excluded classes can win inclusion only one by one is to guarantee that, while individuals may achieve positions of social equality, the group will be forever frozen in a position of second-class status in a white society. . . .
>
> It is time for civil libertarians to acknowledge that the American dream of individual treatment is not wholly compatible with American experience. The day of the true melting pot may yet come, but, until it does, members of racial minority groups are hostages to history. Only those who would blind themselves to the reality of American life would elevate abstract notions of individuality above the obvious collective needs and interests of minority group Americans. (Frank Askin, *Civil Liberties Review*, Spring 1975, p. 95.)
>
> Preference by race is malign. Its malignity has no clearer or more fitting name than racism. Such well-intentioned racism is now widespread, and civil libertarians, however anguished by racial injustice, must not support it. To preclude such racism in striving for racial justice is not to question the need for unrelenting, vigorous affirmative action to right past wrongs. But affirmative action has many species. Some of them, in discriminating by race flatly, infect the wound that they would heal. . . .
>
> I conclude with some brief notes on the counterproductivity of racial preference.

i) Systems of preferential admission do not integrate, they disintegrate the races. However much advocates of such systems may hope for ultimate integration (though some may not share that ideal), the consequences of such systems in practice is ever greater attention to race, agitation about race. The invidious consideration of ethnicity in inappropriate contexts results in rewards and penalties generally thought to be unfair and undeserved. And all with focus on race. No prescription for long-term disharmony among races could be surer of success.

ii) Achieving racial proportionality in the professions through the consideration of race in professional school admission, even where intellectual and other pertinent considerations are counterindicative, must result in the tendency, at least statistical, to yield minority group professionals less well-qualified, less respected, less trusted than their counterparts in the majority. That is a great disservice to minority groups, stigmatizing their members in a most unfortunate way. . . .

iii) One consequence of preferential admissions programs is certain. Fully qualified minority group professionals come to be viewed by many, of all races, as having gained their positions through favor by virtue of their race. No matter their excellence; it is suspected that their credentials were received on a double, lower standard. It is a cruel result. (Carl Cohen, *Civil Liberties Review*, Spring 1975, p. 106.)

AFFIRMATIVE ACTION

Key Questions: Do Affirmative Action Policies Necessarily Lead to Another Form of Racism? Are Affirmative Action Policies Likely to Mean that Preference Will Be Given to Less Qualified Candidates?

▶ *Writing Task:* Summarize the major point of each of the preceding excerpts. Write an essay in which you develop a position supporting one of these perspectives.

The sharpness of these two critiques and the complexity of the division of views only reflects that the Bakke case raised a number of issues and tapped into a variety of different and competing basic beliefs—producing, as such cases often do, some very strange political bedfellows and ironic twists. Among other things, it set up contradictions between peoples' beliefs in such broad concepts as equality, meritocracy, individualism, and compensatory justice.

Meritocratic Perspectives

The Bakke decision violated the meritocratic beliefs of many. Nowhere is this more clearly stated than in the original opinion of the California Supreme Court—

the state level ruling that the university was appealing to the U.S. Supreme Court. The California court argued that Davis's racial preferences would sacrifice "principle for the sake of dubious expediency and would represent a retreat in the struggle to assure that each man and woman shall be judged on the basis of individual merit alone. . . ." The Court's voice was not a new one; it had its American origins in the very beginnings of the country itself when people sought alternatives to European feudal systems where power and rewards went to people based on wealth and birth, not merit. There was talk of building "natural aristocracies" based on "talent and virtue" in the New World. For many, the concept of a meritocracy is their idealized concept of equality and equal opportunity.

Certainly, the California court was not alone in its view. Constitutional scholars like Alexander Bickel added their voice:

> In a society in which men and women expect to succeed by hard work and to better themselves by making themselves better, it is no trivial moral wrong to proceed systematically to defeat this expectation. . . . To reject an applicant who meets established, realistic, and unchanged qualifications in favor of a less qualified candidate is morally wrong, and in the aggregate, practically disastrous.

Some opponents, like Bickel, were not only concerned about the moral issues—that is, the moral violation of meritocratic principles—but also about possible practical consequences, in particular the diminution of academic standards and as Bickel argued in the DeFunis case (a case similar to the Bakke case), "a cost is paid in loss of efficiency." That is, the claim is that racial quotas prevent putting the gifts of the most meritorious individuals in the service of society.

Other Individualistic Perspectives

The meritocratic view is itself an "individualist perspective," because at base its argument is that the individual should get what he/she merits (based on their prior acts); other considerations not based on the individual and their merit are not relevant.

There are other perspectives, however, that also focus on the rights and role of the individual. In particular, there is one that rejects the racial quotas involved in the Bakke case because they create and perpetuate in law a category called "race" that is inimical to the individual. This is to some extent the view being espoused by Cohen in the *Civil Liberties Review* exchange above. It is even more clearly the view adopted by Justice Powell in his rejection of racial quotas in the Bakke decision:

> The "guarantee of equal protection cannot mean one thing when applied to one individual and something else when applied to a person of another color."

The origin of Powell's perspective is in the Brown decision and even further back in the *Plessy* v. *Ferguson* decision of 1896. There Justice Harlan in his impassioned dissent against the separate but equal doctrine had argued that the

Constitution was colorblind and did not countenance race as a classification. In the Brown decision the Court majority affirmed this view. Notably, however, Powell did not reject the concept of the quota itself; he simply rejected the idea that there was a compelling state interest to justify its use in the circumstances at Davis—where, for example, there was no demonstrated history of discrimination.

Why this distinction we might ask? One observation one might make is that it is relatively more consistent with an individualist perspective. That is, Powell is willing to accept what he deems a more "race conscious" remedy like quotas (which he feels does violence to the individual) only in those cases where there is specific past discrimination against an identifiable set of individuals. He was reluctant to consider such actions in order to remedy past discrimination in general.

COMPENSATORY JUSTICE PERSPECTIVES

Key Question: Should Whole Groups of People Be Entitled to Compensation for Past Injustice?

A substantial Court minority of four (Justices Brennan, White, Marshall, and Blackmun) disagreed with Powell and others on this point, adopting a much broader and more liberal concept of compensatory justice. They found that both the Civil Rights Act and the Constitution permitted race-conscious remedies even in cases where there was no demonstrated history of past discrimination. Thus, even though Davis had not itself proven discriminatory, the implication was that racial remedies were permissible in such areas as medicine because minorities had long been underrepresented in that profession. Moreover, there was reason to believe that past societal discrimination was the cause. Further, as Justice Marshall said, "It is not merely the history of slavery alone but also that a whole people were marked as inferior by the law. And that mark has endured. The dream of America as the great melting pot has not been realized by the Negro; because of his skin color he never even made it into the pot."

Considering this and other issues, they felt Davis was justified in acting to right these social wrongs. Moreover, these justices agreed with the defense's argument that in doing so, Davis's racial distinctions were actually "benign" and not subject to the strict scrutiny standards to which Justice Powell and others subjected them. Rather than adopt the "individualist" argument that the Constitution was color blind, they argued that it could be race-conscious in this case without being truly prejudicial. Different treatment is not necessarily prejudicial or discriminatory treatment. The question from their point of view is whether white applicants are deprived of what they are fairly entitled to have because of prejudice. On this point (in language that hearkens back to the Brown decision) Justice Brennan argued the following:

> Nor was Bakke in any sense stamped as inferior by the Medical School's rejection of him. . . . Moreover, there is absolutely no basis for concluding that Bakke's rejection as a result of Davis' use of racial preference will affect him

throughout his life in the same way as the segregation of the Negro school children in Brown I would have affected them. Unlike discrimination against racial minorities, the use of racial preferences for remedial purposes does not inflict a pervasive injury on individual whites in the sense that wherever they go and whatever they do there is a significant likelihood that they will be treated as second class citizens because of their color.

Not only did the Court minority reject Powell's individualist argument as regards race, they elsewhere rejected the meritocratic argument. Not only was Bakke not a victim of racial prejudice, he was also not a person who had been deprived of a place to which he was fairly entitled. Brennan, joined by the other justices argued:

> If it was reasonable to conclude—as we hold that it was—that the failure of minorities to qualify for admission at Davis under regular procedures was due principally to the effects of past discrimination, then there is reasonable likelihood that but for pervasive discrimination, respondent [that is, Bakke] would have failed to qualify for admission even in the absence of Davis' special admissions program." (L 52)

In their view, Bakke's claim that he was deprived of what he was due by virtue of merit was itself sullied by the existence of past discrimination. The justices argue that his merit is purely relative and dependent on the fact that others—as a result of racial discrimination—were not able to advance and demonstrate their own "merit." In a fairer, less racist world there is no reason to believe that he would have demonstrated and been able to claim the same relative merit.

Not surprisingly, Justice Powell took strong exception to this argument:

> The breadth of this hypothesis is unprecedented in our constitutional system. The first step [of acknowledging the fact of past societal discrimination] is easily taken. . . . The second step, however, involves a speculative leap; but for this discrimination by society at large, Bakke 'would have failed to qualify for admission' because Negro applicants would have made better scores. Not one word in the record supports this conclusion. (Liv 52)

Justices Brennan, Blackmun, Marshall, and White, like Justice Powell himself, have their supporters outside the judiciary. In this case John Livingston joined them in an even stronger attack on the meritocratic and individualist perspectives. For example, in the absence of what amounts to an "even playing field" he argues that meritocracy is a system that only ensures that those who have certain advantages to start with continue to have them and along the way are able to use them to acquire more and more "merit," so that in the end they appear to be more "meritorious" than those without such advantages. It is in his view a profoundly unequal approach that is thinly disguised as equality. He rejects Powell's above critique:

> But the undeniable existence of group prejudice and discrimination—which Justice Powell granted—furnishes compelling evidence. At most only a very small

and not very speculative hop (a 'permissible inference,' in the language of the law) is required to make the connection. (Liv 53)

Comparing the Three Perspectives

On the one hand, the differences between the various justices in the Bakke decision seem profound and, indeed, they are. We see coming to the fore often sharply stated differences based on competing and very different views on the concepts of meritocracy, individualism, and compensatory justice. But on the other hand, we can find dramatic similarities in their views.

It is clear that the differences between the various court opinions are not absolute. For example, the proponents of the compensatory justice perspective are by no means opposed to individualism or promotion based on merit *per se.* It would be utterly misguided, based on their remarks, to suggest that they are anti-individualist or antimerit. Similarly, "individualists," like Powell, are by no means opposed to the concept of compensatory justice *per se,* and it would be equally misguided to suggest that they are opposed to such justice.

Closer to the mark would be to suggest that typically the opinion makers in this decision to some extent or another partook of all three tendencies: all valued some kind of meritocratic, individualist, and compensatory justice principles— although not necessarily the same ones, or to the same degree. The decision was problematic for them (and would be so for us) precisely because it forced them to differentiate between these principles and reconcile one with the other. This situation is typical of most difficult decisions that the Court makes (and most that ordinary persons make, for that matter). Thus, the Court often finds itself balancing one principle, interest, or right, against another; the right to free speech versus the right to privacy; or freedom from unreasonable search against the need for public safety.

▶ ***Writing Assignment:*** Assume that you are in Lewis Powell's position in the Bakke case. If yours was the swing vote as his was, how would you have voted on the issues? Would you have granted Bakke admission? How would you have responded to the issue of quotas? Justify your decisions.

Since Bakke

Since the Bakke case, the Court—while not rejecting affirmative action programs— has sought guidelines for their scope. It has generally tended to follow the path that Powell set down. In the Weber case (1979) it approved a voluntarily adopted employment training plan that sought to reduce long-standing imbalances in a company's skilled work force by selecting blacks and whites on a one-for-one basis for the skilled crafts training program—thus, in some cases preferentially choosing blacks for training over whites (even whites with greater seniority).

In *Fullilove* v. *Klutznick* (1980) the Court upheld the use of federal setasides or reserved funds for minority business enterprises as a method of remedying past discrimination on the construction industry. In this case the plaintiffs (a group of nonminority contractors) challenged the Public Works Employment Act of 1977, which had required that at least 10 percent of federal monies designated for local public works be set aside for businesses owned by minorities. The Court (following Powell in the Bakke case) noted that a program that used racial or ethnic criteria was subject to strict scrutiny to determine if there were adequate grounds for using race as a category. However, on review the Court found that Congress had ample evidence of the national scope and longstanding nature of minorities' limited access to public contracts.

In both cases the Court adopted the stance that equal protection allows compensatory policies, but only for groups that have been demonstrably disadvantaged in the past.

Recently, there have been several cases that have sought to test these waters again. One such case—*Martin* v. *Wilks* (1989)—deals with preferential promotion of blacks in an Alabama fire department. In this case the plaintiff—Kenny Wilks, a white fire department officer—sued to overturn an affirmative action plan that promoted a black officer—Jackie Barton—over him, even though Barton's competitive scores were not as good as Wilks'. The case is similar but by no means identical to Bakke and to another Alabama case that was decided in the eighties— U.S. v. Paradise (involving quotas for hiring blacks on the Alabama Highway Patrol).

▶ **Writing Assignment:** Based on this information and on any other you can gather, define the issues and indicate how you would decide them? Justify your decision.

▶ **Writing Assignment:** Reread "The Ethics of Living Jim Crow," by Richard Wright. This autobiographical essay comes from a collection of stories called *Uncle Tom's Children*. Read some of the other stories, and write an essay discussing how these stories reflect the autobiography.

Key Terms

Equal Opportunity

Equal Protection

Separate but Equal

Affirmative Action

Reverse Discrimination

Compensatory Justice

Meritocracy

Fourteenth Amendment

A Citizen Reads the Constitution

E. L. Doctorow

Not including the amendments, it is approximately 5000 words long—about the length of a short story. It is an enigmatically dry, unemotional piece of work, tolling off in its monotone the structures and functions of government, the conditions and obligations of office, the limitations of powers, the means for redressing crimes and conducting commerce. It makes itself the supreme law of the land. It concludes with instructions on how it can amend itself, and undertakes to pay all the debts incurred by the states under its indigent parent, the Articles of Confederation.

It is no more scintillating as reading than I remember it to have been in Mrs. Brundage's seventh-grade civics class at Joseph H. Wade Junior High School. It is 5000 words but reads like 50,000. It lacks high rhetoric and shows not a trace of wit, as you might expect, having been produced by a committee of lawyers. It uses none of the tropes of literature to create empathetic states in the mind of the reader. It does not mean to persuade. It abhors metaphor as nature abhors a vacuum.

One's first reaction upon reading it is to rush for relief to an earlier American document, as alive with passion and the juices of outrage as the work of any single artist:

> We hold these truths to be self-evident, that all men are created equal, that they are endowed by their Creator with certain unalienable Rights, that among these are Life, Liberty and the pursuit of Happiness. That to secure these rights, Governments are instituted among Men, deriving their just powers from the consent of the governed. That whenever any Form of Government becomes destructive of these ends, it is the Right of the People to alter or to abolish it, and to institute new Government..

Here is the substantive diction of a single human mind—Thomas Jefferson's, as it happens—even as it speaks for all. It is engaged in the art of literary revolution, rewriting history, overthrowing divine claims to rule and genealogical hierarchies of human privilege as cruel frauds, defining human rights as universal and distributing the source and power of government to the people governed. It is the radical voice of national liberation, combative prose lifting its musketry of self-evident truths and firing away.

What reader does not wish the Constitution could have been written out of something of the same spirit? Of course, we all know instinctively that it could not, that statute-writing in the hands of lawyers has its own demands, and those are presumably precision and clarity, which call for sentences bolted at all four corners with *wherein*'s and *whereunder*'s and *thereof*'s and *therein*'s and notwithstanding the *foregoing*'s.

Still and all, our understanding of the Constitution must come of an assessment of its character as a composition, and it would serve us to explore further why it is the way it is. . . . It is true but not sufficient to say that the Constitution reads as it does because it was written by a committee of lawyers. Something more is going on here. Every written composition has a voice, a persona, a character of presentation, whether by design of the author or not. The voice of the Constitution is a quiet voice. It does not rally us; it does not call on self-evident truths; it does not arm itself with philosophy or political principle; it does not argue, explain, condemn, excuse, or justify. It is postrevolutionary. Not claiming righteousness, it is, however, suffused with rectitude. It is this way because it seeks standing in the world, the elevation of the unlawful acts of men—unlawful first because the British government has been overthrown, and second because the confederation of the states has been subverted—to the lawful standing of nationhood. All the *herein*'s and *whereas*'s and *thereof*'s are not only legalisms; they also happen to be the diction of the British Empire, the language of the deposed. Nothing has changed that much, the Constitution says, lying; we are nothing that you won't recognize.

But there is something more. The key verb of the text is *shall,* as in "All legislative powers herein granted shall be vested in a Congress of the United States which shall consist of a Senate and a House of Representatives," or "New States may be admitted by the Congress into this Union; but no new State shall be formed or erected within the jurisdiction of any other State." The Constitution does not explicitly concern itself with the grievances that brought it about. It is syntactically futuristic: it prescribes what is to come. It prophesies. Even today, living two hundred years into the prophecy, we read it and find it still ahead of us, still extending itself in time. The Constitution gives law and assumes for itself the power endlessly to give law. It ordains. In its articles and sections, one after another, it offers a ladder to heaven. It is cold, distant, remote as a voice from on high, self-authenticating.

Through most of history kings and their servitor churches did the ordaining, and always in the name of God. But here the people do it: "We the People . . . do ordain and establish this Constitution for the United States." And the word for God appears nowhere in the text. Heaven forbid! In fact, its very last stricture is that "no religious test shall ever be required as a qualification to any office or public trust under the United States."

The voice of the Constitution is the inescapably solemn self-consciousness of the people giving the law unto themselves. But since the Judeo-Christian world of Western civilization all given law imitates God—God being the ultimate lawgiver—in affecting the transhuman voice of law, that dry monotone that disdains persuasion, the Constitution not only takes on the respectable sound of British statute, it more radically assumes the character of scripture.

The ordaining voice of the Constitution is scriptural, but in resolutely keeping the authority for its dominion in the public consent, it presents itself as the sacred text of secular humanism.

I wish Mrs. Brundage had told me that back in Wade Junior High School.

I wish Jerry Falwell's and Jimmy Swaggart's and Pat Robertson's teachers had taught them that back in their junior high schools.

America's Civil Religion
Robert N. Bellah

While some have argued that Christianity is the national faith, and others that church and synagogue celebrate only the generalized religion of "the American Way of life," few have realized that there actually exists alongside of and rather clearly differentiated from the churches an elaborate and well-institutionalized civil religion in America. This article argues not only that there is such a thing, but also that this religion—or perhaps better, this religious dimension—has its own seriousness and integrity and requires the same care in understanding that any other religion does.[1] . . .

THE FOUNDING FATHERS AND CHRISTIANITY

The words and acts of the founding fathers, especially the first few presidents, shaped the form and tone of the civil religion as it has been maintained ever since. Though much is selectively derived from Christianity, this religion is clearly not itself Christianity. For one thing, neither Washington nor Adams nor Jefferson mentions Christ in his inaugural address; nor do any of the subsequent presidents, although not one of them fails to mention God.[2] The God of the civil religion is not only rather "unitarian," he is also on the austere side, much more related to order, law, and right than to salvation and love. Even though he is somewhat deist in cast, he is by no means simply a watchmaker God. He is actively interested and involved in history, with a special concern for America. Here the analogy has much less to do with natural law than with ancient Israel; the equation of America with Israel in the idea of the "American Israel" is not infrequent.[3] What was implicit in the words of Washington . . . becomes explicit in Jefferson's second inaugural when he said: "I shall need, too, the favor of that Being in whose hands we are, who led our fathers, as Israel of old, from their native land and planted them in a country flowing with all the necessaries and comforts of life." Europe is Egypt; America, the promised land. God has led his people to establish a new sort of social order that shall be a light unto all the nations.[4] . . .

What we have, then, from the earliest years of the republic is a collection of

Robert Bellah, "America's Civil Religion" reprinted by permission of *Daedalus,* Journal of the American Academy of Arts and Sciences, from the issue entitled "Religion in America," Winter 1967, Vol. 69/1.

beliefs, symbols, and rituals with respect to sacred things and institutionalized in a collectivity. This religion—there seems no other word for it—while not antithetical to and indeed sharing much in common with Christianity, was neither sectarian nor in any specific sense Christian. At a time when the society was overwhelmingly Christian, it seems unlikely that this lack of Christian reference was meant to spare the feelings of the tiny non-Christian minority. Rather, the civil religion expressed what those who set the precedents felt was appropriate under the circumstances. It reflected their private as well as public views. Nor was the civil religion simply "religion in general." While generality was undoubtedly seen as a virtue by some . . . the civil religion was specific enough when it came to the topic of America. Precisely because of this specificity, the civil religion was saved from empty formalism and served as a genuine vehicle of national religious self-understanding. . . .

CIVIL WAR AND CIVIL RELIGION

Until the Civil War, the American civil religion focused above all on the event of the Revolution, which was seen as the final act of the Exodus from the old lands across the waters. The Declaration of Independence and the Constitution were the sacred scriptures and Washington the divinely appointed Moses who led his people out of the hands of tyranny. The Civil War, which Sidney Mead calls "the center of American history,"[5] was the second great event that involved the national self-understanding so deeply as to require expression in the civil religion. In 1835, Tocqueville wrote that the American republic had never really been tried, that victory in the Revolutionary War was more the result of British pre-occupation elsewhere and the presence of a powerful ally than of any great military success of the Americans. . . .

With the Civil War, a new theme of death, sacrifice, and rebirth enters the civil religion. It is symbolized in the life and death of Lincoln. Nowhere is it stated more vividly than in the Gettysburg Address, itself part of the Lincolnian "New Testament" among the civil scriptures. Robert Lowell has recently pointed out the "insistent use of birth images" in this speech explicitly devoted to "these honored dead": "brought forth," "conceived," "created," "a new birth of freedom." He goes on to say:

> The Gettysburg Address is a symbolic and sacramental act. Its verbal quality is resonance combined with a logical, matter of fact, prosaic brevity. . . . In his words, Lincoln symbolically died, just as the Union soldiers really died—and as he himself was soon really to die. By his words, he gave the field of battle a symbolic significance that it had lacked. For us and our country, he left Jefferson's ideals of freedom and equality joined to the Christian sacrificial act of death and rebirth. I believe this is a meaning that goes beyond sect or religion and beyond peace and war, and is now part of our lives as a challenge, obstacle and hope.[6]

Lowell is certainly right in pointing out the Christian quality of the symbolism here, but he is also right in quickly disavowing any sectarian implication. The earlier symbolism of the civil religion had been Hebraic without being in any specific sense Jewish. The Gettysburg symbolism (". . . those who here gave their lives, that that nation might live") is Christian without having anything to do with the Christian church.

The symbolic equation of Lincoln with Jesus was made relatively early. Herndon, who had been Lincoln's law partner, wrote:

> For fifty years God rolled Abraham Lincoln through his fiery furnace. He did it to try Abraham and to purify him for his purposes. This made Mr. Lincoln humble, tender, forebearing, sympathetic to suffering, kind, sensitive, tolerant; broadening, deepening and widening his whole nature; making him the noblest and loveliest character since Jesus Christ. . . . I believe that Lincoln was God's chosen one. . . .

The new symbolism soon found both physical and ritualistic expression. The great number of the war dead required the establishment of a number of national cemeteries. Of these, the Gettysburg National Cemetery, which Lincoln's famous address served to dedicate, has been overshadowed only by the Arlington National Cemetery. Begun somewhat vindictively on the Lee estate across the river from Washington, partly with the end that the Lee family could never reclaim it,[8] it has subsequently become the most hallowed monument of the civil religion. . . .

Memorial Day, which grew out of the Civil War, gave ritual expression to the themes we have been discussing. As Lloyd Warner has so brilliantly analyzed it, the Memorial Day observance, especially in the towns and smaller cities of America, is a major event for the whole community involving a rededication to the martyred dead, to the spirit of sacrifice, and to the American vision.[9] Just as Thanksgiving Day, which incidentally was securely institutionalized as an annual national holiday only under the presidency of Lincoln, serves to integrate the family into the civil religion, so Memorial Day has acted to integrate the local community into the national cult. Together with the less overtly religious Fourth of July and the more minor celebrations of Veterans Day and the birthdays of Washington and Lincoln, these two holidays provide an annual ritual calendar for the civil religion. The public-school system serves as a particularly important context for the cultic celebration of the civil rituals. . . .

The American civil religion was never anticlerical or militantly secular. On the contrary, it borrowed selectively from the religious tradition in such a way that the average American saw no conflict between the two. In this way, the civil religion was able to build up without any bitter struggle with the church powerful symbols of national solidarity and to mobilize deep levels of personal motivation for the attainment of national goals.

Such an achievement is by no means to be taken for granted. It would seem that the problem of a civil religion is quite general in modern societies and that the way it is solved or not solved will have repercussions in many spheres. One needs only to think of France to see how differently things can go. The French Revolution was anticlerical to the core and attempted to set up an anti-Christian civil religion. Throughout modern French history, the chasm between traditional Catholic symbols and the symbolism of 1789 has been immense. . . .

The civil religion has not always been invoked in favor of worthy causes. On the domestic scene, an American-Legion type of ideology that fuses God, country, and flag has been used to attack nonconformist and liberal ideas and groups of all kinds. Still, it has been difficult to use the words of Jefferson and Lincoln to support special interests and undermine personal freedom. The defenders of slavery before the Civil War came to reject the thinking of the Declaration of Independence. Some of the most consistent of them turned against not only Jeffersonian democracy but Reformation religion; they dreamed of a South dominated by medieval chivalry and divine-right monarchy.[10] For all the overt religiosity of the radical right today, their relation to the civil religious consensus is tenuous, as when the John Birch Society attacks the central American symbol of Democracy itself.

With respect to America's role in the world, the dangers of distortion are greater and the built-in safe guards of the tradition weaker. The theme of the American Israel was used, almost from the beginning, as a justification for the shameful treatment of the Indians so characteristic of our history. It can be overtly or implicitly linked to the idea of manifest destiny which has been used to legitimate several adventures in imperialism since the early-nineteenth century. Never has the danger been greater than today. The issue is not so much one of imperial expansion, of which we are accused, as of the tendency to assimilate all governments or parties in the world which support our immediate policies or call upon our help by invoking the notion of free institutions and democratic values. Those nations that are for the moment "on our side" become "the free world." A repressive and unstable military dictatorship in South Viet Nam becomes "the free people of South Viet Nam and their government." It is then part of the role of America as the New Jerusalem and "the last best hope on earth" to defend such governments with treasure and eventually with blood. When our soldiers are actually dying, it becomes possible to consecrate the struggle further by invoking the great theme of sacrifice. . . .

THE THIRD TIME OF TRIAL

In conclusion it may be worthwhile to relate the civil religion to the most serious situation that we as Americans now face, what I call the third time of trial. The first time of trial had to do with the question of independence, where we should or could run our own affairs in our own way. The second time of trial was over the issue of slavery, which in turn was only the most salient aspect of the more general problem of the full institutionalization of democracy within our country. This second problem we are still far from solving though we have some notable successes to our credit. But we have been overtaken by a third great problem which has led to a third great crisis, in the midst of which we stand. This is the problem of responsible action in a revolutionary world, a world seeking to attain many of the things, material and spiritual, that we have already attained. . . .

Out of the first and second times of trial have come, as we have seen, the major symbols of the American civil religion. There seems little doubt that a successful negotiation of this third time of trial—the attainment of some kind of viable and coherent world order—would precipitate a major new set of symbolic forms. So far the flickering flame of the United Nations burns too low to be the focus of a cult, but the emergence of a genuine transnational sovereignty would certainly change this. It would necessitate the incorporation of vital international symbolism into our civil religion, or, perhaps a better way of putting it, it would result in American civil religion becoming simply one part of a new civil religion of the world. . . .

Behind the civil religion at every point lie Biblical archetypes: Exodus, Chosen People, Promised Land, New Jerusalem, Sacrificial Death and Rebirth. But it is also genuinely American and genuinely new. It has its own prophets and its own martyrs, its own sacred events and sacred places, its own solemn rituals and symbols. It is concerned that America be a society as perfectly in accord with the will of God as men can make it, and a light to all the nations.

It has often been used and is being used today as a cloak for petty interests and ugly passions. It is in need—as is any living faith—of continual reformation, of being measured by universal standards. But it is not evident that it is incapable of growth and new insight.

It does not make any decision for us. It does not remove us from moral ambiguity, from being, in Lincoln's fine phrase, an "almost chosen people." But it is a heritage of moral and religious experience from which we still have much to learn as we formulate the decisions that lie ahead.

---

[1] Why something so obvious should have escaped serious analytical attention is in itself an interesting problem. Part of the reason is probably the controversial nature of the subject. From the earliest years of the nineteenth century, conservative religious and political groups have argued that Christianity is, in fact, the national religion. Some of them have from time to time and as recently as the 1950's proposed constitutional amendments that would explicitly recognize the sovereignty of Christ. In defending the doctrine of separation of church and state, opponents of such groups have denied that the national policy has, intrinsically, anything to do with religion at all. The moderates on this issue have insisted that the American state has taken a permissive and indeed supportive attitude toward religious groups (tax exemption, et cetera), thus favoring religion but still missing the positive institutionalization with which I am concerned. But part of the reason this issue has been left in obscurity is certainly due to the peculiarly Western concept of "religion" as denoting a single type of collectivity of which an individual can be a member of one and only one at a time. The Durkeimian notion that every group has a religious dimension, which would be seen as obvious in southern or eastern Asia, is foreign to us. This obscures the recognition of such dimensions in our society.

[2] God is mentioned or referred to in all inaugural addresses but Washington's second, which is a very brief (two paragraphs) and perfunctory acknowledgment. It is not without interest that the actual word **God** does not appear until Monroe's second inaugural, 5 March 1821. In his first inaugural, Washington refers to God as "that Almighty Being who rules the universe," "Great Author of every public and private good," "Invisible Hand," and "benign Parent of the Human Race." John Adams refers to God as "Providence," "Being who is supreme over all," "Patron of Order," "Foundation of Justice," and "Protector in all ages of the world of virtuous liberty." Jefferson speaks of "that Infinite Power which rules the destinies of the universe," and "that Being in whose hands we are." Madison speaks of "that

Almighty Being whose power regulates the destiny of nations," and "Heaven." Monroe uses "Providence" and "the Almighty" in his first inaugural and finally "Almighty God" in his second. See **Inaugural Addresses of the Presidents of the United States from George Washington 1789 to Harry S. Truman 1949,** 82nd Congress, 2d Session, House Document No. 540, 1952.

[3] For example, Abiel Abbot, pastor of the First Church in Haverhill, Massachusetts, delivered a Thanksgiving sermon in 1790, **Traits of Resemblance in the People of the United States of America to Ancient Israel,** in which he said, "It has been often remarked that the people of the United States come nearer to a parallel with Ancient Israel, than any other nation upon the globe. Hence 'Our American Israel' is a term frequently used; and common consent allows it apt and proper." Cited in Hans Kohn, **The Idea of Nationalism** (New York, 1961), p. 665.

[4] That the Mosaic analogy was present in the minds of leaders at the very moment of the birth of the republic is indicated in the designs proposed by Franklin and Jefferson for a seal of the United States of America. Together with Adams, they formed a committee of three delegated by the Continental Congress on July 4, 1776, to draw up the new device. "Franklin proposed as the device Moses lifting up his wand and dividing the Red Sea while Pharaoh was overwhelmed by its waters, with the motto 'Rebellion to tyrants is obedience to God.' Jefferson proposed the children of Israel in the wilderness 'led by a cloud by day and a pillar of fire at night.'" Anson Phelps Stokes, **Church and State in the United States,** Vol. 1 (New York, 1950), pp. 467–468.

[5] Sidney Mead, **The Lively Experiment** (New York, 1963), p. 12.

[6] Allan Nevins (ed.), **Lincoln and the Gettysburg Address** (Urbana, Ill., 1964) pp. 88–89.

[7] Quoted in Sherwood Eddy, **The Kingdom of God and the American Dream** (New York, 1941), p. 162.

[8] Karl Decker and Angus McSween, **Historic Arlington** (Washington, D.C., 1892), pp. 60–67.

[9] How extensive the activity associated with Memorial Day can be is indicated by Warner: "The sacred symbolic behavior of Memorial Day, in which scores of the town's organizations are involved, is ordinarily divided into four periods. During the year separate rituals are held by many of the associations for their dead, and many of these activities are connected with later Memorial Day events. In the second phase, preparations are made during the last three or four weeks for the ceremony itself, and some of the associations perform public rituals. The third phase consists of scores of rituals held in all the cemeteries, churches, and halls of the associations. These rituals consist of speeches and highly ritualized behavior. They last for two days and are climaxed by the fourth and last phase, in which all the separate celebrants gather in the center of the business district on the afternoon of Memorial Day. The separate organizations, with their members in uniform or with fitting insignia, march through the town, visit the shrines and monuments of the hero dead, and, finally enter the cemetary. Here dozens of ceremonies are held, most of them highly symbolic and formalized." During these various ceremonies Lincoln is continually referred to and the Gettysburg Address recited many times. W. Lloyd Warner, **American Life** (Chicago, 1962), pp. 8–9.

[10] See Louis Hartz, "The Feudal Dream of the South," Part 4, **The Liberal Tradition in America** (New York, 1955).

The Declaration of Independence

In Congress, July 4, 1776. The unanimous Declaration of the thirteen united States of America.

When in the Course of human events, it becomes necessary for one people to dissolve the political bands which have connected them with another, and to assume among the powers of the earth, the separate and equal station to which the Laws of Nature and of Nature's God entitle them, a decent respect to the opinions of mankind requires that they should declare the causes which impel them to the separation.—

We hold these truths to be self-evident, that all men are created equal, that they are endowed by their Creator with certain unalienable Rights, that among these are Life, Liberty and the pursuit of Happiness.—

That to secure these rights, Governments are instituted among Men, deriving their just powers from the consent of the governed,—

That whenever any Form of Government becomes destructive of these ends it is the Right of the People to alter or to abolish it, and to institute new Government, laying its foundation on such principles and organizing its powers in such form, as to them shall seem most likely to effect their Safety and Happiness. Prudence, indeed, will dictate that Governments long established should not be changed for light and transient causes; and accordingly all experience hath shown, that mankind are more disposed to suffer, while evils are sufferable, than to right themselves by abolishing the forms to which they are accustomed. But when a long train of abuses and usurpations, pursuing invariably the same Object evinces a design to reduce them under absolute Despotism, it is their right, it is their duty, to throw off such Government, and to provide new Guards for their future security.—

Such has been the patient sufferance of these Colonies; and such is now the necessity which constrains them to alter their former Systems of Government. The history of the present King of Great Britain is a history of repeated injuries and usurpations, all having in direct object the establishment of an absolute Tyranny over these States. To prove this, let Facts be submitted to a candid world.—

He has refused his Assent to Laws, the most wholesome and necessary for the public good.—

He has forbidden his Governors to pass Laws of immediate and pressing importance, unless suspended in their operation till his Assent should be obtained; and when so suspended, he has utterly neglected to attend to them.—

He has refused to pass other Laws for the accommodation of large districts of people, unless those people would relinquish the right of Representation in the Legislature, a right inestimable to them and formidable to tyrants only.—

He had called together legislative bodies at places unusual, uncomfortable, and distant from the depository of their public Records, for the sole purpose of fatiguing them into compliance with his measures.—

He has dissolved Representative Houses repeatedly, for opposing with manly firmness his invasions on the rights of the people.—

He has refused for a long time, after such dissolutions, to cause others to be elected; whereby the Legislative powers, incapable of Annihilation, have returned to the People at large for their exercise; the State remaining in the mean time exposed to all the dangers of invasion from without, and convulsions within.—

He had endeavoured to prevent the population of these States; for that purpose obstructing the Laws for Naturalization of Foreigners; refusing to pass others to encourage their migrations hither, and raising the conditions of new Appropriations of Lands.—

He has obstructed the Administration of Justice, by refusing his Assent to Laws for establishing Judiciary powers.—

He has made Judges dependent on his Will alone, for the tenure of their offices, and the amount and payment of their salaries.—

He has erected a multitude of New Offices, and sent hither swarms of Officers to harrass our people, and eat out their substance.—

He has kept among us in times of peace, Standing Armies without the Consent of our legislatures.—

He has affected to render the Military independent of and superior to the Civil power.—

He has combined with others to subject us to a jurisdiction foreign to our constitution, and unacknowledged by our laws; giving his Assent to their Acts of pretended Legislation:—

For quartering large bodies of armed troops among us:—

For protecting them, by a mock Trial, from punishment for any Murders which they should commit on the Inhabitants of these States:—

For cutting off our Trade with all parts of the world:—

For imposing Taxes on us without our Consent:—

For depriving us in many cases, of the benefits of Trial by Jury:—

For transporting us beyond Seas to be tried for pretended offences:—

For abolishing the free System of English Laws in a neighbouring Province, establishing therein an Arbitary government, and enlarging its Boundaries so as to render it at once an example and fit instrument for introducing the same absolute rule in these Colonies:—

For taking away our Charters, abolishing our most valuable Laws, and altering fundamentally the Forms of our Governments:—

For suspending our own Legislatures, and declaring themselves invested with power to legislate for us in all cases whatsoever.—

He has abdicated Government here, by declaring us out of his Protection and waging War against us.—

He has plundered our seas, ravaged our Coasts, burnt our towns, and destroyed the lives of our people.—

He is at this time transporting large Armies of foreign Mercenaries to compleat the works of death, desolation and tyranny, already begun with circumstances of Cruelty & perfidy scarcely paralleled in the most barbarous ages, and totally unworthy the Head of a civilized nation.—

He has constrained our fellow Citizens taken Captive on the high Seas to bear Arms against their Country, to become the executioners of their friends and Brethren, or to fall themselves by their Hands.—

He has exicted domestic insurrections amongst us, and has endeavoured to bring on the inhabitants of our frontiers, the merciless Indian Savages, whose known rule of warfare, is an undistinguished destruction of all ages, sexes and conditions.

In every stage of these Oppressions We have Petitioned for Redress in the most humble terms: Our repeated Petitions have been answered only by repeated injury. A Prince, whose character is thus marked by every act which may define a Tyrant, is unfit to be the ruler of a free people.

Nor have We been wanting in attentions to our British brethren. We have warned them from time to time of attempts by their legislature to extend an unwarrantable jurisdiction over us. We have reminded them of the circumstances of our emigration and settlement here. We have appealed to their native justice and magnanimity, and we have conjured them by the ties of our common kindred to disavow these usurpations, which, would inevitably interrupt our connections and correspondence. They too have been deaf to the voice of justice and of consanguinity. We must, therefore, acquiesce in the necessity, which denounces our Separation, and hold them, as we hold the rest of mankind, Enemies in War, in Peace Friends.—

We, therefore, the Representatives of the united States of America, in General Congresss, Assembled, appealing to the Supreme Judge of the world for the rectitude of our intentions, do, in the Name, and by Authority of the good People of these Colonies, solemnly publish and declare, That these United Colonies are, and of Right ought to be, Free and Independent States; that they are Absolved from all Allegiance to the British Crown, and that all political connection between them and the State of Great Britain, is and ought to be totally dissolved; and that as Free and Independent States, they have full Power to levy War, conclude Peace, contract Alliances, establish Commerce, and to do all other Acts and Things which Independent States may of right do.—

And for the support of this Declaration, with a firm reliance on the protection of divine Providence, we mutually pledge to each other our Lives, our Fortunes and our sacred Honor.

The Constitution of the United States

PREAMBLE

We the People of the United States, in Order to form a more perfect Union, establish Justice, insure domestic Tranquility, provide for the common defence, promote the general Welfare, and secure the Blessings of Liberty to ourselves and our Posterity, do ordain and establish this Constitution for the United States of America.

ARTICLE I

SECTION 1. All legislative Powers herein granted shall be vested in a Congress of the United States, which shall consist of a Senate and House of Representatives.

SECTION 2. The House of Representatives shall be composed of Members chosen every second Year by the People of the several States, and the Electors in each State shall have the Qualifications requisite for Electors of the most numerous Branch of the State Legislature.

No Person shall be a Representative who shall not have attained to the age of twenty five Years, and been seven Years a Citizen of the United States, and who shall not, when elected, be an Inhabitant of that State in which he shall be chosen.

Representatives and direct Taxes shall be apportioned among the several States which may be included within this Union, according to their respective Numbers, which shall be determined by adding to the whole Number of free Persons, including those bound to Service for a Term of Years, and excluding Indians not taxed, three fifths of all other Persons. The actual Enumeration shall be made within three Years after the first Meeting of the Congress of the United States, and within every subsequent Term of ten Years, in such Manner as they shall by Law direct. The Number of Representatives shall not exceed one for every thirty Thousand, but each State shall have at Least one Representative; and until such enumeration shall be made, the State of New Hampshire shall be entitled to chuse three, Massachusetts eight, Rhode-Island and Providence Plantations one, Connecticut five, New York six, New Jersey four, Pennsylvania eight, Delaware one, Maryland six, Virginia ten, North Carolina five, South Carolina five, and Georgia three.

When vacancies happen in the Representation from any State, the Executive Authority thereof shall issue Writs of Election to fill such Vacancies.

The House of Representatives shall chuse their Speaker and other Officers; and shall have the sole Power of Impeachment.

SECTION 3. The Senate of the United States shall be composed of two Senators from each State, chosen by the Legislature thereof, for six Years; and each Senator shall have one Vote.

Immediately after they shall be assembled in Consequence of the first Election, they shall be divided as equally as may be into three Classes. The seats of the Senators of the first Class shall be vacated at the Expiration of the second Year, of the second Class at the Expiration of the Fourth Year, and of the third Class at the Expiration of the sixth Year, so that one third may be chosen every second Year; and if Vacancies happen by Resignation, or otherwise, during the Recess of the Legislature of any State, the Executive thereof may make temporary Appointments until the next Meeting of the Legislature, which shall then fill such Vacancies.

No Person shall be a Senator who shall not have attained to the Age of thirty Years, and been nine Years a Citizen of the United States, and who shall not, when elected, be an Inhabitant of that State for which he shall be chosen.

The Vice President of the United States shall be President of the Senate, but shall have no Vote, unless they be equally divided.

The Senate shall chuse their other Officers, and also a President pro tempore, in the Absence of the Vice President, or when he shall exercise the Office of President of the United States.

The Senate shall have the sole Power to try all Impeachments. When sitting for that Purpose, they shall be on Oath or Affirmation. When the President of the

United States is tried the Chief Justice shall preside: And no Person shall be convicted without the Concurrence of two thirds of the Members present.

Judgment in Cases of Impeachment shall not extend further than to removal from Office, and disqualification to hold and enjoy any Office of honor, Trust or Profit under the United States: but the Party convicted shall nevertheless be liable and subject to Indictment, Trial, Judgment and Punishment, according to Law.

SECTION 4. The Times, Places and Manner of holding Elections for Senators and Representatives, shall be prescribed in each State by the Legislature thereof; but the Congress may at any time by Law make or alter such Regulations, except as to the Places of chusing Senators.

The Congress shall assemble at least once in every Year, and such Meeting shall be on the first Monday in December unless they shall by Law appoint a different Day.

SECTION 5. Each House shall be the Judge of the Elections, Returns and Qualifications of its own Members, and a Majority of each shall constitute a Quorum to do Business; but a smaller Number may adjourn from day to day, and may be authorized to compel the Attendance of absent Members, in such Manner, and under such Penalties as each House may provide.

Each House may determine the Rules of its Proceedings, punish its Members for disorderly Behaviour, and, with the Concurrence of two thirds, expel a Member.

Each House shall keep a Journal of its Proceedings, and from time to time publish the same, excepting such Parts as may in their Judgment require Secrecy; and the Yeas and Nays of the Members of either House on any question shall, at the Desire of one fifth of those Present, be entered on the Journal.

Neither House, during the Session of Congress, shall, without the Consent of the other, adjourn for more than three days, nor to any other Place than that in which the two Houses shall be sitting.

SECTION 6. The Senators and Representatives shall receive a Compensation for their Services, to be ascertained by Law, and paid out of the Treasury of the United States. They shall in all Cases, except Treason, Felony and Breach of the Peace, be privileged from Arrest during their Attendance at the Session of their respective Houses, and in going to and returning from the same; and for any Speech or Debate in either House, they shall not be questioned in any other Place.

No Senator or Representative shall, during the Time for which he was elected, be appointed to any civil Office under the Authority of the United States, which shall have been created, or the Emoluments whereof shall have been encreased during such time; and no Person holding any Office under the United States, shall be a Member of either House during his Continuance in Office.

SECTION 7. All Bills for raising Revenue shall originate in the House of Representatives; but the Senate may propose or concur with amendments as on other Bills.

Every Bill which shall have passed the House of Representatives and the Senate, shall, before it becomes a Law, be presented to the President of the United States; If he approve he shall sign it, but if not he shall return it, with his Objections to that House in which it shall have originated, who shall enter the Objections at large on their Journal, and proceed to reconsider it. If after such Reconsideration two thirds of that House shall agree to pass the Bill, it shall be sent, together with the Objections, to the other House, by which it shall likewise be reconsidered, and if approved by two thirds of that House, it shall become a Law. But in all such Cases the Votes of both Houses shall be determined by Yeas and Nays, and the Names of the Persons voting for and against the Bill shall be entered on the Journal of each House respectively. If any Bill shall not be returned by the President within ten Days (Sunday excepted) after it shall have been presented to him, the Same shall be a Law, in like Manner as if he had signed it, unless the Congress by their Adjournment prevent its Return, in which Case it shall not be a Law.

Every Order, Resolution, or Vote to which the Concurrence of the Senate and House of Representatives may be necessary (except on a question of Adjournment) shall be presented to the President of the United States; and before the Same shall take Effect, shall be approved by him, or being disapproved by him, shall be repassed by two thirds of the Senate and House of Representatives, according to the Rules and Limitations prescribed in the Case of a Bill.

SECTION 8. The Congress shall have Power To lay and collect Taxes, Duties, Imposts and Excises, to pay the Debts and provide for the common Defence and general Welfare of the United States; but all Duties, Imposts and Excises shall be uniform throughout the United States;

To borrow Money on the credit of the United States;

To regulate Commerce with foreign Nations, and among the several States, and with the Indian Tribes;

To establish an uniform Rule of Naturalization, and uniform Laws on the subject of Bankruptcies throughout the United States;

To coin Money, regulate the Value thereof, and of foreign Coin, and fix the Standard of Weights and Measures;

To provide for the Punishment of counterfeiting the Securities and current Coin of the United States;

To establish Post Offices and post Roads;

To promote the Progress of Science and useful Arts, by securing for limited Times to Authors and Inventors the exclusive Right to their respective Writings and Discoveries;

To constitute Tribunals inferior to the supreme Court;

To define and punish Piracies and Felonies commited on the high Seas, and Offences against the Law of Nations;

To declare War, grant letters of Marque and Reprisal, and make Rules concerning Captures on Land and Water;

To raise and support Armies, but no Appropriation of Money to that Use shall be for a longer Term than two Years;

To provide and maintain a Navy;

To make Rules for the Government and Regulation of the land and naval Forces;

To provide for calling forth the Militia to execute the Laws of the Union, suppress Insurrections and repel Invasions;

To provide for organizing, arming, and disciplining the Militia, and for governing such Part of them as may be employed in the Service of the United States, reserving to the States respectively, the Appointment of the Officers, and the Authority of training the Militia according to the discipline prescribed by Congress;

To exercise exclusive Legislation in all Cases whatsoever, over such District (not exceeding ten Miles square) as may, by Cession of Particular States, and the Acceptance of Congress, become the Seat of the Government of the United States, and to exercise like Authority over all Places purchased by the Consent of the Legislature of the State in which the Same shall be, for the Erection of Forts, Magazines, Arsenals, dock-Yards, and other needful Buildings;—
And

To make all Laws which shall be necessary and proper for carrying into Execution the foregoing Powers, and all other Powers vested by this Constitution in the Government of the United States, or in any Department or Officer thereof.

SECTION 9. The Migration or Importation of such Persons as any of the States now existing shall think proper to admit, shall not be prohibited by the Congress prior to the Year one thousand eight hundred and eight, but a Tax or duty may be imposed on such Importation, not exceeding ten dollars for each Person.

The Privilege of the Writ of Habeas Corpus shall not be suspended, unless when in Cases of Rebellion or Invasion the public Safety may require it.

No Bill of Attainder or ex post facto Law shall be passed.

No capitation, or other direct, Tax shall be laid, unless in Proportion to the Census of Enumeration herein before directed to be taken.

No Tax or Duty shall be laid on Articles exported from any State.

No Preference shall be given by any Regulation of Commerce or Revenue to the Ports of one State over those of another; nor shall Vessels bound to, or from, one State, be obliged to enter, clear or pay Duties in another.

No Money shall be drawn from the Treasury, but in Consequence of Appropriations made by Law; and a regular Statement and Account of the Receipts and Expenditures of all public Money shall be published from time to time.

No Title of Nobility shall be granted by the United States: And no Person holding any Office of Profit or Trust under them, without the Consent of the Congress, accept of any present, Emolument, Office, or Title, of any kind whatever, from any King, Prince, or foreign State.

SECTION 10. No State shall enter into any Treaty, Alliance, or Confederation; grant Letters of Marque and Reprisal; coin Money; emit Bills of Credit; make any Thing but gold and silver Coin a Tender in Payment of Debts; pass any Bill of Attainder, ex post facto Law, or Law impairing the Obligation of Contracts, or grant any Title of Nobility.

No State shall, without the Consent of the Congress, lay any Imposts or Duties on Imports or Exports, except what may be absolutely necessary for executing it's inspection Laws: and the net Produce of all Duties and Imposts, laid by any State on Imports or Exports, shall be for the Use of the Treasury of the United States; and all such Laws shall be subject to the Revision and Controul of the Congress.

No State shall, without the consent of Congress, lay any Duty of Tonnage, keep Troops, or Ships of War in time of Peace, enter into any Agreement or Compact with another State, or with a foreign Power, or engage in War, unless actually invaded, or in such imminent Danger as will not admit of delay.

ARTICLE II

SECTION 1. The executive Power shall be vested in a President of the United States of America. He shall hold his Office during the Term of four Years, and together with the Vice President, chosen for the same Term, be elected, as follows.

Each State shall appoint, in such Manner as the Legislature thereof may direct, a Number of Electors, equal to the whole Number of Senators and Representatives to which the State may be entitled in the Congress: but no Senator or Representative, or Person holding an Office of Trust or Profit under the United States, shall be appointed an Elector.

The Electors shall meet in their respective States, and vote by Ballot for two Persons, of whom one at least shall not be an Inhabitant of the same State with themselves. And they shall make a List of all the Persons voted for, and of the Number of Votes for each; which List they shall sign and certify, and transmit sealed to the Seat of the Government of the United States, directed to the President of the Senate. The President of the Senate shall, in the Presence of the Senate and House of Representatives, open all the Certificates, and the Votes shall then be counted. The Person having the greatest Number of Votes shall be the President, if such Number be a Majority of the whole Number of Electors appointed; and if there be more than one who have such Majority, and have an equal Number of Votes, then the House of Representatives shall immediately chuse by Ballot one of them for President; and if no Person have a Majority, then from the five highest on the list the said House shall in like Manner chuse the President. But in chusing the President, the Votes shall be taken by States, the Representation from each State having one Vote; a quorum for this Purpose shall consist of a Member or Members from two thirds of the States, and a Majority of all the States shall be necessary to a Choice. In every Case, after the Choice of the President, the Person having the greatest Number of Votes of the Electors shall be the Vice President. But if there should remain two or more who have equal Votes, the Senate shall chuse from them by Ballot the Vice President.

The Congress may determine the Time of chusing the Electors, and the Day on which they shall give their Votes; which Day shall be the same throughout the United States.

No Person except a natural born Citizen, or a Citizen of the United States, at the time of the Adoption of this Constitution, shall be eligible to the Office of President; neither shall any Person be eligible to that Office who shall not have attained to the Age of thirty five Years, and been fourteen Years a Resident within the United States.

In Case of the Removal of the President from Office, or of his Death, Resignation, or Inability to discharge the Powers and Duties of the said Office, the Same shall devolve on the Vice President, and the Congress may by Law provide for the

Case of Removal, Death, Resignation or Inability, both of the President and Vice President, declaring what Officer shall then act as President, and such Officer shall act accordingly, until the Disability be removed, or a President shall be elected.

The President shall, at stated Times, receive for his Services, a Compensation, which shall neither be encreased nor diminished during the Period for which he shall have been elected, and he shall not receive within that Period any other Emolument from the United States, or any of them.

Before he enter on the Execution of his Office, he shall take the following Oath or Affirmation—"I do solemnly swear (or affirm) that I will faithfully execute the Office of President of the United States, and will to the best of my Ability, preserve, protect and defend the Constitution of the United States."

SECTION 2. The President shall be Commander in Chief of the Army and Navy of the United States, and of the Militia of the several States, when called into the actual Service of the United States; he may require the Opinion, in writing, of the principal Officer in each of the executive Departments, upon any Subject relating to the Duties of their respective Offices, and he shall have Power to grant Reprieves and Pardons for Offenses against the United States, except in Cases of Impeachment.

He shall have Power, by and with the Advice and Consent of the Senate, to make Treaties, provided two thirds of the Senators present concur; and he shall nominate, and by and with the Advice and Consent of the Senate, shall appoint Ambassadors, other public Ministers and Consuls, Judges of the supreme Court, and all other Officers of the United States, whose Appointments are not herein otherwise provided for, and which shall be established by Law: but the Congress may by Law vest the Appointment of such inferior Officers, as they think proper, in the President alone, in the Courts of Law, or in the Heads of Departments.

The President shall have Power to fill up all Vacancies that may happen during the Recess of the Senate, by granting Commissions which shall expire at the End of their next Session.

SECTION 3. He shall from time to time give to the Congress Information of the State of the Union, and recommend to their Consideration such Measures as he shall judge necessary and expedient; he may, on extraordinary Occasions, convene both Houses, or either of them, and in Case of Disagreement between them, with Respect to the Time of Adjournment, he may adjourn them to such Time as he shall think proper; he shall receive Ambassadors and other public Ministers; he shall take Care that the Laws be faithfully executed, and shall Commission all the Officers of the United States.

SECTION 4. The President, Vice President and all Civil Officers of the United States, shall be removed from office on Impeachment for, and Conviction of, Treason, Bribery, or other high Crimes and Misdemeanors.

ARTICLE III

SECTION 1. The judicial Power of the United States, shall be vested in one supreme Court, and in such inferior Courts as the Congress may from time to time ordain and establish. The Judges, both of the supreme and inferior Courts, shall hold their Offices during good Behaviour, and shall, at stated Times, receive for their Services, a Compensation, which shall not be diminished during their Continuance in Office.

Section 2. The judicial Power shall extend to all Cases, in Law and Equity, arising under this Constitution, the Laws of the United States, and Treaties made, or which shall be made, under their Authority; to all Cases affecting Ambassadors, other public Ministers and Consuls;—to all Cases of admiralty and maritime Jurisdiction;—to Controversies to which the United States shall be a Party;—to Controversies between two or more States;—between a State and Citizens of another State;—between Citizens of Different States;—beween Citizens of the same State claiming Lands under Grants of different States, and between a State, or the Citizens thereof, and foreign States, Citizens or Subjects.

In all Cases affecting Ambassadors, other public Ministers and Consuls, and those in which a State shall be Party, the supreme Court shall have original Jurisdiction. In all the other Cases before mentioned, the supreme Court shall have appellate Jurisdiction, both as to Law and Fact, with such Exceptions, and under such Regulations as the Congress shall make.

The Trial of all Crimes, except in cases of Impeachment, shall be by Jury; and such Trial shall be held in the State where the said Crimes shall have been committed; but when not committed within any State, the Trial shall be at such Place or Places as the Congress may by Law have directed.

Section 3. Treason against the United States, shall consist only in levying War against them, or in adhering to their Enemies, giving them Aid and Comfort. No Person shall be convicted of Treason unless on the Testimony of two Witnesses to the same overt Act, or on Confession in open Court.

The Congress shall have Power to declare the Punishment of Treason, but no Attainder or Treason shall work Corruption of Blood, or Forfeiture except during the Life of the Person attainted.

Article IV

Section 1. Full Faith and Credit shall be given in each State to the public Acts, Records, and judicial Proceedings of every other State. And the Congress may by general Laws prescribe the Manner in which such Acts, Records and Proceedings shall be proved, and the Effect thereof.

Section 2. The Citizens of each State shall be entitled to all Privileges and Immunities of Citizens in the several States.

A Person charged in any State with Treason, Felony, or other Crime, who shall flee from Justice, and be found in another State, shall on Demand of the executive Authority of the State from which he fled, be delivered up, to be removed to the State having Jurisdiction of the Crime.

No Person held to Service or Labour in one State, under the Laws thereof, escaping into another, shall, in Consequence of any Law or Regulation therein, be discharged from such Service or Labour, but shall be delivered up on Claim of the Party to whom such Service or Labour may be due.

SECTION 3. New States may be admitted by the Congress into this Union; but no new State shall be formed or erected within the Jurisdiction of any other State; nor any State be formed by the Junction of two or more States, or Parts of States, without the Consent of the Legislatures of the States concerned as well as of the Congress.

The Congress shall have Power to dispose of and make all needful Rules and Regulations respecting the Territory or other Property belonging to the United States; and nothing in this Constitution shall be so construed as to Prejudice any Claims of the United States, or of any particular State.

SECTION 4. The United States shall guarantee to every State in this Union a Republican Form of Government, and shall protect each of them against Invasion; and on Application of the Legislature, or of the Executive (when the Legislature cannot be convened) against domestic Violence.

ARTICLE V

The Congress, whenever two thirds of both Houses shall deem it necessary, shall propose Amendments to this Constitution, or, on the Application of the Legislatures of two thirds of the several States, shall call a Convention for proposing Amendments, which, in either Case, shall be valid to all Intents and Purposes, as Part of this Constitution, when ratified by the Legislatures of three fourths of the several States, or by Conventions in three fourths thereof, as the one or the other Mode of Ratification may be proposed by the Congress; Provided [that no Amendment which may be made prior to the Year One thousand eight hundred and eight shall in any Manner affect the first and fourth Clauses in the Ninth Section of the first Article; and] that no State, without its Consent, shall be deprived of its equal Suffrage in the Senate.

ARTICLE VI

All Debts contracted and Engagements entered into, before the Adoption of this Constitution, shall be as valid against the United States under this Constitution, as under the Confederation.

This Constitution, and the Laws of the United States which shall be made in Pursuance thereof; and all Treaties made, or which shall be made, under the Authority of the United States, shall be the supreme Law of the Land; and the Judges in every State shall be bound thereby, any Thing in the Constitution or Laws of any State to the Contrary notwithstanding.

The Senators and Representatives before mentioned, and the Members of the several State Legislatures, and all executive and judicial Officers, both of the United States and of the several States, shall be bound by Oath or Affirmation, to support this Constitution; but no religious Test shall ever be required as a Qualification to any Office or public Trust under the United States.

ARTICLE VII

The Ratification of the Conventions of nine States, shall be sufficient for the Establishment of this Constitution between the States so ratifying the Same.

AMENDMENT I

[First ten amendments ratified December 15, 1791]

Congress shall make no law respecting an establishment of religion, or prohibiting the free exercise thereof; or abridging the freedom of speech, or of the press; or the right of the people peaceably to assemble, and to petition the Government for a redress of grievances.

AMENDMENT II

A well regulated Militia, being necessary to the security of a free State, the right of the people to keep and bear Arms, shall not be infringed.

AMENDMENT III

No Soldier shall, in time of peace be quartered in any house, without the consent of the Owner, nor in time of war, but in a manner to be prescribed by law.

AMENDMENT IV

The right of the people to be secure in their persons, houses, papers, and effects, against unreasonable searches and seizures, shall not be violated, and no Warrants shall issue, but upon probable cause, supported by Oath or affirmation, and particularly describing the place to be searched, and the persons or things to be seized.

AMENDMENT V

No person shall be held to answer for a capital, or otherwise infamous crime, unless on a presentment or indictment of a Grand Jury, except in cases arising in the land or naval forces, or in the Militia, when in actual service in time of War or public danger; nor shall any person be subject for the same offence to be twice put in jeopardy of life or limb; nor shall be compelled in any criminal case to be a witness against himself, nor be deprived of life, liberty, or property, without due process of law; nor shall private property be taken for public use, without just compensation.

AMENDMENT VI

In all criminal prosecutions, the accused shall enjoy the right to a speedy and public trial, by an impartial jury of the State and district wherein the crime shall have been committed, which district shall have been previously ascertained by law, and to be informed of the nature and cause of the accusation; to be confronted with the witnesses against him; to have compulsory process for obtaining witnesses in his favor, and to have the Assistance of Counsel for his defence.

AMENDMENT VII

In Suits at common law, where the value in controversy shall exceed twenty dollars, the right of trial by jury shall be preserved, and no fact tried by a jury, shall be otherwise re-examined in any Court of the United States, than according to the rules of the common law.

AMENDMENT VIII

Excessive bail shall not be required, nor excessive fines imposed, nor cruel and unusual punishments inflicted.

AMENDMENT IX

The enumeration in the Constitution, of certain rights, shall not be construed to deny or disparage others retained by the people.

AMENDMENT X

The powers not delegated to the United States by the Constitution, nor prohibited by it to the States, are reserved to the States respectively, or to the people.

AMENDMENT XI *[Ratified February 7, 1795]*

The Judicial power of the United States shall not be construed to extend to any suit in law or equity, commenced or prosecuted against one of the United States by Citizens of another State, or by Citizens or Subjects of any Foreign State.

AMENDMENT **XII** *[Ratified June 15, 1804]*

The Electors shall meet in their respective states and vote by ballot for President and Vice-President, one of whom, at least, shall not be an inhabitant of the same state with themselves; they shall name in their ballots the person voted for as President, and in distinct ballots the person voted for as Vice-President, and they shall make distinct lists of all persons voted for as President, and of all persons voted for as Vice-President, and of the number of votes for each, which lists they shall sign and certify, and transmit sealed to the seat of the government of the United States, directed to the President of the Senate;—The President of the Senate shall, in the presence of the Senate and House of Representatives, open all the certificates and the votes shall then be counted;—The person having the greatest number of votes for President, shall be the President, if such number be a majority of the whole number of Electors appointed; and if no person have such majority, then from the persons having the highest numbers not exceeding three on the list of those voted for as President, the House of Representatives shall choose immediately, by ballot, the President. But in choosing the President, the votes shall be taken by states, the representation from each state having one vote; a quorum for this purpose shall consist of a member or members from two-thirds of the states, and a majority of all the states shall be necessary to a choice. And if the House of Representatives shall not choose a President whenever the right of choice shall devolve upon them, before the fourth day of March next following, then the Vice-President shall act as President, as in the case of the death or other constitutional disability of the President;—The person having the greatest number of votes as Vice-President, shall be the Vice-President, if such number be a majority of the whole number of Electors appointed, and if no person have a majority, then from the two highest numbers on the list, the Senate shall choose the Vice-President; a quorum for the purpose shall consist of two-thirds of the whole number of Senators, and a majority of the whole number shall be necessary to a choice. But no person constitutionally ineligible to the office of President shall be eligible to that of Vice-President of the United States.

AMENDMENT **XIII** *[Ratified December 6, 1865]*

SECTION 1. Neither slavery nor involuntary servitude, except as a punishment for crime whereof the party shall have been duly convicted, shall exist within the United States, or any place subject to their jurisdiction.

SECTION 2. Congress shall have power to enforce this article by appropriate legislation.

AMENDMENT **XIV** *[Ratified July 9, 1868]*

SECTION 1. All persons born or naturalized in the United States and subject to the jurisdiction thereof, are citizens of the United States and of the State wherein they reside. No State shall make or enforce any law which shall abridge the privileges or immunities of citizens of the United States; nor shall any State deprive any person of life, liberty, or property, without due process of law; nor deny to any person within its jurisdiction the equal protection of the laws.

SECTION 2. Representatives shall be apportioned among the several States according to their respective numbers, counting the whole number of persons in each State, excluding Indians not taxed. But when the right to vote at any election for the choice of electors for President and Vice President of the United States, Representatives in Congress, the Executive and Judicial officers of a State, or the members of the Legislature thereof, is denied to any of the male inhabitants of such State, being twenty-one years of age, and citizens of the United States, or in any way abridged, except for participation in rebellion, or other crime, the basis of representation therein shall be reduced in the proportion which the number of such male citizens shall bear to the whole number of male citizens twenty-one years of age in such State.

SECTION 3. No person shall be a Senator or Representative in Congress, or elector of President and Vice President, or hold any office, civil or military, under the United States, or under any State, who, having previously taken an oath, as a member of Congress, or as an officer of the United States, or as a member of any State legislature, or as an executive or judicial officer of any State, to support the Constitution of the United States, shall have engaged in insurrection or rebellion against the same, or given aid or comfort to the enemies thereof. But Congress may by a vote of two-thirds of each House, remove such disability.

SECTION 4. The validity of the public debt of the United States, authorized by law, including debts incurred for payment of pensions and bounties for services in suppressing insurrection or rebellion, shall not be questioned. But neither the United States nor any State shall assume or pay any debt or obligation incurred in aid of insurrection or rebellion against the United States, or any claim for the loss or emancipation of any slave; but all such debts, obligations and claims shall be held illegal and void.

SECTION 5. The Congress shall have power to enforce, by appropriate legislation, the provisions of this article.

AMENDMENT XV *[Ratified February 3, 1870]*

SECTION 1. The right of citizens of the United States to vote shall not be denied or abridged by the United States or by any State on account of race, color, or previous condition of servitude.

SECTION 2. The Congress shall have power to enforce this article by appropriate legislation.

AMENDMENT XVI *[Ratified February 3, 1913]*

The Congress shall have power to lay and collect taxes on incomes, from whatever source derived, without apportionment among the several States, and without regard to any census or enumeration.

AMENDMENT **XVII** *[Ratified April 8, 1913]*

The Senate of the United States shall be composed of two Senators from each State, elected by the people thereof, for six years; and each Senator shall have one vote. The electors in each State shall have the qualifications requisite for electors of the most numerous branch of the State legislatures.

When vacancies happen in the representation of any State in the Senate, the executive authority of such State shall issue writs of election to fill such vacancies: *Provided,* That the legislature of any State may empower the executive thereof to make temporary appointments until the people fill the vacancies by election as the legislature may direct.

This amendment shall not be so construed as to affect the election or term of any Senator chosen before it becomes valid as part of the Constitution.

AMENDMENT **XVIII** *[Ratified January 16, 1919]*

SECTION 1. After one year from the ratification of this article the manufacture, sale, or transportation of intoxicating liquors within, the importation thereof into, or the exportation thereof from the United States and all territory subject to the jurisdiction thereof for beverage purposes is hereby prohibited.

SECTION 2. The Congress and the several States shall have concurrent power to enforce this article by appropriate legislation.

SECTION 3. This article shall be inoperative unless it shall have been ratified as an amendment to the Constitution by the legislatures of the several States, as provided in the Constitution, within seven years from the date of the submission hereof to the States by the Congress.

AMENDMENT **XIX** *[Ratified August 18, 1920]*

The right of citizens of the United States to vote shall not be denied or abridged by the United States or by any State on account of sex.

Congress shall have power to enforce this article by appropriate legislation.

AMENDMENT **XX** *[Ratified January 23, 1933]*

SECTION 1. The terms of the President and Vice President shall end at noon on the 20th day of January, and the terms of Senators and Representatives at noon on the 3d day of January, of the years in which such terms would have ended if this article had not been ratified; and the terms of their successors shall then begin.

SECTION 2. The Congress shall assemble at least once in every year, and such meeting shall begin at noon on the 3d day of January, unless they shall by law appoint a different day.

SECTION 3. If, at the time fixed for the beginning of the term of the President, the President elect shall have died, the Vice President elect shall become President. If a President shall not have been chosen before the time fixed for the beginning of his term, or if the President elect shall have failed to qualify, then the Vice President elect shall act as President until a President shall have qualified; and the Congress may by law provide for the case wherein neither a President elect nor a Vice President elect shall have qualified, declaring who shall then act as President, or the manner in which one who is to act shall be selected, and such person shall act accordingly until a President or Vice President shall have qualified.

SECTION 4. The Congress may by law provide for the case of the death of any of the persons from whom the House of Representatives may choose a President whenever the right of choice shall have devolved upon them, and for the case of the death of any of the persons from whom the Senate may choose a Vice President whenever the right of choice shall have devolved upon them.

SECTION 5. Sections 1 and 2 shall take effect on the 15th day of October following the ratification of this article.

SECTION 6. This article shall be inoperative unless it shall have been ratified as an amendment to the Constitution by the legislatures of three-fourths of the several States within seven years from the date of its submission.

AMENDMENT XXI *[Ratified December 5, 1933]*

SECTION 1. The eighteenth article of amendment to the Constitution of the United States is hereby repealed.

SECTION 2. The transportation or importation into any State, Territory or possession of the United States for delivery or use therein of intoxicating liquors, in violation of the laws thereof, is hereby prohibited.

SECTION 3. This article shall be inoperative unless it shall have been ratified as an amendment to the Constitution by conventions in the several States, as provided in the Constitution, within seven years from the date of the submission hereof to the States by the Congress.

AMENDMENT XXII *[Ratified February 27, 1951]*

SECTION 1. No person shall be elected to the office of the President more than twice, and no person who has held the office of President, or acted as President, for more than two years of a term to which some other person was elected President shall be elected to the office of the President more than once. But this Article shall not apply to any person holding the office of President when this Article was proposed by the Congress, and shall not prevent any person who may be holding the office of President, or acting as President, during the term within which this Article become operative from holding the office of President or acting as President during the remainder of such term.

SECTION 2. This Article shall be inoperative unless it shall have been ratified as an amendment to the Constitution by the legislatures of three-fourths of the several States within seven years from the date of its submission to the States by the Congress.

AMENDMENT XXIII *[Ratified March 29, 1961]*

SECTION 1. The District constituting the seat of Government of the United States shall appoint in such manner as the Congress may direct:

A number of electors of President and Vice President equal to the whole number of Senators and Representatives in Congress to which the District would be entitled if it were a State, but in no event more than the least populous State; they shall be in addition to those appointed by the States, but they shall be considered, for the purposes of the election of President and Vice President, to be electors appointed by a State; and they shall meet in the District and perform such duties as provided by the twelfth article of amendment.

SECTION 2. The Congress shall have power to enforce this article by appropriate legislation.

AMENDMENT XXIV *[Ratified January 23, 1964]*

SECTION 1. The right of citizens of the United States to vote in any primary or other election for President or Vice President, for electors for President or Vice President, or for Senator or Representative in Congress, shall not be denied or abridged by the United States or any State by reason of failure to pay any poll tax or other tax.

SECTION 2. The Congress shall have power to enforce this article by appropriate legislation.

AMENDMENT XXV *[Ratified February 10, 1967]*

SECTION 1. In case of the removal of the President from office or of his death or resignation, the Vice President shall become President.

SECTION 2. Whenever there is a vacancy in the office of the Vice President, the President shall nominate a Vice President who shall take office upon confirmation by a majority vote of both Houses of Congress.

SECTION 3. Whenever the President transmits to the President pro tempore of the Senate and the Speaker of the House of Representatives his written declaration that he is unable to discharge the powers and duties of his office, and until he transmits to them a written declaration to the contrary, such powers and duties shall be discharged by the Vice President as Acting President.

SECTION 4. Whenever the Vice President and a majority of either the principal officers of the executive departments or of such other body as Congress may by law provide, transmit to the President pro tempore of the Senate and the Speaker of the House of Representatives their written declaration that the President is unable to discharge the powers and duties of his office, the Vice President shall immediately assume the powers and duties of the office as Acting President.

Thereafter, when the President transmits to the President pro tempore of the Senate and the Speaker of the House of Representatives his written declaration that no inability exists, he shall resume the powers and duties of his office unless the Vice President and a majority of either the principal officers of the executive department or of such other body as Congress may by law provide, transmit within four days to the President pro tempore of the Senate and Speaker of the House of Representatives their written declaration that the President is unable to discharge the powers and duties of his office. Thereupon Congress shall decide the issue, assembling within forty-eight hours for that purpose if not in session. If the Congress, within twenty-one days after receipt of the latter written declaration, or, if Congress is not in session, within twenty-one days after Congress is required to assemble, determines by two-thirds vote of both houses that the President is unable to discharge the powers and duties of his office, the Vice President shall continue to discharge the same as Acting President; otherwise, the President shall resume the powers and duties of his office.

AMENDMENT XXVI [Ratified July 1, 1971]

SECTION 1. The right of citizens of the United States, who are eighteen years of age or older, to vote shall not be denied or abridged by the United States or by any State on account of age.

SECTION 2. The Congress shall have power to enforce this article by appropriate legislation.

Two Versions of the Gettysburg Address

VERSION 2

Four score and seven years ago our fathers brought forth, upon this continent, a new nation, conceived in Liberty, and dedicated to the proposition that all men are created equal.

Lincoln wrote five different versions of his famous Gettysburg Address. He held the second version in his hand while he spoke at Gettysburg. The fifth version perhaps represents as exactly as can be known the speech he gave.

Now we are engaged in a great civil war, testing whether that nation, or any nation, so conceived, and so dedicated, can long endure. We are met here on a great battle-field of that war. We have come to dedicate a portion of it as a final resting place for those who here gave their lives that that nation might live. It is altogether fitting and proper that we should do this.

But in a larger sense we can not dedicate—we can not consecrate—we can not hallow this ground. The brave men, living and dead, who struggled here, have consecrated it far above our poor power to add or detract. The world will little note, nor long remember, what we say here, but can never forget what they did here. It is for us, the living, rather to be dedicated here to the unfinished work which they have, thus far, so nobly carried on. It is rather for us to be here dedicated to the great task remaining before us—that from these honored dead we take increased devotion to that cause for which they here gave the last full measure of devotion—that we here highly resolve that these dead shall not have died in vain; that this nation shall have a new birth of freedom; and that this government of the people, by the people, for the people, shall not perish from the earth.

VERSION 5

Four score and seven years ago our fathers brought forth on this continent, a new nation, conceived in Liberty, and dedicated to the proposition that all men are created equal.

Now we are engaged in a great civil war, testing whether that nation, or any nation so conceived and so dedicated, can long endure. We are met on a great battlefield of that war. We have come to dedicate a portion of that field, as a final resting place for those who here gave their lives that that nation might live. It is altogether fitting and proper that we should do this.

But, in a larger sense, we can not dedicate—we can not consecrate—we can not hallow—this ground. The brave men, living and dead, who struggled here, have consecrated it, far above our poor power to add or detract. The world will little note, nor long remember what we say here, but it can never forget what they did here. It is for us the living, rather, to be dedicated here to the unfinished work which they who fought here have thus far so nobly advanced. It is rather for us to be here dedicated to the great task remaining before us—that from these honored dead we take increased devotion to that cause for which they gave the last full measure of devotion—that we here highly resolve that these dead shall not have died in vain—that this nation, under God, shall have a new birth of freedom—and that government of the people, by the people, for the people, shall not perish from the earth.

The Ethics of Living Jim Crow
Richard Wright

AN AUTOBIOGRAPHICAL SKETCH

I

My first lesson in how to live as a Negro came when I was quite small. We were living in Arkansas. Our house stood behind the railroad tracks. Its skimpy yard was paved with black cinders. Nothing green ever grew in that yard. The only touch of green we could see was far away, beyond the tracks, over where the white folks lived. But cinders were good enough for me and I never missed the green growing things. And anyhow cinders were fine weapons. You could always have a nice hot war with huge black cinders. All you had to do was crouch behind the brick pillars of a house with your hands full of gritty ammunition. And the first wooly black head you saw pop out from behind another row of pillars was your target. You tried your very best to knock it off. It was great fun.

I never fully realized the appalling disadvantages of a cinder environment till one day the gang to which I belonged found itself engaged in a war with the white boys who lived beyond the tracks. As usual we laid down our cinder barrage, thinking that this would wipe the white boys out. But they replied with a steady bombardment of broken bottles. We doubled our cinder barrage, but they hid behind trees, hedges, and the sloping embankments of their lawns. Having no such fortifications, we retreated to the brick pillars of our homes. During the retreat a broken milk bottle caught me behind the ear, opening a deep gash which bled profusely. The sight of blood pouring over my face completely demoralized our ranks. My fellow-combatants left me standing paralyzed in the center of the yard, and scurried for their homes. A kind neighbor saw me and rushed me to a doctor, who took three stitches in my neck.

I sat brooding on my front steps, nursing my wound and waiting for my mother to come from work. I felt that a grave injustice had been done me. It was all right to throw cinders. The greatest harm a cinder could do was leave a bruise. But broken bottles were dangerous; they left you cut, bleeding, and helpless.

When night fell, my mother came from the white folks' kitchen. I raced down the street to meet her. I could just feel in my bones that she would understand. I knew she would tell me exactly what to do next time. I grabbed her hand and babbled out the whole story. She examined my wound, then slapped me.

"How come yuh didn't hide?" she asked me. "How come yuh awways fightin'?"

I was outraged, and bawled. Between sobs I told her that I didn't have any trees or hedges to hide behind. There wasn't a thing I could have used as a trench.

And you couldn't throw very far when you were hiding behind the brick pillars of a house. She grabbed a barrel stave, dragged me home, stripped me naked, and beat me till I had a fever of one hundred and two. She would smack my rump with the stave, and, while the skin was still smarting, impart to me gems of Jim Crow wisdom. I was never to throw cinders any more. I was never to fight any more wars. I was never, never, under any conditions, to fight *white* folks again. And they were absolutely right in clouting me with the broken milk bottle. Didn't I know she was working hard every day in the hot kitchens of the white folks to make money to take care of me? When was I ever going to learn to be a good boy? She couldn't be bothered with my fights. She finished by telling me that I ought to be thankful to God as long as I lived that they didn't kill me.

All that night I was delirious and could not sleep. Each time I closed my eyes I saw monstrous white faces suspended from the ceiling, leering at me.

From that time on, the charm of my cinder yard was gone. The green trees, the trimmed hedges, the cropped lawns grew very meaningful, became a symbol. Even today when I think of white folks, the hard, sharp outlines of white houses surrounded by trees, lawns, and hedges are present somewhere in the background of my mind. Through the years they grew into an overreaching symbol of fear.

It was a long time before I came in close contact with white folks again. We moved from Arkansas to Mississippi. Here we had the good fortune not to live behind the railroad tracks, or close to white neighborhoods. We lived in the very heart of the local Black Belt. There were black churches and black preachers; there were black schools and black teachers; black groceries and black clerks. In fact, everything was so solidly black that for a long time I did not even think of white folks, save in remote and vague terms. But this could not last forever. As one grows older one eats more. One's clothing costs more. When I finished grammar school I had to go to work. My mother could no longer feed and clothe me on her cooking job.

There is but one place where a black boy who knows no trade can get a job, and that's where the houses and faces are white, where the trees, lawns, and hedges are green. My first job was with an optical company in Jackson, Mississippi. The morning I applied I stood straight and neat before the boss, answering all his questions with sharp yessirs and nosirs. I was very careful to pronounce my *sirs* distinctly, in order that he might know that I was polite, that I knew where I was, and that I knew he was a *white* man. I wanted that job badly.

He looked me over as though he were examining a prize poodle. He questioned me closely about my schooling, being particularly insistent about how much mathematics I had had. He seemed very pleased when I told him I had had two years of algebra.

"Boy, how would you like to try to learn something around here?" he asked me.

"I'd like it fine, sir," I said, happy. I had visions of "working my way up." Even Negroes have those visions.

"All right," he said. "Come on."

I followed him to the small factory.

"Pease," he said to a white man of about thirty-five, "this is Richard. He's going to work for us."

Pease looked at me and nodded.

I was then taken to a white boy of about seventeen.

"Morrie, this is Richard, who's going to work for us."

"Whut yuh sayin' there, boy!" Morrie boomed at me.

"Fine!" I answered.

The boss instructed these two to help me, teach me, give me jobs to do, and let me learn what I could in my spare time.

My wages were five dollars a week.

I worked hard, trying to please. For the first month I got along O.K. Both Pease and Morrie seemed to like me. But one thing was missing. And I kept thinking about it. I was not learning anything and nobody was volunteering to help me. Thinking they had forgotten that I was to learn something about the mechanics of grinding lenses, I asked Morrie one day to tell me about the work. He grew red.

"Whut yuh tryin' t' do, nigger, get smart?" he asked.

"Naw; I ain' trying' t' git smart," I said.

"Well, don't, if yuh know whut's good for yuh!"

I was puzzled. Maybe he just doesn't want to help me, I thought. I went to Pease.

"Say, are yuh crazy, you black bastard?" Pease asked me, his gray eyes growing hard.

I spoke out, reminding him that the boss had said I was to be given a chance to learn something.

"Nigger, you think you're *white,* don't you?"

"Naw, sir!"

"Well, you're acting mighty like it!"

"But, Mr. Pease, the boss said . . ."

Pease shook his fist in my face.

"This is a *white* man's work around here, and you better watch yourself!"

From then on they changed toward me. They said good-morning no more. When I was just a bit slow in performing some duty, I was called a lazy black son-of-a-bitch.

Once I thought of reporting all this to the boss. But the mere idea of what would happen to me if Pease and Morrie should learn that I had "snitched" stopped me. And after all the boss was a white man, too. What was the use?

The climax came at noon one summer day. Pease called me to his work-bench. To get to him I had to go between two narrow benches and stand with my back against a wall.

"Yes, sir," I said.

"Richard, I want to ask you something," Pease began pleasantly, not looking up from his work.

"Yes, sir," I said again.

Morrie came over, blocking the narrow passage between the benches. He folded his arms, staring at me solemnly.

I looked from one to the other, sensing that something was coming.

"Yes, sir," I said for the third time.

Pease looked up and spoke very slowly.

"Richard, *Mr.* Morrie here tells me you called me *Pease.*"

I stiffened. A void seemed to open up in me. I knew this was the show-down.

He meant that I had failed to call him Mr. Pease. I looked at Morrie. He was gripping a steel bar in his hands. I opened my mouth to speak, to protest, to assure Pease that I had never called him simply *Pease,* and that I had never had any intentions of doing so, when Morrie grabbed me by the collar, ramming my head against the wall.

"Now, be careful, nigger!" snarled Morrie, baring his teeth. "*I* heard yuh call 'im *Pease!* 'N' if yuh say yuh didn't, yuh're callin' me a *lie,* see?" He waved the steel bar threateningly.

If I had said: No, sir, Mr. Pease, I never called you *Pease,* I would have been automatically calling Morrie a liar. And if I had said: Yes, sir, Mr. Pease, I called you *Pease,* I would have been pleading guilty to having uttered the worst insult that a Negro can utter to a southern white man. I stood hesitating, trying to frame a neutral reply.

"Richard, I asked you a question!" said Pease. Anger was creeping into his voice.

"I don't remember calling you *Pease,* Mr. Pease," I said cautiously. "And if I did, I sure didn't mean . . ."

"You black son-of-a-bitch! You called me *Pease,* then!" he spat, slapping me till I bent sideways over a bench. Morrie was on top of me, demanding:

"Didn't yuh call 'im *Pease?* If yuh say yuh didn't, I'll rip yo' gut string loose with this bar, yuh black granny dodger! Yuh can't call a white man a lie 'n' git erway with it, you black son-of-a-bitch!"

I wilted. I begged them not to bother me. I knew what they wanted. They wanted me to leave.

"I'll leave," I promised. "I'll leave right *now.*"

They gave me a minute to get out of the factory. I was warned not to show up again, or tell the boss.

I went.

When I told the folks at home what had happened, they called me a fool. They told me that I must never again attempt to exceed my boundaries. When you are working for white folks, they said, you got to "stay in your place" if you want to keep working.

II

My Jim Crow education continued on my next job, which was portering in a clothing store. One morning, while polishing brass out front, the boss and his twenty-year-old son got out of their car and half dragged and half kicked a Negro woman into the store. A policeman standing at the corner looked on, twirling his night-stick. I watched out of the corner of my eye, never slackening the strokes of my chamois upon the brass. After a few minutes, I heard shrill screams coming from the rear of the store. Later the woman stumbled out, bleeding, crying, and holding her stomach. When she reached the end of the block, the policeman grabbed her and accused her of being drunk. Silently, I watched him throw her into a patrol wagon.

When I went to the rear of the store, the boss and his son were washing their hands at the sink. They were chuckling. The floor was bloody and strewn with wisps of hair and clothing. No doubt I must have appeared pretty shocked for the boss slapped me reassuringly on the back.

"Boy, that's what we do to niggers when they don't want to pay their bills," he said, laughing.

His son looked at me and grinned.

"Here, hava cigarette," he said.

Not knowing what to do, I took it. He lit his and held the match for me. This was a gesture of kindness, indicating that even if they had beaten the poor old woman, they would not beat me if I knew enough to keep my mouth shut.

"Yes, sir," I said, and asked no questions.

After they had gone, I sat on the edge of a packing box and stared at the bloody floor till the cigarette went out.

That day at noon, while eating in a hamburger joint, I told my fellow Negro porters what had happened. No one seemed surprised. One fellow, after swallowing a huge bite, turned to me and asked:

"Huh! Is tha' all they did t' her?"

"Yeah. Wasn't tha' enough?" I asked.

"Shucks! Man, she's a lucky bitch!" he said, burying his lips deep into a juicy hamburger. "Hell, it's a wonder they didn't lay her when they got through."

III

I was learning fast, but not quite fast enough. One day while I was delivering packages in the suburbs, my bicycle tire was punctured. I walked along the hot, dusty road, sweating and leading my bicycle by the handle-bars.

A car slowed at my side.

"What's the matter, boy?" a white man called.

I told him my bicycle was broken and I was walking back to town.

"That's too bad," he said. "Hop on the running board."

He stopped the car. I clutched hard at my bicycle with one hand and clung to the side of the car with the other.

"All set?"

"Yes, sir," I answered. The car started.

It was full of young white men. They were drinking. I watched the flask pass from mouth to mouth.

"Wanna drink, boy?" one asked.

I laughed as the wind whipped my face. Instinctively obeying the freshly planted precepts of my mother, I said:

"Oh, no!"

The words were hardly out of my mouth before I felt something hard and cold smash me between the eyes. It was an empty whisky bottle. I saw stars, and fell backwards from the speeding car into the dust of the road, my feet becoming entangled in the steel spokes of my bicycle. The white men piled out and stood over me.

"Nigger, ain' yuh learned no better sense'n tha' yet?" asked the man who hit me. "Ain' yuh learned t' say *sir* t' a white man yet?"

Dazed, I pulled to my feet. My elbows and legs were bleeding. Fists doubled, the white man advanced, kicking my bicycle out of the way.

"Aw, leave the bastard alone. He's got enough," said one.

They stood looking at me. I rubbed my shins, trying to stop the flow of blood. No doubt they felt a sort of contemptuous pity, for one asked:

"Yuh wanna ride t' town now, nigger? Yuh reckon yuh know enough t' ride now?"

"I wanna walk," I said, simply.

Maybe it sounded funny. They laughed.

"Well, walk, yuh black son-of-a-bitch!"

When they left they comforted me with:

"Nigger, yuh sho better be damn glad it wuz us yuh talked t' tha' way. Yuh're a lucky bastard, 'cause if yuh'd said tha' t' somebody else, yuh might've been a dead nigger now."

IV

Negroes who have lived South know the dread of being caught alone upon the streets in white neighborhoods after the sun has set. In such a simple situation as this the plight of the Negro in America is graphically symbolized. While white strangers may be in these neighborhoods trying to get home, they can pass unmolested. But the color of a Negro's skin makes him easily recognizable, makes him suspect, converts him into a defenseless target.

Late one Saturday night I made some deliveries in a white neighborhood. I was pedaling my bicycle back to the store as fast as I could, when a police car, swerving toward me, jammed me into the curbing.

"Get down and put up your hands!" the policemen ordered.

I did. They climbed out of the car, guns drawn, faces set, and advanced slowly.

"Keep still!" they ordered.

I reached my hands higher. They searched my pockets and packages. They seemed dissatisfied when they could find nothing incriminating. Finally, one of them said:

"Boy, tell your boss not to send you out in white neighborhoods after sundown."

As usual, I said:

"Yes, sir."

V

My next job was a hall-boy in a hotel. Here my Jim Crow education broadened and deepened. When the bell-boys were busy, I was often called to assist them.

As many of the rooms in the hotel were occupied by prostitutes, I was constantly called to carry them liquor and cigarettes. These women were nude most of the time. They did not bother about clothing, even for bell-boys. When you went into their rooms, you were supposed to take their nakedness for granted, as though it startled you no more than a blue vase or a red rug. Your presence awoke in them no sense of shame, for you were not regarded as human. If they were alone, you could steal side-long glimpses at them. But if they were receiving men, not a flicker of your eyelid could show. I remember one incident vividly. A new woman, a huge, snowy-skinned blonde, took a room on my floor. I was sent to wait upon her. She was in bed with a thick-set man; both were nude and uncovered. She said she wanted some liquor and slid out of bed and waddled across the floor to get her money from a dresser drawer. I watched her.

"Nigger, what in hell you looking at?" the white man asked me, raising himself upon his elbows.

"Nothing," I answered, looking miles deep into the blank wall of the room.

"Keep your eyes where they belong, if you want to be healthy!" he said.

"Yes, sir."

VI

One of the bell-boys I knew in this hotel was keeping steady company with one of the Negro maids. Out of a clear sky the police descended upon his home and arrested him, accusing him of bastardy. The poor boy swore he had had no intimate relations with the girl. Nevertheless, they forced him to marry her. When the child arrived, it was found to be much lighter in complexion than either of the two supposedly legal parents. The white men around the hotel made a great joke of it. They spread the rumor that some white cow must have scared the poor girl while she was carrying the baby. If you were in their presence when this explanation was offered, you were supposed to laugh.

VII

One of the bell-boys was caught in bed with a white prostitute. He was castrated and run out of town. Immediately after this all the bell-boys and hall-boys were called together and warned. We were given to understand that the boy who had been castrated was a "mighty, mighty lucky bastard." We were impressed with the fact that next time the management of the hotel would not be responsible for the lives of "trouble-makin' niggers." We were silent.

VIII

One night, just as I was about to go home, I met one of the Negro maids. She lived in my direction, and we fell in to walk part of he way home together. As we passed the white night-watchman, he slapped the maid on her buttock. I turned around, amazed. The watchman looked at me with a long, hard, fixed-under stare. Suddenly he pulled his gun and asked:

"Nigger, don't yuh like it?"

I hesitated.

"I asked yuh don't yuh like it?" he asked again, stepping forward.

"Yes, sir," I mumbled.

"Talk like it, then!"

"Oh, yes, sir!" I said with as much heartiness as I could muster.

Outside, I walked ahead of the girl, ashamed to face her. She caught up with me and said:

"Don't be a fool! Yuh couldn't help it!"

This watchman boasted of having killed two Negroes in self-defense.

Yet, in spite of all this, the life of the hotel ran with an amazing smoothness. It would have been impossible for a stranger to detect anything. The maids, the hall-boys, and the bell-boys were all smiles. They had to be.

IX

I had learned my Jim Crow lessons so thoroughly that I kept the hotel job till I left Jackson for Memphis. It so happened that while in Memphis I applied for a job at a branch of the optical company. I was hired. And for some reason, as long as I worked there, they never brought my past against me.

Here my Jim Crow education assumed quite a different form. It was no longer brutally cruel, but subtly cruel. Here I learned to lie, to steal, to dissemble. I learned to play that dual role which every Negro must play if he wants to eat and live.

For example, it was almost impossible to get a book to read. It was assumed that after a Negro had imbibed what scanty schooling the state furnished he had no further need for books. I was always borrowing books from men on the job. One day I mustered enough courage to ask one of the men to let me get books from the library in his name. Surprisingly, he consented. I cannot help but think that he consented because he was a Roman Catholic and felt a vague sympathy for Negroes, being himself an object of hatred. Armed with a library card, I obtained books in the following manner: I would write a note to the librarian, saying: "Please let this nigger boy have the following books." I would then sign it with the white man's name.

When I went to the library, I would stand at the desk, hat in hand, looking as unbookish as possible. When I received the books desired I would take them home. If the books listed in the note happened to be out, I would sneak into the lobby and forge a new one. I never took any chances guessing with the white librarian about what the fictitious white man would want to read. No doubt if any of the white patrons had suspected that some of the volumes they enjoyed had been in the home of a Negro, they would not have tolerated it for an instant.

The factory force of the optical company in Memphis was much larger than that in Jackson, and more urbanized. At least they liked to talk, and would engage the Negro help in conversation whenever possible. By this means I found that many subjects were taboo from the white man's point of view. Among the topics they did not like to discuss with Negroes were the following: American white women; the Ku Klux Klan; France, and how Negro soldiers fared while there; French women; Jack Johnson; the entire northern part of the United States; the Civil War; Abraham Lincoln; U. S. Grant; General Sherman; Catholics; the Pope; Jews; the Republican Party; slavery; social equality; Communism; Socialism; the 13th and 14th Amendments to the Constitution; or any topic calling for positive knowledge of manly self-assertion on the part of the Negro. The most accepted topics were sex and religion.

There were many times when I had to exercise a great deal of ingenuity to keep out of trouble. It is a southern custom that all men must take off their hats when they enter an elevator. And especially did this apply to us blacks with rigid force. One day I stepped into an elevator with my arms full of packages. I was forced to ride with my hat on. Two white men stared at me coldly. Then one of them very kindly lifted my hat and placed it upon my armful of packages. Now the most accepted response for a Negro to make under such circumstances is to look at the white man out of the corner of his eye and grin. To have said: "Thank you!" would have made the white man *think* that you *thought* you were receiving from him a personal service. For such an act I have seen Negroes take a blow in the mouth. Finding the first alternative distasteful, and the second dangerous, I hit upon an acceptable course of action which fell safely between these two poles. I immediately—no sooner than my hat was lifted—pretended that my packages were about to spill, and appeared deeply distressed with keeping them in my arms. In this fashion I evaded having to acknowledge his service, and, in spite of adverse circumstances, salvaged a slender shred of personal pride.

How do Negroes feel about the way they have to live? How do they discuss it when alone among themselves? I think this question can be answered in a single sentence. A friend of mine who ran an elevator once told me:

"Lawd, man! Ef it wuzn't fer them polices 'n' them ol' lynch-mobs, there wouldn't be nothin' but uproar down here!"

Slick Gonna Learn

Ralph Ellison

AUTHOR'S SYNOPSIS

The Negro, Slick Williams, is laid off from his job at the Hopkins plant shortly after discovering that his wife, Callie, is seriously ill from a condition attending pregnancy. In his effort to obtain money for a doctor, Slick finds himself in the stereotype situation of a "crap" game, in which he loses his last two dollars to the pimp, Bostie. In desperation he asks Bostie for a five dollar loan. Bostie refuses and denies him Callie's humanity, advising him that: "If it's goodnough to marry, it's goodnough to sell. . . ." In the ensuing fight, Slick slashes Bostie with a broken bottle, is knocked senseless by onlookers, and in the stupor of coming to, makes the mistake of knocking out a white policeman who had come to the Negro shine parlor to make arrests. Realizing that he has broken one of the locality's most rigidly enforced taboos—under no situation must a Negro strike a white man—Slick, still confused from the blow on his head, cannot overcome the psychological barrier and loses his power to act. He remains in the room to have the policeman recover and cart him off to jail.

They entered a lighted room. He felt himself being pushed forward to where a white face appeared above a high desk. A lamp cast a shaft of light across the face, giving it a detached appearance. The face turned and looked down upon him. Suddenly it came to him why he should be afraid. Am Ah really afraid? The sound of a throat being cleared caused his feelings to sink. Don't make no difference nohow, now, Po Callie. A voice behind him began speaking.

"This is the nigger, Judge your honor."

"What's the prisoner's name?"

"Slick Williams, Judge your honor."

"Boy, is that your name?"

"Yassuh."

Slick looked up at the red face with its blurred blue eyes behind thick lens. The flesh above the glasses was a network of fine lines. He tried to see past the lens to the eyes, but they were too thick. The face looked down at him silently.

"What are the full charges against this boy, Officer?"

Slick waited for the words that would release the flood of hate that he could feel in the face above him. The room seemed to quiver with hate. His body tensed as though to fight; yet something inside him was surrending to the violence he knew he would receive.

"Fighting, Your Honor. He beat up another nigger and cut him with a bottle."

"Cut up another nigger, eh?"

A pair of hands appeared. Slick watched them toying with a long yellow pencil. A nigguh hater, he thought. Wondah why he don't go on 'n get it over with?

"I understand he gave you some trouble, Officer. Is that true?"

"Well not exactly, Your Honor . . ."

Slick held his breath as the voice hesitated. The policeman moved around to stand beside him.

"You see, Your Honor, they knocked this nigger out. And when I started to pull him up to bring him in he came to fighting and hit me."

"What! Striking a *white* man? Officer you didn't let the boys hear about this?"

"Oh, no sir, Your Honor. I took care of him myself."

Slick stared into the desk, listening.

"Well don't let the boys get hold of this. There's too many reporters in town on account of the shut-downs out to the plants and we cain't afford any more publicity just now."

"Yes sir, Your Honor."

Slick stood in confusion; things were not as they should have been.

"Look at me boy!"

"Yassuh."

"Boy, you ever been in this court before?"

"Nawsuh!"

The head turned to the policeman. Silence. Slick swollered.

"Where did this happen Officer?"

"In a nigger joint over on the West Side, Your Honor."

"You niggers are always fighting, aren't you boy?"

Slick hung his head, remaining silent.

"Boy are you working?"

"Nawsuh."

"Did you *ever* work?"

"Yassuh, but Ah got laid off."

"You have a family?"

"Yassuh."

"Are you married, or just living with one of those high yallas over there on the West Side?"

The policeman laughed. Slick shifted his feet and rubbed his eye with his fist.

"Ahm really married."

"You're really married whut?"

The voice was nasty. He looked up, his eyes wide; the red face frowned down at him.

"Oh," he said. "Ah means Ahm really married *Suh.*"

"That's better. I thought you had forgotten yourself. Now I don't want to see you in this court again. You know what's supposed to happen to you. You look like a tough customer anyway. So you had better confine your fighting to the West Side. Understand what I mean boy?"

"Yassuh!"

"I mean confine your fighting to niggers!"

Slick heard the voice snap off. The blue eyes studied him coldly.

"Boy is your wife working?"

"Nawsuh, she's sick. Gonna have a baby."

"Leave it to niggers to have kids. I should give you some time. But it would be more expense than you're worth. Strikers and Niggers!"

His voice sounded disgusted. Slick saw him nod to the policeman.

"Alright nigger, get going," the policeman said softly.

Slick turned and followed the blue back away from the dim illumination of the desk lamp, down an aisle between rows of empty benches, through the darkened court room. Huge shadows marched before them on the wall. It mus' be late, he thought. His head throbbed painfully and his mind struggled to understand his release.

"Alright nigger, here's the door. You can go now. But don't think we won't find you when we have time!"

Slick was startled. For a moment he had forgotten the man at his side. He came to a sudden stop. He had knocked the hell out of a white man and gotten away with it! The *law* had let him go. Something seemed to surge in his mind. He was going down the steps now. He turned; the cop was standing in the door. He braced himself on the steps:

"Some day yuh gonna learn to leave colored folks alone. 'N if yuh take off that gun 'n star Ah'll show yuh what Ah mean, too."

"Why you black bastard!"

He could hear the voice trail off as he moved up the street. Ah wondah how Callie 'n the kids made out, he thought. His head felt strangely large and high as he walked along, sucking the damp air into his burning lungs. He made his way to the tracks that divided the town and headed for the West Side.

The wind was high now and sent the rain hard and cold against his face. A switch engine with a string of cars puffed behind a building with steam hissing as it poured from its valves, sweeping in a tumbling white cloud against the dark night. His feet crunched in cinders. He turned into a street, walking slow, thoughtfully, beneath bare trees and the smell of damp dried leaves, in the dark.

A car pulled quietly to the curb as he came to a corner, its motor pulsating rhythmically, smoothly. The car blocked his way. Drops of water on the glasses sparkled crystal-like under the rays of the street light as he made to go round the car. Don't give a dam 'bout a man whuts walking, he thought. His glance fell on the door of the car and he was suddenly afraid. Police! The front door was opening and revealing the soft glow of the dash light. He went tense. He wanted to run as he remembered daring the Policeman to fight. But if he ran they would shoot. A head and shoulder framed themselves in the door. He felt the presence of a policeman's cap on the head before his eyes could penetrate the darkness. He swept the glasses with his eyes, his terror rising as he made out three more figures in the car. The round beam of a flashlight glared in his eyes. He raised his arm to his face.

"Drop that arm, nigger!"

He lowered his arm, expecting to feel a club, a bullet.

"Is this the nigger, Tim?"

"Yeah, that's him alright. Dressed just like he told us."

"What the hell do we care if it's the same nigger. Any nigger'll do."

"Get him the hell in here and let's get it over with."

"Goddam you nigger, get in this car!"

Slick reached for the rear door handle.

"Not back there, up here in front!"

The policeman stepped out of the car and was pushing him into the front seat 'long side the driver. As he bent to step inside, the toe of a shoe landed against the end of his spine. He stifled a cry. He felt a blow and they were snatching him back and down into the seat. He closed his eyes in pain. His spine felt as though it had tried to shoot out of his collar. His body was taut with pain and fear as he felt the policeman pressing into the seat against him and closing the door as the car purred off. Someone struck a match in the rear seat. He opened his eyes slightly, seeing a flame and a face drawing on a cigarette mirrored sinisterly in the wind shield. The rain was striking the wind shield and a wiper was sweeping the rain in a half circle, down the glass. They were moving slowly.

"Where'll we take him?"

"Head for the Pike."

"Naw, it's too muddy in that spot."

"Turner's place then. O. K.?"

"Yeah. Turner's place and let's give this nigger the works."

"Suppose he knows where Turner's is and tells?"

"He won't tell. Not when we get through with him."

Slick could hear the motor roar as the machine gained speed. He looked for the speedometer, seeing a row of illuminated dials and nickeled knobs stretched across the dash board. The hands of the meters quivered nerve-like each time the driver shifted gears. The speedometer spun around: 25, 30,40. They swung along through a white residential section. He peered out, trying to find his sense of direction. Row after row of houses flashed past in the rain. He looked down the rapidly approaching street where the traffic lights glowed green in the gloom. He wished to call out to the houses, outlined so complacently behind the stretches of grass he knew now to be dead. He would soon be dead himself. He was already dead. If he could only call out to them in their isolated silence; to call for help; for mercy; not so much for himself as for Callie and the kids. Po Callie. She mus' think Ah took tha' money 'n got drunk, he thought. He could see the cigarette glow in the wind shield each time the policeman took a draw, filling the car with smoke. The one beside him interrupted his feeling of hopelessness as he reached over and turned a gadget on the dash. The grating sound of static filled his ears and died to a low hum as the cop fingered the control. Silence! Why don't they say something? They took a curve. The smooth pulse of the motor filled his ears, punctuated by crashes of static from the droning radio. Ah oughta break outa here 'n pass out fighting. Ahm 'bout to die; on ma way to have these bastards slug ma brains out 'n cain do nothin' . . . He looked out of the sweating window where the swaying of vague shapes told him they were rolling through the country.

"Gawddam ya, nigger, say something!"

A blow struck at the base of his skull, bringing a numbness. He doubled down in the seat.

"Wait 'til we get 'im out of the car," the driver said.

"O. K. Joe. Sit up straight there nigger!"

He sat back in the seat. His body was tense and his mind tried to blot out the world of the car. The rain was white, slanting against the glass. He felt a body pressing against him as the car took a sharp curve. Suddenly he was listening. A slow, toneless voice was calling monotonously: *"Calling car number eleven— Stand by. Calling car number eleven—Stand by."* Slick leaned against the driver as the policeman on his right pushed against him to finger the control. What was happening? *Car eleven—Stand by* . . .

"Slow down Joe, let's take it."

"Car number eleven proceed to the Hopkins plant immediately. Riot call. East gate of factory yard threatened by strikers. Disperse mob. That is all . . . Calling car number fifteen . . . Car . . ."

Slick could hear the switch as the driver snapped off the radio.

"Of all the lousy luck!"

"Swing around and take the short road back."

"But what about the nigger?"

"Yeah; what'll we do with this sonofabitch?"

"Have to forget him tonight, boys. Chief's been expecting this trouble and we gotta be there."

"We'd better go back. He'll probably run the show himself tonight."

Slick watched the driver nose the car around. It groaned.

"What'll we do with him?" a voice said.

"Stop a minute, Joe."

The machine came to a stop. The policeman on his right stepped out and a cold breath of air filled the closed car.

"Alright nigger, get out!"

Slick stepped slowly out. Water seeped through his worn shoes.

"Make it snappy nigger!"

He stood clear of the car. His back was tense and his head held low, expecting a blow from behind. There was a movement inside the car. He stood still, stiff. The policeman caught his throat, choking off his breath.

"Well nigger, you must have your rabbit foot with you tonight."

He tried to breathe. He saw the blow when it started from down around the policeman's knees and rolled with it, striking his arm against the running board as he went down. A kick landed in his ribs. He lay still, silent.

"Come on, come on."

"O. K."

He felt another kick. He bit his lips. The car coughed slightly as it started up; then it was moving off. Suddenly there was an explosion and something was rattling across the concrete where he lay. He rolled frantically, feeling icy water on his hands and face as he flung himself into a ditch alongside the highway. More explosions as he lay in the mud. He could see flashes of fire from the car and showers of sparks as bullets bounced across the highway, trying to find him there. He dug into the mud with his fingers, holding himself flat. Bullets were cutting the weeds down around him, whistling over his head. Another shot; then the sound of the car shifting gears: second, third.

He lay still for hours, it seemed, then pulled slowly to his feet. His hands trembled and his body was damp with the mud. He noticed that the rain had stopped as he wiped the mud from his face. His pants and jumper were soaked. He made his way to the highway and stumbled for where lights cast a blurred glow over the city. He moved by instinct, his mind set upon reaching home. It would be a long walk and the kids would have to go to bed without eating. They *coulda* had some oatmeal, he thought.

A car was coming down the highway behind him, its lights illuminating the trees; flooding the road as it approached. He heard it slowing down as he stepped off the highway to let it pass. It was pulling up beside him. He turned: a truck. The driver was leaning out of the dripping cab, squinting down at him. *Another* one, he said to himself.

"Hey there, are ya alright?"

"Yas Ahm alright."

"Ya sure? Ya wuz stumbling pretty bad just now. What happened?"

Why the hell don't he go on 'n leave me 'lone, he thought. White folks think they can ask you anything.

"Ah got knocked down a while ago but Ahm alright now."

"That's a hell of a thing to have happen. Ya better let me give ya a lift."

Slick looked hard into the man's face, his eyes fingering the furrowed brow, the muscular jaw. There was a row of buttons on his cap.

"Naw," he said. "Ah reckon Ah kin make it."

"But man, you might be hurt inside. Besides, it's a pretty good piece to town."

Slick thought of the distance to the city, the kids, Callie. His body was a mass of pain and he was beginning to feel faint with hunger.

"Ah guess yuh right," he said.

The driver opened the door and he climbed up beside him. He shivered from having rolled in the mud and his elbow was a point of fire. The driver was silently getting the big truck under way. He watched the lights sweeping down the road; it was raining again. He cut his eyes to watch the face of the driver: Irishman. Hope he don't wanta talk.

"Ya picked a helluva night to walk to town, man. Don't you have a car?"

"Ah got one but the carburetor ain' no good," he lied.

"Too bad. On a night like this every man needs a car. It's a hell of a night to walk a highway. A man sure needs a car."

Smoke fumes in the cab irritated Slick. He watched the lights playing on the road and did not answer.

"Say, did ya get the rat's number what hit cha?"

"Nawsuh. He hit me so sudden Ah didn't have no time to look."

The driver was silent, shifting gears as the truck groaned up a steep hill. Then:

"Ya have to be careful, that's all there is to it I guess. Ya have to be careful as hell."

"Yassuh, yuh right."

"Well anyway; you'll soon be in town. I don't usually pick up riders, lose my job if I did. But hell! a man is still a man and it's nasty as hell tonight."

"Ah sho' thank yuh fo' stopping," Slick said. He did not trust the white man and he did not wish to have to say too much to him. Yet he had picked him up. . . . He sat erect. This might be a trap! He looked at the man.

"How far yuh come tonight?" he said.

"All the way from Richberg. Little over two hundred miles. Been on the road since noon and it's been raining most of the time."

Slick sighed and settled back in the seat; then suddenly became rigid again. His eyes swept swiftly over the dash. No, no, there was no radio. He eased himself back.

"How do you feel man? You look like something hurts you?"

"Ahm alright, now. Jus' a lil' shook up Ah guess."

He could feel the cushioned rear of the seat yielding to his flaming back as he watched the rain striking the wind shield; hearing it drumming the top of the cab. Before them the light of the city broke the blackness in a million shimmering glints, throwing a soft glow to meet the rain-swept sky. Soon they would be there. He would be there in the city to face Callie without doctor or money. Them white dawgs! he thought. He turned and watched the man bent over the steering wheel, studying his face and tried to connect him with the experiences of the day as the truck roared through the rain to the city.

---

11 Men and Women in Society
or "Who's Cooking Tonight?"

"Why Can't a Woman Be More Like a Man?"

My Fair Lady

The terms "women's movement" or "women's rights" are probably quite familiar to you. Many of you have grown up during a time of heated activity on behalf of women, and your parents are likely to have strong opinions on this topic. As students, you are likely either to have debated or written about this subject in school or discussed it informally with friends. The notion of a women's "movement" aimed toward the achievement of women's "rights" is likely to arouse strong feelings in both women and men.

This chapter focuses on the changing role of women in contemporary society and on some issues of particular concern to women's struggle for equality. Some of the readings also explore the effect of the women's movement on the role of men. As in all of the chapters which deal with controversial issues, several assignments enable you to explore your own beliefs and values as a means of beginning research. Others require you to learn about the historical and cultural context of the topic, to decide which issues are most important, and to incorporate the views of others into your own thinking.

GENDER ROLE STEREOTYPES: ADVANTAGES AND DISADVANTAGES

Key Question: Does Our Society Provide Advantages for One Sex Over the Other, or Does Each Sex Have Advantages Lacking in the Other?

Within every culture, different expectations are established concerning how men and women "ought" to behave. In some cultures, differences in these expectations are particularly clear. As Chafetz indicates in her article, "Some Individual Costs of Gender Role Conformity," the various Spanish-speaking groups in this country (Mexican-American, Puerto Rican, Cuban) stress domesticity, passivity, and other stereotypical feminine traits, and dominance, aggressiveness, physical prowess, and other stereotypical masculine traits. In other cultures, these differences may be less marked.

The extent to which one adheres to the gender stereotypes of the culture often has an impact on the social and economic opportunities available, and it is recognized that each instance in which one chooses either to accept or reject stereotypical roles brings corresponding advantages and disadvantages. In a society in which gender role stereotypes are clearly defined along traditional lines, a competitive, intellectual, career-oriented woman might experience the personal fulfillment associated with professional success, but might be regarded as an undesirable potential wife. On the other hand, a woman who adheres completely to the passive domestic role assigned to women might find that simply being a good wife does not bring personal fulfillment. Similarly, in such a society, a man who rejects the emotional self-control associated with the "macho" image might enjoy greater freedom to express his feelings, but might also be looked down upon as a weakling. On the other hand, a man who completely embraces the "tight-lipped hero" role might be admired by his mates but might also find himself unable to establish close relationships. Within a given culture, choices concerning adherence to role stereotypes bring associated limits and opportunities.

WRITING TO LEARN

▶ *Exercise: Gender Roles in Today's Society.* Several studies have been conducted to determine whether gender stereotypes can be associated consistently with particular advantages and disadvantages. It will be useful for you and your class to determine for yourselves how you feel about this topic. To generate thinking, then, indicate at the top of a blank sheet of paper whether you are male or female. Then, in the left hand column, indicate what you feel are the disadvantages of your gender role. As a woman, for instance, is there something you feel you are unable to do or are not encouraged to do by society? Does society also impose restrictions on what men can do? Then, in the right hand column, indicate the advantages of your gender role. Thus, if you are female, your sheet will look like this:

Female Disadvantages   Female Advantages

If you are male, your sheet will look like this:

Male Disadvantages   Male Advantages

Once you have filled out the sheet, divide the class according to sex, males in one group and females in the other. Compare lists and create a master list encompassing the advantages and disadvantages noted on each individual list.

▶ *Writing Assignment:* Write a short paper in which you discuss the trends you notice on the master list. Which disadvantages did your group point out? What were the advantages? Do you feel that these advantages and disadvantages have implications for the position of men and women in society?

Comparing Lists Between the Sexes: Each group should make a copy of its master list and give it to the group of the opposite sex. (If you have easy access to a copy machine, you can make a copy for everyone.) Write a short paper in which you compare similarities and differences between the lists.

Key Questions: Where Do We Learn Gender Roles? Were You Socialized to Conform to Gender Role Stereotypes?

How does each individual determine the normal or acceptable behaviors for males and females? Usually, the norms of the culture are transmitted through the family, as well as through schools, the media, etc.

WRITING TO LEARN

▶ *Writing Assignment: Your Own Upbringing.* Think about your own up-bringing, and write an essay in which you discuss the extent to which your own upbringing reflected an adherence to gender role stereotypes. Were you brought up to think that you had to fulfill certain expectations associated with gender roles? What sort of activities were you encouraged to engage in? Did you have role models in your home or community environment that provided possibilities for choice?

▶ *Writing Assignment: The Role of the Media When You Were Growing Up.* Think about the television programs you watched when you were a child. Did they present a stereotypical picture of gender roles? Write an essay in which you discuss the extent to which the media reinforced the gender sterotypes of the culture when you were growing up.

▶ *Writing Assignment: The Media Today.* Look through the television section of the newspaper and at some of the guides to current television programs. Spend a few hours watching some of them, a few during the day, a few at night. (A good excuse, isn't it?) Write an essay in which you discuss the extent to which current programs reinforce stereotypical gender roles. Are there attempts to counteract stereotypes? (In writing this essay, be sure to define for yourself what you mean by a stereotype.)

▶ *Writing Assignment: Conforming to Strictly Defined Male or Female Roles: Benefits and Costs.* Some people claim that adhering to prescribed gender roles of your culture is "easier" than trying to challenge the system. Do you agree with this idea? Or do you feel that conforming to strictly defined male or female behaviors has hidden costs? What are the benefits and costs of not conforming. Write an essay in which you address the following question:

> Which involves greater risk: to adhere to gender role stereotypes or to challenge the system?

To begin to think about this topic, you will have to define for yourself what you mean by "risk."

▶ **Writing Assignment: A Research Study on Gender Role Conformity.**
Read the essay "Some Individual Costs of Gender Role Conformity" by Janet Saltman Chafetz. Summarize Chafetz's main idea. Then write an essay in which you address the following question:

> Janet Chafetz conducted her study of gender roles almost 20 years ago. Some would argue that the intervening years have produced marked changes in male and female roles. Others are less sure. To what extent do you feel her study is dated? You might focus your responses toward the prevailing attitudes and values concerning this issue on your own college campus.

HISTORICAL/CULTURAL CONTEXT

The Women's Movement: An Historical Sketch

Many people are under the impression that until Betty Friedan published *The Feminine Mystique* in 1963, there was no such thing as a "women's movement," and certainly that book did provide the catalyst for a growing consciousness about women's issues. Yet, throughout history, several periods have been characterized by action on behalf of women's "rights." The following very brief discussion is aimed at helping you look at some of these points in history to gain a perspective on how the movement toward women's rights has evolved.

Key Questions: What Is a "Women's" Movement? What Are "Women's Issues"?

It is difficult to discuss or even to define a specifically "feminist" agenda, since, on one hand, what women have agitated for are rights that any human being would want, yet on the other hand, the biological differences between the sexes have generated specific concerns about childbirth, birth control, and abortion, which until recently have been viewed as distinctly women's issues. This difficulty of defining what exactly is meant by a women's movement was just as true 100 years ago as it is today. According to historian Lois Banner, "Before the First World War, all feminists were not of one mind concerning the issues of organization, sexuality, and woman's nature." However, in general, a discussion of "women's rights" historically has been a discussion of a struggle for **equality** with men.

One place to begin the discussion is to look at the role women have played in religious ideology. Women's inferiority can be seen in many religions. In Genesis 3 we read, "Unto the woman God said, I will greatly simplify thy sorrow through thy conception; in sorrow thou shalt bring forth children; and they shall rule over thee." Religious teachings often presented women as inferior and evil. In the Old Testament, God punishes the daughters of Eve for her sin, and, similarly, in the Koran, we read, "Men are superior to women on account of the qualities in which God has given them preeminence." Thus, the predominant religions of the world present woman as an inferior creature to men, although in this chapter, I am limiting the discussion to developments within western culture.

Throughout history, the concept of women as unequal to men frequently manifested itself in the unequal treatment accorded women. Even as late as the eighteenth century, when the issue of human rights was being debated across the world, the rights of women were not considered important. Women's issues were not addressed directly in either the Declaration of Independence or the Constitution of the United States. Until "An Act Concerning the Rights and Liabilities of Husband and Wife" was passed on March 20, 1860, married women did not have control over their own property, they were not legal guardians of their own children, and they were not allowed to engage in civil contracts or business. A woman could not sue her husband, and if she deserted her husband, she could be hunted and reclaimed in the same way as a runaway slave.

If women's condition was so miserable in earlier times, more miserable, many would say, than the condition during the women's movement of the sixties and seventies, why wasn't there agitation on behalf of women earlier? The point to realize is that social movements do not come about necessarily because a problem arises in society at a specific time. Every society has problems at all times, and people may be extremely miserable. But they do not agitate for reform either because they perceive the situation as hopeless or because they lack the energy necessary to organize. Thus, although women's position was always inferior to that of men, only at certain periods in history did women's movements arise. Actually, all movements wax and wane; it is only from the perspective of hindsight that you can discern where they begin and end.

However, even during periods when there was not an organized women's movement, women thought about their position and were aware that reform was necessary. Early literature abounds with references to women's dissatisfaction with their lives, and letters and journals often discuss issues that are remarkably similar to those we discuss today. In March 1776, during the revolutionary period, Abigail Adams wrote to her husband the following remarks concerning women's freedom:

> I long to hear that you have declared an independency. And, by the way, in the new code of laws which I suppose it will be necessary for you to make, I desire you would remember the ladies and be more generous and favorable to them than your ancestors. Do not put such unlimited power into the hands of the husbands. Remember, all men would be tyrants if they could. If particular care and attention is not paid to the ladies, we are determined to foment a rebellion, and will hold ourselves bound by any laws in which we have no voice or representation.

That your sex are naturally tyrannical is a truth so thoroughly established as to admit of no dispute; but such of you as wish to be happy willingly give up the harsh title of master for the more tender and endearing one of friend. Why, then, not put it out of the power of the vicious and the lawless to use us with cruelty and indignity with impunity? Men of sense in all ages abhor those customs which treat us only as the vassals of your sex; regard us then as beings placed by Providence under your protection, and in imitation of the Supreme Being make use of that power only for our happiness. (March 31, 1776)

The Civil War and Beyond

The fight for women's equality is directly linked to the abolitionist movement during the Civil War. Women active in the movement opposing slavery soon began organizing in their own behalf. One woman, Elizabeth Cady Stanton, the wife of an abolitionist and journalist, proposed a women's convention to discuss the tedium and responsibility of a housewife's life. In 1848, a year characterized by revolutions throughout Europe, 260 women and some men attended a convention at Seneca Falls, New York, and drafted the "Seneca Falls Declaration of Sentiments and Resolutions." Stanton was considered quite radical, since she proposed unprecedented reforms, such as granting women the vote, a suggestion that was rejected by most of the moderates in the group. The text of the resolution from Seneca Falls is included at the end of this chapter. Notice how much the language resembles that of the Declaration of Independence.

Key Question: To What Extent Has the Position of Women Improved During the Twentieth Century?

WRITING TO LEARN

▶ **Writing Assignment:** Note all the declarations and resolutions enumerated by Stanton. Has our century dealt effectively with these issues? Or would such a declaration still be appropriate today? Write an essay in which you discuss the relevance of Stanton's declaration to modern times.

▶ **Writing Assignment:** Imitate the style of the declaration choosing another cause, perhaps one that pertains to a situation at home or at school. Try to follow the same pattern that Stanton follows.

Women's Suffrage

Before the passage of the Fifteenth Amendment, the amendment that prohibited racial discrimination in voting, the women's movement fought for suffrage for both blacks and women. Susan B. Anthony said "we [cannot] work in two separate movements to get the ballot for two disenfranchised classes—the negro and the woman—since to do this must be at double cost of time, energy, and money." (Proceedings of the National Women's Rights Convention, May 1866.) However, in 1870, when the Fifteenth Amendment was passed, only black males got the vote; women had to continue fighting until 1920.

The Later Nineteenth Century

Historian Lois Banner calls the 1890s "years of transition." During these years, most states modified the common law doctrine of *"femme couverte,"* whereby wives were considered chattel of their husbands, and many states gave wives control over inherited property and earnings. However, discrimination was still strong. In some states, women could vote only in municipal and school board elections. Some states required a husband's permission before a woman could enter a business partnership. Husbands had the right to decide where a family would live.

The Issue of Pregnancy and Birth

An issue that is still being hotly debated today is that concerning the bearing of children. Although the main concern today is that of abortion (see Chapter 12), many in the early twentieth century fought just as bitterly over the issue of birth control. Margaret Sanger, who established an early birth control clinic in New York City, writes movingly of the horrors she encountered when working with poor women facing continuous unwanted pregnancy and of the difficulties she, herself, had to overcome in order to maintain her clinic.

WRITING TO LEARN

▶ *Reading and Writing Assignment:* Read the selection "My fight For Birth Control." Then find three newspaper articles dealing with confrontations occurring at abortion clinics. Write an essay discussing similarities and differences between the situation in 1912 and that being debated today.

Education

In the United States, we tend to take it for granted that education is equally open to men and women. This, however, was not always the case. In 1789, the public school system was established in Boston and girls were admitted to the schools— but only from April through October. Moreover, until 1825, girls were admitted only in the primary schools. In 1836, Mt. Holyoke Seminary was established, offering women higher education and the curriculum of the seminary, where founder Mary Lyon tried to recreate the mother-daughter bond in teacher-student relationships. The first Mt. Holyoke graduates went on to teach at the most prestigious schools of the time. Mt. Holyoke was originally established as a high school, but gained collegiate status in 1888. Another women's institution, Vassar College, was established in 1865, offering women a full liberal arts curriculum—like the one offered to men in the Ivy League. Oberlin College admitted both men and women on equal terms from its inception in 1833. Slowly, the importance of educating women became an accepted idea in the culture. Yet, until recently, women were the minority at institutions of higher education.

WRITING TO LEARN

▶ *Writing Assignment:* Think about the following statement concerning the treatment of women at the university: "The traditional faculty attitude toward women students . . . is based on the assumption that women students won't finish. And if they do finish, they won't be in the national marketplace as professionals . . . And if they do publish . . . they won't be any good at it. . . . And if by chance they are good, then they're abnormal—they're Amazons."

Consider your own experience, both in high school and in college. Consider the way men and women are treated in the classroom. In a three-page essay, consider whether the attitude toward women students conveyed in the above statement still pertains today.

The Modern Women's Movement

Little remained of an organized women's movement after 1924, since after suffrage was granted, few other issues linked women of different classes, education, and regions. Once the voting victory had been won, there was a general relaxation of effort. Perhaps it was believed that the most important battle had been won. This relaxed attitude was paralleled by an increased emphasis on marriage and motherhood, which became widespread in the 1940s and 1950s. A return to the home and family was romanticized, and women were portrayed either as sex objects or homemakers. In 1947, a book titled *Modern Woman: The Lost Sex* stated that the idea of an "independent woman" is a contradiction in terms because it violates the laws of nature.

The forties and fifties glorified the role of the housewife. Although labor-saving devices such as the freezer, clothes washer, dryer, and dishwasher changed the nature of housework, women still spent as much time involved in housecleaning/beautifying activities as before. This was the era of the gleaming floor and sparkling dishes. As can be imagined, many women found little fulfillment in such tasks.

We tend to date the modern women's movement from 1963 with the publication of Betty Friedan's *The Feminine Mystique*. The book exposed some of women's dissatisfaction with traditional women's roles, particularly those of housewife and mother. According to Friedan, even college women felt that they had to adhere to traditional roles. She estimates that by the mid-1950s, 60 percent of female undergraduates had dropped out of college in order to get married. Marriage rates among professional women were also rising. In 1940, 26 percent of professional women were married; by 1960, the number increased to 45 percent. Yet many of these women found themselves discontented, without understanding the nature of their dissatisfaction.

▶ **Reading and Writing Assignment:** Read the excerpt from *The Feminine Mystique,* "The Problem That Has No Name." Write an essay discussing the extent to which this perspective still pertains to current thinking regarding women. Does Friedan's perspective seem dated?

The Rise of the Women's Movement

The 1960s saw a rise of militant feminism. This was also a time of great social reform. In 1966, National Organization of Women (N.O.W.) was founded by Betty Friedan. The organization has supported legislative measures such as the Equal Rights Amendment and is devoted to the fight for equal opportunity. It is the vehicle that speaks to and for the concerns of American feminists. It is also the subject of a controversy about which issues are most important to women. One question asks whether the concerns of prosperous professional women are related to poorer or blue-collar working women. The organization has been a proponent of affirmative action programs in industry, government, and educational institutions.

With the establishment of N.O.W., modern feminism began to focus its position toward the advocacy of women's rights to full citizenship—that is, political, economic, and social equality with men. Within this position, though, one may find different varieties of feminism including those advocating female separatism. In general, though, most feminists seek equal economic and social rights. They support reproductive rights, including the right to abortion; they criticize traditional definitions of gender roles; and they favor raising children of both genders for equal public and domestic roles and responsibilities. Many wish to reform language so that it does not refer only to "man" as equivalent with humanity. Many also campaign vigorously against violence against women (wife battering, rape) and against the denigration of women in the media. With the rise of feminism, colleges and universities began offering courses in women's studies. Women began speaking out through books, films, and protests. Scholarly journals devoted to women's issues appeared. Feminists set out to prove that the gains made by women in the past were superficial and that there was still work to do, and, on the whole, there was statistical evidence to back them up. Some women adopted extreme behaviors to illustrate their position. Many refused to wear traditional female clothing or makeup, feeling that they reinforced the concept of woman as "object." Bra-burnings represented a dramatic manifestation of this position.

▶ **Writing Assignment:** Interview two women and two men who were mature adults during the beginnings of the women's movement. (You could start with members of your family.) Find out how they felt about the events of that time. Were they aware of *The Feminine Mystique*? How did they feel during the sixties about the terms "women's rights," "women's liberation," or "feminism"? Write an essay in which you present their position. Think about the extent to which it differs from your own.

LEGISLATION FOR WOMEN'S RIGHTS

Key Question: Is There a Need for Legislation on Behalf of Women's Rights?

In 1970, nearly 50 percent of all American women between the ages of 16 and 64 were either working or seeking work. More than 70 percent, however, were employed in the service sector, predominantly in such fields as retail trade, hospital work, and elementary and secondary education. Women in industry tended to be concentrated in clerical and unskilled jobs, or so-called women's jobs. The segregation of jobs by sex had changed little since 1900, despite the great increase in the proportion of women working. Moreover, even when women held the same jobs as men, they were paid substantially less.

During the 1960s and 70s, Congress enacted legislation to combat discrimination in the employment of women. This included the **Civil Rights Act of 1964** and the **Equal Pay Act of 1963.** Federal government agencies were prohibited by presidential executive order from assigning contracts to employers who discriminated against women. **Title VII of the Civil Rights Act of 1964** had an important impact on antidiscrimination legislations. However, since it is open to judicial interpretation, there is considerable variation on how it is enforced. **Title IX of the Education Act Amendments of 1972** covered discrimination in educational programs and prohibited sexual harassment. Most states now also have laws prohibiting discrimination against women, but these vary greatly in scope and effectiveness. In 1981, the Supreme Court ruled that pay equity is a legitimate ground for suit under Title VII of the Civil Rights Act, meaning that persons performing the same work would receive the same salary. Yet a 1985 *Working Women* survey found that a salary bias against women exists. For example, the survey indicated that women professionals earned 75 cents to every dollar earned by a male professional, and that the weekly earning difference between male and female dentists was $269.20.

The Equal Rights Amendment

During recent years, there has been considerable debate concerning the Equal Rights Amendment, a proposed amendment to the Constitution guaranteeing rights to women equal to those of men. Yet, discussion of the Equal Rights Amendment (ERA) actually began in 1920 with the passage of the Nineteenth Amendment, which enabled women to vote. In 1940 the Republican party put the ERA on the party platform. However, in 1963, John Kennedy's Commission on the Status of

Women concluded that "a constitutional amendment need not now be sought in order to establish" equal rights for women.

Finally, in May 1970, Senate hearings on the ERA began. The House passed the Amendment with a vote of 350–15. In the Senate, a provision was added exempting women from the draft. However, women's organizations that had supported the ERA decided that in order for there to be true equality, women had to be drafted and therefore, they could not accept the amended version. This version was never brought to a vote. Senator Birch Bayh, who started the hearings, changed the wording to read, "Neither the United States nor any state shall, on account of sex, deny to any person within its jurisdiction the equal protection of the laws." Bayh said his version allowed for a "flexible standard." Yet, most women's organizations feared too flexible an interpretation of the law and did not support this new version. In 1971, the House Judiciary Committee returned the wording to its original 1970 version but added the "Wiggins Amendment" which stated that the ERA "would not impair the validity of any law of the United States which exempts a person from compulsory military service or any other law of the United States or any state which reasonably promotes the health and safety of the people." The House rejected the "Wiggins Amendment" and voted 354 to 23 to adopt the original ERA.

In the Senate, Senator Sam Ervin introduced eight amendments dealing with subjects such as the draft and marital and family support. All the amendments were voted down. On March 22, 1972, the ERA passed with a vote of 84–8. Then, in order for the amendment to become the law of the land, 38 states were needed to ratify it. However, by 1977, only 35 states had voted positively. Congress then extended the original 1979 deadline until 1982. However, this deadline also ran out, and the ERA died.

The issue of women and the law is complex. Women must ask if equality of the sexes should be based on existing (some say male) terms or on a recognition of what writer Joan Hoff-Wilson calls "equal, but different, patterns of behavior." Wendy Williams of the Georgetown University Law Center asks "Do we want equality of the sexes—or do we want justice for two kinds of human beings who are fundamentally different?"

Key Question: Where Does the Women's Movement Go from Here?

Some people say that the women's movement is over, at least for the time being. The battles have been fought and won, and a new awareness of women's rights has now been achieved for both women and men. Others feel that such awareness is only characteristic of the upper and middle class and that blue collar women still suffer great inequality. They point out that numerous issues still remain to be addressed and that even the issues of the sixties have yet to be resolved.

▶ **Writing Assignment:** Read the excerpts, "The End of the Beginning" and "How to Get the Women's Movement Moving Again." Write a short summary of each of these chapters. Write an essay in which you evaluate whether or not you feel there is still the need for a women's movement. If so, which issues are likely to be predominant?

▶ **Writing Assignment:** Read Gloria Steinem's article, "Why Young Women Are More Conservative" and Kay Mills's article "For Women to Gain in Congress, Parties Ought to Even the Odds." Incorporate these two perspectives into your essay addressing the question of whether or not a women's movement is still needed.

▶ **Writing Assignment:** How does your view of human nature affect your position on whether or not there is still the need for a women's movement? Incorporate that perspective into your essay.

Key Question: Is There a Need for Men's Liberation as Well?

The reevaluation of women's role in society and increased activity on behalf of equality for women was bound to have an important effect on men. Many men are now reexamining their own prescribed roles and discovering that they have been just as limited by such prescriptions as were women. They too feel that they would like to maximize their life choices and they see the women's movement as providing a liberating impetus for men. Other men, of course, resist, feeling that the women's movement has impinged upon their own traditionally defined power base. Still others point out that the women's movement has unfairly relegated men to the position of the enemy; they point out that there is a prevailingly antimale attitude among women, which is just as pervasive as the antifemale prejudice attributed to men.

▶ **Writing Assignment:** Read "Confessions of a Female Chauvinist Sow." Write an essay discussing the male stereotype Roiphe was taught and assessing the extent to which you feel that stereotype still pertains.

▶ **Writing Assignment:** Some people maintain that not only women but also men have been the victims of gender role stereotypes, that they have been unfairly depicted in the culture as morally inferior to women. Read the following essays:

  "Confessions of a Female Chauvinist Sow"

  "Men Need Liberating from Masculine Myths"

  "Men Need Liberating from Unfair Laws"

In a four- to six-page essay, address the following issue:

Men, too, have been disadvantaged by sex role stereotyping.

Remember to define what you mean by "disadvantaged."

Women and Aging

▶ *Reading and Writing Assignments*

1. In her essay, "The Double Standard of Aging," a noted philosopher scholar, Susan Sontag, presents the argument that women suffer more from age discrimination than men and thus are obsessed with aging even when they are young. Read Sontag's article and list her major ideas. Then write an essay in which you discuss the extent to which you feel Sontag's ideas, written in 1972, still pertain to contemporary society.

2. Read the short story, "Good Morning Wardrobe." Write an essay discussing the extent to which that story reflects Sontag's ideas in "The Double Standard of Aging."

3. Sontag makes the point that "most clients for plastic surgery are women." Contact the Association of Plastic Surgeons and find out if this is still true. Are increasing numbers of men now also having plastic surgery? If so, what does that say about the double standard of aging?

4. Write an essay addressing the following question: To what extent are good looks important for men in contemporary society? Refer to the Sontag article in your discussion.

Key Terms

Women's Movement

Women's Rights

Equal Rights Amendment

Gender Roles

Gender Role Stereotypes

The Feminine Mystique

Some Individual Costs of Gender Role Conformity

Janet Saltzman Chafetz

It is probably true that very few individuals conform totally to their sex-relevant stereotypes. Roles of all kinds . . . are sociocultural givens, but this is not to say that people play them in the same way. Indeed, individuals, like stage actors and actresses, interpret their roles and create innovations for their "parts." The fact remains that there is a "part" to be played, and it does strongly influence the actual "performance."

It is also important to recall that the precise definitions of gender role stereotypes vary within the broader culture by social class, region, race and ethnicity, and other subcultural categories. Thus, for instance, more than most other Americans, the various Spanish-speaking groups in this country (Mexican-American, Puerto Rican, Cuban) stress domesticity, passivity, and other stereotypical feminine traits, and dominance, aggressiveness, physical prowess, and other stereotypical masculine traits. Indeed, the masculine gender role for this group is generally described by reference to the highly stereotyped notion of machismo. In fact, a strong emphasis on masculine aggressiveness and dominance may be characteristic of most groups in the lower ranges of the socioeconomic ladder (McKinley, 1964, pp. 89, 93, 112; Yorburg, 1974). Conversely, due to historical conditions beyond its control, black America has had to rely heavily on the female as provider and, more often than in the rest of society, as head of the household. Thus, the feminine stereotype discussed above has traditionally been less a part of the cultural heritage of blacks than that of whites (Staples, 1970; Yorburg, 1974). It is also clear that, at least at the verbal level, both gender role stereotypes have historically been taken more seriously in Dixie than elsewhere (see Scott, 1970, especially chap. 1). Although today this difference is probably declining, along with most other regional differences, personal experience leads me to conclude that it nonetheless remains. The pioneer past of the Far West, where survival relied upon strong, productive, independent females as well as males, may have dampened the emphasis on some aspects of the traditional feminine stereotype in that area of the country.

Much research remains to be done by way of documenting differences in gender role stereotypes between various groups, but there is little doubt that such differences exist. It is important to note, however, that, with the exception of explicitly countercultural groups, such as the "hippies" of the 1960s, even among subcultures with relatively strong traditions of their own the cultural definitions of the dominant society exert substantial pressure toward conformity. Minorities—namely, all those who are not part of the socioculturally dominant white, northern European, Protestant, middle and upper classes—exist within a society that defines them to a greater or lesser extent as inferior. To some degree such definitions are internalized by many members of the various minority groups and accepted as valid, a phenomenon known in the literature on minority groups as racial or ethnic "self-hatred" (Adelson, 1958, pp. 486, 489; Allport, 1958, pp. 147–48; Frazier, 1957, pp. 226, 271; Simpson & Yinger, 1965, pp. 227–29).

To the extent that individual minority members engage in such group self-hatred, they are led to attempt, within the limits of opportunity and the resources allowed by the dominant group, to "live up to" the norms and roles of the dominant society. Given limited economic opportunities, the result is often a parody of the values and behaviors of the dominant society, as exemplified by the strong emphasis on aggression, sexual exploitation, and physical prowess by lower class males of most ethnic groups. Similarly, large numbers of blacks, many highly educated and involved in radical politics, have accepted the negative (and false) description of their family structure as "matriarchal" which has been propounded by Danial Moynihan (1965) and other whites. Moreover, many black males and females are now engaged in efforts to change this structure to conform to the major cultural pattern of male as dominant partner and breadwinner, and female as subservient homemaker. However, less biased research (Hill, 1972; Rhodes, 1971; Stack, 1974; Myers, 1975; Dietrich, 1975) suggests that the traditional black family structure is and has been very functional in enabling the black to survive in this society. This structure is not the pathological, weak, disorganized entity usually conveyed by the term "matriarchy."

Individuals of all levels of society who reject traditional gender role stereotypes are labeled "nonconformist" and subjected to the wrath of most members of the society. The harsh treatment of longhaired males in the 1960s by police, possible employers, and ordinary citizens speaks eloquently of the "cost" of nonconformity, as does the "wallflower" status of competitive, intellectually gifted, or career-oriented females. But costs are also paid by those who generally conform to gender role stereotypes (or any other kind, for that matter), and these are usually more "hidden."

PERCEIVED COSTS AND BENEFITS

In 1971, students in a sex role class were asked to form single-sex groups to discuss the advantages of the other gender role and the disadvantages of their own. This exercise was a replication of the study done by Barbara Polk and Robert Stein at a northern university, using 250 students of highly diverse backgrounds, and the results parallel theirs almost exactly. Results of the class study are reported in Tables 1 and 2.

When the advantages and disadvantages of the gender roles are compared, the most striking finding relates to the relative length of the various lists. There

Table 1: Disadvantages of Same Gender Role and Advantages of Other One as Perceived by Males

Male Disadvantages	Female Advantages
Can't show Emotions (P)	Freedom to express emotions (R)
Must be provider (O)	Fewer financial obligations; parents support longer (S)
Pressure to succeed, be competitive (O)	Less pressure to succeed (P)
Alimony and child support (O)	Alimony and insurance benefits (S)
Liable to draft (O)	Free from draft (S)
Must take initiative, make decisions (O)	Protected (S)
Limit on acceptable careers (P)	More leisure (S)
Expected to be mechanical, fix things (O)	Placed on pedestal; object of courtesy (S)

Note: Letters enclosed in parentheses refer to a fourfold categorization of roles (Polk & Stein, 1972); P = proscription; O = obligation; R = right; S = structural benefit.

Table 2: Disadvantages of Same Gender Role and Advantages of Other One as Perceived by Females

Female Disadvantages	Male Advantages
Job opportunities limited; discrimination; poor pay (P)	Job opportunities greater (S)
Legal and financial discrimination (P)	Financial and legal opportunity (S)
Educational opportunities limited; judged mentally inferior; opinion devalued; intellectual life stifled (P)	Better educational and training opportunities; opinions valued (S)
Single status stigmatized; stigma for divorce and unwed pregnancy (P)	Bachelorhood glamorized (R)
Socially and sexually restricted; double standard (P)	More freedom sexually and socially (R)
Must bear and rear children; no abortions (in many places); responsible for birth control (O)	No babies (S)
Must maintain good outward appearance; dress, make-up (O)	Less fashion demand and emphasis on appearance (R)
Domestic work (O)	No domestic work (R)
Must be patient; give in; subordinate self; be unaggressive; wait to be asked out on dates (P)	Can be aggressive, dating and otherwise (O)
Inhibited motor control; not allowed to be athletic (P)	More escapism allowed (R)

Note: Letters enclosed in parentheses refer to a fourfold categorization of roles (Polk & Stein, 1972): P = proscription; O = obligation; R = right; S = structural benefit.

seem to be many more disadvantages adhering to the feminine role as perceived by females than to the masculine role as perceived by males (or else the females were simply and stereotypically more loquacious!) Conversely, more advantages are seen as accruing to the masculine role by females than to the feminine role by males. More relevant to the question of costs, however, is the finding that the perceived advantages of one sex are the disadvantages of the other. If it is a masculine disadvantage not to be able to show emotions, it is a feminine advantage to be able to do so. Likewise, if it is a feminine disadvantage to face limited job opportunities, the converse is a masculine advantage. Summarizing similar findings, Polk and Stein (1972) conclude: "The extent to which this relationship exists strongly suggests that there is general agreement on the desirable characteristics for any individual, regardless of sex" (p. 16).

Polk and Stein's four-fold categorization of role components as rights, obligations, proscriptions, and structural benefits is useful in examining the nature of specific perceived costs and benefits of the two roles. According to Polk and Stein, "Rights allow the individual the freedom to commit an act or refrain from an act without receiving sanctions for either choice" (p. 19). Obligations and proscriptions are different in that individuals are negatively sanctioned, in the first case for not doing something, in the second for doing it. Structural benefits refer to "advantages derived from the social structure or from actions of others" on the basis of sex alone (p. 21). Each advantage and disadvantage listed in Tables 1 and 2 is followed by a letter in parentheses which represents my judgment as to whether that characteristic is a right (R), a proscription (P), an obligation (O), or a structural benefit (S). Masculine disadvantages consist overwhelmingly of obligations with a few proscriptions, while the disadvantages of the feminine role arise primarily from proscriptions, with a few obligations. Thus females complain about what they can't do, males about what they must do. Females complain that they cannot be athletic, aggressive, sexually free, or successful in the worlds of work and education; in short, they complain of their passivity. Males complain that they must be aggressive and must succeed; in short, of their activity. The (sanctioned) requirement that males be active and females passive in a variety of ways is clearly unpleasant to both.

The nature of the types of advantages seen as accruing to each of the two roles by the other sex supports the stereotyped dichotomy between activity and passivity still further. Females are seen as overwhelmingly enjoying structural benefits, namely, advantages that accrue to them without reference to what they do. Males believe females have only one right. Females believe males also enjoy structural benefits but have considerably more rights, namely, choices of action or inaction. These findings generally agree with those of Polk and Stein, who found that altogether the masculine role had 14 obligations compared to 8 for the feminine role; 6 rights compared to 0; 4 proscriptions compared to 15; and 6 structural benefits compared to 4.

ECONOMIC COSTS AND BENEFITS

How helpful or costly would the masculine or feminine gender role stereotype traits . . . be for a competitor in the highest echelons of our economy and society? One measure of such success is occupation. Robert Hodge, Paul Siegel, and Peter Rossi (1966) studied the relative prestige of a large number of occupations in the United States and found that the four most prestigious were: U.S. Supreme Court Justice, physician, scientist, and state governor. Table 3 summarizes the data on which stereotypical traits are clearly helpful in attaining and performing well in these occupational roles and which are harmful. While the designation as "helpful" or "harmful" for some few traits is debatable, the overall picture probably is not. Stereotypical feminine traits patently do not equip those who might try to live up to them to compete in the world of social and economic privilege, power, and prestige; the exact opposite is the case for masculine characteristics. Where 15 feminine traits are classified as "harmful," only 2 masculine ones are so designated. Conversely, where 17 masculine traits are classified as "helpful," the analogous number of feminine traits is 7. The cost of femininity for those who would enter the world outside the home could scarcely be more clear: The more a female conforms, the less is she capable of functioning in roles that are other than domestic.

Table 3. Gender Role Traits Helpful and Harmful in Acquiring and Performing Well in Prestigious Occupational Roles

Stereotyped Traits	Harmful	Helpful
Masculine	Sloppy	Breadwinner, provider
	Dogmatic	Stoic, unemotional
		Logical, rational, objective, scientific
		Practical
		Mechancial (for scientist and physician)
		Public awareness
		Leader
		Disciplinarian
		Independent
		Demanding
		Aggressive
		Ambitious
		Proud, confident
		Moral, trustworthy
		Decisive
		Competitive
		Adventurous
Feminine	Worry about appearance and age	Compassionate
	Sensual	Intuitive
	Domestic	Humanistic
	Seductive, flirtatious	Perceptive
	Emotional, sentimental	Idealistic
	Nervous, insecure, fearful	Patient
	Scatterbrained, frivolous	Gentle
	Impractical	
	Petty, coy, gossipy	
	Dependent, overprotected	
	Follower, submissive	
	Self-conscious; easily intimidated	
	Not aggressive, passive	
	Tardy	
	Noncompetitive	

Indeed, gender roles are so deeply ingrained that even among successful business executives, women, unlike men, often attribute their success to luck rather than their own hard work and competence. Moreover, women tend to understate the extent of their achievements (Hennig & Jardim, 1977). On the other hand, reared in a culture that emphasizes the myth that hard work and personal worth will result in job success, many males, especially in the middle class, suffer feelings of personal inadequacy and failure if they are not highly successful in a material sense. In short, the feminine role stereotype gears women for economic failure, and if that is not the case, women explain their success in terms external to themselves. The masculine role stereotype gears men for economic success, and if that is not forthcoming men perceive themselves as personally responsible for their "failure."

WORKS CITED IN ARTICLE

Adelson, Joseph. "A Study of Minority Group Authoritarianism." In Marshall Sklare (ed.), *The Jews: Social Patterns of an American Group,* pp. 475–92. Glencoe, Ill.: Free Press, 1958.

Allport, Gordon. *The Nature of Prejudice.* Garden City, N.Y.: Doubleday Anchor books, 1958; first published 1954.

Dietrich, Kathryn. "The Re-examination of the Myth of Black Matriarchy." *Journal of Marriage and the Family* 37 (May 1975): 367–74.

Frazier, E. Franklin. *Black Bourgeoisie.* Glencoe, Ill.: Free Press, 1957.

Hennig, Margaret, and Jardim, Anne. *The Managerial Woman.* New York: Anchor-Doubleday, 1977.

Hill, Robert B. *The Strengths of Black Families.* New York: Emerson Hall Publishers, 1972.

Hodge, Robert; Siegel, Paul; and Rossi, Peter. "Occupational Prestige in the United States: 1925–1963." In Reinhard Bendix and S. M. Lipset (eds.), *Class, Status and Power,* pp. 322–34. 2nd ed. Glencoe, Ill.: Free Press, 1966.

McKinley, Donald G. *Social Class and Family Life.* Glencoe, Ill.: Free Press, 1964.

Moynihan, Daniel P. *The Negro Family: The Case for National Action.* Washington, D.C.: U.S. Department of Labor, 1965.

Myers, Lena Wright. "Black Women and Self-Esteem." In Marcia Millman and Rosabeth Kanter (eds.), *Another Vice,* pp. 240–50. Garden City, N.Y.: Anchor Books, 1975.

Polk, Barbara Bovee, and Stein, Robert B. "Is the Grass Greener on the Other Side?" In Constantina Safilios-Rothschild (ed.), *Toward a Sociology of Women,* pp. 14–23. Lexington, Mass.: Xerox College Publishing Co., 1972.

Rhodes, Barbara. "The Changing Role of the Black Woman." In Robert Staples (ed.), *The Black Family,* pp. 145–49. Belmont, Calif.: Wadsworth Publishing Co., 1971.

Scott, Anne Firor. *The Southern Lady.* Chicago: University of Chicago Press, 1970.

Simpson, George E., and Yinger, J. Milton. *Racial and Cultural Minorities.* 3rd ed. New York: Harper & Row, 1965.

Stack, Carol. *All Our Kin: Strategies for Survival in a Black Community.* New York: Harper & Row, 1974.

Staples, Robert. "The Myth of the Black Matriarchy." *Black Scholar* 1 (January-February, 1970): 8–16.

Yorburg, Betty. *Sexual Identity: Sex Roles and Social Change.* New York: John Wiley & Sons, 1974.

Declaration of Sentiments and Resolutions

Adopted by the Seneca Falls Convention, July 19–20, 1848

When, in the course of human events, it becomes necessary for one portion of the family of man to assume among the people of the earth a position different from that which they have hitherto occupied, but one to which the laws of nature and of nature's God entitle them, a decent respect to the opinions of mankind requires that they should declare the causes that impel them to such a course.

We hold these truths to be self-evident: that all men and women are created equal; that they are endowed by their Creator with certain inalienable rights; that among these are life, liberty, and the pursuit of happiness; that to secure these rights governments are instituted, deriving their just powers from the consent of the governed. Whenever any form of government becomes destructive of these ends, it is the right of those who suffer from it to refuse allegiance to it, and to insist upon the institution of a new government, laying its foundation on such principles, and organizing its powers in such form, as to them shall seem most likely to effect their safety and happiness. Prudence, indeed, will dictate that governments long established should not be changed for light and transient causes; and accordingly all experience hath shown that mankind are more disposed to suffer, while evils are sufferable, than to right themselves by abolishing the forms to which they were accustomed. But when a long train of abuses and usurpations, pursuing invariably the same object, evinces a design to reduce them under absolute despotism, it is their duty to throw off such government, and to provide new guards for their future security. Such has been the patient sufferance of the women under this government, and such is now the necessity which constrains them to demand the equal station to which they are entitled.

The history of mankind is a history of repeated injuries and usurpations on the part of man toward woman, having in direct object the establishment of an absolute tyranny over her. To prove this, let facts be submitted to a candid world.

He has never permitted her to exercise her inalienable right to the elective franchise.

He has compelled her to submit to laws, in the formation of which she had no voice.

He has withheld from her rights which are given to the most ignorant and degraded men—both natives and foreigners.

Having deprived her of this first right of a citizen, the elective franchise, thereby leaving her without representation in the halls of legislation, he has oppressed her on all sides.

He has made her, if married, in the eye of the law, civilly dead.

He has taken from her all right in property, even to the wages she earns.

He has made her, morally, an irresponsible being, as she can commit many crimes with impunity, provided they be done in the presence of her husband. In the covenant of marriage, she is compelled to promise obedience to her husband, he becoming to all intents and purposes, her master—the law giving him power to deprive her of her liberty, and to administer chastisement.

He has so framed the laws of divorce, as to what shall be the proper causes, and in case of separation, to whom the guardianship of the children shall be given, as to be wholly regardless of the happiness of women—the law, in all cases, going upon a false supposition of the supremacy of man, and giving all power into his hands.

After depriving her of all rights as a married woman, if single, and the owner of property, he has taxed her to support a government which recognizes her only when her property can be made profitable to it.

He has monopolized nearly all the profitable employments, and from those she is permitted to follow, she receives but a scanty remuneration. He closes against her all the avenues to wealth and distinction which he considers most honorable to himself. As a teacher of theology, medicine, or law, she is not known.

He has denied her the facilities for obtaining a thorough education, all colleges being closed against her.

He allows her in Church, as well as State, but a subordinate position, claiming Apostolic authority for her exclusion from the ministry, and, with some exceptions, from any public participation in the affairs of the Church.

He has created a false public sentiment by giving to the world a different code of morals for men and women, by which moral delinquencies which exclude women from society, are not only tolerated, but deemed of little account in man.

He has usurped the prerogative of Jehovah himself, claiming it as his right to assign for her a sphere of action, when that belongs to her conscience and to her God.

He has endeavored, in every way that he could, to destroy her confidence in her own powers, to lessen her self-respect, and to make her willing to lead a dependent and abject life.

Now, in view of this entire disfranchisement of one-half the people of this country, their social and religious degradation—in view of the unjust laws above mentioned, and because women do feel themselves aggrieved, oppressed, and fraudulently deprived of their most sacred rights, we insist that they have immediate admission to all the rights and privileges which belong to them as citizens of the United States.

In entering upon the great work before us, we anticipate no small amount of misconception, misrepresentation, and ridicule; but we shall use every instrumentality without our power to effect our object. We shall employ agents, circulate tracts, petition the State and National legislatures, and endeavor to enlist the pulpit and the press in our behalf. We hope this Convention will be followed by a series of Conventions embracing every part of the country.

[The following resolutions were discussed by Lucretia Mott, Thomas and Mary Ann McClintock, Amy Post, Catharine A. F. Stebbins, and others, and were adopted:]

WHEREAS, The great precept of nature is conceded to be, that "man shall pursue his own true and substantial happiness." Blackstone[1] in his Commentaries remarks, that this law of Nature being coeval[2] with mankind, and dictated by God himself, is of course superior in obligation to any other. It is binding over all the globe, in all countries and at all times; no human laws are of any validity if contrary to this, and such of them as are valid, derive all their force, and all their validity, and all their authority, mediately and immediately, from this original; therefore,

Resolved, That such laws as conflict, in any way, with the true and substantial happiness of woman, are contrary to the great precept of nature and of no validity, for this is "superior in obligation to any other."

Resolved, That all laws which prevent woman from occupying such a station in society as her conscience shall dictate, or which place her in a position inferior to that of man, are contrary to the great precept of nature, and therefore of no force or authority.

---

[1] ***Sir William Blackstone (1723–1780)*** The most influential of English scholars of the law. His *Commentaries of the Laws of England* (4 vols., 1765–1769) form the basis of the study of law in England.

[2] ***coeval*** Existing simultaneously.

Resolved, That woman is man's equal—was intended to be so by the Creator, and the highest good of the race demands that she should be recognized as such.

Resolved, That the women of this country ought to be enlightened in regard to the laws under which they live, that they may no longer publish their degradation by declaring themselves satisfied with their present position, nor their ignorance, by asserting that they have all the rights they want.

Resolved, That inasmuch as man, while claiming for himself intellectual superiority, does accord to woman moral superiority, it is pre-eminently his duty to encourage her to speak and teach, as she has an opportunity, in all religious assemblies.

Resolved, That the same amount of virtue, delicacy, and refinement of behavior that is required of woman in the social state, should also be required of man, and the same transgressions should be visited with equal severity on both man and woman.

Resolved, That the objection of indelicacy and impropriety, which is so often brought against woman when she addresses a public audience, comes with a very ill-grace from those who encourage, by their attendance, her appearance on the stage, in the concert, or in feats of the circus.

Resolved, That woman has too long rested satisfied in the circumscribed limits which corrupt customs and a perverted application of the Scriptures have marked out for her, and that it is time she should move in the enlarged sphere which her great Creator has assigned her.

Resolved, That it is the duty of the women of this country to secure to themselves their sacred right to the elective franchise.

Resolved, That the equality of human rights results necessarily from the fact of the identity of the race in capabilities and responsibilities.

Resolved, therefore, That, being invested by the Creator with the same capabilities, and the same consciousness of responsibility for their exercise, it is demonstrably the right and duty of woman, equally with man, to promote every righteous cause by every righteous means; and especially in regard to the great subjects of morals and religion, it is self-evidently her right to participate with her brother in teaching them, both in private and in public, by writing and by speaking, by any intrumentalities proper to be used, and in any assemblies proper to be held; and this being a self-evident truth growing out of the divinely implanted principles of human nature, any custom or authority adverse to it, whether modern or wearing the hoary sanction of antiquity, is to be regarded as a self-evident falsehood, and at war with mankind.

[At the last session Lucretia Mott[3] offered and spoke to the following resolution:]

Resolved, That the speedy success of our cause depends upon the zealous and untiring efforts of both men and women, for the overthrow of the monopoly of

---

[3] ***Lucretia Mott (1793–1880)*** One of the founders of the 1848 convention at which these resolutions were presented. She is one of the earliest and most important of the feminists who struggled to proclaim their rights. She was also a prominent abolitionist.

the pulpit, and for the securing to women an equal participation with men in the various trades, professions, and commerce.

My Fight for Birth Control

Margaret Sanger

AWAKENING AND REVOLT

Early in the year 1912 I came to a sudden realization that my work as a nurse and my activities in social service were entirely palliative and consequently futile and useless to relieve the misery I saw all about me. . . .

Were it possible for me to depict the revolting conditions existing in the homes of some of the women I attended in that one year, one would find it hard to believe. There was at that time, and doubtless is still today, a sub-stratum of men and women whose lives are absolutely untouched by social agencies.

The way they live is almost beyond belief. They hate and fear any prying into their homes or into their lives. They resent being talked to. The women slink in and out of their homes on their way to market like rats from their holes. The men beat their wives sometimes black and blue, but no one interferes. The children are cuffed, kicked and chased about, but woe to the child who dares to tell tales out of the home! Crime or drink is often the source of this secret aloofness, usually there is something to hide, a skeleton in the closet somewhere. The men are sullen, unskilled workers, picking up odd jobs now and then, unemployed usually, sauntering in and out of the house at all hours of the day and night.

The women keep apart from other women in the neighborhood. Often they are suspected of picking a pocket or "lifting" an article when occasion arises. Pregnancy is an almost chronic condition amongst them. I knew one woman who had given birth to eight children with no professional care whatever. The last one was born in the kitchen, witnessed by a son of ten years who, under his mother's direction, cleaned the bed, wrapped the placenta and soiled articles in paper, and threw them out of the window into the court below. . . .

In this atmosphere abortions and birth become the main theme of conversation. On Saturday nights I have seen groups of fifty to one hundred women going into questionable offices well known in the community for cheap abortions. I asked several women what took place there, and they all gave the same reply: a quick examination, a probe inserted into the uterus and turned a few times to disturb the fertilized ovum, and then the woman was sent home. Usually the flow began the next day and often continued four or five weeks. Sometimes an ambulance carried the victim to the hospital for a curetage, and if she returned home at all she was looked upon as a lucky woman.

This state of things became a nightmare with me. There seemed no sense to it all, no reason for such waste of mother life, no right to exhaust women's vitality and to throw them on the scrap-heap before the age of thirty-five.

Everywhere I looked, misery and fear stalked—men fearful of losing their jobs, women fearful that even worse conditions might come upon them. The menace of another pregnancy hung like a sword over the head of every poor woman I came in contact with that year. The question which met me was always the same: What can I do to keep from it? or, What can I do to get out of this? Sometimes they talked among themselves bitterly.

"It's the rich that know the tricks," they'd say, "while we have all the kids." Then, if the women were Roman Catholics, they talked about "Yankee tricks," and asked me if I knew what the Protestants did to keep their families down. When I said that I didn't believe that the rich knew much more than they did I was laughed at and suspected of holding back information for money. They would nudge each other and say something about paying me before I left the case if I would reveal the "secret." . . .

Finally the thing began to shape itself, to become accumulative during the three weeks I spent in the home of a desperately sick woman living on Grand Street, a lower section of New York's East Side.

Mrs. Sacks was only twenty-eight years old; her husband, an unskilled worker, thirty-two. Three children, aged five, three and one, were none too strong nor sturdy, and it took all the earnings of the father and the ingenuity of the mother to keep them clean, provide them with air and proper food, and give them a chance to grow into decent manhood and womanhood.

Both parents were devoted to these children and to each other. The woman had become pregnant and had taken various drugs and purgatives, as advised by her neighbors. Then, in desperation, she had used some instrument lent to her by a friend. She was found prostrate on the floor amidst the crying children when her husband returned from work. Neighbors advised against the ambulance, and a friendly doctor was called. The husband would not hear of her going to a hospital, and as a little money had been saved in the bank a nurse was called and the battle for that precious life began.

It was in the middle of July. The three-room apartment was turned into a hospital for the dying patient. Never had I worked so fast, never so concentratedly as I did to keep alive that little mother. Neighbor women came and went during the day doing the odds and ends necessary for our comfort. The children were sent to friends and relatives and the doctor and I settled ourselves to outdo the force and power of an outraged nature.

Never had I known such conditions could exist. July's sultry days and nights were melted into a torpid inferno. Day after day, night after night, I slept only in brief snatches, ever too anxious about the condition of that feeble heart bravely carrying on, to stay long from the bedside of the patient. . . .

At the end of two weeks recovery was in sight, and at the end of three weeks

I was preparing to leave the fragile patient to take up the ordinary duties of her life, including those of wifehood and motherhood. Everyone was congratulating her on her recovery. All the kindness of sympathetic and understanding neighbors poured in upon her in the shape of convalescent dishes, soups, custards, and drinks. Still she appeared to be despondent and worried. She seemed to sit apart in her thoughts as if she had no part in these congratulatory messages and endearing welcomes. I thought at first that she still retained some of her unconscious memories and dwelt upon them in her silences.

But as the hour for my departure came nearer, her anxiety increased, and finally with trembling voice she said: "Another baby will finish me, I suppose."

"It's too early to talk about that," I said, and resolved that I would turn the question over to the doctor for his advice. When he came I said: "Mrs. Sacks is worried about having another baby."

"She well might be," replied the doctor, and then he stood before her and said: "Any more such capers, young woman, and there will be no need to call me."

"Yes, yes—I know, Doctor," said the patient with trembling voice, "but," and she hesitated as if it took all of her courage to say it, "*what* can I do to prevent getting that way again?"

"Oh ho!" laughed the doctor good naturedly, "You want your cake while you eat it too, do you? Well, it can't be done." Then, familiarly slapping her on the back and picking up his hat and bag to depart, he said: "I'll tell you the only sure thing to do. Tell Jake to sleep on the roof!"

With those words he closed the door and went down the stairs, leaving us both petrified and stunned.

Tears sprang to my eyes, and a lump came in my throat as I looked at that face before me. It was stamped with sheer horror. I thought for a moment she might have gone insane, but she conquered her feelings, whatever they may have been, and turning to me in desperation said: "He can't understand, can he?—he's a man after all—but you do, don't you? You're a woman and you'll tell me the secret and I'll never tell it to a soul."

She clasped her hands as if in prayer, she leaned over and looked straight into my eyes and beseechingly implored me to tell her something—something *I really did not know*. It was like being on a rack and tortured for a crime one had not committed. To plead guilty would stop the agony; otherwise the rack kept turning.

I had to turn away from that imploring face. I could not answer her then. I quieted her as best I could. She saw that I was moved by the tears in my eyes. I promised that I would come back in a few days and tell her what she wanted to know. The few simple means of limiting the family like *coitis interruptus* or the condom were laughed at by the neighboring women when told these were the means used by men in the well-to-do families. That was not believed, and I knew such an answer would be swept aside as useless were I to tell her this at such a time.

A little later when she slept I left the house, and made up my mind that I'd keep away from those cases in the future. I felt helpless to do anything at all. I seemed chained hand and foot, and longed for an earthquake or a volcano to shake the world out of its lethargy into facing these monstrous atrocities.

The intelligent reasoning of the young mother—how to *prevent* getting that way again—how sensible, how just she had been—yes, I promised myself I'd go back and have a long talk with her and tell her more, and perhaps she would not laugh but would believe that those methods were all that were really known.

But time flew past, and weeks rolled into months. That wistful, appealing face haunted me day and night. I could not banish from my mind memories of that trembling voice begging so humbly for knowledge she had a right to have. I was about to retire one night three months later when the telephone rang and an agitated man's voice begged me to come at once to help his wife who was sick again. It was the husband of Mrs. Sacks, and I intuitively knew before I left the telephone that it was almost useless to go.

I dreaded to face that woman. I was tempted to send someone else in my place. I longed for an accident on the subway, or on the street—anything to prevent my going into that home. But on I went just the same. I arrived a few minutes after the doctor, the same one who had given her such noble advice. The woman was dying. She was unconscious. She died within ten minutes after my arrival. It was the same result, the same story told a thousand times before—death from abortion. She had become pregnant, had used drugs, had then consulted a five-dollar professional abortionist, and death followed.

The doctor shook his head as he rose from listening for the heart beat. I knew she had already passed on; without a groan, a sign or recognition of our belated presence she had gone into the Great Beyond as thousands of mothers go every year. I looked at that drawn face now stilled in death. I placed her thin hands across her breast and recalled how hard they had pleaded with me on that last memorable occasion of parting. The gentle woman, the devoted mother, the loving wife had passed on leaving behind her a frantic husband, helpless in his loneliness, bewildered in his helplessness as he paced up and down the room, hands clenching his head, moaning "My God! My God! My God!"

The Revolution came—but not as it has been pictured nor as history relates that revolutions have come. It came in my own life. It began in my very being as I walked home that night after I had closed the eyes and covered with a sheet the body of that little helpless mother whose life had been sacrificed to ignorance.

After I left that desolate house I walked and walked and walked; for hours and hours I kept on, bag in hand, thinking, regretting, dreading to stop; fearful of my conscience, dreading to face my own accusing soul. At three in the morning I arrived home still clutching a heavy load the weight of which I was quite unconscious.

I entered the house quietly, as was my custom, and looked out of the window down upon the dimly lighted, sleeping city. As I stood at the window and looked out, the miseries and problems of that sleeping city arose before me in a clear vision like a panorama: crowded homes, too many children; babies dying in infancy; mothers overworked; baby nurseries; children neglected and hungry—mothers so nervously wrought they could not give the little things the comfort nor care they needed; mothers half sick most of their lives—"always ailing, never failing"; women made into drudges; children working in cellars; children aged six and seven pushed into the labor market to help earn a living; another baby on the way; still another; yet another; a baby born dead—great relief; an older child dies—sorrow, but nevertheless relief—insurance helps; a mother's death—children scattered into institutions; the father, desperate, drunken; he slinks away to become an outcast in a society which has trapped him. . . .

. . . For hours I stood, motionless and tense, expecting something to happen. I watched the lights go out, I saw the darkness gradually give way to the first shimmer of dawn, and then a colorful sky heralded the rise of the sun. I knew a new day had come for me and a new world as well.

It was like an illumination. I could now see clearly the various social strata of our life; all its mass problems seemed to be centered around uncontrolled breeding. There was only one thing to be done: call out, start the alarm, set the heather on fire! Awaken the womanhood of America to free the motherhood of the world! I released from my almost paralyzed hand the nursing bag which unconsciously I had clutched, threw it across the room, tore the uniform from my body, flung it into a corner, and renounced all palliative work forever.

I would never go back again to nurse women's ailing bodies while their miseries were as vast as the stars. I was now finished with superficial cures, with doctors and nurses and social workers who were brought face to face with this overwhelming truth of women's needs and yet turned to pass on the other side. They must be made to see these facts. I resolved that women should have knowledge of contraception. They have every right to know about their own bodies. I would strike out—I would scream from the housetops. I would tell the world what was going on in the lives of these poor women. I *would* be heard. No matter what it should cost. *I would be heard.*

A "PUBLIC NUISANCE"

The selection of a place for the first birth control clinic was of the greatest importance. No one could actually tell how it would be received in any neighborhood. I thought of all the possible difficulties: The indifference of women's organizations, the ignorance of the workers themselves, the resentment of social agencies, the opposition of the medical profession. Then there was the law—the law of New York State.

Section 1142 was definite. It stated that *no one* could give information to prevent conception to *anyone* for any reason. There was, however, Section 1145, which distinctly stated that physicians (*only*) could give advice to prevent conception for the cure or prevention of disease. I inquired about the section, and was told by two attorneys and several physicians that this clause was an exception to 1142 referring only to venereal disease. But anyway, as I was not a physician, it could not protect me. Dared I risk it?

I began to think of the doctors I knew. Several who had previously promised now refused. I wrote, telephoned, asked friends to ask other friends to help me find a woman doctor to help me demonstrate the need of a birth control clinic in New York. None could be found. No one wanted to go to jail. No one cared to test out the law. Perhaps it would have to be done without a doctor. But it had to be done; that I knew.

Fania Mindell, an enthusiastic young worker in the cause, had come on from Chicago to help me. Together we tramped the streets on that dreary day in early October, through a driving rainstorm, to find the best location at the cheapest terms possible. We stopped to inquire about vacant stores of the officials in one of the milk stations. "Don't come over here." "Keep out of this section." "We don't want any trouble over here." These and other pleasantries were hurled at us as we darted in and out of the various places asking for advice, hoping for a welcome.

Finally at 46 Amboy Street in the Brownsville section of Brooklyn, we found a friendly landlord with a good place vacant at fifty dollars a month rental; and Brownsville was settled on. It was one of the most thickly populated sections. It had a large population of working class Jews, always interested in health measures, always tolerant of new ideas, willing to listen and to accept advice whenever the health of mother or children was involved. I knew that here there would at least be no breaking of windows, no hurling of insults into our teeth; but I was scarcely prepared for the popular support, the sympathy and friendly help given us in that neighborhood from that day to this.

The Brownsville section of Brooklyn in 1916 was a hive of futile industry—dingy, squalid, peopled with hard-working men and women, the home of poverty which was steadily growing worse in the tide of increasing responsibilities. Early every morning, weary-eyed men poured from the low tenement houses that crouched together as if for warmth, bound for ten or twelve hours of work. At the same time, or earlier, their women rose to set in motion that ceaseless round of cooking, cleaning, and sewing that barely kept the young generation alive. A fatalistic, stolid, and tragic army of New Yorkers dwelt here, most of them devout Jews or Italians, all of them energetic and ambitious—but trapped by nature's despotism. . . .

We determined to open a birth control clinic at 46 Amboy Street to disseminate information where it was poignantly required by human beings. Our inspiration was the mothers of the poor; our object, to help them.

With a small bundle of handbills and a large amount of zeal, we fared forth each morning in a house-to-house canvass of the district in which the clinic was located. Every family in that great district received a "dodger" printed in English, Yiddish and Italian. . . .

It was on October 16, 1916, that the three of us—Fania Mindell, Ethel Byrne and myself—opened the doors of the first birth control clinic in America. I believed then and do today, that the opening of these doors to the mothers of Brownsville was an event of social significance in the lives of American womanhood.

News of our work spread like wildfire. Within a few days there was not a darkened tenement, hovel or flat but was brightened by the knowledge that motherhood could be voluntary; that children need not be born into the world unless they are wanted and have a place provided for them. For the first time, women talked openly of this terror of unwanted pregnancy which had haunted their lives since time immemorial. The newspapers, in glaring headlines, used the words "birth control," and carried the message that somewhere in Brooklyn there was a place where contraceptive information could be obtained by all overburdened mothers who wanted it.

Ethel Byrne, who is my sister and a trained nurse, assisted me in advising, explaining, and demonstrating to the women how to prevent conception. As all of our 488 records were confiscated by the detectives who later arrested us for violation of the New York State law, it is difficult to tell exactly how many more women came in those few days to seek advice; but we estimate that it was far more than five hundred. As in any new enterprise, false reports were maliciously spread about the clinic; weird stories without the slightest foundation of truth. We talked plain talk and gave plain facts to the women who came there. We kept a record of every applicant. All were mothers; most of them had large families.

It was whispered about that the police were to raid the place for abortions. We had no fear of that accusation. We were trying to spare mothers the necessity of that ordeal by giving them proper contraceptive information. It was well that so many of the women in the neighborhood knew the truth of our doings. Hundreds of them who had witnessed the facts came to the courtroom afterward, eager to testify in our behalf.

One day a woman by the name of Margaret Whitehurst came to us. She said that she was the mother of two children and that she had not money to support more. Her story was a pitiful one—all lies, of course, but the government acts that way. She asked for our literature and preventives, and received both. Then she triumphantly went to the District Attorney's office and secured a warrant for the arrest of my sister, Mrs. Ethel Byrne, our interpreter, Miss Fania Mindell, and myself.

The crusade was actually under way! It is no exaggeration to call this period in the birth control movement the most stirring period up to that time, perhaps the most stirring of all times, for it was the only period during which we had experienced jail terms, hunger strikes, and intervention by the Chief Executive of the state. It was the first time that there was any number of widespread, popular demonstrations in our behalf. . . .

The arrest and raid on the Brooklyn clinic was spectacular. There was no need of a large force of plain clothes men to drag off a trio of decent, serious women who were testing out a law on a fundamental principle. My federal arrest, on the contrary, had been assigned to intelligent men. One had to respect the dignity of their mission; but the New York city officials seem to use tactics suitable only for crooks, bandits and burglars. We were not surprised at being arrested, but the shock and horror of it was that a *woman,* with a squad of five plain clothes men, conducted the raid and made the arrest. A woman—the irony of it!

I refused to close down the clinic, hoping that a court decision would allow us to continue such necessary work. I was to be disappointed. Pressure was brought upon the landlord, and we were dispossessed by the law as a "public nuisance." In Holland the clinics were called "public utilities."

When the policewoman entered the clinic with her squad of plain clothes men and announced the arrest of Miss Mindell and myself (Mrs. Byrne was not present at the time and her arrest followed later), the room was crowded to suffocation with women waiting in the outer room. The police began bullying these mothers, asking them questions, writing down their names in order to subpoena them to testify against us at the trial. These women, always afraid of trouble which the very presence of a policeman signifies, screamed and cried aloud. The children on their laps screamed, too. It was like a panic for a few minutes until I walked into the room where they were stampeding and begged them to be quiet and not to get excited. I assured them that nothing could happen to them, that I was under arrest but they would be allowed to return home in a few minutes. That quieted them. The men were blocking the door to prevent anyone from leaving, but I finally persuaded them to allow these women to return to their homes, unmolested though terribly frightened by it all.

Crowds began to gather outside. A long line of women with baby carriages and children had been waiting to get into the clinic. Now the streets were filled, and police had to see that traffic was not blocked. The patrol wagon came rattling through the streets to our door, and at length Miss Mindell and I took our seats within and were taken to the police station.

As I sat in the rear of the car and looked out on that seething mob of humans, I wondered, and asked myself *what* had gone out of the race. Something had gone from them which silenced them, made them impotent to defend their rights. I thought of the suffragists in England, and pictured the results of a similar arrest there. But as I sat in this mood, the car started to go. I looked out at the mass and heard a scream. It came from a woman wheeling a baby carriage, who had just come around the corner preparing to visit the clinic. She saw the patrol wagon, realized what had happened, left the baby carriage on the walk, rushed through the crowd to the wagon and cried to me: "Come back! Come back and save me!" The woman looked wild. She ran after the car for a dozen yards or so, when some friends caught her weeping form in their arms and led her back to the sidewalk. That was the last thing I saw as the Black Maria dashed off to the station.

The Problem that Has No Name

Betty Friedan

The problem lay buried, unspoken, for many years in the minds of American women. It was a strange stirring, a sense of dissatisfaction, a yearning that women suffered in the middle of the twentieth century in the United States. Each suburban wife struggled with it alone. As she made the beds, shopped for groceries, matched slipcover material, ate peanut butter sandwiches with her children, chauffeured

Cub Scouts and Brownies, lay beside her husband at night—she was afraid to ask even of herself the silent question—"Is this all?"

For over fifteen years there was no word of this yearning in the millions of words written about women, for women, in all the columns, books and articles by experts telling women their role was to seek fulfillment as wives and mothers. Over and over women heard in voices of tradition and of Freudian sophistication that they could desire no greater destiny than to glory in their own femininity. Experts told them how to catch a man and keep him, how to breastfeed children and handle their toilet training, how to cope with sibling rivalry and adolescent rebellion; how to buy a dishwasher, bake bread, cook gourmet snails, and build a swimming pool with their own hands; how to dress, look, and act more feminine and make marriage more exciting; how to keep their husbands from dying young and their sons from growing into delinquents. They were taught to pity the neurotic, unfeminine, unhappy women who wanted to be poets or physicists or presidents. They learned that truly feminine women do not want careers, higher education, political rights—the independence and the opportunities that the old-fashioned feminists fought for. Some women, in their forties and fifties, still remembered painfully giving up those dreams, but most of the younger women no longer even thought about them. A thousand expert voices applauded their femininity, their adjustment, their new maturity. All they had to do was devote their lives from earliest girlhood to finding a husband and bearing children.

By the end of the nineteen-fifties, the average marriage age of women in America dropped to 20, and was still dropping, into the teens. Fourteen million girls were engaged by 17. The proportion of women attending college in comparison with men dropped from 47 per cent in 1920 to 35 per cent in 1958. A century earlier, women had fought for higher education; now girls went to college to get a husband. By the mid-fifties, 60 per cent dropped out of college to marry, or because they were afraid too much education would be a marriage bar. Colleges built dormitories for "married students," but the students were almost always the husbands. A new degree was instituted for the wives—"Ph.T." (Putting Husband Through).

Then American girls began getting married in high school. And the women's magazines, deploring the unhappy statistics about these young marriages, urged that courses on marriage, and marriage counselors, be installed in the high schools. Girls started going steady at twelve and thirteen, in junior high. Manufacturers put out brassieres with false bosoms of foam rubber for little girls of ten. And an advertisement for a child's dress, sizes 3–6x, in the *New York Times* in the fall of 1960, said: "She Too Can Join the Man-Trap Set."

By the end of the fifties, the United States birthrate was overtaking India's. The birth-control movement, renamed Planned Parenthood, was asked to find a method whereby women who had been advised that a third or fourth baby would be born dead or defective might have it anyhow. Statisticians were especially astounded at the fantastic increase in the number of babies among college women. Where once they had two children, now they had four, five, six. Women who had once wanted careers were now making careers out of having babies. So rejoiced *Life* magazine in a 1956 paean to the movement of American women back to the home.

In a New York hospital, a woman had a nervous breakdown when she found she could not breastfeed her baby. In other hospitals, women dying of cancer refused a drug which research had proved might save their lives: its side effects were said to be unfeminine. "If I have only one life, let me live it as a blonde," a larger-than-life-sized picture of a pretty, vacuous woman proclaimed from newspaper, magazine, and drugstore ads. And across America, three out of every ten women dyed their hair blonde. They ate a chalk called Metrecal, instead of food, to shrink to the size of the thin young models. Department-store buyers reported that American women, since 1939, had become three and four sizes smaller. "Women are out to fit the clothes, instead of vice-versa," one buyer said.

Interior decorators were designing kitchens with mosaic murals and original paintings, for kitchens were once again the center of women's lives. Home sewing became a million-dollar industry. Many women no longer left their homes, except to shop, chauffeur their children, or attend a social engagement with their husbands. Girls were growing up in America without ever having jobs outside the home. In the late fifties, a sociological phenomenon was suddenly remarked: a third of American women now worked, but most were no longer young and very few were pursuing careers. They were married women who held part-time jobs, selling or secretarial, to put their husbands through school, their sons through college, or to help pay the mortgage. Or they were widows supporting families. Fewer and fewer women were entering professional work. The shortages in the nursing, social work, and teaching professions caused crises in almost every American city. Concerned over the Soviet Union's lead in the space race, scientists noted that America's greatest source of unused brainpower was women. But girls would not study physics: it was "unfeminine." A girl refused a science fellowship at Johns Hopkins to take a job in a real-estate office. All she wanted, she said, was what every other American girl wanted—to get married, have four children and live in a nice house in a nice suburb.

The suburban housewife—she was the dream image of the young American women and the envy, it was said, of women all over the world. The American housewife—freed by science and labor-saving appliances from the drudgery, the dangers of childbirth and the illnesses of her grandmother. She was healthy, beautiful, educated, concerned only about her husband, her children, her home. She had found true feminine fulfillment. As a housewife and mother, she was respected as a full and equal partner to man in his world. She was free to choose automobiles, clothes, appliances, supermarkets; she had everything that women ever dreamed of.

In the fifteen years after World War II, this mystique of feminine fulfillment became the cherished and self-perpetuating core of contemporary American culture. Millions of women lived their lives in the image of those pretty pictures of the American suburban housewife, kissing their husbands goodbye in front of the picture window, depositing their stationwagonsful of children at school, and smiling as they ran the new electric waxer over the spotless kitchen floor. They baked their own bread, sewed their own and their children's clothes, kept their new washing machines and dryers running all day. They changed the sheets on the beds twice a week instead of once, took the rug-hooking class in adult education, and pitied their poor frustrated mothers, who had dreamed of having a career. Their only dream was to be perfect wives and mothers; their highest ambition to have five children and a beautiful house, their only fight to get and keep their husbands. They had no thought for the unfeminine problems of the world outside the home; they wanted the men to make the major decisions. They gloried in their role as women, and wrote proudly on the census blank: "Occupation: house-wife."

For over fifteen years, the words written for women, and the words women used when they talked to each other, while their husbands sat on the other side of the room and talked shop or politics or septic tanks, were about problems with their children, or how to keep their husbands happy, or improve their chidren's school, or cook chicken or make slipcovers. Nobody argued whether women were inferior or superior to men; they were simply different. Words like "emancipation" and "career" sounded strange and embarrassing; no one had used them for years. When a Frenchwoman named Simone de Beauvoir wrote a book called *The Second Sex,* an American critic commented that she obviously "didn't know what life was all about," and besides, she was talking about French women. The "woman problem" in America no longer existed.

If a woman had a problem in the 1950's and 1960's, she knew that something must be wrong with her marriage, or with herself. Other women were satisfied with their lives, she thought. What kind of a woman was she if she did not feel this mysterious fulfillment waxing the kitchen floor? She was so ashamed to admit her dissatisfaction that she never knew how many other women shared it. If she tried to tell her husband, he didn't understand what she was talking about. She did not really understand it herself. For over fifteen years women in America found it harder to talk about this problem than about sex. Even the psychoanalysts had no name for it. When a woman went to a psychiatrist for help, as many women did, she would say, "I'm so ashamed," or "I must be hopelessly neurotic." "I don't know what's wrong with women today," a suburban psychiatrist said uneasily. "I only know something is wrong because most of my patients happen to be women. And their problem isn't sexual." Most women with this problem did not go to see a psychoanalyst, however. "There's nothing wrong really," they kept telling them-selves. "There isn't any problem."

But on an April morning in 1959, I heard a mother of four, having coffee with four other mothers in a suburban development fifteen miles from New York, say in a tone of quiet desperation, "the problem." And the others knew, without words, that she was not talking about a problem with her husband, or her children, or her home. Suddenly they realized they all shared the same problem, the problem that has no name. They began, hesitantly, to talk about it. Later, after they had picked up their children at nursery school and taken them home to nap, two of the women cried, in sheer relief, just to know they were not alone.

Gradually I came to realize that the problem that has no name was shared by countless women in America. As a magazine writer I often interviewed women about problems with their children, or their marriages, or their houses, or their communities. But after a while I began to recognize the telltale signs of this other problem. I saw the same signs in suburban ranch houses and split-levels on Long Island and in New Jersey and Westchester County; in colonial houses in a small Massachusetts town; on patios in Memphis; in suburban and city apartments; in living rooms in the Midwest. Sometimes I sensed the problem, not as a reporter, but as a suburban housewife, for during this time I was also bringing up my own three children in Rockland County, New York. I heard echoes of the problem in college dormitories and semiprivate maternity wards, at PTA meetings and luncheons of the League of Women Voters, at suburban cocktail parties, in station wagons waiting for trains, and in snatches of conversation overheard at Schrafft's. The groping words I heard from other women, on quiet afternoons when children were at school or on quiet evenings when husbands worked late, I think I understood first as a woman long before I understood their larger social and psychological implications.

Just what was this problem that has no name? What were the words women used when they tried to express it? Sometimes a woman would say "I feel empty somehow . . . incomplete." Or she would say, "I feel as if I don't exist." Sometimes she blotted out the feeling with a tranquilizer. Sometimes she thought the problem was with her husband, or her children, or that what she really needed was to redecorate her house, or move to a better neighborhood, or have an affair, or another baby. Sometimes, she went to a doctor with symptoms she could hardly describe: "A tired feeling . . . I get so angry with the chidren it scares me . . . I feel like crying without any reason." (A Cleveland doctor called it "the housewife's syndrome.") A number of women told me about great bleeding blisters that break out on their hands and arms. "I call it the housewife's blight," said a family doctor in Pennsylvania. "I see it so often lately in these young women with four, five and six children who bury themselves in their dishpans. But it isn't caused by detergent and it isn't cured by cortisone."

Sometimes a woman would tell me that the feeling gets so strong she runs out of the house and walks through the streets. Or she stays inside her house and cries. Or her children tell her a joke, and she doesn't laugh because she doesn't hear it. I talked to women who had spent years on the analyst's couch, working out their "adjustment to the feminine role," their blocks to "fulfillment as a wife and mother." But the desperate tone in these women's voices, and the look in their eyes, was the same as the tone and the look of other women, who were sure they had no problem, even though they did have a strange feeling of desperation.

A mother of four who left college at nineteen to get married told me:

> I've tried everything women are supposed to do—hobbies, gardening, pickling, canning, being very social with my neighbors, joining committees, running PTA teas. I can do it all, and I like it, but it doesn't leave you anything to think about—any feeling of who you are. I never had any career ambitions. All I wanted was to get married and have four children. I love the kids and Bob and my home. There's no problem you can even put a name to. But I'm desperate. I begin to feel I have no personality. I'm a server of food and a putter-on of pants and a bedmaker, somebody who can be called on when you want something. But who am I?

A twenty-three-year-old mother in blue jeans said:

I ask myself why I'm so dissatisfied. I've got my health, fine children, a lovely
new home, enough money. My husband has a real future as an electronics engineer. He doesn't have any of these feelings. He says maybe I need a vacation,
let's go to New York for a weekend. But that isn't it. I always had this idea we
should do everything together. I can't sit down and read a book alone. If the
children are napping and I have one hour to myself I just walk through the
house waiting for them to wake up. I don't make a move until I know where
the rest of the crowd is going. It's as if ever since you were a little girl, there's
always been somebody or something that will take care of your life: your parents, or college, or falling in love, or having a child, or moving to a new house.
Then you wake up one morning and there's nothing to look forward to.

A young wife in a Long Island development said:

I seem to sleep so much. I don't know why I should be so tired. This house
isn't nearly so hard to clean as the cold-water flat we had when I was working.
The children are at school all day. It's not the work. I just don't feel alive.

In 1960, the problem that has no name burst like a boil through the image
of the happy American housewife. In the television commercials the pretty housewives still beamed over their foaming dishpans and *Time*'s cover story on "The
Suburban Wife, an American Phenomenon" protested: "Having too good a time
. . . to believe that they should be unhappy." But the actual unhappiness of the
American housewife was suddenly being reported—from the *New York Times* and
Newsweek to *Good Housekeeping* and CBS Television ("The Trapped Housewife"),
although almost everybody who talked about it found some superficial reason to
dismiss it. It was attributed to incompetent appliance repairmen (*New York Times*),
or the distances children must be chauffeured in the suburbs (*Time*), or too much
PTA (*Redbook*). Some said it was the old problem—education: more and more
women had education, which naturally made them unhappy in their role as
housewives. "The road from Freud to Frigidaire, from Sophocles to Spock, has
turned out to be a bumpy one," reported the *New York Times* (June 28, 1960).
"Many young women—certainly not all—whose education plunged them into a
world of ideas feel stifled in their homes. They find their routine lives out of joint
with their training. Like shut-ins, they feel left out. In the last year, the problem of
the educated housewife has provided the meat of dozens of speeches made by
troubled presidents of women's colleges who maintain, in the face of complaints,
that sixteen years of academic training is realistic preparation for wifehood and
motherhood."

There was much sympathy for the educated housewife. ("Like a two-headed
schizophrenic . . . once she wrote a paper on the Graveyard poets; now she writes
notes to the milkman. Once she determined the boiling point of sulphuric acid;
now she determines her boiling point with the overdue repairman. . . . The
housewife often is reduced to screams and tears. . . . No one, it seems, is appre-

ciative, least of all herself, of the kind of person she becomes in the process of turning from poetess into shrew.")

Home economists suggested more realistic preparation for housewives, such as high-school workshops in home appliances. College educators suggested more discussion groups on home management and the family, to prepare women for the adjustment to domestic life. A spate of articles appeared in the mass magazines offering "Fifty-eight Ways to Make Your Marriage More Exciting." No month went by without a new book by a psychiatrist or sexologist offering technical advice on finding greater fulfillment through sex.

A male humorist joked in *Harper's Bazaar* (July, 1960) that the problem could be solved by taking away woman's right to vote. ("In the pre-19th Amendment era, the American woman was placid, sheltered and sure of her role in American society. She left all the political decisions to her husband and he, in turn, left all the family decisions to her. Today a woman has to make both the family *and* the political decisions, and it's too much for her.")

A number of educators suggested seriously that women no longer be admitted to the four-year colleges and universities; in the growing college crisis, the education which girls could not use as housewives was more urgently needed than ever by boys to do the work of the atomic age.

The problem was also dismissed with drastic solutions no one could take seriously. (A woman writer proposed in *Harper's* that women be drafted for compulsory service as nurses' aides and baby-sitters.) And it was smoothed over with the age-old panaceas: "love is their answer," "the only answer is inner help," "the secret of completeness—children," "a private means of intellectual fulfillment," "to cure this toothache of the spirit—the simple formula of handing one's self and one's will over to God."[1]

The problem was dismissed by telling the housewife she doesn't realize how lucky she is—her own boss, no time clock, no junior executive gunning for her job. What if she isn't happy—does she think men are happy in this world? Does she really, secretly, still want to be a man? Doesn't she know yet how lucky she is to be a woman?

The problem was also, and finally, dismissed by shrugging that there are no solutions: this is what being a woman means, and what is wrong with American women that they can't accept their role gracefully? As *Newsweek* put it (March 7, 1960):

> She is dissatisifed with a lot that women of other lands can only dream of. Her discontent is deep, pervasive, and impervious to the superficial remedies which are offered at every hand. . . . An army of professional explorers have already charted the major sources of trouble. . . . From the beginning of time, the female cycle has defined and confined woman's role. As Freud was credited with saying: "Anatomy is destiny." Though no group of women has ever pushed these natural restrictions as far as the American wife, it seems that she still cannot accept them with good grace. . . . A young mother with a beautiful family, charm, talent and brains is apt to dismiss her role apologetically. "What do I do?" you hear her say. "Why nothing. I'm just a housewife." A good educa-

tion, it seems, has given this paragon among women an understanding of the value of everything except her own worth . . .

And so she must accept the fact that "American women's unhappiness is merely the most recently won of women's rights," and adjust and say with the happy housewife found by *Newsweek:* "We ought to salute the wonderful freedom we all have and be proud of our lives today. I have had college and I've worked, but being a housewife is the most rewarding and satisfying role. . . . My mother was never included in my father's business affairs . . . she couldn't get out of the house and away from us children. But I am an equal to my husband; I can go along with him on business trips and to social business affairs."

The alternative offered was a choice that few women would contemplate. In the sympathetic words of the *New York Times:* "All admit to being deeply frustrated at times by the lack of privacy, the physical burden, the routine of family life, the confinement of it. However, none would give up her home and family if she had the choice to make again." *Redbook* commented: "Few women would want to thumb their noses at husbands, children and community and go off on their own. Those who do may be talented individuals, but they rarely are successful women."

The year American women's discontent boiled over, it was also reported (*Look*) that the more than 21,000,000 American women who are single, widowed, or divorced do not cease even after fifty their frenzied, desperate search for a man. And the search begins early—for seventy per cent of all American women now marry before they are twenty-four. A pretty twenty-five-year-old secretary took thirty-five different jobs in six months in the futile hope of finding a husband. Women were moving from one political club to another, taking evening courses in accounting or sailing, learning to play golf or ski, joining a number of churches in succession, going to bars alone, in their ceaseless search for a man.

Of the growing thousands of women currently getting private psychiatric help in the United States, the married ones were reported dissatisfied with their marriages, the unmarried ones suffering from anxiety and, finally, depression. Strangely, a number of psychiatrists stated that, in their experience, unmarried women patients were happier than married ones. So the door of all those pretty suburban houses opened a crack to permit a glimpse of uncounted thousands of American housewives who suffered alone from a problem that suddenly everyone was talking about, and beginning to take for granted, as one of those unreal problems in American life that can never be solved—like the hydrogen bomb. By 1962 the plight of the trapped American housewife had become a national parlor game. Whole issues of magazines, newspaper columns, books learned and frivolous, educational conferences and television panels were devoted to the problem.

Even so, most men, and some women, still did not know that this problem was real. But those who had faced it honestly knew that all the superficial remedies, the sympathetic advice, the scolding words and the cheering words were somehow drowning the problem in unreality. A bitter laugh was beginning to be heard from American women. They were admired, envied, pitied, theorized over until they were sick of it, offered drastic solutions or silly choices that no one could take seriously. They got all kinds of advice from the growing armies of marriage and child-guidance counselors, psychotherapists, and armchair psychologists, on how to adjust to their role as housewives. No other road to fulfillment was offered to American women in the middle of the twentieth century. Most adjusted to their role and suffered or ignored the problem that has no name. It can be less painful, for a woman, not to hear the strange, dissatisfied voice stirring within her.

It is no longer possible to ignore that voice, to dismiss the desperation of so many American women. This is not what being a woman means, no matter what the experts say. For human suffering there is a reason; perhaps the reason has not been found because the right questions have not been asked, or pressed far enough. I do not accept the answer that there is no problem because American women have luxuries that women in other times and lands never dreamed of; part of the strange newness of the problem is that it cannot be understood in terms of the age-old material problems of man: poverty, sickness, hunger, cold. The women who suffer this problem have a hunger that food cannot fill. It persists in women whose husbands are struggling internes and law clerks, or prosperous doctors and lawyers; in wives of workers and executives who make $5,000 a year or $50,000. It is not caused by lack of material advantages; it may not even be felt by women preoccupied with desperate problems of hunger, poverty or illness. And women who think it will be solved by more money, a bigger house, a second car, moving to a better suburb, often discover it gets worse.

It is no longer possible today to blame the problem on loss of femininity: to say that education and independence and equality with men have made American women unfeminine. I have heard so many women try to deny this dissatisfied voice within themselves because it does not fit the pretty picture of femininity the experts have given them. I think, in fact, that this is the first clue to the mystery: the problem cannot be understood in the generally accepted terms by which scientists have studied women, doctors have treated them, counselors have advised them, and writers have written about them. Women who suffer this problem, in whom this voice is stirring, have lived their whole lives in the pursuit of feminine fulfillment. They are not career women (although career women may have other problems); they are women whose greatest ambition has been marriage and children. For the oldest of these women, these daughters of the American middle class, no other dream was possible. The ones in their forties and fifties who once had other dreams gave them up and threw themselves joyously into life as housewives. For the youngest, the new wives and mothers, this was the only dream. They are the ones who quit high school and college to marry, or marked time in some job in which they had no real interest until they married. These women are very "feminine" in the usual sense, and yet they still suffer the problem.

Are the women who finished college, the women who once had dreams beyond housewifery, the ones who suffer the most? According to the experts they are, but listen to these four women:

My days are all busy, and dull, too. All I ever do is mess around. I get up at eight—I make breakfast, so I do the dishes, have lunch, do some more dishes and some laundry and cleaning in the afternoon. Then it's supper dishes and I get to sit down a few minutes before the children have to be sent to bed. . . . That's all there is to my day. It's just like any other wife's day. Humdrum. The biggest time, I am chasing kids.

Ye Gods, what do I do with my time? Well, I get up at six. I get my son dressed and then give him breakfast. After that I wash dishes and bathe and feed the baby. Then I get lunch and while the children nap, I sew or mend or iron and do all the other things I can't get done before noon. Then I cook supper for the family and my husband watches TV while I do the dishes. After I get the children to bed, I set my hair and then I go to bed.

The problem is always being the children's mommy, or the minister's wife and never being myself.

A film made of any typical morning in my house would look like an old Marx Brothers' comedy. I wash the dishes, rush the older children off to school, dash out in the yard to cultivate the chrysanthemums, run back in to make a phone call about a committee meeting, help the youngest child build a block-house, spend fifteen minutes skimming the newspapers so I can be well-informed, then scamper down to the washing machines where my thrice-weekly laundry includes enough clothes to keep a primitive village going for an entire year. By noon I'm ready for a padded cell. Very little of what I've done has been really necessary or important. Outside pressures lash me through the day. Yet I look upon myself as one of the more relaxed housewives in the neighborhood. Many of my friends are even more frantic. In the past sixty years we have come full circle and the American housewife is once again trapped in a squirrel cage. If the cage is now a modern plate-glass-and-broadloom ranch house or a convenient modern apartment, the situation is no less painful than when her grandmother sat over an embroidery hoop in her gilt-and-plush parlor and muttered angrily about women's rights.

The first two women never went to college. They live in developments in Levittown, New Jersey, and Tacoma, Washington, and were interviewed by a team of sociologists studying workingmen's wives.[2] The third, a minister's wife, wrote on the fifteenth reunion questionnaire of her college that she never had any career ambitions, but wishes now she had.[3] The fourth, who has a Ph.D. in anthropology, is today a Nebraska housewife with three children.[4] Their words seem to indicate that housewives of all educational levels suffer the same feeling of desperation.

The fact is that no one today is muttering angrily about "women's rights," even though more and more women have gone to college. In a recent study of all the classes that have graduated from Barnard College,[5] a significant minority of earlier graduates blamed their education for making them want "rights," later classes blamed their education for giving them career dreams, but recent graduates blamed the college for making them feel it was not enough simply to be a housewife and mother; they did not want to feel guilty if they did not read books or take part in community activities. But if education is not the cause of the problem, the fact that education somehow festers in these women may be a clue.

If the secret of feminine fulfillment is having children, never have so many women, with the freedom to choose, had so many children, in so few years, so willingly. If the answer is love, never have women searched for love with such determination. And yet there is a growing suspicion that the problem may not be sexual, though it must somehow be related to sex. I have heard from many doctors evidence of new sexual problems between man and wife—sexual hunger in wives so great their husbands cannot satisfy it. "We have made woman a sex creature," said a psychiatrist at the Margaret Sanger marriage counseling clinic. "She has no identity except as a wife and mother. She does not know who she is herself. She waits all day for her husband to come home at night to make her feel alive. And now it is the husband who is not interested. It is terrible for the women, to lie there, night after night, waiting for her husband to make her feel alive." Why is there such a market for books and articles offering sexual advice? The kind of sexual orgasm which Kinsey found in statistical plenitude in the recent generations of American women does not seem to make this problem go away.

On the contrary, new neuroses are being seen among women—and problems as yet unnamed as neuroses—which Freud and his followers did not predict, with physical symptoms, anxieties, and defense mechanisms equal to those caused by sexual repression. And strange new problems are being reported in the growing generations of children whose mothers were always there, driving them around, helping them with their homework—an inability to endure pain or discipline or pursue any self-sustained goal of any sort, a devastating boredom with life. Educators are increasingly uneasy about the dependence, the lack of self-reliance, of the boys and girls who are entering college today. "We fight a continual battle to make our students assume manhood," said a Columbia dean.

A White House conference was held on the physical and muscular deterioration of American children: were they being overnurtured? Sociologists noted the astounding organization of suburban children's lives: the lessons, parties, entertainments, play and study groups organized for them. A suburban housewife in Portland, Oregon, wondered why the children "need" Brownies and Boy Scouts out here. "This is not the slums. The kids out here have the great outdoors. I think people are so bored, they organize the children, and then try to hook everyone else on it. And the poor kids have no time left just to lie on their beds and daydream."

Can the problem that has no name be somehow related to the domestic routine of the housewife? When a woman tries to put the problem into words, she often merely describes the daily life she leads. What is there in this recital of comfortable domestic detail that could possibly cause such a feeling of desperation? Is she trapped simply by the enormous demands of her role as modern housewife: wife, mistress, mother, nurse, consumer, cook, chauffeur; expert on interior decoration, child care, appliance repair, furniture refinishing, nutrition, and education? Her day is fragmented as she rushes from dishwasher to washing machine to telephone to dryer to station wagon to supermarket, and delivers Johnny to the Little League field, takes Janey to dancing class, gets the lawnmower fixed and meets the 6:45. She can never spend more than 15 minutes on any one thing; she has no time to read books, only magazines; even if she had time, she has lost the power to concentrate. At the end of the day, she is so terribly tired that sometimes her husband has to take over and put the children to bed.

This terrible tiredness took so many women to doctors in the 1950's that one decided to investigate it. He found, surprisingly, that his patients suffering from "housewife's fatigue" slept more than an adult needed to sleep—as much as ten hours a day—and that the actual energy they expended on housework did not tax their capacity. The real problem must be something else, he decided—perhaps boredom. Some doctors told their women patients they must get out of the house for a day, treat themselves to a movie in town. Others prescribed tranquilizers. Many suburban housewives were taking tranquilizers like cough drops. "You wake up in the morning, and you feel as if there's no point in going on another day like this. So you take a tranquilizer because it makes you not care so much that it's pointless."

It is easy to see the concrete details that trap the suburban housewife, the continual demands on her time. But the chains that bind her in her trap are chains in her own mind and spirit. They are chains made up of mistaken ideas and misinterpreted facts, of incomplete truths and unreal choices. They are not easily seen and not easily shaken off.

How can any woman see the whole truth within the bounds of her own life? How can she believe that voice inside herself, when it denies the conventional, accepted truths by which she has been living? And yet the women I have talked to, who are finally listening to that inner voice, seem in some incredible way to be groping through to a truth that has defied the experts.

I think the experts in a great many fields have been holding pieces of that truth under their microscopes for a long time without realizing it. I found pieces of it in certain new research and theoretical developments in psychological, social and biological science whose implications for women seem never to have been examined. I found many clues by talking to suburban doctors, gynecologists, obstetricians, child-guidance clinicians, pediatricians, high-school guidance counselors, college professors, marriage counselors, psychiatrists and ministers—questioning them not on their theories, but on their actual experience in treating American women. I became aware of a growing body of evidence, much of which has not been reported publicly because it does not fit current modes of thought about women—evidence which throws into question the standards of feminine normality, feminine adjustment, feminine fulfillment, and feminine maturity by which most women are still trying to live.

I began to see in a strange new light the American return to early marriage and the large families that are causing the population explosion; the recent movement to natural childbirth and breastfeeding; suburban conformity, and the new neuroses, character pathologies and sexual problems being reported by the doctors. I began to see new dimensions to old problems that have long been taken for granted among women: menstrual difficulties, sexual frigidity, promiscuity, pregnancy fears, childbirth depression, the high incidence of emotional breakdown and suicide among women in their twenties and thirties, the menopause crises, and so-called passivity and immaturity of American men, the discrepancy between women's tested intellectual abilities in childhood and their adult achievement, the changing incidence of adult sexual orgasm in American women, and persistent problems in psychotherapy and in women's education.

If I am right, the problem that has no name stirring in the minds of so many American women today is not a matter of loss of femininity or too much education, or the demands of domesticity. It is far more important than anyone recognizes. It is the key to these other new and old problems which have been torturing women and their husbands and children, and puzzling their doctors and educators for years. It may well be the key to our future as a nation and a culture. We can no longer ignore that voice within women that says: "I want something more than my husband and my children and my home."

How to Get the Women's Movement Moving Again

Betty Friedan

This is addressed to any woman who has ever said "we" about the women's movement, including those who say, "I'm not a feminist, but . . ." And it's addressed to quite a few men.

It's a personal message, not at all objective, and it's in response to those who think our modern women's movement is over—either because it is defeated and a failure, or because it has triumphed, its work done, its mission accomplished. After all, any daughter can now dream of being an astronaut, after Sally Ride, or running for President, after Geraldine Ferraro.

I do not think that the job of the modern women's movement is done. And I do not believe the movement has failed. For one thing, those of us who started the modern women's movement, or came into it after marriage and children or from jobs as "invisible women" in the office, still carry the glow of "it changed my whole life," an aliveness, the satisfaction of finding our own voice and power, and the skills we didn't have a chance to develop before.

I do believe, though, that the movement is in trouble. I was too passionately involved in its conception, its birth, its growing pains, its youthful flowering, to acquiesce quietly to its going gently so soon into the night. But, like a lot of other mothers, I have been denying the symptoms of what I now feel forced to confront as a profound paralysis of the women's movement in America.

I see as symptoms of this paralysis the impotence in the face of fundamentalist backlash; the wasting of energy in internal power struggles when no real issues are at stake; the nostalgic harking back to old rhetoric, old ideas, old modes of action instead of confronting new threats and new problems with new thinking; the failure to mobilize the young generation who take for granted the rights we won and who do not defend those rights as they are being taken away in front of our eyes, and the preoccupation with pornography and other sexual diversions that do not affect most women's lives. I sense an unwillingness to deal with the complex realities of female survival in male-modeled careers, with the new illusions of having it all in marriage and equality in divorce, and with the basic causes of the grim feminization of poverty. The potential of women's political power is slipping away between the poles of self-serving feminist illusion and male and female opportunism. The promise of that empowerment of women that enabled so many of us to change their own lives is being betrayed by our failure to mobilize the next generation to move beyond us.

Evidence of the movement's paralysis has been impinging on my own life in many ways:

• Over the last few years, I've noticed how the machinery for enforcing the laws against sex discrimination in employment and education has been gradually dismantled by the Reagan Administration, and how the laws' scope has been narrowed by the courts, with little public outcry. Professional lobbyists for women's organizations objected, of course, but there have been no mass protests from the women in the jobs and professions that those laws opened to them. In the early days of the National Organization for Women, nearly 20 years ago, we demanded and won an executive order banning government contracts to companies or institutions guilty of sex discrimination; it was the first major weapon women could use to demand jobs. Some officials in the Administration are proposing the order's elimination. The Reagan Administration is also urging the courts to undo recent movement victories regarding equal pay for work of comparable value.

• The crusade against women's right to choice in the matter of childbirth and abortion, preached from the pulpits of fundamentalist churches and by the Catholic hierarchy, first achieved a ban on Federal aid to poor women seeking abortion, then the elimination of United States Government aid to third-world family-planning programs that counsel abortion. The Attorney General announced in the summer of 1985 that he would seek to reverse the historical Supreme Court decision, Roe v. Wade, which in 1973 decreed that the right of a woman to decide according to her own conscience when and whether and how many times to bear a child was as basic a right as any the Constitution originally spelled out for men. At a recent meeting to mobilize women in mass communications to help save that right, I was amazed to hear a one-time radical feminist suggest that abortion should not be defended in terms of a woman's right. "Women's rights are not chic in America anymore," she argued.

• The main interest of many feminist groups in various states in recent years seems to be outlawing pornography. Laws prohibiting pornography as a form of sex discrimination and violation of civil rights have been proposed in Minnesota, Indiana, California and New York. A former NOW leader who practices law in upstate New York was startled, when she dropped in on a feminist fund-raiser, to be asked to support a nationwide ban on sexually explicit materials. When she warned, "A law like that would be far more dangerous to women than the most obscene pornography," she was greeted with incomprehension and hostility.

- At a black-tie banquet at the Plaza Hotel in New York in September 1985, I proudly watched a sparkling parade of champion women athletes as they entertained the corporate donors who sponsor their games and scholarships through the 11-year-old Women's Sports Foundation. The women champions in basketball, judo, gymnastics, tennis, skiing, swimming, boxing, running and sports-car and dogsled racing paraded down the runway in sequined miniskirts and satin jumpsuits, clasping their hands over their heads in the victory gesture. They gave credit to parents and teachers, but not one mentioned the recent Supreme Court decision regarding Grove City College in Pennsylvania. That decision threatens to remove school athletic programs from the protection of the law banning sex discrimination in Federally assisted education—which is what provided crucial athletic training to these new female champions in the first place.

- At another reception, one of the many new networks of women corporate executives, a woman in her late thirties, holding a job a woman had never been given before in a large insurance company, told me: "If my slot became open today, they wouldn't give it to a woman. Not because I haven't done a good job— I keep getting raises. But they've stopped talking about getting more women on the board—or in the company. The word has gone out from the White House: They don't have to worry anymore about women and blacks. Its over." . . .

- At one company, executives who faced class-action suits a decade ago now boast that their best new employees are the women. They were shocked when one of their star superwomen, on a rung very near the top, became pregnant with her second child and announced she was quitting. The boss even offered her an extended maternity leave, which is not required by law or union contract, but she quit anyway. "You may never have another chance like this," her colleagues, male and female, protested. "I'll never have these years with my chidren again," she answered. Most of them did not understand. They figured that whatever guilt or pressure she suffered trying to juggle baby and demanding job was her peculiar "personal problem." That sort of thing is not discussed as a woman's movement problem, requiring a political solution, in her professional network.

- Another longtime feminist mother, with three "yuppie" daughters—banker, lawyer, talent agent—says, regretfully, "They're not feminists . . . they take all that for granted." She goes on to tell me that "Janey's problem is her love life and her job, and Ann's is her kids and her job, and Phyllis thinks maybe she should go back and get an MBA. With all that and exercise class, they don't have time for the meetings we used to go to. Why do they have to be feminists when they never had to suffer like we did?" . . .

. . . Aware of these symptoms, and yet denying my own sense that the American women's movement was over, not ready to admit defeat but wanting to move on to other things myself, I went to Kenya in the summer of 1985 out of a sheer sense of historic duty to see the thing through to its end. Most card-carrying American feminists were not even bothering with the meeting in Nairobi. NOW had scheduled its own convention in New Orleans at the same time as the United Nations World Conference of Women.

Ten years earlier, when the modern women's movement was spreading from America to the world, I had joined women wanting to organize in their countries in appealing to the UN to call a world assembly of women. At the first two world women's meetings, in Mexico in 1975 and Copenhagen in 1980, I had seen the beginnings of international networking among women broken up by organized disrupters led by armed gunmen shouting slogans against "imperialism" and "Zionism." I had been appalled at the way the official male delegates from Arab countries and other third-world and Communist nations that control the UN showed contempt for women's rights, using those conferences mainly to launch a new doctrine of religious and ethnic hate, equating Zionism and racism. And I had been repelled by the way the delegates from Western countries, mostly male officials or their wives and female flunkies, let them thereby rob those conferences of the moral and political weight they might have given to the advance of women worldwide. This year, the United States delegation had instructions from President Reagan to walk out if the question of Zionism was included in the conclusions reached at Nairobi.

To my amazement, the women's movement emerged in Nairobi with sufficient strength worldwide to impose its own agenda of women's concerns over the male political agenda that had divided it before. Despite, or because of, the backlash and other problems they face at home, nearly 17,000 women from 159 nations assembled, some 14,000 having paid their own way or been sent by volunteer, church or women's groups to the unofficial forum that is part of every such UN conference. Some traveled by plane three and four days, or by bus from African villages.

Whole new worlds of women's skills, strength, expertise and a new confidence in themselves and each other became visible in 1800 workshops at the unofficial world forum on the Nairobi University campus. Women in saris and African Kangas, blue jeans and summer dresses, overflowed into the corridors, discussing "New Dimensions of Women's Spirituality," "Women as the Driving Force in Development," "The Economic Value of Women's Unpaid Work," "Getting Benefits for Part-time Workers," "Female Sexuality in Different Religious Traditions." The new women lawyers and jurists from Asia, Africa and Latin America used international law, backed up by the media skills of black and white veterans of American civil rights and women's movements, to force the Kenyan government to let us double up and stay in the hotel rooms from which they were going to evict us because of the unexpected numbers of official delegates and journalists. The scholars from centers of women's studies that now exist in 32 nations got beyond "defining everything in terms of our subordination to men" to new feminist thinking, based on women's own experience, "embracing rather than denying biological differences between the sexes," as a brilliant woman scholar from Trinidad put it. New women theologians compared notes in the way their scriptures (Bible, Talmud, Koran) have been distorted by the fundamentalists trying to use every religion's authority to put women down. Across the lines of capitalism, communism, socialism and different levels of development, we found common roots of economic discrimination against women in the unpaid and undervalued housework and child care which women everywhere are still expected to do on top of paid work, for which women everywhere are still paid less than work of comparable value done by men.

There was a bypassing, or bridging, of the old, abstract ideological conflicts that had seemed to divide women before—a moving beyond the old rhetoric of career versus family, equality versus development, feminism versus socialism, religion versus feminism, or feminism as an imperialist capitalist arrogance irrelevant to poor third-world women. What took the place of all this was a discussion of concrete strategies for women to acquire more control of their lives. Third-world revolutionaries, Arab and Israeli women, as well as Japanese, Greeks and Latins, gathered under a baobab tree where, every day at noon, like some African tribal elder, I led a discussion on "Future Directions of Feminism." . . .

. . . I and other Americans—as many black as white among the 2,000 of us at Nairobi—went home strengthened, resolved not to accept backward-nation status for American women. For though we had gone to Nairobi subdued by our own setbacks and sophisticated enough not to offer Western feminism as the answer to the problems of women of the third world, it was truly humiliating to discover that we are no longer the cutting edge of modern feminism or world progress toward equality. Even Kenya has an equal rights clause in its Constitution!

How can we let the women's movement die out here in America when what we began is taking hold now all over the world? I would like to suggest 10 things that might be done to break the blocks that seem to have stymied the women's movement in America:

1. Begin a new round of consciousness-raising for the new generation. These women, each thinking she is alone with her personal guilt and pressures, trying to "have it all," having second thoughts about her professional career, desperately trying to have a baby before it is too late, with or without husband, and maybe secretly blaming the movement for getting her into this mess, are almost as isolated, and as powerless in their isolation, as those suburban housewives afflicted by "the problem that had no name" whom I interviewed for "The Feminine Mystique" over 20 years ago. Those women put a name to their problem; they got together with other women in the feminist groups and began to work for political solutions and began to change their lives.

That has to happen again to free a new generation of women from its new double burden of guilt and isolation. The guilts of less-than-perfect motherhood and less-than-perfect professional career performance are real because it's not possible to "have it all" when jobs are still structured for men whose wives take care of the details of life, and homes are still structured for women whose only responsibility is running their families. I warned five years ago that if the women's movement didn't move into a second stage and take on the problems of restructuring work and home, a new generation would be vulnerable to backlash. But the movement has not moved into that needed second stage, so the women struggling with these new problems view them as purely personal, not political, and no longer look to the movement for solutions. . . .

2. Mobilize the new professional networks and the old established volunteer organizations to save women's rights. We can't fight fundamentalist backlash with backward-looking feminist fundamentalism. Second-stage feminism is itself pluralistic, and has to use new pluralist strengths and strategies. The women who have been 30 and 40 percent of the graduating class from law school or business school and 47 percent of the journalism school classes, the ones who've taken women's studies, the women who grew up playing Little League baseball and cheered on those new champion women athletes, the new professional networks of women in every field, every woman who has been looking to those networks only to get ahead in her own field, must now use her professional skills to save the laws and execute orders against sex discrimination in education and employment. They must restore the enforcement machinery and the class-action suits that opened up all these opportunities to her in the first place.

The last time the ladies with briefcases went to Washington from the "new girl" networks like Women's Forum was to get the deadline for ERA extended, nearly a decade ago. The dismantling of the laws of sex discrimination shows how much we need that Constitutional underpinning. But new symbolic marches for ERA are not what we need now but urgent, immediate concrete strategies to save the laws themselves. And this can't be left to the few professional lobbyists on feminist organization payrolls. . . .

. . . America's first movement for women's rights died out after winning the vote, four generations ago, because women didn't tackle the hard political tasks of restructuring home and work so that women who married and had children could also earn and have their own voice in the decision-making mainstream of society. Instead, those women retreated behind a cultural curtain of female "purity," focusing their energies on issues like prohibition, much like the pornographic obsession of some feminists today.

3. Get off the pornography kick and face the real obscenity of poverty. No matter how repulsive we may find pornography, laws banning books or movies for sexually explicit content could be far more dangerous to women. The pornography issue is dividing the women's movement and giving the impression on college campuses that to be a feminist is to be against sex. More important, it is diverting energies that need to be spent in saving the basic rights now being destroyed and in facing the new problems of economic and emotional survival, for young women and old. And feminists joining forces with the Far Right to outlaw pronography are strengthening the Right's campaign to weaken constitutional protections of all our freedoms and rights, including women's basic right to control her own body. . . .

. . . 4. Confront the illusion of equality in divorce. Economists and feminists have been talking a lot lately about "the feminization of poverty" in theoretical terms, but the American women's movement has not developed concrete strategies that get at its root cause. It's not just a question of women earning less than men— though as long as women do not get equal pay for work of comparable value, or earn Social Security or pensions for taking care of children and home, they are both economically dependent on marriage and motherhood and pay a big economic price for it. And this is as true for divorced aging yuppies as for welfare mothers. Not many women or men want to face the fact that the overwhelming majority of the truly poor in this country, regardless of race, religion or husband's economic status, are women alone, and children in families headed by women.

A startling new book by the sociologist Lenore J. Weitzman, "The Divorce Revolution: The Unexpected Social and Economic Consequences for Women and Children in America," reveals that in the 1970s, when 48 states adopted "no-fault" divorce laws treating men and women "equally" in divorce settlements—laws feminists originally supported—divorced women and their children suffered an immediate 73 percent drop in their standard of living, while their ex-husbands enjoyed a 42 percent rise in theirs. The legal profession, including women lawyers, sought and won passages in those laws that merely enjoined the judge to "equitable" distribution of property, requiring the wife to "prove" that her contribution was equal to her husband's. (Feminists like myself were almost alone then in demanding truly equal division.)

In dividing "marital property," Lenore Weitzman reports, judges have systematically overlooked the major assets of many marriages—the husband's career assets that the wife helped make possible, his professional education that she may have helped support, the career on which he was able to concentrate because she ran the home, and his salary, pension, health insurance and earning power that resulted. They have also ignored the wife's years of unpaid housework and child care (not totally insured by Social Security in the event of divorce) and her drastically diminished job prospects after divorce. And, for most, the "equal" division of property means the forced sale of the family home—which used to be awarded to the wife and children. Child support, which has often been inadequate, unpaid and uncollectible, usually ends when the child is 18, just as college expenses begin. Thus the vicious cycle whereby an ever-increasing majority of the truly poor in America are families headed by women.

When those "no fault" divorce "reform" laws were first passed, feminists in the first brave flush of "independence" repudiated women's need for alimony; a generation of "displaced housewives" paid a bitter price.

A new generation of feminist lawyers and judges has now drafted, and must get urgent grass-roots political support for, the kind of law needed, a law that treats marriage as a true economic partnership—and includes fairer standards of property division, maintenance and child support. It should be a law that does not penalize women who have chosen family over, or even together with, professional career.

5. Return the issue of abortion to the matter of women's own responsible choice. I think feminists have been so traumatized by the fundamentalist crusade against abortion and all the talk of fetuses and when life begins that they are in danger of forgetting the values that make abortion a feminist issue in the first place. Those pictures of revived fetuses raise new moral questions. And, in fact, hard new thinking is being done in the medical and religious communities about the use of technology to keep unwanted life alive at both extremes of the life

cycle. New, hard thinking is required here of feminist theories and leaders generally, as well as the new women doctors and midwives. . . .

I think women who are young, and those not so young, today must be able to choose when to have a child, given the necessities of their jobs. They will indeed join their mothers, who remember the humiliations and dangers of back-street butcher abortions, in a march of millions to save the right of legal abortion. I certainly support a march for women's choice of birth control and legal abortion. NOW has called for one in the spring of 1986.

6. Affirm the differences between men and women. New feminist thinking is required if American women are to continue advancing in a man's world, as they must, to earn their way, and yet "not become like men." This fear is heard with more and more frequency today from young women, including many who have succeeded, and some who have failed or opted out of male-defined careers. More books, like Carol Gilligan's *In a Different Voice,* and consciousness-raising sessions are needed. First-stage feminism denied real differences between women and men except for the sexual organs themselves. Some feminists still do not understand that true equality is not possible unless those differences between men and women are affirmed and until values based on female sensitivities to life begin to be voiced in every discipline and profession, from architecture to economics, where, until recently, all concepts and standards were defined by men. This is not a matter of abstract theory alone but involves the restructuring of hours of work and patterns of professional training so that they take into account the fact that women are the people who give birth to children. It must lead to concrete changes in medical practice, church worship, the writing of history, standards of ethics, even the design of homes and appliances.

7. Breakthrough for older women. Though the great majority of Americans living vitally now through their sixties, seventies and eighties are women (men still die prematurely, part of the price they seem to pay for machismo dominance), the women's movement has never put serious energy into the job that must be done to get women adequately covered by Social Security and pensions, especially those women now reaching sixty-five who spent many years as housewives and are ending up alone. The need for more independent and shared housing for older women now living alone in suburban houses they can't afford to sell, or lonely furnished rooms—and the need for services and jobs or volunteer options that will enable them to keep on living independent, productive lives—has never been a part of the women's movement agenda. But that first generation of feminist mothers, women now in their sixties, is a powerful political resource for the movement as these women retire from late or early professional or volunteer careers. Women in their fifties and sixties are shown by the polls to be more firmly committed than their daughters to the feminist goals of equality. Let the women's movement lead the rest of society in breaking the spell of the youth cult and drawing on the still enormous energies and the wisdom that may come to some of us in age. Or will we have to start another movement to break through the age mystique, and affirm the personhood of women and men who live beyond that dread ceiling of sixty-five—my own next birthday!

8. Bring in the men. It's passé, surely, for feminists now to see men only as

the enemy, or to contemplate separatist models for emotional or economic survival. Feminist theorists like Barbara Ehrenreich cite dismal evidence of the "new men" opting out of family responsibilities altogether. But in my own life I seem to see more and more young men, and older ones—even former male chauvinist pigs—admitting their vulnerability and learning to express their tenderness, sharing the care of the kids, even though most of them may never share it equally with their wives.

And as men let down their masks of machismo, and admit their dependence on the women in their lives, women may admit a new need to depend on men, without fear of sinking back into the old abject subservience. After all, even women who insist they are not, and never will be, feminists have learned to defend themselves against real male brutality. Look at Charlotte Donahue Fedders, the wife of that Security and Exchange commissioner, who testified in divorce court about his repeated abuse—his repeated beatings caused black eyes and a broken eardrum. At one time, a woman in her situation would have kept that shame a secret. The Reagan Administration had to ask him to resign, because wife-beating is no longer politically acceptable, even in conservative America in 1985.

I don't think women can, or should try to, take the responsibility for liberating men from the remnants of machismo. But there has to be a new way of asking what do men really want, to echo Freud, a new kind of dialogue that breaks through or gets behind both our masks. Women cannot restructure jobs or homes just by talking to themselves. As a movement, we have to figure out a new kind of second stage consciousness-raising and a new kind of political organization that bring men in as organic partners.

9. Continue to fight for real political power. Feminists do not now, and in fact never really did support a woman just because she is a woman. In the '82 elections, NOW actually opposed Millicent Fenwick's Senate race in New Jersey and Margaret Heckler in Massachusetts because, though they had supported ERA, they went along with Reagan's nuclear missile buildup and cuts in social programs and legal protections for women. The "gender gap" that emerged in American politics, when women, for the first time voting independently of men, defeated governors, senators and congressmen who seemed to threaten their values of peace and social concerns, did not operate as strongly in '84 against Reagan as it did in '80, despite the presence of Ferraro on the ticket. Did the onslaught of the bishops and the attempt to tarnish her for collusion in her husband's brutally exposed business dealings rule her out as an embodiment of women's hopes? Did she fail to raise that "different voice" for women in that disastrous campaign? Or did the male backlash against Democratic values prevail also, or sufficiently, among women to offset what had seemed to be her stunning significance.

There is no substitute for having women in political offices that matter. Women are discovering that they have to fight, as men do, in primaries where victory is not certain, and not just wait for an "open seat." . . .

. . . 10. Move beyond single-issue thinking. Even today, I do not think women's rights are the most urgent business for American women. The important thing is somehow getting together with men who also put the values of life first to break through the paralysis that fundamentalist backlash has imposed on all our movements. It is not only feminism that is becoming a dirty word in America, but also liberalism, humanism, pluralism, environmentalism and civil liberties. The very freedom of political dissent that enabled the women's movement to start here has been made to seem unsafe for today's young men as well as young women. I think the yuppies are afraid to be political.

Women may have to think beyond "women's issues" to join their energies with men to redeem our democratic tradition and turn our nation's power to the interests of life instead of the nuclear arms race that is paralyzing it. I've never, for instance, seen the need for a separate women's peace movement. I'm not really sure that women, by nature, are more peace-loving than men. They were simply not brought up to express aggression the way men do (they took it out covertly, on themselves and on their men and children, psychologists would say). But the human race may not survive much longer unless women move beyond the nurture of their own babies and careers to political decisions of war and peace, and unless men who share the nurture of their children take responsibility for ending the arms race before it destroys all life. . . .

End of the Beginning

Betty Friedan

I did not intend to write another book on the woman question. I have already started a major new quest that is taking me way beyond my previous concerns, opening strange doors. I am tired of the pragmatic, earthbound battles of the women's movement, tired of rhetoric. I want to live the rest of my life.

But these past few years, fulfilling my professional and political commitments, and picking up the pieces of my personal life, for which the women's movement has been the focus for nearly twenty years, I have been nagged by a new, uneasy urgency that won't let me leave. Listening to my own daughter and sons, and others of their generation whom I meet, lecturing at universities or professional conferences or feminist networks around the country and around the world, I sense something *off,* out of focus, going wrong, in the terms by which they are trying to live the equality we fought for.

From these daughters—getting older now, working so hard, determined not to be trapped as their mothers were, and expecting so much, taking for granted the opportunities we had to struggle for—I've begun to hear undertones of pain and puzzlement, a queasiness, an uneasiness, almost a bitterness that they hardly dare admit. As if with all those opportunities that we won for them, and envy them, how can they ask out loud certain questions, talk about certain other needs they aren't supposed to worry about—those old needs which shaped our lives, and trapped us, and against which we rebelled?

● In California, in the office of a television producer who prides himself on being an "equal opportunity employer," I am confronted by his new "executive assistant." She wants to talk to me alone before her boss comes in. Lovely, in her late twenties and "dressed for success" like a model in the latest *Vogue,* she is not just a glorified secretary with a fancy title in a dead-end job. The woman she replaced has just been promoted to the position of "creative vice-president."

"I know I'm lucky to have this job," she says, defensive and accusing, "but you people who fought for these things had your families. You already had your men and children. What are we supposed to do?"

She complains that the older woman vice-president, one of the early radical feminists who vowed never to marry or have children, didn't understand her quandary. "All she wants," the executive assistant says, "is more power in the company."

● A young woman in her third year of Harvard Medical School tells me, "I'm going to be a surgeon. I'll never be a trapped housewife like my mother. But I would like to get married and have children, I think. They say we can have it all. But how? I work thirty-six hours in the hospital, twelve off. How am I going to have a relationship, much less kids, with hours like that? I'm not sure I can be a superwoman. I'm frightened that I may be kidding myself. Maybe I can't have it all. Either I won't be able to have the kind of marriage I dream of or the kind of medical career I want."

● In New York, a woman in her thirties who has just been promoted says, "I'm up against the clock, you might say. If I don't have a child now, it will be too late. But it's an agonizing choice. I've been supporting my husband while he gets his Ph.D. We don't know what kind of job he'll be able to get. There's no pay when you take off to have a baby in my company. They don't guarantee you'll get your job back. If I don't have a baby, will I miss out on life somehow? Will I really be fulfilled as a woman?"

Mounting the barricades yet again in the endless battle for the Equal Rights Amendment—in Illinois, at the national political conventions—I also sensed a political bewilderment, a frustration, a flagging, finally, of energy for battle at all. It is hard to keep summoning energy for battles like ERA, which, according to all the polls and the public commitment of elected officials and political parties, should have been won long ago; or for the right to choose when and whether to have a child, and thus to safe, legal, medical help in abortion—won eight years ago and decreed by the Supreme Court more basic than many of the rights guaranteed in the Constitution and the Bill of Rights as it was written of, by and for men—only to be fought over and over again, until even the Supreme Court in 1980 took that right away for poor women.

I sense other victories we thought were won yielding illusory gains; I see new dimensions to problems we thought were solved. As, for instance, the laws against sex discrimination in employment and education, and the affirmative action programs and class-action suits that have given women access to professions and executive jobs held only by men before. Yet, after fifteen years of the women's movement, the gap between women's earnings and men's is greater than ever, women earning on the average only fifty-nine cents to every dollar men earn, the average male high school dropout today earning $1,600 more a year than female college graduates. An unprecedented majority of women have entered the work force in these years, but the overwhelming majority of women are still crowded into the poorly paid service and clerical jobs traditionally reserved for females. (With the divorce rate exceeding 50 percent, it turns out that 71 percent of divorced women are now working compared to only 78 percent of divorced men; the women must be taking jobs the men won't touch.)

What will happen in the eighties as inflation, not just new aspirations, forces women to keep working, while unemployment, already reaching 7.8 percent, hits women the worst? Growing millions of "discouraged workers," who are no longer counted among the unemployed because they have stopped looking for jobs, were reported in 1980, two thirds of them women.

It becomes clear that the great momentum of the women's movement for equality will be stopped, or somehow transformed, by collision or convergence with basic questions of survival in the 1980s. Is feminism a theoretical luxury, a liberal or radical notion we could toy with in the late soft age of affluence, in the decadence of advanced capitalist society, but in the face of 10 percent inflation, 7.8 percent unemployment, nuclear accident at home, and mounting terrorism from Right and Left abroad, something we must put aside for the grim new realities of economic and national survival? Or is equality itself becoming a question of basic human survival? . . .

. . . Of course, the women's movement has for some years been the scapegoat for the rage of threatened, insecure housewives who can no longer count on husbands for lifelong support. Recently I've been hearing younger women, and even older feminists, blame the women's movement for the supposed increase of male impotence, the inadequacy or unavailability of men for the "new women." Some even suggest that the recent explosion of rape, "battered wives," "battered children" and violence in the family is a reaction to, or byproduct of, feminism.

The women's movement is being blamed, above all, for the destruction of the family. Churchmen and sociologists proclaim that the American family, as it has always been defined, is becoming an "endangered species," with the rising divorce rate and the enormous increase in single-parent families and people—especially women—living alone. Women's abdication of their age-old responsibility for the family is also being blamed for the apathy and moral delinquency of the "me generation."

Can we keep on shrugging all this off as enemy propaganda—"their problem, not ours"? I think we must at least admit and begin openly to discuss feminist denial of the importance of family, of women's own needs to give and get love and nurture, tender loving care.

What worries me today is the agonizing conflicts young and not-so-young women are facing—or denying—as they come up against the biological clock, at thirty-five, thirty-six, thirty-nine, forty, and cannot "choose" to have a child. I fought for the right to choose, and will continue to defend that right, against reactionary forces who have already taken it away for poor women now denied Medicaid for abortion, and would take it away for all women with a constitutional amendment. But I think we must begin to discuss, in new terms, the choice to *have* children.

What worries me today is "choices" women have supposedly won, which are not real. How can a woman freely "choose" to have a child when her paycheck is needed for the rent or mortgage, when her job isn't geared to taking care of a child, when there is no national policy for parental leave, and no assurance that her job will be waiting for her if she takes off to have a child?

What worries me today is that despite the fact that more than 45 percent of the mothers of children under six are now working because of economic necessity due to inflation, compared with only 10 percent in 1960 (and, according to a Ford Foundation study, it is estimated that by 1990 only one out of four mothers will be at home full time), no major national effort is being made for child-care services by government, business, labor, Democratic or Republican parties—or by the women's movement itself.

Another troubling sign: When President Carter proposed registering young women as well as men for the draft, it was clear that most young women, and a lot of older feminists, as well as middle Americans generally, would oppose such a draft of women. Phyllis Schlally seized on the draft, of course, to sow new hysteria against the ERA. But I got long-distance calls from young women across the country, blaming the women's movement for a draft they didn't want. What becomes of the feminist axiom that equal rights and opportunity have to mean equal responsibility? Did the women's movement really mean equal opportunity for women to fire ballistic missiles in another Vietnam? . . .

. . . Though the women's movement has changed our lives and surpassed our dreams in its magnitude, and our daughters take their own personhood and equality for granted, they—and we—are finding that it's not so easy to *live,* with or without men and children, solely on the basis of that first feminist agenda. I think, in fact, that the women's movement has come just about as far as it can in terms of women alone. The very choices, options, aspirations, opportunities that we have won for women—no matter how far from real equality—and the small degree of new power women now enjoy, or hunger for, openly, honestly, as never before, are converging on and into new economic and emotional urgencies. Battles lost or won are being fought in terms that are somehow inadequate, irrelevant to this new personal, and political, reality. I believe it's over, that first stage: the women's movement. And yet the larger revolution, evolution, liberation that the women's movement set off, has barely begun. How do we move on? What are the terms of the second stage?

In the first stage, our aim was full participation, power and voice in the mainstream, inside the party, the political process, the professions, the business world. Do women change, inevitably discard the radiant, inviolate, idealized feminist dream, once they get inside and begin to share that power, and do they then operate on the same terms as men? Can women, will women even try to, change the terms?

What are the limits and the true potential of women's power? I believe that the women's movement, in the political sense, is both less and more powerful than we realize. I believe that the personal is both more and less political than our own rhetoric ever implied. I believe that we have to break through our own *feminist* mystique now to come to terms with the new reality of our personal and political experience, and to move into the second stage.

All this past year, with some reluctance and dread, and a strange, compelling relief, I've been asking new questions and listening with a new urgency to other women again, wondering if anyone else reads these signs as beginning-of-the-end, end-of-the-beginning. When I start to talk about them, it makes some women, feminists and antifeminists, uncomfortable, even angry.

There is a disconcerted silence, an uneasy murmuring, when I begin to voice my hunches out loud:

The second stage cannot be seen in terms of women alone, our separate personhood or equality with men.

The second stage involves coming to new terms with the family—new terms with love and with work.

The second stage may not even be a women's movement. Men may be at the cutting edge of the second stage.

The second stage has to transcend the battle for equal power in institutions. The second stage will restructure institutions and transform the nature of power itself.

The second stage may even now be evolving, out of or even aside from what we have thought of as our battle.

I've experienced before the strange mix of shock and relief these hunches arouse. It happened twenty years ago when I began to question the feminine mystique. It happened before when I put into words uncomfortable realities women had been avoiding because they meant we'd have to change. Even the makers of change, self-proclaimed revolutionaries, women no less than men, resist change of the change that has become their security, their power. . . .

. . . "How can you talk about the second stage when we haven't even won the first yet?" a woman asks me at a Catholic college weekend for housewives going back to work. "The men still have the power. We haven't gotten enough for ourselves yet. We have to fight now just to stay where we are, not to be pushed back."

But that's the point. Maybe we have to begin talking about the second stage to keep from getting locked into obsolete power games and irrelevant sexual battles that never can be won, or that we will lose by winning. Maybe only by moving into the second stage, and asking the new questions—political and personal—confronting women and men trying to live the equality we fought for, can we transcend the polarization that threatens even the gains already won, and keep alive the national commitment to women's rights, equal opportunity and choice through this time of economic turmoil and reaction. . . .

. . . The feminine mystique was obsolete. That's why our early battles were won so easily, once we engaged our will. It was, is, awesome—that quantum jump in consciousness. A whole new literature, a new history, new dimensions in every field are now emerging, as the larger implications of women's personhood and equality are explored. The women's movement, which started with personal truth, not seen or understood by the experts, or even by women themselves, because it did not fit the accepted image, has, in the span of a single generation, changed life, and the accepted image.

But the new image, which has come out of the women's movement, cannot evade the continuing tests of real life. That uneasiness I have been sensing these past few years comes from personal truth denied and questions unasked because they do not fit the new accepted image—the *feminist* mystique—as our daughters live what we fought for. It took many centuries of social evolution, technological revolution, to disturb "the changeless face of Eve." That immutable, overshadowing definition of woman as breeder of the race, once rooted in biological, historical necessity, only became a mystique, a defense against reality, as it denied the possibilities and necessities of growth opened by women's new life span in advanced technological society. . . .

. . . At the Harvard commencement in June 1980, class speaker Diana Shaw criticized the feminists who have paved the way for her graduation from that venerable arrogant university on equal terms, with the same diploma, as men. "Contemporary feminism," she said, "has taught us to reject the values conventionally associated with our sex. We are expected to pursue the male standards of success, while remaining 'feminine' according to male standards."

Her words hit a sensitive nerve in one of those earlier feminists, Ellen Goodman, who graduated from the same college, when Radcliffe women were separate from and not quite equal to Harvard men, class of 1963, the year *The Feminine Mystique* was published. "We were to be the first generation of superwomen," she writes (*Washington Post,* June 7, 1980).

> We were the women who would—in fact, should—have dazzling careers and brilliant, satisfied husbands, and remarkable, well-adjusted children.
>
> The half-formed feminism of the early 1960's . . . taught us that to find fulfillment we would have to fit in—fit in to family life . . . fit in to career ladders . . . fit in to our husband's goals . . . fit in to the basic ideas of womanhood. . . .
>
> Through the 1970's, we argued about what kind of equality we wanted. Did we want equal access to the same system or the power to change it? Can you change the system only by becoming a part of it? Once you are in it, does it change you instead?
>
> We discovered that it is easier to fit in than to restructure. When the "male" standard is regarded as the "higher" one, the one with the most tangible rewards, it is easier for women to reach "up" than to convince men of the virtues of simultaneously reaching "down."
>
> It has proved simpler—though not simple, God knows—for women to begin traveling traditional (male) routes than to change those routes. It is simpler to dress for success than to change the definition of success. . . .

"I'm suffering from feminist fatigue," writes Lynda Hurst, a columnist on the *Toronto Star,* in a new non- or antifeminist sheet started in Canada in June 1980 called *Breakthrough.* "After the last dazzle of the [feminist] fireworks, there was deeper darkness. You are perhaps more enslaved now than you have ever been."

She says defiantly:

I've been letting sexist cracks slip past with barely a shrug. I haven't read *Ms.* magazine in months. I can sleep nights without worrying about my lack of a five-year career plan. I can even watch "I Love Lucy" reruns without tsk-tsking over the rampant sexism of the Ricardo marriage.

Don't get me wrong. It's not the women's movement I'm fed up with. . . . It's the "feminist" label—and its paranoid associations—that I've started to resent. I'm developing an urge to run around telling people that I still like raindrops on roses and whiskers on kittens, and that being the local easy-to-bait feminist is getting to be a bore.

I'm tired of having other people (women as well as men) predict my opinion on everything from wedding showers to coed hockey. . . .

I don't want to be stuck today with a feminist label any more than I would have wanted to be known as a "dumb blonde" in the fifties. The libber label limits and short-changes those who are tagged with it. And the irony is that it emerged from a philosophy that set out to destroy the whole notion of female tagging.

I write this book to help the daughters break through the mystique I myself helped to create—and put the right name to their new problems. They have to ask new questions, speak the unspeakable again, admit new, uncomfortable realities, and secret pains and surprising joys of their personal truth that are hard to put into words because they do not fit either the new or old images of women, or they fit them disconcertingly.

These questions come into consciousness as personal ones, each daughter thinking maybe she alone feels this way. The questions have to be asked personally before they become political. Or rather, these simple, heartfelt questions I've been hearing from young women all over the country this past year seem to me to indicate a blind spot in feminism that is both personal and political in its implications and consequences. The younger women have the most questions:

"How can I have it all? Do I *really* have to choose?"

"How can I have the career I want, and the kind of marriage I want, and be a good mother?"

"How can I get him to share more responsibility at home? Why do I always have to be the one with the children, making the decisions at home?"

"I can't count on marriage for my security—look what happened to my mother—but can I get all my security from my career?"

"Can I make it in a man's world, doing it the man's way? What other way is there? But what is it doing to me? Do I want to be like men?"

"What do I have to give up? What are the tradeoffs?"

"Will the jobs open to me now still be here if I stop to have children?"

"Does it really work, that business of 'quality, not quantity' of time with the children? How much is enough?"

"How can I fill my loneliness, except with a man?"

"Do men really want an equal woman?"

"Why are men today so gray and lifeless, compared to women? How can I find a man I can really look up to?"

"How can I play the sex kitten now? Can I ever find a man who will let me be myself?"

"If I put off having a baby till I'm thirty-eight, and can call my own shots on the job, will I ever have kids?"

"How can I juggle it all?"

"How can I put it all together?"

"Can I risk losing myself in marriage?"

"Do I have to be a superwoman?"

Among ourselves, the mothers, I also sense new uneasiness, new questions even harder to put into words lest they evoke those old needs, long since left behind, by us who fought so hard to change the terms of our own lives:

"I have made it, far beyond my dreams. If I put everything else aside, I can see myself as president of the company in ten years. It's not impossible for a woman now. But is that what I really want?"

"My marriage didn't work. I value my independence. I don't want to get married again. But how can I keep on taking care of my kids and myself, on what I earn, and have any kind of life at all, with only myself to depend on? All I do is work to pay the bills."

This is the jumping-off point to the second stage, I believe: these conflicts and fears and compelling needs women feel about the choice to have children now and about success in the careers they now seek—and the concrete practical problems involved (which have larger political implications). I believe daughters and mothers hold separate pieces of the puzzle. I think of my own uneasiness, being called "mother" of the women's movement—not because of modesty, but because of the way I felt about being a mother altogether. An uneasiness, an unsureness, a fear about being a mother because I certainly didn't want to be like my mother. How many generations of American women have felt like that? Until recently I've sensed that same uneasiness with my daughter, an agonizing love-fear-dread, as we see ourselves in each other and do not want to see the pain of it.

With my own daughter now, and so many others, I sense that we have begun to break some seemingly endless vicious cycle. "Another one like me!" "Don't let me be like her!" What we did, we had to do, to break that cycle. But it is not finished yet. It won't be finished until our daughters can freely, joyously choose to have children. They, and we, are beginning to be afraid—and some of our fears are false shadows of dangers past, and some are presently real—because the cycle we broke, and have to embrace again, is basic to life.

From their new place, the daughters can deny their fears and confusions until exaggerated dangers and unrecognized real problems turn them back. The daughters can't make a map from their own experience alone—they might not even recognize the same old traps, dead ends, that we had such a hard time finding our way out of, or the feel of firm ground we were looking for. They never knew the necessity that drove us. But the daughters cannot get their map from us because they truly start from a different place, that assumption of their own personhood and semblance of equal opportunity we won.

Daughters moving ahead where mothers could not go may be, in fact, not so much in danger of being trapped as their mothers were as they are in danger of wasting, avoiding life in unnecessary fear. But even the map we piece together from our bridged experience as women—our daughters and ourselves, moving proudly now as women through the first stage, breaking the chains that kept us out of man's world—is not enough for the next stage. For women may be in new danger of falling into certain deadly traps that men are now trying to climb out of to save their own lives. We can't traverse the next stage and reembrace the cycle of life as women alone.

I have been hearing from men this past year warning signs of certain dead ends for women. Surprising clues of the second stage can be found in the new questions men are asking.

- A Vietnam veteran, laid off at the auto plant where he thought he was secure for life, decides: "There's no security in a job. The dollar's not worth enough any more to live your life for. I'll work three days a week at the garage and my wife will go back to nursing nights, and between us we'll take care of the kids."

- A man on his way up in a New York bank quits to sell real estate on the tip of Long Island for part of his groceries, and to grow the rest himself. "I asked myself one day whether, if my career continued going well and I really made it up the corporate ladder, did I want to be there, fifteen years from now, with the headaches of the senior executives I saw being pushed off to smaller offices, their staff, secretaries, status taken away, or having heart attacks, strokes. Men who had been loyal to the company twenty-five years, it consumed their whole lives—to what end? Did I want to live my life to wind up like them?"

- A hotshot MBA in Chicago balks at the constant traveling and the sixty-to-eighty-hour weeks he is expected to work, assigned to troubleshoot an aerospace company in Texas. "I'm supposed to leave Sunday night and get back Friday. My wife and I are getting to be strangers. Besides, I want to have a family. There are other things I want in life besides getting ahead in this company. But how can I say I won't travel like that when the other guys are willing to? They'll get ahead, and I won't. How can I live for myself, not just for the company?"

- A sales engineer in New Jersey, struggling to take equal responsibilities for the kids now that his wife has gone to work in a department store, says: "For ten years now, all you hear is women talking about what it means to be a woman, how can she fulfill herself as a woman, even forcing men to talk about women. It's over, the man sitting down with his paper, the wife keeping the kids out of his way. The women's movement forced us to think it through—the presumption that the house and the children were the women's responsibility, the shopping, the cooking, even if both were working. Now you're going to see more men asking, What am I doing with my life, what about my fulfillment, what does it mean being a man? What do I have but my job? I think you're going to see a great wave of men dropping out from traditional male roles. Our sense of who we are was profoundly based on work, but men are going to begin to define themselves in ways other than work. Partly because of the economy, partly because men are beginning to find other goodies at the table, like the children, where men have been excluded before. Being a daddy has become very important to me. Why shouldn't she support the family for a while and let *me* find myself?"

Are men and women moving in opposite directions, chasing illusions of liberation by simply reversing roles that the other sex has already found imprisoning? Maybe there are some choices we, they, don't want to face, or shouldn't have to face. Maybe they are not real choices—not yet, not the way society is structured now; or not ever, in terms of basic human reality. Do we have to transcend the very terms of these choices in the second stage?

I think we can only find out by sharing our new uncertainties, the seemingly insoluble problems and unremitting pressures, our fears and shameful weaknesses, and our surprising joys and strengths as we each have been experiencing them, the daughters, ourselves, and the men, as we begin to live the quality we fought for. Even though we know it's not really all that equal yet, even if we have some new thoughts about what equality really means—for women and men. We had better admit these feelings, or more and more women and men will lose heart and say they do not want equality after all. . . .

. . . There is no going back. The women's movement was necessary. But the liberation that began with the women's movement isn't finished. The equality we fought for isn't livable, isn't workable, isn't comfortable in the terms that structured our battle. The first stage, the women's movement, was fought within, and against, and defined by that old structure of unequal, polarized male and female sex roles. But to continue reacting against that structure is still to be defined and limited by its terms. What's needed now is to transcend those terms, transform the structure itself. Maybe the women's movement, as such, can't do that. The experts of psychology, sociology, economics, biology, even the new feminist experts, are still engaged in the old battles, of women versus men. The new questions that need to be asked—and with them, the new structures for the new struggle—can only come from pooling our experience: the agonies and ecstasies of our own transition as women, our daughters' new possibilities, and problems, and the confusion of the men. We have to break out of feminist rhetoric, go beyond the assumptions of the first stage of the women's movement and test life again—with personal truth—to turn this new corner, just as we had to break through the feminine mystique twenty years ago to begin our modern movement toward equality.

Saying no to the feminine mystique and organizing to confront sex discrimination was only the first stage. We have somehow to transcend the polarities of the first stage, and even the rage of our own "no," to get on to the second stage: the restructuring of our institutions on a basis of real equality for women and men, so we can live a new "yes" to life and love, and can *choose* to have children. The dynamics involved here are both economic and sexual. The energies whereby we live and love, and work and eat, which have been so subverted by power in the past, can truly be liberated in the service of life for all of us—or diverted in fruitless impotent reaction.

How do we surmount the reaction that threatens to destroy the gains we thought we had already won in the first stage of the women's movement? How do we surmount our own reaction, which shadows our feminism and our femininity (we blush even to use that word now)? How do we transcend the polarization between women and women and between women and men, to achieve the new human wholeness that is the promise of feminism, and get on with solving the concrete, practical, everyday problems of living, working and loving as equal persons? This is the personal and political business of the second stage.

Why Young Women Are More Conservative

Gloria Steinem

If you had asked me a decade or more ago, I certainly would have said the campus was the first place to look for the feminist or any other revolution. I also would have assumed that student-age women, like student-age men, were much more likely to be activist and open to change than their parents. After all, campus revolts have a long and well-publicized tradition, from students of medieval France, whose "heresy" was suggesting that the university be separate from the church, through the anticolonial student riots of British India; from students who led the cultural revolution of the People's Republic of China, to campus demonstrations against the Shah of Iran. Even in this country, with far less tradition of student activism, the populist movement to end the war in Vietnam was symbolized by campus protests and mistrust of anyone over thirty.

It has taken me many years of traveling as a feminist speaker and organizer to understand that I was wrong about women; at least, about women acting on their own behalf. In activism, as in so many other things, I had been educated to assume that men's cultural pattern was the natural or the only one. If student years were the peak time of rebellion and openness to change for men, then the same must be true of women. In fact, a decade of listening to every kind of women's group—from brown-bag lunchtime lectures organized by office workers to all-night rap sessions at campus women's centers; from housewifes' self-help groups to campus rallies—has convinced me that the reverse is more often true. Women may be the one group that grows more radical with age. Though some students are big exceptions to this rule, women in general don't begin to challenge the politics of our own lives until later.

Looking back, I realize that this pattern has been true for my life, too. My college years were full of uncertainties and the personal conservatism that comes from trying to win approval and fit into the proper grown-up and womanly role, whether that means finding a well-to-do man to be supported by or a male radical to support. Nonetheless, I went right on assuming that brave exploring youth and cowardly conservative old age were the norms for everybody, and that I must be just an isolated and guilty accident. Though every generalization based on female culture has many exceptions, and should never be used as a crutch or excuse, I think we might be less hard on ourselves and each other as students, feel better about our potential for change as we grow older—and educate reporters who announce feminism's demise because its red-hot center is not on campus—if we figured out that for most of us as women, the traditional college period is an unrealistic and cautious time. Consider a few of the reasons. . . .

As young women, whether students or not, we're still in the stage most valued by male-dominant cultures: we have our full potential as workers, wives, sex partners, and childbearers.

That means we haven't yet experienced the life events that are most radical-izing for women: entering the paid-labor force and discovering how women are treated there; marrying and finding out that it is not yet an equal partnership; having children and discovering who is responsible for them and who is not; and aging, still a greater penalty for women than for men.

Furthermore, new ambitions nourished by the rebirth of feminism may make young women feel and behave a little like a classical immigrant group. We are determined to prove ourselves, to achieve academic excellence, and to prepare for interesting and successful careers. More noses are kept to more grindstones in an effort to demonstrate new-found abilities, and perhaps to allay suspicions that women still have to have more and better credentials than men. This doesn't leave much time for activism. Indeed, we may not yet know that it is necessary.

In addition, the very progress into previously all-male careers that may be revolutionary for women is seen as conservative and conformist by outside critics. Assuming male radicalism to be the measure of change, they interpret any concern with careers as evidence of "campus conservatism." In fact, "dropping out" may be a departure for men, but "dropping in" is a new thing for women. Progress lies in the direction we have not been. . . .

Then there is the female guilt trip, student edition. If we're not sailing along as planned, it must be our fault. If our mothers didn't "do anything" with their educations, it must have been their fault. If we can't study as hard as we think we must (because women still have to be better prepared than men), and have a substantial personal and sexual life at the same time (because women are supposed to care more about relationships than men do), then we feel inadequate, as if each of us were individually at fault for a problem that is actually culture-wide.

I've yet to be on a campus where most women weren't worrying about some aspect of combining marriage, children, and a career. I've yet to find one where many men were worrying about the same thing. Yet women will go right on suffering from the double-role problem and terminal guilt until men are encour-aged, pressured, or otherwise forced, individually and collectively, to integrate themselves into the "women's work" of raising children and homemaking. Until then, and until there are changed job patterns to allow equal parenthood, children will go right on growing up with the belief that only women can be loving and nurturing, and only men can be intellectual or active outside the home. Each half of the world will go on limiting the full range of its human talent.

Finally, there is the intimate political training that hits women in the teens and early twenties: the countless ways we are still brainwashed into assuming that women are dependent on men for our basic identities, both in our work and our personal lives, much more than vice versa. After all, if we're going to enter a marriage system that's still legally designed for a person and a half, submit to an economy in which women still average about fifty-nine cents on the dollar earned by men, and work mainly as support staff and assistants, or co-directors and vice-presidents at best, then we have to be convinced that we are not whole people on our own.

In order to make sure that we will see ourselves as half-people, and thus be addicted to getting our identity from serving others, society tries hard to convert us as young women into "man junkies"; that is, into people who are addicted to regular shots of male-approval and presence, both professionally and personally. We need a man standing next to us, actually and figuratively, whether it's at work, on Saturday night, or throughout life. (If only men realized how little it matters which man is standing there, they would understand that this addiction depersonalizes them, too.) Given the danger to a male-dominant system if young women stop internalizing this political message of derived identity, it's no wonder that those who try to kick the addiction—and, worse yet, to help other women do the same—are likely to be regarded as odd or dangerous by everyone from parents to peers.

With all that pressure combined with little experience, it's no wonder that younger women are often less able to support each other. Even young women who espouse feminist goals as individuals may refrain from identifying themselves as "feminist": it's okay to want equal pay for yourself (just one small reform) but it's not okay to want equal pay for women as a group (an economic revolution). Some retreat into the safe middle ground of "I'm not a feminist but . . ." Still others become politically active, but only on issues that are taken seriously by their male counterparts.

The same lesson about the personal conservatism of younger women is taught by the history of feminism. . . . In this country, for instance, the nineteenth-century wave of feminism was started by older women who had been through the radicalizing experience of getting married and becoming the legal chattel of their husbands (or the equally radicalizing experience of not getting married and being treated as spinsters). Most of them had also worked in the antislavery movement and learned from the political parallels between race and sex. In other countries, that wave was also led by women who were past the point of maximum pressure toward marriageability and conservatism.

Looking at the first decade of the second wave, it's clear that the early feminist activist and consciousness-raising groups of the 1960s were organized by women who had experienced the civil rights movement, or homemakers who had discovered that raising kids and cooking didn't occupy all their talents. While most campuses of the late sixties were still circulating the names of illegal abortionists privately (after all, abortion could damage our marriage value), slightly older women were holding press conferences and speak-outs about the reality of abortions (including their own, even though that often meant confessing an illegal act) and demanding reformer repeal of antichoice laws. Though rape had been a quiet epidemic on campus for generations, younger women victims were still understandably fearful of speaking up, and campuses encouraged silence in order to retain their reputation for safety with tuition-paying parents. It took many off-campus speak-outs, demonstrations against laws of evidence and police procedures, and testimonies in state legislatures before most student groups began to make demands on campus and local cops for greater rape protection. In fact, "date rape"—the common campus phenomenon of a young woman being raped by someone she knows, perhaps even by several students in a fraternity house—is just now being exposed. Marital rape, a more difficult legal issue, was taken up several years ago. As for battered women and the attendant expose of husbands and lovers as more statistically dangerous than unknown muggers in the street, that issue still seems to be thought of as a largely noncampus concern, yet at many of the colleges and universities where I've spoken, there has been at least one case within current student memory of a young woman beaten or murdered by a jealous lover.

This cultural pattern of youthful conservatism makes the growing number of older women going back to school very important. They are life examples and pragmatic activists who radicalize women young enough to be their daughters. Now that the median female undergraduate age in this country is twenty-seven because so many older women have returned, the campus is becoming a major place for cross-generational connections.

None of this should denigrate the courageous efforts of young women, especially women on campus, and the many changes they've pioneered. On the contrary, they should be seen as even more remarkable for surviving the conservative pressures, recognizing societal problems they haven't yet fully experienced, and organizing successfully in the midst of a transient student population. Every women's history course, rape hot line, or campus newspaper that is finally covering all the news; every feminist professor whose job has been created or tenure saved by student pressure, or male administrator whose consciousness has been permanently changed; every counselor who's stopped guiding women one way and men another; every lawsuit that's been fueled by student energies against unequal athletic funds or graduate school requirements: all those accomplishments are even more impressive when seen against the backdrop of the female pattern of activism. . . .

Young women have a big task of resisting pressures and challenging definitions. Their increasing success is a miracle of foresight and courage that should make us all proud. But they should know that they, too, may grow more radical with age.

For Women to Gain in Congress, Parties Ought to Even the Odds

Kay Mills

In 1960 there were two women in the U.S. Senate. Today, nearly three decades and one feminist movement later, there are two women in the Senate. This is progress?

In 1960 there were 17 women in the House. In the new 101st Congress there are 25. They include two new Democrats—Nita Lowey, who beat incumbent Joseph DioGuardi in New York, and Jolene Unsoeld, who won a close and caustic contest in Washington state. At this rate, says long-time activist Eleanor Smeal, it will take 345 years to achieve parity on Capitol Hill.

So what? What difference would it make if there were double the current number of women ready to be sworn in as members of Congress? And, if their presence is such a big deal, what can be done to ensure better representation of women?

Rep. Patricia Schroeder (D-Colo.) concludes that even doubling the number of women would make little difference. She says the theory is that you need to have about one-fourth of the members of any organization to make any difference. One-fourth of the House's 435 members is 109, four times the current membership.

But she believes that if there were significantly more women the tone would change on everything from combatting sexual harassment on Capitol Hill to determining how the government spends money. With more women in Congress, the bill that would have vastly expanded child-care programs would have had a far better chance of passing last year. The family medical-leave act might be law now, too.

Women in politics tend to pay more attention than men to issues that especially affect other women—whether it's child care, money for breast-cancer research or better pay for jobs traditionally held by women. Women also tend to put other women on their staffs, thus further opening the process, says Ruth Mandel, who has been studying the subject for years at Rutgers University's Center for the American Woman and Politics.

Women now fill 15% of the seats in state legislatures and have even higher representation in local government. In West Virginia last year, women in the Legislature got their colleagues to override the governor's veto of a bill providing medical care for poor pregnant women and poor children. Mandel reports in a new study that, to win that battle, the female legislators threatened to filibuster in the closing days of the session and called a candlelight protest outside the Capitol.

Smeal, who has been comparing the political representation of women in European parliaments with our own dismal scene, reports that 8 of the 18 Cabinet members in Norway are women. When the country faced budget cuts recently, those female Cabinet members made sure that child-care programs were not affected.

Smeal, former president of the National Organization for Women, heads the Fund for the Feminist Majority, a new group that is trying to improve women's representation in elective offices. Where, she was asked recently, do you start? On the college campuses and in the law schools. Smeal's organization, backed financially by Los Angeles feminist Peg Yorkin, has been telling young women that they shouldn't buy the notion that they have to wait or that they have to be better than the men. Young men don't wait to run.

But women need some help from the system, help that they rarely get now because that system supports incumbents. Smeal wants the political parties to engage in some affirmative action. She wants them to require that a certain portion—maybe half—of the party's candidates be female, and many of them should be black or Latina. We now have a national legislature with only one black woman—Cardiss Collins (D-Ill.)—and no Latinas. How representative is that?

At first blush, Smeal's proposal seems like an idea that no one in power would buy. But the political parties have already taken some steps down that road. Internally, the Democrats have already guaranteed parity. They require equal representation by sex on all party committees and commissions and at the national convention (which of course doesn't mean all that much any more). The Supreme Court has upheld the delegate-selection rule.

Smeal hopes that women and sympathetic men in each party will see the advantages, in terms of both politics and social programs, in requiring that more women get party encouragement in primaries, are selected as candidates for open seats and get solid party backing in general elections. The 1988 Democratic platform endorses the idea, and the Republican platform says that the party should move toward this equality.

It has become obvious that women playing by the existing rules will achieve political office no faster than I can run a 10K. Trust me—that is not fast. That brings to mind a scene in the ultimate runners' film, "Chariots of Fire." The Ben Cross character, who works at running to prove himself in a prejudiced world, has just lost a race. He's sitting in the grandstand, and his girlfriend—you remember, the beautiful singer—finds him. He says that if he can't win, he won't run. She replies that if you don't run, you can't win. Women can win, too, if they run with a little more help from their friends in the parties.

Confessions of a Female Chauvinist Sow

Anne Roiphe

I once married a man I thought was totally unlike my father and I imagined a whole new world of freedom emerging. Five years later it was clear even to me— floating face down in a wash of despair—that I had simply chosen a replica of my handsome daddy-true. The updated version spoke English like an angel but— good God!—underneath he was my father exactly: wonderful, but not the right man for me.

Most people I know have at one time or another been fouled up by their childhood experiences. Patterns tend to sink into the unconscious only to reappear, disguised, unseen, like marionette strings, pulling us this way or that. Whatever ails people—keeps them up at night, tossing and turning—also ails movements no matter how historically huge or politically important. The women's movement cannot remake consciousness, or reshape the future, without acknowledging and shedding all the unnecessary and ugly baggage of the past. It's easy enough now to see where men have kept us out of clubs, baseball games, graduate schools, it's easy enough to recognize the hidden directions that limit Sis to cake-baking and Junior to bridge-building, it's now possible for even Miss America herself to identify what *they* have done to us, and, of course, *they* have and *they* did and *they* are. . . . But along the way we also developed our own hidden prejudices, class assumptions and an anti-male humor and collection of expectations that give us, like all oppressed groups, a secret sense of superiority (co-existing with a poor self-image—it's not news that people can believe two contradictory things at once).

Listen to any group that suffers materially and socially. They have a lexicon with which they tease the enemy: ofay, goy, honky, gringo. "Poor pale devils," said Malcolm X loud enough for us to hear, although blacks had joked about that to each other for years. Behind some of the women's liberation thinking lurk the rumors, the prejudices, the defense systems of generations of oppressed women whispering in the kitchen together, presenting one face to their menfolk and another to their card clubs, their mothers and sisters. All this is natural enough but potentially dangerous in a revolutionary situation in which you hope to create a future that does not mirror the past. The hidden anti-male feelings, a result of the old system, will foul us up if they are allowed to persist.

During my teen years I never left the house on my Saturday night dates without my mother slipping me a few extra dollars—mad money, it was called. I'll explain what it was for the benefit of the new generation in which people just sleep with each other: the fellow was supposed to bring me home, lead me safely through the asphalt jungle, protect me from slithering snakes, rapists, and the like.

But my mother and I knew young men were apt to drink too much, to slosh down so many rye-and-gingers that some hero might well lead me in front of an oncoming bus, smash his daddy's car into Tiffany's window or, less gallantly, throw up on my new dress. Mad money was for getting home on your own, no matter what form of insanity your date happened to evidence. Mad money was also a wallflower's rope ladder; if the guy you came with suddenly fancied someone else, well, you didn't have to stay there and suffer, you could go home. Boys were fickle and likely to be unkind, my mother and I knew that, as surely as we knew they tried to make you do things in the dark they wouldn't respect you for afterwards, and in fact would spread the word and spoil your rep. Boys like to be flattered, if you made them feel important they would eat out of your hand. So talk to them about their interests, don't alarm them with displays of intelligence— we all knew that, we groups of girls talking into the wee hours of the night in a kind of easy companionship we thought impossible with boys. Boys were prone to have a good time, get you pregnant, and then pretend they didn't know your name when you came knocking on their door for finances or comfort. In short, we believed boys were less moral than we were. They appeared to be hypocritical, self-seeking, exploitative, untrustworthy and very likely to be showing off their precious masculinity. I never had a girl friend I thought would be unkind or embarrass me in public. I never expected a girl to lie to me about her marks or sports skill or how good she was in bed. Altogether—without anyone's directly coming out and saying so—I gathered that men were sexy, powerful, very inter-esting, but not very nice, not very moral, humane and tender, like us. Girls played fairly while men, unfortunately, reserved their honor for the battlefield.

Why are there laws insisting on alimony and child support? Well, everyone knows that men don't have an instinct to protect their young and, given half a chance, with the moon in the right phase, they will run off and disappear. Everyone assumes a mother will not let her child starve, yet it is necessary to legislate that a father must not do so. We are taught to accept the idea that men are less than decent; their charms may be manifold but their characters are riddled with faults. To this day I never blink if I hear that a man has gone to find his fortune in South America, having left his pregnant wife, his blind mother and taken the family car. I still gasp in horror when I hear of a woman leaving her asthmatic infant for a rock group in Taos because I can't seem to avoid the assumption that men are naturally heels and women the ordained carriers of what little is moral in our dubious civilization.

My mother never gave me mad money thinking I would ditch a fellow for some other guy or that I would pass out drunk on the floor. She knew I would be considerate of my companion because, after all, I was more mature than the boys that gathered about. Why was I more mature? Women just are people-oriented, they learn to be empathetic at an early age. Most English students (students interested in humanity, not artifacts) are women. Men and boys—so the myth goes—conceal their feelings and lose interest in anybody else's. Everyone knows that even little boys can tell the difference between one kind of a car and another—proof that their souls are mechanical, their attention directed to the nonhuman.

I remember shivering in the cold vestibule of a famous men's athletic club. Women and girls are not permitted inside the club's door. What are they doing in there, I asked? They're naked, said my mother, they're sweating, jumping up and down a lot, telling each other dirty jokes and bragging about their stock market exploits. Why can't we go in? I asked. Well, my mother told me, they're afraid we'd laugh at them.

The prejudices of childhood are hard to outgrow. I confess that every time my business takes me past that club, I shudder. Images of large bellies resting on massage tables and flaccid penises rising and falling with the Dow Jones average flash through my head. There it is, chauvinism waving its cancerous tentacles from the depths of my psyche.

Minorities automatically feel superior to the oppressor because, after all, they are not hurting anybody. In fact, they feel morally better. The old canard that women need love, men need sex—believed for too long by both sexes—attributes moral and spiritual superiority to women and makes of men beasts whose urges send them prowling into the night. This false division of good and bad, placing deforming pressures on everyone, doesn't have to contaminate the future. We know that the assumptions we make about each other become a part of the cultural air we breathe and, in fact, become social truths. Women who want equality must be prepared to give it and to believe in it, and in order to do that it is not enough to state that you are as good as any man, but also it must be stated that he is as good as you and both will be humans together. If we want men to share in the care of the family in a new way, we must assume them as capable of consistent loving tenderness as we.

I rummage about and find in my thinking all kinds of anti-male prejudices. Some are just jokes and others I will have a hard time abandoning. First, I share an emotional conviction with many sisters that women given power would not create wars. Intellectually I know that's ridiculous, great queens have waged war before; the likes of Lurleen Wallace, Pat Nixon and Mrs. General Lavelle can be depended upon in the future to guiltlessly condemn to death other people's children in the name of some ideal of their own. Little girls, of course, don't take toy guns out of their hip pockets and say "Pow, pow" to all their neighbors and friends like the average well-adjusted little boy. However, if we gave little girls the six-shooters, we would soon have double the pretend body count.

Aggression is not, as I secretly think, a male-sex-linked characteristic: brutality is masculine only by virtue of opportunity. True, there are 1,000 Jack the Rippers for every Lizzie Borden, but that surely is the result of social forms. Women as a group are indeed more masochistic than men. The practical result of this division is that women seem nicer and kinder, but when the world changes, women will have a fuller opportunity to be just as rotten as men and there will be fewer claims of female moral superiority.

Now that I am entering early middle age, I hear many women complaining of husbands and ex-husbands who are attracted to younger females. This strikes the older woman as unfair, of course. But I remember a time when I thought all boys around my age and grade were creeps and bores. I wanted to go out with an older man: a senior or, miraculously, a college man. I had a certain contempt for my coevals, not realizing that the freshman in college I thought so desirable was some older girl's creep. Some women never lose that contempt for men of their own age. That isn't fair either and may be one reason why some sensible men of middle years find solace in young women.

I remember coming home from school one day to find my mother's card game dissolved in hysterical laughter. The cards were floating in black rivers of running mascara. What was so funny? A woman named Helen was lying on a couch pretending to be her husband with a cold. She was issuing demands for orange juice, aspirin, suggesting a call to a specialist, complaining of neglect, of fate's cruel finger, of heat, of cold, or sharp pains on the bridge of the nose that might indicate brain involvement. What was so funny? The ladies explained to me that all men behave just like that with colds, they are reduced to temper tantrums by simple nasal congestion, men cannot stand any little physical discomfort—on and on the laughter went.

The point of this vignette is the nature of the laughter—us laughing at them, us feeling superior to them, us ridiculing them behind their backs. If they were doing it to us we'd call it male chauvinist pigness; if we do it to them, it is inescapably female chauvinist sowness and, whatever its roots, it leads to the same isolation. Boys are messy, boys are mean, boys are rough, boys are stupid and have sloppy handwriting. A cacophony of childhood memories rushes through my head, balanced of course, by all the well-documented feelings of inferiority and envy. But the important thing, the hard thing, is to wipe the slate clean, to start again without the meanness of the past. That's why it's so important that the women's movement not become anti-male and allow its most prejudiced spokesmen total leadership. The much-chewed-over abortion issue illustrates this. The women's-liberation position, insisting on a woman's right to determine her own body's destiny, leads in fanatical extreme to a kind of emotional immaculate conception in which the father is not judged even half-responsible—he has no rights, and no consideration is to be given to his concern for either the woman or the fetus.

Woman, who once was abandoned and disgraced by an unwanted pregnancy, has recently arrived at a new pride of ownership or disposal. She has traveled in a straight line that still excludes her sexual partner from an equal share in the wanted or unwanted pregnancy. A better style of life may develop from an assumption that men are as human as we. Why not ask the child's father if he would like to bring up the child? Why not share decisions, when possible, with the male? If we cut them out, assuming an old-style indifference on their part, we perpetuate the ugly divisiveness that has characterized relations between the sexes so far.

Hard as it is or many of us to believe, women are not really superior to men in intelligence or humanity—they are only equal.

Men Need Liberating from Unfair Laws

Richard F. Doyle

Objective examination demonstrates that over the past 30 years antimale discrimination has become far greater, in scope, in degree and in damage, than any which may exist against women. It takes the form of violations of law, decency and common sense that can be described as unconscionable at best. It is most evident in the areas of domestic relations, employment, and crime and punishment, and denigration of the very male image itself.

The social repercussions are predictable and catastrophic. They include:

a. The male image is becoming that of "Jack-the-Ripper" or "Dagwood Bumstead."

b. The female image is emerging supreme, almost to the point of canonization.

c. Women and bureaucracies are usurping male roles and functions in family and industry.

d. The sexes are becoming indistinguishable. More and more persons are becoming sexual nonentities and homosexuals.

e. Fifty percent of marriages end in divorce.

f. A large percentage of children therefore are being deprived of normal family lives, due to divorce.

g. Defeated, emasculated men, in ever-increasing numbers, are matriculating into the flotsam and jetsam of skid row.

h. Immorality, neurotic instability, drug addiction, delinquency, crime, and other aberrations are being spawned at a disastrous rate.

i. The resultant welfare, corrections and mental institution burdens are becoming staggering, actually, intolerable. . . .

We have attempted to identify the causes. Summarized, they seem to be: distortion of sexual identity and function, displacement and subordination of the male, a perversion of chivalry, and plain old greed. . . .

A "Sacred Cow" syndrome regarding women permeates our society. An example is the great concern in wars and disasters over the killing and maiming of women and children. The killing and maiming of men is of less, if any, importance.

Men are treated like second class citizens throughout the entire spectrum of crime and punishment. Operating under the assumption that two wrongs make a right, government, business and industry discriminate against men in employment and promotion through "Affirmative Action" programs.

The roles of family provider, protector, disciplinarian, and co-rearer of children, traditionally within the functions of husband and father, are being usurped by women, by the welfare department, by other agencies and by the legal fraternity.

GOVERNMENTAL RESPONSIBILITY

The foregoing philosophies, and the more vicious anti-male attitudes covered later, have been assimilated by government offices. Government employees, from judges to legal aid lawyers, are like self-appointed Galahads, who can't, or don't, distinguish between ladies and women. They eagerly welcome opportunities to rescue damsels in distress and to enforce men's responsibilities. Men's rights must be purchased by hiring expensive lawyers. . . .

Probably the most extensive and outrageous manifestation of anti-male prejudice is in divorce. . . . Divorce courts are frequently like slaughter-houses, with about as much compassion and talent. They function as collection agencies for lawyer fees, however outrageous, stealing children and extorting money from men in ways blatantly unconstitutional. Job havens for the incompetent and catchpolls, the arrogance and archaic mentalities permeating so many are unspeakable. Men are regarded as mere guests in their homes, evictable any time at the whims of wives and judges. Men are driven from home and children against their wills, then when unable to stretch paychecks far enough to support two households are termed "runaway fathers." Contrary to all principles of justice, men are thrown into prison for inability to pay alimony and support, however unreasonable or unfair the "obligation." Dispel all notion that written "law" controls divorce. It has very little impact. Indeed, few judges are even aware of statutory provisions. Judicial whim, or (to grant the pretense of respectability) "discretion," is the actual basis on which decisions are made. Recourse to legal remedies is practically nonexistent.

In custody and property disposition morality and fitness are insignificant. Sex-gender is the primary criteria. Women, regardless of merit—whether they're unstable, tramps, lesbians, or whatever, are routinely awarded almost everything—especially custody of children (in 95% of cases) and continuing financial sustenance. . . .

The next largest area of male subordination is crime and punishment; from decision to arrest, amount of bail required, guilt or innocence in judgement, severity of sentences, physical conditions of imprisonment, to release on parole.

Men are jailed on offenses for which women would be winked at. They receive stiffer sentences for similar, or lesser, crimes than women. For example, if a man looks into a home in which a woman is undressing, he will be arrested for window peeping. Reverse the situation, with the woman looking in, again the man will be arrested—this time for indecent exposure. Women are murdering husbands or boyfriends and getting off scott-free, by simply pleading "brutality." It's a near epidemic. Often the victims were sound asleep or even living separately. That these women could simply pack up and leave doesn't even occur to the courts. On the other hand, men may receive 50 year sentences for rapes wherein the victim suffers no physical damage. Contrast the sentences received by Patti Hearst and William James Runnel (whose life sentence by the State of Texas for theft of $299.11 was upheld by the U.S. Supreme Court) and Robert Earl May Jr. (a 14 year old Brookhaven, Mass. boy who got 48 years for armed robbery). Men's Rights Ass'n files are bursting with such examples.

Consider how many men are in jail as opposed to women. According to a recent survey by the U.S. Law Enforcement Assistance Administration, 94% of prisoners are male. Does anyone suggest this to be the proportion of evil in men to that in women? Consider the condition of men's prisons vis a vis those of women's prisons. The former are like dungeons, with cages of steel and concrete. The latter are usually like campuses, with furnished, TV-equipped cottages and grounds for strolling. . . .

WOMEN'S LIB

Normal women are the most pampered creatures in western society. In fact, bluntly put, many are parasites, living off the production of men and doing little more to justify their existence than cooking and cleaning a few hours a week, and perhaps computing the value of these services as if the husband were the only beneficiary. This is called biting the hand that feeds you. The alleged discrimination against women in employment, abortion, and miscellaneous areas is insignificant compared to that against men in crime and punishment, employment, and domestic relations. Braying, irrational, but widely heard neo-feminists are cluttering the women's cause with emotional trash, non-issues, impractical solutions and some dangerous policies. They need only perch glasses atop their head and babble "newspeak." People, especially the liberal press, take them seriously. . . .

The very term, "feminists," is misleading. Most adherents are attempting to destroy all traces of femininity. Hence we shall term them "neo-feminists."

Neo-feminists demand to become employed at work men can do best in numbers equal to their population. Government and industry, taking the line of least resistance, are giving women preference in hiring and promotion, regardless of qualification. This is causing hardship to male family breadwinners, especially the emerging Blacks. The military and police forces are becoming weakened by an influx of women, seriously threatening this country's security. Yet not one neo-feminist in a hundred is prepared to sacrifice the privileges routinely accorded women by virtue of their sex, or to demand equal treatment with men in the areas where men are discriminated against. One never sees them clamoring for the dirty jobs men must perform or for equal representation in jails or skid row. It's a "have their cake and eat it too" situation. . . .

But this is not to imply that all blame lies on the shoulders of women, judges, lawyers and institutions. Males themselves are largely responsible for allowing this sorry condition to develop, by gradually surrendering their rights, shirking their responsibilities and abdicating their trousers. Fuzzy-headed housemales, purporting to represent "men's liberation," but sponsored by NOW, are denouncing their masculinity while groping at each other in "consciousness raising" sessions. The bleats of these eunuchs have been hailed as representative of men's liberation. Nothing could be further from the truth. . . . Men's liberation means establishing the right of males *to be* men; not to liberate them *from being* men.

In the face of their treatment most men lie down and roll over in the manner of submissive dogs. This only encourages further tyranny. Protest must be made.

Male dignity and men's rights must be restored, preserved and protected against the excesses of society, legalists, and bureaucrats. Just and competent administration of law must be implemented.

Men Need Liberating from Masculine Myths

Herb Goldberg

Women bend and men break. The blueprint for masculinity is a blueprint for self-destruction. It is a process so deeply embedded in the male consciousness, however, that awareness of its course and its end has been lost. The masculine imperative, the pressure and compulsion to perform, to prove himself, to dominate, to live up to the "masculine ideal"—in short, to "be a man"—supersedes the instinct to survive. His psychological fragility and volatility may even cause him to destroy a lifetime of work and relationships in a momentary impulse.

The diagnosis of chauvinism is superficial. More often it is a gross and misleading distortion. Closer examination of a man's behavior reveals a powerfully masochistic, self-hating and often pathetically self-destructive style.

The brittle male conducts his life by his *ideas* about masculinity. Living up to the *image* is the important thing. Though the moment-to-moment experience may be painful and generally unsatisfying for him, his mind is continually telling him *what he is supposed to be.* As long as he is able to be that way, he can fend off the inner demons that threaten him with accusations of not being "a man."

As his isolation and distrust, the hallmarks of "successful" masculinity, increase, so do his drive for power and control and his inner rage and frustration. He senses the human experience drifting beyond his reach forever. By trying to control the world, even "improve" it or change it, he may simply be trying to make it a place in which he can safely become human—more loving and less aggressive. But the plan fails. His great hunger to prove himself, plus his anger and distrust, drive the possibilities of intimacy away. As his life unfolds and he is well into living up to masculine expectations, his behavior and choices for emotional nourishment may very well become more desperate and bizarre.

Herb Goldberg, "Men Need Liberating from Masculine Myths." From "The Cardboard Goliath" from *The New Male: From Self-Destruction to Self-Care* by Herb Goldberg, Copyright © 1979 by Herb Goldberg. Reprinted by permission of William Morrow & Company, Inc.

DRIVEN BY IDEA OF MANHOOD

Traditional masculinity is largely a psychologically defensive operation rather than an authentic and organic process. A man's psychological energy is used to defend *against,* rather than to express, what he really is. His efforts are directed at proving to himself and others what *he is not*: feminine, dependent, emotional, passive, afraid, helpless, a loser, a failure, impotent and so on. He burns himself out in this never-ending need to prove, because he can *never* sufficiently prove it. To his final day he is driven to project himself as "a man," whether on the battlefield, behind the desk, in lovemaking, on the hospital operating table, in a barroom or even on his deathbed. And when he fails, his self-hate and humiliation overwhelm him.

He would sooner die than acknowledge the things that threaten him most. And yet his deepest imprint is feminine, for it was a woman, not a man, who was his lifeline and his deepest source of identification when he was a baby and a young boy. The femininity is therefore naturally a part of his core. The stronger that identification is and the more it threatens, the more powerfully will he need to deny it. Prisons, as well as violent street gangs, are filled with men who have "Mother" tattooed on their arm. . . .

In the traditional contemporary American home, the feminine imprint is particularly deep because the father sees himself as an incompetent, bumbling parent whose only legitimate territory is the office or the factory. He defers to the innate "maternal wisdom" of his wife in the early child-rearing process. Or he is by necessity simply minimally present, consumed by economic pressures. He is a father in name rather than in behavior, his role is to keep the bills paid and provide for the necessities of life. In many cases, divorce has made him largely a stranger to his family.

A Real Man

Real men have always lived by one simple rule: never settle with words what you can accomplish with a flame thrower.

But if you want to see what's happening to us now, look at today's movies. Instead of having John Wayne fight Nazis and Commies for peace and democracy, we've got Dustin Hoffman fighting Meryl Streep for a six-year-old in *Kramer vs. Kramer.* It's no wonder things are so mixed up. Thirty years ago the Duke would have slapped the broad around and shipped the kid off to military school. Not anymore. I'm convinced things were better in the past.

All a Real Man had to do was abuse women, steal land from Indians and find some place to dump toxic waste. . . . Now you're expected to be sympathetic, sensitive and to split the household chores. (Bruce Feinstein, *Real Men Don't Eat Quiche,* New York: Pocket Books, 1981, from *Reader's Digest,* Dec. '82.)

The emotions are there, but the admonitions against expressing them have progressively caused them to be blocked out of consciousness. As a boy the message he received was clear: Feelings are taboo.

REPRESSION OF FEELINGS

Recently I conducted a marathon therapy group for married couples in a small city in the Midwest, where most of the men still behave in gender-traditional ways. I began by asking each man to write about his feelings, about his life as it was for him, and about his marriage. Five of the eight men insisted that they had *no feelings* inside themselves at all. With assistance, they eventually began to get in touch with their emotions, and it was not hard to understand why they had been blocked. Feelings of frustration, resentment, conflict, loneliness and of not being cared for lay underneath. The men were afraid of these emotions and would not know how to deal with them if they acknowledged them. On the surface, in self-protection, all of these men were "macho"—detached, hyperrational and tough—in short, machinelike. Of course, all of them drank before coming home each day after work, and heavily on weekends. They were burning out rapidly in every way.

The feminist movement has brought the man's rigidity forth in maximal relief. If his fear of change weren't so powerful, he would embrace the movement for the lifegiving and life-expanding possibilities it offers him: a release from age-old guilt and responsibility toward women and from many onerous burdens. And if he could redefine himself and perceive women differently, he could begin to achieve the rebirth in heterosexual relationships that would come from equal responsibility and comfortable self-expression. However, unable to change, he is afraid of women's changing, too. As a result of his rigidity, the transformation in women only spells danger in the form of abandonment and potential emotional starvation.

It is my interpretation that on the deepest archetypal level the feminist movement is partially fueled by an intuitive sensing of the decay and demise of the male. Women are rushing in to take men's places, as much for survival's sake as for any sociological or philosophical reasons. He has become a hyperactive, hyper-cerebral, hyper-mechanical, rigid, self-destructive machine out of control.

In 1910 there were 106.2 men for every 100 women in the population at large. By 1970, about the time when the feminist movement began to develop momentum, there were approximately 94.8 men for every 100 women. In 1978, by age sixty-five, there were only 75 men left for every 100 women. Little boys fall prey to major illnesses, such as hyperkinesis, autism, stuttering and so on, at rates several hundred percent higher than little girls. The suicide rate for men is also several times higher than for women, to say nothing of the many indirect and less obvious ways in which men kill themselves. And the behavior of the up-and-coming generations of men suggests that the self-destructive trend may be accelerating. . . .

UNRECOGNIZED HAZARD

The nature of masculinity is such that the male is unable even to recognize that he is in hazard. His life seems to him to be totally within his control. Unaccustomed to self-examination, he blocks out awareness of the way he lives and the conditioning that created it. He stoically accepts his lot as a given, or at best a challenge that the "real man" will accept and cope with and only the "sissy" will not. . . .

The repression of emotion, the denial and suppression of vulnerability, the compulsive competitiveness, the fear of losing, the anxiety over touching or any other form of sensual display, the controlled intellectualizing, and the general lack of spontaneity and unself-conscious playfulness serve to make the companionship of most men unsatisfying and highly limited. Men are at their best when a task has to be completed, a problem solved, or an enemy battled. Without such a structure, however, anxiety and self-consciousness accelerate too rapidly to allow for a sustained pleasurable experience.

This is also what makes feminist independence a threat. If a man cannot turn to other men in a crisis; if there is no support available to see him through periods of transition and change; if he can only bond comfortably with other men in pursuit of a tangible goal or to defeat a common enemy, he has no basis of intimacy for reaching out to them. It is particularly uncomfortable in moments of weakness, vulnerability, humiliation or pain.

His relationship with his woman is suffocated by the heavy weight of his dependency and draining demandingness, as he turns to her for everything. If she abandons him, his emotional lifeline will have been cut. At the same time, he never clearly defines what it is that he needs or wants from her. He detaches himself, with occasional moments of explosiveness, to control the torrent of unexpressed feelings. She will in turn either come to hate him for it or "suffer through it" masochistically.

Finally, there will be rapid physical decline, because health-giving things are mainly feminine. To take care is not masculine.

Before the age of liberation and feminism he could rationalize this self-destructiveness: He was doing it for his wife and family. That made it all valid and worthwhile. Today the enlightened and honest woman is owning up. "You're not doing it for me: you're doing it for yourself. And if you're doing it for me, please stop, because I'm not getting anything from it. It's boring. It's dead and I hate it."

But the sham is revealed. In spite of the fact that she no longer wants what he is giving her, he can't stop giving it. . . .

As a cardboard Goliath, the male cannot easily shift direction. It was recently reported by Dr. Sandra Bem, based on her extensive research, that "while high masculinity in males has been related to better psychological adjustment during adolescence, it is often accompanied during adulthood by high anxiety, high neuroticism and low self-acceptance. . . . Boys who are strongly masculine and girls who are strongly feminine tend to have lower overall intelligence, lower spatial ability, and show lower creativity."

If he continues to cling to the traditional masculine blueprint, he will be a victim of himself. He will end his life as a pathetic throwaway, abandoned and asleep.

Are Working Wives Hazardous to Their Husbands' Mental Health?

Zick Rubin

Social-science research has, by and large, pointed up the psychological advantages of two-worker families. When wives work outside the home, according to the preponderance of evidence, their self-esteem rises, their marriages become more equal, and their children do not suffer. New evidence suggests, however, that when wives are employed, their husbands can be the losers.

The finding, published last year in the *American Sociological Review,* comes from a major interview study of American men and women conducted in 1976 by the University of Michigan's Institute for Social Research. In a resourceful analysis of these national data, sociologists Ronald Kessler and James McRae Jr. found that although married women who were employed tended to have a better mental health than homemakers, the husbands of employed wives tended to have lower self-esteem and to be more depressed. The husbands of employed wives were less likely than the husbands of homemakers to agree with such statements as "I am a person of worth" and "I can do things as well as most people."

The correlation between a man's self-esteem and whether or not his wife is employed is not a large one. With the husband's age and income held constant, the correlation is .21—significant statistically, but too small (with a sample of about 500 men) to be of much help in predicting the mental health of any particular husband. Moreover, the fact that wives' employment is *correlated* with husbands' low self-esteem does not prove that her employment *causes* his distress. When one looks at it closely, it is hardly the sort of finding that advocates of housewifery should be writing home about.

Nevertheless, the finding deserves to be considered carefully. For lurking behind Kessler and McRae's modest .21 correlation is a more complex state of affairs. I am convinced that having a working wife can indeed be stressful for husbands, but that it can have emotional benefits as well. An important task for researchers is to determine more fully what factors underlie these different results.

Kessler and McRae have started to uncover these fctors. Their analysis argues against one possible explanation for the negative effects of a wife's employment on her husband's well-being—the notion that when wives work, husbands must spend more time on housekeeping and child-rearing tasks for which they are not equipped. As it turns out, wives' employment is more highly associated with ill health and anxiety among husbands who seldom or never help to care for their children than among husbands who help more often. Kessler and McRae suggest that those men who are supportive enough of their wives to take on child-care responsibilities tend to be the men who are the most comfortable with a two-worker family.

The ISR data also argue against the notion that the more money a wife makes, the more threatened the husband will be. Indeed, among those men whose wives are working, there is a small *positive* relationship between the wives' income and the husbands' self-esteem. While the loss of a man's status as sole provider for his family may take a psychological toll, once that status is lost, men seem to feel better about the situation—and about themselves—if the wife is bringing in a respectable income. A husband may be more upset, though, if his wife actually earns more than he does—a state of affairs that was extremely rare in the ISR sample. (See "Real Men Don't Earn Less Than Their Wives," *Psychology Today*, November 1982.)

Why, then, do some men wilt when their wives work? Although the ISR data do not permit a probing examination of individual cases, I suspect that several different factors are involved. Especially among working-class couples in which the wife works out of economic necessity, the husband may take the wife's employment as a sign of his own failure as a provider—and, by extension, as a man. As the sociologist and therapist Lillian Rubin writes in *Worlds of Pain,* her portrait of working-class families: "Many men and women still feel keenly that it's his job to support the family, hers to stay home and care for it. For her to take a job outside the house would be, for such a family, tantamount to a public acknowledgment of his failure."

When wives do work outside the home, moreover, the husbands often feel that they have lost their authority as heads of the household. "I think our biggest problem is her working," one husband told Rubin. "She started working and she started getting too independent. I never did want her to go to work, but she did anyway. I don't think I had the say-so I should have." With this loss of authority within the home—which has historically been the only place where the working-class man has had much authority at all—can come a tumbling of self-esteem.

These relatively affluent husbands whose wives work by choice rather than by necessity may experience another sort of loss: that of the wife's emotional support. While homebound wives have traditionally depended on their husbands' achievements for much of their sense of worth, husbands have been at least as dependent on their wives—as listeners, consolers, and ego-builders—for their emotional sustenance. When the wife has a career of her own, however, the exchange is altered. The wife is less dependent on her husband for her own self-esteem, and she may also be less attentive to his needs and problems.

For example, a Los Angeles public-relations man told Mary Bralove, a reporter for *The Wall Street Journal,* how he was shaken by his wife's indifference to his work now that she had her own real-estate career. On one occasion he asked for her opinion of a press kit that he had spent many hours preparing. "I asked her the next morning if she had looked at it, and she said, 'No.' I was extremely hurt. She had plenty of time if she had wanted to." Another professional man attributed his divorce to his wife's employment. "I could handle Kris working okay," he told organizational researchers Francine and Donald Hall, "but I couldn't handle being second in her life."

The George Gilders of the world, who have been warning for years about such unfortunate results of changing sex roles, might take all of this as vindication. Subvert the biological ground plan for the sexes at your own risk, Gilder cautioned in *Sexual Suicide*. Tamper with the roles of men and women only at the cost of having people take on assignments for which they are by nature unsuited.

But the data at hand do not provide support for such biological determinism. The fact that the correlation between wives' employment and husbands' distress is small suggests that while there are many men who are depressed by the wives' employment, there are many others who are heartened by it. Not only can the added income give the husband a psychological boost, but so can the wife's development of her own sense of competence in the world of work. A wife's financial independence can also give some husbands a feeling of security. "I know that she is staying with me out of choice rather than because she couldn't make a better deal," one husband told Mary Bralove.

Clinical psychologist Paul Fiddleman remarks on the emotional benefits that he has derived from his wife's journey from full-time housewife to a career in pediatric nursing. Her enhanced sense of confidence and autonomy has also enhanced his, Fiddleman writes in Peter Filene's collection, *Men in the Middle*. "I no longer feel obligated to 'entertain' or stimulate her with news of the outside world, and I no longer have to consider the time away from home as somehow taking from her the only stimulation she has in life."

The Double Standard of Aging

Susan Sontag

"How old are you?" The person asking the question is anybody. The respondent is a woman, a woman "of a certain age," as the French say discreetly. That age might be anywhere from her early twenties to her late fifties. If the question is impersonal—routine information requested when she applies for a driver's license, a credit card, a passport—she will probably force herself to answer truthfully. Filling out a marriage license application, if her future husband is even slightly her junior, she may long to subtract a few years; probably she won't. Competing for a job, her chances often partly depend on being the "right age," and if hers isn't right, she will lie if she thinks she can get away with it. Making her first visit to a new doctor, perhaps feeling particularly vulnerable at the moment she's asked, she will probably hurry through the correct answer. But if the question is only what people call personal—if she's asked by a new friend, a casual acquaintance, a neighbor's child, a co-worker in an office, store, factory—her response is harder to predict. She may side-step the question with a joke or refuse it with playful indignation. "Don't you know you're not supposed to ask a woman her age?" Or, hesitating a moment, embarrassed but defiant, she may tell the truth. Or she may lie. But neither truth, evasion, nor lie relieves the unpleasantness of that question. For a woman to be obliged to state her age, after "a certain age," is always a miniature ordeal.

If the question comes from a woman, she will feel less threatened than if it comes from a man. Other women are, after all, comrades in sharing the same potential for humiliation. She will be less arch, less coy. But she probably still dislikes answering and may not tell the truth. Bureaucratic formalities excepted, whoever asks a woman this question—after "a certain age"—is ignoring a taboo and possibly being impolite or downright hostile. Almost everyone acknowledges that once she passes an age that is, actually, quite young, a woman's exact age ceases to be a legitimate target of curiosity. After childhood the year of a woman's birth becomes her secret, her private property. It is something of a dirty secret. To answer truthfully is always indiscreet.

The discomfort a woman feels each time she tells her age is quite independent of the anxious awareness of human mortality that everyone has, from time to time. There is a normal sense in which nobody, men and women alike, relishes growing older. After thirty-five any mention of one's age carries with it the reminder that one is probably closer to the end of one's life than to the beginning. There is nothing unreasonable in that anxiety. Nor is there any abnormality in the anguish and anger that people who are really old, in their seventies and eighties, feel about the implacable waning of their powers, physical and mental. Advanced age is undeniably a trial, however, stoically it may be endured. It is a shipwreck, no matter with what courage elderly people insist on continuing the voyage. But the objective, sacred pain of old age is of another order than the subjective, profane pain of aging. Old age is a genuine ordeal, one that men and women undergo in a similar way. Growing older is mainly an ordeal of the imagination—a moral disease, a social pathology—intrinsic to which is the fact that it afflicts women much more than men. It is particularly women who experience growing older (everything that comes *before* one is actually old) with such distaste and even shame.

The emotional privileges this society confers upon youth stir up some anxiety about getting older in everybody. All modern urbanized societies—unlike tribal, rural societies—condescend to the values of maturity and heap honors on the joys of youth. This revaluation of the life cycle in favor of the young brilliantly serves a secular society whose idols are ever-increasing industrial productivity and the unlimited cannibalization of nature. Such a society must create a new sense of the rhythms of life in order to incite people to buy more, to consume and throw away faster. People let the direct awareness they have of their needs, of what really gives them pleasure, be overruled by commercialized *images* of happiness and personal well-being; and, in this imagery designed to stimulate ever more avid levels of consumption, the most popular metaphor for happiness is "youth." (I would insist that it is a metaphor, not a literal description. Youth is a metaphor for energy, restless mobility, appetite: for the state of "wanting.") This equating of well-being with youth makes everyone naggingly aware of exact age—one's own and that of other people. In primitive and pre-modern societies people attach much less importance to dates. When lives are divided into long periods with stable responsibilities and steady ideals (and hypocrisies), the exact number of years someone has lived becomes a trivial fact; there is hardly any reason to mention, even to know, the year in which one was born. Most people in nonindustrial societies are not sure exactly how old they are. People in industrial societies are haunted by numbers. They take an almost obsessional interest in keeping the score card of aging, convinced that anything above a low total is some kind of bad news. In an era in which people actually live longer and longer, what now amounts to the latter *two-thirds* of everyone's life is shadowed by a poignant apprehension of unremitting loss.

The prestige of youth afflicts everyone in this society to some degree. Men, too, are prone to periodic bouts of depression about aging—for instance, when feeling insecure or unfulfilled or insufficiently rewarded in their jobs. But men rarely panic about aging in the way women often do. Getting older is less profoundly wounding for a man, for in addition to the propaganda for youth that puts both men and women on the defensive as they age, there is a double standard about aging that denounces women with special severity. Society is much more permissive about aging in men, as it is more tolerant of the sexual infidelities of husbands. Men are "allowed" to age, without penalty, in several ways that women are not.

This society offers even fewer rewards for aging to women than it does to men. Being physically attractive counts much more in a woman's life than in a man's, but beauty, identified, as it is for women, with youthfulness, does not stand up well to age. Exceptional mental powers can increase with age, but women are rarely encouraged to develop their minds above dilettante standards. Because the wisdom considered the special province of women is "eternal," an age-old, intuitive knowledge about the emotions to which a repertoire of facts, worldly experience, and the methods of rational analysis have nothing to contribute, living a long time does not promise women an increase in wisdom either. The private skills expected of women are exercised early and, with the exception of a talent for making love, are not the kind that enlarge with experience. "Masculinity" is identified with competence, autonomy, self-control—qualities which the disappearance of youth does not threaten. Competence in most of the activities expected from men, physical sports excepted, increases with age. "Femininity" is identified with incompetence, helplessness, passivity, noncompetitiveness, being nice. Age does not improve these qualities.

Middle-class men feel diminished by aging, even while still young, if they have not yet shown distinction in their careers or made a lot of money. (And any tendencies they have toward hypochondria will get worse in middle age, focusing with particular nervousness on the specter of heart attacks and the loss of virility.) Their aging crisis is linked to that terrible pressure on men to be "successful" that precisely defines their membership in the middle class. Women rarely feel anxious about their age because they haven't succeeded at something. The work that women do outside the home rarely counts as a form of achievement, only as a way of earning money; most employment available to women mainly exploits the training they have been receiving since early childhood to be servile, to be both supportive and parasitical, to be unadventurous. They can have menial, low-skilled jobs in light industries, which offer as feeble a criterion of success as housekeeping. They can be secretaries, clerks, sales personnel, maids, research assistants, waitresses, social workers, prostitutes, nurses, teachers, telephone operators—public transcriptions of the servicing and nurturing roles that women have in family life. Women fill very few executive posts, are rarely found suitable for large corporate or political responsibilities, and form only a tiny contingent in the liberal professions (apart from teaching). They are virtually barred from jobs that involve an expert, intimate relation with machines or an aggressive use of the body, or that carry any physical risk or sense of adventure. The jobs this society deems appropriate to women are auxiliary, "calm" activities that do not compete with, but aid, what men do. Besides being less well paid, most work women do has a lower ceiling of advancement and gives meager outlet to normal wishes to be powerful. All outstanding work by women in this society is voluntary; most women are too inhibited by the social disapproval attached to their being ambitious and aggressive. Inevitably, women are exempted from the dreary panic of middle-aged men whose "achievements" seem paltry, who feel stuck on the job ladder or fear being pushed off it by someone younger. But they are also denied most of the real satisfactions that men derive from work—satisfactions that often do increase with age.

The double standard about aging shows up most brutally in the conventions of sexual feeling, which presuppose a disparity between men and women that operates permanently to women's disadvantage. In the accepted course of events a woman anywhere from her late teens through her middle twenties can expect to attract a man more or less her own age. (Ideally, he should be at least slightly older.) They marry and raise a family. But if her husband starts an affair after some years of marriage, he customarily does so with a woman much younger than his wife. Suppose, when both husband and wife are already in their late forties or early fifties, they divorce. The husband has an excellent chance of getting married again, probably to a younger woman. His ex-wife finds it difficult to remarry. Attracting a second husband younger than herself is improbable; even to find someone her own age she has to be lucky, and she will probably have to settle for a man considerably older than herself, in his sixties or seventies. Women become sexually ineligible much earlier than men do. A man, even an ugly man, can remain eligible well into old age. He is an acceptable mate for a young, attractive woman. Women, even good-looking women, become ineligible (except as partners of very old men) at a much younger age.

Thus, for most women, aging means a humiliating process of gradual sexual disqualification. Since women are considered maximally eligible in early youth, after which their sexual value drops steadily, even young women feel themselves in a desperate race against the calendar. They are old as soon as they are no longer very young. In late adolescense some girls are already worrying about getting married. Boys and young men have little reason to anticipate trouble because of aging. What makes men desirable to women is by no means tied to youth. On the contrary, getting older tends (for several decades) to operate in men's favor, since their value as lovers and husbands is set more by what they do than how they look. Many men have more success romantically at forty than they did at twenty or twenty-five; fame, money, and, above all, power are sexually enhancing. (A woman who has won power in a competitive profession or business career is considered less, rather than more, desirable. Most men confess themselves intimidated or turned off sexually by such a woman, obviously she is harder to treat as just a sexual "object.") As they age, men may start feeling anxious about actual sexual performance, worrying about a loss of sexual vigor or even impotence, but their sexual eligibility is not abridged simply by getting older. Men stay sexually possible as long as they can make love. Women are at a disadvantage because their sexual candidacy depends on meeting certain much stricter "conditions" related to looks and age.

Since women are imagined to have much more limited sexual lives than men do, a woman who has never married is pitied. She was not found acceptable, and it is assumed that her life continues to confirm her unacceptability. Her presumed lack of sexual opportunity is embarrassing. A man who remains a bachelor is judged much less crudely. It is assumed that he, at any age, still has a sexual life— or the chance of one. For men there is no destiny equivalent to the humiliating condition of being an old maid, a spinster. "Mr.," a cover from infancy to senility, precisely exempts men from the stigma that attaches to any woman, no longer young, who is still "Miss." (That women are divided into "Miss" and "Mrs.," which calls unrelenting attention to the situation of each woman with respect to marriage, reflects the belief that being single or married is much more decisive for a woman than it is for a man.)

For a woman who is no longer very young, there is certainly some relief when she has finally been able to marry. Marriage soothes the sharpest pain she feels about the passing years. But her anxiety never subsides completely, for she knows that should she re-enter the sexual market at a later date—because of divorce, or the death of her husband, or the need for erotic adventure—she must do so under a handicap far greater than any man of her age (*whatever* her age may be) and regardless of how good-looking she is. Her achievements, if she has a career, are no asset. The calendar is the final arbiter.

To be sure, the calendar is subject to some variations from country to country. In Spain, Portugal, and the Latin American countries, the age at which most women are ruled physically undesirable comes earlier than in the United States. In France it is somewhat later. French conventions of sexual feeling make a quasi-official place for the woman between thirty-five and forty-five. Her role is to initiate an inexperienced or timid young man, after which she is, of course, replaced by a young girl. (Colette's novella *Chéri* is the best-known account in fiction of such a love affair; biographies of Balzac relate a well-documented example from real life.) This sexual myth does make turning forty somewhat easier for French women. But there is no difference in any of these countries in the basic attitudes that disqualify women sexually much earlier than men.

Aging also varies according to social class. Poor people look old much earlier in their lives than do rich people. But anxiety about aging is certainly more common, and more acute, among middle-class and rich women than among working-class women. Economically disadvantaged women in this society are more fatalistic about aging; they can't afford to fight the cosmetic battle as long or as tenaciously. Indeed, nothing so clearly indicates the fictional nature of this crisis than the fact that women who keep their youthful appearance the longest—women who lead unstrenuous, physically sheltered lives, who eat balanced meals, who can afford good medical care, who have few or no children—are those who feel the defeat of age most keenly. Aging is much more a social judgment than a biological eventuality. Far more extensive than the hard sense of loss suffered during menopause (which, with increased longevity, tends to arrive later and later) is the depression about aging, which may not be set off by any real event in a woman's life, but is a recurrent state of "possession" of her imagination, ordained by society—that is, ordained by the way this society limits how women feel free to imagine themselves.

There is a model account of the aging crisis in Richard Strauss's sentimental-ironic opera *Der Rosenkavalier,* whose heroine is a wealthy and glamorous married woman who decides to renounce romance. After a night with her adoring young lover, the Marschallin has a sudden, unexpected confrontation with herself. It is toward the end of Act I; Octavian has just left. Alone in her bedroom she sits at her dressing table, as she does every morning. It is the daily ritual of self-appraisal practiced by every woman. She looks at herself and, appalled, begins to weep. Her youth is over. Note that the Marschallin does not discover, looking in the mirror, that she is ugly. She is as beautiful as ever. The Marschallin's discovery is moral—that is, it is a discovery of her imagination; it is nothing she actually *sees.* Nevertheless, her discovery is no less devastating. Bravely, she makes her painful, gallant decision. She will arrange for her beloved Octavian to fall in love with a girl his own age. She must be realistic. She is no longer eligible. She is now "the old Marschallin."

Strauss wrote the opera in 1910. Contemporary operagoers are rather shocked when they discover that the libretto indicates that the Marschallin is all of thirty-four years old; today the role is generally sung by a soprano well into her forties or in her fifties. Acted by an attractive singer of thirty-four, the Marschallin's sorrow would seem merely neurotic, or even ridiculous. Few women today think of themselves as old, wholly disqualified from romance, at thirty-four. The age of retirement has moved up, in line with the sharp rise in life expectancy for everybody in the last few generations. The *form* in which women experience their lives remains unchanged. A moment approaches inexorably when they must resign themselves to being "too old." And that moment is invariably—objectively—premature.

In earlier generations the renunciation came even sooner. Fifty years ago a woman of forty was not just aging but old, finished. No struggle was even possible. Today, the surrender to aging no longer has a fixed date. The aging crisis (I am speaking only of women in affluent countries) starts earlier but lasts longer; it is diffused over most of a woman's life. A woman hardly has to be anything like what would reasonably be considered old to worry about her age, to start lying (or being tempted to lie). The crises can come at any time. Their schedule depends on a blend of personal ("neurotic") vulnerability and the swing of social mores. Some women don't have their first crisis until thirty. No one escapes a sickening shock upon turning forty. Each birthday, but especially those ushering in a new decade—for round numbers have a special authority—sounds a new defeat. There is almost as much pain in the anticipation as in the reality. Twenty-nine has become a queasy age ever since the official end of youth crept forward, about a generation ago, to thirty. Being thirty-nine is also hard; a whole year in which to meditate in glum astonishment that one stands on the threshhold of middle age. The frontiers are arbitrary, but not any less vivid for that. Although a woman on her fortieth birthday is hardly different from what she was when she was still thirty-nine, the day seems like a turning point. But long before actually becoming a woman of forty, she has been steeling herself against the depression she will feel. One of the greatest tragedies of each woman's life is simply getting older; it is certainly the *longest* tragedy.

Aging is a movable doom. It is a crisis that never exhausts itself, because the anxiety is never really used up. Being a crisis of the imagination rather than of "real life," it has the habit of repeating itself again and again. The territory of aging (as opposed to actual old age) has no fixed boundaries. Up to a point it can be defined as one wants. Entering each decade—after the initial shock is absorbed—an endearing, desperate impulse of survival helps many women to stretch the boundaries to the decade following. In late adolescence thirty seems the end of life. At thirty, one pushes the sentence forward to forty. At forty, one still gives oneself ten more years.

I remember my closest friend in college sobbing on the day she turned twenty-one. "The best part of my life is over. I'm not young any more." She was a senior, nearing graduation. I was a precocious freshman, just sixteen. Mystified, I tried lamely to comfort her, saying that I didn't think twenty-one was *so* old. Actually, I didn't understand at all what could be demoralizing about turning twenty-one. To me, it meant only something good: being in charge of oneself, being free. At sixteen, I was too young to have noticed, and become confused by, the peculiarly loose, ambivalent way in which this society demands that one stop thinking of oneself as a girl and start thinking of oneself as a woman. (In America that demand can now be put off to the age of thirty, even beyond.) But even if I thought her distress was absurd, I must have been aware that it would not simply be absurd but quite unthinkable in a *boy* turning twenty-one. Only woman worry about age with that degree of inanity and pathos. And, of course, as with all crises that are inauthentic and therefore repeat themselves compulsively (because the danger is largely fictive, a poison in the imagination), this friend of mine went on having the same crisis over and over each time as if for the first time.

I also came to her thirtieth birthday party. A veteran of many love affairs, she had spent most of her twenties living abroad and had just returned to the United States. She had been good-looking when I first knew her; now she was beautiful. I teased her about the tears she had shed over being twenty-one. She laughed and claimed not to remember. But thirty, she said ruefully, that really is the end. Soon after, she married. My friend is now forty-four. While no longer what people call beautiful, she is striking-looking, charming, and vital. She teaches elementary school; her husband, who is twenty years older than she, is a parttime merchant seaman. They have one child, now nine years old. Sometimes, when her husband is away, she takes a lover. She told me recently that forty was the most upsetting birthday of all (I wasn't at that one), and although she has only a few years left, she means to enjoy them while they last. She has become one of those women who seize every excuse offered in any conversation for mentioning how old they really are, in a spirit of bravado compounded with self-pity that is not too different from the mood of women who regularly lie about their age. But she is actually fretting much less about aging than she was two decades ago. Having a child, and having one rather late, past the age of thirty, has certainly helped to reconcile her to her age. At fifty, I suspect, she will be ever more valiantly postponing the age of resignation.

My friend is one of the more fortunate, sturdier casualties of the aging crisis. Most women are not as spirited, nor as innocently comic in their suffering. But almost all women endure some version of this suffering: A recurrent seizure of the imagination that usually begins quite young, in which they project themselves into a calculation of loss. The rules of this society are cruel to women. Brought up to be never fully adult, women are deemed obsolete earlier than men. In fact, most women don't become relatively free and expressive sexually until their thirties. (Women mature sexually this late, certainly much later than men, not for innate biological reasons but because this culture retards women. Denied most outlets for sexual energy permitted to men, it takes many women *that* long to wear out some of their inhibitions.) The time at which they start being disqualified as sexually attractive persons is just when they have grown up sexually. The double standard about aging cheats women of those years, between thirty-five and fifty, likely to be the best of their sexual life.

That women expect to be flattered often by men, and the extent to which their self-confidence depends on this flattery, reflects how deeply women are psychologically weakened by this double standard. Added on to the pressure felt by everybody in this society to look young as long as possible are the values of "femininity," which specifically identify sexual attractiveness in women with youth. The desire to be the "right age" has a special urgency for a woman it never has for a man. A much greater part of her self-esteem and pleasure in life is threatened when she ceases to be young. Most men experience getting older with regret, apprehension. But most women experience it even more painfully: with shame. Aging is a man's destiny, something that must happen because he is a human being. For a woman, aging is not only her destiny. Because she is that more *narrowly* defined kind of human being, a woman, it is also her vulnerability.

To be a woman is to be an actress. Being feminine is a kind of theater, with its appropriate costumes, *décor,* lighting, and stylized gestures. From early childhood on, girls are trained to care in a pathologically exaggerated way about their appearance and are profoundly mutilated (to the extent of being unfitted for first-class adulthood) by the extent of the stress put on presenting themselves as physically attractive objects. Women look in the mirror more frequently than men do. It is, virtually, their duty to look at themselves—to look often. Indeed, a woman who is not narcissistic is considered unfeminine. And a woman who spends literally *most* of her time caring for, and making purchases to flatter, her physical appearance is not regarded in this society as what she is: a kind of moral idiot. She is thought to be quite normal and is envied by other women whose time is mostly used up at jobs or caring for large families. The display of narcissism goes on all the time. It is expected that women will disappear several times in an evening—at a restaurant, at a party, during a theater intermission, in the course of a social visit—simply to check their appearance, to see that nothing has gone wrong with their make-up and hairstyling, to make sure that their clothes are not spotted or too wrinkled or not hanging properly. It is even acceptable to perform this activity in public. At the table in a restaurant, over coffee, a woman opens a compact mirror and touches up her make-up and hair without embarrassment in front of her husband or her friends.

All this behavior, which is written off as normal "vanity" in women, would seem ludicrous in a man. Women are more vain than men because of the relentless pressure on women to maintain their appearance at a certain high standard. What makes the pressure even more burdensome is that there are actually several standards. Men present themselves as face-and-body, a physical whole. Women are split, as men are not, into a body and a face—each judged by somewhat different standards. What is important for a face is that it be beautiful. What is important for a body is two things, which may even be (depending on fashion and taste) somewhat incompatible: first, that it be desirable and, second, that it be beautiful. Men usually feel sexually attracted to women much more because of their bodies than their faces. The traits that arouse desire—such as fleshiness—don't always match those that fashion decrees as beautiful. (For instance, the ideal woman's body promoted in advertising in recent years is extremely thin: the kind of body that looks more desirable clothed than naked.) But women's concern with their appearance is not simply geared to arousing desire in men. It also aims at fabricating a certain image by which, as a more indirect way of arousing desire, women state their value. A woman's value lies in the way she *represents* herself, which is much more by her face than her body. In defiance of the laws of simple sexual attraction, women do not devote most of their attention to their bodies. The well-known "normal" narcissism that women display—the amount of time they spend before the mirror—is used primarily in caring for the face and hair.

Women do not simply have faces, as men do; they are identified with their faces. Men have a naturalistic relation to their faces. Certainly they care whether they are good-looking or not. They suffer over acne, protruding ears, tiny eyes; they hate getting bald. But there is a much wider latitude in what is esthetically acceptable in a man's face than what is in a woman's. A man's face is defined as something he basically doesn't need to tamper with; all he has to do is keep it clean. He can avail himself of the options for ornament supplied by nature: a beard, a mustache, longer or shorter hair. But he is not supposed to disguise himself. What he is "really" like is supposed to show. A man lives through his face; it records the progressive stages of his life. And since he doesn't tamper with his face, it is not separate from but is completed by his body—which is judged attractive by the impression it gives of virility and energy. By contrast, a woman's face is potentially separate from her body. She does not treat it naturalistically. A woman's face is the canvas upon which she paints a revised, corrected portrait of herself. One of the rules of this creation is that the face *not* show what she doesn't want it to show. Her face is an emblem, an icon, a flag. How she arranges her hair, the type of make-up she uses, the quality of her complexion—all these are signs, not of what she is "really" like, but of how she asks to be treated by others, especially men. They establish her status as an "object."

For the normal changes that age inscribes on every human face, women are much more heavily penalized than men. Even in early adolescence, girls are cautioned to protect their faces against wear and tear. Mothers tell their daughters (but never their sons): You look ugly when you cry. Stop worrying. Don't read too much. Crying, frowning, squinting, even laughing—all these human activities make "lines." The same usage of the face in men is judged quite positively. In a man's face lines are taken to be signs of "character." They indicate emotional strength, maturity—qualities far more esteemed in men than in women. (They show he has "lived.") Even scars are often not felt to be unattractive; they too can add "character" to a man's face. But lines of aging, any scar, even a small birthmark on a woman's face, are always regarded as unfortunate blemishes. In effect, people take character in men to be different from what constitutes character in women. A woman's character is thought to be innate, static—not the product of her experience, her years, her actions. A woman's face is prized so far as it remains unchanged by (or conceals the traces of) her emotions, her physical risk-taking. Ideally it is supposed to be a mask—immutable, unmarked. The model woman's face is Garbo's. Because women are identified with their faces much more than men are, and the ideal woman's face is one that is "perfect," it seems a calamity when a woman has a disfiguring accident. A broken nose or a scar or a burn mark, no more than regrettable for a man, is a terrible psychological wound to a woman; objectively, it diminishes her value. (As is well known, most clients for plastic surgery are women.)

Both sexes aspire to a physical ideal, but what is expected of boys and what is expected of girls involves a very different moral relation to the self. Boys are encouraged to *develop* their bodies, to regard the body as an instrument to be improved. They invent their masculine selves largely through exercise and sport, which harden the body and strengthen competitive feelings; clothes are of only secondary help in making their bodies attractive. Girls are not particularly encouraged to develop their bodies through any activity, strenuous or not; and physical strength and endurance are hardly valued at all. The invention of the feminine self proceeds mainly through clothes and other signs that testify to the very effort of girls to look attractive, to their commitment to please. When boys become men, they may go on (especially if they have sedentary jobs) practicing a sport or doing exercises for a while. Mostly they leave their appearance alone, having been trained to accept more or less what nature has handed out to them. (Men may start doing exercises again in their forties to lose weight, but for reasons of health—there is an epidemic fear of heart attacks among the middle-aged in rich countries—not for cosmetic reasons.) As one of the norms of "femininity" in this society is being preoccupied with one's physical appearance, so "masculinity" means *not* caring very much about one's looks.

This society allows men to have a much more affirmative relation to their bodies than women have. Men are more "at home" in their bodies, whether they treat them casually or use them aggressively. A man's body is defined as a strong body. It contains no contradiction between what is felt to be attractive and what is practical. A woman's body, so far as it is considered attractive, is defined as a fragile, light body. (Thus, women worry more than men do about being overweight.) When they do exercises, women avoid the ones that develop the muscles, particularly those in the upper arms. Being "feminine" means looking physically weak, frail. Thus, the ideal woman's body is one that is not of much practical use in the hard work of this world, and one that must continually be "defended." Women do not develop their bodies, as men do. After a woman's body has reached its sexually acceptable form by late adolescence, most further development is viewed as negative. And it is thought irresponsible for women to do what is normal for men: simply leave their appearance alone. During early youth they are likely to come as close as they ever will to the ideal image—slim figure, smooth firm skin, light musculature, graceful movements. Their task is to try to maintain that image, unchanged, as long as possible. Improvement as such is not the task. Women care for their bodies—against toughening, coarsening, getting fat. They *conserve* them. (Perhaps the fact that women in modern societies tend to have a more conservative political outlook than men originates in their profoundly conservative relation to their bodies.)

In the life of women in this society the period of pride, of natural honesty, of unself-conscious flourishing is brief. Once past youth women are condemned to inventing (and maintaining) themselves against the inroads of age. Most of the physical qualities regarded as attractive in women deteriorate much earlier in life than those defined as "male." Indeed, they perish fairly soon in the normal sequence of body transformation. The "feminine" is smooth, rounded, hairless, unlined, soft, unmuscled—the look of the very young; characteristics of the weak, of the vulnerable; eunuch traits, as Germaine Greer has pointed out. Actually, there are only a few years—late adolescence, early twenties—in which this look is physiologically natural, in which it can be had without touching-up and covering-up. After that, women enlist in a quixotic enterprise, trying to close the gap between the imagery put forth by society (concerning what is attractive in a woman) and the evolving facts of nature.

Women have a more intimate relation to aging than men do, simply because one of the accepted "women's" occupations is taking pains to keep one's face and body from showing the signs of growing older. Women's sexual validity depends, up to a certain point, on how well they stand off these natural changes. After late adolescence women become the caretakers of their bodies and faces, pursuing an essentially defensive strategy, a holding operation. A vast array of products in jars and tubes, a branch of surgery, and armies of hairdressers, masseuses, diet counselors, and other professionals exist to stave off, or mask, developments that are entirely normal biologically. Large amounts of women's energies are diverted into this passionate, corrupting effort to defeat nature: to maintain an ideal, static appearance against the progress of age. The collapse of the project is only a matter of time, Inevitably, a woman's physical appearance develops beyond its youthful form. No matter how exotic the creams or how strict the diets, one cannot indefinitely keep the face unlined, the waist slim. Bearing children takes its toll: the torso becomes thicker; the skin is stretched. There is no way to keep certain lines from appearing, in one's mid-twenties, around the eyes and mouth. From about thirty on, the skin gradually loses its tonus. In women this perfectly natural process is regarded as a humiliating defeat, while nobody finds anything remarkably unattractive in the equivalent physical changes in men. Men are "allowed" to look older without sexual penalty.

Thus, the reason that women experience aging with more pain than men is not simply that they care more than men about how they look. Men also care about their looks and want to be attractive, but since the business of men is mainly being and doing, rather than appearing, the standards for appearance are much less exacting. The standards for what is attractive in a man are permissive; they conform to what is possible or "natural" to most men throughout most of their lives. The standards for women's appearance go against nature, and to come anywhere near approximating them takes considerable effort and time. Women must try to be beautiful. At the least, they are under heavy social pressure not to be ugly. A woman's fortunes depend, far more than a man's, on being at least "acceptable" looking. Men are not subject to this pressure. Good looks in a man is a bonus, not a psychological necessity for maintaining normal self-esteem.

Behind the fact that women are more severely penalized than men are for aging is the fact that people, in this culture at least, are simply less tolerant of ugliness in women than in men. An ugly woman is never merely repulsive. Ugliness in a woman is felt by everyone, men as well as women, to be faintly embarrassing. And many features or blemishes that count as ugly in a woman's face would be quite tolerable on the face of a man. This is not, I would insist, just because the esthetic standards for men and women are different. It is rather because the esthetic standards for women are much higher, and narrower, than those proposed for men.

Beauty, women's business in this society, is the theater of their enslavement. Only one standard of female beauty is sanctioned: the *girl*. The great advantage men have is that our culture allows two standards of male beauty: the *boy* and the *man*. The beauty of a boy resembles the beauty of a girl. In both sexes it is a fragile kind of beauty and flourishes naturally only in the early part of the life-cycle. Happily, men are able to accept themselves under another standard of good looks—heavier, rougher, more thickly built. A man does not grieve when he loses the smooth, unlined, hairless skin of a boy. For he has only exchanged one form of attractiveness for another: the darker skin of a man's face, roughened by daily shaving, showing the marks of emotion and the normal lines of age. There is no equivalent of this second standard for women. The single standard of beauty for women dictates that they must go on having clear skin. Every wrinkle, every line, every grey hair, is a defeat. No wonder that no boy minds becoming a man, while even the passage from girlhood to early womanhood is experienced by many women as their downfall, for all women are trained to want to continue looking like girls.

This is not to say there are no beautiful older women. But the standard of beauty in a woman of any age is how far she retains, or how she manages to simulate, the appearance of youth. The exceptional woman in her sixties who is beautiful certainly owes a large debt to her genes. Delayed aging, like good looks, tends to run in families. But nature rarely offers enough to meet this culture's standards. Most of the women who successfully delay the appearance of age are rich, with unlimited leisure to devote to nurturing along nature's gifts. Often they are actresses. (That is, highly paid professionals at doing what all women are taught to practice as amateurs.) Such women as Mae West, Dietrich, Stella Adler, Dolores Del Rio, do not challenge the rule about the relation between beauty and age in women. They are admired precisely because they *are* exceptions, because they have managed (at least so it seems in photographs) to outwit nature. Such miracles, exceptions made by nature (with the help of art and social privilege), only confirm the rule, because what makes these women seem beautiful to us is precisely that they do not look their real age. Society allows no place in our imagination for a beautiful old woman who does look like an old woman—a woman who might be like Picasso at the age of ninety, being photographed outdoors on his estate in the south of France, wearing only shorts and sandals. No one imagines such a woman exists. Even the special exceptions—Mae West & Co.—are always photographed indoors, cleverly lit, from the most flattering angle and fully, artfully clothed. The implication is they would not stand a closer scrutiny. The idea of an old woman in a bathing suit being attractive, or even just acceptable looking, is inconceivable. An older woman is, by definition, sexually repulsive— unless, in fact, she doesn't look old at all. The body of an old woman, unlike that of an old man, is always understood as a body that can no longer be shown, offered, unveiled. At best, it may appear in costume. People still feel uneasy, thinking about what they might see if her mask dropped, if she took off her clothes.

Thus, the point for women of dressing up, applying make-up, dyeing their hair, going on crash diets, and getting face-lifts is not just to be attractive. They are ways of defending themselves against a profound level of disapproval directed toward women, a disapproval that can take the form of aversion. The double standard about aging converts the life of women into an inexorable march toward a condition in which they are not just unattractive, but disgusting. The profoundest terror of a woman's life is the moment represented in a statue by Rodin called *Old Age:* a naked old woman, seated, pathetically contemplates her flat, pendulous, ruined body. Aging in women is a process of becoming obscene sexually, for the flabby bosom, wrinkled neck, spotted hands, thinning white hair, waistless torso, and veined legs of an old woman are felt to be obscene. In our direst moments of the imagination, this transformation can take place with dismaying speed—as in the end of *Lost Horizon,* when the beautiful young girl is carried by her lover out of Shangri-La and, within minutes, turns into a withered, repulsive crone. There is no equivalent nightmare about men. This is why, however much a man may care about his appearance, that caring can never acquire the same desperateness it often does for women. When men dress according to fashion or now even use cosmetics, they do not expect from clothes and make-up what women do. A face-lotion or perfume or deodorant or hairspray, used by a man, is not part of a disguise. Men, as men, do not feel the need to disguise themselves to fend off morally disapproved signs of aging, to outwit premature sexual obsolescence, to cover up aging as obscenity. Men are not subject to the barely concealed revolution expressed in this culture against the female body—except in its smooth, youthful, firm, odorless, blemish-free form.

One of the attitudes that punish women most severely is the visceral horror felt at aging female flesh. It reveals a radical fear of women installed deep in this culture, a demonology of women that has crystallized in such mythic caricatures as the vixen, the virago, the vamp, and the witch. Several centuries of witch-phobia, during which one of the cruelest extermination programs in Western history was carried out, suggest something of the extremity of this fear. That old women are repulsive is one of the most profound esthetic and erotic feelings in our culture. Women share it as much as men do. (Oppressors, as a rule, deny oppressed people their own "native" standards of beauty. And the oppressed end up being convinced that they *are* ugly.) How women are psychologically damaged by this misogynistic idea of what is beautiful parallels the way in which blacks have been deformed in a society that has up to now defined beautiful as white. Psychological tests made on young black children in the United States some years ago showed how early and how thoroughly they incorporate the white standard of good looks. Virtually all the children expressed fantasies that indicated they considered black people to be ugly, funny looking, dirty, brutish. A similar kind of self-hatred infects most women. Like men, they find old age in women "uglier" than old age in men.

This esthetic taboo functions, in sexual attitudes, as a racial taboo. In this society most people feel an involuntary recoil of the flesh when imagining a middle-aged woman making love with a young man—exactly as many whites flinch viscerally at the thought of a white woman in bed with a black man. The banal drama of a man of fifty who leaves a wife of forty-five for a girlfriend of twenty-eight contains no strictly sexual outrage, whatever sympathy people may have for the abandoned wife. On the contrary. Everyone "understands." Everyone knows that men like girls, that young women often want middle-aged men. But no one "understands" the reverse situation. A woman of forty-five who leaves a husband of fifty for a lover of twenty-eight is the makings of a social and sexual scandal at a deep level of feeling. No one takes exception to a romantic couple in which the man is twenty years or more the woman's senior. The movies pair Joanne Dru and John Wayne, Marilyn Monroe and Joseph Cotten, Audrey Hepburn and Cary Grant, Jane Fonda and Yves Montand, Catherine Deneuve and Marcello Mastroianni; as in actual life, these are perfectly plausible, appealing couples. When the age difference runs the other way, people are puzzled and embarrassed and simply shocked. (Remember Joan Crawford and Cliff Robertson in *Autumn Leaves*? But so troubling is this kind of love story that it rarely figures in the movies, and then only as the melancholy history of a failure.) The usual view of why a woman of forty and a boy of twenty, or a women of fifty and a man of thirty, marry is that the man is seeking a mother, not a wife; no one believes the marriage will last. For a woman to respond erotically and romantically to a man who, in terms of his age, could be her father is considered normal. A man who falls in love with a woman who, however attractive she may be, is old enough to be his mother is thought to be extremely neurotic (victim of an "Oedipal fixation" is the fashionable tag), if not mildly contemptible.

The wider the gap in age between partners in a couple, the more obvious is the prejudice against women. When old men, such as Justice Douglas, Picasso, Strom Thurmond, Onassis, Chaplin, and Pablo Casals, take brides thirty, forty, fifty years younger than themselves, it strikes people as remarkable, perhaps an exaggeration—but still plausible. To explain such a match, people enviously attribute some special virility and charm to the man. Though he can't be handsome, he is famous; and his fame is understood as having boosted his attractiveness to women. People imagine that his young wife, respectful of her elderly husband's attainments, is happy to become his helper. For the man a late marriage is always good public relations. It adds to the impression that, despite his advanced age, he is still to be reckoned with; it is the sign of a continuing vitality presumed to be available as well to his art, business activity, or political career. But an elderly woman who married a young man would be greeted quite differently. She would have broken a fierce taboo, and she would get no credit for her courage. Far from being admired for her vitality, she would probably be condemned as predatory, willful, selfish, exhibitionistic. At the same time she would be pitied, since such a marriage would be taken as evidence that she was in her dotage. If she had a conventional career or were in business or held public office, she would quickly suffer from the current of disapproval. Her very credibility as a professional would decline, since people would suspect that her young husband might have an undue influence on her. Her "respectability" would certainly be compromised. Indeed, the well-known old women I can think of who dared such unions, if only at the end of their lives—George Eliot, Colette, Edith Piaf—have all belonged to that category of people, creative artists and entertainers, who have special license from society to behave scandalously. It is thought to be a scandal for a woman to ignore that she is old and therefore too ugly for a young man. Her looks and a certain physical condition determine a woman's desirability, not her talents or her needs. Women are not supposed to be "potent." A marriage between an old woman and a young man subverts the very ground rule of relations between the two sexes, that is: whatever the variety of appearances, men remain dominant. Their claims come first. Women are supposed to be the associates and companions of men, not their full equals—and never their superiors. Women are to remain in the state of a permanent "minority."

The convention that wives should be younger than their husbands powerfully enforces the "minority" status of women, since being senior in age always carries with it, in any relationship, a certain amount of power and authority. There are no laws on the matter, of course. The convention is obeyed because to do otherwise makes one feel as if one is doing something ugly or in bad taste. Everyone feels intuitively the esthetic rightness of a marriage in which the man is older than the woman, which means that any marriage in which the woman is older creates a dubious or less gratifying mental picture. Everyone is addicted to the visual pleasure that women give by meeting certain esthetic requirements from which men are exempted, which keeps women working at staying youthful-looking while men are left free to age. On a deeper level everyone finds the signs of old age in women esthetically offensive, which conditions one to feel automatically repelled by the prospect of an elderly woman marrying a much younger man. The situation in which women are kept minors for life is largely organized by such conformist, unreflective preferences. But taste is not free, and its judgments are never merely "natural." Rules of taste enforce structures of power. The revulsion against aging in women is the cutting edge of a whole set of oppressive structures (often masked as gallantries) that keep women in their place.

The ideal state proposed for women is docility, which means not being fully grown up. Most of what is cherished as typically "feminine" is simply behavior that is childish, immature, weak. To offer so low and demeaning a standard of fulfillment in itself constitutes oppression in an acute form—a sort of moral neo-colonialism. But women are not simply condescended to by the values that secure the dominance of men. They are repudiated. Perhaps because of having been their oppressors for so long, few men really *like* women (though they love individual women), and few men ever feel really comfortable or at ease in women's company. This malaise arises because relations between the two sexes are rife with hypocrisy, as men manage to love those they dominate and therefore don't respect. Oppressors always try to justify their privileges and brutalities by imagining that those they oppress belong to a lower order of civilization or are less than fully "human." Deprived of part of their ordinary human dignity, the oppressed take on certain "demonic" traits. The oppressions of large groups have to be anchored deep in the psyche, continually renewed by partly unconscious fears and taboos, by a sense of the obscene. Thus, women arouse not only desire and affection in men but aversion as well. Women are thoroughly domesticated familiars. But, at certain times and in certain situations, they become alien, untouchable. The aversion men feel, so much of which is covered over, is felt most frankly, with least inhibition, toward the type of woman who is most taboo "esthetically," a woman who has become—with the natural changes brought about by aging—obscene.

Nothing more clearly demonstrates the vulnerability of women than the special pain, confusion, and bad faith with which they experience getting older. And in the struggle that some women are waging on behalf of all women to be treated (and treat themselves) as full human beings—not "only" as women—one of the earliest results to be hoped for is that women become aware, indignantly aware, of the double standard about aging from which they suffer so harshly.

It is understandable that women often succumb to the temptation to lie about their age. Given society's double standard, to question a woman about her age is indeed often an aggressive act, a trap. Lying is an elementary means of self-defense, a way of scrambling out of the trap, at least temporarily. To expect a woman, after "a certain age," to tell exactly how old she is—when she has a chance, either through the generosity of nature or the cleverness of art, to pass for being somewhat younger than she actually is—is like expecting a landowner to admit that the estate he has put up for sale is actually worth less than the buyer is prepared to pay. The double standard about aging sets women up as property, as objects whose value depreciates rapidly with the march of the calendar.

The prejudices that mount against women as they grow older are an important arm of male privilege. It is the present unequal distribution of adult roles between the two sexes that gives men a freedom to age denied to women. Men actively administer the double standard about aging because the "masculine" role awards them the initiative in courtship. Men choose; women are chosen. So men choose younger women. But although this system of inequality is operated by men, it could not work if women themselves did not acquiesce in it. Women reinforce it powerfully with their complacency, with their anguish, with their lies.

Not only do women lie more than men do about their age but men forgive them for it, thereby confirming their own superiority. A man who lies about his age is thought to be weak, "unmanly." A woman who lies about her age is behaving in a quite acceptable, "feminine" way. Petty lying is viewed by men with indulgence, one of a number of patronizing allowances made for women. It has the same moral unimportance as the fact that women are often late for appointments. Women are not expected to be truthful, or punctual, or expert in handling and repairing machines, or frugal, or physically brave. They are expected to be second-class adults, whose natural state is that of a grateful dependence on men. And so they often are, since that is what they are brought up to be. So far as women heed the stereotypes of "feminine" behavior, they *cannot* behave as fully responsible, independent adults.

Most women share the contempt for women expressed in the double standard about aging—to such a degree that they take their lack of self-respect for granted. Women have been accustomed so long to the protection of their masks, their smiles, their endearing lies. Without this protection, they know, they would be more vulnerable. But in protecting themselves as women, they betray themselves as adults. The model corruption in a woman's life is denying her age. She symbolically accedes to all those myths that furnish women with their imprisoning securities and privileges, that create their genuine oppression, that inspire their real discontent. Each time a woman lies about her age she becomes an accomplice in her own underdevelopment as a human being.

Women have another option. They can aspire to be wise, not merely nice; to be competent, not merely helpful; to be strong, not merely graceful; to be ambitious for themselves, not merely for themselves in relation to men and children. They can let themselves age naturally and without embarrassment, actively protesting and disobeying the conventions that stem from this society's double standard about aging. Instead of being girls, girls as long as possible, who then age humiliatingly into middle-aged women and then obscenely into old women, they can become women much earlier—and remain active adults, enjoying the long, erotic career of which women are capable, far longer. Women should allow their faces to show the lives they have lived. Women should tell the truth.

Good Morning Wardrobe

Edith Campion

'I'll wear the beige.' Mrs Crimpton spoke largely to the small room. She sat back in bed as if she expected an obedient servant, black-dressed, white-aproned, to appear with the breakfast tray.

Her eyes commanded the room to increase its size. The large unwieldy furniture settled more comfortably into the new dimensions.

'I had a very good night's rest,' she addressed the wardrobe. 'Perhaps I shall pop into town later.'

Mrs Crimpton's life fell from hangers in the larger, be-mirrored wardrobe. The styles suggested a short opulent span commencing in the forties and ending abruptly in the fifties.

'Tea,' she commanded; and moved to her kitchen, a large, rather common table. Her long hands wove a spell above the colourful plastic cloth, plugging in the jug, warming the worthy silver teapot, then casting the gritty black leaves within.

She caught a shadow glance of herself in one of the mirrors. 'A model figure, Norma—you have a model figure.' Someone had once said that many years ago and it would often sing in her mind. 'A model figure. . . .'

She smiled at the distant figure. Raw-boned, she had become a tall old mare, not a good doer.

Her hand grasped the teapot handle, her nails spots of blood against the white skin. She tilted the silver pot, filling her cup, the sound was comforting.

'Ah. . . .'

She pulled the curtain across and craned her neck to look at the sky. Blue. A patch of blue. She cast open the curtains upon a dark grey concrete wall.

'I shall wear the beige,' she told the wardrobe. She placed the large delicate bone china cup by the bed and returned to its warmth. She examined her wristwatch. Nine-fifteen, plenty of time. She didn't want to be there until twelve, but there was much to be accomplished before that hour.

She sighed and reached up a hand to touch one of the rollers screwing her chestnut hair tightly to her head. She began to unroll it and its companions. Each released curl sprang back to caress her head. When they were all at liberty, she shook her head and the curls danced, giving her the look of an aged Shirley Temple. She tumbled her hair happily with her fingers.

'You haven't hair, Norma. It's like a wild mane,' sang her memory.

She wiped the night cream from her face. What was today? She had 'bath rights' Tuesday, Thursday and Saturday; and sometimes she managed to sneak one on Sunday. She moved to the basin and washed carefully, powdering her body. She slipped into her padded bra, white embroidered slip, suspender belt and stockings. She could never bring herself to wearing stocking tights, they seemed to her unfeminine. She slipped on her dressing-gown.

Seated before the dressing-table mirror she examined her face—this was the one moment that shook her day. Her hand trembled as it reached for the first magic pot. Moisture cream. Her fingers tenderly smoothed her cheeks and fluttered across her brow. An olive base followed. The fingers paused, seeking colour for cheeks and finally lipstick. Her confidence returned. She smiled and nodded to herself. She trapped her eyelashes in the curler. They lay clamped, her eye bald, vulnerable. Skilfully she blacked the lashes and darkened her eyebrows. She sat quite still regarding her art. Had she made the chestnut hair too dark last time?

'No,' she assured the mirror. 'It's perfect.'

Nearly eleven. She would be late. She slipped on her white sling-back shoes and took out the beige dress. It fitted snugly at the waist; she ignored current fashion, the childish smocks and tiny skirts; they had no dignity.

She turned back to the mirror, took up her brush and attacked the tight bobbing curls. They bounced rebelliously. She tamed them with the comb. She reached up to the shelf in the wardrobe and drew out a ginger, long-furred hat. Carefully she placed it on the even-spaced curls, securing it with a hat-pin.

She smiled, almost laughed with pleasure. She opened the drawer and picked out a pair of gloves, took up her purse and a beige umbrella that was almost a parasol, paused before the long wardrobe mirror, fumbled in her bag and produced a pair of dark glasses.

'I'll be back after lunch,' she told the mirror.

She teetered down the stairs, clinging to the bannister-rail. She wove her way down many levels to the street. At the door she blinked and covered her eyes with the dark glasses, which she wore, sunshine, cloud-dark.

She moved carefully through the street, switching back the years. Heads turned. The rare bird moved through the jeans and mini-skirts. It was as if a Spanish galleon had sailed into Wellington Harbour.

She enjoyed the attention. She could still turn heads. She smiled contentedly to herself and strolled on to James Smith's. She entered the doors at twelve. Took the lift.

'How are you today?' The attendant had known her for many years.

'Wonderful. It's a perfect day outside. Thank you.' She swept into her second-floor world, looked about and took a chair outside the tea-rooms.

She waited expectantly. An old woman lowered herself carefully into the chair beside her.

'How are you today?'

'Getting a bit slower all the time.'

She smiled at age. Someone took the chair on her other flank. Nicely dressed—but those short skirts were common.

'Have you the time, please?' she asked the new arrival.

'Twelve-fifteen.'

'What a very charming watch.'

'A present from my fiancé.' The young woman sounded as if this was a new situation and she wanted to test 'my fiancé,' caress it with her tongue, let it hang in the air and command admiration. 'I'm waiting for him, for lunch.'

Mrs Crimpton nodded, a queen in approval.

'How wonderful for you both. I'm waiting for my husband. We've been married a very long time, most happily. I hope you will be just as happy.'

Mrs Crimpton disappeard from the girl's consciousness as she rose and moved towards the fiancé.

A woman in middle years caught Mrs Crimpton's eye. She was dressed elegantly in black. She was very smart, Mrs Crimpton had to admit. She touched her fur hat fondly and rummaged in her purse for her mirror. She bent her eyes and felt a pang of disappointment in the silver image that looked critically back at her. Perhaps the lipstick was too heavy. The woman in black stood and moved towards a friend—taking Mrs Crimpton's sense of failure with her.

A mother with a large shopping bag and a small child sank thankfully into a chair. Her face pink, her breathing fussed.

'What a gorgeous child.' Mrs Crimpton removed her dark glasses and made her brown eyes warm. 'You have the deepest, warmest brown eyes I have ever seen,' sang memory.

'Thank you,' said the mother. 'But she is tiring to shop with.'

'Ah—but they are such companions. I do envy you. I had no children.' She replaced the dark glasses, a symbol of mourning for lack of offspring; and to hide the self-pity welling in her eyes.

The mother was too tired to deal with this confession of failure. Gratefully she perceived her husband pushing towards her, and thrust herself from the chair, almost toppling child and shopping in her desire to escape.

'Nice little woman,' said Mrs Crimpton to the old lady.

A rather military man now sat at attention in the vacant chair, looking sternly at people. Who would dare be late for him? thought Mrs Crimpton; and didn't attempt conversation.

'Darling, I'm sorry.' She was beautiful. The rigidity fell from the man as he stood beside her. He took her arm and they moved away. Mrs Crimpton was glad, and sad. She looked at her watch. One-fifteen.

'Isn't it beautiful out?' A large woman tossed the words to Mrs Crimpton like flowers.

'Just like spring,' she agreed.

'The harbour looked beautiful from the bus.'

'Yes,' said Mrs Crimpton. 'My house looks down on it and it was perfect this morning.'

'You are lucky to have a harbour view.'

Mrs Crimpton nodded: "I've just had lunch with my husband and I'm getting my shopping list together.' She returned to the handbag and produced pen and notebook.'

'I've only myself to shop for, so it's easy remembered,' said her companion.

'It is harder when you have a husband and a family,' smiled Mrs Crimpton, attacking her list. She glanced at the clock on the wall. 'I must rush. It's been delightful talking to you.' She rose and moved towards the lift.

'Ground, please.'

'Pleasant lunch?' asked her attendant.

'Lovely—the grills are always good. Thank you.'

She moved with dignity through the crowded shop and into the open air. She crossed the street in a river of people.

At the Sanitarium she bought two sandwiches and carefully placed them in her bag. She moved jauntily up Cuba Street.

Home. She paused at the door. It was good to be home, but the thought of the stairs to be climbed daunted. She took the banister-rail firmly in a gloved hand and started the ascent. Outside she paused, short-breathed, fumbled for the key and opened the door.

'I'm back,' she informed the room.

She sat at the dressing-table, stripped off the gloves and removed the fur hat, shaking her hair loose. She smiled happily at herself—the dressing-table—and the wardrobe.

'I was right to wear the beige,' she confided. 'I've had a lovely day.'

---

12 *Understanding the Abortion Controversy or "How Can I Decide?"*

Not too long ago, people spoke in whispers when discussing the topic of abortion. Prohibited by law and regarded by many as unconditionally immoral, the subject was considered inappropriate to introduce in polite company, particularly if both sexes were present. Today, of course, abortion is no longer considered a taboo subject by most people. On the contrary, it is now the subject of numerous public debates and private discussions, among men as well as women. However, although people are willing, in fact anxious, to talk about abortion, it is difficult for them to reach agreement about if or when abortions ought to be available. Issues associated with the subject of abortion today generate a great deal of controversy; thus, these issues are well suited for a researched paper.

Of course, some of you may already be saying, "Hey, I already have an opinion on abortion and nothing is going to change it. No matter what I read and no matter what anyone might say, my feelings about this subject will always stay the same." Recognizing that you may already feel strongly about abortion, I have developed assignments that do not require you to take a strong position either for or against abortion. Instead, the readings and assignments will enable you to clarify your own position on the subject and to become familiar with some of the central issues so that you can better understand the contemporary controversy.

Key Question: What Are the Two Extreme Positions on the Abortion Issue?

One position on abortion is simply that it is murder and thus morally wrong in any situation. This position, currently held by the Roman Catholic Church, considers the fetus as a living human being from the moment of conception. The Church's 1974 Declaration on Procured Abortions states that "The First Right of the Human Person is his life. Never, under any pretext, may a woman resort to abortion. Nor can one exempt women from what nature demands of them." Thus, their argument rests on moral grounds according to the definition of what constitutes human life.

The other extreme position is that a woman has complete rights over what happens to her own body and can therefore have an abortion on demand, even if she so decides in her eighth month of pregnancy. Of course, most people would not be in favor of such a position, even if they strongly support women's rights.

A **compromise** position maintains that although abortion involves the destruction of human life, certain medical and social issues must be taken into consideration when deciding if an abortion can be justified. For example, according to this view, if a woman is raped, an abortion would be a morally acceptable action because the pregnancy was the result of the woman being made a victim of a social crime. She did not become pregnant because of her own promiscuous sexual activities and therefore should not be held morally accountable for the life created within her. Also, many who advocate this position consider the woman's life and/or health to be of primary importance, more important than that of the fetus (see definitions of terms). If the woman's life is jeopardized (and some others would include mental health here too), then abortion is justifiable.

Another compromise position maintains that abortion is justified as long as it is performed in the early months of pregnancy and is not treated trivially. Thus, this position emphasizes the importance of using birth control responsibly and not viewing abortion as an alternative to birth control.

Clearly the issue of just what is moral and immoral is uncertain for many people. While the Roman Catholic Church's official position is absolute and clear, it is not necessarily accepted by all other religions (even those within the Judeo-Christian tradition) and not practiced by all Catholics. Moreover, there is also a "secular morality" to consider. Secular morality refers to the norms and conventions of society; that is, moral notions generally shared by a culture. For example, polls show that Americans tend to favor a woman's right to choose whether or not to have an abortion. Secular morality also relates to moral philosophies which hold that an embryo or a fetus is a part of a woman's body and lacks any morally significant potential to develop outside of her body. Since the embryo or fetus is not a "person," then it is not entitled to the rights accorded a fully developed individual.

PRO-LIFE VERSUS PRO-CHOICE

The abortion issue may be thought of as divided into two sides: pro-life and pro-choice. Pro-lifers are concerned with the rights of the fetus over the rights of the mother. They believe that abortion constitutes murder, and stress that society has deemed murder as immoral. Pro-choice advocates believe that women have the right to control their bodies and hence make their own private decisions on whether or not to have an abortion. These people assert that the question of abortion does not involve the fetus but a woman's right to choose and have control over her own body. In other words, the life of the woman should come before that of the fetus. In fact, many pro-choice advocates do not believe that the fetus even is a human life until it becomes viable at between 24 and 28 weeks of pregnancy.

Often, the pro-choice position is associated with the feminist position because it symbolizes sexual and reproductive self-determination. On a sociopolitical level, feminists claim that women have been (and in some respects still are) dominated and controlled, and that forbidding or limiting abortion guarantees the continuation of women's subordination, restricting them to the realm of the home and childrearing. Feminists, then, view abortion regulation as denying a woman's right to privacy and individual choice because the state is allowed to intervene and decide her fate for her. They feel that relegating women to the home inhibits their personal, social, and economic development and gains, reinforcing society's view of women as second class citizens.

MEN AND ABORTION

Key Question: Are Men Entitled to a Position on Abortion?

More recently, the abortion issue has been raised as a concern of men as well. Some men feel that whether or not a child is to be born has almost, if not as much, impact on them as on women. They assert that many men now welcome a major role in childrearing; in fact, many men are now assuming full responsibility for the care of their children. Men also are concerned about instances in which a woman has decided for herself to have an abortion even if the decision went against the wishes of the father or sometimes without even telling the father that she was pregnant. If women wish to have social and political equality, men ask, shouldn't that equality be granted to men when it comes to the issue of abortion?

THE COMPLEXITY OF THE ABORTION ISSUE

Key Question: How Does One's Position on When Life Begins Relate to the Abortion Controversy?

Issues concerning abortion are not easy to decide. Many argue that in the early months, an embryo is simply a lump of tissue and that to give a shapeless lump precedence over an already functioning human being cannot be morally justified. They cite numerous instances of women, particularly poor women, already burdened with too many children. Who is to support unwanted children of the poor? What sort of life can one expect for an unwanted child born into a ghetto? These people feel that the abortion question needs to focus on the needs of society. They stress that if the poor are ever to improve their position in the culture, they must not be burdened with more children than they can afford to raise.

Others are not so sure of when life actually begins. They argue that the question of when an embryo or fetus should be considered human life with all rights accorded it, has changed with medical advances. One argument in favor of abortion maintains that human life does not begin until the fetus can survive on its own outside of the mother's body. However, with new medical technology, premature infants that once were beyond medical assistance can now be kept alive and can ultimately survive. What does this mean for the definition of life? Then, of course, the question of the circumstances under which conception occurred also raises many questions. If one regards abortion simply as murder, why should the circumstances of conception (i.e., rape or incest) become grounds for that "murder"? After all, if you discover that a classmate had been born as the result of a rape, that surely does not give you the right to kill him.

HISTORICAL/CULTURAL CONTEXT

As with other issues, your understanding of the abortion issue will deepen with a historical perspective. It is known that abortion has been practiced worldwide for centuries, because techniques for abortion can be found in the oldest of medical texts. And if abortion did not occur, infanticide did. Unwanted pregnancies and the problems related to them are by no means new. *Collier's Encyclopedia* notes that "Aristotle and Plato advocated abortions to limit the population and to maintain an economically healthy society" (*Collier's,* 1988: 25). And even the Roman Catholic Church once accepted abortions. Pope Gregory XIV for instance condoned abortions up to 40 days after conception in a pronouncement made in 1591. Only as late as 1869 did Pope Pius IX forbid all abortions, and it is only in the nineteenth century that abortion laws were passed, making abortion a criminal act in England and the United States.

Real regulation of abortion only began in the latter half of the nineteenth century. Some theorize that abortion became an issue at this time because of a steady drop in population due to abstinence, birth control, and abortion in the years preceding the Civil War. Others connect the country's industrial growth to a change in social and ideological views toward motherhood.

The state laws and popular ideology that made abortion a criminal act in the late nineteenth century continued into the twentieth century until the 1960s, when it became a major political issue. This increased attention was due to a changing attitude among doctors, who resented legal interference in decisions they felt should be based solely on professional medical opinion. Consequently, lawyers became concerned that since abortion was considered a criminal act, doctors could be punished for following through on their own professional medical recommendations. Despite the law, abortions continued to occur since it was difficult to enforce the law against them. Most illegal abortions occurred in secrecy, and family relations were not likely to want to prosecute.

But medical and psychological complications often arise in illegal abortions, unlike in legal ones done in sanitary conditions by a licensed physician. And so some of the same reasons—medically, legally, and socially—that led doctors to a more open opinion regarding abortion affected the general public's opinion too. The ACLU began to sponsor court challenges to abortion laws in the late 1960s. In addition to the ACLU, the National Association for the Repeal of the Abortion

Laws (known after the Roe decision as NARAL, or National Abortion Rights Action League) was founded by Lawrence Lader in 1969. Twelve states "enacted laws permitting abortion on broader medical grounds, including considerations of mental health, anticipated physical or mental defects of the child to be born, and in the cases of rape or incest" (*Collier's,* 1988: 25). In 1970, Alaska, Hawaii, and New York enacted laws that in effect permitted abortion on request.

Roe v. Wade

On January 22, 1973, the United States Supreme Court ruled in the *Roe* v. *Wade* case that women had a constitutional right, in conjunction with their doctors, to choose to have abortions. The basis of the Court's decision rests on the issue of privacy. But the Supreme Court also saw that individual rights were balanced with states' interest in human health and potential human life. Dividing pregnancy into three stages, the Court decided that only the woman has a right to decide whether to have an abortion. During the second trimester, however, the Court recognized states' interest in protecting maternal health, and ruled that states can exercise their rights to regulate in order to protect it. Finally, the Court also acknowledged states' interest in protecting potential human life by allowing states the power to prohibit abortions during the third trimester of pregnancy, except where a woman's life or health was jeopardized. In addition to the Roe case, the Supreme Court ruled on the same day in *Doe* v. *Bolton* that the consent of a woman's husband or parents was not needed.

Challenges to the Roe decision immediately followed. Many critics objected to the Court's broad interpretation of privacy. In 1976, the Hyde Amendment was enacted as a way of circumventing at least some of the force of the Roe decision. The Hyde Amendment prohibits federal funding for abortions. Although challengers of the Hyde decision argued that this lack of funding would in effect deny poor women the right to choose to have an abortion, and that the amendment makes abortion the exception to the government's policy of subsidizing of all medical services to the poor, the Court maintained its decision by denying that economic and social realities were within their realm of concern in this decision. Some states do have policies, however, that provide funding for poor women's abortions. With the exception of the Hyde Amendment, the Supreme Court's response to the continued challenges and testing of parameters by various states has been to uphold its substantial restrictions on the kinds of regulations a state may adopt.

Medically speaking, a legal abortion performed by a knowledgeable physician is safer than giving birth to a full-term baby. Abortion procedures vary and the type used is primarily determined by gestational state (which trimester the pregnancy is in). In the United States, the "suction curettage" is the preferred method for first trimester abortions but the traditional D & C (sharp curettage) is also sometimes used. In the second trimester, the D & E (dilation and evacuation) is the preferred method. The first trimester suction method is the safest, and hence most preferred abortion procedure, but regardless of the method, death following legal abortions is extremely rare. Such was not the case before legalized abortion, where non-doctors with little medical knowledge frequently administered abortions in unsanitary conditions. Illegal abortion horror stories abound.

The question for the funding of abortions is still being debated, as are issues concerned with its mortality. Pro-lifers would like a substantial revision in the *Roe* v. *Wade* decision, making abortions less available on demand. The newspapers abound with incidents occurring at abortion clinics, where emotions are often highly charged.

Webster v. Reproductive Health Services

On July 3, 1989, the United States Supreme Court decided the case of *Webster* v. *Reproductive Health Services,* a case which could possibly have a profound effect on the availability of abortions. In broad terms, the 5 to 4 decision granted states the right to legally enact restrictions on abortion. More specifically, the ruling allowed states to ban any public employee (doctor, nurse, or other health care worker) or public hospital from performing an abortion not necessary to save a woman's life, as well as to ban the use of tax money for "encouraging or counseling" women to have abortions that are not necessary to save their lives. The Webster decision also permits states to require doctors to determine whether a fetus is capable of surviving outside the womb. A viable fetus may not have any abortion procedure performed that may hurt its chances for survival. This provision, in effect, did away with the trimester system established by *Roe* v. *Wade,* which forbid states to regulate abortions during the first trimester or first three months of pregnancy.

Although the sharply divided court (Rehnquist, O'Connor, Scalia, White, and Kennedy for the majority; Blackmun, Stevens, Marshall, and Brennan, dissenting) stopped short of overturning *Roe* v. *Wade* (1973), Scalia called for the outright reversal of the decision, and the majority's remaining four justices implied that Roe could be overturned in the future. Indeed, Blackman's dissent provided that the stage was set for overturning the Roe decision.

The court's majority decision and Blackmun's dissenting comments show that the abortion debate is far from over. In fact, the Court's new emphasis on the rights of the unborn and its granting states new authority to regulate abortions is certain to increase the efforts of both the pro-life and pro-choice sides and to shift the debate to the state political arena.

The pro-life movement already is lobbying for new restrictive state laws as well as investigating old state statutes for possible revival. Some of these attempts to reenact and enforce old statutes restricting abortions and to create new ones will undoubtedly be challenged in the courts, paving the way for the Supreme Court's further reconsideration of the Roe decision.

With so much lobbying going on in state legislatures, no candidate for political office will be able to avoid taking a public position on abortion. It is quite possible that a candidate's position on abortion will be the pivotal factor in whether he or she gets elected. In other words, a political candidate may win or lose solely on his/her publically stated opinion on abortion and any candidate who refuses to take a stand will almost surely not be elected.

Clearly, the abortion controversy in this country is far from over. The Webster decision guarantees that both sides of the abortion debate will renew and redouble their efforts, keeping the issue in the forefront of the legislative and political scenes, on both the state and federal level for years to come.

WRITING ABOUT ABORTION

Using the Key Terms

In order to understand the abortion issue, you must be sure that you understand the terms about which people debate. At the end of this chapter, therefore, I have not only provided you with a list of key terms, but also with definitions for them. Be sure you understand these terms before you read what others have to say on this issue.

Clarifying Your Own Position

In the past, because it was regarded as too emotional a topic, abortion was not considered suitable for a writing assignment. The idea was that either students were in favor of it, or they weren't, and that their ideas were based on belief, not on logic. Some of you may, indeed, have profound religious beliefs about the morality of abortion, and those beliefs would lead you to say that you, yourself, would never get an abortion, or, if you are male, that you would never approve of one for your own wife or female partner. However, what must be emphasized here is that simply because you, yourself, do not approve of a particular action for yourself, it does not mean, necessarily, that you are in favor of laws preventing others from engaging in that action. The extent to which you feel that laws ought to prevent people from having abortions rests on your conception of what an abortion is and of what you believe are likely to be the consequences of enacting laws against abortion.

WRITING TO LEARN

▶ ***Writing Assignment:*** Thoughtful persons in a pluralistic society acknowledge that there are actions of which one morally disapproves that ought not to be legislated by law to prevent them from occurring. In a small group, discuss what actions (other than abortion) you, yourself, disapprove of, but which are not currently against the law. Do you feel that such actions *ought* to be against the law?

Write a short paper discussing this idea.

► *Writing Assignment: The Concept of the Embryo or Fetus.* Read Joan Callahan's essay, "The Fetus and Fundamental Rights," Sidney Callahan's essay "Abortion and the Sexual Agenda," and Daniel Maguire's "A Catholic Theologian at an Abortion Clinic." Write a summary of each of these essays. Then write a researched paper addressing the following question: To what extent is one's position on abortion influenced by the way in which one regards the fetus or embryo? Incorporate ideas from your readings into your essay.

Key Question: How Does the Abortion Issue Relate to the Concept of the Good Society?

Some have argued that whatever moral dilemmas might exist within the abortion issue, the fact remains that if a law were passed prohibiting abortion, a rich woman would be able to get one anyway. Therefore, it is argued that any abortion law would be most likely to affect the poor, who often have more babies to care for than they can afford. Pro-choice advocates maintain that abortion should be available on demand, simply because the alternative would be too costly, i.e., it would not be beneficial for society if abortion were to be made illegal.

► *Writing Assignment:* Write a researched paper in which you consider the extent to which you agree with the following statement: Issues of practicality ought to be considered when deciding on the availability of abortion. Use at least three sources to help develop your position (suggestions: "Babies, Anyone?" "The Right to Life and the Restoration of the American Public," and "A Catholic Theologian at an Abortion Clinic").

Understanding Some of the Arguments

► *A Sequence of Assignments*

Several articles concerned with abortion make extensive use of metaphor and analogy to develop a position. Judith Thomson in "A Defense of Abortion," uses these devices with particular effectiveness in order to argue that even if the fetus is a person, it does not follow that a woman is required to carry it to term. Read the article, noting the following analogies: the unconscious violinist, the house, the coat, the house and the burglars, the boys and the box of chocolates, the Kitty Genovese case, the story of the good Samaritan. Jot down some notes about how these analogies are used. Then in small groups, discuss which analogies you find the most effective.

► *Writing Assignment:* Write a short paper discussing how Thomson uses analogies in her essay.

► *Writing Assignment:* Write a three- to five-page paper discussing how analogies are used to develop arguments concerned with abortion. Choose some of the analogies used in the Thomson article and compare them with the slavery analogy in "The Right to Life and the Restoration of the American Republic" and the analogy about oppressed women in "Abortion and the Sexual Agenda." Consider which analogies you find most effective.

▶ **Writing Assignment: *Abortion and the Feminist Perspective.*** Use the readings to develop a four- to six-page paper addressing the following question: To what extent is abortion mainly a feminist issue?

▶ **Writing Assignment: *Abortion and Men.*** In recent times, men have felt that they have not had an adequate role in deciding questions concerned with abortion. Read the essays "Men and Abortion" and "Abortion and the Sexual Agenda." Write a three- to five-page paper addressing the following question: To what extent is abortion also a men's issue?

Key Terms:

Abortion: (induced or voluntary abortion) the willful termination of a pregnancy by the removal of an embryo or fetus from a woman's uterus.

Embryo: "the young of . . . a mammal, in the early stages of development within the womb, in humans up to the end of the second month" (*Random House Dictionary,* 1987).

Fetus: "the young of an animal in the womb or egg, esp. in later stages of development when the body structures are in the recognizable form of its kind, in humans after the end of the second month of gestation" (*Random House Dictionary,* 1987).

Fourteenth Amendment: In the abortion issue, this amendment is important for its protection of human life. It states that no person shall be deprived of life without due process of law. Moralists apply this guarantee to the fetus.

Human Life Bill: Introduced in 1981 by Senator Jessie Helms, this was an attempt to overrule the Roe decision by attempting to establish that human life scientifically begins at conception and then applying this "fact" to the Fourteenth Amendment.

Hyde Amendment: Prohibits federal funding for abortions. Some states have nevertheless found a way to provide funding to poor women for abortions anyway. An attempt to severely limit the impact of the Roe decision. However, Hyde's impact is limited to the poor.

Pro-choice: "supporting or advocating legalized abortion"; a women's right to decide whether or not to have an abortion.

Pro-life: "opposed to legalized abortion; right-to-life" (*Random House Dictionary,* 1987).

Roe v. Wade: The 1973 landmark Supreme Court decision determining that a woman has the constitutional right to a legal abortion.

Viability of fetus: whether life can be sustained outside the uterus. In humans, viability usually begins at between the 24th to 28th weeks of pregnancy.

The Fetus and Fundamental Rights

Joan C. Callahan

THE CONSISTENCY PROBLEM

Although the 1984 presidential election is history, the campaigns raised a number of questions which have not been resolved, and which need more public discussion. Not the least among these are the questions that surrounded Geraldine Ferraro's position on abortion—a position that significantly disrupted her campaign, and which, during the early fall of 1984, put all liberal Democratic Catholic politicians into political trouble from which they have not yet escaped.[1]

The trouble was focused on the question of abortion, but the problem is deeper than any single issue. The problem is one of consistency: How can a politician believe that something is profoundly morally wrong, yet insist that he or she will not use political power to right the wrong? The reply from the Geraldine Ferraros and the Edward Kennedys was that it is not the proper business of the politician to impose his or her religious beliefs on members of a pluralistic society. Although this is surely true, it was an inadequate response. It was inadequate because it missed the point; and it missed the point because it seemed to treat matters like our public policy on abortion as if they were the same in kind as eating meat on Friday or making one's Easter Duty. The Catholic politicians may not have been making a category mistake, but they certainly sometimes sounded as if they were. Bishop James Timlin of Scranton did not have to be a bishop, a Roman Catholic, or even a Christian to say with understandable astonishment that Geraldine Ferraro's position on abortion is like saying "I'm personally opposed to slavery, but I don't care if people down the street want to own slaves."[2] The Catholic liberal Democrats thought and think this analogy fails. But *why* it fails was never made clear. In what follows, I want to address Bishop Timlin's analogy and hence, the particular question of abortion, as well as the larger question of appropriate reasons for a politician's policy choices. My purpose is to get clearer on both the morality of elective abortion and the question of moral consistency in political life.

RELIGIOUS V. PHILOSOPHICAL REASONS

Bishop Timlin's analogy is faulty in at least three ways. First, refusing to use the law to fight a practice one believes is immoral does not imply that one does not *care* if people engage in that practice. Mario Cuomo, in his thoughtful, if not wholly adequate, speech at Notre Dame made that very clear.[3] There is no doubt that Mr. Cuomo cares deeply about abortion. But we can cite any number of examples (e.g., the selfish breaking of promises, the telling of lies to friends for bad reasons, etc.) of actions we believe are morally wrong and about which we care, but which we do not (and should not) attempt to eradicate by law. Thus, it does not follow from the fact that someone is unwilling to pursue a legal prohibition on some kind of activity that the person does not care if people engage in that activity. Nor does it follow from the fact that one believes that some kind of action is morally wrong that one is morally obligated to seek a legal prohibition on that kind of action.

Bishop Timlin's analogy is also faulty because it fails to recognize that the *reasons* one has for holding something to be wrong are of the utmost importance when one is trying to decide whether to pursue a legal prohibition on individual liberty. In a pluralistic society, the fact that a religious institution, or a religious contingency (no matter how large), holds something to be wrong is simply not a good reason for setting a public policy prohibiting or requiring action on the part of all citizens. Insofar as a Catholic politician's reason for holding that abortion is wrong is that this is church doctrine, there can be no obligation to try to institute a prohibition on abortion on those who do not share the same religious affiliation. Indeed, part of the politician's obligation in a pluralistic society is to guard against just such impositions by religious groups. In the vice-presidential debate, Congresswoman Ferraro made it clear that her reason for being "personally" opposed to abortion is that her church holds this as doctrine. If this is indeed *why* she is opposed to abortion, then it ought to be clear to all of us that she has no more duty (or right) to try to capture her opposition to abortion in law than she has to try to force Americans who do not share her religious affiliation to attend Roman Catholic Mass weekly. And the same is true for any other politician who is opposed to abortion *because* this is a doctrine of his or her faith.[4]

But there are other reasons for being opposed to abortion—philosophical reasons which appeal to the laws of logic and to moral rights—which might be shared by the most ardent atheist. Many who are opposed to abortion have these kinds of reasons for holding that abortion is wrong, and so profoundly wrong that it might be rightly prohibited by law, even in a pluralistic society. We need, then, to make a distinction between those who hold that abortion is wrong simply because their religion says so, and those who think that abortion is wrong because they believe that the philosophical reasons compel us to accept that human fetuses have a right not to be killed which is comparable to your right and my right not to be killed.

Reasons of the first kind (i.e., purely religious reasons) are excellent reasons for acting or not acting in certian ways in one's own life, but they are bad reasons for imposing legal requirements or legal restraints on those who do not share the same religious commitments. We all know this. If some new, large religious contingency were to come to believe that zero population growth is the will of God, and if the government set out to capture this belief in law, Roman Catholics and other Christians would lead the ranks of civil disobedients. But reasons of the second kind (i.e., reasons appealing to the logic of human rights) are of the appropriate kind to justify or even require someone's working for legal prohibitions on certain actions or practices. The problem in the abortion debate is that there is a profound disagreement about the relative strengths of the philosophical reasons given for and against holding that elective abortion is the killing of an unconsenting innocent person for inadequate moral reasons. If an elective abortion *is* the killing of an unconsenting innocent person for reasons which would not justify killing an adult person, then it is wrongful killing, and a policy allowing elective abortion cannot be morally justified. But *are* human fetuses persons? The question is a sensible one, and there are responsible philosophical reasons for saying yes and there are responsible philosophical reasons for saying no. And that's the rub.

FETAL RIGHTS AND THE LOGICAL WEDGE

Those who oppose elective abortion often insist that human life begins at conception. But this is just wrong. Human life begins long before conception. The sperm and egg are alive, and they are not bovine or feline or canine—they are living human gametes. To couch the question in terms of the beginning of human life is to muddle the issue. It is to make the question of the morality of abortion sound like one that can be answered by a very clever biologist. But the issue is not when human life begins. Unquestionably, human fetuses are, from the earliest stages, alive. What we *really* want to know is whether the living human fetus should be recognized as a bearer of the same range of fundamental moral rights that you and I have, among them the right not to be killed without *very* good reason. And the most clever biologist in the world cannot answer this for us, since the question is simply not a biological one.

But it might be objected that although some who are opposed to abortion and who have not thought carefully enough about the issue do make the mistake of thinking that the question is when biological life begins, it is also true that not everyone who talks in terms of the beginning of human life is making this mistake. For surely many who are opposed to elective abortion mean to contend that the life of a *unique* human being, of a distinct *person,* begins at conception, and that is why a policy allowing elective abortion is wrong.

The problem with this response, however, is that it is not a single claim. For one can grant that the life of a unique human being begins at conception, yet not grant that a distinct person emerges at conception, since the two claims are not equivalent unless one begs the question in favor of fetal personhood. That is, if we mean by "human being" "a member of the biological species, *homo sapiens,*" then (if we ignore the problem of identical twins) it is uncontroversially true that the life of a unique human being begins at conception. This is merely a scientific claim, and it is one that can be conclusively defended by scientists as such. But the claim that a distinct *person* emerges at conception is not a scientific one; for to call something "a person" is already to assert that it is a bearer of the strongest moral rights—fundamental rights comparable to yours and mine, among them the right not to be killed except for the most compelling of moral reasons. If in asserting that "a human life begins at conception" the opponent of elective abortion means to assert the biological claim, that can be granted immediately. But if he or she means to assert that "a person emerges at conception," that is a very different claim—it is a moral claim. Indeed, it is the very claim that is at issue in the abortion debate. What those who oppose retaining a policy of elective abortion need to tell us is *why* we must accept that the truth of the biological claim commits us to accepting the moral claim.

But those opposed to elective abortion might still respond that those who admit that the life of a unique human being (in the biological sense) begins at conception are indeed committed to granting that (insofar as human fetuses become distinct persons) the life of a distinct person begins here as well. For where did the life of any adult person begin but at conception?

There are, however, at least two responses to this. The first is simply to make the logical point that one can allow that the life of a person begins at conception without allowing that the (biological human) being present at conception is yet a person. That is, just as one can allow that the first tiny bud in an acorn is the beginning of the life of a (future) oak tree without being committed to saying that the bud is already an oak tree, one can allow that conception marks the beginning of the life of a (future) person without being committed to saying that the conceptus is already a person.

This logical point leads to the second, more substantive, response: namely, that we think the tiny bud in the acorn is quite clearly *not* an oak tree. And we think this because the bud does not yet have the characteristics of oak trees. Indeed, acorns with tiny buds are very *unlike* oak trees, even though every oak tree began as a bud in an acorn. In just the same way, the new conceptus is very unlike beings who have the kinds of characteristics which compel us to recognize them as persons. What kinds of characteristics are these? I cannot offer a full account here. But perhaps it will be enough to point out that if we came across a being like E.T. (who is not biologically human), we would surely think him a person—a being with fundamental moral rights comparable to yours and mine. And this would be because we would recognize that he has certain characteristics—the capacity to suffer mental and physical pain, the ability to make plans, a sense of himself as an ongoing being, and so on—which are sufficient to compel us to hold that he must (and must not) be treated in certain ways. (And, of course, the film, *E.T.*, turns on precisely this point.) A conceptus, however, has none of these characteristics. Indeed, like the mystery of the acorn and the oak, what is amazing is that such radically *different* beings emerge from such beginnings. But it needs to be clearly recognized that in the case of the acorn and in the case of the conceptus, at the end of the process, we do have beings *very* unlike those at the beginning of the process.[5]

When, then, must we say of a developing human being that we must recognize it as a person? If we are talking about when we have a being with the kinds of characteristics we take to be relevant to compelling a recognition of personhood, it seems that persons (at least human persons) are, like oak trees, emergent beings, and that deciding when to classify a developing human being as a person is like deciding when to call a shoot a tree. Young trees do not have all the characteristics of grown trees—for example, children cannot safely swing from them. But when a shoot begins to take on at least some of the characteristics of full-fledged trees, we think we are not confused in beginning to call that shoot a tree. Similarly, there is no clear distinction between where the Mississippi River ends and the Gulf of Mexico begins. But settle the issue by setting a *convention* which does not seem counterintuitive. We are faced with quite the same kind of question when it comes to the manner of persons. Since fetuses do not have the kinds of characteristics which compel us to recognize beings as persons, we must, whether we like it or not, sit down and *decide* whether fetuses are to be recognized as full-fledged persons as a matter of public policy. And we must decide the question on the basis of the appropriate kinds of reasons. That is, for the purposes of setting public policy in a religiously heterogeneous society, we must decide it on the basis of the nonreligious, philosophical arguments, some of which urge us to accept that we must recognize human fetuses as having the same range of fundamental rights that you and I have, and some of which hold that this is just not so.

One possible convention is to set the recognition of personhood at birth. Another is to set it at conception. Still others might be at various stages of prenatality or at various points after birth. Those who oppose elective abortion insist that we *must* recognize personhood at conception, and central to the position is most frequently an argument known as "the logical wedge." This argument holds that if we are going to recognize older children as having the same fundamental rights that you and I have, then logic compels us to recognize that, from the moment of conception, all human beings must have those same rights. The argument proceeds by starting with beings everyone recognizes as having the rights in question and then by pointing out that a child (say) at fifteen is not radically different from one at fourteen and a half; and a child at fourteen and a half is not radically different from one at fourteen, and so on. The argument presses us back from fourteen to thirteen to twelve—to infancy. From infancy, it is a short step to late-term fetuses, because (the argument goes) change in location (from the womb to the wider world) does not constitute an essential change in the being itself. *You* do not lose *your* right not to be killed simply by walking from one room to another. Similarly, it is argued, mere change of place is not philosophically important enough to justify such a radical difference in treatment between infants and late-term fetuses. The argument then presses us back to early-term fetuses—back to conception. Logic and fairness, then, force us to accept that even the new conceptus has the same fundamental right to life that you and I have.

But those who support retaining a policy of elective abortion often point out that this kind of argument for fetal rights is faulty, since if we accept that we can never treat beings who are not radically different from one another in radically different ways, we shall be unable to justify all sorts of public policies which we want to keep and which we all believe are fair. It is argued, for example, that this kind of argument for fetal rights entails that we cannot be justified in setting driving or voting ages, since withholding these privileges until a certain age discriminates against those close to that age: An eighteen-year-old is not radically different from a seventeen-and-a-half-year-old, and so on. Thus, the implication of this kind of argument is that setting ages for the commencement of certain important societal privileges cannot be morally justified. We must give the five-year-old the right to vote, the six-year-old the right to drink, the nine-year-old the right to drive. But these implications, it is argued, show that this kind of argument for fetal rights is unsound.[6]

The response to this criticism of the logical wedge argument, however, is that the granting of societal privileges is not a matter of arbitrariness, even if there is some arbitrariness in selecting ages for the commencement of such privileges. Proper use of these rights, it may be argued, requires a certain degree of maturity—responsibility, background knowledge, experience, independence, and, in the case of driving, a certain degree of developed physical dexterity. Thus, it is because certain changes normally occur as a child matures into an adult that it is appropriate to set policies which acknowledge those changes. But this, it may be argued, is not the case when it comes to recognizing the right to life. That is, those who oppose retaining a policy of elective abortion insist that after conception *no* changes occur that are relevant to recognizing the personhood (and thus the right to life) of a human being.

But this immediately takes us back to the acorn and the oak. The bud and the tree simply *are* significantly different kinds of beings. And you and I *are* significantly different from a conceptus, which has *none* of the characteristics which morally compel us to recognize it as a being with rights. It will not do simply to deny that there are significant changes between the time of conception and the time when we have a being which we simply *must* recognize as a bearer of rights. Thus, we are once again confronted with the question of deciding where we shall set the convention of recognizing personhood.

At this point, however, there is yet another response open to the opponent of elective abortion—namely, that the kind of reasoning used to defeat the argument for fetal rights cannot be correct, since it will not only rule out our being committed to the rights of fetuses, it also entails that we are not compelled to accept that human infants are beings of a kind which must be recognized as having the full range of fundamental moral rights, since infants are, it might be suggested, more like very young kittens in regard to the characteristics in question than they are like paradigm cases of persons.

But this objection is not devastating. For, again, the question before us is a question of deciding what convention we shall adopt. And one can allow that even if infants do not (yet) have the characteristics which compel us to accept a being as a person, there are other considerations which provide excellent reasons for taking birth as the best place to set the convention of recognizing personhood and the full range of fundamental moral rights, despite the fact that infants as such are far more like very young kittens than they are like beings whose characteristics compel us to accept them as full members of the moral community.

Chief among these considerations are the facts that persons other than an infant's biological mother are able to care for the infant and have an interest in doing so. There is no radical change in the characteristics of a human being just before birth and just after birth. But once a human being emerges from the womb and others are able to care for it, there are radical changes in what is involved in preserving its life. And the crucial change is that sustaining its life violates no right of its biological mother. Thus birth, which marks this change, is not an arbitrary point for commencing recognition of personhood.

It is important to notice here that to hold that a woman has a right to terminate a pregnancy is not to hold that she also has a right to the death of her fetus if that fetus can survive, and quite the same reasons that can justify a proscription on infanticide can justify a requirement to sustain viable fetuses that survive abortion. What we are not entitled to do, it may be argued, is force a woman to complete a pregnancy because others have an interest in having her fetus. But it does not follow from this that a woman may kill a born infant that can be cared for by others. Thus, it does not follow from the kind of reasoning I have sketched above that the defender of a policy allowing elective abortion is committed to a policy allowing infanticide. Indeed, the position is fully consistent with holding that even though infants do not yet possess the kinds of characteristics which compel recognition of a being as a person, the fact that they are now biologically independent beings that can be sustained without forcing an unwilling woman to serve as a life support provides an excellent reason for setting the convention of a right to life at birth, that is, viable emergence.[7]

Perhaps it should be pointed out here that the view I have just sketched can also allow that even kittens have *some* moral rights. I, for one, believe that as sentient beings—being capable of suffering pain—they have a strong moral right not to be treated cruelly, that is, not to have pain wantonly imposed on them. Insofar as fetuses can suffer pain, the defender of elective abortion can quite coherently hold that any pain imposed on a fetus in abortion must be justified. To say this, however, is not to be committed to holding that fetuses must be recognized as having the same full range of fundamental rights that you and I have. It is, rather, to allow fetuses (at the very least) the moral standing of any being of comparable sentience, and, hence, to hold that there is always a moral obligation not to wantonly impose pain on fetuses. But given the exquisite intimacy of pregnancy, any woman who does not want to bring a child to term has a strong reason for seeking an abortion. Thus, if pain is imposed on the fetus in abortion, it is not wantonly imposed.[8]

But it will surely still be objected that human fetuses and human infants are beings that are potentially like paradigm cases of persons, and this makes them very *unlike* other beings of comparable sentience. Kittens, after all, will never develop the kinds of characteristics that compel us to recognize them as full-fledged members of the moral community, and because of this, we must recognize human fetuses as having a far more significant moral standing than other beings of comparable sentience. Sometimes opponents of elective abortion point this out, saying that from the moment of conception a fetus is a *potential* person, and must, therefore, be granted the right to life. But the problem here is that to say that a being is a potential person is just to say that it is a person-not-yet, which is, of course, to deny that it is now a person. And this is to give the defender of retaining choice in this area the very point that is crucial to his or her argument against the argument for fetal rights, and to thereby turn the question back to the question of deciding on a convention.

ACTUAL AND POTENTIAL PERSONS

The crucial question, then, is whether we should recognize the fetus as a person now or whether we should recognize the fetus as a potential person—as a person-not-yet. If we take the first choice, then the full range of fundamental moral rights attaches to the fetus. If we take the second choice, it remains an open question what moral duties we might have toward the fetus. Either way, our *reasons* for deciding as we do must be more than religious ones if the purpose of deciding is to set policy in a pluralistic society. Bishop Timlin's analogy to slavery fails yet a third time because there are no such open questions about involuntary slavery. Enslaving a person against his or her will is a paradigm case of injustice. But we haven't anything like the same sort of moral certainty about the injustice of abortion. And since we haven't, those who recognize the complexity of the question can hold, without being heartless or inconsistent, that *they* believe abortion is wrong, but also that they are unprepared to impose that view on those who remain reflectively unconvinced by the arguments that the human fetus must be recognized as having the full moral status of a person.

Does it follow from all this that there is some serious doubt about the personhood of fetuses—that is, that the fetus might be a person? Sometimes those who support retaining a policy of elective abortion say things like this—that the fetus *might* be a person, but that the evidence just is not conclusive. But if this is the position one holds, those who oppose allowing elective abortion have a strong response. That response is that we should give the fetus the benefit of the doubt. After all, if a hunter hears a movement in the bushes and shoots without making sure she is not shooting a person, and it turns out that she has killed or injured a person, we charge her with gross recklessness. And her saying that it was possible that what she shot at was not a person is no defense. She simply should not have shot if there were even a remote possibility that she would injure a person. In just the same way, the opponent of allowing elective abortion argues that if there is *any* possibility that the fetus is a person, we have a duty to act as if it were a person—a duty to avoid acting recklessly. And part of what *that* means is that another person may not kill it for reasons less than self-defense.

This is an interesting argument, but it misses an important point. For the real doubt is not whether a fetus is a person. Rather, if there is a doubt it is about whether we should treat something which is obviously a potential person (in the sense that it has potentially the characteristics of paradigm cases of persons) as if it were a person already. And this is not something that can be decided by going and looking at the fetus, as one might go and look in the bushes. For (again) in looking, we shall find that although fetuses are quite wonderful beings, they lack the kinds of characteristics that morally compel us to accept a being as a person. The question to be resolved, then, is whether we should accept that these beings which will emerge as persons if their lives are supported ought, at this stage of their development, be treated as if they were persons already—as beings with a moral right to life comparable to yours and mine, comparably protected by the coercive power of the law.

When we are trying to resolve the real doubt, a large part of what we need to ask is what deciding to treat fetuses as beings with the full range of fundamental moral rights would really involve in pratice, and whether our shared moral views about paradigm cases of persons will allow us to accept these things. Let us, then, look for a moment at just two of the implications of deciding to admit human fetuses into the class of full-fledged persons with full-fledged fundamental rights.

SOME IMPLICATIONS OF RECOGNIZING FETUSES AS PERSONS

If we decide to recognize fetuses as full persons, the first thing that follows (as Mr. Reagan has recognized) is that abortion in cases of rape or incest must be ruled out. Suppose that I were to discover that you are the product of rape or incest. You would not think (and none of us would think) that it followed from this that I could just kill you. Fundamental rights are not a consequence of where someone came from. If we allow that human fetuses are persons, we could not consistently allow abortion for (say) an eighteen-year-old woman who had been raped by her father. What is more, if this woman were to perform an abortion on herself and be found out, we must treat her as we treat any murderer. In some jurisdictions, this might well lead to life imprisonment or even execution. During the 1984 campaigns, President Reagan was asked in the first debate with Mr. Mondale whether he believed we should treat women who abort for reasons less than self-defense as murderers, with all that might entail. He avoided the question, saying that this would be a matter for the states to decide. But the opponent of elective abortion needs to confront this question squarely and honestly. Precisely what *are* we to do with women who abort? Could we accept that states may decide to imprison them or execute them? Just what are we to do with them? If the proponent of a prohibition on elective abortion confronts this question earnestly and *cannot* comfortably hold that jurisdictions *should* treat these women as they typically treat murderers, then he or she needs to begin to think carefully about *why*. When asked in the first debate to explain his position on abortion, Mr. Mondale (echoing Governor Cuomo) said of the prohibitive policy espoused by Mr. Reagan, "It won't work." This is a woefully inadequate response. But I suspect that what Mr. Mondale had in mind was that accepting the fetus as a full-fledged person commits us to measures in practice that even those who are deeply opposed to elective abortion cannot fully accept, among them that the eighteen-year-old who aborts a fetus resulting from rape by her father is to be treated as any murderer of a helpless, innocent person. We are not, even in this pluralistic society, free to kill others for reasons less than the immediate defense of our own lives, and if we do, we are subject to the most severe legal penalties, including possible execution. If fetuses are to be recognized as full-fledged persons, then justice requires that those who abort them for reasons less than self-defense must be recognized as full-fledged murderers and treated as such. Those who are rigorously opposed to retaining a policy of elective abortion on the ground that fetuses are persons must confront this implication sincerely and sensitively, and they must be explicit on what they are willing to accept as the practical implications of their position. If they are not willing to accept that those who abort should be subject to exactly the same treatment as others who murder innocent persons, then they do not *really* believe that the fetus has precisely the same moral status as you and I.

There is yet another potent implication of recognizing fetuses as full-fledged persons. Mr. Reagan and Mr. Bush would both allow abortion in cases of self-defense—that is, in cases where the woman's life is threatened. But there is a problem with this position that generally goes unnoticed. For if our public policy is to recognize that the fetus is genuinely an innocent person, then its threat to a woman's life is an innocent threat, and the state can have no legitimate reason for systematically preferring the life of the woman to the life of the fetus.[9] That is, the argument from self-defense simply cannot justify the state's allowing a woman the use of medical specialists who will systematically prefer her life to the life of the fetus. If the fetus is a person who has precisely the same moral status as the woman, the state must, as a matter of fairness to the fetus, do nothing that would involve it in giving the woman an unfair advantage over the fetus. And, again, this means that the state should not permit the use of technologically advanced institutions or the use of technologically advanced practitioners which give the woman an unfair advantage in this battle for life between moral equals. The argument from self-defense, then, seems to entail far greater restrictions on abortion than even the most fervent opponents of elective abortion tend to want to allow, Mr. Reagan among them. If opponents of elective abortion want to allow abortions in cases where the woman's life is at stake, then they must realize that implicit in their position is the view that the woman and the fetus are *not* of equal moral stature after all.

MORAL SENSITIVITY AND SETTING PUBLIC POLICY

My own view is that there are insurmountable difficulties to finding an argument for the recognition of fetuses as persons which is cogent and compelling enough to justify imposing on women the exquisitely intimate burden of bearing an unwanted child. But even if this view is correct, it does not follow that we can do just anything to human fetuses. Kittens are not persons, but we are not at moral liberty to wantonly impose pain on them. Natural resources are not persons, but we are not at moral liberty to wantonly destroy them. Several years ago, Patrick Buchanan wrote of an experiment on human fetuses, discussed in *The Second American Revolution,* by John Whitehead. Six months after *Roe v. Wade,* Dr. A. J. Adam of Case Western Reserve University reported to the American Pediatric Research Society that he and his associates had conducted an experiment on twelve fetuses, up to twenty weeks old, delivered alive by hysterectomy abortion. Adam and his associates cut the heads off these fetuses and cannulated the internal carotid arteries. They kept the heads alive, much as the Russians kept dogs' heads alive during the 1950s. When challenged, Dr. Adam's response was that society had decided that these fetuses would die, thus they had no rights. Said Adam, "I don't see any ethical problem." I find Dr. Adam's failure to see any ethical problem chilling and morally repugnant, even though these fetuses had no real chance of long-term survival *ex utero*. One of the legitimate worries of those who are opposed to abortion is that this kind of ghoulish insensitivity will become more and more prevalent in our society, spilling over to a cavalier attitude toward human life in general. One need not be opposed to allowing elective abortion to share that worry, and one need not think nonviable fetuses are persons to be astonished at Dr. Adam's failure to see *any* ethical problem.

When asked in the 1984 campaign debate about his position on abortion, Vice President Bush replied that he had changed his view (which previously had been more liberal) because of the number of legal abortions that have taken place in this country. But the problem with this reason for disallowing elective abortion is that it misses the very point of those who have traditionally opposed abortion; for if fetuses have the same range of moral rights that you and I have, then even one abortion for reasons less than those which would justify killing an adult person is too many. Determining moral rights is not a numbers game. We don't have laws against murder because there are too many murders—we have laws against murder because every single person has a compelling moral right not to be murdered. Because that right is so compelling, the state comes forward to protect it. When one understands that persons have a compelling moral right not to be murdered, one also understands that numbers of murders are irrelevant to the question of whether society should have laws against murder. One murder is simply one too many. Mr. Bush's position, then, misses the very strong position on fundamental fetal rights that has been the moral centerpiece of the movement against elective abortion.

Still, there is much to be said for Mr. Bush's discomfort with the use of abortion as a form of birth control. Although I believe that defenders of retaining a policy of elective abortion who have thought carefully and sensitively about the issue are more than willing to admit that abortion, however well-justified, is never a happy moral choice, some who favor elective abortion angrily talk about fetuses as being, like tumors, morally equivalent to parasites. Such talk is inexcusably cavalier; and those who believe that the human fetus is of significant moral worth are understandably infuriated when they hear it or read it. Language like that does not help get us to reasonable, sensitive discussion. And it is precisely reasonable, sensitive discussion that we now most need on this difficult question of morality and public policy.

It should go without saying that public policy should not be set by those who shout the loudest—that it should not be set by those who carry the most emotively charged posters, or by those who use the most emotively charged language. But neither should it be carelessly set by an unreflective commitment to a woman's right to self-direction which fails to take into serious account the genuine moral costs of giving absolute priority to such a right. Public policy must be set by sitting down and coming to understand the legitimate concerns on both sides of hard issues. It must be set with an eye toward what *all* morally sensitive persons in a pluralistic society can live with.

The abortion issue is one about which reasonable people can disagree. We all need to realize this, and we need to do more talking instead of shouting. Deliberation in the philosophy of moral rights involves much more than repeating bumper sticker slogans; and rational agreement in such deliberation is often hard-won, and will only succeed when each side can see clearly why the other side begins from the position it does. It will not do, then, for those who are opposed to retaining a policy of elective abortion to call themselves "prolife" and to call fetuses "babies" and take the issue to be settled. And it will not do for those who believe we must retain abortion as an option for women to call fetuses "parasites" and take the issue to be settled. Trying to decide public policy must involve refusing to use language which implies that the opposition is against something that any morally reasonable person would support or which simply begs the question against the other side. It must involve sensitive deliberation which takes carefully into account the deeply felt and morally reasonable concerns of a variety of perspectives. And the effort must lead to decisions that thoughtful persons in a pluralistic society can respect, no matter what policies they would prefer to see. Defenders and opponents of a policy of elective abortion must realize that we share a large common moral ground. We must begin to work from that common ground to come to an agreement on policies that can respectfully govern us all.

The liberal Catholic politicians are in trouble, and they will stay in trouble until they more adequately explain their reasons for not seeking a moratorium on elective abortion. Mario Cuomo began that explanation at Notre Dame. But there is much more to be said if all morally concerned Americans are to understand why politicians like Geraldine Ferraro and Mario Cuomo are neither necessarily inconsistent, nor rabid moral relativists, nor insensitive moral thugs.

Notes

1. An edited version of this essay appeared in *Commonweal* 11 (April 1986) 203–9. I am deeply indebted to Peter Steinfels for his extensive and enormously helpful comments and questions on an earlier draft. For an expanded discussion of fetal rights, see James W. Knight and Joan C. Callahan, *Preventing Birth: Contemporary Methods and Related Moral Controversies* (Salt Lake City: University of Utah Press, 1989) chaps. 7 and 9.

2. *Newsweek,* Sept. 24, 1984.

3. Governor Cuomo's speech was given on Sept. 13, 1984. It has been reprinted in this volume on pp. 202–16.

4. I offer a more detailed account of what it means to be "personally" opposed to some kind of action in "Religion and Moral Consistency in Politics," in progress.

5. For a fuller discussion of the kinds of characteristics morally relevant to compelling a recognition of beings (including nonhuman beings) as persons see, e.g., Mary Anne Warren, "On the Moral and Legal Status of Abortion," in *Today's Moral Problems,* ed. Richard Wasserstrom (New York: Macmillan, 1975) 120–36. See also Jane English, "Abortion and the Concept of a Person," *Canadian Journal of*

Philosophy 5, no. 2 (1975) 233–43, for an even more detailed discussion of the cluster of features that enter into our concept of a person.
6. For a more detailed treatment of this response to the logical wedge, see, e.g., Jonathan Glover, *Causing Death and Saving Lives* (New York: Penguin, 1977), chap. 12.
7. Again, see Warren for a version of this line of reasoning.
8. I deal with the question of fetal sentience (as well as several related issues) in more detail in *"The Silent Scream:* A New, Conclusive Argument Against Abortion?" *Philosophy Research Archives* 11 (1986) 181–95. On the question of fetal sentience, see also L. W. Sumner, *Abortion and Moral Theory* (Princeton: Princeton University Press, 1981) chap. 4. A revised version of that chapter appears as "A Third Way," in *The Problem of Abortion,* ed. Joel Feinberg, 2nd ed. (Belmont, CA: Wadsworth, 1984) 71–93.
9. This point is argued in detail by Nancy Davis in "Abortion and Self-Defense," *Philosophy and Public Affairs* 13, no. 3 (Summer 1984) 175–207.

Abortion and the Sexual Agenda

Sidney Callahan

The abortion debate continues. In the latest and perhaps most crucial develop-ment, pro-life feminists are contesting pro-choice feminist claims that abortion rights are prerequisites for women's full development and social equality. The outcome of this debate may be decisive for the culture as a whole. Pro-life feminists, like myself, argue on good feminist principles that women can never achieve the fulfillment of feminist goals in a society permissive toward abortion.

These new arguments over abortion take place within liberal political circles. This round of intense intra-feminist conflict has spiraled beyond earlier right-versus-left abortion debates, which focused on "tragic choices," medical judgments, and legal compromises. Feminist theorists of the pro-choice position now put forth the demand for unrestricted abortion rights as a *moral imperative* and insist upon women's right to complete reproductive freedom. They morally justify the present situation and current abortion practices. Thus it is all the more important that pro-life feminists articulate their different feminist perspective.

These opposing arguments can best be seen when presented in turn. Perhaps the most highly developed feminist arguments for the morality and legality of abortion can be found in Beverly Wildung Harrison's *Our Right to Choose* (Beacon Press, 1983) and Rosalind Pollack Petchesky's *Abortion and Woman's Choice* (Longman, 1984). Obviously it is difficult to do justice to these complex arguments, which draw on diverse strands of philosophy and social theory and are often interwoven in pro-choice feminists' own version of a "seamless garment." Yet the fundamental feminist case for the morality of abortion, encompassing the views of Harrison and Petchesky, can be analyzed in terms of four central moral claims:

Sidney Callahan, "Abortion and the Sexual Agenda," *Commonweal*, April 18, 1986. Reprinted by permission.

(1) the moral right to control one's own body; (2) the moral necessity of autonomy and choice in personal responsibility; (3) the moral claim for the contingent value of fetal life; (4) the moral right of women to true social equality.

1. The moral right to control one's own body. Pro-choice feminism argues that a woman choosing an abortion is exercising a basic right of bodily integrity granted in our common law tradition. If she does not choose to be physically involved in the demands of a pregnancy and birth, she should not be compelled to be so against her will. Just because it is *her* body which is involved, a woman should have the right to terminate any pregnancy, which at this point in medical history is tantamount to terminating fetal life. No one can be forced to donate an organ or submit to other invasive physical procedures for however good a cause. Thus no woman should be subjected to "compulsory pregnancy." And it should be noted that in pregnancy much more than a passive biological process is at stake.

From one perspective, the fetus is, as Petchesky says, a "biological parasite" taking resources from the woman's body. During pregnancy, a woman's whole life and energies will be actively involved in the nine-month process. Gestation and childbirth involve physical and psychological risks. After childbirth a woman will either be a mother who must undertake a twenty-year responsibility for childrearing, or face giving up her child for adoption or institutionalization. Since hers is the body, hers the risk, hers the burden, it is only just that she alone should be free to decide on pregnancy or abortion.

This moral claim to abortion, according to the pro-choice feminists, is especially valid in an individualistic society in which women cannot count on medical care or social support in pregnancy, childbirth, or childrearing. A moral abortion decision is never made in a social vacuum, but in the real life society which exists here and now.

2. The moral necessity of autonomy and choice in personal responsibility. Beyond the claim for individual *bodily* integrity, the pro-choice feminists claim that to be a full adult *morally,* a woman must be able to make responsible life commitments. To plan, choose, and exercise personal responsibility, one must have control of reproduction. A woman must be able to make yes or no decisions about a specific pregnancy, according to her present situation, resources, prior commitments, and life plan. Only with such reproductive freedom can a woman have the moral autonomy necessary to make mature commitments, in the area of family, work, or education.

Contraception provides a measure of personal control, but contraceptive failure or other chance events can too easily result in involuntary pregnancy. Only free access to abortion can provide the necessary guarantee. The chance biological proces of an involuntary pregnancy should not be allowed to override all the other personal commitments and responsibilities a woman has: to others, to family, to work, to education, to her future development, health, or well-being. Without reproductive freedom, women's personal moral agency and human consciousness are subjected to biology and chance.

3. The moral claim for the contingent value of fetal life. Pro-choice feminist exponents like Harrison and Petchesky claim that the value of fetal life is contingent upon the woman's free consent and subjective acceptance. The fetus must be invested with material valuing in order to become human. This process of "humanization" through personal consciousness and "sociality" can only be bestowed by the woman in whose body and psychosocial system a new life must mature. The meaning and value of fetal life are constructed by the woman; without this personal conferral there only exists a biological, physiological process. Thus fetal interests or fetal rights can never outweigh the woman's prior interest and rights. If a woman does not consent to invest her pregnancy with meaning or value, then the merely biological process can be freely terminated. Prior to her own free choice and conscious investment, a woman cannot be described as a "mother" nor can a "child" be said to exist.

Moreover, in cases of voluntary pregnancy, a woman can withdraw consent if fetal genetic defects or some other problem emerges at any time before birth. Late abortion should thus be granted without legal restrictions. Even the minimal qualifications and limitations on women embedded in *Roe v. Wade* are unacceptable—repressive remnants of patriarchal unwillingness to give power to women.

4. The moral right of women to full social equality. Women have a moral right to full social equality. They should not be restricted or subordinated because of their sex. But this morally required equality cannot be realized without abortion's certain control of reproduction. Female social equality depends upon being able to compete and participate as freely as males can in the structures of educational and economic life. If a woman cannot control when and how she will be pregnant or rear children, she is at a distinct disadvantage, especially in our male-dominated world.

Psychological equality and well-being is also at stake. Women must enjoy the basic right of a person to the free exercise of heterosexual intercourse and full sexual expression, separated from procreation. No less than males, women should be able to be sexually active without the constantly inhibiting fear of pregnancy. Abortion is necessary for women's sexual fulfillment and the growth of uninhibited feminine self-confidence and ownership of their sexual powers.

But true sexual and reproductive freedom means freedom to procreate as well as to inhibit fertility. Pro-choice feminists are also worried that women's freedom to reproduce will be curtailed through the abuse of sterilization and needless hysterectomies. Besides the punitive tendencies of a male-dominated healthcare system, especially in response to repeated abortions or welfare pregnancies, there are other economic and social pressures inhibiting reproduction. Genuine reproductive freedom implies that day care, medical care, and financial support would be provided mothers, while fathers would take their full share in the burdens and delights of raising children.

Many pro-choice feminists identify feminist ideals with communitarian, ecologically sensitive approaches to reshaping society. Following theorists like Sara Ruddick and Carol Gilligan, they link abortion rights with the growth of "maternal thinking" in our heretofore patriarchal society. Maternal thinking is loosely defined as a responsible commitment to the loving nurture of specific human beings as they actually exist in socially embedded interpersonal contexts. It is a moral perspective very different from the abstract, competitive, isolated, and principled rigidity so characteristic of patriarchy.

How does a pro-life feminist response to these arguments? Pro-life feminists grant the good intentions of their pro-choice counterparts but protest that the pro-choice position is flawed, morally inadequate, and inconsistent with feminism's basic demands for justice. Pro-life feminists champion a more encompassing moral ideal. They recognize the claims of fetal life and offer a different perspective on what is good for women. The feminist vision is expanded and refocused.

1. From the moral right to control one's own body to a more inclusive ideal of justice. The moral right to control one's own body does apply to cases of organ transplants, mastectomies, contraception, and sterilization; but it is not a conceptualization adequate for abortion. The abortion dilemma is caused by the fact that 266 days following a conception in one body, another body will emerge. One's own body no longer exists as a single unit but is engendering another organism's life. This dynamic passage from conception to birth is genetically ordered and universally found in the human species. Pregnancy is not like the growth of cancer or infestation by a biological parasite; it is the way every human being enters the world. Strained philosophical analogies fail to apply: having a baby is not like rescuing a drowning person, being hooked up to a famous violinist's artificial life-support system, donating organs for transplant—or anything else.

As embryology and fetology advance, it becomes clear that human development is a continuum. Just as astronomers are studying the first three minutes in the genesis of the universe, so the first moments, days, and weeks at the beginning of human life are the subject of increasing scientific attention. While neonatology pushes the definition of viability ever earlier, ultrasound and fetology expand the concept of the patient in utero. Within such a continuous growth process, it is hard to defend logically any demarcation point after conception as the point at which an immature form of human life is so different from the day before or the day after, that it can be morally or legally discounted as a non-person. Even the moment of birth can hardly differentiate a nine-month fetus from a newborn. It is not surprising that those who countenance late abortions are logically led to endorse selective infanticide.

The same legal tradition which in our society guarantees the right to control one's own body firmly recognizes the wrongfulness of harming other bodies, however immature, dependent, different looking, or powerless. The handicapped, the retarded, and newborns are legally protected from deliberate harm. Pro-life feminists reject the suppositions that would except the unborn from this protection.

After all, debates similar to those about the fetus were once conducted about feminine personhood. Just as women, or blacks, were considered too different, too underdeveloped, too "biological," to have souls or to possess legal rights, so the fetus is now seen as "merely" biological life, subsidiary to a person. A woman was once viewed as incorporated into the "one flesh" of her husband's person; she too was a form of bodily property. In all patriarchal unjust systems, lesser orders of human life are granted rights only when wanted, chosen, or invested with value by the powerful.

Fortunately, in the course of civilization there has been a gradual realization that justice demands the powerless and dependent be protected against the uses of power wielded unilaterally. No human can be treated as a means to an end without consent. The fetus is an immature, dependent form of human life which only needs time and protection to develop. Surely, immaturity and dependence are not crimes.

In an effort to think about the essential requirements of a just society, philosophers like John Rawls recommend imagining yourself in an "original position," in which your position in the society to be created is hidden by a "veil of ignorance." You will have to weigh the possibility that any inequalities inherent in that society's practices may rebound upon you in the worst, as well as in the best, conceivable way. This thought experiment helps ensure justice for all.

Beverly Harrison argues that in such an envisioning of society everyone would institute abortion rights in order to guarantee that if one turned out to be a woman one would have reproductive freedom. But surely in the original position and behind the "veil of ignorance," you would have to contemplate the possibility of being the particular fetus to be aborted. Since everyone has passed through the fetal stage of development, it is false to refuse to imagine oneself in this state when thinking about a potential world in which justice would govern. Would it be just that an embryonic life—in half the cases, of course, a female life—be sacrificed to the right of a woman's control over her own body? A woman may be pregnant without consent and experience a great many penalties, but a fetus killed without consent pays the ultimate penalty.

It does not matter (*The Silent Scream* notwithstanding) whether the fetus being killed is fully conscious or feels pain. We do not sanction killing the innocent if it can be done painlessly or without the victim's awareness. Consciousness becomes important to the abortion debate because it is used as a criterion for the "personhood" so often seen as the prerequisite for legal protection. Yet certain philosophers set the standard of personhood so high that half the human race could not meet the criteria during most of their waking hours (let alone their sleeping ones). Sentience, self-consciousness, rational decision-making, social participation? Surely no infant, or child under two, could qualify. Either our idea of person must be expanded or another criterion, such as human life itself, be employed to protect the weak in a just society. Pro-life feminists who defend the fetus empathetically identify with an immature state of growth passed through by themselves, their children, and everyone now alive.

It also seems a travesty of just procedures that a pregnant woman now, in effect, acts as sole judge of her own case, under the most stressful conditions. Yes, one can acknowledge that the pregnant woman will be subject to the potential burdens arising from a pregnancy, but it has never been thought right to have an interested party, especially the more powerful party, decide his or her own case when there may be a conflict of interest. If one considers the matter as a case of a powerful versus a powerless, silenced claimant, the pro-choice feminist argument can rightly be inverted: since hers is the body, hers the risk, and hers the greater burden, then how in fairness can a woman be the sole judge of the fetal right to life?

Human ambivalence, a bias toward self-interest, and emotional stress have always been recognized as endangering judgment. Freud declared that love and hate are so entwined that if instant thoughts could kill, we would all be dead in the bosom of our families. In the case of a woman's involuntary pregnancy, a complex, long-term solution requiring effort and energy has to compete with the immediate solution offered by a morning's visit to an abortion clinic. On the simple, perceptual plane, with imagination and thinking curtailed, the speed, ease, and privacy of abortion, combined with the small size of the embryo, tend to make early abortions seem less morally serious—even though speed, size, technical ease, and the private nature of an act have no moral standing.

As the most recent immigrants from non-personhood, feminists have traditionally fought for justice for themselves and the world. Women rally to feminisn as a new and better way to live. Rejecting male aggression and destruction, feminists seek alternative, peaceful, ecologically sensitive means to resolve conflicts while respecting human potentiality. It is a chilling inconsistency to see pro-choice feminists demanding continued access to assembly-line, technological methods of fetal killing—the vacuum aspirator, prostaglandins, and dilation and evacuation. It is a betrayal of feminism, which has built the struggle for justice on the bedrock of women's empathy. After all, "maternal thinking" receives its name from a mother's unconditional acceptance and nurture of dependent, immature life. It is difficult to develop concern for women, children, the poor and the dispossessed— and to care about peace—and at the same time ignore fetal life.

2. From the necessity of autonomy and choice in personal responsibility to an expanded sense of responsibility. A distorted idea of morality overemphasizes individual autonomy and active choice. Morality has often been viewed too exclusively as a matter of human agency and decisive action. In moral behavior persons must explicitly choose and aggressively exert their wills to intervene in the natural and social environments. The human will dominates the body, overcomes the given, breaks out of the material limits of nature. Thus if one does not choose to be pregnant or cannot rear a child, who must be given up for adoption, then better to abort the pregnancy. Willing, planning, choosing one's moral commitments through the contracting of one's individual resources becomes the premier model of moral responsibility.

But morality also consists of the good and worthy acceptance of the unexpected events that life presents. Responsiveness and response-ability to things unchosen are also instances of the highest human moral capacity. Morality is not confined to contracted agreements of isolated individuals. Yes, one is obligated by explicit contracts freely initiated, but human beings are also obligated by implicit compacts and involuntary relationships in which persons simply find themselves. To be embedded in a family, a neighborhood, a social system, brings moral obligations which were never entered into with informed consent.

Parent-child relationships are one instance of implicit moral obligations arising by virtue of our being part of the interdependent human community. A woman, involuntarily pregnant, has a moral obligation to the now-existing dependent fetus whether she explicitly consented to its existence or not. No pro-life feminist would dispute the forceful observations of pro-choice feminists about the extreme difficulties that bearing an unwanted child in our society can entail. But the stronger force of the fetal claim presses a woman to accept these burdens; the fetus possesses rights arising from its extreme need and the interdependency and unity of humankind. The woman's moral obligation arises both from her status as a human being embedded in the interdependent human community and her unique lifegiving female reproductive power. To follow the pro-choice feminist ideology of insistent individualistic autonomy and control is to betray a fundamental basis of the moral life.

3. From the moral claim of the contingent value of fetal life to the moral claim for the intrinsic value of human life. The feminist pro-choice position which claims that the value of the fetus is contingent upon the pregnant woman's bestowal—or willed, conscious "construction"—of humanhood is seriously flawed. The inadequacies of this position flow from the erroneous premises (1) that human value and rights can be granted by individual will; (2) that the individual woman's consciousness can exist and operate in an *a priori* isolated fashion; and (3) that "mere" biological, genetic human life has little meaning. Pro-life feminism takes a very different stance to life and nature.

Human life from the beginning to the end of development *has* intrinsic value, which does not depend on meeting the selective criteria or tests set up by powerful others. A fundamental humanist assumption is at stake here. Either we are going to value embodied human life and humanity as a good thing, or take some variant of the nihilist position that assumes human life is just one more random occurrence in the universe such that each instance of human life must explicitly be justified to prove itself worthy to continue. When faced with a new life, or an involuntary pregnancy, there is a world of difference in whether one first asks, "Why continue?" or "Why not?" Where is the burden of proof going to rest? The concept of "compulsory pregnancy" is as distorted as labeling life "compulsory aging."

In a sound moral tradition, human rights arise from human needs, and it is the very nature of a right, or valid claim upon another, that it cannot be denied, conditionally delayed, or rescinded by more powerful others at their behest. It seems fallacious to hold that in the case of the fetus it is the pregnant woman alone who gives or removes its right to life and human status solely through her subjective conscious investment or "humanization." Surely no pregnant woman (or any other individual member of the species) has created her own human nature by an individually willed act of consciousness, nor for that matter been able to guarantee her own human rights. An individual woman and the unique individual embryonic life within her can only exist because of their participation in the genetic inheritance of the human species as a whole. Biological life should never be discounted. Membership in the species, or collective human family, is the basis for human solidarity, equality, and natural human rights.

4. The moral right of women to full social equality from a pro-life feminist perspective. Pro-life feminists and pro-choice feminists are totally agreed on the moral right of women to the full social equality so far denied them. The disagreement between them concerns the definition of the desired goal and the best means to get there. Permissive abortion laws do not bring women reproductive freedom, social equality, sexual fulfillment, or full personal development.

Pragmatic failures of a pro-choice feminist position combined with a lack of moral vision are, in fact, causing disaffection among young women. Middle-aged pro-choice feminists blamed the "big chill" on the general conservative backlash. But they should look rather to their own elitist acceptance of male models of sex and to the sad picture they present of women's lives. Pitting women against their own offspring is not only morally offensive, it is psychologically and politically destructive. Women will never climb to equality and social empowerment over mounds of dead fetuses, numbering now in the millions. As long as most women choose to bear children, they stand to gain from the same constellation of attitudes and institutions that will also protect the fetus in the woman's womb—and they stand to lose from the cultural assumptions that support permissive abortion. Despite temporary conflicts of interest, feminine and fetal liberation are ultimately one and the same cause.

Women's rights and liberation are pragmatically linked to fetal rights because to obtain true equality, women need (1) more social support and changes in the structure of society, and (2) increased self-confidence, self-expectations, and self-esteem. Society in general, and men in particular, have to provide women more support in rearing the next generation, or our devastating feminization of poverty will continue. But if a woman claims the right to decide by herself whether the fetus becomes a child or not, what does this do to parental and communal responsibility? Why should men share responsibility for child support or child-rearing if they cannot share in what is asserted to be the woman's sole decision? Furthermore, if explicit intentions and consciously accepted contracts are necessary for moral obligations, why should men be held responsible for what *they* do not voluntarily choose to happen? By pro-choice reasoning, a man who does not want to have a child, or whose contraceptive fails, can be exempted from the responsibilities of fatherhood and child support. Traditionally, many men have been laggards in assuming parental responsibility and support for their children; ironically, ready abortion, often advocated as a response to male dereliction, legitimizes male irresponsibility and paves the way for even more male detachment and lack of commitment.

For that matter, why should the state provide a system of day-care or child support, or require workplaces to accommodate women's maternity and the needs of childrearing? Permissive abortion, granted in the name of women's privacy and reproductive freedom, ratifies the view that pregnancies and children are a woman's private individual responsibility. More and more frequently, we hear some version of this old rationalization: if she refuses to get rid of it, it's her problem. A child becomes a product of the individual woman's freely chosen investment, a form of private property resulting from her own cost-benefit calculation. The larger community is relieved of moral responsibility.

With legal abortion freely available, a clear cultural message is given: conception and pregnancy are no longer serious moral matters. With abortion as an acceptable alternative, contraception is not as responsibly used; women take risks, often at the urging of male sexual partners. Repeat abortions increase, with all their psychological and medical repercussions. With more abortion there is more abortion. Behavior shapes thought as well as the other way round. One tends to justify morally what one has done; what becomes commonplace and institutionalized seems harmless. Habituation is a powerful psychological force. Psychologically it is also true that whatever is avoided becomes more threatening; in phobias it is the retreat from anxiety-producing events which reinforces future avoidance. Women begin to see themselves as too weak to cope with involuntary pregnancies. Finally, through the potency of social pressure and the force of inertia, it becomes more and more difficult, in fact almost unthinkable, *not* to use abortion to solve problem pregnancies. Abortion becomes no longer a choice but a "necessity."

But "necessity," beyond the organic failure and death of the body, is a dynamic social construction open to interpretation. The thrust of present feminist pro-choice arguments can only increase the justifiable indications for "necessary" abortion; every unwanted fetal handicap becomes more and more unacceptable. Repeatedly assured that in the name of reproductive freedom, women have a right to specify which pregnancies and which children they will accept, women justify sex selection, and abort unwanted females. Female infanticide, after all, is probably as old a custom as the human species possesses. Indeed, all kinds of selection of the fit and the favored for the good of the family and the tribe have always existed. Selective extinction is no new program.

There are far better goals for feminists to pursue. Pro-life feminists seek to expand and deepen the more communitarian, maternal elements of feminism—and move society from its male-dominated course. First and foremost, women have to insist upon a different, woman-centered approach to sex and reproduction. While Margaret Mead stressed the "womb envy" of males in other societies, it has been more or less repressed in our own. In our male-dominated world, what men don't do, doesn't count. Pregnancy, childbirth, and nursing have been characterized as passive, debilitating, animal-like. The disease model of pregnancy and birth has been entrenched. This female disease or impairment, with its attendant "female troubles," naturally handicaps women in the "real" world of hunting, war, and the corporate fast track. Many pro-choice feminists, deliberately childless, adopt the male perspective when they cite the "basic injustice that women have to bear the babies," instead of seeing the injustice in the fact that men cannot. Women's biologically unique capacity and privilege has been denied, despised, and suppressed under male domination; unfortunately, many women have fallen for the phallic fallacy.

Childbirth often appears in pro-choice literature as a painful, traumatic, life-threatening experience. Yet giving birth is accurately seen as an arduous but normal exercise of lifegiving power, a violent and ecstatic peak experience, which men can never know. Ironically, some pro-choice men and women think and talk of pregnancy and childbirth with the same repugnance that ancient ascetics displayed toward orgasms and sexual intercourse. The similarity may not be accidental. The obstetrician Niles Newton, herself a mother, has written of the extended threefold sexuality of women, who can experience orgasm, birth, and nursing as passionate pleasure-giving experiences. All of these are involuntary processes of the female body. Only orgasm, which males share, has been glorified as an involuntary function that is nature's great gift; the involuntary feminine processes of childbirth and nursing have been seen as bondage to biology.

Fully accepting our bodies as ourselves, what should woman want? I think women will only flourish when there is a feminization of sexuality, very different from the current cultural trend toward masculinizing female sexuality. Women can never have the self-confidence and self-esteem they need to achieve feminist goals in society until a more holistic, feminine model of sexuality becomes the dominant cultural ethos. To say this affirms the view that men and women differ in the domain of sexual functioning, although they are more alike than different in other personality characteristics and competencies. For those of us committed to achieving sexual equality in the culture, it may be hard to accept the fact that sexual differences make it imperative to talk of distinct male and female models of sexuality. But if one wants to change sexual roles, one has to recognize pre-existing conditions. A great deal of evidence is accumulating which points to biological pressures for different male and female sexual functioning.

Males always and everywhere have been more physically aggressive and more likely to fuse sexuality with aggression and dominance. Females may be more variable in their sexuality, but since Masters and Johnson, we know that women have a greater capacity than men for repeated orgasm and a more tenuous path to arousal and orgasmic release. Most obviously, women also have a far greater sociobiological investment in the act of human reproduction. On the whole, women as compared to men possess a sexuality which is more complex, more intense, more extended in time, involving higher investment, risks, and psychosocial involvement.

Considering the differences in sexual functioning, it is not surprising that men and women in the same culture have often constructed different sexual ideals. In Western culture, since the nineteenth century at least, most women have espoused a version of sexual functioning in which sex acts are embedded within deep emotional bonds and secure long-term commitments. Within these committed "pair bonds" males assume parental obligations. In the idealized Victorian version of the Christian sexual ethic, culturally endorsed and maintained by women, the double standard was not countenanced. Men and women did not need to marry to be whole persons, but if they did engage in sexual functioning, they were to be equally chaste, faithful, responsible, loving, and parentally concerned. Many of the most influential women in the nineteenth-century women's movement preached and lived this sexual ethic, often by the side of exemplary feminist men. While the ideal has never been universally obtained, a culturally dominant demand for monogamy, self-control, and emotionally bonded and committed sex works well for women in every stage of their sexual life cycles. When love, chastity, fidelity, and commitment for better or worse are the ascendant cultural prerequisites for sexual functioning, young girls and women expect protection from rape and seduction, adult women justifiably demand male support in childrearing, and older women are more protected from abandonment as their biological attractions wane.

Of course, these feminine sexual ideals always coexisted in competition with another view. A more male-oriented model of erotic or amative sexuality endorses sexual permissiveness without long-term commitment or reproductive focus. Erotic sexuality emphasizes pleasure, play, passion, individual self-expression, and romantic games of courtship and conquest. If is assumed that a variety of partners and sexual experiences are necessary to stimulate romantic passion. This erotic model of the sexual life has often worked satisfactorily for men, both heterosexual and gay, and for certain cultural elites. But for the average woman, it is quite destructive. Women can only play the erotic game successfully when like the "*Cosmopolitan* woman," they are young, physically attractive, economically powerful, and fulfilled enough in a career to be willing to sacrifice family life. Abortion is also required. As our society increasingly endorses this male-oriented, permissive view of sexuality, it is all too ready to give women abortion on demand. Abortion helps a woman's body be more like a man's. It has been observed that *Roe v. Wade* removed the last defense women possessed against male sexual demands.

Unfortunately, the modern feminist movement made a mistaken move at a critical juncture. Rightly rebelling against patriarchy, unequal education, restricted work opportunities, and women's downtrodden political status, feminists also rejected the nineteenth-century feminine sexual ethic. Amative, erotic, permissive sexuality (along with abortion rights) became symbolically identified with other struggles for social equality in education, work, and politics. This feminist mistake also turned off many potential recruits among women who could not deny the positive dimensions of their own traditional feminine roles, nor their allegiance to the older feminine sexual ethic of love and fidelity.

An ironic situation then arose in which many pro-choice feminists preach their own double standard. In the world of work and career, women are urged to grow up, to display mature self-discipline and self-control; they are told to persevere in long-term commitments, to cope with unexpected obstacles by learning to tough out the inevitable sufferings and setbacks entailed in life and work. But this mature ethic of commitment and self-discipline, recommended as the only way to progress in the world of work and personal achievement, is discounted in the domain of sexuality.

In pro-choice feminism, a permissive, erotic view of sexuality is assumed to be the only option. Sexual intercourse with a variety of partners is seen as "inevitable" from a young age and as a positive growth experience to be managed by access to contraception and abortion. Unfortunately, the pervasive cultural conviction that adolescents, or their elders, cannot exercise sexual self-control, undermines the responsible use of contaception. When a pregnancy occurs, the first abortion is viewed in some pro-choice circles as a *rite de passage*. Responsibly choosing an abortion supposedly ensures that a young woman will take charge of her own life, make her own decisions, and carefully practice contraception. But the social dynamics of a permissive, erotic model of sexuality, coupled with permissive laws, work toward repeat abortions. Instead of being empowered by their abortion choices, young women having abortions are confronting the debilitating reality of *not* bringing a baby into the world; *not* being able to count on a committed male partner; *not* accounting oneself strong enough, or the master of enough resources, to avoid killing the fetus. Young women are hardly going to develop the self-esteem, self-discipline, and self-confidence necessary to confront a male-dominated society through abortion.

The male-oriented sexual orientation has been harmful to women and children. It has helped bring us epidemics of venereal disease, infertility, pornography, sexual abuse, adolescent pregnancy, divorce, displaced older women, and abortion. Will these signals of something amiss stimulate pro-choice feminists to rethink what kind of sex ideal really serves women's best interests? While the erotic model cannot encompass commitment, the committed model can—happily encompass and encourage romance, passion, and playfulness. In fact, within the security of long-term commitments, women may be more likely to experience sexual pleasure and fulfillment.

The pro-life feminist position is not a return to the feminine mystique. That espousal of "the eternal feminine" erred by viewing sexuality as so sacred that it cannot be humanly shaped at all. Women's *whole* nature is supposed to be opposite to man's, necessitating complementary and radically different social roles. Followed to its logical conclusion, such a view presumes that reproductive and sexual experience is necessary for human fulfillment. But as the anti-feminists insisted, no woman has to marry or engage in sexual intercourse to be fulfilled, nor does a woman have to give birth and raise children to be complete, nor must she stay home and function as an earth mother. But female sexuality does need to be deeply respected as a unique potential and trust. Since modern contraceptives and sterilization procedures really do involve only the woman's body rather than destroying new life, they can be an acceptable and responsible moral option.

With sterilization available to accelerate the inevitable natural ending of fertility and childbearing, a woman confronts only a limited number of years in which she exercises the reproductive trust and may have to respond to unplanned pregnancy. Responsible use of contraception can lower the probabilities even more. Yet abortion is not decreasing. The reason is the current permissive attitude embodied in the law, not the "hard cases" which constitute 3 percent of today's abortions. Since attitudes, the law, and behavior interact, pro-life feminists conclude that unless there is an enforced limitation of abortion, which currently confirms the sexual and social status quo, alternatives will never be developed.

For women to get what they need in order to combine childbearing, education, and careers, society has to recognize that female bodies come with wombs. Women and their reproductive power, and the children women have, must be supported in new ways. Another and different round of feminist consciousness-raising is needed in which all of women's potential is accorded respect. This time, instead of humbly buying entrée by conforming to male lifestyles, women will demand that society accommodate to them.

New feminist efforts to rethink the meaning of sexuality, femininity, and reproduction are all the more vital as new techniques for artificial reproduction, surrogate motherhood, and the like present a whole new set of dilemmas. In the long run, the very long run, the abortion debate may be merely the opening round in a series of far-reaching struggles over the role of human sexuality and the ethics of reproduction. Significant changes in the culture, both positive and negative in outcome, may begin as local storms of controversy. We may be at one of those vaguely realized thresholds when we had best come to full attention. What kind of people are we going to be? Pro-life feminists pursue a vision for their sisters, daughters, and granddaughters. Will their great-granddaughters be grateful?

A Catholic Theologian at an Abortion Clinic

Daniel C. Maguire

I should not have been nervous the first day I drove to the abortion clinic. After all, I wasn't pregnant. There would be no abortions done this day. I would see no patients and no picketers. And yet tremors from a Catholic boyhood wrenched my usually imperturbable stomach. I was filled with dread and foreboding.

What was it that brought this Philadelphia Irish-Catholic male moral theologian to the clinic door? Abortion has not been my academic obsession. My wife and I have had no personal experience with abortion, although it once loomed as a possible choice in our lives. Our first son, Danny, was diagnosed as terminally ill with Hunter's syndrome when Margie was three months pregnant with our second child. However, amniocentesis revealed that the fetus, now Tommy, was normal.

The stimulus for my visit was the woman who agonized with Margie and me over the decision she had rather conclusively made, and asked us, as ethicists, to ponder with her all the pro's and con's. She was almost six weeks pregnant. Her life situation was seriously incompatible with parenting and she could not bear the thought of adoption. After her abortion, she told us she had made the right decision, but she paid the price in tears and trauma.

More generally, I was drawn to this uneasy experience by women. I have often discussed abortion with women in recent years, been struck by how differently they viewed it. I experienced their resentment at the treatment of the subject by the male club of moral theologians. One woman, an author and professor at a Chicago seminary, wrote me after reading my first article on abortion ("Abortion: A Question of Catholic Honesty," *The Christian Century,* September 14–21, 1983) thanking me and surprising me. She said she found it difficult to use the American bishops' pastoral letter on nuclear war because these *men* could agonize so long over the problems of *men* who might decide to end the world, but had not a sympathetic minute for the moral concerns of a woman who judges that she cannot bring her pregnancy to term.

I knew that my visit would not give me a woman's understanding of the abortion decision, but I hoped it might assist me, in the phrase of French novelist Jean Sulivan, to "lie less" when I write this subject and to offend less those women who come this way in pain.

Those who write on liberation theology go to Latin America to learn; those who write on abortion stay at their desks. Until recently, all churchly writing on abortion has been done by desk-bound celibate males. If experience is the plasma of theory, the experience obtained in a clinic three blocks from Marquette, where I teach and have done research on abortion, could only enhance my theological ministry.

MEETING THE CLINIC STAFF

One day last May, I called the Milwaukee Women's Health Organization and spoke to its director, Elinor Yeo, an ordained minister of the United Church of Christ. I was afraid she would find my request to spend time at her clinic unseemly and out of order. She said she would call back when she finished an interview with a patient and spoke to her staff. She called later to tell me that the staff was enthusiastic about my prospective visits, adding the ironic note that the patient she was interviewing when I first called was a Marquette University undergraduate.

The clinic door still had traces of red paint from a recent attack. The door was buzzed open only after I was identified. A sign inside read: PLEASE HELP OUR GUARD. WE MAY NEED WITNESSES IF THE PICKETS GET OUT OF CONTROL. YOU CAN HELP BY OBSERVING AND LETTING HIM/HER KNOW IF YOU SEE TROUBLE. I realized that these people live and work in fear of "pro-life" violence. In the first half of this year there have been 58 reported incidents of criminal violence at clinics, including bombing, arson, shootings, and vandalism.

Elinor Yeo sat with me for more than an hour describing the clinic's activities. Half of its patients are teenagers; half, Catholic; and 20 percent, black. Of the 14 patients seen on a single day the previous week, one was 13 years old; one, 14; and, one 15. Nationally, most abortions are performed within eight weeks of conception, at which point the *conceptus* is still properly called an embryo; 91 percent are within 12 weeks. At this clinic, too, most abortions are performed in the first two months. Most of the patients are poor; the clinic is busiest at the time when welfare checks come in. The normal cost for an abortion here is $185. For those on public assistance, it is $100.

I asked Elinor about the right-to-lifers' claim that most women who have abortions are rich. She replied: "The typical age of an abortion patient at this clinic is 19 years." In what sense is a 19-year-old woman with an unwanted pregnancy rich?

I asked about the charge that doing abortions makes doctors rich. She assured me that, given their budget, all the doctors who work for them would make more if they remained in their offices. These doctors are also sometimes subject to harassment and picketing at their homes. Their care of patients is excellent, and they often end up delivering babies for these same women at some later date.

Each patient is given private counseling. About half want their male partners with them for these sessions. If there is any indication that the man is more anxious for the abortion than the woman, private counseling is carefully arranged. Every interested woman is offered the opportunity to study charts on embryonic and fetal development, and all women are informed of alternatives to abortion. The consent form, to be signed at the end of the interview and counseling sessions, includes the words: "I have been informed of agencies and services available to assist me to carry my pregnancy to term should I desire. . . . The nature and purposes of an abortion, the alternatives to pregnancy termination, the risks involved, and the possibility of complications have been fully explained to me."

All counselors stress reproductive responsibility. Two of the counselors have worked with Elinor for 14 years. One is the mother of five children, the other, of three. Free follow-up advice on contraception is made available. It is the explicit goal of the counselors not to have the woman return for another abortion. According to Yeo, those most likely to have repeat abortions are women who reject contraceptive information and say they will never have sex again until they are married. It became ironically clear to me that the women working in this abortion clinic prevent more abortions than the zealous pickets demonstrating outside.

Yeo says that only 5 percent of the patients have ever seriously considered adoption as an alternative. *Abortion* or *keeping* are the two options considered by these young women. (Ninety-five percent of teenagers who deliver babies keep them, according to Elinor Yeo.)

Adoption is, of course, the facile recommendation of the bumper-sticker level of this debate. One patient I spoke to at a subsequent visit to the clinic told me how unbearable the prospect was of going to term and then giving up the born baby. For impressive reasons she found herself in no condition to have a baby. Yet she had begun to take vitamins to nourish the embryo in case she changed her mind. "If I continued this nurture for nine months, how could I hand over to someone else what would then be my baby?" It struck me forcefully how aloof and misogynist it is not to see that the adoption path is full of pain. Here is one more instance of male moralists prescribing the heroic for women as though it were simply moral and mandatory.

The surgery lasts some 5 to 15 minutes. General anesthesia is not needed in these early abortions. Most women are in and out of the clinic in two and one half hours. They return in two weeks for a checkup. These early abortions are done by suction. I was shown the suction tube that is used and was surprised to find that it is only about twice the width of a drinking straw. This was early empirical information for me as to *what* it is that is aborted at this stage.

All patients are warned about pregnancy aftermath groups that advertise and offer support but actually attempt to play on guilt and recruit these women in their campaign to outlaw all abortions, even those performed for reasons of health. One fundamentalist Protestant group in Milwaukee advertises free pregnancy testing. When the woman arrives, they subject her to grisly slides on abortions of well-developed fetuses. They take the woman's address and phone number and tell her they will contact her in two weeks at home. The effects of this are intimidating and violative of privacy and often lead to delayed abortions of more developed fetuses.

MEETING THE WOMEN

My second visit was on a Saturday when the clinic was busy. I arrived at 8:30 in the morning. The picketers were already there, all men, except for one woman with a boy of 10. A patient was in the waiting room, alone. We greeted each other, and I sat down and busied myself with some papers, wondering what was going on in her mind. I was later to learn that she was five to six weeks pregnant. I was told that she was under psychiatric care for manic-depression, and receiving high doses of lithium to keep her mood swings under control. However, lithium in high doses may be injurious to the formation of the heart in embryos and early fetuses.

Pro-life? Pro-choice? How vacuous the slogans seemed in the face of this living dilemma. What life options were open to this woman? Only at the expense of her emotional well-being could a reasonably formed fetus come to term. This woman had driven alone a long distance that morning to get to the clinic and she would have to return home alone afterward. She had to walk to the door past demonstrators showing her pictures of fully formed fetuses and begging her: "Don't kill your baby! Don't do it." However well-intentioned they may be, in what meaningful moral sense were those picketers in this instance pro-life?

As I watched this woman I thought of one of my colleagues who had recently made a confident assertion that there could be no plausible reason for abortion except to save the physical life of the woman or if the fetus was anencephalic. This woman's physical life was not at risk and the embryo would develop a brain. But saving *life* involves more than cardiopulmonary continuity. How is it that in speaking of women we so easily reduce human life to physical life? What certitudes persuade theologians that there are only two marginal reasons to justify abortion?

Why is the Vatican comparably sure that while there may be *just* wars with incredible slaughter, there can be no *just* abortions? Both need to listen to the woman on lithium as she testifies that life does not always confine itself within the ridges of our theories.

With permission I sat in on some of the initial interviews with parents. The first two were poor teenagers, each with an infant at home, and each trying to finish high school. One was out of work. Elinor Yeo let her know that they were now hiring at "Wendy's." I was impressed that the full human plight of the patients was of constant concern to the staff. The other young woman had just gotten a job after two years and would lose it through pregnancy. One woman counted out her $100 and said: "I hate to give this up; I need it so much."

The staff told me about the various causes of unwanted pregnancies. One staff member said that it would seem that most young men have "scorn for condoms." "Making love" does not describe those sexual invasions. For these hostile insem-inators nothing is allowed to interfere with their pleasure. Often there is contra-ceptive failure. One recent case involved a failed vasectomy. Sometimes conception is admittedly alcohol- and drug-related. A few women concede that they were "testing the relationship." Often it is a case of a broken relationship where the woman, suddenly alone, feels unable to bring up a child. Economic causes were most common. Lack of job, lack of insurance, a desire to stay in school and break out of poverty.

I wondered how many "pro-lifers" voted for Ronald Reagan because of his antiabortion noises, even though Reaganomics decreased the income of the lowest fifth of society's families by 8 percent while increasing the income of the rich. More of this could only be more poverty, more ruin, more social chaos, more unwanted pregnancies, and more women at clinic doors.

MEETING THE PICKETERS

The picketers are a scary lot. Because of them a guard has to be on duty to escort the patients from their cars. Before the clinic leased the adjacent parking lot—making it their private property—some picketers used to attack the cars of the women, screaming and shaking the car. The guard told me he was once knocked down by a picketer. Without the guard, some of the demonstrators surround an unescorted woman and force her to see and hear their message. Other picketers simply carry placards and pray. One day, 20 boys from Libertyville, Illinois, were bused in to picket. They were not passive. They had been taught to shout at the women as they arrived. One staff member commented: "Statistically, one quarter to one third of these boys will face abortion situations in their lives. I wonder how this experience will serve them then."

A reporter from the Milwaukee *Journal* arrived, and I followed her when she went out to interview the picketers. Two picketers recognized me. Since I have been quoted in the press in ways that did not please, I am a persona non grata to this group. I had a chance to feel what the women patients endure. "You're in the right place, Maguire. In there, where they murder the babies." I decided they were not ripe for dialogue, so I remained silent and listened in on the interview.

I learned that some of these men had been coming to demonstrate every Saturday for nine years. Their language was filled with allusions to the Nazi Holocaust. Clearly, they imagine themselves at the ovens of Auschwitz, standing in noble protest as innocent *persons* are led to their death. There could hardly be any higher drama in their lives. They seem not to know that the Nazis were antiabortion too—for Aryans. They miss the anti-Semitism and insult in this use of Holocaust imagery. The 6 million murdered Jews and more than 3 million Poles, Gypsies, and homosexuals were actual, not potential, persons who were killed. Comparing their human dignity to that of prepersonal embryos is no tribute to the Holocaust dead.

Sexism too is in bold relief among the picketers. Their references to "these women" coming here to "kill their babies" are dripping with hatred. It struck me that for all their avowed commitment to life, these are the successors of the witch-hunters.

MEETING THE EMBRYOS

On my third visit to the clinic, I made bold to ask to see the products of some abortions. I asked in such a way as to make refusal easy, but my request was granted. The aborted matter is placed in small cloth bags and put in jars awaiting disposal. I asked to see the contents of one of the bags of a typical abortion—a six- to nine-week pregnancy—and it was opened and placed in a small metal cup for examination. I held the cup in my hands and saw a small amount of unidentifiable fleshy matter in the bottom of the cup. The quantity was so little that I could have hidden it if I had taken it into my hand and made a fist.

It was impressive to realize that I was holding in the cup what many people think to be the legal and moral peer of a woman, if not, indeed, her superior. I thought too of the Human Life Amendment that would describe what I was seeing as a citizen of the United States with rights of preservation that would countermand the good of the woman bearer. I have held babies in my hands and now I held this embryo. I know the difference.

CONCLUSIONS

• My visits to the clinic made me more anxious to maintain the legality of abortions for women who judged they need them. There are no moral grounds for political consensus against this freedom on an issue where good experts and good people disagree. It also made me anxious to work to reduce the need for abortion by fighting the causes of unwanted pregnancies: *sexism* enforced by the institutions of church, synagogue, and state that diminishes a woman's sense of autonomy; *poverty* induced by skewed budgets; *antisexual* bias that leads to eruptive sex; and the other *macro* causes of these micro tragedies.

● I came to understand that abortion can be the *least* violent option facing a woman. It is brutally insensitive to pretend that for women who resort to abortion, death is the only extremity they face.

● I came away from the clinic with a new longing for a moratorium on self-righteousness and sanctimonious utterances from Catholic bishops on the subject of abortion. An adequate Catholic theology of abortion has not yet been written. But the bishops sally forth as though this complex topic were sealed in a simple negative. Bishops like New York's John O'Connor, who use tradition as though it were an oracle instead of an unfinished challenge, are not helping at all. A position like O'Connor's has two yields: (a) it insults the Catholic intellectual tradition by making it look simplistic, and (b) it makes the bishops the allies of a right wing that has been using its newfound love of embryos as an ideological hideaway for many who resist the bishop's call for peace and social justice.

● Finally, I come from the abortion clinic with an appeal to my colleagues in Catholic moral theology. Many theologians (especially clerics) avoid this issue or behave weirdly or skittishly when they touch it. How do Catholic theologians justify their grand silence when they are allowing physicalism, crude historical distortions, and fundamentalistic notions of "Church teaching" to parade as "the Catholic position"? Why are ethical errors that are thoroughly lambasted in the birth-control debate tolerated when the topic is abortion? Geraldine Ferraro and Governor Mario Cuomo of New York are taking the heat and trying to do the theology on this subject. Their debts to American Catholic theologians are minis-cule. What service do we Church teachers give when errors, already corrected in theology, are allowed to roam unchallenged in the pastoral and political spheres? Why are nonexperts, church hierarchy or not, allowed to set the *theological* terms of this debate? What service is it to ecumenism to refuse serious dialogue not only with women but with main-line Jewish and Protestant theologians on this issue? Vatican II said that "ecumenical dialogue could start with discussions concerning the application of the gospel to moral questions." That dialogue has not happened on abortion, and our brothers and sisters from other communions are waiting for it.

I realize, as do my colleagues in Catholic ethics, that abortion is not a pleasant topic. At its best, abortion is a negative value, unlike the positive values of feeding the poor and working for civil rights. On top of that it has become the litmus test of orthodoxy, and that spells danger in the Catholic academe. But, beyond all this, we in the Catholic family have been conditioned against an objective and empathic understanding of abortion. We are more sensitized to embryos than to the women who bear them. I claim no infallibility on this subject, but I do insist that until we open our affections to enlightenment here, we will none of us be wise.

Babies, Anyone?

Katha Pollitt

"I oppose abortion, and I favor adoption," said George Bush in the Sunday debate. He then went on to suggest that although he hadn't yet "sorted out" the matter, "we" would have to "come to grips with the penalty side" were abortion to be made a crime, and left open the possibility of jailing women who have them. By the next day, Bush's handlers had figured out that 1.6 million abortions a year added up to a lot of criminals—and a lot of votes. And so the women who had been murderers the night before were upgraded to "victims" (of card-carrying members of the A.C.L.U., perhaps?), and their doctors took their place as candidates for striped loungewear.

Given the tea-party politesse of the media where the Vice President is concerned, Bush may succeed in his efforts at damage control. So far he has escaped connection with the appalling Republican Party platform, which rejects abortion even to save the mother's life. "Adoption not abortion" is a clever stroke. Just as "pro-life" implies that the opposition is "pro-death," this sound bite implies that pro-choicers would prefer to send a little soul shivering into limbo rather than find it "a family where there will be love."

Once again the pregnant woman has been excised from the abortion debate, as though bearing a child against her will in order to turn it over to strangers were no big deal. Nevertheless, let's consider how the Bush adoption program might work. Say there are about 1 million couples who seriously want to adopt a baby and 1.6 million women who have abortions each year. If abortion became illegal on, say, January 1, 1990, every couple currently in the adoption market would have its bundle of joy by around July 4. Then what? Presumably, the Bush Administration would call upon the "thousand points of light," those little stars of volunteerism bravely twinkling in the Republican night. Thanks to a "take two, they're small" campaign, a fever of altruistic childmania would sweep the land and every family that has ever fantasized about adopting a child would throw caution to the winds and sign up for two. I figure that would bring us up to Labor Day. Then what? Would Jerry Falwell demand that his faith partners take babies as premiums instead of white leather Bibles?

The fact is, adoption cannot be the solution to the problem of unwanted children. The numbers are simply too overwhelming, and would be so even if all the children born after abortion became illegal were the white healthy infants many would-be adoptive parents want. The only way to make a real dent in the abortion rate—legal or illegal—is to lower the unwanted pregnancy rate, the third highest in the industrialized West. The only way to do that is to conquer our national squeamishness about birth control and sex while also providing a full menu of social benefits to mothers and children. I'd like to hear both candidates address these issues in detail but, needless to say, they won't. It wouldn't make a sound bite.

The Right to Life and the Restoration of the American Republic

Lewis E. Lehrman

The Declaration of Independence and the Constitution of the United States inaugurated not only the American experiment, but also one of the great economic booms in history. Americans moved West and South, labored North and East to till the soil, build roads, finance banks, invest in new technologies, discover new methods of farming, mining, and manufacture. "We made the experiment," Lincoln wrote during the prosperity of 1854. In America "we proposed to give all a chance." Now "the fruit is before us. Look at it—think of it. Look at it in its aggregate grandeur, of extent of country and numbers of population—of ship and steamboat and rail."

In 1854, almost four score years had gone by since the Founding, and nearly as many years divided the abject poverty of Thomas Lincoln from the prosperity of his son Abraham, the "lone Whig star" of Illinois. In twenty years of hard work before 1854, Lincoln had been preoccupied with personal advance in law and politics, during which time he had focused on the great issues of economic nationalism: the tariff, the National Bank, and internal improvements. It is true that he was only one among thousands of apostles of national development and economic growth; but he was utterly devoted to their cause.

In 1853, all America basked in the glow of a prosperity Americans took as their just deserts. The period stretching from the inauguration of James Monroe in 1817 through the early 1850s has gone down in American history as the Era of Good Feeling and of Manifest Destiny—an era during which, despite the great perils faced by the infant nation at the turn of the century, America had conquered a continent and established her independence of Europe. The new nation had finally settled down.

Then, out of the Great Plains, the Kansas-Nebraska Act of 1854 blew in upon

American politics with the force of a tornado, sweeping aside the economic issues paramount in the immediate past. The old Whig Party disintegrated under the pressure of the new politics, and so in all but name did the Old Democracy, the party of Jefferson and Jackson—both parties swept aside by the gale force of a single moral issue, or what our pundits today would call a social issue. That issue, the extension of slavery to the territories, led ineluctably to the great national debate over the "unalienable right to liberty" of the black slave. It was neither the first nor the last, but it was, up to that time, the greatest debate over the first principles of the American Republic.

At first, Americans—Democrats and Whigs alike—refused to believe that the work and wealth of recent decades, not to mention the pocketbook politics of the era, would be swallowed up in a moral struggle over a single issue. But, in opening all the Western lands to slaveholding, Kansas-Nebraska shattered the spirit of the Missouri Compromise of 1820, which had limited slavery to states south of 36°30'. If it were true, as Lincoln would later say, that eventually the nation must be all slave or all free, there could be little doubt in which direction the new act was taking us.

In the words of one distinguished historian of the period, Professor Gabor Borritt of Gettysburg College, Kansas-Nebraska shook national politics like Jefferson's "firebell in the night." So abrupt was the transition from preoccupation with economics and national security ("Manifest Destiny" and "Western Lands") that Abraham Lincoln, himself one of the most knowledgeable of Whig leaders on tax, tariff, and banking issues, abandoned further discussion of them. After 1854, he became almost mute on economic issues, claiming in the year he stood for President that "just now [tax, tariff, and financial affairs] cannot even obtain a hearing . . . for, whether we will or not, the question of slavery is *the* question, the all-absorbing topic of the day."

Today, six years after President Reagan's first victory, we are far along with economic expansion and just as far along with rebuilding our national defense. Financial markets have risen to new highs. Employment levels and new business formations have reached new peaks. In Libya and Grenada we have successfully, if ever so cautiously, tested our willingness once again to use force in defense of our national principles and interests. Politicians of both parties still speak as if they expect Americans, riding the wave of new prosperity at home and restored prestige abroad, to continue to focus on economic and defense issues as they have for a generation. As Vice President Bush declared in an interview in June, "Today, people vote their pocketbooks." We shall see.

For I believe that today the American people are prepared to put their pocketbooks back into their pockets. I believe that Americans once again are preparing to ask fundamental questions, about life and death, about our special purpose as a nation, and about the first principles and fundamental law by which, as a nation under God, we have dedicated ourselves to live. I believe that national politics during the late 1980s and the 1990s will be dominated by the great constitutional, moral, and social issues of our time.

Chief among these issues will be the right to life. Thirteen years ago, in *Roe v. Wade,* the Supreme Court overthrew the common law of centuries and the statute law of fifty states, authorized abortion on demand, and thereby severed the child-about-to-be-born from the Declaration of Independence. It was in the Declaration, the organic law of the American Founding, that the Fathers of our country proclaimed the self-evident truths of our fundamental moral and constitutional law: that all men are created equal, and that all men are created by God with the unalienable right to life, liberty, and the pursuit of happiness. It was this original charter of the nation that the Supreme Court violated in *Roe,* without even the mandate of an election or a vote in Congress.

Five thousand days and twenty million lives later, abortion on demand has buried a nation of children as big as the whole of Canada. But far from resolving the issue of the right to life, as the Justices intended, the Court has stirred up all America and ignited the moral tinder deep in the souls of our countrymen. The Court, by creating a great debate over our fundamental law and essential character as a people, has guaranteed that abortion will surely sweep away all more mundane political considerations.

I suggest not merely that the issues of slavery and abortion are historically analogous. Rather I say that they are, in a crucial sense, the same issue. Both are but particular cases of the recurring challenge to the first principles of the American Revolution, which forbid the violation of the God-given rights of any person, no matter how convenient such a violation might be for some powerful individual or faction, or even a majority.

In the normal course of our politics we do not experience this challenge in its starkest terms. Our fundamental law, our fundamental purpose as a nation is not fully articulated in the positive law by which we govern our daily affairs. The Declaration of Independence, in which our nation's fundamental principles are stated, is not phrased in such a way as to give perfect guidance to the resolution of everyday political disputes. In the normal course of events the American people are content to let the Declaration's unalienable rights be secured by the more intricate structure of the Constitution, which by the genius of the Founding Fathers transformed the play of political interests into a dynamic balance wheel of human and civil rights. Nevertheless, the Declaration gave birth to America as an independent nation and best expresses our ultimate reason for national being.

From time to time, our ordinary politics fails us in ways too dramatic to ignore. An impasse develops in the constitutional process. A weakness shows up in the architecture of liberty. Our positive law (including even the Constitution, or its interpreters) can fail in some critical way to uphold the first principles of our national Founding. It is at such times that it becomes necessary for Americans—who seem now, as they seemed in 1854, too concerned with progress and payrolls—to reconsider the organic law written in their hearts. It is then that American politics again becomes a struggle over the meaning of the Declaration of Independence.

In our time, most leading politicians and intellectuals argue that such philosophical struggles, turning ultimately on moral and religious questions, should be excluded from American politics. With Senator Stephen Douglas, Lincoln's great opponent, who held that Kansas-Nebraska and the *Dred Scott* decision (1857) made the black man forever a slave in America, they hold that the Supreme Court can settle and has settled forever the abortion issue. They are content to accept, paraphrasing Judge Taney, that the child in the womb has no rights which Americans are bound to respect. They argue, with Supreme Court Justice John Paul Stevens, that only "secular interests" are fit subjects of national debate. Some even argue that the resurgence of religion and moral issues in American politics is but a passing fad, safely scorned by sophisticated pragmatists concerned with the weightier matters of wealth and weaponry.

These opinions are as unsurprising as they are unconvincing. What we hear rolling across the Potomac are the hollow, haunting echoes of the great slavery debates of the 1850s. For decades the battle over slavery has been stayed by the timely intervention of grave Whigs and eloquent Democrats who foresaw what passions would be loosed when men ceased to struggle for gain and ground and sought instead to live faithfully by the Divine standards Americans had set themselves in the Declaration. Webster and Clay, Calhoun and Douglas, prudently had sought to guide the energies of the people into economic growth and westward expansion, to mitigate, even to avoid the supervening moral and religious issues raised by the debate over slavery. The remarkable thing is how successful they were for so long in convincing Americans that slavery could be countenanced if its extent could be compromised.

But the insurgent noise would not be silenced. For the muffled murmur throughout the land was the sound of the slave, his tortured breathing rustling the pages of the Declaration of Independence, scaring up from the dry parchment the great truths placed there by Jefferson. For the needs of nation-building, for the sake of a union between slave and free states, slavery may have been legalized in the Constitution. But it was the Creator, as the Founders proclaimed in the Declaration, Who gave men the unalienable right to life and liberty. This contradiction, like a house divided, could not stand.

Just three years after the Kansas-Nebraska Act, the *Dred Scott* decision gave meaning to Lincoln's warnings; it declared the U.S., in effect, a slave nation. *Dred Scott* held that the black slave was not a person under the Constitution, and it made inviolate the property rights of slaveowners. In the very next election, the nation responded by choosing a President who had proclaimed *Dred Scott* unbinding as a "rule of political action" in virtue of the fundamental law of the Declaration and the power of Congress to prohibit slavery in the territories. Six hundred thousand men and boys, the flower of American youth, perished in a war over the meaning of a religious and moral principle—or, in the words of "The Battle Hymn of the Republic": "As He died to make men holy, we shall die to make men free."

There is then no need to be surprised that in the battle over *Roe* v. *Wade*—wherein we deal not only with life and liberty, as in *Dred Scott,* but with life and death—moderate men and women should wish to put the fundamental issues aside. There is no reason to be astonished that so many leading intellectuals wish to believe that the Supreme Court has settled the matter. Nothing should be easier to understand than that the political, business, and academic establishments are embarrassed by the issue and affect to scorn those who raise it. After all, if the modern followers of Lincoln are right, no material bounty America bestows on her people or the world can excuse her crime. If the party of Lincoln is right, there is only one road to national rededication: to fight the evil of abortion until it is extinguished, a fight that may make the divisions of the 1960s, from which we are barely recovered, look like a family reunion.

One way of scorning the issue—one popular tune to whistle past the grave-yard—is to deride abortion as a "single issue" pursued by fanatics to the detriment of the common good. Those who take this tack understand neither the issue nor their countrymen. The unalienable right to life is not, for America, a single issue, but a first principle, a self-evident truth established at its Founding. Nothing is more striking about American history than our willingness to take principles of truth and right seriously. Americans know that neither blood, nor culture, nor even locality is what binds us together. Uniquely among nations we are bound together and defined by our founding principles. It is the pragmatic politicians of the pocketbook who do not know their countrymen.

July 4, 1776, was an event of worldwide significance, not because a new nation was founded on the shores of the Atlantic, but because a new nation, the very first of its kind, was founded "under God," begotten, as Thomas Jefferson wrote, according to the "Laws of Nature and of Nature's God," a nation dedicated, in fact, to a religious proposition, a principle of natural theology. Consider again the phrasing: "We hold these truths to be self-evident, that all men are created equal, that they are endowed by their Creator with certain unalienable Rights," to life, liberty, and the pursuit of happiness. This proposition, the great Emancipator proclaimed, is "the Father of all moral principle" among Americans, the animating spirit of our laws. By reason of this founding principle, Lincoln called his coun-trymen "the almost chosen people"; and it was Jefferson himself who proposed that the national seal portray Moses leading the chosen people to the promised land.

The Founders' principles of equality and unalienable rights are characterized by their universality and claim to Divine sanction. The universality of the principles makes it clear that the Founders did not mean that all human beings are or ought to be equal in all respects—height, weight, beauty, wealth. They meant instead that no person has to another the relation God has to him: Thus the rights enumerated in the Declaration are God-given, and hence "unalienable." Neither the weight of tradition nor the exigencies of statecraft can rationalize the false claim that the unalienable rights of the Declaration are a gift of the state or of the people. As Professor Harry Jaffa would put it: No man has a natural right to rule over any other man, as God does over man; thus a man may rule over another, his equal, only with his consent. This is the essential meaning of our founding law. If there were ever any doubt that we are bound by it—and the Declaration is still put at the head of the statutes-at-large of the U.S. Code and described therein as organic law—Lincoln's testimony and the general assent given it by Americans then and later should have laid that doubt permanently to rest.

But while most Americans take the Declaration seriously, we do have a ten-dency to fix upon its assertions of equality and liberty, quickly passing over its guarantee of an unalienable right to life as if it were merely a glittering generality. The truth is that life, liberty, and the pursuit of happiness are a logically ordered sequence. The rights to liberty and to the pursuit of happiness derive from every man's right to his own life and are meaningless without it.

Life precedes liberty in the words of the Declaration because liberty was made for life, not life for liberty. If the right to life is omitted, then liberty is a right contingent upon force and without moral substance, and the Declaration is a nullity. Moreover, it is by reason of the unalienable right to life that all men hold the right to the fruits of their labor. A free society dissolves into an absurdity if the right to life is denied.

Abortion, like slavery, allows equals to rule over equals without their consent, depriving the child in the womb not only of the right to liberty, but of the right to life as well. But there is a disputed point: Do unborn children hold these rights? There can be no denial that they have life and have had it from the very first moment of conception: That is true in medicine as in law. But what is more important is that, as our fundamental law affirms, they hold life as a gift of the Creator—Who "created" them "equal" and "endowed them" at creation "with certain unalienable rights"—from the moment of conception. Creation does not occur at the second trimester, or at the third, or at viability, but at the very beginning of life. The usual arguments about viability, intelligence, pain, quickening, meaningful life, or unwanted children are as irrelevant as earlier arguments that the poor, black slaves were better off under the rule of a benevolent master. Under the Declaration, under the Divine and natural law by which we have promised to live, the child about to be born, no less than the black slave, holds rights unconditional upon the convenience of others, rights that cannot be altered because other men place a lesser value on the life of a child in the womb.

It is no use, in extenuation, to invoke the pluralism of opinions, or the absence of consensus, as if, in the struggle over *Roe* v. *Wade,* all disagreements were merely part of a friendly historical debate; as if no lives were at stake and there were no ultimate judge to whom to make an appeal. The organic law of the American nation and the Divine law prevail over all positive law, and thus over the litigious subtleties of politicians and judges.

Our task is easier than Lincoln's, and its strain on the country will be less. In the Constitution Lincoln faced an explicit, if time-bound, sanction for slavery, which is lacking in the case of abortion. Each in its own time, slavery and abortion have masqueraded as the law of the land; and the abortion masquerade is utterly transparent. There is an inescapable absurdity in the Supreme Court's argument that the same Fourteenth Amendment that made the black slave a person can be used to deny the personhood of the child about to be born. In 1868, when the Fourteenth Amendment was passed, 28 of the 37 states held abortion to be a criminal act, even prior to quickening. (Over the next 15 years seven more states made abortion a crime. By the time of *Roe* v. *Wade,* in 1973, nearly all the states had criminalized abortion. There *was* a national consensus on abortion: that it is wrong.) In view of the near universality of the laws against abortion at the time of the Fourteenth Amendment was passed, there can be no doubt about its intent or the meaning of the amendment today. The Court's decision in *Roe* v. *Wade* had absolutely no basis, literal or implied, in the Fourteenth Amendment. If the Fourteenth Amendment calls for anything, it calls for reversal of *Roe* v. *Wade*.

Roe v. *Wade* may for now be a legal decision of the Supreme Court; but it is unlawful in the full sense of the word. It is without any identifiable source of authority in constitutional law. In the light of logic, the moral law, and American history, *Roe* v. *Wade* is absurd; it comes to just nothing—nothing but "raw judicial power." It requires no irreverence for the letter or the spirit of the Constitution to declare that the decision must be overturned, by a subsequent Supreme Court decision if possible, but if not, then by constitutional amendment or congressional act. There is in the *Federalist Papers,* the original handbook of constitutional interpretation, a clear warrant for such a rebuke of the Court. *Federalist* Number 81 declares that if judicial "misconstructions and contraventions of the will of the Legislature" do create constitutional defects, there is a constitutional remedy. Even if the legislature cannot "reverse a [judicial] determination once made, in a particular case," it can "prescribe a new rule for future cases." Above all, and despite recent judicial imperialism, the three branches of the Federal Government are co-equal, and all subordinate to "the people" who "ordained" the Constitution to fulfill the promises of the Declaration.

Yet this argument does not end the debate. For the ultimate charge against those who would push the right to life to the top of our political agenda is that they are mixing religion and politics, trying to impose a single set of religious values on the nation. But the link between religion and American politics is indissoluble, for, at the very beginning, in the Declaration, the nation was founded upon the principle of natural religion; it would collapse without them. Jefferson himself, often falsely described as a completely secular man, acknowledged this link, writing that "The God Who gave us life, gave us liberty . . . Can the liberties of a nation be secure when we have removed a conviction that these liberties are the gift of God?"

Those who fear the intrusion of religion into politics are not all wrong. We have been well served by the consensus that excludes sectarian passions from ordinary political disputes. But when fellow Americans of good will ask us to grow quiet on the painful but fundamental issues of abortion, prayer, or pornography, for fear of starting a divisive debate over religious and moral principles, they make a rule of thumb into a rule of life. The truth is not that religion never belongs in American politics. The truth is instead, as Lincoln argued, that religion belongs in American politics only when our politics have been forced back upon first principles.

By nature Lincoln was as much politician as prophet. He was a moderate and judicious man, certainly not inclined to fanaticism. Neither was he a natural candidate for a martyr's crown. But when the crucial issue was joined, Lincoln exposed the counsels of moderation for the well-meaning sophistries they were. And he died a martyr.

Some of us, dreading the great moral conflict Lincoln faced, might have sided with Douglas. But now, more than a century later, who laments the reversal of *Dred Scott* or would rewrite history to keep the slave in chains? Who now holds up the memory of Chief Justice Taney for the honor of the ages? Who now wishes that Lincoln had used the Court's decision as an excuse to turn to other matters?

Who can ever forget what Lincoln, against all polite opinion, and borne up by his faith in a just God, did for free men?

We know it intuitively. It is the Declaration's principles and Lincoln's example we must follow. Certainly not to violence. There will be no need, for, as I said at the outset, the law to which we appeal is inscribed on the hearts of all Americans, more deeply now than ever. The abyss of civil war does not lie before us. If we fail, we will have been overcome by nothing but false opinion and the petty demon of polite society—because we are afraid of the elite consensus and the inelegance of moral commitment, afraid to take on the establishment by naming the national sin, unwilling to bear witness to first principles while the party of prosperity is going so well. But to name these considerations is to know how shameful it is to hold back. We must be bold; so that for now and for all time to come, the unalienable rights to life and liberty, the promises of the Declaration of Independence, shall not perish from this earth.

A Defense of Abortion

Judith Jarvis Thomson

Most opposition to abortion relies on the premise that the fetus is a human being, a person, from the moment of conception. The premise is argued for, but, as I think, not well. Take, for example, the most common argument. We are asked to notice that the development of a human being from conception through birth into childhood is continuous; then it is said that to draw a line, to choose a point in this development and say "before this point the thing is not a person, after this point it is a person" is to make an arbitrary choice, a choice for which in the nature of things no good reason can be given. It is concluded that the fetus is, or anyway that we had better say it is, a person from the moment of conception. But this conclusion does not follow. Similar things might be said about the development of an acorn into an oak tree, and it does not follow that acorns are oak trees, or that we had better say they are. Arguments of this form are sometimes called "slippery slope arguments"—the phrase is perhaps self-explanatory—and it is dismaying that opponents of abortion rely on them so heavily and uncritically.

I am inclined to agree, however, that the prospects for "drawing a line" in the development of the fetus look dim. I am inclined to think also that we shall probably have to agree that the fetus has already become a human person well

Judith Jarvis Thomson, "A Defense of Abortion." Reprinted by permission of the publishers from *Rights, Restitution, and Risk: Essays in Moral Theory* by Judith Jarvis Thomson, Cambridge, Mass.: Harvard University Press, Copyright © 1986 by the President and Fellows of Harvard College.

before birth. Indeed, it comes as a surprise when one first learns how early in its life it begins to acquire human characteristics. By the tenth week, for example, it already has a face, arms and legs, fingers and toes; it has internal organs, and brain activity is detectable. On the other hand, I think that the premise is false, that the fetus is not a person from the moment of conception. A newly fertilized ovum, a newly implanted clump of cells, is no more a person than an acorn is an oak tree. But I shall not discuss any of this. For it seems to be of great interest to ask what happens if, for the sake of argument, we allow the premise. How, precisely, are we supposed to get from there to the conclusion that abortion is morally impermissible? Opponents of abortion commonly spend most of their time establishing that the fetus is a person, and hardly any time explaining the step from there to the impermissibility of abortion. Perhaps they think the step too simple and obvious to require much comment. Or perhaps instead they are simply being economical in argument. Many of those who defend abortion rely on the premise that the fetus is not a person, but only a bit of tissue that will become a person at birth; and why pay out more arguments than you have to? Whatever the explanation, I suggest that the step they take is neither easy nor obvious, that it calls for closer examination than it is commonly given, and that when we do give it this closer examination we shall feel inclined to reject it.

I propose, then, that we grant that the fetus is a person from the moment of conception. How does the argument go from here? Something like this, I take it. Every person has a right to life. So the fetus has a right to live. No doubt the mother has a right to decide what shall happen in and to her body; everyone would grant that. But surely a person's right to life is stronger and more stringent than the mother's right to decide what happens in and to her body, and so outweighs it. So the fetus may not be killed; an abortion may not be performed.

It sounds plausible. But now let me ask you to imagine this. You wake up in the morning and find yourself back to back in bed with an unconscious violinist. A famous unconscious violinist. He has been found to have a fatal kidney ailment, and the Society of Music Lovers has canvassed all the available medical records and found that you alone have the right blood type to help. They have therefore kidnapped you, and last night the violinist's circulatory system was plugged into yours, so that your kidneys can be used to extract poisons from his blood as well as your own. The director of the hospital now tells you, "Look, we're sorry the Society of Music Lovers did this to you—we would never have permitted it if we had known. But still, they did it, and the violinist now is plugged into you. To unplug you would be to kill him. But never mind, it's only for nine months. By then he will have recovered from his ailment, and can safely be unplugged from you." Is it morally incumbent on you to accede to this situation? No doubt it would be very nice of you if you did, a great kindness. But do you *have* to accede to it? What if it were not nine months, but nine years? Or longer still? What if the director of the hospital says, "Tough luck, I agree, but you've now got to stay in bed, with the violinist plugged into you, for the rest of your life. Because remember this. All persons have a right to life, and violinists are persons. Granted you have a right to decide what happens in and to your body, but a person's right to life outweighs your right to decide what happens in and to your body. So you cannot ever be unplugged from him." I imagine you would regard this as outrageous, which suggests that something really is wrong with the plausible-sounding argument I mentioned a moment ago.

In this case, of course, you were kidnapped; you didn't volunteer for the operation that plugged the violinist into your kidneys. Can those who oppose abortion on the ground I mentioned make an exception for a pregnancy due to rape? Certainly. They can say that persons have a right to life only if they didn't come into existence because of rape; or they can say that all persons have a right to life, but that some have less of a right to life than others, in particular, that those who came into existence because of rape have less. But these statements have a rather unpleasant sound. Surely the question of whether you have a right to life at all, or how much of it you have, shouldn't turn on the question of whether or not you are the product of a rape. And in fact the people who oppose abortion on the ground I mentioned do not make this distinction, and hence do not make an exception in case of rape.

Nor do they make an exception for a case in which the mother has to spend the nine months of her pregnancy in bed. They would agree that would be a great pity, and hard on the mother; but all the same, all persons have a right to life, the fetus is a person, and so on. I suspect, in fact, that they would not make an exception for a case in which, miraculously enough, the pregnancy went on for nine years, or even the rest of the mother's life.

Some won't even make an exception for a case in which continuation of the pregnancy is likely to shorten the mother's life; they regard abortion as impermissible even to save the mother's life. Such cases are nowadays very rare, and many opponents of abortion do not accept this extreme view. All the same, it is a good place to begin: a number of points of interest come out in respect to it.

1. Let us call the view that abortion is impermissible even to save the mother's life "the extreme view." I want to suggest first that it does not issue from the argument I mentioned earlier without the addition of some fairly powerful premises. Suppose a woman has become pregnant, and now learns that she has a cardiac condition such that she will die if she carries the baby to term. What may be done for her? The fetus, being a person, has a right to life, but as the mother is a person too, so has she a right to life. Presumably they have an equal right to life. How is it supposed to come out that an abortion may not be performed? If mother and child have an equal right to life, shouldn't we perhaps flip a coin? Or should we add to the mother's right to life her right to decide what happens in and to her body, which everybody seems to be ready to grant—the sum of her rights now outweighing the fetus' right to life?

The most familiar argument here is the following. We are told that performing the abortion would be directly killing the child, whereas doing nothing would not be killing the mother, but only letting her die. Moreover in killing the child, one would be killing an innocent person, for the child has committed no crime, and is not aiming at his mother's death. And then there are a variety of ways in which this might be continued. (1) But as directly killing an innocent person is always and absolutely impermissible, an abortion may not be performed. Or, (2) as directly killing an innocent person is murder, and murder is always and absolutely impermissible, an abortion may not be performed. Or, (3) as one's duty to refrain from directly killing an innocent person is more stringent than one's duty to keep a person from dying, an abortion may not be performed. Or, (4) if one's only options are directly killing an innocent person or letting a person die, one must prefer letting the person die, and thus an abortion may not be performed.

Some people seem to have thought that these are not further premises which must be added if the conclusion is to be reached, but that they follow from the very fact that an innocent person has a right to life. But this seems to me to be a mistake, and perhaps the simplest way to show this is to bring out that while we must certainly grant that innocent persons have a right to life, the theses in (1) through (4) are all false. Take (2), for example. If directly killing an innocent person is murder, and thus is impermissible, then the mother's directly killing the innocent person inside her is murder, and thus is impermissible. But it cannot seriously be thought to be murder if the mother performs an abortion on herself to save her life. It cannot seriously be said that she *must* refrain, that she *must* sit passively by and wait for her death. Let us look again at the case of you and the violinist. There you are, in bed with the violinist, and the director of the hospital says to you, "It's all most distressing, and I deeply sympathize, but you see this is putting an additional strain on your kidneys, and you'll be dead within the month. But you *have* to stay where you are all the same. Because unplugging you would be directly killing an innocent violinist, and that's murder, and that's impermissible." If anything in the world is true, it is that you do not commit murder, you do not do what is impermissible, if you reach around to your back and unplug yourself from that violinist to save your life.

The main focus of attention in writings on abortion has been on what a third party may or may not do in answer to a request from a woman for an abortion. This is in a way understandable. Things being as they are, there isn't much a woman can safely do to abort herself. So the quesiton asked is what a third party may do, and what the mother may do, if it is mentioned at all, is deduced, almost as an afterthought, from what it is concluded that third parties may do. But it seems to me that to treat the matter in this way is to refuse to grant to the mother that very status of person which is so firmly insisted on for the fetus. For we cannot simply read off what a person may do from what a third party may do. Suppose you find yourself trapped in a tiny house with a growing child. I mean a very tiny house, and a rapidly growing child—you are already up against the wall of the house and in a few minutes you'll be crushed to death. The child on the other hand won't be crushed to death; if nothing is done to stop him from growing he'll be hurt, but in the end he'll simply burst open the house and walk out a free man. Now I could well understand it if a bystander were to say, "There's nothing we can do for you. We cannot choose between your life and his, we cannot be the ones to decide who is to live, we cannot intervene." But it cannot be concluded that you too can do nothing, that you cannot attack it to save your life. However innocent the child may be, you do not have to wait passively while it crushes you to death. Perhaps a pregnant woman is vaguefly felt to have the status of house, to which we don't allow the right of self-defense. But if the woman houses the child, it should be remembered that she is a person who houses it.

I should perhaps stop to say explicitly that I am not claiming that people have a right to do anything whatever to save their lives. I think, rather, that there are drastic limits to the right of self-defense. If someone threatens you with death unless you torture someone else to death, I think you have not the right, even to save your life, to do so. But the case under consideration here is very different. In our case there are only two people involved, one whose life is threatened, and one who threatens it. Both are innocent: the one who is threatened is not threatened because of any fault, the one who threatens does not threaten because of any fault. For this reason we may feel that we bystanders cannot intervene. But the person threatened can.

In sum, a woman surely can defend her life against the threat to it posed by the unborn child, even if doing so involves its death. And this shows not merely that the theses in (1) through (4) are false, it shows also that the extreme view of abortion is false, and so we need not canvass any other possible ways of arriving at it from the argument I mentioned at the outset.

2. The extreme view could of course be weakened to say that while abortion is permissible to save the mother's life, it may not be performed by a third party, but only by the mother herself. But this cannot be right either. For what we have to keep in mind is that the mother and the unborn child are not like two tenants in a small house which has, by an unfortunate mistake, been rented to both: the mother *owns* the house. The fact that she does adds to the offensiveness of deducing that the mother can do nothing from the supposition that third parties can do nothing. But it does more than this: it casts a bright light on the supposition that third parties can do nothing. Certainly it lets us see that a third party who says "I cannot choose between you" is fooling himself if he thinks this is impartiality. If Jones has found and fastened on a certain coat, which he needs to keep him from freezing, but which Smith also needs to keep him from freezing, then it is not impartiality that says "I cannot choose between you" when Smith owns the coat. Women have said again and again "This body is *my* body!" and they have reason to feel angry, reason to feel that it has been like shouting into the wind. Smith, after all, is hardly likely to bless us if we say to him, "Of course it's your coat, anybody would grant that it is. But no one may choose between you and Jones who is to have it."

We should really ask what it is that says "no one may choose" in the face of the fact that the body that houses the child is the mother's body. It may be simply a failure to appreciate this fact. But it may be something more interesting, namely the sense that one has a right to refuse to lay hands on people, even where it would be just and fair to do so, even where justice seems to require that somebody do so. Thus justice might call for somebody to get Smith's coat back from Jones, and yet you have a right to refuse to be the one to lay hands on Jones, a right to refuse to do physical violence to him. This, I think, must be granted. But then what should be said is not "no one may choose," but only "*I* cannot choose," and indeed not even this, but "*I* will not *act*," leaving it open that somebody else can or should, and in particular that anyone in a position of authority, with the job of securing people's rights, both can and should. So this is no difficulty. I have not been arguing that any given third party must accede to the mother's request that he perform an abortion to save her life, but only that he may.

I suppose that in some views of human life the mother's body is only on loan to her, the loan not being one which gives her any prior claim to it. One who held this view might well think it impartiality to say "I cannot choose." But I shall simply ignore this possibility. My own view is that if a human being has any just, prior claim to anything at all, he has a just, prior claim to his own body. And perhaps this needn't be argued for here anyway, since, as I mentioned, the arguments against abortion we are looking at do grant that the woman has a right to decide what happens in and to her body.

But although they do grant it, I have tried to show that they do not take seriously what is done in granting it. I suggest the same thing will reappear even more clearly when we turn away from cases in which the mother's life is at stake, and attend, as I propose we now do, to the vastly more common cases in which a woman wants an abortion for some less weighty reason than preserving her own life.

3. Where the mother's life is not at stake, the argument I mentioned at the outset seems to have a much stronger pull. "Everyone has a right to life, so the unborn person has a right to life." And isn't the child's right to life weightier than anything other than the mother's own right to life, which she might put forward as ground for an abortion?

This argument treats the right to life as if it were unproblematic. It is not, and this seems to me to be precisely the source of the mistake.

For we should now, at long last, ask what it comes to, to have a right to life. In some views having a right to life includes having a right to be given at least the bare minimum one needs for continued life. But suppose that what in fact *is* the bare minimum a man needs for continued life is something he has no right at all to be given? If I am sick unto death, and the only thing that will save my life is the touch of Henry Fonda's cool hand on my fevered brow, then all the same, I have no right to be given the touch of Henry Fonda's cool hand on my fevered brow. It would be frightfully nice of him to fly in from the West Coast to provide it. It would be less nice, though no doubt well meant, if my friends flew out to the West Coast and carried Henry Fonda back with them. But I have no right at all against anybody that he should do this for me. Or again, to return to the story I told earlier, the fact that for continued life that violinist needs the continued use of your kidneys does not establish that he has a right to be given the continued use of your kidneys. He certainly has no right against you that *you* should give him continued use of your kidneys. For nobody has any right to use your kidneys unless you give him such a right; and nobody has the right against you that you shall give him this right—if you do allow him to go on using your kidneys, this is a kindness on your part, and not something he can claim from you as his due. Nor has he any right against anybody else that *they* should give him continued use of your kidneys. Certainly he had no right against the Society of Music Lovers that they should plug him into you in the first place. And if you start to unplug yourself, having learned that you will otherwise have to spend nine years in bed with him, there is nobody in the world who must try to prevent you, in order to see to it that he is given something he has a right to be given.

Some people are rather stricter about the right to life. In their view, it does not include the right to be given anything, but amounts to, and only to, the right not to be killed by anybody. But here a related difficulty arises. If everybody is to refrain from killing that violinist, then everybody must refrain from doing a great many different sorts of things. Everybody must refrain from slitting his throat, everybody must refrain from shooting him—and everybody must refrain from unplugging you from him. But does he have a right against everybody that they shall refrain from unplugging you from him? To refrain from doing this is to allow him to continue to use your kidneys. It could be argued that he has a right against us that *we* should allow him to continue to use your kidneys. That is, while he had no right against us that we should give him the use of your kidneys, it might be argued that he anyway has a right against us that we shall not now intervene and deprive him of the use of your kidneys. I shall come back to third-party interventions later. But certainly the violinist has no right against you that *you* shall allow him to continue to use your kidneys. As I said, if you do allow him to use them, it is a kindness of your part, and not something you owe him.

This difficulty I point to here is not peculiar to the right to life. It reappears in connection with all the other natural rights, and it is something which an adequate account of rights must deal with. For present purposes it is enough just to draw attention to it. But I would stress that I am not arguing that people do not have a right to life—quite to the contrary, it seems to me that the primary control we must place on the acceptability of an account of rights is that it should turn out in that account to be a truth that all persons have a right to life. I am arguing only that having a right to life does not guarantee having either a right to be given the use of a right to be allowed continued use of another person's body— even if one needs it for life itself. So the right to life will not serve the opponents of abortion in the very simple and clear way in which they seem to have thought it would.

4. There is another way to bring out the difficulty in the most ordinary sort of case, to deprive someone of what he has a right to is to treat him unjustly. Suppose a boy and his small brother are jointly given a box of chocolates for Christmas. If the older boy takes the box and refuses to give his brother any of the chocolates, he is unjust to him, for the brother has been given a right to half of them. But suppose that, having learned that otherwise it means nine years in bed with that violinist, you unplug yourself from him. You surely are not being unjust to him, for you gave him no right to use your kidneys, and no one else can have given him such right. But we have to notice that in unplugging yourself, you are killing him; and violinists, like everybody else, have a right to life, and thus in the view we were considering just now, the right not to be killed. So here to do what he supposedly has a right you shall not do, but you do not act unjustly to him in doing it.

The emendation which may be made at this point is this: the right to life consists not in the right not to be killed, but rather in the right not to be killed unjustly. This runs a risk of circularity, but never mind: it would enable us to square the fact that the violinist has a right to life with the fact that you do not act unjustly toward him in unplugging yourself, thereby killing him. For if you do not kill him unjustly, you do not violate his right to life, and so it is no wonder you do him no injustice.

But if this emendation is accepted, the gap in the argument against abortion stares us plainly in the face: it is by no means enough to show that the fetus is a person, and to remind us that all persons have a right to life—we need to be shown also that killing the fetus violates its right to life, i.e., that abortion is unjust killing. And is it?

I suppose we may take it as a datum that in a case of pregnancy due to rape the mother has not given the unborn person a right to the use of her body for food and shelter. Indeed, in what pregnancy could it be supposed that the mother has given the unborn person such a right? It is not as if there were unborn persons drifting about the world, to whom a woman who wants a child says "I invite you in."

But it might be argued that there are other ways one can have acquired a right to the use of another person's body than by having been invited to use it by that person. Suppose a woman voluntarily indulges in intercourse, knowing of the chance it will issue in pregnancy, and then she does become pregnant; is she not in part responsible for the presence, in fact the very existence, of the unborn person inside her? No doubt she did not invite it in. But doesn't her partial responsibility for its being there itself give it a right to the use of her body? If so, then her aborting it would be more like the boy's taking away the chocolates, and less like your unplugging yourself from the violinist—doing so would be depriving it of what it does have a right to, and thus would be doing it an injustice.

And then, too, it might be asked whether or not she can kill it even to save her own life: If she voluntarily called it into existence, how can she now kill it, even in self-defense?

The first thing to be said about this is that it is something new. Opponents of abortion have been so concerned to make out the independence of the fetus, in order to establish that it has a right to life, just as its mother does, that they have tended to overlook the possible support they might gain from making out that the fetus is *dependent* on the mother, in order to establish that she has a special kind of responsibility for it, a responsibility that gives it rights against her which are not possessed by any independent person—such as an ailing violinist who is a stranger to her.

On the other hand, this argument would give the unborn person a right to its mother's body only if her pregnancy resulted from a voluntary act, undertaken in full knowledge of the chance a pregnancy might result from it. It would leave out entirely the unborn person whose existence is due to rape. Pending the availability of some further argument, then, we would be left with the conclusion that unborn persons whose existence is due to rape have no right to the use of their mothers' bodies, and thus that aborting them is not depriving them of anything they have a right to and hence is not unjust killing.

And we should also notice that it is not at all plain that this argument really does go even as far as it purports to. For there are cases and cases, and the details make a difference. If the room is stuffy, and I therefore open a window to air it, and a burglar climbs in, it would be absurd to say, "Ah, now he can say, she's given him a right to the use of her house—for she is partially repsonsible for his presence there, having voluntarily done what enabled him to get in, in full knowledge that there are such things as burglars, and that burglars burgle." It would be still more absurd to say this if I had had bars installed outside my windows, precisely to prevent burglars from getting it, and a burglar got in only because of a defect in the bars. It remains equally absurd if we imagine it is not a burglar who climbs in, but an innocent person who blunders or falls in. Again, suppose it were like this: people-seeds drift about in the air like pollen, and if you open your windows, one may drift in and take root in your carpets or upholstery. You don't want children, so you fix up your windows with fine mesh screens, the very best you can buy. As can happen, however, and on very, very rare occasions does happen, one of the screens is defective; and a seed drifts in and takes root. Does the person-plant who now develops have a right to the use of your house? Surely not—despite the fact that you voluntarily opened your windows, you knowingly kept carpets and upholstered furniture, and you knew that screens were sometimes defective. Someone may argue that you are responsible for its rooting, that it does have a right to your house, because after all you *could* have lived out your life with bare floors and furniture, or with sealed windows and doors. But this won't do—for by the same token anyone can avoid a pregnancy due to rape by having a hysterectomy, or anyway by never leaving home without a (reliable!) army.

It seems to me that the argument we are looking at can establish at most that there are *some* cases in which the unborn person has a right to the use of its mother's body, and therefore *some* cases in which abortion is unjust killing. There is room for much discussion and argument as to precisely which, if any. But I think we should sidestep this issue and leave it open, for at any rate the argument certainly does not establish that all abortion is unjust killing.

5. There is room for yet another argument here, however. We surely must all grant that there may be cases in which it would be morally indecent to detach a person from your body at the cost of his life. Suppose you learn that what the violinist needs is not nine years of your life, but only one hour: all you need do to save his life is to spend one hour in that bed with him. Suppose also that letting him use your kidneys for that one hour would not affect your health in the slightest. Admittedly you were kidnapped. Admittedly you did not give anyone permission to plug him into you. Nevertheless it seems to me plain you *ought* to allow him to use your kidneys for that hour—it would be indecent to refuse.

Again, suppose pregnancy lasted only an hour, and constituted no threat to life or health. And suppose that a woman becomes pregnant as a reuslt of rape. Admittedly she did not voluntarily do anything to bring about the existence of a child. Admittedly she did nothing at all which would give the unborn person a right to the use of her body. All the same it might well be said, as in the newly emended violinist story, that she *ought* to allow it to remain for that hour—that it would be indecent in her to refuse.

Now some people are inclined to use the term "right" in such a way that it follows from the fact that you ought to allow a person to use our body for the hour he needs, that he has a right to use your body for the hour he needs, even though he has not been given that right by any person or act. They may say that it follows also that if you refuse, you act unjustly toward him. This use of the term is perhaps so common that it cannot be called wrong, nevertheless it seems to me to be an unfortunate loosening of what we would do better to keep a tight rein on. Suppose that box of chocolates I mentioned earlier had not been given to both boys jointly, but was given only to the older boy. There he sits, stolidly eating his way through the box, his small brother watching enviously. Here we are likely to say "You ought not to be so mean. You ought to give your brother some of those chocolates." My own view is that it just does not follow from the truth of this that the brother has any right to any of the chocolates. If the boy refuses to give his brother any, he is greedy, stingy, callous—but not unjust. I suppose that the people I have in mind will say it does follow that the brother has a right to some of the chocolates, and thus that the boy does act unjustly if he refuses to give his brother any. But the effect of saying this is to obscure what we should keep distinct, namely the difference between the boy's refusal in this case and the boy's refusal in the earlier case, in which the box was given to both boys jointly, and in which the small brother thus had what was from any point of view clear title to half.

A further objection to so using the term "right" that from the fact that A ought to do a thing for B, it follows that B has a right against A that A do it for him, is that it is going make the question of whether or not a man has a right to a thing turn on how easy it is to provide him with it; and this seems not merely unfortunate, but morally unacceptable. Take the case of Henry Fonda again. I said earlier that I had no right to the touch of his cool hand on my fevered brow, even though I needed it to save my life. I said it would be frightfully nice of him to fly in from the West Coast to provide me with it, but that I had no right against him that he should do so. But suppose he isn't on the West Coast. Suppose he has only to walk across a room, place a hand briefly on my brow—and lo, my life is saved. Then surely he ought to do it, it would be indecent to refuse. Is it to be said "Ah, well, it follows that in this case she has a right to the touch of his hand on her brow, and so it would be an injustice in him to refuse"? So that I have a right to it when it is easy for him to provide it, though no right when it's hard? It's rather a shocking idea that anyone's rights should fade away and disappear as it gets harder and harder to accord them to him.

So my own view is that even though you ought to let the violinist use your kidneys for the one hour he needs, we should not conclude that he has a right to do so—we should say that if you refuse, you are, like the boy who owns all the chocolates and will give none away, self-centered and callous, indecent in fact, but not unjust. And similarly, that even supposing a case in which a woman pregnant due to rape ought to allow the unborn person to use her body for the hour he needs, we should not conclude that he has a right to do so; we should conclude that she is self-centered, callous, indecent, but not unjust, if she refuses. The complaints are no less grave; they are just different. However, there is no need to insist on this point. If anyone does wish to deduce "he has a right" from "you ought," then all the same he must surely grant that there are cases in which it is not morally required of you that you allow that violinist to use your kidneys, and in which he does not have a right to use them, and in which you do not do him an injustice if you refuse. And so also for mother and unborn child. Except in such cases as the unborn person has a right to demand it—and we were leaving open the possibility that there may be such cases—nobody is morally *required* to make large sacrifices, of health, of all other interests and concerns, of all other duties and commitments, for nine years, or even for nine months, in order to keep another person alive.

6. We have in fact to distinguish between two kinds of Samaritan: the Good Samaritan and what we might call the Minimally Decent Samaritan. The story of the Good Samaritan, you will remember, goes like this:

> A certain man went down from Jerusalem to Jericho, and fell among thieves, which stripped him of his raiment, and wounded him, and departed, leaving him half dead.
>
> And by chance there came down a certain priest that way; and when he saw him, he passed by on the other side.
>
> And likewise a Levite, when he was at the place, came and looked on him, and passed on the other side.
>
> But a certain Samaritan, as he journeyed, came where he was; and when he saw him he had compassion for him.
>
> And went to him, and bound up his wounds, pouring in oil and wine, and set him on his own beast, and brought him to an inn, and took care of him.
>
> And on the morrow, when he departed, he took out two pence, and gave them to the host, and said unto him, "Take care of him, and whatsoever thou spendest more, when I come again, I will repay thee."   (Luke 10:30–35)

The Good Samaritan went out of his way, at some cost to himself, to help one in need of it. We are not told what the options were, that is, whether or not the priest and the Levite could have helped by doing less than the Good Samaritan did, but assuming they could have, then the fact they did nothing at all shows they were not even Minimally Decent Samaritans, not because they were not Samaritans, but because they were not even minimally decent.

These things are a matter of degree, of course, but there is a difference, and it comes out perhaps most clearly in the story of Kitty Genovese, who, as you will remember, was murdered while thirty-eight people watched or listened, and did nothing at all to help her. A Good Samaritan would have rushed out to give direct assistance against the murderer. Or perhaps we had better allow that it would have been a Splendid Samaritan who did this, on the ground that it would have involved a risk of death for himself. But the thirty-eight not only did not do this, they did not even trouble to pick up a phone to call the police. Minimally Decent Samaritanism would call for doing at least that, and their not having done it was monstrous.

After telling the story of the Good Samaritan, Jesus said "Go, and do thou likewise." Perhaps he meant that we are morally required to act as the Good Samaritan did. Perhaps he was urging people to do more than is morally required of them. At all events it seems plain that it was not morally required of any of the thirty-eight that he rush out to give direct assistance at the risk of his own life, and that it is not morally required of anyone that he give long stretches of his life—nine years or nine months—to sustaining the life of a person who has no special right (we were leaving open the possibility of this) to demand it.

Indeed, with one rather striking class of exceptions, no one in any country in the world is *legally* required to do anywhere near as much as this for anyone else. The class of exceptions is obvious. My main concern here is not the state of the law in respect to abortion, but it is worth drawing attention to the fact that in no state in this country is any man compelled by law to be even a Minimally Decent Samaritan to any person, there is no law under which charges could be brought against the thirty-eight who stood by while Kitty Genovese died. By contrast, in most states in this country women are compelled by law to be not merely Minimally Decent Samaritans, but Good Samaritans to unborn persons inside them. This doesn't by itself settle anything one way or the other, because it may well be argued that there should be laws in this country—as there are in many European countries—compelling at least Minimally Decent Samaritanism. But it does show that there is a gross injustice in the existing state of the law. And it shows also that the groups currently working against liberalization of abortion laws, in fact working toward having it declared unconstitutional for a state to permit abortion, had better start working for the adoption of Good Samaritan laws generally, or earn the charge that they are acting in bad faith.

I should think, myself, that Minimally Decent Samaritan laws would be one thing, Good Samaritan laws quite another, and in fact highly improper. But we are not here concerned with the law. What we should ask is not whether anybody should be compelled by law to be a Good Samaritan, but whether we must accede to a situation in which somebody is being compelled—by nature, perhaps—to be a Good Samaritan. We have, in other words, to look now at third-party interventions. I have been arguing that no person is morally required to make large sacrifices to sustain the life of another who has no right to demand them, and this even where the sacrifices do not include life itself; we are not morally required to be Good Samaritans or anyway Very Good Samaritans to one another. But what if a man cannot extricate himself from such a situation? What if he appeals to us to extricate him? It seems to be plain that there are cases in which we can, cases in which a Good Samaritan would extricate him. There you are, you were kidnapped, and nine years in bed with that violinist lie ahead of you. You have your own life to lead. You are sorry, but you simply cannot see giving up so much of your life to the sustaining of his. You cannot extricate yourself, and ask us to do so. I should have thought that—in light of his having no right to the use of your body—it was obvious that we do not have to accede to your being forced to give up so much. We can do what you ask. There is no injustice to the violinist in our doing so.

7. Following the lead of the opponents of abortion, I have throughout been speaking of the fetus merely as a person, and what I have been asking is whether or not the argument we began with, which proceeds only from the fetus being a person, really does establish its conclusion. I have argued that it does not.

But of course there are arguments and arguments, and it may be said that I have simply fastened on the wrong one. It may be said that what is important is not merely the fact that the fetus is a person, but that it is a person for whom the woman has a special kind of responsibility issuing from the fact that she is its mother. And it might be argued that all my analogies are therefore irrelevant—for you do not have that special kind of responsibility for that violinist, Henry Fonda does not have the special kind of responsibility for me. And our attention might be drawn to the fact that men and women both *are* compelled by law to provide support for their children.

I have in effect dealt (briefly) with this argument in section 4 above; but a (still briefer) recapitulation now may be in order. Surely we do not have any such "special responsibility" for a person unless we have assumed it, explicitly or implicitly. If a set of parents do not try to prevent pregnancy, do not obtain an abortion, and then at the time of birth of the child do not put it out for adoption, but rather take it home with them, then they have assumed responsibility for it, they have given it rights, and they cannot *now* withdraw support from it at the cost of its life because they now find it difficult to go on providing for it. But if they have taken all reasonable precautions against having a child, they do not simply by virtue of their biological relationship to the child who comes into existence have a special responsibility for it. They may wish to assume responsibility for it, or they may not wish to. And I am suggesting that if assuming responsibility for it would require large sacrifices, then they may refuse. A Good Samaritan would not refuse—or anyway, a Splendid Samaritan, if the sacrifices that had to be made were enormous. But then so would a Good Samaritan assume responsibility for that violinist; so would Henry Fonda, if he is a Good Samaritan, fly in from the West Coast and assume responsibility for me.

8. My argument will be found unsatisfactory on two counts by many of those who want to regard abortion as morally permissible. First, while I do argue that abortion is not impermissible, I do not argue that it is always permissible. There may well be cases in which carrying the child to term requires only Minimally Decent Samaritanism of the mother, and this is a standard we must not fall below. I am inclined to think it a merit of my account precisely that it does *not* give a general yes or a general no. It allows for and supports our sense that, for example, a sick and desperately frightened fourteen-year-old schoolgirl, pregnant due to rape, may *of course* choose abortion, and that any law which rules this out is an insane law. And it also allows for and supports our sense that in other cases resort to abortion is even positively indecent. It would be indecent in the woman to request an abortion, and indecent in a doctor to perform it, if she is in her seventh month, and wants the abortion just to avoid the nuisance of postponing a trip abroad. The very fact that the arguments I have been drawing attention to treat all cases of abortion, or even all cases of abortion in which the mother's life is not at stake, as morally on a par ought to have made them suspect at the outset.

Second, while I am arguing for the permissibility of abortion in some cases, I am not arguing for the right to secure the death of the unborn child. It is easy to confuse these two things in that up to a certain point in the life of the fetus it is not able to survive outside the mother's body; hence removing it from her body guarantees its death. But they are importantly different. I have argued that you are not morally required to spend nine months in bed, sustaining the life of that violinist; but to say this is by no means to say that if, when you unplug yourself, there is a miracle and he survives, you then have a right to turn round and slit his throat. You may detach yourself even if this costs him his life; you have no right to be guaranteed his death, by some other means, if unplugging yourself does not kill him. There are some people who will feel dissatisfied by this feature of my argument. A woman may be utterly devastated by the thought of a child, a bit of herself, put out for adoption and never seen or heard of again. She may therefore want not merely that the child be detached from her, but more, that it die. Some opponents of abortion are inclined to regard this as beneath contempt— thereby showing insensitivity to what is surely a powerful source of despair. All the same, I agree that the desire for the child's death is not one which anybody may gratify, should it turn out to be possible to detach the child alive.

At this place, however, it should be remembered that we have only been pretending throughout that the fetus is a human being from the moment of conception. A very early abortion is surely not the killing of a person, and so is not dealt with by anything I have said here.

Men and Abortion

Kathleen McDonnell

While some criticize feminists for ignoring the fetus in the abortion issue, others (often the same people) do so for ignoring men as well. And indeed, with our steady insistence that "abortion is a woman's right," we may sometimes forget, or appear to forget, that abortion always occurs in the context of sexual contact between a woman and a man. (Except, of course, in the rare case of an abortion where the pregnancy is the result of artificial insemination. Even then there is male involvement, but not *sexual* involvement.)

Often the man is no longer in the picture by the time the abortion takes place, or the woman has chosen not to tell the man that she is pregnant, or she may not even know for certain who the father is. But whether or not the man is present within the orbit of persons and events surrounding an abortion, the fact remains that men as a group are intimately and inextricably connected to abortion. Like making a baby, it takes two to create an unwanted pregnancy.

In dealing with abortion and other reproductive matters, feminists have gone a long way toward eradicating the sexist notion that unwanted pregnancy is the fault of the woman, a kind of punishment for sexual activity that men are not expected to share. But while fostering the notion that men should bear an equal share of responsibility in reproductive matters, feminists have been reluctant to accord them anything more than a minor role in reproductive decisions, especially where abortion is concerned. There are some perfectly good reasons for this. Women are the ones who bear children. Women are the ones, still, who are largely responsible for their care and nurturing. It is our bodies and our lives that are at issue, so the decisions must be ours as well. Besides, ample evidence over the centuries has shown us that we have been prudent not to accord men much say in reproductive matters, especially abortion, because on the whole they have not acquitted themselves well in this area.

The most common male response to unwanted pregnancy when it occurs outside of marriage has been to "take off," leaving the woman to bear the physical, the emotional and, often, the financial brunt of either having an abortion or carrying the pregnancy to term. Studies of abortion and its aftermath reveal that, more often than not, relationships do not survive an abortion: the majority of unmarried couples break up either before or soon after an abortion.[1] In many cases, of course, the breakup is at the instigation of the woman, or the decision is a mutual one. But the most frequent scenario is that the man terminates the relationship on being told of the pregnancy or shortly after the abortion, or he just gradually fades out of the picture. Male reluctance to accept responsibility in reproductive matters extends far beyond pregnancy and abortion, of course. The majority of men still regard the use of contraception as a woman's problem, for example. And men are increasingly disowning responsibility for their own biological children, as Barbara Ehrenreich demonstrates in her book *The Hearts of Men*. Over the past decade and a half men have begun to "take off" in unprecedented numbers, abandoning their traditional breadwinner roles, defaulting on support payments and leaving women to be the sole financial support of their children.

Often men take the opposite tack when confronted with an unplanned pregnancy: they stick around and demand that the woman not abort "their" child. This demand is rarely accompanied by an offer to raise and support the child, however. Personal accounts of abortion reveal this particular scenario with an astounding frequency: the man will say he is "against abortion" or forbid the woman to abort "his" child, without the slightest awareness of the responsibility that this position logically demands of him. A woman in one study even felt that her lover was "more logical and more correct" in his contention that "she should have the child and raise it without either his presence or his financial support."[2] Another, a fifteen-year-old, acceded to her boyfriend's wish not to "murder his child." But after she decided against having an abortion, he left her to raise the child alone and "ruined my life," she said.[3]

This extraordinary attitude stems from a number of factors. First, there is the simple fact that, for many men, making a woman pregnant is a proof of virility, and they are unable to think beyond that to the consequences. One recent study of male and female attitudes toward childbearing showed that men tend to view it as a kind of testament to their "immortality," rather than in terms of a personal relationship with a particular child, as women tend to do.[4] And, as we saw in the last chapter, men are more likely to take "principled" stands on moral issues without any regard for the human circumstances. Simone de Beauvoir notes that

> Men universally forbid abortion, but individually they accept it as a convenient solution of a problem; they are able to contradict themselves with careless cynicism.[5]

Even when men have supported our right to abortion, it has not always been for the best reasons. Since the late sixties, the Playboy Foundation has been one of the chief funding agencies for abortion reform efforts in the United States. As some feminists have pointed out, Playboy's support has much more to do with the fact that abortion makes women sexually available to men without the inconvenience of unwanted pregnancy than it has to do with any philosophical commitment to women's rights. In fact, in the hands of such an ideologue of sexism as Hugh Hefner, abortion does seem like another of those freedoms won by the so-called sexual revolution of the sixties and seventies that has, so far at least, benefited men much more than women. Widely available contraception and legal abortion have made it possible, for the fist time in history, for women to have sex with men without the fear of unwanted childbearing. Whether women are actually enjoying the fruits of this new-found freedom and getting what they need from men is another matter altogether.

Of course, there are many individual men who do not fall into any of these categories—men who support their partners through an abortion, men who take their parenting responsibilities very seriously, men who believe that women, like men, have the right to control their own bodies. But on the whole, our reluctance to "let men in" on our reproductive decisions has been well-founded, because men as a *group* have always sought to wrest control of reproduction from women. In fact, as we shall see in Chapter Seven of this book, the whole history of the patriarchy is in one sense the story of this struggle by men to take control of reproduction and make it theirs. We see this in a variety of cultural practices, which are only now being called into question: the naming of children with the father's surname, the male medical control of childbirth, contraceptive technology and abortion.

Though feminism has never actually worked out a position on the role of men in abortion, in practice we have designated only one appropriate role for them, that of the "supportive man." In this scenario the man is to provide emotional support to a woman facing an unwanted pregnancy, and to help her carry out her choice, whatever it may be. In fostering this role we may give men the message, intentionally or not, that they should put aside whatever feelings or preferences they might have and just "be there" for the woman. Some progressive, "feminist" men, who are sympathetic to the goals of the women's movement and who in many cases actively work to support them, have particularly gravitated toward this role in their relationships with women. (A lot of other men are, of course, not so cooperative!) So, to a large extent, what we have encouraged in men is a passive, auxiliary role in abortion, allow them to participate in a way that is helpful, but perhaps not, in some important sense, truly meaningful. Perhaps this is just what we want. Abortion is, after all, a woman's choice.

But there is a problem here. In every area of reproduction we are encouraging just the opposite behaviour in men: we want them to take equal responsibility for contraception. We want them to be actively and intimately involved in every aspect of pregnancy, labour and delivery. And we want them to take an active, equal role in child care and parenting. We have fostered this trend toward greater male participation with some ambivalence, always remembering men's oft-demonstrated tendency to try to take control in reproductive and other matters. But in the end we recognize that we must do so if we want to eradicate coercive sex roles. By encouraging male participation in all aspects of reproduction and parenting we chip away at the notion that bearing and caring for children is woman's "natural" function in life, that woman's place is in the home, and man's is out in the world. We also make a true and equal partnership in childbearing and parenting a real possibility for women and men.

We have to acknowledge, then, that there is a grave inconsistency between our eagerness to involve men in all other aspects of reproduction and our unwillingness to allow them a similar role in abortion. This means we must acknowledge and validate men's role in the act of procreation. It really does take two. This isn't to suggest that men's and women's part in creating life are somehow equivalent, as some maintain. They obviously are not. Nature involves women in the reproductive process in a total physical and emotional way. We go through pregnancy, labour, birth, postpartum and breastfeeding, with all their attendant physical, hormonal and psychological changes. By contrast, nature does not even provide us with a sure way of verifying which man has fathered which child. But, if we are serious in our efforts to, in a sense, right nature's imbalance and make reproduction a truly joint effort, it behooves us to make more room for men in the abortion process, to allow them a meaningful role that acknowledges their part in procreation.

This stance poses, of course, a veritable minefield of problems, which we must traverse carefully if we are to maintain our hard-fought struggle for control of our bodies. The Right-to-Life movement has long argued for male involvement in abortion decisions—as long as the men involved are against abortion. On Father's Day, 1984, a group of anti-abortionists picketed a number of Toronto hospitals to dramatize their contention that men should have the right to veto abortions. Some of the participants interviewed used arguments that were uncomfortably close to the feminist view that reproduction should be a shared responsibility. Raising children "is not woman's work, it's humanity's work," said one man.[6] We should have no illusions about the fact that our arguments for greater male involvement can and will be used against us. This does not mean that we should reject them altogether, but only that we must be continually clarifying and strengthening our position.

Another pitfall lies in the fact that, to many men, "meaningful involvement" equals control. The only power they know is power over others. They do not understand how to participate in truly cooperative decision-making. As a rule women are much more schooled in the art of cooperation, of sharing power and encouraging others to offer input, whether we agree with it or not. So when we call for greater male involvement in abortion and other reproductive matters, we must do so with the regettable understanding that many men, perhaps most men, are not yet capable of this kind of power-sharing, and we must act accordingly.

We can say that we support male involvement in abortion decisions, but, as always, life presents us with complex, unwieldy situations where hard-and-fast rules can't be applied. For example, if the man withdraws from the relationship as soon as he finds out about the pregnancy, there is no question of his continued involvement in the process—he has made his choice. But what about women who don't tell their partners they are pregnant, who simply go off and quietly have an abortion? Are we dictating to them that they must involve their partners? Obviously we cannot do so. Most often when a woman does this, she has good reason to believe that telling her lover about the pregnancy may have bad repercussions. She may fear that he will try to prevent her from having the abortion, or may actually physically harm her. It is an uncomfortable fact that pregnancy is one of the situations in which wife battering is most likely to occur, and some men have been known to respond to the news of an unwanted pregnancy with rage and violence because they feel "tricked" or blame the woman.

In the end we must come back to our starting point: abortion is still a woman's right, a woman's choice. This means that when push comes to shove, when a man and a woman cannot come to agreement, it is the woman's wishes that must prevail. We cannot allow men any kind of absolute veto over our abortion decisions. Further, we must fight any attempts to enshrine such a veto power in law. One such attempt occurred in Toronto in the spring of 1984, when a husband, Alexander Medhurst, tried to block his wife's abortion with a court injunction. Although his application was ultimately denied and the Supreme Court of Ontario ruled that the father of an unborn child has no legal right to prevent it from being aborted, Medhurst succeeded in delaying his wife's abortion by several weeks, causing her increased health risk and considerable anguish. We shall undoubtedly see more such cases: although Medhurst was not against abortion in principle and had no discernible ties to anti-abortion groups, pro-life organizations in the U.S. and Canada have taken a keen interest in such cases and have supported them financially and politically.

What about instances where the man agrees to take and raise the child himself? The woman's right to choose abortion should be no different in this situation than in any other, though it is hoped that she would give full and honest consideration to such an offer in making her decision. In fact, however, such instances are exceedingly rare. Although some men may voice such intentions during the pregnancy, few are able or willing to carry through on the commitment. Usually the men are simply not serious, or are deluding themselves in some way. Medhurst, for example, admitted to a reporter that his real hope in seeking to block his wife's abortion was that having the baby would heal his crumbling marriage.[7]

By the same token, we cannot allow men to force us into abortions we don't want. This happens more often than many people realize, not because men force women kicking and screaming into hospitals and abortion clinics, but because women's economic and emotional dependence on men can make them unable to carry out their own wishes. Forced abortion can have as devastating consequences for women as denied abortion. Naomi, whose own abortion is touched on in Chapter Two, gives this account of her hospital roommate:

> [The woman] was perhaps thirty, a recent immigrant to Canada. She had one child, and had been forced by her husband to have this abortion, her second in six months. She kept repeating that she wanted to die. She felt that she had killed her child. She had not been allowed a choice, and her anxiety was tremendous.[8]

How, then, can we create a greater space, a more substantive role in abortion decisions for men, without surrendering our legitimate right to control our own bodies? To begin with we have to go beyond the fairly one-dimensional notion of the "supportive man" and allow for a more complex process that acknowledges men's role in procreation. An important part of this is acknowledging that men, too, have feelings about abortion. Their ambivalence has to be dealt with, their wishes have to be allowed expression and listened to, even if they are not agreeable to us, and even if we ultimately don't go along with them.

Just what is men's emotional response to abortion? It is a testament to the extent to which reproduction is seen as exclusively a woman's concern that there is such a dearth of literature on the subject. Roger Wade, a counsellor at a Colorado abortion clinic, has produced one of the few substantive resources on the subject. His booklet, *For Men About Abortion,* is based on his experience of counselling more than 1,200 men accompanying women to abortions. According to Wade, the first concern of most men is for the physical safety of their partners—as it is for women themselves. Any surgical procedure is accompanied by fears that some kind of harm will result. After that fear is assuaged, men exhibit a range of emotions as wide as women's. But there are some fairly typical responses. Men commonly adopt the role of the strong, silent protector, what Wade calls the "John Wayne" role. They may focus on the woman's emotional state while hiding their own feelings. Naomi described this reaction in her partner:

> Michael was very supportive. But he felt that he had to deny his own feelings in order to be there for me, which turned out to be a way of blocking his emotions.[9]

A variant of the John Wayne role that Wade identifies is the "jester" role, where the man tries to keep things light by making jokes and cheering his partner up. Men understandably gravitate to these kinds of roles because they are consistent with the male sex-role expectations of our society—men are tough, they don't give in to their emotions. It is, in a sense, safer for a man to play a role and thus keep his emotional distance from a painful situation, but by doing so he may be robbing himself of an important human experience as well as unfairly expecting his partner to shoulder the emotional burden for both of them.

Men sometimes, with the best of intentions, keep silent about their preference and withdraw from the abortion decision in the belief that it is "all up to her." This is true in a sense, but, Wade says, such a withdrawal can also be interpreted by the woman as a "Pontius Pilate" response, a disavowal of responsibility and an abandonment of her to the lonely process of soul-searching. Men also attempt to take on the whole responsibility for the pregnancy, berating themselves for "failing to protect their woman" and saying things like "*I* got you pregnant." Again, this kind of paternalistic response fits in with the prescribed male role, but is not very helpful for either party.

Like women, men may experience profound ambivalence and sadness surrounding an abortion. They may on one level want to continue with the pregnancy, even while knowing that to do so would be a grave mistake. They may also experience grief after the abortion, though often their grief is not simply for a child lost, but for a potential *son*. And men's failure to work through their feelings around an abortion can occasionally have devastating consequences. One man who did not make clear to his wife the strength of his desire that she carry through with the pregnancy suffered severe emotional repercussions. Even several years after the abortion he told writer Linda Bird Francke, "I'm still not sure I have buried that fetus."[10]

The feelings of the men quoted here and those counselled by Wade may not be typical: these are men who, after all, did *not* "take off," who were aware and committed enough to support their partners through the abortion process. But they do give a hint of the potential depth and breadth of male involvement in abortion and indeed the whole range of reproductive experiences. But as it stands now, men's needs are in no way being addressed in the way abortion services are provided in Canada. They are treated as largely peripheral to the whole process, when in fact their role is a central one, particularly as a strong source of emotional sharing and support for women. Some have suggested, in fact, that men's role in abortion is analogous to their growing role in the birth process. Once shut out there, too, men are now becoming deeply involved in their partners' labours and are physically present at their children's births. (Male presence at abortion procedures is, however, probably an idea whose time has not yet come. One progressive administrator at a U.S. abortion clinic began allowing men in the procedure room and claims that the fainting rate forced her to terminate the experiment almost immediately. Interestingly, this is precisely the same as the old objections to having men in hospital delivery rooms.) Counselling services and support groups, while scanty for women seeking abortion, are virtually non-existent for men. According to Wade, "Feeling excluded is the most frequently expressed complaint" of men involved in an abortion.[11] And it may be that by allowing so little space for men to explore their response to abortion, we are perpetuating the polarization between men and women around the issue. In the Medhurst case mentioned earlier, for example, it is possible that the husband would never have taken such extreme legal measures if his feelings about the decision had been properly acknowledged. He had been present at the birth of an earlier child, and his anguish over the loss of another was undeniably real. And he complained, with some bitterness, about the fact that nowhere in the process involving his wife, the doctors and the hospital abortion committee were his wishes taken into account.

Feminists should, with caution, re-assess our perspective on the male role in abortion. We should ask whether, by keeping men's role circumscribed, we are actually discouraging them from real emotional involvement, and from a full sense of shared responsibility in reproduction. Women are now faced with agonizing, unprecedented choices. We should not have to make them alone.

The Abortion Ruling: What Has the Court Done?

Walter R. Mears

This time, the election returns may follow the Supreme Court, onto an abortion battlefield no candidate is likely to escape without scars.

President Bush expressed confidence that Americans will handle the issue "within the bounds of civility and our legal institutions."

That may be wishful confidence.

Abortion is not a subject that fosters civil discourse. Not even in the chambers of the Supreme Court, where black-robed justices bitterly denounced one another in the July 3 decision permitting state restrictions on abortion. And certainly not in the streets.

Chief Justice William Rehnquist said dissenting colleagues had accused his 5–4 majority of cowardice and illegitimacy. In angry dissent, Justice Harry Blackmun said the decision invites constitutional crisis for the nation and brutal consequences for women who would defy laws against abortion.

The shouting and shoving started almost at once, in demonstrations scattered around the country, with confrontations that can only escalate.

Both sides said they would demand that every state legislator, indeed every candidate for office, take a public position on abortion. To the rival activists, that single issue overrides everything else in judging a candidate.

Turn-of-the-cuntury columnist Finley Peter Dunne wrote that the Supreme Court follows the election returns.

That observation may be reversed on abortion. There is no safe side for officeholders, office seekers, even for judges.

Justice Antonin Scalia said the court should overturn its 1973 abortion rights ruling, get out of the way and let the political system deal with the issue.

For 16 years, since the court held that a woman has a right to terminate a pregnancy, opponents of abortion have been campaigning intensively, sometimes defying the law to barricade abortion clinics, sometimes shouting down candidates.

Now the court has opened another path to their objective, permitting state restrictions and hinting that it may eventually reverse its 1973 abortion decision. So they will lobby and demonstrate for restrictive state laws and also will put the issue before the courts in as many versions as possible.

Abortions rights organizations saw the handwriting of an increasingly conservative Supreme Court and began mobilizing in anticipation of court setbacks. Now they will try to make the issue central in every legislature and every election.

The first arenas will be the closely divided Florida Legislature, to be summoned to special session by a Republican governor bent on restricting abortion; and the Nov. 7 elections in New Jersey and Virginia, which are electing governors and legislators.

The Supreme Court will consider three more abortion cases later this year.

That probably will escalate the battle. But perhaps, eventually, the political system will shape answers acceptable to the majority of Americans.

Acknowledging and Documenting Sources

When a writing assignment requires the inclusion of outside sources, it is important that these sources be **acknowledged** and **documented.** The following material focuses on incorporating material from outside sources into the body of your text and on acknowledging sources properly according to the MLA (Modern Language Association) and the APA (American Psychological Association) systems. Writing assignments for a researched paper usually require the MLA system. However, it is important to keep in mind that the method of documentation varies according to discipline, and that when you are writing papers for courses in other departments, you should check with your instructor about which method to use. Your campus writing center may have several textbooks that outline different methods of acknowledging and documenting sources, and your library has many different manuals you will be able to use, among them

> *MLA Handbook for Writers of Research Papers,* 3rd edition. New York: MLA, 1988. This outlines the MLA system, which is preferred in most disciplines in the Humanities, including philosophy, religion and history.

> *Publication Manual of the American Psychological Association,* 3rd edition. Washington, D.C.: APA, 1983. This outlines the APA system, which is preferred in most disciplines in the social sciences, including sociology, political science, and economics.

> Kate L. Turabian. *A Manual for Writers,* 5th edition. Chicago: University of Chicago Press, 1987.

AVOIDING PLAGIARISM

Learning to acknowledge and document sources properly will enable you to avoid being charged with plagiarism, which not only can be embarrassing but can also prevent you from reaching educational and professional objectives. Some plagiarism is actually unintentional—students do not acknowledge their sources simply because they are unaware of the importance of doing so and are unacquainted with scholarly methods. The following material, then, will help you avoid plagiarism, either deliberate or inadvertent. Of course, proper documentation of sources is also important for helping your readers locate your references, if they are interested in doing so. It also indicates that you are a serious student who knows what has been written about the topic and who understands the importance of acknowledging other people's work.

Documentation: A Two-Part System

To document a paper means to provide information about the sources the writer used in order to write the paper. A documentation system consists of two parts:

- parenthetical references within the body of the text
- a list at the end of the paper, which provides bibliographic information about works that were consulted and cited.

All papers using outside sources include both parts. However, the specific method of documentation can vary according to discipline, since disciplines have become specialized and therefore place emphasis on different types of knowledge. For example, in the Works Cited section, the MLA system places the date of publication as one of the later elements in the citation, since knowledge in the humanities does not become dated as quickly as it might in the social or the hard sciences (a 1920 edition of a Shakespeare play, for example, would be just as valid as a 1965 edition). However, in the social sciences, which use the APA system, more recent findings might contradict older findings; therefore, in that system, the date is given toward the beginning of the citation.

Differences in documentation styles are also based on what is deemed convenient or efficient. Therefore, in its "References" list, the APA style does not use quotation marks around the title of an article, nor does it capitalize major words in the title.

Some variations, though, are simply due to the conventions of different disciplines, and if you are writing for a particular discipline, you must demonstrate that you are familiar with its documentation practices. The information below provides some basic information about acknowledging and documenting sources according to the MLA and APA formats. You should also keep in mind the following tips:

1. **Be scrupulous about acknowledging secondary source material.** Do not risk plagiarizing either deliberately or inadvertently.

2. **Form is important.** Always check to see that you have the proper form for referring to outside material within the body of your text and for listing on the Works Cited or References page. Remember that proper form includes spacing and punctuation. If you are writing for a course within a specific discipline, look over the journals for that discipline. Note the system of documentation within those journals. Understanding

the form requires concentration, so leave sufficient time for documenting your sources correctly.

3. It is almost impossible to memorize every specific rule about documenting sources. **Keep a set of rules handy** when you polish your final draft.

THE MLA SYSTEM

Parenthetical Reference and a Works Cited Page

According to the new MLA system, information that is referred to in your paper must be acknowledged by **parenthetical reference** within the body of the paper and through a **"Works Cited"** page at the end. The parenthetical reference provides your reader with enough information to locate the full reference in the "Works Cited" section. Remember that all information or points of view that you obtained from an outside source must be acknowledged, whether it is a quotation, a summary, or a paraphrase. It is better to be over-scrupulous about acknowledging your sources than to plagiarize unintentionally.

Parenthetical Documentation in the MLA System

In the MLA system, you should refer to outside sources within the body of your text by including enough information so that the reader will be able to locate a source in the "Works Cited" page at the end of the paper. Each citation consists of the author's name (or a short title if the author's name is missing) and a page number. Here is an example:

> Snodgrass points out that "young men these days are as concerned about their weight as young women" (237).

Note that you would not need to include Snodgrass's name in parentheses because it already appears in the text; that is, the reader is already aware of the author's name and would be able to find the rest of the information about the source in the Works Cited section. Note also the placement of the quotation marks, the parentheses, and the period. These are conventions that must be observed correctly.

In the example below, however, Snodgrass's name is not mentioned; therefore, it would be important to include his name as well as the page number within parentheses:

> What is often overlooked is that "young men these days are as concerned about their weight as young women" (Snodgrass 237).

Note that there is no comma between the name, "Snodgrass" and the page number.

Now suppose that your Works Cited section included two works by Snodgrass. In this case, in order for the reader to locate the source within the Works Cited section, you would have to include the title as well as the author and page number within the parentheses. Here is an illustration:

> What is often overlooked is that "young men these days are as concerned about their weight as young women" (Snodgrass, *Men and Appearance* 237).

The use of parenthetical documentation has made it much easier for writers to refer to outside materials. Not too long ago, students who were writing even relatively short papers had to use an elaborate system of footnotes when they included information from a secondary source.

Long Quotations

For quotations of more than four typed lines, use block quotations, indented ten lines and double spaced. The parenthetical reference should appear two spaces after the punctuation at the end of the block. Here is an example:

The following charming description of a day in Prague refutes the common stereotype of the bleakness of Eastern Europe:

> The crowd of shoppers, strollers, and office workers was standing around to-
>
> gether listening—as best I could figure out—to a comedian who must have
>
> been performing in an auditorium inside. I don't understand Czech but I
>
> guessed that it was a comedian—and a very funny one—because the staccato
>
> rhythm of his monologue, the starts, stops, and shifts of tone, seemed con-
>
> sciously designed to provide the crowd into spasms of laughter that ripened
>
> into a rich roar. (Roth 106)

THE MLA SYSTEM: THE WORKS CITED PAGE

There are three main components in a Works Cited page, the title, the author, and the publication information (city, publisher, publication date). Here is some basic information about the Works Cited page:

1. All items are arranged in alphabetical order by the last name of the author. If no author is listed, use the first significant word of the title.
2. Each citation should begin at the left margin and additional lines in each citation should be indented five spaces.

3. Double-space between each line and double-space between each citation. The title, "Works Cited," should be placed one inch down from the top of the page. Then double-space between the title and the first citation.

James D. Lester suggests the following scheme for including information in a Works Cited page (note that 1, 3, and 8 are required):

1. Author
2. Chapter or part of a book
3. Title of the book
4. Editor, translator, or compiler
5. Edition
6. Number of volumes
7. Name of the series
8. Place, publisher, and date
9. Volume number of this book
10. Page numbers

Here are some examples you can use as models:

A Book with One Author

Snodgrass, Stanley. *Men and Appearance.* Los Angeles: Vanity Press, 1985.

Two or More Books by the Same Author

If you are citing two or more books by the same author, do not repeat the author's name with each entry. Instead, insert a three-hyphen line flush with the left margin. Then type a period. Below is an example.

Snodgrass, Stanley. *Men and Appearance.* Los Angeles: Vanity Press, 1985.
---. *Women and Appearance.* Los Angeles: Vanity Press, 1986.

A Book with Two Authors

Johnson, Zachary, and Sandra Stone. *Living with Lunatics.* New York: Bayberry

   Scott, 1975.

A Book with Three Authors

Smith, Jason, Leonard Luden and Marjory Vicks. *Cough Remedies For the Nineties.*

   Coldwater Springs: Harper, 1990.

A Book with Four or More Authors

Fieldstone, Jerome, et al. *Conservatism on the Rise.* Boston: Hillman, 1987.

A Book with a Translator or Editor

Lagerscrantz, Olof. *From Hell to Paradise: Dante and His Comedy.* Trans. Alan

   Blair. New York: Washington Square Press, 1966.

A Chapter that is Part of an Anthology or Collection

Updike, John "A&P." *Fiction 100*. Ed. James E. Pickering. 4th ed. New York:

Macmillan, 1982. 1086–1089.

An Introduction, Preface, Foreword, or Afterword

Flintstone Fred. Introduction. *Life in Bedrock*. By Wilma Flintstone. Little Rock:

Stone Age, 1982. i–ix.

Note here the use of the word "by" to distinguish the author from the writer of the preface.

THE WORK'S CITED PAGE: PERIODICALS

James D. Lester suggests the following sequence for listing references to periodicals on the Works Cited page.

1. Author.
2. Title of the article
3. Name of periodical
4. Volume, issue, and page number

Enter the **author's last name** at the margin, followed by a comma, then the author's first name, followed by a period.

The **title of the article** should be enclosed in quotation marks followed by a period placed inside the closing quotation marks.

The **name of the periodical** is then underlined with no following punctuation.

References to volume, dates, issue, and page number depend on the type of periodical you are citing.

MAGAZINES AND JOURNALS

In general, magazines begin with page one in each issue, whereas journals tend to have continuous pagination for an entire year, and this distinction between separate and continuous pagination determines the sort of information you should include. A volume number, year, and page numbers are sufficient for journal entries, since they are paginated continuously. However, for magazines, omit the volume number and provide a month or even a specific day in the case of weekly publications. Here are some examples.

Magazine (Monthly)

Crickmer, Barry. "Can We Control Spending?" *Nation's Business* Apr. 1982: 22–24.

Magazine (Weekly)

von Hoffman, Nicholas. "The White House News Hole." *The New Republic* 6

   Sept. 1982: 19–23.

   Note that there is no mark of punctuation between the name of the magazine and the date. Also note that if the magazine does not indicate the name of the author, begin with the title of the article as shown below:

"Chaos in Television." *Time* 12 Mar. 1979: 60–61.

JOURNAL ENTRIES

For journal entries, you should include the volume number, the year within a parentheses, followed by a colon, and include page numbers. Here is an example:

Barker, James R. "Living with a Pit Bull and Loving It." *The Canine Courier* 20

   (1989): 262–69.

   If the journal begins each issue with number one, add an issue number following the volume number. Separate the volume number from the issue number with a period. Here is an example:

Hiss, Stephanie. "Declawing Your Cat: Pros and Cons." *The Feline Fancier* 9.6

   (1988): 9–12.

Note that arabic, not roman numerals are used.

NEWSPAPER

For newspaper entries provide the author's name, the title of the article, the name of the newspaper as it appears on the front page (*Daily News,* not *The Daily News*) and the complete date (day, month, year). Page numbers should be listed according to how they actually appear on the page. If the article does not continue on the next page, that is, if it is not printed consecutively, write only the first page number and add a + sign. Thus, if the article begins on page 15 and continues on page 36, you should write 15+.

Here is an example of a newspaper citation:

James, Noah. "The Comedian Everyone Loves to Hate." *New York Times* 22 Jan.

   1984: 23.

OTHER TYPES OF SOURCES

Some sources are neither books nor periodicals. Here are some other possibilities:

An Inteview

If the interview is published, treat it as a work in a collection:

Shaw, Robert. Interview. *Interviews with Robert Shaw.* By John Schaffer. Chicago:

Brentwood, 1989.

If you are citing a personal interview, identify it by date.

Smith, James. Personal interview. 6 Nov. 1988.

A Broadcast Interview

Schwarzkopf, Norman. Interview. Morning Edition. National Public Radio. KCRW,

Los Angeles. 4 Jan. 1991.

Material from a Computer Service

"Affirmative Action." *Grolier's On-Line Encyclopedia.* 1987.

THE APA SYSTEM

Parenthetical Citation

In the APA system, you should also refer to outside sources within the body of your text by including enough information so that the reader will be able to locate a source in the References page at the end of the paper. When using the APA system, you should write the year of publication in parentheses immediately following the author's name. If you do not mention the author by name in the text, then you should include the author's name (or a short title if the author's name is missing) and the year of publication, separated by a comma enclosed in parentheses. If you quote from your source, you must also add the page number in your parentheses, with "p." preceding the page number. Here are some examples:

> Snodgrass (1988) points out that "young men these days are as concerned about their weight as young women" (p. 4).

Note, as in the MLA system, that you would not need to include Snodgrass's name in parentheses because it already appears in the text; that is, the reader is already aware of the author's name and would be able to find the rest of the information about the source in the References section. Note also the placement of the quotation marks, the parentheses, and the period.

In the example below, however, Snodgrass's name is not mentioned; therefore, it would be important to include his name as well as the page number within the parentheses:

What is often overlooked is that "young men these days are as concerned about their weight as young women" (Snodgrass, 1988, p. 237).

Note the use of commas.

A Work with Two or More Authors

If a work has two authors, refer to both within the text. Here is an example:

In a recent study of obese corporate executives (James & Jones, 1989), it was stated . . .

or

James and Jones (1989) state that . . .

Note that the "&" sign is used only in parentheses.

If a work has several authors (fewer than six), they should all be mentioned in the first reference:

James, Jones, Smith, Jeeves, and Raskovsky (1987) argue that . . .

However, in subsequent references, you can use "et al." as in

James et al. (1987) argue that . . .

APA System: The References Page

Like the Works Cited page in MLA form, there are also three main components in a References page, the title, the author, and the publication information (city, publisher, publication date). Here are some points to remember about the References page in the APA system:

1. All items are arranged in alphabetical order by the last name of the author. If no author is listed, use the first significant word of the title.
2. Each citation should begin at the left margin and additional lines in each citation should be indented three spaces.
3. Double-space between each line and double-space between each citation. Two spaces follow a period, one space follows a comma, semicolon, or colon.
4. The title, "References," should be placed one and a half inches down from the top of the page. Then double-space between the title and the first citation.

Here are some significant differences between the APA style and the MLA style:

1. Initials, instead of full first names, are used for authors.
2. Titles of books and articles do not use capital letters, except for the first word.
3. Titles of articles do not use quotation marks.
4. There is a greater emphasis on the year of publication.

Here are some examples you can use as models:

A Book with One Author

Snodgrass, S. (1985). *Men and appearance*. Los Angeles: Vanity Press.

Note that the author's first name is indicated only by an initial, that the date appears in parentheses, and that only the first word of the title begins with a capital letter.

Two or More Books by the Same Author

List two or more books by the same author in chronological order.

Snodgrass, S. (1985). *Men and appearance*. Los Angeles: Vanity Press.

Snodgrass, S. (1986). *Women and appearance*. Los Angeles: Vanity Press.

A Book with Two Authors

Reverse all authors' names and separate them with commas. Use an ampersand (&) before the last author.

Johnson, Z., & Stone, S. (1975). *Living with lunatics*. New York: Bayberry Scott.

A Book with a Translator or Editor

Lagerscrantz, O. (1966). *From hell to paradise: Dante and his comedy*. (Alan Blair,

Trans.). New York: Washington Square Press.

A Chapter That is Part of an Anthology or Collection

Updike, J. (1982). A&P. In James E. Pickering (Ed.). *Fiction 100* (pp. 1086–1089).

New York: Macmillan.

APA STYLE PERIODICALS

Article in a Journal with Continuous Pagination

Crickmer, B. (1982). Can we control spending? *Nation's Business, 12*, 22–24.

The number following the title is the volume number. Notice that it is italicized. Note also that commas separate the journal title, volume number, and page numbers.

Article in a Journal Paginated Separately in Each Issue

von Hoffman, N. (1982). The White House news hole. *The New Republic 6* (4),

19–23.

In this case you follow the volume number "6" with the issue number (4), which is placed in parentheses.

If the journal does not indicate the name of the author, begin with the title of the article as shown below:

Chaos in television. (1979, Mar. 12). *Time,* pp. 60–61.

General Interest Magazines

General interest magazines, which are frequently published either monthly or weekly, often cite the date of publication, rather than the volume number. Here is an example:

Barker, James R. (1989, April). Living with a pit bull and loving it. *The Canine*

Courier, pp. 262–269.

NEWSPAPER

For newspaper entries, provide the author's name, the title of the article, the name of the newspaper as it appears on the front page (*Daily News,* not *The Daily News*) and the complete date (day, month, year). Page numbers should be listed according to how they actually appear on the page.

Here is an example of a newspaper citation:

James, Noah. (1984, Jan. 22). The comedian everyone loves to hate. *The New York*

Times, p. 23.

OTHER TYPES OF SOURCES

Interviews

Under the APA system, personal interviews are not entered in the reference list, but are cited in the body of the paper. Here is an example of how it is done:

James Kohl (personal communication, June 20, 1990) indicated that . . .

Published interviews are cited as works in a book or periodical. Here is an example:

Smith, J. (1988, May). Predictions for the eighties (Interview). *Futurist,* pp. 16–20.

Material from a Computer Service

Affirmative Action. (1987) *Grolier's Online Encyclopedia,* New York.

USING OUTSIDE SOURCES: SOME ADDITIONAL POINTS TO CONSIDER

In addition to knowing how to acknowledge and document sources, students also need to be able to use them competently. Here are some additional points to consider in working with outside sources:

1. **Distinguish between primary and secondary sources.** In order to select sources for papers utilizing outside sources, you should be aware of the difference between primary and secondary sources. A **primary source** provides primary knowledge of your topic—it is most often used to refer to an original document, such as the Declaration of Independence or the Constitution. If you are writing about a work of literature, then the work itself is the primary source; if you are writing about a particular person, a statement made by that person is a primary source.

   A **secondary source** is a statement or comment about the primary source. Thus, an article analyzing the Fourth Amendment to the Constitution is a secondary source. Commentary on a work of literature is a secondary source. A statement about a person who is the subject of your paper is a secondary source. Thus, if you were writing about President George Bush's feelings about the Persian Gulf War, his own statements on the war are a primary source, but newspaper articles commenting on his statements are a secondary source.

   In incorporating primary and secondary source material in your paper, you should be careful that you differentiate between the two so as not to confuse your reader. The following sentence was written by an observer and is therefore a secondary source:

   > The Chief of Police seemed concerned about allegations of police brutality of minorities.

   However, the next sentence was spoken directly by the Chief of Police in a press interview and is therefore a primary source:

   > "These allocations of police brutality to minorities are a source of great concern to me," the Chief of Police indicated in a statement to the press.

2. **Decide *why* you are using an outside source.** In deciding to use a source, you should first consider why that source would be helpful to

your paper. Does it serve as a useful example? Does it support your own position or represent the opposing viewpoint? Does it provide needed authority or an important definition?

3. **Determine if information is common knowledge.** Many students are confused about what sort of information to document, since some information may be considered "common knowledge"; that is, everyone already knows this information, even if it is also written in a source. For example, the statement that Thomas Jefferson was the third president of the United States is considered common knowledge, so you would not have to document the source of this fact if you mentioned it in a paper. However, if you referred to the perspective of a social historian that Jefferson was not as egalitarian a statesman as he is often credited for, then it is important that you acknowledge that point of view through a citation. Of course, some students may argue that what is common knowledge for one person is new information for another, and that is certainly true. In general, though, well-known facts are considered common knowledge; opinions and expert observations must be documented.

4. **Blend sources smoothly into your text to avoid the "crouton" effect.** Students often experience difficulty incorporating their sources smoothly within their text. Instead of introducing the sources and then commenting on them, they just throw them in, as in the following typical example:

> Love is an important theme in Shakespeare's sonnets. "Let me not to the marriage of true minds admit impediments."

Note here that the writer has not introduced the quotation and that there is no commentary following. The quotation is simply sprinkled in, with the result that there is no blend between the quotation and the writer's own words. Like croutons in a salad, the reader crunches on the quotations from time to time and may enjoy the flavor, but the information from outside sources always stands out. Unless you deliberately wish to create this effect, you should aim for a smooth blend of quoted material with your prose.

How Many Sources to Use?

Students frequently are concerned with how many sources to incorporate into writing a researched paper. Many are under the impression that "more is better"— that is, that the more sources one uses, the more learned and impressive the paper will be. My feeling, though, is that if you try to include too many sources, too many quotations, too many summaries and paraphrases, your own personal voice will be lost. The paper will be a tissue of quotations from other people, and your own position will be hard to determine. Remember that in a researched paper, you are incorporating sources in order to support a position that you, yourself, have formulated after thinking, reading, and writing; you are not using sources simply for the sake of showing how much information you have found.

In deciding to use a source, then, you should first consider why that source would be helpful to your paper. Does it serve as a useful example? Does it support your own position or represent the opposing viewpoint? Does it provide needed authority? These questions should help you decide how many sources to use, but for those of you who are looking for a specific number, I would suggest that you use at least four and not more than ten. But, of course, flexibility is the key word here. You should include enough sources to support your position, not so many that your own writing is lost.

Subject Index

Webster v. Reproductive Health Services, 542.
  See also Abortion
Weeks v. United States, 318. *See also* Exclusion-
  ary rule
Wolf v. Colorado, 318. *See also* Exclusionary rule
Women, 440-447
  education, 443-444
  Legislation for women's rights, 446-448
    Civil Rights Act of 1964, 446
    Equal Pay Act of 1963, 446
    Equal Rights Amendment (ERA), 446-447

Title VII of the Civil Rights Act of 1964, 446
Title IX of the Education Act Amendments
  of 1972, 446
Women's Movement, History of. *See* Women
  Civil War, 442
  Feminine Mystique, 444-445
  National Organization for Women, 445
  Seneca Falls Declaration, 442
  suffrage movement, 442-443
  revolutionary period, 441-442